THE

ANTI-SLAVERY CRUSADE

IN AMERICA

AM I NOT A MAN AND A BROTHER?

MEMOIR AND LETTERS OF
CHARLES SUMNER

Edward L. Pierce

Volume I

ARNO PRESS
&
THE NEW YORK TIMES
New York · 1969

Reprint edition 1969 by Arno Press, Inc.

*

Library of Congress Catalog Card No. 78–82211

*

Reprinted from a copy in
The State Historical Society of Wisconsin Library

*

Manufactured in the United States of America

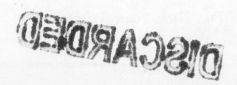

MEMOIR AND LETTERS OF
CHARLES SUMNER

Ever Yours,
Charles Sumner

MEMOIR AND LETTERS

OF

CHARLES SUMNER.

BY

EDWARD L. PIERCE.

VOL. I.

1811—1838.

BOSTON:

ROBERTS BROTHERS.

1877.

CAMBRIDGE:

PRESS OF JOHN WILSON AND SON.

NOTE.

THE first article of Mr. Sumner's will is as follows : — "I bequeath to Henry W. Longfellow, Francis V. Balch, and Edward L. Pierce, as trustees, all my papers, manuscripts, and letter-books, to do with them what they think best ; with power to destroy them, to deposit them in some public library, or to make extracts from them for publication." With the facilities afforded by this trust, and the aid of Mr. Sumner's early friends, who have kindly contributed their recollections of him and such letters as they had preserved, the biographer has prepared two volumes of his Memoir and Letters for the period closing with the Oration on " The True Grandeur of Nations," July 4, 1845, which is the first production included in the edition of his Works as revised by himself, and marks the beginning of his public career.

E. L. P.

MILTON, MASSACHUSETTS,
September 22, 1877.

CONTENTS OF VOL. I.

CHAPTER I.

PAGE

ANCESTRY 1

CHAPTER II.

PARENTAGE AND FAMILY. — THE FATHER 11

CHAPTER III.

1811–26.

BIRTH AND EARLY EDUCATION 35

CHAPTER IV.

September, 1826, to September, 1830.

COLLEGE LIFE 45

CHAPTER V.

September, 1830, to September, 1831.

YEAR AFTER COLLEGE 71

CHAPTER VI.

September, 1831, to December, 1833.

LAW SCHOOL 90

CHAPTER VII.

January, 1834, to September, 1834.

STUDY IN A LAW OFFICE. — VISIT TO WASHINGTON 123

CHAPTER VIII.
September, 1834, to December, 1837.

EARLY PROFESSIONAL LIFE 146

CHAPTER IX.
December, 1837.

GOING TO EUROPE 196

CHAPTER X.
December, 1837, to January, 1838.

THE VOYAGE AND ARRIVAL 213

CHAPTER XI.
January and February, 1838.

PARIS, ITS SCHOOLS 226

CHAPTER XII.
March to May, 1838.

PARIS. — SOCIETY AND THE COURTS 261

CHAPTER XIII.
June, 1838, to March, 1839.

ENGLAND 298

CHAPTER XIV.
June and July, 1838.

FIRST WEEKS IN LONDON 312

CHAPTER XV.
August to October, 1838.

THE CIRCUITS — VISITS IN ENGLAND AND SCOTLAND 341

MEMOIR AND LETTERS

OF

CHARLES SUMNER.

CHAPTER I.

ANCESTRY.

THE SUMNER FAMILY is of English origin. The name was at first Summoner or Somner, — the title of officers whose duty it was to summon parties into courts. Roger Sumner died at Bicester, in the county of Oxford, and was buried in the church of St. Edburg, Dec. 4, 1608. William, his only son and heir, from whom descended Charles Sumner, in the seventh generation, was baptized in St. Edburg, Jan. 27, 1604–5. About 1635, he came, with his wife Mary and his three sons, William, Roger, and George, to Dorchester,[1] Massachusetts, and became the founder of an American family, now widely spread.

Many of the first settlers of Dorchester were from the southwestern counties of England. They arrived in 1630, less than ten years after the settlement of the Pilgrims at Plymouth. They were attracted to the particular site by the salt-marsh, which lay along the bay and the Neponset River. This furnished an immediate supply of hay, and dispensed with the necessity of clearing at once large tracts of forest land. Among them were expert fishermen, who were pleased to find at hand this means of support. The territory which they selected for their new home presented one of the fairest of landscapes, — diversified with upland and meadow, the Blue Hills and the river.

At first, the organization of the settlement was imperfect. In 1633, a local government was organized; and the next year the town sent delegates to the first general court or legislature. The community was still in its infancy, when William Sumner joined

---

[1] Annexed to Boston, 1870.

it. Four children were born to him after his arrival. The early records show that he entered actively on his duties as a citizen. He became at once a grantee of land. " He was made a freeman in 1637 ; admitted to the church in 1652 ; was for twelve years a deputy to the general court; a selectman twenty-three years, nearly half the time from 1637 to 1688; was a rater for five years, and a commissioner ' to try and issue small causes ' for nine years, from 1663 to 1671 inclusive. In 1645, he was ' appointed one of a committee for building a new meeting-house,' and in 1663 was chosen ' clerk of ye training band.' "

Roger, the second son [1] of the emigrant ancestor, was baptized at Bicester, Aug. 8, 1632. Marrying Mary Josselyn, of Hingham, he had seven children. In 1660, he removed from Dorchester to Lancaster, " that he might, with other Christians at Lancaster, join together for the gathering of a church; " but, after the destruction of that town by the Indians, he removed to Milton (set off from Dorchester and incorporated in 1662), where he became the deacon of the first church, and died in 1698. His fourth son, William, who was born about 1673, had, for his seventh child, Seth, who was born in 1710, and became, by two marriages, the father of thirteen children. By the first marriage he had Seth, the grandfather of Major-General Edwin V. Sumner, who was an officer of the regular army, served in the Mexican War, commanded in Kansas during a part of the controversy between the free-state and the pro-slavery men, and bore a distinguished part in the war of the Rebellion. By the second marriage [2] he had Job, his ninth child, who was the father of Charles Pinckney Sumner, and the grandfather of Charles Sumner.[3]

The Sumners who remained in Dorchester and Milton during the seventeenth and eighteenth centuries were generally farmers,

[1] From his third son, George, who lived on Brush Hill, Milton, descended, in the fifth generation, Increase Sumner; an associate justice of the Supreme Judicial Court, 1782-97, and the successor of Samuel Adams, in 1797, as governor of the Commonwealth.

[2] By the same marriage he had, as his thirteenth and last child, Jesse, who was the father of Harriot, the second wife of Nathan Appleton of Boston, a member of Congress in 1831-33, and again in 1842. It may be noted, that one of Mr. Appleton's daughters, by his first marriage, married Robert J. Mackintosh, who was the son of Sir James, the English publicist and historian; and another married Henry W. Longfellow, the poet.

[3] The following are reliable authorities concerning the genealogy of the Sumner Family : "Memoir of Increase Sumner," Governor of Massachusetts, by his son, William H. Sumner: together with a genealogy of the Sumner Family, prepared by William B. Trask ; Boston, 1854. "New England Historical and Genealogical Register," April, 1854, and October, 1855. "History of East Boston," by William H. Sumner; Boston, 1858; pp. 278-307 (with a drawing of the St. Edburg Church). "History of Dorchester;" Boston, 1859.

owning considerable estates in fee-simple, and blessed beyond the usual measure with large families of children.

The Jacob or Jacobs family, — the maternal ancestors of Charles Sumner, — begins with Nicholas Jacob, who came to this country from Hingham, England, in 1633, settled in Watertown, and removed two years later to Hingham.[1] His son John was the father of David, the grandfather of Joshua, and the great-grandfather of David, Sr., who was born in Scituate in 1729, and died in 1808. David Jacob, Sr., the grandfather of Relief Jacob, who became the wife of Charles Pinckney Sumner, owned ample estates, held public offices, and served on the Committee of Public Safety in the Revolution. The house, which he built and used for an inn, is now the residence of Rev. Robert L. Killam. It is situated in the part of Hanover known as Assinippi. His son David, Jr., who was born in Hanover in 1763, married Hannah Hersey,[2] of Hingham, and died in 1799, at the age of thirty-six. His home was but a short distance from his father's, and its site is now occupied by the residence of Perez Simmons. The first child of David, Jr., and Hannah (Hersey) Jacob was Hannah R., who died in 1877. Their second was Relief, who was born, Feb. 29, 1785, and became the mother of Charles Sumner. The Jacob family were generally farmers, residing in Hingham, Scituate, South Scituate, and Hanover. They were marked by good sense and steady habits, and some of them discharged important civic trusts.

THE GRANDFATHER OF CHARLES SUMNER.

Job Sumner was born in Milton, April 23, 1754. The house on Brush Hill, Milton, in which he was born is the home of one of

---

[1] For the genealogy of the Jacob family, see "History of Hanover," by J. S. Barry, pp. 319–335; and for that of the Simmons family, pp. 371–374.

[2] She was a descendant of William Hersey, an emigrant from England, who was in Hingham as early as 1635. To him a numerous family, largely still resident in that town, trace their lineage. His great-grandson, Joshua, married a descendant of Governor William Bradford, from whom Charles Sumner is thus descended. Martha Hersey, a sister of Mrs. Relief Sumner's mother, married Elisha Simmons, of Hanover, who died, in 1825, at the age of eighty. The site of his residence is near that of Perez Simmons, but on the opposite side of the way. One of his sons was William Simmons, a graduate of Harvard College, of the class of 1804, a judge of the police court of Boston, and the father of William H. Simmons, a graduate of Harvard College, of the class of 1831, and of Rev. George F. Simmons, of the class of 1832. Judge Simmons and Charles Pinckney Sumner were faithful friends, and their families maintained an intimacy. Joshua Hersey, a brother of Mrs. Relief Sumner's mother, lived on Prospect Street in South Hingham, under Prospect Hill, a well-known landmark. Upon this estate now live his children.

his nephews, being near the residence of the Hon. James M. Robbins. His father died in 1771, leaving a widow and twelve children; and, two years later, Thomas Vose was appointed his guardian. Job was employed, after his father's death, upon the farm of Daniel Vose[1] of that town; and one day, when eighteen years of age, he made known, with some emphasis, his purpose to abandon that occupation and to obtain a liberal education. When twenty years old, he joined the Freshman Class of Harvard College. He entered in November, 1774, not being sufficiently qualified in the preparatory studies to enter in July, at the time of the regular examination for admission.

It appears by the records of the college on the fourth of that month, that "Job Sumner of Milton, having applied for admission to Harvard College, after examination had, voted that upon condition that he pay into the college the sum of £6, to comply with the second law of the first chapter of the college laws, he be admitted into the present Freshman Class."

His most distinguished classmate was Nathan Dane, who reported in Congress the ordinance of 1787 for the government of the North-west Territory, by which a vast domain was saved to freedom. Rev. Samuel Langdon had become president of the college, July 18, 1774. Immediately after the battle of Lexington (April 19, 1775), Cambridge became the head-quarters of the troops for the siege of Boston, then held by the British. The students were ordered to leave the buildings, which were turned into barracks. The institution was temporarily removed to Concord. Washington arrived, July 2; and on the next day took command of the patriot army under the ancient elm which still attracts many a pilgrim. Sumner did not follow his teachers to Concord, but, in May, joined the army at Cambridge, with the rank of an ensign. He had already acquired some knowledge of the drill in a college company, called the "Marti-Mercurian Band," which existed in the years 1770–87,[2] and was afterwards revived as the Harvard Washington Corps.

The good soldier, though his text-books had been for ever laid

---

[1] At Mr. Vose's house, still standing at the Lower Mills Village in Milton, adjacent to the railway station, were passed, in September, 1774, the Suffolk Resolves, which have been regarded as the earliest organized demonstration for Independence in the American colonies. The centenary of this event was commemorated in this historic house, by proper ceremonies, Sept. 9, 1874.

[2] "Reminiscences of the Old College Company, or Marti-Mercurian Band," in "Columbian Centinel," Boston, April 2, 1828, by Charles Pinckney Sumner. References to this company and its uniform may be found in "The Harvard Book," Vol. I. pp. 42, 67.

aside, was kindly remembered by his college. On June 13, 1777, it was "voted that all the charges in Sumner's quarterly bills, since the end of the first quarter in the year 1775, be abated, as he has been engaged in the army ever since the commencement of the war, though he never appeared to give up his relation to the college."

Again, July 7, 1785, two years after Independence was acknowledged, it was voted by the President and Fellows (present the President, Governor Bowdoin, Mr. Lowell, Dr. Harvard, Dr. Lathrop, and the Treasurer), that "Major Job Sumner, who was admitted into the University A. D. 1774, and who entered the service of his country in the army, by leave from the late President, early in the contest between Great Britain and the United States of America, and who, during the war, behaved with reputation as a man and as an officer, be admitted to the degree of Master of Arts at the next commencement, and have his name inserted in the class to which he belonged." This vote alone entitled him to registration with his class in the catalogues of the alumni.

He served as lieutenant in Moses Draper's company of Thomas Gardner's Massachusetts regiment at Bunker Hill,[1] and in Bond's (25th) regiment at the siege of Boston and the invasion of Canada; was commissioned captain in the Second Massachusetts regiment, April 7, 1779, to date from July 1, 1776 (commission signed by John Jay, President of Congress); captain in the Third (Greaton's) Massachusetts regiment, Sept. 29, 1779, to date from Jan. 1, 1777; and again, Sept. 16, 1782, to date from Jan. 1, 1777; and major, March 4, 1783, to date from Oct. 1, 1782. His several commissions are preserved.

The following sketch of Major Sumner is combined from two manuscript sketches left by his son, with some abridgment: —

On the 21st of April, 1776, the regiments under Colonels Greaton, Patterson, Bond, and Poor were sent, after the evacuation of Boston by the British, to succor the remnants of Montgomery's army, then hard pressed and on their retreat from Canada. In one of these regiments Sumner was a lieutenant, — healthful, active, and intelligent. By the invitation of his general officers, Schuyler and Arnold, he was induced to quit for a while his station in the line and enter the flotilla of gunboats, which those generals found it necessary to equip on Lake Cham-

---

[1] Memorials of the Massachusetts Society of the Cincinnati, by Francis S. Drake.

plain.[1] In this service, in which he was appointed captain, July
1, 1776, by General Arnold, he distinguished himself as commander of one of the armed vessels. On this account, by recommendation of the Board of War, which reported that in this
service he had, "in several actions, behaved with great spirit
and good conduct," Congress voted, April 7, 1779, that he have
a commission as captain in the army, to rank as such from
July 1, 1776.[2]

Captain Sumner was placed at the head of a company of
light infantry. He was attached to the division of the army,
whose head-quarters were at or near West Point. His company was frequently, for weeks and months together, some miles
in advance of the division, either up or down the North River, in
some exposed position, at Verplanck's Point, Fishkill, or Peeks-
kill. His command involved constant activity.

While serving under General Heath, he was impressed with
the characteristic difference between that officer and General
Arnold, under whom he had served on the northern frontier in
1776. He said to General Heath, one day, that he hoped at some
time to see more of the hazards of war, and to meet them on a
larger theatre. The general, who was a prudent rather than an
adventurous officer, replied: "I am placed here to retain the
fortress of West Point, and not to seek battles. You have as
exposed a duty as can be assigned to you, — the separate command of a company at an advanced post. If the officers of such
posts are known to relax in their vigilance, we may expect a
general battle very soon; which I hope you will have no share
in bringing on. If my division enjoys an unusual exemption
from the clash of arms, it is what I want; and I am thankful
that I have such active and faithful outposts."

For some days Sumner had charge of the guard of Major
André, while he was under arrest and sentence of death; held
frequent conversations with him, and conceived sincere respect
for that unfortunate officer.

Lieutenant-Colonel (afterwards General) William Hull commanded a detachment of light infantry, cavalry, and artillery,
which guarded New York in the autumn of 1783, during the
evacuation of the city by the British troops. Major Sumner

1 An account of this flotilla may be found in Marshall's "Life of Washington," Vol. III.
pp. 4–10; Irving's "Life of Washington," Vol. II. p. 384, ch. xxxix.
2 Journals of Congress, Vol. V. p. 140.

was his second in command.[1] The force was necessary for the
protection of the city while the British soldiers and partisans
were embarking in the ships, and the former proprietors were
resuming possession of their homes.[2]

The command of the detachment, during the evacuation and
for some time afterwards, devolved largely upon Major Sumner.
General Washington, Dec. 4, 1783, immediately after taking
leave of his officers at Fraunces' Tavern, passed through this
battalion of light infantry, and received from it the last military
salute of the Revolutionary army.

One regiment, formed from the disbanded army, was continued
in service at West Point a few months after the discharge of the
rest. In this regiment, Colonel Henry Jackson was first in rank,
Lieutenant-Colonel William Hull the second, Major Caleb Gibbs
the third, and Major Sumner the fourth. On July 1, 1784, his
military career finally closed.

Major Sumner was about five feet and ten inches in height,
rather stout in person, and walked rapidly, bending forward and
seemingly intent on some errand. He was quick in observation,
frank in his intercourse with men, and liable to be deceived.
He adapted himself readily to society of various kinds, and was
widely acquainted with persons of every grade in the army. He
was fond of a soldier's life, and never repined at its hardships.
He had an ear and voice for music, and delighted in hunting-songs
and marches rather than in psalmody. " He enjoyed books,"
we are told, " such as military dictionaries, State constitutions,
Shakspeare, ' Don Quixote,' and Smith's ' Wealth of Nations.' "
One or more of these were the companions of his travels, and
all of them he owned. Two relics of his handwriting remain, —
copies of lines of poetry, one from Home's " Douglass," and the
other, Othello's apology.

In the autumn of 1785, he was appointed by Congress a commissioner for settling the accounts between the Confederation
and the State of Georgia. He remained in that State until his

---

[1] General Hull, in a letter to Charles Pinckney Sumner, dated March 12, 1825, says:
"Your father was my particular friend, and we served together in those memorable scenes
which never will be forgotten. At the close of the war he was my second in command, in
a corps of light infantry, whose fortune it was to escort General Washington into New York,
take possession of that city, at the time it was evacuated by the British army, and pay the
last salutations to our beloved general when he took his final farewell of that army which had
followed his fortunes through the trials and dangers of the Revolutionary contest."

[2] Sir Guy Carleton had reported to Washington the suspicion of a plot to plunder the
city.

death, with occasional visits to his friends in New York and Boston, and his relatives in Milton. When in Massachusetts, he was usually the guest of Daniel Vose, at whose house in Milton he had lived before he entered college.

In 1787, Governor John Hancock appointed him a justice of the peace, — a distinction then less common than now.

Before Major Sumner entered upon his duties as commissioner, he was publicly presented by the Governor of Georgia to the General Assembly. Shortly before his death, he is said to have been voted for as Governor of that State in the General Assembly, and to have failed of success by only a few votes. He maintained there an expensive style of living, keeping his horse and servant, and enjoying the best and most fashionable company. He became embarrassed by his improvident loans to his friends at home and in the South. From 1784 to 1789, poverty and debt prevailed. In a letter from Savannah, of July 16, 1788, he says : " There never was a man, under such fair prospects as I had three years ago, so dreadfully cut up. I have been robbed by almost every man I have put any confidence in. They have taken all." His last visit to Boston was in the summer of 1788. It was then observed that his health had been impaired by his southern residence. Early in September, 1789, having lately experienced a severe attack of a fever, from the effects of which he had but imperfectly recovered, he embarked on board a vessel bound from Savannah to New York. While at sea, he was poisoned, we are told, by eating a dolphin, caught off the copper banks of Cape Hatteras. The vessel made a rapid passage to New York, reaching there on the 14th, and he was taken on shore without delay. He was already in the height of a fever, and bereft of reason ; and he died on the morning of Wednesday, Sept. 16, at the age of thirty-five. He was buried the next day with the respect due to his memory. His funeral was attended by the Vice-President (John Adams), the Secretary of War (Henry Knox), and the Senators and Representatives in Congress from Massachusetts.[1] His pall was upheld by eight officers of the late army : General Webb, and Colonels Bauman, Walker, Hamilton, Willet, Platt, Smith, and White. The hearse was preceded by a regiment of artillery and the Society of the Cincinnati.[2]

[1] The first Congress under the Constitution was then in session in New York.
[2] New York Journal and Weekly Register, Sept. 16, 1789; Gazette of the United States, Sept. 19, 1789; Massachusetts Centinel, Sept. 26, 1789.

The tombstone of Major Sumner is in the centre of St. Paul's Churchyard, on Broadway. It is by the side of that of Major John Lucas of the Georgia line, who died the month preceding. Both stones, — lying horizontally, with hardly any space between them, and the two closing lines of poetry running across from one to the other, — were doubtless erected by the Society of the Cincinnati. That of Major Sumner gives his age incorrectly, — it being thirty-five instead of thirty-three.

The inscriptions are as follows: —

THIS TOMB IS ERECTED TO THE MEMORY OF **MAJOR JOHN LUCAS,** OF THE GEORGIA LINE OF THE ARMY OF THE REVOLUTION, AND TREASURER OF THE SOCIETY OF THE CINCINNATI OF THAT STATE. HE BORE A SEVERE AND LINGERING DECAY WITH THAT FORTITUDE WHICH EVER MARKED HIS CHARACTER AS A SOLDIER, AND DIED IN THIS CITY ON TUESDAY THE 18TH AUGUST, 1789, AGED 33 YEARS. *Alike in arms they rang'd* *Alike in turn to Death*	AND THIS TOMB CONTAINS THE REMAINS OF **MAJOR JOB SUMNER,** OF THE MASSACHUSETTS LINE OF THE SAME ARMY, WHO, HAVING SUPPORTED AN UNBLEMISHED CHARACTER THROUGH LIFE AS THE SOLDIER, CITIZEN, AND FRIEND, DIED IN THIS CITY, AFTER A SHORT ILLNESS, UNIVERSALLY REGRETTED BY HIS ACQUAINTANCES, ON THE 16TH DAY OF SEPT., 1789, AGED 33 YEARS. *the Glorious Field,* *the victors yeild.*

In 1799, Charles Pinckney Sumner sought information as to the tomb from a correspondent in New York. In 1829, at his request, his son Charles visited the yard and wrote, with a rough sketch, an account of its site, condition, and surroundings. Sheriff Sumner caused it, soon after, to be repaired, through the good offices of his friend, Colonel Josiah H. Vose.

Major Sumner's estate was valued at about $12,000. It consisted chiefly of land-warrants, one of which was for forty-six hundred acres, and of securities of the United States and of the State of Georgia, which had risen in value with the adoption of the National Constitution. The most interesting items of the inventory were a Shakspeare in eight volumes, Smith's "Wealth of Nations," "Don Quixote," "Junius," "Adventures of Ferdinand Count Fathom," "Boswell's Tour," "Anecdotes of Dr. Johnson," and a "History of England." Among other books left by him was Lord Chesterfield's "Letters to his Son."

His traits of character appear quite clearly in his son's manuscript records and the traditions of his birthplace. He was a man of genuine courage, adventurous spirit, and capacity for affairs; generous with his money, and faithful in all trusts. He took life merrily, and rejected the severity of the Puritan standards. His love of knowledge was attested in his youth by his seeking a liberal education without the direction of a parent or guardian, and in his manhood by his solicitude for the careful training of his son.

CHAPTER II.

PARENTAGE AND FAMILY. — THE FATHER.

CHARLES PINCKNEY SUMNER, the son of Major Job Sumner, was born in Milton, a suburb of Boston. His name was at first Job, but was afterwards changed to Charles Pinckney by his father, who probably had friendly relations with the South Carolina statesman.[1] The boy passed his early childhood on the farm of the parish sexton, working hard, and attending in winter the public school.[2] He then entered Phillips Academy, Andover, Mass., at that time under the charge of Ebenezer Pemberton, and was placed in the family of Rev. Jonathan French, the minister of the South Parish of that town.

Mr. Pemberton was a graduate of Princeton College. James Madison and Aaron Burr are supposed to have been his pupils. It has been said of him that "no teacher had a higher character for scholarship, manners, elegance, and piety." While of a kindly nature and beloved by his pupils, he maintained discipline and respect for authority after the old style. He died, June 25, 1835, at the age of eighty-nine.[3] Rev. Mr. French was of Braintree nativity. He was, in early life, a soldier and subal-

---

[1] Charles Pinckney Sumner contributed, with the signature of "An Elderly Man," a sketch of Charles Pinckney to the "Patriot and Mercantile Advertiser," March 4, 1828.

[2] On Aug. 15, 1829, he wrote, "I had but little time to enjoy the society of anybody. I scarcely remember the time from my eighth to my twelfth year, when all the summer long I did not perform half the labor of a man in the field from sunrise to nearly sundown, in the long summer days, and after that go every night about a mile, all over the Milton Church land, for the cows."

[3] History of Andover, by Abiel Abbot, Andover, 1829; Allen's American Biographical Dictionary. Edmund Quincy, in his "Life of Josiah Quincy," p. 28, says of Mr. Pemberton: "This gentleman lived till 1836, and was past ninety when he died. I well remember the handsome old man, and the beautiful picture of serene and venerable age which he presented, seeming in old-world courtesy and costume to have stepped out of the last century into this, and the pride with which he spoke of the eminent men who had been his pupils, and especially of his having offered two presidents — Kirkland and Quincy — to Harvard." A sketch of Mr. Pemberton, written by Charles Pinckney Sumner, is printed in the "Daily Advertiser and Patriot," July 15, 1835.

tern officer in the colonial army. While so engaged, he applied himself, in leisure hours, to medical studies. He began to practise as a physician; but, changing his plan of life, he prepared for college, entered Harvard, and, graduating with the class of 1771, became a clergyman. He maintained zealously the patriot cause during the Revolution. Taking with him his gun and surgical instruments, he rode on horseback to Bunker Hill and shared in the battle. While a clergyman, he was accustomed to receive students of the academy into his family. At the suggestion of Washington, when President, Colonel William Augustus Washington sent his two sons, Bushrod and Augustine, to the academy; and Charles Lee also sent the two sons of his deceased brother, Richard Henry Lee. The young Washingtons were received into the family of Rev. Mr. French.[1] Josiah Quincy was, from 1778 to 1786, an inmate of Mr. French's family, while pursuing his studies at the academy under Mr. Pemberton and his predecessor, Dr. Eliphalet Pearson, afterwards Hancock Professor at Harvard College.[2] Mr. French has been commended for his fidelity and success as a Christian teacher. He died, July 28, 1809.[3]

To both Mr. Pemberton and Rev. Mr. French Major Sumner wrote with earnestness concerning the education of his son, laying much stress on his manners as well as his progress in knowledge. To the former he wrote, Aug. 26, 1787: —

" It rests with you, sir, entirely, to form his mind while young, and lead him into the paths of virtue, of education, and good breeding; which will redound to your glory and his felicity. He is now brought into a new line of life, and will probably finish his education under your direction. Do with him, in all respects, as you shall think most proper. . . . I wish the child's manners to be particularly attended to, and that he may see and be introduced to as much company, in the house where he may live and others, as may be consistent with a proper attention to his studies."

The letter also referred to " the army, the law, physic, or merchandise," as the boy's future occupation, to be determined by his capacity and choice. In a letter written in October of the same year to Rev. Mr. French, he enjoined upon him to correct

---

[1] Memoir of Hon. Samuel Phillips, LL.D, by Rev. John L. Taylor. Boston, 1856. pp. 253–256.

[2] Life of Josiah Quincy, by his son, Edmund Quincy, Boston, 1867, p. 26, where an account is given of Mr. French's family life.

[3] Sprague's Annals (Trinitarian and Congregational), Vol. II. pp. 42–48, containing an account by Josiah Quincy. Memorial of Abigail Stearns. Boston, 1859.

Master Charles's " mode of speaking, his spelling, and manner of address," and " to hold frequent discourse of reason with him, and treat him as you would a child of your own."　On Nov. 6, 1787, he wrote from New York, and on July 16, 1788, from Savannah, anxious letters in relation to the funds for the boy's maintenance, which he had expected his friend and debtor, General (afterwards Governor) Brooks, to advance.　Disappointed in this resource, and lamenting his own pecuniary misfortunes, he relied upon a loan from a friend.　But, soon after, the boy was taken from the school.　On Oct. 9, 1788, Major Sumner, then in Boston, wrote to Mr. Pemberton, —

" I like the appearance and improvement of Master Charles, for the short time he has been with you, very much; and am happy to hear you are also pleased with him.　I lament his having been from you so long.　I hope no circumstance in future will prevent his being with you continually.　I desire you would put him into all the studies he is fit for.　I think he had better go into Latin, as though he was designed for college, if you judge this study proper for him.　Whether he will be sent there or not will depend entirely on his disposition for study and your opinion of his genius.　However, for the present, I would have you neglect nothing towards him necessary for a boy so intended.　If he discovers an active, capable mind, I shall either send him there, into a counting-house, or to France for his education, according to his disposition and my ability to support him.　In short, I mean to give him every opportunity to fit him for a gentleman and scholar that he himself is capable of receiving.　To you, sir, I consign him as though he were your son, and beg from my heart you will consider him as such.　On himself will depend his fate.　I hope he will do you honor."

On Dec. 14, 1788, eight months before his death,[1] he wrote from Savannah to his agent in Boston, expressing great pleasure at Charles's return to school, and providing carefully for his future expenses, so that no further interruption might occur in his studies.　In this letter he wrote, —

" Should any thing take place that I should not make you regular remittances, I desire you to call on my friend, General Henry Jackson.　I know he will advance thirty or fifty dollars at any time, after hearing the circumstances, rather than see Charles taken from school.　Remittances are hard to be forwarded from this place, but not the less certain; and all advances made by any friend of mine on this score, I will repay with interest and gratitude.　Give my love to Charles, and tell him I expect he will be a studious, good boy, and learn eloquence and manners, as well as wisdom and the languages, at the academy.　These are the grand pillars of all great objects and great

---

[1] A few months after Major Sumner's death, his brother, Dr. Seth Sumner, was appointed guardian of the boy.

men. I lay great stress on the two first acquirements, because I think them
very essential, and by far the most difficult for Charles to attain."

These letters prove the writer's love of learning, which often
descends with the blood. The patriotism and scholarly tastes of
the soldier, who closed his books to enter his country's service
at the first drum-beat of the Revolution, were to be the inheri-
tance of his illustrious grandson.

The boy remained at Phillips Academy till 1792,[1] studying
Cheever's Latin Accidence, Nepos, Cæsar, and Virgil. Late in
life he visited Andover, and recalled those early days in a letter
to Mrs. Abigail Stearns, the daughter of Rev. Mr. French : —

"I went to Andover a few weeks ago, to look at the places which I began
to know, 28 August, 1787. That was the day, fifty-one years ago, when I first
entered your father's house and became a student at Phillips Academy. How
changed is every thing now! Fifty-one years ago Andover was a pleasant,
noiseless town: now it is a bustling manufacturing village. I saw no old
face that I knew. I looked over and about the land that was once your
father's parsonage. It is now divided into house-lots, and much of it is covered with buildings. The railroad goes close to your native mansion. The
large rock and the grape-vine that were in the garden still remain, but the
garden is no more a garden. There are no currant bushes; nor is that lead-
lined, square box to be found in which your father caught the rain as it fell,
and measured its depth and noted it down in his meteorological table. The
fence of your front yard is entirely gone. Those beautiful elms are cut down,
and no trace of them remains. From the summer of 1787 to that of 1792,
the house, the elms, the woodland (half-way up the road to the academy),
and the fields around, all looked beautiful to my eye. That pump is gone
that stood in the low ground of the common, between your house and the
meeting-house. How often have I seen your mother, your brother, and your
sister go by that pump or near it, in your orderly walk together on the Sabbath, to and from the meeting-house!"[2]

Charles Pinckney Sumner entered Harvard College in 1792,
and graduated in 1796. The members of his class who became
most widely known were Dr. James Jackson, the eminent physician, who survived till 1867 ; Rev. Dr. Leonard Woods; and
John Pickering.[3] His college quarterly-bills, including board

[1] A medal which was awarded him in 1789 is preserved.

[2] Josiah Quincy, on the occasion of the death, in December, 1858, of Mrs. Stearns, whose
senior he was by four years, gave pleasant reminiscences of her childhood, and of his residence in Mr. French's family in his boyhood. "Memorial of Madam Abigail Stearns, with
Funeral Discourses of Rev. Samuel Sewall, and of her son, Rev. Jonathan F. Stearns."
Boston, 1859.

[3] Charles Sumner's tributes to Mr. Pickering are well known. "Biographical Sketch
of the late John Pickering," Works, Vol. I. p. 214; "The Scholar (Mr. Pickering), the
Jurist, the Artist, the Philanthropist," Works Vol. I. p. 241.

in commons and tuition, varied from twenty-eight to thirty-six dollars.

In college his compositions were largely poetical. Among his themes of this kind were, " Non omnia possumus omnes," " Winter," and a " Dialogue between Churchill the Warrior and Churchill the Poet." At the end of his Junior year, he delivered before the Speaking Club a valedictory poem, on the occasion of his classmates leaving it. At the exhibition in September, 1795, his part was a poem, entitled " The Compass," which was printed in a pamphlet. It contains these lines : —

> " More true inspir'd, we antedate the time
> When futile war shall cease thro' every clime;
> No sanction'd slavery Afric's sons degrade,
> But equal rights shall equal earth pervade." [1]

When his class had completed their studies, he delivered (June 21, 1796) a valedictory poem in the College Chapel, in the presence of the officers and students, in which his muse, after the style of such performances, recognized gratefully the instructions of President Willard and Professors Tappan, Pearson, and Webber.

His part at Commencement was a poem on " Time." Two years later, he delivered a poem before the Phi Beta Kappa Society. This taste for versification lasted during most of his life. He wrote many odes for the anniversaries of benevolent societies, and for patriotic or festive occasions, and New-Year's addresses for the carriers of newspapers.

One of his best passages in verse is the following, given as a sentiment at the Doric Hall of the State House, July 4, 1826: " The United States, one and indivisible ! "

> " Firm, like the oak, may our blest Union rise;
> No less distinguished for its strength than size;
> The unequal branches emulous unite,
> To shield and grace the trunk's majestic height;
> Through long succeeding years and centuries live,
> No vigor losing from the aid they give." [2]

It was then the fashion for aspiring youth to attempt verses after the style of Pope's grave and sonorous periods. But there

---

[1] As a grateful acknowledgment of this poem, his college friends presented him with copies of Shakspeare and Young's " Night Thoughts."

[2] This is quoted by Charles Sumner at the close of his address, " Are We a Nation," delivered Nov. 19, 1867: Works, Vol. XII. p. 249.

was little of genuine inspiration in American poetry prior to the period which gave to it Bryant, Longfellow, Whittier, Holmes, and Lowell.

Leaving college, young Sumner accepted the place of an assistant in the Billerica Academy, of which his former teacher, Mr. Pemberton, had become the principal. While here he received a playful letter from his classmate, Leonard Woods, then at Cambridge, who had been enlivening his theological studies, which he had pursued at Princeton, with the reading of "Don Quixote," "Cecilia," and other novels; Shakspeare, Ossian, Pope, and the "Spectator;" and 'admiring "Belfield" in "Cecilia," and "the character of Sancho, Esq." Remaining at Billerica but a short time, he obtained, through the influence of Rev. Dr. Freeman and Colonel Samuel Swan, of Dorchester, a place as assistant in the private school of Rev. Henry Ware at Hingham, on a salary of £150, with special reference to the instruction of two lads, one of whom was John Codman, afterwards the pastor of the second church in Dorchester.

An intimate friendship had grown up in college between Sumner and Joseph Story, of Marblehead, who was two years his junior in the course. A correspondence ensued. Their letters are playful, and hopeful of the future. Sumner's letters refer to books and poems he had read, as "Hogarth Moralized," Roberts' "Epistle to a Young Gentleman on leaving Eton School," Masson's "Elegy to a Young Nobleman leaving the University," Pope's "Eloisa to Abelard," Goldsmith's "Edwin and Angelina," Shenstone's "Pastoral Ballad," and some pieces in Enfield's "Speaker."

Sumner did not persevere as a teacher. In 1797–98 he passed nearly a year in the West Indies. He then began the study of law with Judge George R. Minot, an historical writer and effective public speaker. As early as 1799 he accepted an invitation from Josiah Quincy to a desk in his law-office; and was, while the relation continued, accustomed to have charge of the office, and to sleep in Mr. Quincy's house on Pearl Street during his absences from the State.

Mr. Quincy was soon absorbed in politics, as a leader of the Federal party, and severed his active connection with the profession; but he remained the friend of his pupil, notwithstanding their differences in politics, which made sharp divisions in society in those days. Mr. Sumner, in company with Richard Sullivan and Holder Slocum, was proposed as an attorney in the Court of Common Pleas in Boston, at the April Term, 1801 (May 7); and admitted to practice at the July Term (July 11), before Chief Justice Shearjashub Bourne and his associates, William Dennison and Samuel Cooper. His office was at one time on Court Street, at number ten and a half, on the north side; and later at number ninety, according to the numbers of that period.

For some time in 1802–3 he was at the South, attending to business which grew out of his father's estate. He remained three months at Savannah, in the early part of 1803, and was present at trials in which John M. Berrien, then a young man, won his first distinction.

He delivered, Feb. 22, 1800, when twenty-four years of age, a eulogy on Washington, then recently deceased. The occasion was a commemorative service at Milton, his native town, where he spoke upon the invitation of the selectmen. Pieces of music were performed, and a prayer was offered by Rev. Joseph McKean. The eulogy was printed, at the request of the selectmen and other citizens.

The following passages are specimens : —

" Americans! what a vast weight of your revolution did this mighty man sustain! Taxes were indeed great, were burdensome; but think how often your army was obliged to evade a decisive blow; think of the complicated hardships they endured (the relation of which might make you shudder) because the flame of public spirit too soon died away, and the resources of the country had become inaccessible. What must Washington have often felt! Every eye in America, in wondering, doubtful Europe, was fixed on him. He was a man of humanity; not a sentinel felt a grievance he did not painfully commiserate. He was a man of consummate bravery; and, to add to the full measure of his calamity, the country, whose fate was hourly in his hand, began to murmur, to reproach him with delay. Delicate situation! Unconquerable greatness of soul! His reputation, dearer to a soldier than life, he sacrificed to your good. . . .

" For a life devoted to your service, what does Washington deserve ? The rising trophied column shall from far attract the admiring eye. The enduring statue, with emulative care, will present to revering posterity his august attitude and awful form. History shall be immortal, as just to his worth. Poesy shall robe him in unborrowed charms. A city, after the majestic model of his mind, bearing his name, shall concentrate our national glory, as he does our affection. These a grateful empire will voluntarily pay; but he deserves more : he deserves that you be faithful to yourselves, that you be free, united, and happy; that party asperity from this memorable day subside; and all, with liberal eye, seek private interest in the common weal."

Mr. Sumner did not become actively interested in politics till 1803, near the close of Mr. Jefferson's first administration.[1] The antagonism between the Federal party, which opposed Mr. Jefferson, and the Republican or Democratic party, which sustained him, was at its height. The Federalists, as a minority, had departed from the traditions of Washington's administration, and to a great degree had become the partisans of State sovereignty and a New England confederacy. These notions repelled the sympathies of many who had borne their name, and led to the secession of John Quincy Adams from the party.

Mr. Sumner's first political address was delivered at Milton, March 5, 1804. It was a plea for the integrity of the Union, for a common love of all its sections, for faith in popular government, and for confidence in the national administration, and in Mr. Jefferson, its head. The young orator said : —

"And has it come to this, that the Union must be dissolved ? Because a particular set of men cannot engross the government, must there be no government at all ? Shall party attachments supersede national allegiance ? Shall State jealousies be summoned from the dead to overthrow the magnificent structure of the Union, which we have fondly hoped to see founded on their tomb?"

On July 4, 1808, he delivered an address in the Third Baptist Meeting-house in Boston. It was an earnest defence of Mr. Jefferson's administration, and a protest against any national alliance with England against France, which the Federal party was charged with favoring. It rebuked, with great emphasis, sectional jealousies : —

"There is, indeed, no diversity of interest between the people of the North and the people of the South; and *they* are no friends to either who endeavor to stimulate and embitter the one against the other. What if the sons of Massachusetts rank high on the roll of Revolutionary fame ? The wisdom and heroism for which they have been distinguished will never permit them to indulge an inglorious boast. The independence and liberty we possess are the result of ' joint councils and joint efforts, of common dangers, sufferings,

---

[1] Letter of Charles Pinckney Sumner, published Aug. 29, 1811, in the "Commercial Gazette," Boston, dated Aug. 23, 1811, replying to the charge that he is an "apostate." This letter was copied in the "National Intelligencer." In another letter he denied having been at any time a member of "a Jacobin club."

and successes;' and God forbid that those who have every motive of sympathy and interest to act in concert should ever become the prey of petty bickerings among themselves!"

In a similar spirit he wrote, in 1812: —

"De Witt Clinton, I fear, will be the advocate for State sovereignty and State supremacy more than any President we have yet had. If so, and he should be President from March 3, 1813, to March 3, 1817, we shall be far advanced on the road to confusion by the time his administration expires. The Federal party seems to be disposed to erect New England into a separate government. But where would be the boundaries of this fragment of our continent? What will be the benefit of a separation? Would not this fragment soon be split into other fragments; and if the process of separation is begun, where will it end?"

Mr. Sumner's public efforts belong to the least interesting period of American literature, the first quarter of the present century. It followed the generation which was illustrated by the orators and writers of the Revolution, and the authors of the " Federalist;" and it preceded the demonstration of Mr. Webster's marvellous forensic powers. It was an interval in which political speeches and writings showed little originality of thought, depth of feeling, or terseness and vigor of expression. There was a manifest effort to use words of Latin derivation, and to elaborate lengthened and swelling periods, after the style of Johnson and Gibbon. Letter-writing, too, had the same defects. The correspondence of friends had the stateliness of a page of history.

Mr. Sumner enjoyed the confidence of his party. He was chosen Clerk of the House of Representatives of Massachusetts, for the years 1806–7, and 1810–11. The last two years he was associated with his college friend, Joseph Story, who was the Speaker. Story, on resigning the office, soon after his appointment as Judge of the Supreme Court of the United States, wrote him a letter, stating it to be his last official act, and expressing his "perfect conviction of the ability, the correctness, and impartiality with which you have discharged the important duties of your office." In 1808, he desired Mr. Sumner to become the editor of a Republican newspaper in Boston, and pressed his excellent qualifications for the position. In 1815, Mr. Sumner urged Judge Story to deliver a series of law lectures in Boston, but the judge declined, for the reason that the Royall Professorship was about to be established at Cambridge, and a course, delivered by himself, would be considered to be in competition with it.

Mr. Sumner's earnestness and activity as a partisan were confined to this early period of his life. When he became sheriff, he ceased to exert political influence, or to cherish any strong preference for one party over another. After that he seldom voted, and did not sympathize with the partisan bitterness of the day. His favorite notion, for the rest of his life, was that it was the duty of a good citizen to speak well of, and to sustain, the powers that be.

He was admitted, in 1803, into the Society of the Cincinnati, as the successor of his father.

Mr. Sumner was married, April 25, 1810, to Relief Jacob, of Hanover. They had formed an acquaintance while both were boarding with Captain Adams Bailey, on South-Russell Street. Miss Jacob, at the time of her marriage, was living with Shepard Simonds, on the corner of May (Revere) and South-Russell Streets. She had, since leaving Hanover, been earning her livelihood with her needle, upon work received at her room. Crossing the street from the Simonds house, they were married by Justice Robert Gardner, in their new home, a frame house which they had hired, situated at the West End, on the southeast corner of May (Revere) and Buttolph (Irving) Streets, occupying a part of what is now the site of the Bowdoin schoolhouse. Here eight of their children, all but the youngest, Julia, were born. Mr. Sumner occupied this house, as a tenant, till 1825, or early in 1826, when, soon after his appointment as sheriff, he hired number sixty-three (then fifty-three) Hancock Street, opposite the site of the Reservoir. In 1830, he purchased number twenty Hancock Street, which was occupied at the time by Rev. Edward Beecher. He removed to this house in November, and resided in it during the rest of his life. The family retained the estate until it was sold, in 1867, to Judge Thomas Russell.

Mr. Sumner was a well-read lawyer. His memorandum-books, which are preserved, contain, in his handwriting, copies of the rules of court, forms of pleading, references to authorities on various points of law and practice, and careful digests of law in different branches, showing him to have been faithful and painstaking in his profession. But he did not, for some reason, succeed in it. His mind lacked, perhaps, the vigor and aggressiveness which qualify for forensic controversies, or even the aptitude for affairs which is needed in office business. His professional work was mainly the collection of bills, and these rarely of large amounts. He appears, as early as 1808, to have desired some official post, with a view to increasing his revenues.

In 1819, he left the bar to become a deputy-sheriff, a transition which then subjected a lawyer to less comment than it would now. He was impressed with his inability to increase his professional income, so as to educate his children, then five in number. His condition of health, as he stated at the time, advised a less sedentary occupation than he had been following. To Josiah Quincy, whom he called his "master," he wrote an apologetic note, stating his proposed change of life. William Minot, and other members of the bar who knew his worth, volunteered to be his sureties. The revenues of his office proved to be less than a thousand dollars a year. In 1823, he declined the office of City Marshal, tendered him by Mr. Quincy, then Mayor.

In 1825, his affairs took a favorable turn. On Sept. 6, by appointment of Governor Levi Lincoln, he became sheriff of Suffolk County; succeeding Joseph Hall, who had been appointed Judge of Probate. This office he continued to hold till April 11, 1839, thirteen days before his death. His first commission was during pleasure. Under a later statute, which fixed a term of five years for the office, he was reappointed by Governor Lincoln, March 14, 1831, and afterwards by Governor Edward Everett, March 23, 1836. To relieve them from fancied embarrassment, he at different times volunteered a resignation, which they declined to accept. The letters and action of Governor Everett, particularly at the time of the Sheriff's last appointment, which met with some opposition, are highly creditable to him. They show how careful the Governor was, in his consideration of personal questions, not to do injustice to any one.

The office of sheriff, to which is attached the custody of the jail, brought Mr. Sumner an annual revenue varying from $2,000 to $3,000, and once or twice considerably exceeding the larger sum. With this assured income he had, in 1828, accumulated $17,000; in 1830, $27,000; and at his decease, in 1839, his property was valued at nearly $50,000. The office enabled him to give his son Charles a liberal education. He always entertained

the liveliest gratitude to Governor Lincoln, accounting him, in
a letter to him, Jan. 21, 1834, his "greatest earthly benefactor,"
as, without his favor, he "should not probably have sent a son
to college." Governor Lincoln answered, as he retired from
office, in terms appreciative of the sheriff's personal and official
character.

The sheriff's sureties, on his official bond, were William
Sullivan, William Minot, Samuel Hubbard, William Prescott,
John Heard, Jr., Timothy Fuller, and Asaph Churchill. These
well known names show his high standing in the confidence of
the community.

Mr. Sumner's home life, which before his appointment as
sheriff had been regulated with severe economy, was now more
generously maintained. Twice a year, at the opening of the
Supreme Judicial Court, he gave a dinner to the judges, the
chaplain, and members of the bar and other gentlemen. He
gathered, on these festive occasions, such guests as Chief Justices
Parker and Shaw, Judges Prescott, Putnam, Wilde, Morton,
Hubbard, Thacher, Simmons, Solicitor General Davis, Governor
Lincoln, Josiah Quincy, John Pickering, Harrison Gray Otis,
William Minot, Timothy Fuller, Samuel E. Sewall; and, among
the clergy, Gardiner, Tuckerman, Greenwood, Pierpont, and Lyman Beecher. His son Charles, and his son's classmates, Hopkinson and Browne, were, once at least, among the youngest
guests. He gave a dinner, in 1831, to surviving classmates; at
which were present Pickering, Jackson, Thacher, Mason, and
Dixwell.

He made the duties and history of his office the subject of
elaborate research. He read to the bar, and published in the
"American Jurist," July, 1829, a learned exposition of the
points of difference between the office in England and in Massachusetts, stating clearly its duties in each jurisdiction, and giving
sketches of his predecessors in office. No sheriff in this country,
probably, has ever pursued studies of this kind to the same
extent.

An incident, which illustrates his professional learning and
his independence of character, may be fitly given here.

In 1829, the Supreme Court of the Commonwealth held that
an officer serving a writ, which directs him to attach the property of the defendant, may be resisted, as a trespasser, by another
party, whose goods he undertakes to seize, honestly but errone-

ously supposing them to be the defendant's.[1] The decision
imposed on executive officers a serious responsibility, and subjected them to personal peril. The sheriff regarded it as contrary
to the precedents and policy of the law, and as depriving the
officer of the protection to which he is entitled. So earnest
were his convictions, that he did what would now hardly be
thought deferential to the court. Besides communicating the
decision to the sheriffs of other counties, with strong terms of
disapproval, he addressed to Chief Justice Parker and his associates, before the printing of the opinion, an elaborate argument
in writing, supported by a review of the English authorities and
by reasons of public policy, with the view to obtain a recon-
sideration of the doctrine as held by the court. He failed to
convince the judges; but his conclusion is in accord with the
later authorities in other States, where it is held that the true
owner, whose property an officer in good faith undertakes to
seize, with a process against another, cannot lawfully obstruct
or assault the officer, but must resort to a writ of replevin, or
other civil remedy.[2]

Sheriff Sumner performed his duties with scrupulous fidelity
and exactness. His fearlessness was remarked on the occasion
of the riot in Broad Street, June 11, 1837, between the Irish and
an engine company, when under the statute it became his duty
to read the riot act. In the latter part of his life the perplexities of his office annoyed him. He was too formal and punctilious, too reserved, and too little pliant to the ways of men to
please the general public. His last appointment drew out some
opposition, but his sterling worth overcame it.

He participated in the controversy concerning Masonry, which
was carried on with greater or less zeal during the decade of
1825–35. He co-operated with the leading opponents of the
order in the State, — John Quincy Adams, Pliny Merrick, Benjamin F. Hallett, Henry Gassett, and Amasa Walker. He had
been himself initiated, about 1799, when quite a young man, and
had become a master-mason in 1802. A year later he was the
eulogist of the order, in a poem and an address before the Grand
Lodge of the State. In 1806, however, he discontinued his attendance on its meetings. In 1829, he renounced his connection

---

[1] Commonwealth *v.* Kennard, 8 Pickering's Reports, p. 133.

[2] State *v.* Donner, 8 Vermont Reports, 424; State *v.* Buchanan, 17 *id.* 573; State *v.* Fifield,
18 New Hampshire Reports, 34; Faris *v.* State, 3 Ohio State Reports, 159.

with it. The same year, he wrote a paper on "Speculative Free-Masonry," in the form of a letter to gentlemen who had solicited his views. It was published as a pamphlet, and provoked against him much hostility and many newspaper attacks. The memorandum-books left by him show his sustained earnestness in the question. One of them was appropriated exclusively to his thoughts upon it from time to time. He attributed to his connection with this controversy some unkind treatment which he received.

Sheriff Sumner, while not participating publicly in the abolition movement, was always an antislavery man. His forecast discerned the conflict in which his son was to bear his great part. Tradition and his papers give abundant evidence of his opinions on this subject.

About 1820, in a conversation relating to slavery, he said to a neighbor: " Our children's heads will some day be broken on a cannon-ball on this question." At another time, rebuking the social aversion to the negro, he said he should be entirely willing to sit on the bench with a negro judge ; and when complaint was made of the presence in the schools, of children with colored blood, he protested that there was no objection to such association. He recorded himself against the law which prohibited the intermarriage of the two races. He saluted colored persons on the street with his customary bow, and made special efforts in behalf of prisoners of this class, to enable them to procure the witnesses for their defence. He wrote in the album of the daughter of his friend, Colonel Josiah H. Vose, Cowper's familiar lines, beginning with, —

" I would not have a slave to till my ground."

At one time he wrote: " The South will say, in less than one hundred years, ' Who shall deliver us from the body of this death?' " His memorandum-books contain numerous passages showing his sympathy with the antislavery movement. At one time he recorded his conviction that Congress ought to abolish slavery in the District of Columbia. He denounced the proslavery riots which took place in Boston, New York, Philadelphia, and Alton. Indeed, there was no topic on which he was more thoughtful and earnest.

His relation to an attempted reclamation of some fugitive slaves deserves a record. On July 30, 1836, two colored women, alleged to be slaves, were held on board a brig in Boston Harbor, by one Turner, the agent of a Maryland slaveholder, with the intent to carry them to that State. On that day, a writ of *habeas corpus* was granted, at the instance of some philanthropic persons. A deputy-sheriff served the writ on the master of the vessel, and took the women into custody. They were brought into court, and the legality of their detention was heard on August 1. A large number of people, chiefly colored, were in attendance. Chief Justice Shaw, after hearing the affidavits, remarked that the captain had not sufficient authority to detain the women. At this stage of the proceedings, before any formal order of discharge had been given, and while the claimant was preparing other papers in order to obtain a new process for their detention, the counsel of the petitioners, Samuel E. Sewall, said to the women that they were discharged. The colored people present at once made a rush; and, in spite of the officers, carried off the women, who were pursued as far as Framingham, where all traces of them were lost. They were not recovered. The Chief Justice was displeased with the premature announcement of the discharge and the breach of decorum. The conduct of the sheriff, who was not present, but was at the time engaged in attendance on the Municipal Court, was called in question by the newspaper press of the city, then much in sympathy with the enforcement of the Fugitive Act of 1793.[1] He had previously offered the deputy in charge of the process to undertake himself the duty; but the offer being declined, he did not concern himself further with the matter, and went to the Municipal Court. He seems to have been in no official default, even on the theory that his duties were the same as in the custody of a party accused of crime. He was charged with having, out of sympathy with the alleged slaves, intentionally neglected to provide an adequate force, and with expressing that sympathy to Mr. Sewall in the remark that he wished him success in his cause. In his published letter of vindication, he thus answers this last accusation: "Whether I addressed Mr. Sewall, as it is said, I cannot tell; but I should be ashamed of myself if I did not wish that every person claimed as a slave might be proved to be a freeman, which is the purport of the words attributed to me." The sheriff, in consequence of the adverse expressions of opinion on his action,

---

[1] Evening Transcript, Aug. 3 and 13, 1836; Evening Gazette, Aug. 6, 1836; Morning Post, Aug. 5, 1836; Centinel and Gazette, Aug. 15, 1836.

tendered his resignation to Governor Everett, who declined to accept it.

To George T. Davis, of Greenfield, then editor of the " Franklin Mercury," he wrote a note of thanks for an article in that paper, Aug. 9, 1836, which had " served as a breakwater to turn aside the strong tide of reproach, which, for a few days, had been setting against him ; " in which he said, —

" It seems to me as if there were some persons in Boston who would have been gratified to see those women (after being liberated from one unlawful detention) seized in the court-house, in the presence of the judge, and confined till proof could be sent for to Baltimore, and from thence be sent to Boston, to make them slaves. I hope the walls of a Massachusetts court-house will never be the witnesses of such a spectacle. What would the late Judge Sedgwick have said, if a human being had been seized in his presence, in the court-house, while he was on the bench, for the purpose of having him sentenced and certified as a slave? Though dead, he yet lives and speaks in the opinion he gave in the case of Greenwood v. Curtis, 6 Mass. Rep. 362–378 n."

It is interesting to note, in Sheriff Sumner's correspondence, how nearly alike were the questions of 1833 and those of 1861, between the government and slavery. His relative, Edwin V. Sumner, a lieutenant of the regular army in 1833, and a major-general of volunteers in the Civil War, wrote to him from Fort Niagara, Jan. 11, 1833, —

" What think you of the nullifiers? Our affairs begin to assume a very gloomy appearance in that quarter. If South Carolina stood alone, there would be less cause of apprehension; but is there not every reason to fear that it will result in a controversy between North and South? We are ready at this post to move instantly; but we hope and trust that the difficulty will be quietly and happily adjusted without an interruption."

The sheriff replied, under date of Feb. 3, regretting that he could not call his country "a nation," enforcing the need of a government of greater strength and uniformity of pressure and of less regard for State lines, and expressing his fear that, " in an emergency, its authority will be aided but little by the militia south of the Potomac ; and that Virginia, North and South Carolina, Georgia, Florida, and Alabama will sooner or later unite and bid defiance to the North." He added : " In the course of this year, 1833, I trust we are to see whether we are a nation or a confederacy." He had before this, Jan. 20, 1830, written to Mr. Webster, acknowledging the receipt of a copy of his speech

on Foote's resolution, saying that "the debate will be noticed in
the history of our Union; and in that history you will appear as
a man fulfilling the duty of your station, faithful to your country
and to your own character."

Sheriff Sumner was in favor of a strong government both for
the nation and the State. He was greatly disturbed by the mobs
which were frequent in American cities from 1834 to 1838, and
which usually grew out of Slavery, religious antipathies, or
criminal trials; and he insisted often on a more vigorous police.

As early as 1830, he took an active interest in the temperance
question;[1] and, in the years immediately succeeding, delivered
lectures, in which he enforced the duty of sobriety.[2] He favored
the restrictive legislation of 1837–38, and insisted on the immor-
ality of licensing the sale of ardent spirits.

He promoted the improvement of public schools. In 1818,
when there were only five such schools in Boston, and these were
crowded, he published several newspaper articles, in which he
urged additional schools and an increase in the number of teachers for each.[3]

Sheriff Sumner attended, in his early manhood, the services
of the Protestant Episcopal Church, at Trinity Church, of which
Rev. Dr. Gardiner was the rector. He was at one time the
clerk; and, after the English style, had an elevated seat near
the chancel, from which he made responses. About 1825, he
began to attend at King's Chapel (Unitarian), of which Rev.
F. W. P. Greenwood was the pastor. Here the family retained
their pew till the death of his widow, in 1866. His religious
belief was quite indefinite. He was indulgent to all shades of
doctrine. He welcomed the Catholics when there were few in
Boston. Once he discontinued a newspaper, on account of its
attacks upon them. His feelings were strongly excited by the
destruction of the Ursuline Convent at Charlestown by a mob, in
August, 1834; and he sent thirty dollars, the amount he had
received for a special official service, to Bishop Fenwick, to be
used in aid of the sufferers. While disinclined to attend public
dinners, he accepted an invitation to attend one given by the
Irish Charitable Society, in 1830, at the Exchange Coffee-House,
on St. Patrick's Day. When called on to respond to a sentiment,

1 Article on exclusion of bars from theatres, in "Commercial Gazette," Nov. 8, 1830.
2 At Holliston, May 4, 1831; Boston, June 2, 1833.
3 Boston Yankee, May 15, June 11 and 18, July 2, 9, and 23.

he paid a tribute to Lord Baltimore, the founder of Maryland. His reply is a specimen of his efforts on such occasions : —

" There is a name that was of great note between one and two hundred years ago, which does not seem to be remembered in this part of our country with sufficient respect. I mean the name of Calvert, Lord Baltimore, the founder of Maryland. He was a worthy son of Ireland, and an ornament of the age in which he lived. He was a Catholic and a statesman. As governor of Maryland, he received with open arms all who came to him suffering from the hand of religious intolerance. He studied the things that made for peace, and used his authority to inspire his followers with the love of it, always acting upon that maxim of political wisdom, — ' By agreement a colony may rise to greatness; while by dissension an empire must come to nothing.' Sir, I offer a sentiment dear to my heart, — Respect to the name of Calvert."

He observed with scrupulous exactness the rules of good breeding, and taught them to his children. His thought on this subject was embodied in a sentiment which he gave, in August, 1827, at the customary public-school festival, in Faneuil Hall, — " Good learning and good manners; two good companions. Happy when they meet, they ought never to part."

Sheriff Sumner was a scholarly man for his time. He read history like a student, using charts and writing out in memorandum-books tables of events in English and American history. He had a fancy for collating those which had occurred in different periods on the same day. He also noted down current events in war and diplomacy, and applied to them historical precedents. He transcribed choice extracts from English and Latin authors. His diligence in these respects was remarkable. His public addresses and newspaper articles, and also his letters to friends and his conversation — though in no respect brilliant or epigrammatic — were carefully worded, every sentence well weighed and spoken, or written out in his fair, clerkly hand. He took pains to lead his son Charles and his other children to the studies which he had himself pursued, teaching them, as their minds developed, to love history and all knowledge. Other homes enjoyed more of luxury; but his was enriched at least with the atmosphere of culture.

He was rigidly conscientious in his dealings with his fellow-men. His fidelity to trust, even in the smallest items, was never doubted. It was easy for him to procure, among his neighbors, the best sureties on his official bond, although his known integrity, rather than his acquired property, was the guarantee of his trustworthiness. He was genuine in character, and would not consent to receive any undeserved consideration. In early life he declined invitations, the acceptance of which might imply a claim to a social position higher than he held, and even went out of his way by quaint methods to prevent any impression that his household life was more luxurious than it really was. His conviction that equal justice was due to all, without favor to any, was strong; and when a near relative, for whom he had the tenderest regard, had violated the law, and he was desired to intervene in his behalf, he answered, with Roman firmness, "The law must take its course." He applied the same high standard to corporate and public affairs as to private life. In October, 1837, during the suspension of specie payments, he moved, as a stockholder of the State Bank, that no dividends be paid till its bills were redeemable in specie. The motion was lost, but he recorded his determination to renew it the next year.

Sheriff Sumner's health was feeble in his later years. He became quite ill early in January, 1839, and after that month was confined to his house. He resigned his office, March 14. Governor Everett delayed action, hoping for his recovery; but relieved him, April 11, by the appointment of Joseph Eveleth as his successor. The judges of the Supreme Judicial Court, by a formal letter, drawn by Chief Justice Shaw, gratefully recognized his uniform kindness and attention during his administration. He died, April 24, at the age of sixty-three, the period which he had often designated as his probable end. In length of life, he and his son Charles differed less than one month.

His will, signed a few days before his death, after gifts to some of his children, to equalize advances to others, bequeathed a life-estate in his house, on Hancock Street, to his wife, and the fee equally to his children; and the residue of his property to her, for her own disposal, adding these words: —

"I have made the foregoing devises and bequests to my wife, confiding in her disposition to carry into effect my wishes, and in her affection for our children, and that she will, from time to time, and finally by her last will, make such disposition of the property given her as justice and the condition of the children shall require." This trust was faithfully administered, and the estate more than doubled in value during the period which intervened between his death and hers.

Sheriff Sumner was very formal in his manners and punctilious in etiquette, not only in public, but in his family. In salutations he was somewhat excessive, bowing low, touching his mouth with his hand, and waving it back to his side. He was reserved to a marked degree, and was rarely seen in public to smile, at least in his later years. He had during his life, but more towards its close, a grave and sombre tone of mind. His rigid and cheerless nature was not one which makes a happy home. He was loyal to ancient friends, and grateful to those who had in any way befriended him; but he did not mingle easily with men to whom he was not allied by any tie of kin or early association. From natural kindness, and not from a desire to win favor, he was accustomed, in letters and personal greetings, to say pleasant things, in the way of compliment, to those whom he respected. His *conscientiousness*, — his fixedness of purpose in doing his duty, as he understood it, no matter what others might say or think, — was the prominent trait of his character. With this was associated love of learning, of social order, and of good morals. If he was wanting in the lighter moods, he had the sterling qualities which children respect and imitate. If he was not himself great, he had in him elements of character which are essential to greatness.

In person he was of average height, five feet and eight or nine inches. He was slender in form, and not well favored in countenance. No portrait of him is preserved.[1]

THE MOTHER.

Mrs. Sumner was a woman of excellent sense, and of unusual skill in domestic economies. By her own toil, and the prudent management of the household, she succeeded, even before he became sheriff, in keeping the family expenses within the income of her husband. In the care of the estate and the nurture of the children, after his decease, she justified the confidence which his will placed in her. She was equable, even imperturbable, in her temperament. She survived her husband twenty-seven years, and all her children, save Charles and Julia. She was the constant nurse, night as well as day, of three daughters, during wasting

[1] The papers left by Sheriff Sumner are the chief sources of this sketch. Information has been sought from those who knew him, and "The Hundred Boston Orators," by James S. Loring, has been consulted.

disease which ended in death, and of her son Charles, during a severe illness in 1844.   Her early education was that of the common-school only.   She found little time for liberal studies during the season when maternal cares pressed heavily upon her, although encouraging them in her children; but her good sense and native understanding always insured her the respect of the best people.

One will observe the larger space which is almost always given to the father of any subject of biography.   The life of the man is various, illustrated by adventure and incident; while the life of the woman is in her home, monotonous and undistinguished.   She may have had, by force of her innate qualities or her nurture, an equal or greater share in the character and fortunes of her child, but the story of her life will be briefly told : —

> " Her lot to bear, to nurse, to rear,
>   To love, — and then to lose."

In person, Mrs. Sumner was tall and slender.   She enjoyed health and cheerful spirits during her prolonged life.   She died, June 15, 1866, at the age of eighty-one.

BROTHERS AND SISTERS.

Sheriff Sumner had nine children.   Of these, Charles and *Matilda*, twin brother and sister, were the eldest.   She died, March 6, 1832, of consumption, after a year's sickness, at the age of twenty-one.

Albert was born, Aug. 31, 1812; passed through a regular course in the public schools, and served some time in a counting-room.   He sailed, at the age of seventeen, from New Bedford for the Pacific, on a whaling voyage, which lasted three years; and afterwards, as mate or captain in different ships, for South America and Europe.   He retired from maritime service on his marriage, in 1840, to the widow of Thomas Barclay, of New York, and from that time resided in New York and Newport. He had a fine presence, cultivated the habits and tastes of a gentleman, and gave a generous welcome to friends at his fireside and table.   He met an untimely fate in 1856.   With his wife and their only daughter, Catharine, a girl of fourteen years, for whose health the journey was planned, he sailed, Nov. 1,

from New York for Havre, in the French steamer "Lyonnais."
On the following day, near midnight, she was disabled by
a collision with the bark "Adriatic," of Belfast, Me., bound
for Savannah, when some sixty miles off the Nantucket light.
The day after the collision, the passengers and crew left the ship,
in the midst of a storm, for the boats and a raft. Of the one
hundred and fifty persons on board, eighteen only were saved,
two of whom floating on a raft and sixteen in a life-boat were
picked up a week after. Captain Sumner and his family had
entered another boat, which was seen the day after and then
disappeared in a fog.

It appears to have been established that the mother and child
died first, and that the father inherited their property. Mrs.
Sumner's estate thus descended to the heirs of her husband, —
his mother and surviving brothers, Charles and George, and his
sister Julia. The Sumners surrendered voluntarily, and without
the assertion of an adverse claim, to the heirs of Albert's wife
all her property ; and the Barclays certified in a formal letter
to George Sumner, the administrator of Albert, that "the Barclays had no legal claim to the property, and this fact was known
both to yourself and to the other heirs-at-law. Such conduct
merits the esteem and approbation of every honorable man."

Henry was born, Nov. 22, 1814, and died in South Orange,
N. J., May 5, 1852. He received a mercantile education, travelled in the Southern States, and visited the West Indies and
South America. In 1838, he held for a few months the office
of deputy-sheriff, by his father's appointment.

George was born, Feb. 5, 1817, and died, Oct. 6, 1863. He
was trained in the public schools and a counting-house. He developed in his youth the spirit of adventure ; and, at the age of
twenty-one, sailed as the supercargo of a ship for Russia, where
he received many civilities from the Czar Nicholas and his
court. From this time until 1852, he travelled, without the
interval of any visit to his country, in the East and in Europe ;
studying languages, politics, and institutions, observing with rare
diligence contemporary events, and profiting by a large acquaintance with scholars and public men. He made Paris his home,
and knew French affairs well, — better, probably, than most
Frenchmen. He was commended both by Tocqueville and Alexander von Humboldt for his intelligence and researches. During
his residence abroad, he contributed to foreign reviews, and also

to American periodicals and newspapers. His themes concerned history, philanthropy, and the existing state of nations, including affairs in the East. After his return to this country, he was, for some years, an acceptable lecturer before lyceums in the Western as well as Eastern States. On July 4, 1859, he delivered the oration before the municipal authorities of Boston, taking for his topic the services rendered by Spain to the United States during our Revolution. Some of his friends and relatives, and particularly his brother Charles, regretted that he tarried so long in Europe, and desired him rather to concentrate his mind on some definite literary work or occupation.[1]

Jane was born, April 28, 1820, and died, Oct. 7, 1837. She did not recover from a typhoid fever, which seized her two years before her death, and afterwards was afflicted with a spinal disease. Her delicate conscientiousness and religious thoughtfulness appear in a paper, written at the age of sixteen, in which she recorded a severe self-examination. Her father wrote of her: "She was tall, well proportioned and graceful, intelligent and discreet. Her light was clear and cheering. She was never impatient or irritated She was well informed for one of her years. She understood English well, and had some knowledge of Latin and French. She was tolerably proficient in music, and could sing and play well. She could dance well, and walk with strength, agility, and grace. But whatever were her accomplishments, goodness was her chief characteristic; and this, at all times, beamed forth from her clear, dark-colored, benignant eyes."

Mary was born, April 28, 1822, and died, Oct. 11, 1844. She was a lovely character, and in person the fairest among the daughters. Her disease was pulmonary. She was the darling sister of her brother Charles, whose grief at her wasting sickness and death later pages will record.

Horace was born, Dec. 25, 1824, and was lost, July 19, 1850, in the wreck of the ship "Elizabeth," on Fire Island, near New York. At two in the afternoon he left the ship to swim ashore, and was not seen again. The Marchioness Ossoli, *née* Margaret Fuller, perished in the same disaster. Horace, for some time an invalid, was returning from a voyage to Italy, which had been undertaken for his health. He was a gentle, unaspiring youth,

---

[1] A sketch of George Sumner may be found in Allibone's "Dictionary of English Literature."

not marked by any strong qualities, and with less intellectual vigor than the other children. He was placed on a farm for his health, and was at one time with the Brook-Farm Community, a well-known fraternity of social reformers. It was remarkable that two brothers, not at the time sea-faring men, should end their lives in different shipwrecks.[1]

Julia was born, May 5, 1827, and died, May 29, 1876; the last survivor of the nine children, and the only one who outlived Charles. She married, in 1854, Dr. John Hastings, of San Francisco. Her children, Alice, Edith, and Julia, are the only living issue of Charles Pinckney Sumner. She was an invalid for many years. She was beloved for her sweetness of nature and her true womanliness. Her last visit to the Atlantic States was in 1862, and her ill-health did not permit her to make a later one. She visited Washington at that time. Charles accompanied her to New York, and parted with her at the steamer, as she sailed on her return. " I shall never forget," she afterwards wrote, " his tender care at that time. My last sight of him was standing on the wharf as the steamer moved off."

---

[1] For a detailed account of the shipwreck, see "Memoir of Margaret Fuller Ossoli," by R. W. Emerson, W. H. Channing, and J. F. Clarke, Vol. II. pp. 341–351.

CHAPTER III.

BIRTH AND EARLY EDUCATION. — 1811-26.

CHARLES and Matilda, the eldest and twin children of Charles Pinckney and Relief Sumner, were born in Boston, Jan. 6, 1811. Their birthplace was the frame-house on the south-east corner of Revere (then May) and Irving (then But-tolph) Streets, the site of which is now occupied by the rear part of the Bowdoin Schoolhouse. The neighbors, who took a kindly interest in the event, remember that they weighed, at the time of birth, only three and a half pounds each, and were not dressed for some days. At first, the tiny babes gave little promise of living many hours ; but, surviving the first struggle for existence, they soon began to thrive. The boy was retained by his mother, and the girl was provided with another nurse. The parents re-joiced in their first-born. To the father, whose heart was full of gladness, it seemed as if the whole town knew his good fortune as soon as he knew it himself. Indeed, children, as they came one after the other, were always welcomed in that household.

Charles was first taught in a private infant school, kept by his maternal aunt, Miss Hannah R. Jacob, in the upper room of his father's house. Perry's and Webster's Spelling Books and the "Child's Assistant" were then the primary school-books. It is not likely that he remained at his aunt's school when he was older than six or seven. For some time before his admission to the Latin School he attended the West Writing-School, afterwards known as the Mayhew School, which was kept in a building now used as a stable, at the corner of Hawkins and Chardon streets. Not only writing but the other common English branches were taught in the school. Benjamin Holt, who lived to an advanced age, was the master in the writing department, and Hall J. Kelley in the reading. James Robinson, of Cambridge, who died in 1877, was an usher. Charles is remembered by persons still living as large for his age, amiable and quiet, and maturer than most of the other scholars. The boys liked him, and even those older than himself looked up to him. He was taught writing before entering the Latin School, by a well-known master of the art, Elmer Valentine, whose rooms were at 3 Cornhill Square, now known as Joy's Building. From him, Feb. 17, 1821, he received a merit-card, handsomely executed in pen-and-ink.

The father, deeming it necessary to prepare his son as soon as might be to earn his livelihood and assist in the support of the family, intended to have him taught in the English branches only, and not in Latin and Greek. The boy, however, with a kind of instinct for classical culture, bought, with some coppers he had saved, a Latin Grammar and " Liber Primus " of an older boy, who had no further use for them. He studied them privately out of school, and one morning surprised his father by appearing with the books, and showing his ability to recite from them. His father, impressed perhaps by this incident, decided to put him in the classical course provided by the public schools.[1]

Charles, having passed the required examination, was admitted with his next younger brother, Albert, as a member of the Boston Latin School, near the close of August, 1821. This public school, and the private academies at Exeter, N. H., and Andover, Mass., have for a long time maintained a high repute both as to quality of instruction and lists of pupils eminent in all professions.[2] The Latin School was, from 1821–26, under the charge of Benjamin A. Gould as head-master, and Jonathan Greely Stevenson and Frederick P. Leverett, his assistants. Joseph Palmer, the necrologist of Harvard College, and for many years connected with the " Boston Advertiser," was an usher. Mr. Leverett, the author of an excellent Latin Lexicon, was the teacher whose thorough drill added much to the character of the school at that time. Charles continued his attendance at Mr. Valentine's writing school until December of the next year.[3]

The course at the Latin School was then one of five years, and the school was divided into five classes, according to the years of study. Each class was distributed into three divisions, gener-

---

[1] Mr. Sumner, in September, 1854, related this incident in presence of some friends, one of whom was Richard H. Dana, Jr.

[2] The centennial anniversary of the re-opening of the Latin School, after the evacuation of Boston by the British, was celebrated by a reunion, Nov. 8, 1876.

[3] His father recorded in his almanac, Sept. 17, 1821, " Charles and Albert began at Mr. Valentine's again, from 11 to 1; " on July 3, 1822, " Exhibition at Mr. Valentine's; " and, on Dec. 17, 1822, " Paid Mr. Elmer Valentine, and withdrew Charles and Albert."

ally with some reference to proficiency in the appointed studies. Charles and his brother and their kinsman, William H. Simmons, belonged to the third or lowest division. The class had forty-five members the first year; but three years later it had only twenty-nine. While he was in the school, there were in older classes Robert C. Winthrop, George S. Hillard, George T. Bigelow, James Freeman Clarke, and Samuel F. Smith; and in the succeeding one, Wendell Phillips.

The curriculum at the Latin School comprehended more than was then or is now required for admission to Harvard College. It included, in Latin, Adam's " Latin Grammar," " Liber Primus," " Epitome Historiæ Græcæ " (Siretz), " Viri Romæ," " Phædri Fabulæ," " Cornelius Nepos," Ovid's " Metamorphoses," Sallust's " Catiline " and " Jugurthine War," Cæsar, Virgil, Cicero's " Select Orations," the " Agricola " and " Germania " of Tacitus, and the " Odes " and " Epodes " of Horace. In Greek, it included Valpy's " Greek Grammar," the " Delectus Sententiarum Græcarum," Jacob's " Greek Reader," the " Four Gospels," and two books of Homer's " Iliad." Tooke's " Pantheon of the Heathen Gods " introduced the pupil to mythology. In arithmetic, Lacroix was used; and in reading, Lindley Murray's " English Reader." [1]

In 1824, Charles won a third prize for a translation from Ovid, and a second prize for a translation from Sallust; and, in 1826, second prizes for a Latin hexameter poem and an English theme. He received, for the two prizes last named, an English edition of Gibbon's History in twelve volumes. A *detur*, awarded to him, Feb. 1, 1823, probably as a recognition of good conduct and attention to studies, is preserved, running thus : —

" Scholæ Latinæ in Aula.

Detur Carolo Sumner.

Juveni ingenuo atque laude digniori.

Qui cupit [2] optatam cursu contingere metam,
Multa tulit fecitque puer."

Some of his attempts at Latin poetry, at this time, are preserved, — two hexameters, one of June 26, 1825, *Ad Inferos*

---

[1] On the fly-leaf of many of his text-books which he used in the Latin School and in College he wrote the motto, " *Me jure tenet.*"

[2] Qui studet, &c., Ars Poet. 412.

Orpheos descensus, and the other of January, 1826, *Hectoris mors,* and an ode of June 15, 1826, *Ad ver,* in eight verses.

While at the Latin School, he did not distance the greater number of the pupils in the prescribed course; but his general knowledge and occasional efforts in composition, as well as fair standing in recitations, insured him a respectable rank as a scholar. He gave no promise of a remarkable career; and yet both teachers and pupils respected his qualities of mind and his disposition.

The exhibition, or annual visitation, of the Latin and other schools at the close of the five-years' course, in 1826, took place Wednesday, Aug. 23. The occasion, at the Latin School, was graced by distinguished guests, — John Quincy Adams, then President of the United States, Nicholas Biddle, the President of the Bank of the United States, Leverett Saltonstall, of Salem, and Admiral Sir Isaac Coffin, a native of Boston and an officer in the British navy. The sixth part — not a prominent one — was "A Discussion on the Comparative Merits of the Present Age and the Age of Chivalry. — C. Sumner and H. W. Sargent."

Six scholars, of whom Charles was one, each received a Franklin medal. His is still preserved, with the same blue ribbon which was then attached to it. In the afternoon, there was the customary dinner at Faneuil Hall, attended by the mayor, Josiah Quincy, the distinguished guests, the school-committee, and four hundred and fifty other city officers. The scholars who had been on that day decorated with the medals also attended. President Adams, who had since his father's recent death abstained from participation in festivities, made the occasion an exception. He was present at the dinner, and spoke with his usual energy and aptness. After a tribute to the worthies of Massachusetts in other days, and a reference to the recent commemoration of the lives of Adams and Jefferson, he closed his inspiring speech with the sentiment, "The blooming youth! May the maturity of the fruit equal the promise of the blossom!" His wish was to be fulfilled in at least one of the scholars who heard him.

On August 2, three weeks before these festivities, Daniel Webster delivered, at Faneuil Hall, his oration on Adams and Jefferson. Early in the morning of that day, the young men of Boston, having formed in procession at the State House, went to the First Church in Chauncy Place, where, with solemn services, they commemorated the deceased ex-Presidents. The scholars of the Latin School were assigned a place in the procession. At a later hour, Faneuil Hall was not large enough to contain the multitude which pressed for admission. Charles at length forced his way in, just in time to hear the imagined speech of John Adams in favor of the Declaration of Independence, which, according to the newspapers of the day, was the most impressive passage of the oration. Never has a youth, when passing from one interesting period of study to another, had a more precious opportunity than was enjoyed by this boy of fifteen, who was then fortunate enough to listen to such orators as Daniel Webster and John Quincy Adams.

One who was in the same division of his class relates an incident which illustrates his acquisitions and tastes at this time:

" He was not always attentive to his studies at school; that is, to the specially appointed lessons in Latin, Greek, and mathematics. For the first two years of our course we studied nothing whatever but Latin and Greek. But we boys felt the superiority of his mind and education, though we could get above him, at times, in school rank. I used to look at him with wonder as I heard him talk on subjects I knew nothing of. The first I ever learned of the *Labarum* of the Romans was from a discussion he had, in common talk, with one of his mates. He had a full sense of his knowledge, yet he never obtruded it upon his fellows, or showed any self-conceit. When we had been less than two years in the school, he fell into a dispute one day, in the middle of the class exercises, with an ill-natured teacher, who undertook to put him down for ignorance on some point of geography, — a branch not studied in the school, or made the subject of examination on admission. Sumner, then about eleven years of age, replied, with spirit, that he could answer any question which the teacher might put to him. The teacher bethought himself a moment, and, going to his table, and looking up what he esteemed a difficulty, asked him where *Cumana* was. The boy replied instantly, with a full and correct answer; and no further question was asked."

Other pupils at the school do not recall any characteristics, as distinguishing him from his fellows.

He was a thoughtful, studious youth, always fond of reading. His mother, in later life, often spoke of this trait of his boyhood. He enjoyed history most of all, reading it not in an easy, careless way, but with earnest attention, sitting on a low seat, and with maps spread out before him. When fourteen years of age, he wrote a compendium of English history, from Cæsar's conquest to 1801, which filled a manuscript-book of eighty-six pages.

The penmanship is elaborate in the early part, but less careful towards the end. The events are succinctly narrated, in good English, and dates are given, with the year and often with the month and day. With a boy's humor he begins with this title: "A Chronological Compendium of English History, by Charles Sumner. Copyright secured. Boston, 1825." This abstract, probably begun at his father's suggestion, was a discipline in composition and study, which prepared the way for larger acquisitions. In 1826, when fifteen years old, he read Gibbon's History, copying at the same time the extracts which pleased him. Some of these he re-copied into a commonplace-book, which he began in his Senior year in college. His inquisitive mind sought knowledge as well in conversation as in books; and he plied with many questions travelled persons, and his father's friends who had served as army officers in the unsettled territory of the West. This trait survived boyhood, and he always listened well to those who could tell him aught worthy of note that they had seen or heard.

As a boy he was little given to sports. It is remembered that he was rarely seen playing with his mates. He was not addicted to games. Once he was sent, with his twin sister and his brother Albert, to a dancing-school, but while enjoying well enough the sight of others engaged in the pastime, he had no fancy for sharing in it himself, and soon ceased to attend. Other boys of the same school met out of school hours, on playgrounds or at their father's houses, but he was seen chiefly at the school. Swimming was the sport which he enjoyed most.

While thoughtful and somewhat reserved, he was in no respect severe or unsympathetic. He was liked by his fellows, relished fun in a quiet way, and laughed heartily at a good story. He was never vulgar or profane. His æsthetic as well as his moral nature repelled indecency and irreverence. Soon after he entered the Latin School, a classmate of rather diminutive size was attempting a juvenile oath, when Charles called the attention of the boys and turned the laugh on him, by saying, with a comical expression of face, "Hear little ——. He says 'damn.'" The rebuke sufficed.

His features were at this time strongly marked, and were less attractive than in later years. He was slender and tall. He did not carry himself easily, and, as the phrase is, did not know what to do with his limbs. It was the habit of the boys in the Latin School to give nicknames to each other, significant of something in their appearance or ways, by which they were uniformly called, without however intending or giving offence. One was applied to him, as expressive of his awkwardness.

His growth was rapid, and his constitution rather delicate than robust; but his only illness in early life occurred when he was six years old. The fare of the family table was quite simple, but Charles was entirely content with it.

Boston, which with its growth in space and numbers is now a city of nearly 350,000 inhabitants,[1] contained in Sumner's early boyhood only about 40,000. It retained its town organization until 1822, its citizens electing selectmen and voting upon municipal affairs in Faneuil Hall. Within its limits, then quite narrow, were many open spaces, now covered by warehouses and dwellings. Ample gardens were spread out on streets since lined with blocks. Families most regarded for lineage and wealth lived near the Common and the State House, and also on Fort Hill, which after being deserted by this class was levelled in 1871, and is now a thoroughfare of business. Copp's Hill, the North End, and the West End were inhabited generally by citizens who enjoyed a competency or were raised above poverty by their earnings. The suburbs were occupied by villages and large farms, with estates here and there of merchants who drove daily to their counting-rooms in Boston.

The people were generally primitive in their mode of living. A few were moderately rich, but equality of condition was the general feature of society. The streets were not as yet filled with the metropolitan life which one now meets in them. The town was more like a large village than a city. It combined the advantages of a well-appointed community, but its character was that of repose rather than rapid movement. One was humble, indeed, not to be personally known to most of his fellow-citizens. Harvard College diffused an atmosphere of culture among a people distinguished for a traditional love of learning. Charles's father, being a lawyer and liberally educated, ranked with the intelligent class, but he had not the fortune to place him in the more exclusive society. He had also separated himself from the political party which attracted the wealth and culture of New England. Among such a people,

---

[1] The suburban cities of Cambridge and Chelsea together contain, in addition, nearly 70,000 inhabitants.

and with such surroundings, the boyhood of Charles Sumner was passed.

The boy's life was not wholly within the city; he sometimes visited his maternal relatives at South Hingham, where, with others of the family, he was the guest of his mother's uncle. Here he could enjoy the view from Prospect Hill, near by. Once, he and his brother Albert took a long walk, from South Hingham to Nantasket Beach. He was fond of going with the cow-boy for the cattle, at evening, and had a fancy for watching the dairy-work in the kitchen. Later in life, he spoke with interest of these early days. His surviving kinsfolk recall him, on these visits, as fond of reading, well behaved, helpful in doing chores, and never mischievous. He made visits also to his father's relatives in the district of Dorchester, now comprehended in Hyde Park.

His father did not expect to send him to college until after the last year of his five-years' course at the Latin School had begun. With his limited means, he had designed him for some occupation in which he could earn his livelihood sooner than in one of the learned professions. Charles had desired a cadetship at West Point, but no way opened for admission to the National Military Academy.[1] The father began inquiries in relation to the "American Literary, Scientific, and Military Academy," under the charge of Captain Alden Partridge, which was first established at Norwich, Vt., and had recently been removed to Middletown, Conn. The school was conducted on a military system, and enrolled cadets from nineteen States. In 1829 it was discontinued, and the present Wesleyan University was established on its site. The father's letter to Captain Partridge gives an interesting description of his son: —

BOSTON, 15 August, 1825.

SIR, — I have read the prospectus which you issued, in 1821, at Norwich, and I have recently read a notice, in the "Palladium," that you wish to *employ* some lads in your institution at Middletown.

I have a son, named Charles Sumner, in his fifteenth year, and large of his age, but not of so firm and solid a constitution as I should wish to have him.

---

[1] Charles Pinckney Sumner, in a letter to Colonel Sylvanus Thayer, commanding at West Point, dated July 14, 1829, in which he introduces his son, says: "It was once my son's wish to become a member of your institution, but I perceived it to be a hopeless undertaking to procure his admission." The thought of a military education was probably prompted by the circumstance that a relative, Edwin V. Sumner, and a friend of the family, Josiah H. Vose, were of the regular army.

He has no immoral practices or propensities known to me; he has acquired a pretty good knowledge of Latin and Greek; understands the fundamental rules of arithmetic, and has a superficial knowledge of the whole. He is well acquainted with geography and history, both ancient and modern; in fine, he has been four years at the public Latin School in Boston, sustaining a good standing in the class, which will be qualified for admission at Cambridge college in 1826, for which I do not design him. The life of a scholar would be too sedentary and inactive for him.

I have eight children, of whom this boy is the oldest, to all of whom I wish to give a useful, but not what is commonly called a learned, education. My means enable me only to think of usefulness. I wish him to learn all of agriculture, arithmetic, and book-keeping he conveniently can by a year's attendance, service, and study at your institution; also something, and as much as you think proper, in the elements of soldiership. I wish him, if convenient, to hold his own in Latin and Greek; and to make some progress in the preliminary branches of mathematics. And, if consistent with rules applicable to lads of humble acquirements and standing, I wish he may be admitted to hear your instructions on ancient and modern warfare, your comparison between the phalanx and the legion, and some of those orations and lectures that I heard you deliver, a few winters since, in Boston, to silent, instructed, and delighted auditories. His knowledge of geography and history is sufficiently extensive and minute to give him a relish for such ennobling instruction and entertainment. I think I should like to send him about the first of September; but, Sir, if I send him at all, it must be on a footing of those who seek *employment*, according to that notice of yours which I have recently read. And I wish to know, before you see him, on what terms he would probably be received, and to what employment he would probably be put that would be serviceable to you and not disagreeable to his feelings; feelings that do not incline him to become improperly a burden on you or on me, or to ordinary menial services that would injure him in the estimation of those lads who are now his associates, among whom he is destined to earn his living, and, I hope, to sustain a respectable rank.

The notice I have above alluded to has seemed to me to lay you open to such inquiries as I have thus taken the liberty to make. I do not expect you to descend to minutiæ in your reply. I shall be content with the shortest answer that it will čomport with your continually usefully occupied time to make; and, as it is my affair more than yours, I request that your answer, if it shall be found consistent and agreeable to send one, may not be postpaid.

The above is in the handwriting of my son. I will only add that I am, Sir,

Your respectful and obedient servant and well-wisher,

CHARLES P. SUMNER,

A Deputy-sheriff of Suffolk.

ALDEN PARTRIDGE, Esquire.

The father's plan for the education of his son, who entered heartily into it, was changed by the improvement in his own fortunes which took place three weeks after his letter to Captain Partridge. On Sept. 6, he was appointed Sheriff of Suffolk County; an office whose revenues enabled him to dispense with the rigid economy he had hitherto been compelled, with his narrow income and large family, to practise. A few months later he determined upon a college-course for his son.[1]

At the beginning of September, 1826, Charles entered upon his studies as a member of the Freshman Class of Harvard College. A week later, his father gratefully acknowledged to Mr. Gould, the head-master of the Latin School, the value of the services rendered by its instructors to his son, and particularly those of Mr. Leverett, to whose accuracy, he wrote, Charles had often borne his testimony, and whose faithful attentions he had received during the whole of his five-years' course in the school.

[1] His letter to Governor Lincoln, who appointed him, attributed to this appointment his ability to send his son to college. *Ante*, p. 22.

NOTE. — Since this chapter was stereotyped, there has been found among the files of the War Department a letter of Charles Pinckney Sumner to the Secretary of War, dated Nov. 22, 1825, in which he applies for a cadetship for his son Charles at West Point. This letter shows that the father's purpose to send his son to college was not formed immediately after his appointment as sheriff. The interesting part of the letter (in which he gives Mr. Webster and Judge Story as his own references) is as follows: —

"My oldest son, Charles Sumner, is desirous of being admitted a member of the Military Academy at West Point. He will be fifteen years old in January next. He is of a good constitution and in good health, although unusually studious. He is well acquainted with Latin and Greek; is somewhat acquainted with arithmetic and algebra, and French. He is exceedingly well acquainted with history and geography, both ancient and modern. He knows the scenes of many of the distinguished battles of ancient and modern times, and the characters of the heroes who figured in them. He has a strong sense of patriotic pride, and a devotion to the welfare and glory of his country. He is now at the Latin School in Boston, and in August next will be qualified to enter the University at Cambridge. He prefers the Academy at West Point."

CHAPTER IV.

COLLEGE LIFE. — SEPTEMBER, 1826, TO SEPTEMBER, 1830. — AGE, 15–19.

SUMNER began his studies as a Freshman at Harvard College, Sept. 1, 1826.[1] Its undergraduates, now increased to more than eight hundred, numbered at that period not quite two hundred. Rev. John T. Kirkland was the president. Among the professors were Edward T. Channing in rhetoric, George Ticknor in French and Spanish literature, John S. Popkin in Greek, George Otis in Latin, Levi Hedge in logic and metaphysics, and John Farrar in mathematics and natural philosophy. Francis Sales[2] was the instructor in French and Spanish, and Charles Follen in German and the civil law. Of the corps of teachers then in service, none survive. In 1829, Josiah Quincy succeeded Dr. Kirkland in the presidency of the college.

Sumner occupied, in his Freshman year, the room numbered 17 Hollis Hall; in his Sophomore and Junior years, 12 Stoughton; and in his Senior, 23 Holworthy. This last room, of which the ceiling has since been raised, is situated in the fourth story, and contains two dormitories and one study-room. Holworthy had superior accommodations, and was at that time reserved chiefly for Seniors. The classmates with whom he associated most were John W. Browne, of Salem, his chum in the Sophomore and Senior years; Jonathan F. Stearns, of Bedford, his chum in the Freshman year; Thomas Hopkinson, of New Sharon, Me.; and Charlemagne Tower, of Paris, N. Y. Of these, only Stearns and Tower survive.

Browne studied law, opening an office in Salem, and afterwards removing to Boston. His mind and character were of an original cast, and he made a strong impression on the friends who knew

---

[1] A letter of his father, written to him a few days after, admonished him as to behavior and associates, and recalled Professor Pearson's warning to each Freshman class of his time at his first meeting with it, of "*Procul o, procul este, profani.*"

[2] Mr. Sumner, some years later, was active in promoting a subscription for the benefit of Mr. Sales.

him well. Sumner was in closer intimacy with him at this
period than with any other companion, and felt the spell of his
peculiar character and temperament.

" Of all my classmates," said Sumner, in a tribute to him at the time of
his death, in 1860, "I think he gave in college the largest promise of future
eminence; mingled, however, with uncertainty whether the waywardness of
genius might not betray him. None then imagined that the fiery nature,
nursed upon the study of Byron, and delighting always to talk of his poetry
and life, would be tamed to the modest ways which he afterwards adopted.
The danger seemed to be, that, like his prototype, he would break loose from
social life, and follow the bent of lawless ambition, or at least, plunge with
passion into the strifes of the world. His earnestness at this time bordered
on violence, and in all his opinions he was a partisan. But he was already
thinker as well as reader, and expressed himself with accuracy and sententious force. Voice harmonizes with character, and his was too apt to be
ungentle and loud. They who have known him only latterly will be surprised at this glimpse of him in early life. A change so complete in sentiment,
manner, and voice as took place in him, I have never known. It seemed like
one of those instances in Christian story, where the man of violence is soft-
ened suddenly into a saintly character. I do not exaggerate in the least. So
much have I been impressed by it at times, that I could hardly believe in his
personal identity, and I have recalled the good Fra Cristoforo, in the exquisite
romance of Manzoni, to prove that the simplest life of unostentatious goodness may succeed a youth hot with passion of all kinds." [1]

Stearns was the grandson of Rev. Jonathan French, of Andover, whose care for Sumner's father as a boy has already been
mentioned. Formerly a clergyman in Newburyport, he is now
the pastor of a Presbyterian church in Newark, N. J. He took
high rank in college, and has fulfilled his early promise.

Hopkinson received the highest honors in the class. He was
as a student quite mature, and was older than most of his classmates. He practised law in Lowell, became a judge of the Court
of Common Pleas, and was afterwards president of the Boston
and Worcester Railroad Corporation. He died in 1856.

Tower practised law for a time, and then diverged from the
profession. He removed to Pottsville, Pa., and has been identified with the management of railroads.

Sumner was one of the youngest members of his class. With
the advantage of the thorough discipline of the Latin School, he
took rank among its best classical scholars. He excelled in
translations, and entered into the spirit of the authors so sympa-

[1] Works, Vol. V. pp. 236–239.

thetically that their best passages became fixed in his memory, and were ever after available for use. His facility in remembering and quoting choice extracts — too great, perhaps — was thus early developed. He stood among the best in forensics.

In history and *belles lettres* he was also among the foremost. An illustration of his industry in this department may here be given. The students attending Professor Ticknor's lectures were each provided with a printed syllabus of leading dates and events. Sumner attended, in his Sophomore year, the French course, beginning Jan. 21, and ending March 22, 1828. After each lecture, he wrote out from brief memoranda full notes, to which he added an index, the whole filling a book of one hundred and fifty pages.[1] The lectures are reported with such clearness and fulness, and such fidelity to the instructor's style, that they might be now read with advantage to a class. Professor Ticknor, hearing of the notes, requested Sumner's father to send them to him. On returning them, July 7, 1828, he wrote: "I return your son's notes, with many thanks. They have gratified me very much, for I am always pleased when I find a student disposed to get as much out of me as he can. If your son continues as diligent as he has been, he will go far in the ways of reputation and success." The student was encouraged by the teacher's praise, and his taste for Continental literature was stimulated at this early period by the instructions of this accomplished scholar.

But while succeeding in these branches, he entirely failed in mathematics. He had no faculty for the science, and he became disheartened and disgusted with the study. The elective system had not then been introduced, and there was no escape from the prescribed course. He is reported by one classmate to have said that he had not cut the leaves of some of the text-books in this department.[2] His difficulty extended, of course, more or less, to applied mathematics under whatever name. With downright frankness he said, one day, in the recitation-room, to the professor who was pursuing him with questions, "I don't know; you know I don't pretend to know any thing about mathematics." Quickly, but good-humoredly, the professor replied, getting the laugh on the pupil, "Sumner! Mathematics! mathe-

---

[1] His memorandum-book, and also his copy of the syllabus of the lectures on Spanish literature with his pencil interlineations of the lecturer's points, are preserved.

[2] Dec. 27, 1829, he wrote to Stearns, who was then teaching at Weymouth, "Browne went home and escaped the mathematical examination. *That* I attended. All I can say about myself is, *gratia Deo,* I escaped with life."

matics! Don't you know the difference? This is not *mathematics*. This is *physics*." His failure in mathematics lowered
very much his general standing, and excluded any hope of successful competition for the higher parts. If, when entering college, he aspired, as there is reason to believe, to high rank in his
class, he soon gave up any ambition of this kind. He studied
well such text-books as he liked, neglecting the rest. If he did
not outrank others in the appointed studies, he had no rival in
his devotion to miscellaneous literature. He delighted in Scott's
novels, but most of all in Shakspeare, from whom he was perpetually quoting in conversation and letters. No student of his
class, when he left college, had read as widely. His memory,
both of thought and language, was remarkable; and he imitated
with ease an author's style. Most of Sumner's classmates do not
appear to have anticipated for him more than ordinary success
in life; but those who knew him best were impressed with his
love of books, and with something in his tone and manner which
gave assurance that he would "make his mark in the world."
This feeling grew stronger near the end of his college course,
and particularly after the announcement of his successful competition for a Bowdoin prize.

Early in his Senior [1] year he provided himself with a commonplace-book. He copied into it extracts from authors and condensed statements of their narrations or opinions. The larger
number are from the " Retrospective Review," a London magazine, first issued in 1820, and devoted chiefly to early English
literature. Some are from Sir John Beaumont's Elegy on the
" Lady Marquesse of Winchester," printed in Chalmers's " English Poets ; " Massinger's " Fatal Dowry ; " Marston's " Antonio
and Mellida," and " What You Will ; " Sir Thomas Browne's
" Vulgar and Common Errors ; " Butler's " Reminiscences ; "
Southey's " Book of the Church ; " Scott's " Stories taken from
Scottish History," and his " Life of Swift ; " and Bulwer's " Paul
Clifford." He enjoyed at this time the old English writers, particularly the dramatists. He wrote in his commonplace-book
brief sketches (drawing the material chiefly from the " Retro-
spective Review ") of Owen Feltham, John Marston, James
Howell, Thomas Fuller, Sir John Suckling, and Robert South.

---

[1] In his Senior year (Sept. 26, 1829), he gave to the College library a copy of Homer,
printed in 1531, the first of a series of contributions which ended with his bequest of one-half
of his estate and his library and autographs.

The notice of the autobiography of Jerome Cardan, in the "Retrospective Review," specially interested him. Some of the extracts from these authors reappear in his subsequent writings and speeches. One from Beaumont, copied March 16, 1830, was applied to the Mt. Auburn Cemetery, in his tribute to Judge Story.[1] One from Marston —

> " O, a faire cause stands firme and will abide.
> Legions of angels fight upon her side!" —

was introduced, Aug. 22, 1848, in his speech in Faneuil Hall.[2]

On March 8, 1830, he wrote thus of the "Old English Writers:" —

" I admire the old English authors. In them is to be found the pure well of English undefiled. There is a richness of expression with them to which we moderns are strangers; but, above all, there is a force and directness which constitute their chief merit. They are copious without being diffuse, and concise without being obscure. They had not then learned — or, if they had learned, they had not practised — the art of wire-drawing a sentence into a page, and a page into a book. Learning was then confined to fewer than at present, and consequently there must have been fewer authors. There were then no would-be authors, who sprung up like mushrooms, and died as soon. Few attempted to play the part who were not competent to its performance. They did not write till the spirit within forced them to; and when they did, they wrote with all that energy and expansion of thought which sincerity and earnestness could not fail to give. Their illustrations and figures are most striking; there is a simplicity, a grandeur, and, withal, a pertinency, about them which we look for in vain amongst the ' exquisites ' of our ' degenerate days.' Their works are not scattered over with flowers, which only serve to deck and adorn them without adding to their strength or clearness. Their figures rather resemble pillars, which are at once ornaments and supports of the fabric to which they are attached. Witness the beauty and strength of Shakspeare's allusions, and also those of Jeremy Taylor and Bacon. The latter of these comes among the last of those who can be numbered in that iron phalanx which we denominate the ' old English writers.'

" How can we account for this great superiority that they possessed over us in point of real strength and beauty? It was because they depended more upon their own resources; because they thought. Yet many of their works are most curious examples of pedantry, which none of the dullest dogs of our dull days could hope to equal even in this particular. Who has ever produced a work more pedantic and yet more pregnant with sound thought and beautiful allusion than Burton? His ' Anatomy of Melancholy ' is a perfect

---

[1] Works, Vol. I. p. 136. For other extracts from the old English writers in his addresses, see Vol. I. pp. 10, 141, 401; Vol. II. pp. 14, 36, 42, 127.

[2] Orations and Speeches, Boston, 1850, Vol. II. p. 270.

mass of pedantry, yet the genius of the author shines like a bright star through the night which would have obscured a luminary of less magnitude."

On Jan. 15, 1830, he copied several extracts from Carlyle's article on Burns, in the "Edinburgh Review." [1] Not knowing its author, he prefaced his extracts with a note, that in the number "is a most elegant article on the life and character of Robert Burns, the Scotch poet. It is written with a great deal of force and beauty of imagery, and shows a masterly knowledge of the character it is describing."

Sumner allowed himself but little recreation, much preferring his room and his books. He took no part in the sports of the Delta. Cards and chess he played, but not often. Unlike most students with his opportunities, he did not go into society. He seldom took walks during term-time, except, on Saturday, to visit the family in Boston. A classmate (Dr. Jonathan W. Bemis) recalls an excursion made with him in the Freshman year, contrary to the regulations, to the Brighton cattle-fair. The fathers of the two, who also had been classmates, happened to be there together, and met their sons. This colloquy occurred: —

"Why, Charles," said Sumner's father, "how came you here?" "I thought," Charles replied, "that we could leave without detriment to our studies, and could see how things were going on." The fathers advised the sons to return speedily. Sumner's father took young Bemis aside for the moment, and inquired, "How is Charles in mathematics?" "Very good indeed, sir," said young Bemis, unwilling to compromise his classmate. "I'm glad of it," said Mr. Sumner. "He then is doing better than I did; for I let drop the links and lost the chain, and have never been able to take it up again."

Sumner escaped the moral dangers which beset a student's life. He was never profane, and rarely indulged in expletives of any kind. He was kindly to all, and took the best view of the conduct and purposes of others. He was very social, enjoyed pleasantry and good cheer, and was a favorite in his class.[2]

---

[1] Vol. XLVIII. (December, 1828), pp. 267–312.

[2] His classmate, Frost (afterwards a Unitarian clergyman), wrote to him, July 29, 1833, regretting that he had missed him on a recent visit to Cambridge, and lost the opportunity of "drinking in some of the invigorating influences of your buoyant spirits and refreshing sociality." Tower wrote to him, Feb. 3, 1833, "It is an unusual pleasure that one of your letters always calls up in the remembrance of our intercourse. It was always harmonious and rich with innocent enjoyment. And our stolen chats in Farrar's recitation-room. I believe, were about as keen of relish as any in the whole history of classmate pleasures."

He had none of the coarseness and indifference to the feelings of others which boys are apt to have, and was quick to beg pardon when he found that he had unconsciously wounded them. He always relished a happy quotation from an author, suggested by some incident or remark. When the conversation turned one day on Zerah Colburn's precocious powers as a mathematician, he repeated with zest the couplet, —

> " As yet a child, nor yet a fool to fame,
> He lisped in numbers, for the numbers came."

As muscular youths delight in a wrestle, he enjoyed the intellectual exercise of a debate with his friends upon vexed questions in literature and history, and sometimes pressed his view aggressively.

Three of his letters while in college are preserved. They were written in the winter of 1829–30, to his classmate, Stearns, then teaching a school at Weymouth.[1] Two of them relate in a light mood the incidents and gossip of college life; the affairs of the Hasty-Pudding Club; its annual meeting, with the oration and poem; its new catalogue, prepared by a committee of which he was a member; the election of Wendell Phillips as its president; the meetings of " The Nine;" the issue of the new magazine, " The Collegian;" the examination in mathematics; the love-affairs of students; and a trial in which he had heard Samuel Hoar make "a most excellent and ingenious plea." The letter of Dec. 12, 1829, begins with a sentence filling nearly a page, — a parody on the style of Dr. Thomas Brown's " Philosophy of the Human Mind," an abridgment of which, by Professor Hedge, was a text-book for the Senior Class, — and it closes thus : —

" Have told you every thing new in college now. Every thing here is always the same, — the same invariable round of bells and recitations, of diggings and of deads! Mathematics piled on mathematics! Metaphysics murdered and mangled! Prayer-bells after prayer-bells; but, worse than all, commons upon commons! Clean, handsome plates, and poor food! By the way, the commons bell rung fifteen minutes ago. If I don't stop, I shall lose the invaluable meal. Accordingly, adieu.

" CHARLES SUMNER.

---

[1] The letter of Dec. 27, 1829, speaks of his purpose, in company with his classmate, Frost, to make a pedestrian trip to Weymouth. Tower remembers him as wearing in college a " cloak of blue camlet lined with red," and, in a letter written soon after they left college, recalled him as " muffled in his ample camlet."

108009

"N. B. — Spare me! Oh. spare me! *Eheu me miserum!* αἲ αἲ δύστανος ἐγώ!¹ I arrived too late; lost my breakfast; got to University, however, soon enough to be present at one of Follen's lectures. ' This was the unkindest cut of all.' Again, adieu.   C. S."

The third, beginning with an extract from Shakspeare, contains a full narrative of the suicide of a student, who shot himself " about a third of a mile from the colleges, on the Craigie Road, about where the bushes are." It moralizes on the evil courses and fatalistic notions of the young man, and the rather heroic style which he affected in the fatal deed. " There is more of the old Roman in his end than in that of any suicide since the days of Cato. How differently is he now regarded from what he would have been, if he had lived in those days when self-murder was admired and considered the most noble exit from the earthly stage!" These three letters of Sumner, the earliest preserved, do not distinguish his correspondence from that of most undergraduates. The frequent quotations which appear in them are alone suggestive of a habit of his life.

His pertinacity in his opinions and purposes was then a prominent feature of his character. His classmate, Rev. Dr. Samuel M. Emery, says: —

" Sumner was not in the habit of changing his opinions or purposes. He adhered to them as long as he could. If he had an idea that A and B stood the highest of any in the class, nothing could change his opinion except their having the third or fourth part at Commencement. If he appointed a certain evening to go into Boston, he would go even in a violent snow-storm. Being a lover of truth, if he conceived he had reached the truth on any subject, — *e. g.* the slavery question, — he would not yield to the exigency of the times, or to any authority, however high. His persistency in whatever he undertook was immovable. It is well illustrated by an incident which occurred, I believe, in the Sophomore year."

The incident related by Dr. Emery was this: The college rules at this time prescribed an undergraduate's uniform dress; and, as one of the details, a waistcoat of " black-mixed, or black; or, when of cotton or linen fabric, of white." Sumner wore a buff-colored waistcoat, which encountered the observation of the " Parietal Board." He maintained that it was white, or nearly enough so to comply with the rule. He persisted in his position, and was summoned several times to appear for disobedience; but to no purpose. The Board, wearied with the con-

¹ Soph. Oed. Tyr. 1307, 1308.

troversy, at length yielded.   Other classmates do not recall
the incident; but Dr. Emery is corroborated by a memorandum
on Sumner's college-bill for the first term of his Junior year,
— "admonition for illegal dress."

He, however, in general conformed gracefully to the college
régime, and rarely encountered the criticism of the administration.   He was regular in attendance on recitations; and during
his first year he was observant of the rule which required the
students to be present at daily worship in the chapel, though
afterwards somewhat negligent in this respect.

His college bills did not exceed the average bills of his class.
Including instruction, board in commons, rent and care of room,
fuel, use of class-books, and other fees, they amounted for the
four years to less than eight hundred dollars, which is now quite
a moderate expenditure for a single year.   These were carefully
filed at the time, and preserved by him.

In his Sophomore year (May 13, 1828), eighteen members of
the class received *deturs;* but his name is not among them.

At the Junior exhibition (April 28, 1829), Frost, Andrews,
and Sumner were assigned parts in a Greek dialogue, respectively
as mathematician, linguist, and orator.   Sumner was reluctant to
take his part, but yielded to the entreaty of his father, who was
anxious that he should have the good opinion of Mr. Quincy,
recently elected President of the College.   Greek dialogues are
ordinarily mere spectacles on such occasions; the language unin-
telligible to most of the audience, and the thought little regarded
by those who sustain the characters: and this one was no exception to the rule.   Sumner, in maintaining the superior claims of
the orator, was unconsciously somewhat prophetic of his future.
His English translation of the dialogue gives the following as
the reply with which he concluded: "You may both despise my
profession, but I will yet pursue it.   Demosthenes and Pericles,
examples of former days, will be like stars to point out the path-
way to glory; and their glory will always be the object of my
desire."

At the Senior exhibition (May 4, 1830), Bryant, Gardiner,
Kerr, and Sumner had parts in a conference; namely, "A Comparative Estimate of Alexander, Cæsar, Cromwell, and Bonaparte
as Statesmen and Warriors."   Sumner's part is well written and
spirited.   While admitting the selfish ambition of the French
emperor, and his subversion of the liberties of his country, he

insisted that he had exhibited high intellectual power, and had rendered most important services to France. Some years later, his view of Napoleon corresponded more with that which Rev. Dr. William E. Channing set forth in papers published in 1827, 1828. In his part he said, —

" It is too much in fashion to depreciate the abilities and to misrepresent the actions of Napoleon. All the criminalities and missteps of a life of great temptation and power have been raked up against him, while the innumerable benefits he conferred upon his country, and the glorious actions he performed, have all been forgotten. . . . Yet this man, who could lead an army on to victory, organize the government of a great nation, form and digest the Code Napoleon, — this man, whose works are not written upon leaves which can be scattered by the winds, but indelibly stamped on the whole face of Europe and of the age in which he lived, — this man has been denied the possession of high intellectual powers ! "

At the Commencement, Aug. 25, 1830, twenty-four of the forty-eight members of his class were awarded parts. The highest honors were borne by Hopkinson, Stearns, Tower, and Andrews. Sumner's was an inferior part, not equal to his general ability or merits as a scholar, nor what his classmates thought he deserved, but all that his standing in the regular course strictly admitted. He was one of four in a conference on " The Roman Ceremonies, the System of the Druids, the Religion of the Hindoos, and the Superstition of the American Indians." The different systems were set forth in their order by " John Bryant, of Boston, Isaac A. Jewett, of Columbus, Ohio, John B. Kerr, of Talbot County, Md., and Charles Sumner, of Boston." Sumner treated with sympathy and respect the religious belief of the Indians. He wrote on his manuscript that the programme had miscalled the part, which should have been " The Religious Notions of the North American Indians." He seems to have been somewhat sensitive about his part. Anticipating his place on the programme, he had proposed to decline in advance any share in the public exercises of Commencement. His father interfered with an earnest protest against this course. " You have gained," he wrote to his son, May 16, 1830, " credit by the parts you have performed ; and I do not doubt you could sustain your reputation amid any competition. You have never been associated with any but honorable compeers on exhibition days, and the esteem in which the Faculty hold you is to me a source of satisfaction." The next day, his father wrote to President Quincy, expressing the hope that conferences which were usually assigned to students ranking from twenty to thirty in the scale would be hereafter discontinued, for want of time, and as the less interesting performances.

Sixteen of the forty-eight members of Sumner's class were elected into the Phi Beta Kappa Society, half in the Junior and half in the Senior year. The elections required a unanimous vote, and were made by the undergraduates already admitted. A student's rank in his class was considered to give the best title, though the preference was sometimes accorded, on account of general merits, to a student whose rank was somewhat below that of another classmate. Sumner was not one of the sixteen.[1] With his admitted superiority in general literature and the favor which he enjoyed among the students, it is fair to infer that he was not near enough in marks to the first third of his class to justify his election into the society. His place was probably within the first half, but not within the first third. The scales which determined the rank of the students at that time do not now exist.

Sumner belonged to the " Hasty-Pudding Club," — one of the oldest and the most popular of the college clubs. He was initiated, Dec. 18, 1828. He served as a judge in one of its moot courts, held March 19, 1829. On his motion, its first catalogue of past and present members was made and printed ; and he was one of the committee appointed to prepare it. He was, when a Senator, accustomed to send books to its library.

Some of his class, in their Senior year, formed a private society for mutual improvement, keeping even its existence a secret, and calling it " The Nine," from their number. They were Hopkinson, Stearns, Sumner, Browne, Warren, Worcester, Appleton, Carter, and McBurney. They met in each other's rooms, read essays, and each in turn made up a record, generally of an amusing kind, to be read at the next meeting. On Nov. 2, 1829, Sumner read, in 22 Holworthy,[2] an essay on the English Universities of Cambridge and Oxford, which he had just published in a newspaper, with the signature of "Amicus." [3] It is a historical account of their origin and methods of administration and instruction. On the evening of March 1, 1830, he read the

---

1 He was chosen an honorary member at the anniversary meeting of Aug. 31, 1837.

2 Hopkinson's and Carter's room.

3 Independent Chronicle and Boston Patriot, Oct. 29, 31.

record of the previous meeting, which he had prepared. It gives a humorous account of a " bore," who, by his presence, had unconsciously obstructed for a while a meeting of " The Nine ; " and notes the attitude of two members, who lay during the evening on the bed, " like Abelard and Eloisa on their monument."

Sumner competed for the Bowdoin prize in his Senior year, the subject being, " The Present Character of the Inhabitants of New England, as Resulting from the Civil, Literary, and Religious Institutions of the First Settlers." In June, he sent in his dissertation, signed, " A Son of New England ; " and, in August, received the second prize of thirty dollars. The committee of award were John Pickering, George Ticknor, and Rev. John G. Palfrey. The tradition is that Sumner's dissertation suffered in the comparison from its great length. Its style, while well-formed, lacks the felicity of expression and fastidiousness in the choice of language which mark his compositions in mature life. In method, it is manly and serious, never trivial, but wanting in condensation. He was, as a living classmate remarks, too " full of matter." His citations and extracts show that he left nothing unread which could illustrate the subject, and that his reading in English literature was beyond that of most undergraduates. On the whole, the dissertation, while creditable to his industry and thoughtfulness, does not foreshadow a distinguished career as a writer. Although doing justice to the Puritans in many respects, he dwells with some impatience on their narrowness and religious eccentricities.[1] Later in life, when dealing with the great issues of right and duty, he looked with a kindlier eye on even the rugged and imperfect features of their character. Among the many tributes which grateful patriotism has paid to their memory in recent years, none is warmer and more sympathetic than his " Finger-Point from Plymouth Rock." [2]

Two first prizes were given for dissertations on this subject, — one to his classmate Tower, and the other to Benjamin R. Curtis, who was then a member of the Law School, and afterwards became distinguished as a lawyer and judge. In the case of Curtis, more than in Sumner's, the style of manhood agrees with that of

---

[1] Curiously enough, Macaulay's article on "Milton," published in 1825, is referred to in the dissertation, without its author being known, as "the apotheosis of the Puritans in the pages of one of the British journals."

[2] Speech at the Plymouth Festival, Aug. 1, 1853. Works, Vol. III. pp. 269-275.

youth.   The former had been one year out of college, and was advanced in his legal course, — a decided advantage at a period of study when intellectual powers develop rapidly.

The fortunate competitors were required to read their dissertations in the chapel before the students and officers.   Sumner read his in the usual indifferent way, very rapidly, and omitting the greater part.   He invested his prize-money in books, among which were Byron's Poems, the " Pilgrim's Progress," Burton's " Anatomy of Melancholy," Hazlitt's " Select British Poets," and Harvey's " Shakspeare."   The last two were kept during life on his desk or table, ready for use; and the Shakspeare was found open on the day of his death, as he had left it, with his mark between the leaves, at the Third Part of Henry VI., pp. 446, 447.   His pencil had noted the passage, —

> " 'Would I were dead! if God's good will were so :
> For what is in this world, but grief and woe ? "

Some of Sumner's classmates have, since his death, sketched his character as a student.   At an immature period of life one's individuality is only partially developed, and any portrait retained in the mind becomes dim after an interval of nearly half a century.   The subsequent career, too, will to some extent tinge the coloring.   There is, however, a substantial identity in the outlines as drawn by his classmates.

Hon. Samuel T. Worcester, of Nashua, N. H., writes : —

" Though reasonably attentive to his college studies, and rarely absent from the recitations, I do not think that, as an undergraduate, he was distinguished for close application to his college studies.   Having been much better fitted for college, especially in Latin and Greek, than the majority of his class, he continued to maintain a very high rank in both the ancient and modern languages through his whole collegiate course.   He stood, also, very well in elocution, English composition, and the rest of his rhetorical pursuits. In the last year of his college course, he failed in all the more abstruse and difficult mathematics.   His memory was uncommonly retentive; and it was sometimes said of him that he committed to memory, so as to be able to repeat by rote, some of the more difficult problems in mathematics with but little apprehension of their import.   Morally, so far as I have ever heard, his character while a member of college was without reproach.   At the time of entering college, he was quite tall of his age, and rather thin and slender for a youth of his height.   In manner he was somewhat awkward, and at times seemed diffident.   He grew taller as he grew older; and upon graduating, though not then arrived at his full height, he was among the tallest of his class.   Socially, as I remember him, he was amiable and gentlemanly in his intercourse with his classmates, and uniformly respectful to the College Faculty."

Rev. Dr. Samuel M. Emery, of Newburyport, writes: —

"The classes in college at that time, as I suppose is the case still, were divided into divisions alphabetically. Of course, as I was nearer the beginning of the alphabet, I was not in Sumner's sections, except when, for sake of variety, two sections would for a time recite together; and then I could not help noticing that he acquitted himself among the best in his class, especially in construing, reading, and translating Greek and Latin. In mathematics, his recitations were not up to mediocrity. He was so well prepared for college at the Boston Latin School, that the lessons in the classical department were mere boy's play to him; and he would have a perfect lesson with half the study, apparently at least, which most of the class would expend upon it. While he hardly attained average rank in mathematical studies, he was not exceeded in the Greek and Latin classics, in themes and forensics, and in English literature generally, by any in his class. In the Junior and Senior years, public declamations were attended in the chapel, when any of the classes could be present. In his declamations I always noticed a great degree of earnestness, with an entire freedom from any effort to make a *dash*. I looked upon him as one of the best declaimers in the class. It was the same type of subdued eloquence, inseparable from the man, which he has often put forth on real and important actions in his public life.

"Sumner had been accustomed to literary society from his youth, and was brought up among books; so that study was with him a kind of second nature. He never studied, as many young men do, for college honors, but for love of study and for cultivating his mind, — well disciplined and refined at that early age. He was by no means what, in our college days, was denominated a *dig*, — one who has to study from morning till night and bring nothing to pass. He could abstract his mind so as to accomplish in a short time what others would employ hours upon.

"Sumner, having always lived in Boston, and knowing all the boys in the Latin School for a succession of years, had friends in all the classes in college, and his circle of acquaintance was therefore much larger than that of other students who prepared for college in schools remote from the capital. His intercourse with the other classes was as intimate almost as with his own. He was cordial to all, having a kind word for all, and ready for a joke with any one whom he chanced to meet: *e. g.*, he met a classmate the morning after the parts had been announced for exhibition, and congratulated him thus: 'Good morning, I am happy to meet with a man of *parts*.' He was more dignified than most young students, but genial at all times; and would perpetrate a joke with as much gusto as any others of his class. His good taste, if nothing else, kept him from the company of fast young men, from any bad habits, and generally from a disregard of the college rules and the strict proprieties expected of students. I do not remember a single instance of his being called before the Faculty for any impropriety, and only one instance in which the Parietal Board took him in hand; and that was more for a joke on his part than any thing serious.

" In the Junior year I had a room in the same entry with his, — the north entry of Stoughton Hall. Mine was in the second story, and his at the head of the stairs in the third story. Of course, I then saw more of him than at any previous time in the college course. We were often in each other's rooms. He was always engaged in his studies, or more frequently spending his time in general reading; indeed, his greatest pleasure seemed to be found in attending to his favorite studies, — works relating to the humanities or the arts. He was generally ready to play a game of chess, or take a turn at foils, in both which he was sure to come out first. Many a time have I known him to rush down to my room and begin a speech, in which he would introduce quotations from Virgil, Horace, and Juvenal. He had many parts of those authors at his tongue's end, and his quotations from them were always accurate; and, if they were quoted by others, he would detect the least inaccuracy. I recollect accompanying him to an ecclesiastical council (*ex parte*), held in the old court-house in Cambridge, and convened for the purpose of dismissing the Rev. Dr. Holmes. Mr. Samuel Hoar, a distinguished lawyer of Concord, was counsel for the party opposed to Dr. Holmes. Never having heard him in a set speech, Sumner and myself went for the purpose of hearing his plea, in which he quoted the familiar verse, ' Tempora mutantur, nos et mutamur in illis.' But, instead of *in illis*, he said *cum illis*. Sumner was greatly disturbed by this slight lapse of the tongue or memory; and, turning to me, said, ' A man ought to be ashamed who quotes an author and does not quote correctly.' I heard him repeat the expression *cum illis* several times afterwards, intimating that he knew better than to use the wrong word in quoting from Latin or Greek.

" Sumner was a person of remarkable readiness and self-possession. As to the former, I have no doubt that even then, if called upon to make a speech when he least expected it, he would not have been disturbed as most other persons would have been, but would have acquitted himself creditably. I do not remember any instance of this, but I have no doubt he could have done it. As to the latter, — self-possession, — it seems to have been a trait which he inherited from his father, who, when Sheriff of Suffolk County, was called upon to read the riot act, on occasion of a riot in the Federal-Street Theatre. It is said he coolly went upon the stage, and read it amidst a shower of brick-bats. The son was like him in that respect. He seemed as much at home in declaiming on public declamation days as if speaking a piece in his own room. To me, and to many, public declamation days were a terror; and it always seemed a mystery to me how he could be so cool while I trembled like an aspen-leaf.

" From my first acquaintance with Sumner until I left Cambridge, in December, 1835, to assume the charge of a parish in the Episcopal Church, he was always careful to lead an exemplary and blameless life, full of kindly feelings and ready to say a pleasant word to all; and punctilious in all the proprieties which refined society is accustomed to observe. . . . I do not remember to

have seen him since the morning of the day on which he delivered his Phi
Beta Kappa oration, in 1846. I have always regarded him as a true man,
high-minded, who would never stoop to any meanness for any purpose whatever. Till he entered upon public life, I never knew that he had an enemy,
being kind and cordial to all, both high and low alike, and free from all
fawning to gain the favor of any. His greatness was not, in my opinion,
the result of ambition to become known and distinguished above most other
men, but to do his duty faithfully in whatever he took in hand, seeking the
right and pursuing it without regard to public opinion. He was thoroughly
equipped for the station which he reached; and the world knows how well
he acquitted himself.''

In his vacations, Sumner saw something of country life, walking once to Hanover, with his friend William H. Simmons, and
occasionally passing a few days with his father's uncle, William
Sumner, who lived on what is now River Street, in Hyde Park,
then a part of Dorchester. This relative died in 1836, at the age
of eighty-seven. The Neponset River flows just in the rear of
his house. Near by were then forests and pastures, where now
are streets and dwelling-houses. Sumner rowed on the river,
strolled over the fields, took long walks to Scots' Woods, the sea-
shore at Squantum, and once, at least, made the ascent of Blue
Hill. He joined the farmers when, with their hay-carts, they
went for the salt hay they had cut on the marshes of the Neponset. He seems to have had a boy's passion for a gun, and urged
his uncle to let him have one. The tradition that he succeeded
in his appeal is confirmed by a sketch which he made of himself
at the time, and which is preserved in one of his school-books.
It is marked with his initials and the date of January, 1828. He
is accompanied by a dog, and the birds are flying from a tree, all
safe from the shot of his flint-lock gun, which he has just fired.
"Charles's first attempt. Ha! ha! ha!" is written at the foot
of it.

In those days it was the fashion for parents to give children
formal advice more than now. His father wrote to him, during
the vacation following his Junior year, hoping that his behavior
would be in every way respectful to Mr. William Sumner, on
account of his age and character, — advice which was hardly
needed. He says, in his letter: "Charles, upon your discretion
and good deportment the happiness of my life will in no trifling
degree depend. If any persons entertain a favorable opinion of
you, I hope you will never disappoint them."

In his Junior year, in company with four classmates, Frost,

Babcock,[1] Penniman, and Munroe, of whom only the last survives, he made a pedestrian trip to Lake Champlain. This was
his first absence from Boston and its suburbs. He kept a journal
of the excursion, from which the following account is abridged :

The party left Cambridge, July 14, 1829, at four P. M., "with
knapsacks on their backs and umbrellas in their hands, and in
high spirits," and walked on "singing and laughing, and attracting considerable attention." Refreshing themselves in the early
evening, at Lincoln, with "a hearty supper of brown-bread and
milk," they passed their first night at a small inn in Concord.
Rising before four the next morning (15th), they went through
Sudbury, Stow, and Bolton, and lodged that night at Sterling,
enduring severe heat during the day. From Sterling, which they
left before five A. M. (16th), they walked up the steep hill to the
village of Princeton, where they enjoyed breakfast at a well-kept
hotel. Then, giving up the ascent of Mt. Wachusett on account
of the weather, they kept on their way through a hilly and
uncultivated country ; and picking raspberries which served for
luncheon and dinner, and refreshed once by a shower, they arrived at Barre village, sixty-five[2] miles from Boston, "single-file,
umbrellas up, and singing." "We usually stopped to talk with
the farmers whom we passed, asked them about the hay, and
heard some of the stories which they had to tell about pieces
of land which they owned. One of them told us that he was
the son of the first man who was born in Princeton. In this
manner we passed through the towns, gaining information about
the state of the country, and health and strength by our exercise. Most of the persons whom we passed, and with whom
we stopped, seemed to think that we were doing wonders.
They frequently said that they should like to take the same
route, in the same way, but thought they could not go on
at the rate we did. Barre, where we are now waiting for our
supper, is a very pretty village. The town is famous for its
dairies, making more butter and cheese than any other in the
State." Passing the night at Dana, which they reached after an
evening walk, they rose as usual, at four A. M. (17th), and walked
through Greenwich, "a very pretty and pleasant town, situated
on a plain," observing Mt. Pomroy and Mt. Liz ; thence to Enfield, and arrived at Amherst "after a most toilsome journey

---

[1] Rev. Samuel B. Babcock, rector of a parish in Dedham. He died in 1873.
[2] The distances are given as in the journal.

through the hottest part of the day." "The people in most of the towns through which we passed were perfectly astonished, and utterly at a loss what to make of us. At Barre we were taken for United States officers, and at Dana we were asked if we were on a 'peddling-voyage.' In another place we were taken for factory-boys." The sight of Amherst and its college buildings, and the students, who were not yet relieved from their tasks, was grateful to the weary Harvard lads. Fatigued more than before by the heat and the hilly roads, they still, before resting, sought the chapel, to attend evening prayers. Next, they visited the recitation-rooms, the libraries, the Mt.-Pleasant School, and the chapel tower, where they enjoyed " a very fine view of the whole country round about." The journal describes the college buildings and the scenery. The next morning (18th), waked by the college bell at five, they attended prayers, which were conducted by the President, in the chapel. After the devotions, Sumner and Babcock set out, leaving their comrades to follow. Here the journal records a hazardous adventure of the advanced party : —

" It was our determination to visit Mt. Holyoke. On our arrival at the bottom of the hill, we went into a poor house and got a cheap breakfast. We then started to ascend the mountain by an old and at present unfrequented path. After going some ways, we came to a place where there were two roads. It was our ill luck to choose the one which proved to be only a wood-cutter's track. After we had followed it for some time, we arrived at the end. Then, not wishing to turn back and tread the ground over again, we pushed right into the brush and wood, aiming directly for the summit. We proceeded with considerable difficulty through these impediments, till we arrived at the upper part, which was an almost perpendicular ascent to the summit. This part we made great exertions to ascend, now catching hold of the loose rocks and now of the trees, and every moment fearing lest we should tumble over the precipice. Our situation was indeed very precarious. The least slip would have been sufficient to place our lives in imminent jeopardy, and expose us to almost certain destruction. After a hard struggle and many desponding thoughts, we at last arrived at the top, where Frost and a couple of Amherst students had already been some time. Here we passed a considerable time in looking upon the surrounding country. The prospect was most beautiful, embracing a view of the Connecticut, winding its way through the most delightful fields, without a fence on the road or in the fields; but all presenting the appearance of one extensive field. Our descent from the mountain was not so unfortunate as our ascent. There was a road, consisting, part of the way, of steps, which made it very easy. On our arrival at the bottom, we bathed in the Connecticut, which runs at its base."

Crossing the river by "the first ferry in which horses and teams were carried over" that Sumner had ever seen, "the boat being moved by two horses on deck," the travellers entered Northampton, where they admired the fine houses on its main street, visited the Round-Hill School, and took supper at the Coffee House. Then they pressed on to Hatfield, where they were to lodge. Here their attention was attracted by a house with large pillars on both sides, and apparently built of marble. At this place, for the sake of "a better road and easier travelling," they changed their original purpose of striking directly across the mountains, and decided to go northward, following the river further up. On Sunday morning (19th), they walked before breakfast some six or seven miles, in a rain, to Deerfield, whose "brick meeting-house and a long street shaded by elms" were observed. The traditions of Indian warfare in the vicinity of Bloody Brook were recalled. "We are now at Deerfield, and in the neighborhood of a spot famous for a massacre by the Indians. In fact, all these towns have been the scene of bloody battles between the Indians and the first settlers."

Sumner, in the afternoon, went on to Greenfield, riding about "half a mile in a wagon;" his first ride since he left Boston. The next morning (20th), the party journeyed on "a most delightful road, with a brook running by its side, and through a beautiful wood" to Coleraine, where they paused for breakfast. They met, near the border-line of Massachusetts and Vermont, a farmer from Milton, who entertained them with "beer and milk," and they eat raspberries on the very spot where the two States divide. Thence they proceeded through an uncleared, rocky, and hilly country, with no habitations but a few log huts. After "a fine country supper of brown-bread and milk, at a small village secluded among the mountains" which they reached about dusk, they went on to the next public house, five miles off.

"We were told, beforehand, that the whole road was through a perfect forest, without a single house on the way. This we found to be too true. It was beginning to be dark when we started, and we had proceeded scarcely a mile before we found ourselves enveloped in total darkness. The forest through which we were passing was one of great extent, stretching over all the neighboring country. It was infested by wolves, bears, and wildcats. The road had been made through it but in the preceding spring, and had not yet been thrown open. One step would be upon a smooth and slippery rock, and another into a deep slough. Stumps of trees were in the middle of the road, and the high woods by the side shut out the small light that the moon would otherwise have afforded.   Every step was made upon an uncertainty.   After the longest five miles that I ever went, I arrived at the tavern, which happened to be immediately at the end of the road.   This forest was in Readsboro.   It was thirty-three miles that I went to-day."

Early the next morning (21st), after a walk " through another forest of eight miles, with but one house in the whole distance," they breakfasted at a tavern in the neighborhood of which a wolf had been shot the week previous.   Here, as before, the young men excited the curiosity of the people.   " At one of the houses we passed we were taken for play-actors, on their way to Bennington to perform.   The reason assigned for this belief was that we had ' pale faces.'   One of our company, being taken for a pedler, was asked ' what trinkets he had to sell.' "   They passed over the summit of the Green Mountains, " about the highest eminence " on which Sumner had ever stood, with a view extending " from sixty to one hundred miles," and descended the long hill, two or three miles in length, to Bennington, where, after taking a view of the iron-works and the unattractive streets, they set off for the Revolutionary battle-field, six miles distant.   " Here Munroe left us, not being able to keep up."   They passed the night on the very site of the battle between the English and the colonists, in the house of Mr. Barnet, who cordially welcomed the visitors and refused compensation for their entertainment.   " It was not to visit the iron-works or to see the condition of the village, that we were induced to come in this direction.   We came to visit a spot hallowed in American history, — to tread that field sacred to liberty, where the cause of the colonies first began to brighten.   We came upon a pilgrimage, not to the shrine of a prophet, but to one of the shrines of our country's glory." [1]   Very early the next morning (22d), their host explained to them, on the ground, the positions and movements of the hostile forces; and these Sumner recorded with particularity.   Leaving the house of Mr. Barnet, as early as six in the morning, the party breakfasted, after a walk of six miles, at Whitecreek, in New York.   " For three successive nights we have slept in three different States, Massachusetts, Vermont, and New York; as well as for three successive mornings we have breakfasted in these three States."   A few miles further, Penniman took the stage for Saratoga, as he had pre-

[1] The journal of July 21, 22, and 23, varied and added to, was printed in the "Boston Patriot and Mercantile Advertiser," Nov. 20 and Dec. 3, 1829.

viously designed. It was Frost's purpose to continue the journey on foot, but "the sight of the stage had such an effect upon him that he, too, immediately jumped aboard and rode off for the Springs. Babcock and myself are thus left alone to perform the excursion to the Lakes." The two passed through Cambridge and Union Village, to Fort Miller, on the Hudson River, where they arrived at a late hour in the evening.

"It was here that we first saw the Champlain canal, which communicates with Lake Champlain and Albany. This is one of the vast undertakings which have given New York such a superiority in point of enterprise and wealth over her sister States. By means of this, the immense expenses of teaming formerly incurred in carrying the productions of the northern part of the State to the southern marts have been avoided. It is, as it were, a new road to wealth. Yet it was astonishing to see how some of the people were prejudiced against it. . . . Every great undertaking always finds opponents; and the New York canals are not free from this common lot. The perseverance displayed by Clinton, in the planning and making these canals, cannot be too much admired. . . . After all the opposition he met with, he at length succeeded, and he has left behind him a more durable monument than a sculptured bust or marble tomb, — the gratitude of his country. No one in the most distant ages could look upon these canals without calling to his remembrance the name of their designer and executor. Alexander wished for a Homer to celebrate his actions. Clinton will need none; his works will speak for themselves." [1]

The next day (23d) they walked to Fort Edward and Sandy Hill, — "rightly so called," — going over localities associated with the ill-fated Jane McCrea, resting at Fort Ann, and arrived at Whitehall, "the southern extremity of Lake Champlain," after a day's journey of thirty-one miles, and tiresome travelling through a hilly and rough country. "Whitehall is by far the most business-like place we have seen since we left Boston. Most of the houses are built of brick or stone, which gives it much of a city-like appearance. Besides, the continual passing and repassing of the canal-boats adds to the bustle. We can also discern the masts of vessels lying at the wharves. The situation at the foot of the lake made it a good place for embarkation of troops destined for Canada. This advantage of situation however, it is hoped will no longer be valuable for that purpose, but rather for the cultivation of the mild arts of peace, for the advancement of trade, and the means it affords for a

[1] Boston Patriot and Mercantile Advertiser, Dec. 3, 1829.

quick and easy communication between the Canadas and the
United States." At this point, the plan of the travellers was to
take the steamer for Ticonderoga. The next morning (24th),
as the steamer " Congress " was not to leave till one in the afternoon, they indulged in a sleep longer than usual; "it being the
first time that we have not risen before, or at least with, the
sun since we started." " Our pedestrian journey, most probably,
with the exception of some few miles, ends at this place. It is
now nine days since we left home, and in that time we have
travelled between two and three hundred miles on foot." Arriving by the steamer at a landing on the Vermont side of the
lake, and being ferried across to a place a mile above Fort Ticonderoga, they inspected the remains of the fortifications. " Ticonderoga is now in ruins; but there are still sufficient remains to
convince us of its former strength. Situated as it is on a prom-
ontory, it has complete command over that part of the lake; and,
were it not for Mt. Defiance, which overlooks it, would rightly
be deemed impregnable. The sides toward the water are of
massive rock, partly the work of Nature and partly of art. In
fact, the whole fortress is built upon a rock. The walls of the
buildings connected with the fort still remain, and present quite
a castellated appearance. There are also several cellars and
magazines under ground. The form of the fort we could not
distinctly discern, as several parts of it were entirely wanting.
Its great extent, however, was very evident."

Thence they walked about three miles to the hotel at the head
of Lake George, and visited both the Lower and the Greater
Falls. The last " were a most splendid sight. The water came
dashing over the rocks in a complete foam, and making a roaring
noise. From this I can have a pretty good idea of a cataract."
The next day (25th), Sumner alone ascended Mt. Defiance, to
obtain a view of the fortress beneath. The adventure cost him a
severe effort. He wondered how field-pieces were ever carried up
its sides to surprise General St. Clair. He was unable to trace the
British works on the summit; but enjoyed the fine view. The
two classmates embarked at one in the afternoon. " The scenery
all the way through Lake George was most beautiful, and the
number of islands with which the water was interspersed very
much heightened it." Arriving at Caldwell at six in the evening, they at once walked to Glenn Falls, seeing, on their way,
the remains of the forts William Henry and George; " pass-

ing over a level plain, frequently the battle-field of contending armies, and the scene of the alternate triumphs of the English and French;" skirting "Bloody Pond, the place where the dead bodies of all who were slain in the battle between Dieskau and Williams were buried," and lodging at "a country tavern, situated almost immediately upon one of the battle-fields, under a hill, which we were told was called French Hill from the circumstance of the French being posted there." The next morning (26th) they rose before four, and walked over ground they had in part traversed on their way up, going by Glenn Falls to Sandy Hill, where they attended the Presbyterian Church in the forenoon. Resuming in the afternoon their journey, they pressed on to Schuylerville, fifteen miles distant, and "stopped under the very tree to which Miss McCrea was tied when she was shot," and drank from the neighboring spring. Thence they passed through the village of Fort Edward, finishing the day's journey (Babcock being lame) with a pleasant ride on a canal-boat. The next morning (27th) they left Schuylerville, where they had lodged at a hotel opposite Fort Hardy. Babcock went directly to Saratoga Springs; but Sumner, persevering in sight-seeing, repaired alone to the scenes of Burgoyne's retreat and surrender, and visited the fort, the battle-field, the house occupied by Burgoyne as head-quarters, the room where Frazier died, and the place where he was reputed to have been buried. Thence, in the heat of the day, he walked to the Springs, where, joining Babcock, he took lodgings at Montgomery Hall, instead of Congress Hall, which was then chief among the hotels. The next morning (28th), he subscribed for a day at the Reading Room. Leaving Saratoga on the 29th, at four in the morning, they walked to Ballston, where Babcock took the stage for Schenectaday, on his way to Utica. Sumner, now left alone, still persevered, "arriving at the Erie Canal, about two o'clock, just at the famous aqueduct over the Mohawk;" thence walking on the tow-path, passing Cohoes Falls, numerous locks, and the junction of the Erie and Champlain Canals, and reaching Troy about six P. M., and (still following the canal) Albany about sundown, — making thirty-seven miles on foot during the day. Lodging for the night at the Eagle Tavern, the next morning (30th) he took a view quite early of the State House, "a building far inferior to our Massachusetts one, and in my opinion unworthy of so great a State as New York;" observing also the great number

of spires in the city, and "the vast number of canal and steamboats." At seven A. M. he left by the steamboat, and was landed
at Catskill in three hours. The rain and bad condition of the
road prevented a walk to the mountain, and in the afternoon he
took the stage, — the first time he had travelled on a coach since
he left home, — and arrived after dark at the Catskill House, —
the passengers all walking for the last three miles, and reaching
an elevation "about three thousand feet above the level of the
Hudson." The next morning (31st) he "arose before sunrise,
in order to have a view from such a height." The prospect was
soon overclouded, and a storm set in. Disappointed, he took the
coach, which ran in connection with the boat. "My excursion
to the mountain has been almost entirely fruitless. Of the two
great objects of coming, — the prospects and the falls, — the
former I saw very little of, and of the latter nothing. So that
all I have gained is to say I have been on the Catskill Mountain, and seen the clouds at my feet." Taking the steamer at
ten A. M., he arrived in four hours at West Point, — a distance
of seventy or eighty miles. "The scenery before reaching West
Point is sublime, consisting of rough cliffs and mountains."
Here he presented to Colonel Sylvanus Thayer, then commanding at this military station and academy, his father's letter of
introduction. This letter, dated July 14, 1829, contains the
following : —

"About twenty years ago, it was my happiness to have some conversation
with you in Boston. . . . I am desirous that my son, Charles Sumner, the
bearer of this, should have the honor of touching your hand. His own
reading and my conversation have taught him to respect you. He is about
to commence a pedestrian tour from Boston to the Springs, to view the battle-
grounds of Bennington and Saratoga, and on his way home by the steamboat
to touch at West Point. He is a student at Harvard College, and sets out
with two of his classmates, one of whom, Mr. Frost, will probably accompany
him to West Point. I request you, if convenient and consistent with your
regulations, to let these young men have a foothold on your ground during
the few hours they may be inclined to stay. It was once my son's wish to
become a member of your institution; but I perceived it to be a hopeless
undertaking to procure his admission, and he must now content himself with
barely taking a transient view of that of which he once had a desire to
make a part. He is now a tall stripling, somewhat deficient in strength and
consistency. Had he been under your orders for the three years past that he
has spent under merely literary men, he would, perhaps, now have been as
strong as a soldier of Bonaparte on the bridge of Lodi."

The journal says : —

" I visited Colonel Thayer, and presented the letter I had to him. He received me very kindly, showed me the rooms of his house, which were very neatly furnished, and also his library, and presented me with a map of West Point. I left him for a little while, and visited the ruins of Fort Putnam, — that impregnable fortress. There are a number of the old cells still remaining, and also loop-holes for the musketry. It is to my eye the strongest of any of the fortresses I have visited. On my return, Colonel Thayer conducted me around, showed me the library and the drawing-room, and then invited me home to drink tea. This I accepted. We talked about Arnold and about fortifications, and particularly those round Boston. He explained to me the meaning of *defilading*. About seven, I left him in order to view the parade, and then immediately to take the boat for New York, which was expected shortly to arrive. The parade was the finest military show, without exception, I ever beheld. The extreme nicety and regularity of the movements was astonishing. Every hand moved at the same moment, and every arm made the same angle."

Here the preserved sheets of the journal end. There were probably others which were mislaid. It is only known further that at New York he visited, at his father's request, the grave of Major Job Sumner, in St. Paul's Churchyard, and wrote a description and drew a sketch of the memorial stone.

The notes of this excursion on foot show how simple were Sumner's tastes and mode of living in his early life. He enjoyed the primitive fare of the farm-house and of the obscure inn. He made no complaint of his food or of the hardships of a traveller on foot.

He observed every thing as he went, — farms, fences, crops, style of buildings, landscapes, canals, and trade. But his journal was the fullest and his interest the greatest when he visited places which were associated with events, whether purely local or connected with Indian hostilities, the Revolutionary period, or the earlier wars of France and England. He sought these with enthusiasm, carefully studied their topography, and recalled, in connection with them, all that tradition and history had narrated. One sees even in these early adventures the same ardor with which, nine years later, he trod scenes memorable in the world's history.

His perseverance was also thus early tested. His companions, wearied with the toils of a journey on foot, left him, one after the other ; but he adhered to his original plan until it was fully accomplished. Here, too, was developed a characteristic which he always retained: what he undertook, he would not give up.

Many years after, he made a public allusion to this journey. At a dinner of the Hampshire County Agricultural Society, at Northampton, Oct. 14, 1862, he said, as he began his remarks: [1]

"I cannot forget the first time that I looked upon this beautiful valley, where river, meadow, and hill contribute to the charm. It was while a youth in college. With several of my classmates I made a pedestrian excursion through Massachusetts. Starting from Cambridge, we passed, by way of Sterling and Barre, to Amherst, where, arriving weary and footsore, we refreshed ourselves at the evening prayer in the college chapel. From Amherst we walked to Northampton, and then, ascending Mount Holyoke, saw the valley of the Connecticut spread out before us, with river of silver winding through meadows of gold. It was a scene of enchantment, and time has not weakened the impression it made. From Northampton we walked to Deerfield, sleeping near Bloody Brook, and then to Greenfield, where we turned off by Coleraine through dark woods and over hills to Bennington in Vermont. The whole excursion was deeply interesting, but no part more so than your valley. Since then I have been a traveller at home and abroad, but I know no similar scene of greater beauty. I have seen the meadows of Lombardy, and those historic rivers, the Rhine and the Arno, and that stream of Charente, which Henry the Fourth called the most beautiful of France, — also those Scottish rivers so famous in legend and song, and the exquisite fields and sparkling waters of Lower Austria; but my youthful joy in the landscape which I witnessed from the neighboring hill-top has never been surpassed in any kindred scene. Other places are richer in the associations of history; but you have enough already in what Nature has done, without waiting for any further illustration."

[1] Works, Vol. VII. p. 249.

CHAPTER V.

YEAR AFTER COLLEGE. — SEPTEMBER, 1830, TO SEPTEMBER, 1831.—
AGE, 19–20.

SUMNER left Cambridge with grateful recollections of college
life.   Revisiting, as the new academic year opened, the familiar scenes, he saw the Seniors taking possession of the rooms
which his class had vacated, and described, in a letter to Browne,
the desolation of 23 Holworthy.   He kept up his interest in the
exhibitions, parts, prizes, clubs, and personal incidents of the
college, and reported them to the distant classmates with whom
he corresponded.   Harvard never sent forth a son whose affection was warmer at the parting, or endured more faithfully to
the end.

He passed the next year at home,[1] without daily cares and
with his time fully at his command.   He was uncertain what
path of life to pursue, his associations drawing him to the law,
but as yet no strong current of his nature carrying him to a
decisive choice.   If he were to study law, he would be content
only with the best advantages, — those offered by the Law School
at Cambridge; and he was anxious — almost morbidly so — not
to subject his father to any further expense in his education.
But while postponing the choice of a profession, he was not
idle.   He rose at quarter-past five in the morning, and retired at
midnight, often later.   Having no private room for the purpose,
he used as a study one of the parlors, where he was much interrupted by the children.   He took but little exercise, and did not
go into society.   His readings were, in the classics, Tacitus, Juvenal, Persius ; in poetry and general literature, Shakspeare and
Milton,[2] Burton's "Anatomy of Melancholy," " The Correspondence of Gilbert Wakefield with Charles James Fox, Chiefly on

---

[1] The family moved, in November, from No. 53 (now 63) Hancock Street to 20 Hancock
Street.

[2] Finished, Oct. 12.

Subjects of Classical Literature," Moore's " Life of Byron," Butler's " Reminiscences," Hume's " Essays ; " and in history, Hallam,
Robertson, and Roscoe. He copied at great length into his commonplace-book — soon after laid aside — the narrations and reflections of these historians. He read both the " Lorenzo de
Medici " and the " Leo X." of Roscoe ; and on completing the
former, Oct. 29, he wrote : —

" The character of Lorenzo de Medici appears to be one of the most estimable which history records. A man with so great an ambition, and yet
with one so well controlled and directed, with so much power in his hands
and so little disposition to increase it by any infringement of the rights of his
countrymen, with so many temptations in his path, and so firm and Hercules-
like always in his choice; so great a statesman and magistrate, so strict a
scholar, and so fine a poet; so great a friend of the ingenious, and patron of
talent in every shape, — the annals of no country but Florence can show. In
him seemed to centre all those talents which Heaven scatters singly; and
these were moulded and directed by a temper soft and amiable. He united
in himself the almost diverse professions of a merchant and a scholar, super-
intending at the same time his ships and his studies, and receiving in the
same keel merchandise and manuscripts.

" ' Advectus Romam quo pruna et cottana vento.' [1]

" Lorenzo is fortunate in a historian who is his most ardent admirer;
whether the truth has been warped or concealed in any parts I cannot tell,
but Roscoe surely presents us with an elegant character. His work to me is
not so attractive in point of composition as Hume or Gibbon. It has not the
charming ease of the former or the commanding periods of the latter; but it
is chaste, ornate, classical, rather deficient in spirit and in philosophy, and
unsound in several instances in the general reflections or propositions deduced
from particular cases. It is deficient in dates."

At this time he set himself to a study, always disagreeable to
those who, like him, have for it no natural aptitude. Mathematics, to which, as already stated, he gave very little attention
in college, he now felt to be a necessary part of a complete education, and determined to overcome his deficiencies in the neglected science. He at once entered with zeal on the study of
geometry, and found it less difficult than before. From geometry
he passed to algebra, the abstruseness of which he was less able
to overcome. It is seldom that a young man to whom mathematics has been an uncongenial study returns to it merely for
the purpose of supplying a defect in his education. His classmates were much impressed with the resolution which he showed

[1] Juvenal, Sat. III. 83.

in his private studies, and particularly with his grappling with the branch which had annoyed him so much in college.

Frost wrote, Sept. 25, " Before closing, I cannot omit expressing my strong approbation of the rigid discipline to which you have subjected yourself. Such voluntary sacrifices in a man of your age and circumstances augur well of his coming years. Persevere!" Browne wrote, Sept. 28, "You have begun well. Quarter-past five in the morning is auspicious. *Macte!* Walker's geometry, with its points, lines, angles, &c., is a good employment for an adept in mathematics, like yourself. . . . Read your course of history by all means. If you mean to grapple with the law, dissect the feudal system. Your reading is a fortune." Stearns wrote, Oct. 8, "Hopkinson tells me you are all absorbed in mathematics, and are making rapid progress in the study of that long neglected science. I am glad to hear this news." Tower wrote, Nov. 1, recommending Dibdin's "Introduction to the Greek and Latin Classics," and said, "I should certainly think it indispensable to every one who loves the old Latin and Greek writers and venerable tomes as you do, as soon as he begins to form his library."

Soon after leaving college, Sumner sought an ushership in the Boston Latin School, but did not succeed in obtaining it. He was pressed by Stearns, then teaching an academy at Northfield, to become his assistant, and afterwards to take the sole charge of the institution; the latter urging that, with his attainments in the classics, he would have ample leisure to pursue his reading; but he was unwilling to separate himself from Boston and Cambridge, and declined the offer. In January, he taught for three weeks at Brookline, filling a temporary vacancy in the school of Mr. L. V. Hubbard (where his classmate McBurney was an usher), which was kept in a stone building modelled after the Greek style, and is still standing on Boylston Street. This brief experience as a school-teacher, while not attended with any unpleasant occurrence, did not give him a taste for the occupation.

In the latter part of December he composed an essay on commerce, the subject of a prize, limited to minors, which had been offered by the " Boston Society for the Diffusion of Useful Knowledge," — a society formed after the example of the famous English association. Its president at that time was Daniel Webster, and its vice-president, John Pickering. The society gave public notice that, on April 1, the envelope corresponding to the manuscript which had been approved as the best would be opened at the Athenæum Hall. On the evening appointed, at the close of a lecture by Chief-Justice Shaw, Mr. Webster opened the envelope in presence of the audience, and announced " Charles Sumner " as the name enclosed. He requested Sumner to come forward ; and, taking him by the hand, called him his " young friend," adding the remark that the public held a pledge of him, and other kindly words. Little thought the great orator that he was greeting one who was to succeed him in the Senate, with a longer term and, as time may show, a more enduring fame than his own. The prize was given in Lieber's " Encyclopædia Americana," valued at thirty dollars. The books were afterwards sent to Sumner, with a note signed by Mr. Webster, certifying that they were awarded as a premium for the essay.

His classmates were greatly pleased with his success. Tower wrote, June 5, " I rejoice with you, Sumner, in your late success. I wish I could take you by the hand, and assure you by look and sensibly how glad I am for the new honor you have won. It is a good thing ; and, I hope, only one of many laurels which are to garland your life. I *hope* so, — I know so ; and not I alone. One of our friends has predicted high places for Sumner. Therefore, on ! on ! Follow your spirit."

Browne wrote, in reference to the prize, to Stearns, April 5 :

" I had a letter from friend Charles on Saturday. He has stepped to the pinnacle of fame. Our friend outstrips all imagination. He will leave us all behind him; and, for my single self, I care not how far he may leave me. He is a good man; and, so far as a mortal may speak with confidence, my joy at his success would be unalloyed with envy. He has been working hard to lay a foundation for the future. I doubt whether one of his classmates has filled up the time since Commencement with more, and more thorough labor; and to keep him constant he has a pervading ambition, — not an intermittent, fitful gust of an affair, blowing a hurricane at one time, then subsiding to a calm, but a strong, steady breeze, which will bear him well on in the track of honor."

Sumner neglected no opportunity to listen to the best public speakers. In September, he heard Josiah Quincy's address in the Old South Church, in commemoration of the close of the second century from the first settlement of Boston.[1] He attended

---

[1] An account of this occasion, with an extract from the address, is given in Mr. Quincy's Life, pp. 443–448.

a course of lectures given under the auspices of the "Society for the Diffusion of Useful Knowledge." Among the lectures, of which he wrote out full notes, were those of Judge Davis on "Natural History," James T. Austin on the "History of Massachusetts," and John Pierpont on "Useful Knowledge the Ally of Religion."

The great orator of the period, Daniel Webster, was then in his prime. Aspiring young men spared no pains to obtain sitting or standing room at political meetings and in court-rooms where he was to speak. Sumner, accompanied by Browne, who came from Salem for the purpose, heard Webster's tariff speech, which was begun at Faneuil Hall, Oct. 30, and concluded the next (Sunday) evening at Quincy Hall. A few days later, Sumner went to Salem, as Browne's guest, and attended the trial of Joseph J. Knapp, as accessory to the murder of Stephen White. He heard Mr. Webster's closing argument for the government. It was in this address, which according to the newspapers of the day ended with "a peroration of surpassing pathos," that Mr. Webster, alluding to the suggestion that the jury should have compassion on the prisoner, said that their compassion should be for his internal, not his external, condition; "it is," he added, "his greatest misfortune to be what he is, not where he is." Knapp was convicted and executed.[1]

Rev. Dr. Emery, a classmate of Sumner, writes: —

"Immediately after graduating, I opened a private school in Beverly; and, while residing in that town, the great trial of Knapp, as an accomplice of Crowninshield in the murder of Mr. White, took place in Salem. Mr. Franklin Dexter and Mr. W. H. Gardiner were Knapp's counsel, and Webster was on the side of the State. The trial attracted many from the neighboring towns, — law-students and young lawyers. Among them Sumner was present. I recollect how delighted he was with the keenness of Dexter in worming the truth out of witnesses on their cross-examination, and especially in summing up the evidence in the prisoner's behalf. I met him at the trial several times, and he seemed to take as much interest in it as if he were one of the lawyers. He was not a member of the Law School at the time; and I could not help thinking that, if he had not decided what profession to study, the dignity and even solemnity of that trial, conducted by the ablest counsel to be found, must have decided him to study law."

[1] The points contested at this trial between Franklin Dexter, the defendant's counsel, and Mr. Webster are given in Commonwealth *v.* Knapp, 10 Pickering's Reports, p. 477. The celebrated argument of Mr. Webster on the earlier trial of John F. Knapp as principal is printed in his Works, Vol. II. pp. 41–105. See Curtis's "Life of Webster," Vol. I. pp. 378–385.

Soon after leaving college, Sumner became warmly interested in the Anti-masonic movement, then at its height.[1] He resented the annoyances and unfriendly criticisms to which his father had been subjected on account of his participation in this controversy. He was a diligent reader of the newspapers and pamphlets on the subject, with which the period abounded, particularly of Mr. Hallett's "Free Press," which he frequently posted to his friends. He is supposed to have contributed articles to this newspaper, and even to have had charge of it for a short time, during the editor's absence. He was an admirer of eminent Anti-masons, like Richard Rush and William Wirt, the latter of whom he hoped to see elected President at the next election, of 1832. He pressed "the great and good cause" of Anti-masonry, as he called it, on his favorite classmates, Browne, Hopkinson,[2] Tower, Stearns, and Frost; but, while they were not partisans of the Order, they did not sympathize with his ardent support of its political opponents. When he portrayed in his letters the dangers which the Order threatened to liberty and the administration of justice, they quite coolly reproved what they regarded as an intense and exaggerated view. Browne, who always dealt very plainly with him, rallied him for his "knight-errantry." Sumner himself, as the season of professional study drew near, was persuaded that he had allowed the exciting topic to occupy his thoughts more than would be consistent with the student's work which was to be his first duty; and, while not appearing to undergo any change of opinion, abstained from any further participation in the controversy. Perhaps the direction then given to his mind led him afterwards to favor publicity in the proceedings of the Phi Beta Kappa Society, and the discontinuance of the secret sessions of the United States Senate. "The genius of our institutions," he said in the Senate, "requires publicity. The ancient Roman, who bade his architect so to construct his house that his guests and all that he did could be seen by the world, is a fit model for the American people."[3]

[1] Browne wrote to Stearns, May 23, 1831. "Sumner feels unutterably on the subject, and he is pricked on by the wrongs done his father by Masons. His resentment is worthy of all commendation. I wish it had exploded in a different way." And again, July 12: "He holds to it [Anti-masonry] as to the ark of the nation's safety. I saw him in Boston last month, very well in body, low in spirits."

[2] Hopkinson wrote, May 10, "Leave off reading newspapers, and forget politics till you are thirty; by so doing you may redeem the pledge which Webster says 'the public hold of you.'"

[3] Speech in the Senate, April 6, 1853. Works, Vol. III. pp. 212–214.

Sumner and the classmates with whom he had been intimate kept up their interest in each other. Gifts of books were interchanged. He gave a Byron to Browne, and a Milton to Hopkinson; and received from Browne Sterne's "Sentimental Journey," and from Hopkinson a polyglot Bible.[1] Having access to bookstores and libraries, he was often the agent of his classmates in borrowing and purchasing books. He maintained a frequent correspondence with Browne, who was studying law with Rufus Choate at Salem; with Hopkinson, who was first a tutor at Cambridge and then a law-student at Groton; with Tower, who was teaching school at Waterville, N. Y., and afterwards studying law with Hermanus Bleecker, in Albany; and with Stearns and Frost, — who were teaching, the former at Northfield, and the latter at Framingham. The letters which they wrote to him are familiar and affectionate, usually addressing him by his Christian name, and most of them quite extended. Of these he kept during his life more than fifty, written from Sept., 1830, to Sept., 1831.

Once a week, or oftener, he sent long letters to Browne.[2] Browne was fearless in his treatment of received opinions, but his radical notions were under the control of good sense. The two friends discussed political topics, like Masonry, and the public men of the day; literary themes, like the characters of Shakspeare, Milton's poetry, and Moore's "Biography of Byron;" Hallam's "History of the Middle Ages," and the historical characters of Francis I. and Charles V. They criticised for mutual improvement each other's style of writing so plainly and unreservedly, that only their assured confidence in each other's sincerity and friendliness prevented their keen words from leaving a sting behind. Sumner thought Browne's style "Byronic," and invited a criticism of his own. Browne, while appreciating Sumner's as one which "every man not a critic and many who are would be delighted with," and as "flowing smoothly, rapidly, clearly, and full of bright images," objected to it as "too ornate and embellished, too exuberant, and too full of figures and figurative language; and, while correct and not violating the proprieties of nature, as wanting generally in

---

[1] Sumner gave his classmate Kerr, in their Senior year in college, the "Apothegms of Paulus Manutius," an edition printed in Venice in 1583.

[2] Of the letters to Browne and Hopkinson, the two classmates to whom he wrote most confidentially, none exist; but the letters written to him at that period were carefully preserved by him.

simplicity and directness." He wrote, March 6, " Either send
me a Lemprière, or be less lavish of your classical allusions;
for so thickly was your epistle, especially the first page, bediz-
ened with gems, that my mineralogy was all at fault. I could
neither measure nor sort them." Three weeks later, he wrote,
" Your last letter was full of bone and muscle and figures, — of
the last an excess, though invariably bold and strong, remarkably
and unusually so. I am right glad to see this improvement in
your style. It was a desideratum; almost the only one. *Macte
nova virtute !* "

Sumner's letters to Tower and Stearns, which are preserved,
are playful, abound in Latin phrases and other quotations, and
are rather carelessly written. Neither in thought nor in style
are they superior to the similar compositions of most young men
of his age and education.

As the summer of 1831 waned, Sumner felt seriously that he
must, without delay, begin in earnest the study of a profession,
or take up some occupation which would be at once remunerative.
He was very reluctant to draw any further on his father, who had
now to provide for the education of younger sons and daughters.
He questioned, too, his chances of success in the legal profession,
or at least of attaining his ideal in it. His thoughts turned to
school-keeping for a time, as assuring immediate revenues; but a
teacher's duties did not attract him. He was troubled in spirit,
even unhappy; and he opened his heart frankly to Hopkinson,
— a young man of mature reflection and six years his senior.
The classmate replied at length, reviewing Sumner's difficulties,
which he thought exaggerated, and mingling gentle reproof with
good counsel. The father, he thought, with his improved fortunes, could not spend money better than in educating a son of
promise; and he added, " If, then, you really wish to go on
immediately with the profession, there is no lion in the way.
You may do it with strong grounds to hope for success, and
with a clear conscience and cheerful heart." Sumner feared
that an engagement as teacher for a few years would consume
time which ought to be appropriated to preparation for his
life-work, whatever that was to be; but his classmate thought
well of such a temporary experience, as it would occupy his
mind, promote cheerfulness, and give him a knowledge of the
world, which, with his too great seclusion, he much needed;
and besides it would not conflict with his admission to the bar

at as early a period as was desirable. "You would," he said, "then come to the sturdy science with nerves and muscles hardened for the combat, and with a mind better stored than that of any of your class." Hopkinson rebuked Sumner's apprehension of failure in life, his indecision, his chosen abstinence from society, which had brought on an unhealthy gloominess of mind, and his too absorbing contemplation of extraordinary characters in history, which are not, except in rare instances, attainable ideals. "That vague ambition which looks at ends and overlooks means is the cause of half your troubles, and is caused by your overmuch reading and ignorance of men. Your thoughts have conversed only with kings, generals, and poets. Come down to this tame world and this tame reality of things." Hopkinson thus closed this thoughtful letter, which must have affected Sumner's immediate purpose, and probably his whole future: "Be assured of my high regard, of my high opinion of your talents; and if you do not make a strong man of yourself, on you rests the sin of throwing away talents and education which I might envy, and which might make your name familiar in men's mouths. The following passage I transcribe from a letter of our Salem friend [Browne]. You know he does not calculate highly on puny geniuses. Speaking of your prize lately obtained, he writes: 'Charles looms in the world. We glory in his present success. May we not assuredly hope that it is but the beginning of the end?' This I send because the circumstances are a warranty of his sincerity. Had he said as much of me, I should have respected myself the more for it."

Among other expressions of interest in his career which belong to this transition period of life are the following: Browne wrote, July 26, "Do you go to Cambridge next year? You have put your hand to the plow, you have even broken ground, and now look back. There is no going back, and you have duty and all hope to draw you forward." And, a few weeks later, he wrote: "Did you ever read Dean Swift's life? If you have not, — but you have: you have read every thing. Have you brought your Law-School resolution to a focus, and made preparation for next year in any way?" Stearns wrote, Aug. 3, "What are your plans for the coming year? I hope you mean to grapple with the law. That is the profession you are made for, and the sooner you prepare for it the better."

After a considerable period of perplexity and indecision, Sumner chose the law. He made the choice without enthusiasm; but, when once made, he formed a plan of severe and comprehensive study, which he pursued with patience and enthusiasm. The question of a profession being determined, he was vexed with no hesitation as to the place where he should prepare himself for its duties, but was drawn irresistibly to Cambridge, where he had passed four happy years.

This year at home, intervening between College and Law School, Sumner himself did not, at its close, regard as profitably spent. It began with the study of mathematics, which does not seem to have been kept up more than five months. He read much, but in a desultory way. What he wrote was wanting in careful reflection and finish of style. His mind, as he saw the year in retrospect, had been prematurely agitated with political strifes which were not likely to be of permanent interest. Manhood had now come with its work and duties, and he entered upon it in a serious and resolute spirit.

LETTERS TO CLASSMATES.

TO CHARLEMAGNE TOWER, WATERVILLE, N.Y.

BOSTON, Sept. 27, 1830.

Scene. — Fourth-story, House 53 Hancock Street, half-past ten in the evening.

MY FRIEND, —

" Truditur dies die,
Novaeque pergunt interire Lunae." [1]

Yes, a month has now passed since we bade adieu to college pleasures and labors; and, if I mistake not, just a month since I last saw you in Holworthy, 4. You and I, I believe, had some sympathies with one another on departure; we both of us looked upon Cambridge with rather warmer feelings than most, and dreaded to sunder ourselves from so many kindly associations. One month " hath not a whit altered *me;* " my mind is still full of those feelings of affection which bound me to the place and the friends I there enjoyed. I find it hard to untie the spell that knits me so strongly to college life. I never had a more melancholy time in my life than for the four hours after I last saw you. I went to my room, and found it usurped by a " new race," and my furniture on the road to Boston. Like Noah's dove, then, with nowhere to rest the sole of my foot, I went from room to room, and saw

1 Horace, Ode II. xviii. 15, 16.

everywhere the signs of approaching departure.   Juniors were parading round, the almost "undisputed lords and masters" of what we Seniors a day before alone enjoyed.   Excuse this sentimentality.

Two days after you had read your dissertation, the fame whereof was in the land when I arrived, I underwent the most unwelcome drudgery of reading mine, — namely, of going through the form, — in order to satisfy the requisitions of the will.   Be assured it was only a form.   I did not read in all more than a third, and that I cantered through as fast as my tongue (naturally a "fast goer") could carry me.   I did not read along in course, but took shreds and patches from one page and another through the whole forty-five.   How absurd to make us thus murder our own children!   The whole dissertation ought to be read, for it cannot be properly judged except as a whole.   The pedant of olden times, who offered a brick as a specimen of a house he had for sale, acted about as wisely as the Faculty in this particular, thus forcing us to slice off a few bits and offer them as the successful Bowdoin dissertations. . . . Just a week ago yesterday, I commenced Walker's Geometry, and have now got nearly half through.   All those problems, theorems, &c., which were such stumbling-blocks to my Freshman-year career, unfold themselves as easily as possible now.   You would sooner have thought, I suppose, that fire and water would have embraced than mathematics and myself; but, strange to tell, we are close friends now.   I really get geometry with some pleasure.   I usually devote four hours in the forenoon to it.   I have determined not to study any profession this year, and I have marked out to myself a course of study which will fully occupy my time, — namely, a course of mathematics, Juvenal, Tacitus, a course of modern history, Hallam's "Middle Ages" and "Constitutional History," Roscoe's "Leo" and "Lorenzo," and Robertson's "Charles V.;" with indefinite quantities of Shakspeare, Burton, British poets, &c., and writing an infinite number of long letters.   I have doomed myself to hard labor, and I shall try to look upon labor as some great lawyer did, as pleasure, — " *Labor ipse voluptas.*"   And the gratification from labor is, indeed, the surest and most steadfast pleasure. . . . President Quincy has been completely successful; has done himself, the city, the State, honor.[1] Webster, I understood, said it was the best discourse he ever heard from a *pulpit* in his life.   It was two hours long; the whole of this time he held the attention of a most numerous audience, among whom was myself, squeezed and pushed round amidst the crowd of groundlings in one of the aisles, standing up during all the two performances, about three hours.   The first part of Quincy's oration, I thought, was not well digested; but he grew better and better the more he got heated with his subject, and held the attention of the audience better the last hour than he did the first.   His vindication of the bigotry and intolerance of our ancestors was the best I ever heard, and was too good for them.   His delivery, also, was fine, — full, loud, energetic, frequently eloquent.   Sprague's poem was beautiful; its most prominent parts were on the Indians.   There was an immense procession to the

[1] Centennial Oration, *ante*, p. 74.

meeting-house, in which our friend Hopkinson walked amongst the corporation, professors, and tutors of Harvard University. . . .

I should have liked to roam round with you through those New York bookstores. In fact, a bookstore or a library is my paradise. I have been doing something here, as you did in New York, to invest my prize-money; and, depend upon it, I often sighed from the bottom of my spirit when I felt the hollowness of my pockets. I bought me a Burton's "Anatomy of Melancholy," a Hazlitt's "British Poets," a Byron, and a fine one volume 8vo Shakspeare, called the London "Stage Edition," with which I am much pleased. It contains Shakspeare's poems, in addition to his plays. I should like to know what some of those fine editions were which you saw at New York. I take such an interest in books that I like to hear about them though I do not see them. I presume from your habits that you have been accustomed to keep a commonplace-book or scrap-book or something of the kind. I wish you to tell me whether you kept it on any philosophical plan, and what that plan was, — *si tibi placeat.* I wish you to draw upon me for information about what is going on, to any amount whatever, and be assured I shall answer your bills most cheerfully. My father is full of good wishes for your well-doing and happiness.[1]   C. S.

TO CHARLEMAGNE TOWER.

NOVEMBER 4, 1830.

. . . The exhibition took place at the College on Oct. 19. I had little desire to hear all the performances, so I did not get there till about twelve o'clock, when, as I was ascending the steps with Hopkinson, Browne presented himself before us. The exhibition for the time was deserted, and we repaired to Hopkinson's proctorial room, there to have a short, friendly chat, which was prolonged till the oration came on. The subject of that was "Specks in the Literary Horizon." Simmons[2] did nobly. His oration was over half an hour in length. It was marked by a plenitude of thought and a strength of expression, and showed an ease of composition, which in a painter we should call a "free pencil." . . . I know you will wish you were here during this last week. The election for member of Congress has taken place, and, as it turned upon the tariff and anti-tariff, it produced a considerable excitement. Nathan Appleton, father of Appleton in the present Senior class, was the tariff candidate, and Henry Lee the anti-tariff one, both merchants. The Tariffites held one caucus just a fortnight ago, at which Evarts, author of "William Penn," J. B. Davis, A. H. Everett, J. T.

---

[1] The letters which Sumner wrote at this period, and also those which he wrote at the Law School, contain many references to his classmates and other students, with details of their experiences and plans of life, most of which it has seemed proper to omit. They show a friendly, and in many instances an affectionate, interest in those with whom he had been associated as a student.

[2] William H. Simmons.

Austin, Ben. Gorham (present Representative), and William Sullivan spoke; and lastly the huge leviathan of New England, Webster himself. He spoke but a few minutes, simply expressing his wish to address his fellow-citizens at length on this subject; and, as it was then late, moving an adjournment to Saturday, Oct. 30. On Saturday evening, the hall [Faneuil] was crowded to excess an hour before the time (to which the meeting adjourned) had arrived. Never had the "Cradle of Liberty" more within its sides than on that evening. He spoke three and a half hours, and then had not concluded his remarks; when the meeting adjourned to Quincy Hall for Sunday evening. When Sunday evening arrived, Quincy Hall was crowded to overflowing, and Mr. Webster concluded. His peroration brought to my mind the admirable one in his speech in the Senate. Between every one of about the last four sentences he was greeted with three cheers by that immense audience; and when he had finished, with repeated cheers, wavings of hats, kerchiefs, &c. What a day of glory to him! I cannot paint the impression he made, neither can I the strong, convincing argument and eloquence he displayed. I leave it to your imagination. Webster was followed by H. G. Otis, who spoke about two hours, beautifully, of course. His voice was melodious and liquid; but the whole character of his oratory was a contrast to the bold, nervous delivery of Webster. He plainly showed that age had slackened his fires, and that he was no longer what he was twenty years ago, when he might almost be said to have

> "Wielded at will the fierce democratie"

of Boston. The caucus of the Anti-tariffites was nothing. The result of these great exertions of the Tariffites was the election of Appleton. You can well imagine that this rich feast of eloquence relished well, and with no one better than myself. . . .   Your friend,

SUMNER.

TO JONATHAN F. STEARNS, NORTHFIELD, MASS.

BOSTON, Nov. 24, 1830.

MY FRIEND, — Here I am fairly located in house No. 20, Hancock Street, on the opposite side and lower down than that where I have had the pleasure of seeing you occasionally. For the last month, the thoughts of moving and a visit to Salem to see John,[1] and attend the notorious trials, completely filled my mind. Besides, mathematics, my chiefest foe, buckles on daily more impenetrable armor. I am now digging among the roots of algebra, and believe your opinion will bear me out when I say that these roots, when obtained, are but bitter. If I had accepted your kind invitation and posted up to Northfield, it would have been a month before I could have got my mind again into the right train to have prosecuted all the studies I am bear-

---

[1] Browne.

ing up under. I fear that mathematics will yet conquer me. Browne appears in as good spirits as I ever knew him to be. I spent three days with him, the greater part of which time was spent both by him and myself in the court-room. While there, he gave me a "Sterne's Sentimental Journey," neatly bound. . . .

Your friend,   C. S.

TO CHARLEMAGNE TOWER.

BOSTON, Dec. 8, 1830.

Never, my friend, when the heavens have been dressed in their scorching robes of brass for weeks, was a drop of rain more grateful than your most timely epistle. It found me about one and a half o'clock to-day mired among the roots of algebra, clawing around in vain, involved in Cimmerian darkness, looking and finding no dawn. Algebra was closed, and myself was deposited safely in the chair, whence my mathematical exertions had abstracted me, to read and re-read, and read again the letter of a friend. . . .

My study! *mehercle!* it would require the graphic pencil of Hogarth to set it before you, — children and chairs, bores and books, andirons and paper, sunlight and Sumner; in short, a common resting-place for all the family. I often think of you and your neat premises when I am sitting, like Chance amidst the little chaos around. . . . I was sorry not to find on your table Juvenal, one of the first poets and moralists the world ever saw, the Roman Shakspeare in the ripeness of his thoughts and the strength of his expressions, in his expanded views of human nature and intensity of conception. Juvenal I shall make my Latin text-book; I study him every afternoon, reading about one hundred lines at a time. I frequently find it hard to unfold his meaning; but the richness of the fruit will repay any labor in gathering. . . . I have just read "Fox and Wakefield's Correspondence, Chiefly on Subjects of Classical Literature." How could a man in Fox's situation, with so many diverse and enfolding cares, surrender himself so devotedly to the study of the classics, rivalling an old scholiast in astuteness and critical inquiry, and seemingly as conversant with *all* as any man who had made them the study of his life? And yet this man was then employed upon a portion of English history, and was supporting the Atlantean weight of a party which held divided empire with the king himself. Tower, you and I are both young, and the world is all before us. You are ambitious, I know; and I am not ashamed to confess, though "by that sin fell the angels," that I also am guilty. We are then fellow-laborers in the same field; we are both striking our sickles at the same harvest. Its golden sheaves are all pointing to you. You have been laborious, and I have not. I have trod the primrose, and you the thorny, path. . . . There is no railway to fame. Labor, labor must be before our eyes; nay, more, its necessity must sink deep in our hearts. This is the most potent alchemy to transmute lead into gold.

One o'clock at night!   C. S.

TO JONATHAN F. STEARNS.

SUNDAY, Feb. 13, 1831.

MY FRIEND, — . . . I have for three weeks been trying to rear the tender thought, as an assistant to our old friend, McBurney, at Mr. Hubbard's school. Mr. H. had to go to Vermont, and he engaged me to assist in the duties of instruction during his absence. And oh! — *quorum magna pars fui* — the harassing, throat-cutting, mind-dissolving duties: pounding knowledge into heads which have no appetency for it, and enduring the *arguing* of urchin boys, and all those other ills to which schoolmaster-flesh is heir. . . . But the cares of Mr. H.'s school are more severe than those of most schools, on account of the want of classification in the boys, and the being obliged to drudge through lessons with single boys without any of the excitement of hearing a large class, and also the attention bestowed on them out of school. You must see that my experiences are rather unfavorable. Shall I, then, take the responsibility of a school like that of which you are the head, — an academy upon which many look with an eye of jealousy, and others with an interest which would keep a watchful eye upon the instructor, and feel itself wronged if his exertions and abilities did not come up to a standard already fixed? Further, I have a natural aversion to keeping school. Yet again, it does not seem right that I should stand all the day idle, dependent upon my father for support and a profession, when the means are placed before me of gaining a little of that *aliquid immensum infinitumque*, not of the Roman but of the modern. Which of the two to choose? Here I am wavering, veering from point to point as of old, distrustful of myself. I feel unsettled in my condition. My age begins to tell me I ought to stand on my own legs, and loosen the chain which has ever held me to home. I see no means of making money or reputation anywhere, with the exception of the former, as a schoolmaster.

The *secrets* of the Φ. B. K. are shortly to be published. I have seen the manuscript myself, in the handwriting of one of the oldest ministers of this State, initiated in 1790. . . . A gentleman told me he had conversed with J. Q. Adams, and he said he was opposed to all secret societies, and should like to assist in removing the secrecy from the Φ. B. K. It will not hurt it; it will benefit it. There is nothing for which they need blush.

McBurney and Hopkinson were here last evening, and spent in my room a kind of old college evening. I shall expect to pass a like time with you soon.   C. S.

TO CHARLEMAGNE TOWER, ALBANY, N.Y.

BOSTON, Friday Evening, May 27, 1831.

" Quid? quasi magnum
Nempe diem donas?" [1]

. . . Your method and application are to me an assurance that the studies of the law office will be fruitful; but excuse the impertinence of a friend. I

[1] Persius, Sat. V. 66, 67; quoted with reference to Tower's remissness in correspondence.

fear that Blackstone and his train will usurp your mind too much, to the exclusion of all cultivation of polite letters.   The more I think of this last point, the more important it seems to me in the education of a lawyer. " Study law hard," said Pinckney, " but study polite letters as hard."   So also says Story.   The fact is, I look upon a *mere* lawyer, a reader of cases and cases alone, as one of the veriest wretches in the world.   Dry items and facts, argumentative reports, and details of pleadings must incrust the mind with somewhat of their own rust.   A lawyer must be a man of polish, with an *omnium gatherum* of knowledge.   There is no branch of study or thought but what he can betimes summon to his aid, if his resources allow it.   What is the retailer of law-facts by the side of the man who invests his legal acquisitions in the fair garments of an elegantly informed mind ?   Every argument of the latter is heightened by the threads of illustration and allusion which he weaves with it.   Besides, it is more profitable as to legal knowledge for a student to devote but a portion of his time to the law.   A continual application to it would jade the mind, so that it would falter under the burden imposed by its own ardor.   There must be a relaxation.   And the best relaxation for a scholar will be found in a change of studies. . . .   Your ambition has kept you employed and happy all this winter, I will engage, while lassitude and negligence have been preying upon me. . . .   One little feat I did, which I now tell in the fulness of friendship rather than vanity. The "Boston Society for the Diffusion of Useful Knowledge," — D. Webster, President, John Pickering, V. P., — offered a premium in books to the author (a minor) of the best dissertation on any thing relating to commerce, trade, and manufactures, to be handed up Jan. 1.   It popped into your friend's head, about a week before Jan. 1, that he might spend a day or two in throwing together some ideas on commerce, and the time would not be lost, whether he was successful or not.   I wrote about thirty pages, and handed it up, Bowdoin-like, anonymously.   After several months, a committee of twelve unanimously awarded the premium to me, or rather to my signature, — my name not being known till the night the premium was presented; when the envelope inclosing it was opened (after Judge Shaw had finished the evening lecture) by Mr. Webster himself, in presence of the society, and found to contain my name.   I had to step out and receive some compliments from the "godlike man," and the information that the society awarded to me Lieber's "Encyclopædia Americana," price thirty dollars. Surely the prize and praise were most easily gained.   Mind you, I tell this with no vanity.   It requires, though, the eye of a friend not to read in the foregoing lines a self-praising disposition.   With you I trust them. . . .

From your true friend,   C. S.

TO CHARLEMAGNE TOWER.

BOSTON, Friday, June 10, 1831.

MY DEAR FRIEND, — . . . Your letter, just handed to me by my father, has called me from a most listless, fruitless perusal of Hallam's "History of

the Middle Ages." The book now lies open on the sofa, where I was loung-
ing. My paper is before me, and pen in hand. The past has gone through
my mind with its thronging associations. . . . You have quite introduced
me to your master [Mr. Bleecker]. I should like him for his law, his literature; and should not dislike him for the singleness of his life. My own
reflections though, and the advice of others, tell me that it is better to study
with one whose business is other than that of a counsellor; the drudgery,
writ-making, &c., of an office is what a young student ought to undergo.
Give me my first year and a half in the entirely theoretical studies of a law-
school and my remainder in a thronged business office, where I can see the
law in those shapes in which a young lawyer can alone see and practise it.
It is years which make the counsellor.

I have just read Persius. I value him little. My mind, like yours, is
full of plans of study, few of which I am ever able to compass. My reflection calls up such a multitude of books unread, that I am lost, — like
Spenser's Una and the Redcrosse Knight, —

> "So many pathes, so many turnings seene,
> That which of them to take, in diverse doubt they been." [1]

I wish to read the principal classics, particularly Latin ones. I fear I shall
never reach the Greek. I have thought of Thucydides, the hardest but
completest historian. I shall not touch him probably. Tell me your experiences of Herodotus. . . .

From your true friend,   C. S.

TO JONATHAN F. STEARNS, BEDFORD, MASS.

Sunday Eve, Aug. 7, 1831.

My Friend, my old College Friend, — . . . You ask if I hold fast
to Anti-masonry? When I do not, pronounce me a recreant. I hold fast to
it through some ridicule, and, I dare say, slurs upon my sense. Truth has
ever been reviled when she first appeared, whether as the bearer of a glorious
system of religion, or of the laws which govern this universe. *Time* is her great
friend. I do not hardly understand from your letter whether you join with
me or no. Dr. Beecher has come out manfully. At the celebration in Boston,
he prayed that the great and good cause in which we are engaged might find
acceptance above; and if ever cause did find that acceptance, this will.

I think of hitching upon the law at Cambridge this coming Commencement. I am grateful for the encouraging word you give me. I am rather
despondent, and I meet from none of my family those vivifying expressions
which a young mind always heartily accepts. My father says nought by way
of encouragement, He seems determined to let me shape my own course, so
that if I am wise, I shall be wise for myself; and if I am foolish, I alone shall
bear it. It may be well that it is so. I do not revolt from taking my fate

---

[1] The Faerie Queene.

into my own hands. I shall go to Cambridge with a cartload of resolves, and
I believe with enough of the firmness of a man to abide by a five-hundredth
part. Law, classics, history, and literature; all of them shall meet my
encounter. Methinks I must read some of the Greek tragedians. . . .

Your friend truly,   C. S.

TO CHARLEMAGNE TOWER, WATERVILLE, N.Y.

BOSTON, Monday Evening, Aug. 29, 1831.

MY DEAR FRIEND, — . . . I can fully sympathize in your feelings arising from the severance from your studies.[1] Yet I see in it much room for
hope. Your mind will be brought at once into the hard conflict of the world.
You will transact *business;* and get initiated into those perplexities which,
sooner or later, all of the sons of Adam must meet. You will confirm yourself in a knowledge of the world, and wear off the academic rust with which
exclusive students are covered. Time will allow you, I know (for I know
you will lose no time), to prosecute your law with profit; and you will find
in your newly assumed cares a grateful change, perhaps, from the abstract
speculations in which Blackstone and Kent and Fearne will engage you.
And more than all, you will have the consciousness that you are forwarding
the wishes of your father, and giving up your time, perhaps, that it may
be added to his days.

It is now two days before Commencement. I am stiff in the determination to commence the coming year in the study of law at Cambridge. . . . I
intend to give myself to the law, so as to read satisfactorily the regular and
parallel courses, to take hold of some of the classics, —Greek, if I can possibly
gird up my mind to the work, — to pursue historical studies, — to read Say
and Stewart;[2] all mingled with those condiments to be found in Shakspeare
and the British poets. All empty company and association I shall eschew,
and seek in the solitariness of my own mind the best (because the least
seducing from my studies) companion. Can I hold fast to these good determinations? I fear much the rebellious spirit of the mortal. However,
I will try. I must endeavor to redress by future application my past remissness. The latter part of this year has been given up to unprofitableness. I
have indeed studied, or passed my eyes over books; but much of my time,
and almost my whole mind, have been usurped by newspapers and politics.
I have reached in anxiety for the latest reports from Washington, and watched
the waters in their ebb and rise in different parts of the country. No more
of this though. With Boston I shall leave all the little associations which
turned aside my mind from its true course.

---

[1] Tower had been obliged to suspend his studies in order to take charge of the mercantile
business of his father, who was then ill.

[2] J. B. Say's "Treatise on Political Economy," and Dugald Stewart's "Elements of the
Philosophy of the Human Mind."

In the way of classics, I wish to read Tacitus, Lucretius, Virgil, Ovid, Sallust, Cicero, Horace, Homer, Thucydides, and choice plays of the great tragedians. Do you start? I only say I *wish* to do it; but I *mean* to do it if impossibility is not written upon it. I wish also to reacquaint myself with political economy and intellectual philosophy. I find myself *nonplussed* daily in my own reflections by my ignorance of these subjects. . . .

J. Q. Adams has written a letter on Masonry. I will send it to you as soon as I can lay my hands upon it. Rumor says something on this may be expected soon from Webster. He is an Anti-mason, and in this I speak from more than report.[1]　　Your true friend,

CHARLES SUMNER.

[1] Curtis's Life of Webster, Vol. I., pp. 391–393, 508–511, refers to Mr. Webster's course on this question.

CHAPTER VI.

LAW SCHOOL. — SEPTEMBER, 1831, TO DECEMBER, 1833. — AGE, 20–22.

SUMNER joined the Law School of Harvard University, Sept. 1, 1831.[1] This school grew out of the Royall Professorship of Law, which was established in 1815. It was organized as a distinct department two years later; but its vigorous life began in 1829, with the appointment of Judge Story and John H. Ashmun as professors. The character of Story as jurist and teacher, his immense learning, copious speech, great enthusiasm, and kindly interest in students have been often commemorated.[2] Ashmun was remarkable for his acumen and logical method; and the two professors were well mated. At that time the method of teaching was, not only to illustrate the topic of study by decided or supposed cases, and to comment upon and criticise the text-book, but also to examine most of the students quite closely upon the lesson of the day. The exercise was a recitation rather than a lecture, — a mode of instruction which becomes inconvenient when a professional school is largely attended.

Professor Ashmun was the sole instructor when Judge Story was absent on judicial duty at Washington, or on his circuit. His service as teacher was cut short by his death, April 1, 1833. Sumner alone was with him when he died, his sole watcher for the night.[3] He afterwards collected the funds for a monument to his teacher, and revised his manuscripts for posthumous publication in the "American Jurist." He was admitted to the pro-

---

[1] Sumner was the author of two sketches of the Law School, —one, an article in the "American Jurist," Jan., 1835, Vol. XIII. pp. 107–130; and the other, "A Report of the Committee of Overseers," Feb., 1850. Works, Vol. II. pp. 377–392. Another history of the school, by Professor Emory Washburn, may be found in "The Harvard Book," Vol. I. pp. 223–231.

[2] Judge Story's method as a teacher is described in his "Life and Letters," edited by his son, Vol. II. pp. 35–39.

[3] Judge Story's funeral discourse on Professor Ashmun was printed in the "American Jurist," July, 1833, Vol. X. pp. 40–52. An extract is copied in Story's "Life and Letters," Vol. II. pp. 143–148. Sumner was "the interesting friend" referred to in the discourse.

fessor's confidence, and received peculiar help from his severe method of legal investigation. Ashmun insisted always on definiteness of thought and exactness of expression, and was in the habit of testing the knowledge of his favorite pupils by close scrutiny and criticism. This was a healthy discipline for one of Sumner's tastes and habits of study, and he profited much by it.

Professor Ashmun was succeeded, in July, by Simon Greenleaf,[1] the author of the treatise on "The Law of Evidence;" the vacancy being filled during the intervening period by James C. Alvord, of Greenfield, a young lawyer of marked ability. Both saw in Sumner a student of large promise, and became at once his friends. Professor Greenleaf's interest in him was hardly second to Judge Story's, and was prolonged after the close of Sumner's connection with the school as pupil or instructor.

Judge Story was at first attracted to Sumner by a long-existing friendship with his father; and he had been in the school but a short time before a very close intimacy was established between them. Biography gives no instance of a more beautiful relation between teacher and pupil. The judge admired Sumner's zeal in study, enjoyed his society, and regarded him like a son. Sumner conceived a profound respect for the judge's character and learning, and was fascinated by his personal qualities. This friendship entered very largely into Sumner's life, and for many years gave direction to his thoughts and ambition. The eloquent tributes which he afterwards paid to the memory of his master and friend are the witnesses of his veneration and love.[2]

Sumner, during the early part of his course at the Law School, occupied room Number 10 Divinity Hall, the most retired of the college buildings, and took his meals in commons. Afterwards, he became librarian of the school, and, as one of the privileges of his office, occupied as a dormitory room Number 4 Dane Hall, from the time that building was opened for use in Oct., 1832.[3]

The Law School then numbered forty students,[4] and was divided into three classes, — the Senior, Middle, and Junior. There were three terms a year, corresponding to the college terms; and the instruction was given, prior to the erection of Dane

---

[1] 1783–1853; practised law in Maine, 1806–1833; professor at Cambridge, 1833–1848.

[2] Tribute of Friendship, Works, Vol. I. pp. 133–148; "The Jurist," Works, Vol. I. pp. 258–272.

[3] When Dane Hall was removed a few feet, in 1871, to its present site, its portico and columns were taken down and an enclosed brick porch substituted.

[4] It now numbers one hundred and eighty-seven.

Hall, in College House, Number 1, nearly opposite to its present site. Of the law-students, Sumner associated most with his college classmate Browne, who, entering at the same time, was, on account of a year's study in an office, advanced to the Middle Class; with Wendell Phillips, who, graduating from college a year later than Sumner, now entered with him the Junior Class; with Henry W. Paine, of Winslow, Me.,[1] who entered Sumner's class in the spring of 1832, and whose acquaintance he then made; and with his classmate Hopkinson, who joined the school in the autumn of that year.[2] With each of these he discussed common studies and plans of life, in his room and in occasional walks. Sumner and Phillips had been fellow-students, though in different classes, at the Latin School and in college; but their familiar acquaintance dates from their connection with the Law School.[3]

Sumner had now attained the full height of his manhood, — six feet and two inches. He was tall and gaunt, weighing only one hundred and twenty pounds. His hair was dark-brown; his eyes hazel, and inflamed by excessive use; his face sharp-featured; his teeth gleaming with whiteness; his complexion dark and not clear; his visage and person not attractive to the eye, and far unlike his presence in later life, when with full proportions and classic features he arrested attention in the Senate and on the street. He was never disabled by illness, and seemed exempt from the physical limitations which beset others, denying himself the exercise and sleep which Nature commands. He was swift on his feet, striding from Boston to Cambridge at the pace of nearly five miles an hour, and putting out of breath any companion who had been unlucky enough to undertake the walk with him. His voice was strong, clear, and sonorous. His countenance was lighted up with expression, and his genial smile won friends upon an introduction. His spirits were buoyant

---

[1] Mr. Paine practised his profession for several years in Hallowell, Me., and removed, in 1854, to Boston, where he is still one of the leaders of the bar.

[2] Among other friends in the Law School were Charles C. Converse and George Gibbs. Converse became a judge of the Supreme Court of the State of Ohio. He resided at Zanesville, and died in 1860. Gibbs was a nephew of Rev. Dr. William E. Channing. He was the author of the "Memoirs of the Administrations of Washington and John Adams." He resided at Washington during our Civil War, and died April 9, 1873. He assisted Sumner in procuring and arranging the materials for his speech on the purchase of Alaska. His manuscripts, containing researches on the Indians of the Northwest, are deposited in the Smithsonian Institution. Sumner, in his "Sketch of the Law School," referred to Gibbs's "Judicial Chronicle," prepared when the latter was under the age of majority. "American Jurist," Jan., 1835, Vol. XIII. p. 120.

[3] Mr. Phillips is the author of the sketch of Sumner in Johnson's Encyclopædia.

in company, and his laugh was loud and hearty. But, whatever were his physical characteristics, there was a charm in his perfect simplicity and naturalness, his absolute sincerity of heart, his enthusiasm and scholarly ambition, his kindness to fellow-students, his respect for older people, his friendliness for all, — qualities which never fail to win interest and affection. Many who knew him in early days, parted afterwards by divergent tastes or sharp political antagonisms, now recall the memory of this period only to speak pleasantly and even tenderly of him.

The beginning of his studies in the Law School marks a distinct transition in Sumner's early life. To the classmates who were nearest to him in sympathy he frankly confessed his ambition. It had, while in college and the year after, been stirred by the great names of history; but, until he decided to study at the Law School, it was vague and unsettled. Having chosen his profession, the *jurist* became his ideal. He aspired to know the law as a science, and not merely to follow it as a lucrative occupation. Such names as those of Grotius, Pothier, Mansfield, and Blackstone dwelt much in his thoughts. Fascinated by Story's learning and fame, he looked probably to the bench or the professor's chair as the highest reward of his unwearied toils.[1]

He entered on his chosen study with the greatest ardor and enthusiasm. To a classmate he wrote of the law as " a noble profession, an immense field." He husbanded his time, and grudged every moment of diversion. Early and late at his books, limiting personal associations to a narrow circle, abstaining from needful recreation even in vacations, chary of evenings spared for amusements, and only yielding to the attractions of some eminent actor, he devoted himself to his studies, not only during the day and evening, but prolonged them past midnight till two in the morning, — his usual hour of retiring. Once, when poring over his books, he was startled by the janitor's tread and the breaking daylight. He knew the place of each book in the library so well, that he could readily find it in the dark. No monk ever kept his vigils with more absorbing devotion. The tone of his letters changed perceptibly at this time; no longer light and sportive as before, they are altogether serious, and relate chiefly to his studies, with only brief references to the incidents of college life and tidings from classmates.

[1] In his oration on " The Scholar, the Jurist, the Artist, the Philanthropist," he draws, with illustrations, the distinction between the jurist and the lawyer. Works, Vol. I. pp. 263-268.

Shortly after he entered the Law School, he procured a " Lawyer's Commonplace-Book," in which he wrote out tables of English kings and lord-chancellors, with dates of reigns and terms; sketches of lawyers, drawn largely from Roscoe's "Lives;" extracts from Sir Matthew Hale's "History of the Common Law;" and the definitions and incidents of " Estates," as laid down by Blackstone.

The list of books read by him at the school, as noted in his commonplace-books, is remarkable for its wide range, and begins with this memorandum and extract from Coke's First Institute: " Law reading commenced Sept., 1831, at Cambridge. 'Holding this for an undoubted verity, that there is no knowledge, case, or point in law, seeme it of never so little account, but will stand our student in stead at one time or other.' 1 Inst. 9." Besides his common-law studies, he read widely in French law.

Sumner's memory was not less extraordinary than his industry. Students applied to him for guidance in their investigations, and even lawyers in practice sought, in a few instances at least, his aid in the preparation of briefs.

While his friends admired his zeal and enthusiasm, they were not altogether pleased with his excessive application, and advised greater moderation in his studies. There was reason in their caution. It is possible to task the receptive capacity of the mind to the injury of its creative power; and Sumner, perhaps, gathered his knowledge too fast for the best intellectual discipline.

His notes of the moot-court cases heard by the professors, in several of which he was counsel,[1] are preserved. In Feb., 1833, he maintained (Wendell Phillips being of counsel on the other side) the negative of the question, whether a Scotch bond, assignable by the law of Scotland, can be sued by the assignee in his own name in our courts. He seems to have been dissatisfied with his argument, and wrote to Browne, stating his hesitation in public speaking, and his difficulty in selecting fit language for his thoughts. Browne replied, saying that he had overstated the difficulty, which was not peculiar to him; and advising a simpler style, with less effort and consciousness, and the rejection of large words, — *sesquipedalia verba* (" to which you know you are addicted "), — and " uncommon, brilliant, and Gibbonic phrases." " You do not stumble," he said; " you utter rapidly enough.

---

[1] Cases heard Oct. 22, Nov. 22, and Dec. 13, 1832; and Jan. 14, Feb. 18, June 5, July 5, and Oct. 20, 1833.

To be sure, you have not the *torrens dicendi*, and that is a very fortunate thing."

Sumner competed successfully for a Bowdoin prize offered to resident graduates for the best dissertation on the theme, " Are the most important Changes in Society effected Gradually or by Violent Revolutions?" His manuscript bore a motto from the "Agricola" of Tacitus: "Per intervalla ac spiramenta temporum." It was written in a fortnight, without interfering with his regular studies, and covered fifty pages. Some of its quotations may be traced in his orations. The early part is elaborate, but the latter hurriedly written. Much space is taken with a review of the condition of Europe in the " Dark Ages," and of the agencies which promoted modern civilization, — a line of thought probably suggested by his recent reading of Hallam's " Middle Ages." This progressive development, he maintained, shows that the improvement of society is effected by gradual reforms, often unobserved, rather than by revolutions. The former are always to be encouraged; the latter become necessary when society has outgrown its institutions, and peaceful changes are resisted by the governing power. The dissertation bears the marks of haste in composition, and is marred by digressions and wanting in compactness.[1] He did not then apply the labor of assiduous and repeated revision, which was afterwards habitual with him. While not falling below the similar efforts of clever young men, it is not prophetic of future distinction. One passage is interesting, when read in the light of his subsequent career: —

" Times like these (when revolutions become necessary) call for the exertions of the truly brave man. The good citizen may revolt at violence and outrage, and all the calamities which thicken upon a people divided with itself; but if he be true to his country, he will incur the risk for the prize in store. ' For surely, to every good and peaceable citizen,' said Milton,[2] himself an actor in scenes like these to which I am referring, ' it must in nature needs be a hateful thing to be the displeaser and molester of thousands. But when God commands to take the trumpet and blow a dolorous or a jarring blast, it lies not in man's will what he shall say or what he shall conceal.' The question is one upon which hangs the prosperity and happiness of his country for years to come. A great battle is to be fought; but the fruits of the victory are not to him alone. The honor and garland are his; but the benefit goes

1 President Quincy wrote him a note, requesting an interview in relation to the dissertation, — with what particular purpose it is not now definitely known, but perhaps with reference to some digressions which are still noted with pencil-marks, made at the time.

2 " Reason of Church Government urged against Prelatry."

down to the latest posterity. The toil and danger are his; but, in Milton's words again, ' he shall have his charter and freehold of rejoicing to him and his heirs.' "

It was Sumner's purpose to leave the Law School in July, 1833, at the end of a two years' course; but he yielded to the persuasions of Judge Story, who urged him to remain during the next term, which would close with the year. The judge wrote to him from Washington, July 12: " I am very glad that you have concluded to remain at the Law School another term. It will, I think, be very profitable to you, and not in the slightest degree affect your means of practical knowledge. Let nothing induce you to quit the law. You will, as sure as you live, possess a high rank in it, and need not fear the frowns of fortune or of power."

While Judge Story was absent at Washington, Sumner was his correspondent at Cambridge, and served him in forwarding books, distributing presentation copies of his works, and in similar good offices. The judge wrote, Feb. 6, 1833,[1] " There are not many of whom I would venture to ask the favor of troubling themselves in my affairs; but I feel proud to think that you are among the number, and I have, in some sort, as the Scotch would say, a heritable right to your friendship." And again, on Feb. 4, 1834: " You must begin to be chary of your intellectual as well as physical strength, or it may be exhausted before you reach the fair maturity of life."

During the summer and autumn of 1833, while serving as librarian, Sumner prepared a catalogue of the library of the Law School. His work, for which he was voted one hundred and fifty dollars by the corporation, was carefully done and much approved at the time. It contains, besides the list of books, an interesting sketch of the growth of the library, and of the gifts of the second Thomas Hollis, of Lincoln's Inn, which was republished in the " American Jurist."[2]

In 1833, he contributed two articles to the " American Monthly Review: "[3] one, a review of the impeachment trials before the Senate of the United States, and particularly that of Judge Peck; and the other, a notice of an edition of Blackstone's " Commentaries," with special reference to the notes of Chris-

---

[1] Story's Life and Letters, Vol. II. pp. 119, 120.
[2] Jan., 1834, Vol. XII. pp. 263–268.   [3] April and May.

tian and Chitty. Browne wrote to him in relation to the former
article : —

"It is learned without a show of learning. To have been able to accomplish such a matter is no small subject of rejoicing. I am glad to see you
grow. You have improved your style in proportions and muscle. It bears
in that article a favorable comparison with a strong, healthy, well-built man.
Did you get that Latin quotation from Persius? That was the only thing
I would ask to strike out. It was far-fetched, knotty, and hard to be
translated."

Near the close of his second year in the Law School, he began
to write for the "American Jurist," a law periodical which maintained a high rank, and numbered among its contributors Theron
Metcalf, Simon Greenleaf, Luther S. Cushing, George S. Hillard,
and Dr. I. Ray. Some of its series of articles — notably, Judge
Metcalf's on Contracts — afterwards grew into treatises. Willard Phillips — author of the treatise on "The Law of Insurance " — was the editor. Sumner's first contribution was to the
number for July, 1833, — a notice of a lecture before King's College, London, by Professor J. J. Park, on "Courts of Equity." [1]
The article defines at some length and with happy illustrations
the distinction between law and equity, then much misconceived.
Judge Story noted it, in his "Equity Jurisprudence," as "a forci-
ble exposition of the prevalent errors on the subject," and as
"full of useful comment and research." [2] It is a thoughtful and
well-written paper, entirely worthy of a lawyer who had added
practice to his professional studies.

Sumner's method of composition changed perceptibly while he
was in the Law School. His style became more compact, his
vocabulary more select, his thought clearer and more exact. His
topics exercised the critical faculty, and the discipline of legal
studies counteracted his tendency to diffuseness. He was, more
than before, the master of his material. There was not as yet
the glow, the earnestness, or the moral inspiration which were
afterwards the peculiar traits of his writings; these were reserved for a period when his life was to be among events rather
than among books. His freedom of thought, and his sympathy
with new ideas and reforms, checked probably in some measure
by his association with conservative teachers, appear thus early

[1] Vol. X. pp. 227-237. The English professor died shortly after, too soon to read this
notice of his lecture.
[2] Vol. I. § 23, note.

warm and active.[1] His intellect lacked subtlety; it was generally repelled by abstruse and technical questions, and, led by Story's example, sought the more congenial domains of international and commercial law. Some of his surviving fellow-students recall that he was not thought to have what is called " a legal mind; " though Story and Greenleaf, each of whom counted on him as colleague or successor, do not appear to have observed this defect. His classmate Browne took exception at the time to his articles in the " Jurist," as being speculative rather than practical in their topics; and certainly his contributions to that magazine, then and later, show that he preferred to write upon the literature of the law rather than upon the law itself. One with his qualities of mind would be more likely to find his place in the profession as author or teacher, than among the details of office-business or the hand-to-hand contests of the court-room.

Contemporaneous letters, written chiefly by his classmates, show his habits at this time, and the expectations entertained as to his future. His father wrote to him, April 4, 1832, " Charles, while you study law, be not too discursive. Study your prescribed course well. That is enough to make you a lawyer. You may bewilder your mind by taking too wide a range."

Stearns, in a similar tone, wrote, Sept. 19, 1831, " *You* were cut out for a lawyer. . . . I cannot altogether applaud your resolution to include so much in your system of study for the coming year. 'Law, classics, history, and literature' is certainly too wide a range for any common mind to spread over at one time. Better follow Captain Bobadil's example; take them man by man, and 'kill them all up by computation.'" Hopkinson, Jan. 6, 1832, calls him " the indefatigable, ever-delving student, and amorous votary of antiquity; " and refers, May 12, " to the study and diligence for which the world gives you credit."

Browne wrote from Cambridge to Stearns, May 6, 1832: —

" We, in Cambridge here, are studying law at a trot, or rather I should say, reciting it. Some study hard, — among them your good friend Charles, hater of mathematics; but as to your other friend [himself], he studies the books but little. Sumner will be a vast reservoir of law, if he lives to be at the bar; which, if you take the bodings of a harsh, constant cough and a most pale face, might seem doubtful. Yet his general health seems perfect. He eats well, sleeps well, and so through all the functions of the animal man.

[1] Hopkinson wrote, Oct. 28, 1831, taking him to task for assuming positions because of their novelty, and for depreciating authority and prescription.

We often laugh together in speaking of the time to come, when I tell him I will send to him for law when I have a case to look up. He is to the law what he used to be to history, — a repertory of facts to which we might all resort. Let him speed in his studies, increase in the color of his cheeks, expel his cough from a dominion whose title is almost confirmed by prescription, and he will hold himself higher than his legal brethren by the head and shoulders."

Stearns wrote, May 14 : —

" Browne tells me you are studying law with all the zeal and ardor of a lover. But by all means do not sacrifice your health. You must take care of that. You owe it as a duty to yourself, a duty to your friends and country, a duty to your God. It will be too late to think of this when disease has taken a firm grapple on the body. . . . You cannot be a man and reach the lawful height to which your intellect is capable of being raised, unless you carefully watch over and preserve your health. You may think these remarks are frivolous, but I consider them as serious truths. I look forward to the time, if you do not kill yourself prematurely, when I shall see you a decided, powerful champion of the cause of justice, patriotism, and the true Christian faith."

Hopkinson wrote, July 17 : —

" Congratulations are matter of course; but I hope you will consider it equally a matter of course that a friend should feel great joy in your success.[1] Your pen was always that of a ready writer, once indeed racy and loose. But words were always your obedient slaves. They came and ranged themselves at your bidding; nay, seemed often to outrun your swift intent, and marshal you the way. But I have for two years been observing your pen to grow stiffer. Your crude troops have been growing more disciplined and forming in straighter lines, till you have a numerous and well-ordered army. . . . Be this a foretaste of many successes in laudable undertakings."

Again, on July 30 : —

" You never think of bodily health. Do you have the folly to spend this vacation in poring? For shame! Take a country tour, — a long pedestrian tour. It will be the best way to further your intellectual progress. Give that pallid face a little color, those lean limbs a little muscle, and the bow of your mind a greater elasticity."

Again, on May 9, 1833, Hopkinson wrote from Lowell, where he was practising law as the partner of Mr. Luther Lawrence :

" Had I but your application, I might consider myself in a good way. Not, indeed, that I could grasp such honors as are within your reach; not that I could walk over the heads of all young practitioners, and be in fact a counsellor during my attorneyship: but I could take an immediate practice and

[1] Bowdoin prize.

profit. Your chance at Cambridge, had I your fitness for the place, would tempt me more than a tour to Washington, which has so kindled your imagination. . . . As to your despondency, or whatever other name you please to give it, take exercise! — exercise! — exercise! — and it will vanish like the morning dew.''

Henry W. Paine, having left the Law School, wrote from Winslow, Me., March 12, 1833: —

" There is not one among my friends in whom I feel a more lively interest, whose prosperity would more essentially contribute to my happiness. Be careful of your health, my friend, and the day is not distant when I shall have the proud satisfaction of saying that ' Sumner was once my classmate.' ''

Again, on May 25 : —

" Since my last, you have been called to mourn the departure of poor Ashmun. Indeed, we all mourned the event; but you must have felt it more sensibly than the rest of us, situated so near him as you were, and so intimate with him as you had been for the past two years. You were present, too, at the last solemn scene, performing those acts of kindness which you must now reflect upon with satisfaction. . . . If you could realize what a treat is one of your letters, you have too much of the milk of human kindness to withhold the favor. I seem to see in them once more Old Harvard, and to be seated again in the librarian's room of Dane Law College. But you are soon to leave, and thus the strongest chain that binds me to the ' sacred ' spot is to be severed. I have always supposed that the place of your ultimate destination was certain. Surely you cannot hesitate. You were made for Boston. There your talents and attainments will be appreciated, and cannot fail of securing you that reputation which all who know you would rejoice to see you attain. But, as you have been so incessant in your application, I am sincerely concerned for your health; and, if my poor advice could avail, you would spend your coming vacation in journeying. Come ' down East.' Dismiss your books and the toils of study. You may think this ' interested advice; ' and in part it is, though not wholly so. I feel it would be beneficial to you. It would be a joyous event to me.''

Hopkinson wrote from Lowell, July 13 : —

" Dear Charles, — I regret to learn that you are to stay yet a term further at Cambridge, for I had calculated on your coming here this fall. Yet nothing is so like yourself as to stay to please your friend [Judge Story], — and *such* a friend! I most earnestly congratulate you on having gained the confidence, esteem, and friendship of that truly great man. It will fix your life's direction, and I would not have you forego the advantages which that situation and that intercourse will secure to you for my pleasure or gratification. You will find your employment probably in the science of the law, and will escape its drudgery.''

In March, 1833, a temperance society was formed in the college, which included members of the professional schools, as well as undergraduates. It was a period of special interest in this reform. The pledge of this society admitted the use of wines, excluding only that of spirituous liquors, and was binding only during the signer's connection with the college. The meeting for organization was held in a room in University Hall, which was used for commons.[1] Sumner was chosen President; Abiel A. Livermore, of the Divinity School, Vice-President; and Samuel Osgood, of the Divinity School, Secretary. Among the members of the Executive Committee were Barzillai Frost, of the Divinity School, and Richard H. Dana, Jr., of the Sophomore Class. Public meetings were held in the City Hall, or one of the churches; at one of which Rev. John G. Palfrey delivered an impressive address, still well remembered for its effective reference to graduates of the college who had fallen victims to the vice. He then, for the first time, met Sumner, who presided; and was attracted by his manly presence and genial smile. In the autumn of 1833, Sumner invited George S. Hillard to repeat before the society a temperance lecture which he had delivered in other places.

Rev. A. A. Livermore, of Meadville, Penn., a living officer of the society, writes : —

" A peculiar life-and-death earnestness characterized even then all that Sumner did and said. His voice had a trumpet tone, and he was a good leader to rally under; but temperance was not popular."

Rev. Dr. Osgood, of New York, also writes : —

" Sumner was then a law-student, and I saw a good deal of him. He talked much of ethics and international law. He had great strength of conviction on ethical subjects and decided religious principle; yet he was little theological, much less ecclesiastical."

He was connected, at least during his first year in the Law School, with a debating society, and bore his part in discussions which related to the utility of trial by jury and of capital punishment, and the value of lyceums. He was not fluent in speech, but he prepared himself with care, as his minutes still preserved show.

One attraction at this time proved stronger with Sumner than

1 The first meeting was held March 6, and the officers were chosen March 14. "Mercantile Journal," March 16, 1833.

even his books. Miss Frances A. Kemble, the daughter of Charles Kemble, the English actor, and the niece of Mrs. Siddons, came with her father to this country in 1832, three years after her *début* at Covent Garden in the character of Juliet. She was then but twenty-one years old; and her youth added to the fascination of her brilliant talents. Wherever she played, her acting was greatly admired; and by no class so much as by students. After fulfilling engagements in New York and other cities, she made her first appearance in Boston in April, 1833. Sumner was an enthusiast in his devotion, walking again and again to the city during her engagement at the Tremont Theatre, witnessing her acting with intense admiration, and delighting to talk of her with his friends.[1] He did not know her personally at this time, but greatly enjoyed her society some years afterwards, during a visit to Berkshire County.

Sumner visited, while a student in the Law School, but few families. He was a welcome guest at the firesides of the two professors, and Mrs. Story and Mrs. Greenleaf took an interest in him almost equal to that of their husbands. His friendship with the family of President Quincy, which began at this period, remained unbroken through life; and from them, in all the vicissitudes of his career, he never failed to receive hearty sympathy and support. While he entered sympathetically into the household life of his friends, he was, at this period, — which is marked by an absorbing, almost ascetic, devotion to the pursuit of knowledge, — indifferent to the society of ladies whose charms were chiefly those of person and youth; and his preference for the conversation of scholarly persons gave at times much amusement to others; but, as some lifelong friendships attest, no one was ever more appreciative of women of superior refinement and excellence.

Mrs. Waterston, a daughter of President Quincy, writes: —

"Charles Sumner entered his Senior year in 1830. The son of an old friend of my father's, he must have had an early invitation to our house. The first distinct remembrance I have of him personally was on one of my mother's reception evenings, held every Thursday during the winter, and

---

[1] Browne wrote, April 18, "You speak rapturously of the girl." Judge Story's enthusiasm for Miss Kemble quite equalled Sumner's. He was charmed with her acting, and addressed some verses to her: —

"Go! lovely woman, go! Enjoy thy fame!
A second Kemble, with a deathless name."

Life and Letters, Vol. II. pp. 114–117.

open to all acquaintances and the students. I was standing at the end of one of the long, old-fashioned rooms, and saw, among a crowd of half-grown youths and towering above them, the tall, spare form and honest face of Charles Sumner. Years after we recalled that evening; and from his wonderful memory he mentioned a little fact. 'A three-cornered note was brought to you,' said he, 'and you said to the gentlemen round you, " it is from Miss M.; she cannot be here this evening." ' ' Why were you not introduced to me?' said I. ' Oh, I did not dare to be; I only looked at you from afar with awe.' I was, in fact, a year younger than himself; but in those simple days the chasm was wide between a raw collegian, as he then was, and a young lady in society. I recall him very distinctly in his seat on Sundays. It was in the old chapel in University Hall, before any alteration had been made. The President's pew was in the gallery, on the right of the pulpit. Perched there, I looked down, first on good Dr. Ware, Sr., in his professor's gown; and, while he discoursed ' furthermore,' I looked beyond and below on the very young Sophomores, and saw Sumner's long proportions in the front seat of the Seniors.

" It was during his residence as a law-student that he was most frequently at our house. I do not think he ever sought ladies' society much, though I remember we always enjoyed his conversation, and that my mother foresaw a future for Charles Sumner. It was during his law-studies that Judge Story and my father recognized his uncommon abilities. On one of those memorable Sunday evenings, when the judge, seated by my mother, drew all present around them, he spoke of Sumner, and said: ' He has a wonderful memory; he keeps all his knowledge in order, and can put his hand on it in a moment. This is a great gift.' On July 28, 1833, the new First Parish church was in progress; and the steeple, after being finished inside, was to be raised entire and placed on the tower. I give an extract from my journal: ' We sent Horace to ask Mr. Sumner, the law-student, to let us come over to the Law School and see the raising. In a few moments, mamma, Margaret, and myself were joined by Mr. Sumner, who escorted us not only to the Law School, but all over the building, even into his own room, as, being librarian, he lives there. This youth, though not in the least handsome, is so good-hearted, clever, and real, that it is impossible not to like him and believe in him. Judge and Mrs. Story and several other ladies joined us, and we sat on the portico; for Judge Story, fearing some accident would occur, would not let any of us go over to the church to see how the raising was managed. The steeple went up so slowly that mamma and my sister could not wait for it; but I staid with Mrs. Story until it rose to its full height and was safely moored on the tower. Mr. Sumner walked home with me arm in arm.' This latter clause is underlined, as I suppose it was a very remarkable attention; at least he had now no ' awe ' of the young lady.

" It was in the preceding April, 1833, that John Hooker Ashmun died, — the Royall Professor of Law, — and Sumner must have been present at Judge Story's eulogy on Mr. Ashmun. In my journal of that day I write: ' After the services closed and the men came forward to remove the body, a number of Mr. Ashmun's students, as if moved by an irresistible impulse, pressed forward and surrounded him for the last time. They were to see his face no more.'

"Mr. Alvord took Mr. Ashmun's place as professor, but, in the summer of 1833, he also was taken very ill. During the weeks after the notice of the steeple-raising, I find Mr. Sumner's name mentioned constantly, coming in to report Mr. Alvord's state, as he visited him daily. One extract more from the journal: 'Charles Sumner came to give his account of Mr. Alvord, which is more favorable. He paid me a long visit, and we talked at the rate of nine knots an hour. He gave a curious account of a young man who has been studying Latin and Greek in a lighthouse, to prepare for college. The reason of his choosing a lighthouse is to save the expense of oil! We agreed that he deserved all success. Mamma returned from Dedham while Mr. Sumner was still here, and he staid and had a good long talk with her.' "

His classmate, Rev. Dr. Emery, writes: —

"In Oct., 1833, I returned to Cambridge and became a resident graduate. I found Sumner in the Law School, pursuing his studies with great enthusiasm, and we were often in each other's rooms. He was the same scholarly person then as when in college, and he lived, as it were, in intimate converse with the learned of ancient and modern times. I have no doubt his mind was better stored with accurate and critical knowledge than that of any other student in the school. He occupied as librarian one of the front rooms in the second story of Dane Hall, 'the pleasantest room in Cambridge,' as he told me. If he had at that time any thought of being one of the foremost public men in the country beyond that of an eminent lawyer, he certainly kept it to himself, for he seemed to take but little interest in political matters. He came one day to my room in Massachusetts Hall, and told me how he had unfortunately just congratulated a professor, recently resigned, on his election to the State Senate, not knowing that he had been defeated. His mind was wholly absorbed in other pursuits, which, perhaps unconsciously to himself, were preparing him for the lofty stand he attained in after life."

Professor William C. Russell, of Cornell University, who saw much of Sumner at Cambridge in 1832-33, writes: —

"He was a tall, thin, bent, ungainly law-student; his eyes were inflamed by late reading, and his complexion showed that he was careless of exercise. I was from New York, and he had less experience of life; and from that cause, I suppose, liked to talk to me. He certainly was very kind, very simple, and very easily pleased. I rather think, however, that I owed a great deal of the kindness with which he treated me to the fact that I was personally acquainted, though very slightly, with 'Fanny Kemble,' as we boys used to call her. He was, as much as any of us, infatuated by her acting; and I remember his one day stopping me in the street, and drawing me out of the thoroughfare, and saying, 'Come, Russell, tell me something about Fanny Kemble,' with all the interest of a lover.

"His personal kindness never ceased while I remained at Cambridge, and he helped me on one occasion when I needed a friend, with the tenderness of a girl. When I left, in 1834, to no one of the friends whom I had gained there was I more attached."

A lady, then a *fiancée* of one of his most intimate classmates, writes : —

" As a young law-student, I remember very well the first impression he made upon me of a certain dignity and strength. which supplied the want of grace, and which was as perceptible in his conversation as in his person. You would have said then that he was a man of ideas, and that the ideas of other people would never be trammels, only steps, for him."

William W. Story writes from Rome : —

" I was a mere boy when I first knew him, but the affectionate kindness which he then showed me remained unclouded by the slightest shadow until the day of his death. His father was in a class two years before my father at Harvard; and when Charles Sumner entered the Law School, my father took an interest in him at first, because of his father, and this interest soon ripened into a warm affection. My first recollections of him are at this period. He used to come to our house some two or three evenings in the week, and to his long conversations I used to listen night after night with eager pleasure. His simplicity and directness of character, his enthusiasm and craving for information, his lively spirit and genial feeling, immediately made a strong impression on me. My father was very fond of him, always received him with a beaming face, and treated him almost as if he were a son; and we were all delighted to welcome him to our family circle. He was free, natural, and *naïve* in his simplicity, and plied my father with an ever-flowing stream of questions; and I need not say that the responses were as full and genial as heart and mind could desire. When I heard that he was in the room, I quitted all occupations to see and hear him, though for the most part I only played the *rôle* of listener. When other persons came in, he would turn to me and make inquiries as to my studies, and endeavor to help me in them; and at last, out of pure good nature, he proposed to me to come to his room in the Dane Law College, and read Latin with him and talk over the ancient authors. I gladly accepted the offer, and many an evening I used to spend with him in half study, half talk. He had the art to render these evenings most agreeable. He talked of Cicero and Cæsar; of Horace, Virgil, Tacitus, Sallust, and indeed of all the old Latin writers; of the influence they had on their age, and their age had on them; of the characteristics of their poetry and prose; of the peculiarities of their style; of the differences between them and our modern authors: and he so talked of them as to interest and amuse me, and bring them before me as real and living persons out of the dim, vague mist in which they had hitherto stood in my mind. We used then, also, to cap Latin verses; and he so roused my ambition not to be outdone by him that I collected from various authors a book full of verses, all of which I committed to memory. Of course he beat me always, for he had a facile and iron memory which easily seized and steadily retained every thing he acquired.

"English poetry was also a constant subject of our talks; and he used to quote and read favorite passages which we earnestly discussed together. Among all the poets, at this time certainly, Gray was his favorite;[1] and I have still a copy of his poems, presented to me by him, and full of annotations, many of which are due to these conversations. I shall never cease to feel grateful to him for these happy evenings, so full of interest and instruction.

"Then, as afterwards, his judgment in respect to poetry was not a keen one. The higher flights of the imagination, or the rapid ranges of fancy, were above him; and I think his noblest idea of poetry was embodied in Gray's 'Elegy,' which he would repeat with sonorous tones. But poetry was with him more an acquired taste than a natural one. He had himself little imagination or fancy, and better loved strong manly sentiments and thoughts within the range of the understanding, and solid facts and statements of principles. When he could steady himself against a statement by an ancient author he felt strong. His own moral sense, which was very high, seemed to buttress itself with a passage from Cicero or Epictetus. He seemed to build upon them as upon a rock, and thence defy you to shake him.

"He was then, as ever in after life, an indefatigable and omnivorous student. He lived simply, was guilty of no excesses of any kind, went very little into society, and devoted his days and nights to books. Shortly after my first acquaintance with him, he became librarian of the Dane Law School, and I think there was scarcely a text-book in the library of the contents of which he had not some knowledge. Nor was this a superficial knowledge, considering its extent and his youth. He had acquainted himself, also, with the lives, characters, and capacity of most of the authors, and could give a fair *résumé* of the contents of most of their works. His room was piled with books: the shelves overflowed and the floor was littered with them. Though a devoted student of law, he did not limit his reading to it, but ranged over the whole field of literature with eager interest. He was at this time totally without vanity, and only desirous to acquire knowledge and information on every subject. Behind every work he liked to see and feel the man who wrote it, and, as it were, to make his personal acquaintance. Whenever a particular question interested him, he would come to my father and talk it over with him, and discuss it by the hour.

"He had no interest in games and athletic sports; never, so far as I know, fished or shot or rowed; had no fancy for dogs and horses; and, in a word, was without all those tastes which are almost universal with men of his age. As for dancing, I think he never danced a step in his life. Of all men I ever knew at his age, he was the least susceptible to the charms of women. Men he liked best, and with them he preferred to talk. It was in vain for the loveliest and liveliest girl to seek to absorb his attention. He would at once

---

[1] W. W. Story gave Sumner, Jan. 1, 1834, a copy of Milton, inscribed with, "From his grateful friend."

desert the most blooming beauty to talk to the plainest of men. This was a constant source of amusement to us, and we used to lay wagers with the pretty girls, that with all their art they could not keep him at their side a quarter of an hour. Nor do I think we ever lost one of these bets. I remember particularly one dinner at my father's house, when it fell to his lot to take out a charming woman, so handsome and full of *esprit* that any one at the table might well have envied him his position. She had determined to hold him captive, and win her bet against us. But her efforts were all in vain. Unfortunately, on his other side was a dry old *savant*, packed with information; and within five minutes Sumner had completely turned his back on his fair companion, and engaged in a discussion with the other, which lasted the whole dinner. We all laughed. She cast up her eyes deprecatingly, acknowledged herself vanquished, and paid her bet. Meantime, Sumner was wholly unconscious of the jest or of the laughter. He had what he wanted, — sensible men's talk. He had mined the *savant* as he mined every one he met, in search of ore, and was thoroughly pleased with what he got.

" Though he was an interesting talker, he had no lightness of hand. He was kindly of nature, interested in every thing, but totally put off his balance by the least *persiflage;* and, if it was tried on him, his expression was one of complete astonishment. He was never ready at a retort, tacked slowly, like a frigate when assaulted by stinging feluccas, and was at this time almost impervious to a joke. He had no humor himself, and little sense of it in others; and his jests, when he tried to make one, were rather cumbrous. But in 'plain sailing' no one could be better or more agreeable. He was steady and studious, and, though genial, serious in his character; while we were all light, silly, and full of animal spirits, which he sympathized with but could not enter into.

" He was, as a young man, singularly plain. His complexion was not healthy. He was tall, thin, and ungainly in his movements, and sprawled rather than sat on a chair or sofa. Nothing saved his face from ugliness but his white gleaming teeth and his expression of bright intelligence and entire amiability. None could believe that he was thus plain in his youth, who only knew him in his full and ripened manhood. As years went on, his face and figure completely changed; and at last he stood before us a stalwart and imposing presence, full of dignity and a kind of grandeur. Age added to his appearance as well as to his influence. His genial illuminating smile he never lost; and at fifty years of age he was almost a handsome, and certainly a remarkable, man in his bearing and looks.

" I do not think, in his early years, he had any great ambition. *That* developed itself afterwards. Circumstances and accidents forced him forward to the van, and he became a leader terribly in earnest. He had the same high-mindedness, the same single aim at justice and truth, the same inflexible faith and courage then that ever after characterized him." [1]

1 Mr. Story contributed an " In Memoriam " tribute to Sumner, in forty-one verses, to "Blackwood's Magazine," Sept., 1874, Vol. CXVI. pp. 342–346.

In an address to the students — colored — of Howard University, Washington, D. C., Feb. 3, 1871, Sumner said : —

These exercises " carry me back to early life, when I was a student of the Law School of Harvard University as you have been students in the Law School of Howard University. I cannot think of those days without fondness. They were the happiest of my life. . . . There is happiness in the acquisition of knowledge, which surpasses all common joys. The student who feels that he is making daily progress, constantly learning something new, — who sees the shadows by which he was originally surrounded gradually exchanged for an atmosphere of light, — cannot fail to be happy. His toil becomes a delight, and all that he learns is a treasure, — with this difference from gold and silver, that it cannot be lost. It is a perpetual capital at compound interest."

LETTERS TO CLASSMATES.

TO JONATHAN F. STEARNS, BEDFORD, MASS.

SUNDAY, Sept. 25, 1831. Div. 10.

To Cambridge,[1] — your missile hit the mark; though, from its early date and late coming, one would think that the post-office powder was not of the best proof. To Cambridge, — yes; it has come to me here — Law School. Yester afternoon presented me with it, as I looked in at the office on my return from sweet Auburn, where Judge Story had been, in Nature's temple, set around with her own green and hung over with her own blue, dedicating to the dead a place well worthy of their repose. The general subject was the claims of the dead for a resting-place amongst kindred; the fondness of their living friends for seemly sepulchres in which to bury them, and where a tear can be shed unseen but by the waving grass or sighing trees; and the customs of nations in honors to the dead, — all naturally arising from the occasion.[2]

Your objections to the Anti-masonic party, and not to Anti-masonry, are perhaps good, though rather too strong. What party ever showed uniform placidness; and especially what young party? The blood is too warm to beat slowly or healthfully; sores and ulcers show themselves. And so it is with Anti-masonry. Some there are with more zeal than knowledge, and whose rabid philosophy will not suffer them to judge in candor and truth. They strain the principles of their party to such a tension that they almost crack (as in the case you instanced); but pray set this down to the infirmity

1 Stearns, not knowing where Sumner was, wrote, Sept. 18, "Where art thou ? At Cambridge, I presume."

2 An account of the services at the consecration of the Mt. Auburn Cemetery, with extracts from Judge Story's address, is given in his "Life and Letters," Vol. II. pp. 61–67.

of man. They, poor men, have their consciences on their side; and with
that ally need we admire that they are insensible to those feelings which
would make them stop? For myself, my mind is made up: I shall never
give back. Yet may this hand forget its cunning, if ever aught shall come
from me savoring of intolerance or unwarrantable exclusion. I have been
scourged into my present opinions by the abuse which my father has met
with, — namely, my mind was brought by this to see what Masonry did, and
to inquire what it could do. Anti-masonry has rather a ridiculous, repulsive
air, of which no one is more conscious than myself; and had not the circumstances of my father's relation to it brought me into close contact (almost
perforce) with it, I should probably have been an unbeliever to this day.
Anti-masonry cannot claim its due proportion of talent for the numbers of its
professors; and there is nothing strange in this, for it is *new*. The religion
you profess drew to it none but fishermen when it first came down with
the Son of the Father. Truth always walks lame when she first starts. It
is *time* which habits her in the wings that bear her upward. I have said
more upon this than I wished to; for I care not to have it in my mind. I
feel so strongly upon it, that when it is called before me my mind engages
itself too much, to the detriment of more profitable thoughts.

Come to Cambridge and see me. I room at Divinity Hall, No. 10, on
the lower floor; and you shall have half of the couch which is mine. Come,
and we will have an evening's chat. You will not disturb me; for, though I
try to seize every moment of time, yet our law-studies are so indefinite that no
number of hours cut out will be missed. We recite but three times a week;
and one forenoon will master our lesson, though days can be given to it with
profit. Come, then, and bring with you "The Nine" book, and Browne
and yourself and myself will renew old scenes and live happy times over
again. I like living here, for I can be by myself. I know hardly an individual in the school. Days of idleness must be atoned for; the atoning offering is at hand, and it is a steady devotion to *study*. Late to bed and early to
rise, and full employment while up, is what I am trying to bind myself to.
The *labor ipse voluptas* I am coveting. I had rather be a toad and live upon
a dungeon's vapor than one of those lumps of flesh that are christened lawyers, and who know only how to wring from quibbles and obscurities that
justice which else they never could reach; who have no idea of law beyond
its letter, nor of literature beyond their Term Reports and Statutes. If I am
a lawyer, I wish to be one who can dwell upon the vast heaps of law-matter,
as the temple in which the majesty of right has taken its abode; who will
aim, beyond the mere letter, at the spirit, — the broad spirit of the law, —
and who will bring to his aid a liberal and cultivated mind. Is not this an
honest ambition? If not, reprove me for it. A lawyer is one of the best or
worst of men, according as he shapes his course. He may breed strife, and
he may settle dissensions of years. But when I look before me and above
me, and see the impendent weight, — *molem ingentem et perpetuis humeris sus-
tinendam*, — I incontinently shrink back. Book peers above book; and one
labor of investigation is gone only to show a greater one. The greatest lawyers, after fifty years of enfolding study, have confessed, with the Wise Man,

that they only knew that they knew nothing. And what a discomfiting expression is here, that all the piled-up grains of human wisdom will raise one not at all from this earth; that he may labor and heap his acquirements, and yet they are as nothing! He begins with nothing, and ends where he began. If it is so, yet knowledge and acquirements are relative; and the man who knows that he knows nothing is yet more wise than the herd of his fellow-men, — even as much more wise, as wisdom itself is wiser than he is. And here is the place for hope, — though we cannot mount to the skies or elevate ourself from mother earth, yet can we reach far above those around us, and look with a far keener gaze. "What man has done, man can do;" and in these words is a full fountain of hope. And again, hear Burke: "There is nothing in the world really beneficial that does not lie within the reach of an informed understanding and a well-directed pursuit. There is nothing that God has judged good for us that He has not given us the means to accomplish, both in the natural and the moral world." [1] What a sentiment! how rich in expression, how richer in truth!

A lawyer must know every thing. He must know law, history, philosophy, human nature; and, if he covets the fame of an advocate, he must drink of all the springs of literature, giving ease and elegance to the mind and illustration to whatever subject it touches. So experience declares, and reflection bears experience out.

I have not yet methodized my time, — and, by the way, method is the life of study, — but I think of something like the following: The law in the forenoon; six hours to law is all that Coke asks for (*sex horas des legibus æquis*), and Matthew Hale and Sir William Jones and all who have declared an opinion; though, as to that matter, I should be influenced little more than a tittle by any opinions of others. [2] We all of us must shape our own courses; no two men will like the same hours or manner of study. Let each one assist himself from the experience of others; but let him not put aside his own judgment. Well, six hours, — namely, the forenoon wholly and solely to law; afternoon to classics; evening to history, subjects collateral and assistant to law, &c. I have as yet read little else than law since I have been here; but the above is the plan I have chalked out. Recreation must not be found in idleness or loose reading. "Le changement d'occupation est mon seul délassement," says Chancellor D'Aguesseau, one of the greatest lawyers France ever saw.

And now have I blackened enough paper? Have you read to this spot? If you have, you are a well-doing servant, and shalt surely have your reward. But pray visit upon these sheets the heretic's fate, — fire, fire, fire. And now I stop. "Dabit deus his quoque finem." [3]

Your true friend,

C. S.

---

[1] Speech on the "Plan for Economical Reform."

[2] The authority of these eminent jurists as to the distribution of the hours of the day is cited in Mr. Sumner's lecture on "The Employment of Time," delivered in 1846. This lecture may be read with interest in connection with the letters of this period, which emphasize the value of time. Works, Vol. I. pp. 184-213.

[3] Virgil, Æneid I. 199.

TO CHARLEMAGNE TOWER, WATERVILLE, N. Y.

LAW SCHOOL, DIVINITY HALL, No. 10, Sept. 29, 1831.

A new curtain has arisen. I am treading another scene of life. I behold new objects of study, and am presented with new sources of reflection. I have left Boston and the profitless thoughts which its streets, its inhabitants, its politics, and its newspapers ever excite. I find myself again in loved Cambridge, where are sociability and retirement, and where those frittering cares and thoughts which every city inflicts upon its unlucky sojourners do not intrude. I feel differently, very differently, from what I did when I enjoyed this town, in all the *nonchalance* of an undergraduate, heedless of *time*, — that property more valuable than silver and gold, — and seeking, in the main, a pleasant way to throw away hours and minutes. I now feel that every moment, like a filing of gold, ought to be saved. But in the acting up to this feeling, strong as it may be, will lie the failure. Labor, though we all acknowledge its potency, still has too repulsive a front. Be it my duty to see in its appearance nothing but invitation and incentive. Yes, duty shall gird me for its endurance. But, to stop this vague sermonizing, I am now a regular member of the Law School, have read a volume and a half of Blackstone, and am enamored of the law. Tower, we have struck the true profession; the one in which the mind is the most sharpened and quickened, and the duties of which, properly discharged, are most vital to the interests of the country, — for religion exists independent of its ministers; every breast feels it: but the law lives only in the honesty and learning of lawyers. Let us feel conscious, then, of our responsibility; and, by as much as our profession excels in interest and importance, give to it a corresponding dedication of our abilities. And yet I give back in despair when I see the vast weight which a lawyer must bear up under. Volumes upon volumes are to be mastered of the niceties of the law, and the whole circle of literature and science and history must be compassed. . . .

Tell me what law-books you have read and are reading, and whether you have taken notes of or " commonplaced " any of your study. I have taken some notes from Blackstone of the different estates, contingent remainders, &c. As to Blackstone, I almost feel disposed to join with Fox, who pronounced him the best writer in the English language. He is clear, fluent, and elegant, with occasionally a loose expression and a bad use of a metaphor; but what a good thing for our profession that we can commence our studies with such an author. His commentaries unfold a full knowledge by themselves of the law, — a knowledge to be filled out by further study, but which is yet a whole by itself. . . .

The lower floor of Divinity Hall, where I reside, is occupied by law-students. There are here Browne and Dana of our old class, with others that I know nothing of, — not even my neighbor, parted from me by a partition-wall, have I seen yet; and I do not wish to see him. I wish no acquaintances, for they eat up time like locusts. The old classmates are enough. . . . I admire that filial piety which would make you give up formed plans and professional studies for cares with which your mind has little sympathy. It will result in good.   Your friend in truth,

CHARLES SUMNER.

TO CHARLEMAGNE TOWER.

CAMBRIDGE, LAW SCHOOL, Jan. 31, 1832.

MY DEAR FRIEND, — I never receive a letter from one of my old college friends without experiencing a most pleasing melancholy. Memory is always at hand, with her throng of recollections and associations, the shadows of past joys, — joys gone as irrevocably as time. Youth and college feelings have given way to manhood and its sterner avocations. The course is fairly commenced in the race of life, and every intellectual and corporal agency is bent to exertion. There are now no Saturdays bringing weekly respites from drudgery, allowing a momentary stop in the path of duty. All is labor. It mattereth not the day or hardly the hour, for duty is urgent all days and all hours. What, then, could bring up more pleasing recollections, and yet tinged with melancholy (because they are never more to be seen, except in memory's mirror) than a letter from one who was present and active in those scenes to which the mind recurs? I sometimes let a whole hour slip by unconsciously, my book unvexed before me, musing upon old times, feelings, and comrades. My eye sees, as exactly as if I had left it but yesterday, the old recitation-room and all its occupants. My ear seems yet to vibrate with the sound of the various voices which we heard so often. But the reverie has its end, for the present and future drive from the mind musings of the past.

Judge Story is at Washington, with the Supreme Court, for the winter. Of course the school misses him. Our class, as yet, has had nothing to do with him. Those who do recite to him love him more than any instructor they ever had before. He treats them all as gentlemen, and is full of willingness to instruct. He gives to every line of the recited lesson a running commentary, and omits nothing which can throw light upon the path of the student. The good scholars like him for the knowledge he distributes; the poor (if any there be), for the amenity with which he treats them and their faults. Have you determined never again to return to the shadows of Cambridge? By the way, the judge has a book in press, which will be published within a week, which you must read. I mention this because I doubted whether you would hear of it immediately. It is called "Commentaries on Bailments," and will entirely supersede the classic work of Jones. The title of "Bailments" is of but a day's growth. It is hardly known to the common law. Jones's work was written about forty years ago. Since then it has gained a much completer conformation. Story's work will supply all deficiencies, and, I suspect, be an interesting book; certainly a useful one.

I am now upon Kent's second volume. He is certainly the star of your State. I like his works, though less than most students. To me he is very indistinct in his outlines. This, perhaps, is the more observable, stepping, as I do, from the well-defined page of Blackstone. Truly, the English commentator is a glorious man; he brings such a method, such a flow of language and allusion and illustration to every topic! I have heard a sensible lawyer place Kent *above* him; but, in my opinion, sooner ought the earth to be above the clear and azure-built heavens! And yet the character of Kent, as told to me, bewitches me. His works, in fact, are crude, and made to publish and get money from (he has already cleared twenty thousand dollars from them) rather than to be admired and to last. A revision may put them in a little better plight for visiting posterity, and I understand he is giving them this.[1]

When you write, tell me all the law you have read. I wish to compare "reckonings" with you occasionally, as we are voyaging on the same sea.

This is written in the vexation of a cough,

By your true friend,

CHAS. SUMNER.

TO CHARLEMAGNE TOWER.

CAMBRIDGE, Friday Morning, May 11, 1832.

MY DEAR FRIEND, — The moment I saw the black seal of your letter my mind anticipated the sorrowful intelligence it bore.[2] Permit me to join with you in grief. I offer you my sincere sympathies. The loss of a father I can only imagine: may God put far distant the day when that affliction shall come over me! You have been a faithful son; and, I know, a joy to his eyes. I reverence the spirit with which you have sacrificed all your professional and literary predilections. You did that for your father's sake; and the thought that you did it on his account must be to you a spring of satisfaction and consolation as hallowed as the grief which you feel. You follow duty: what nobler object can man follow; and what can bring him to a nobler end? The professions or walks of life in which we may tread are of but little consequence, so that the way we take is well trod. I promise that your sacrifice will be ever unrepented; not that I undervalue the study of the law, or the means which it affords of advancement and honor, but because your sacrifice was one of duty and piety.

You kindly mentioned my sister.[3] I owe every one thanks and regard who speaks of her with respect. But my grief, whatever it may be, has not the source that yours has. A Persian matron, oppressed by a tyrant king, had the leave of the monarch to save from death *one* of her family and relatives. She had many children and a husband; but she had also a father, old and decrepit. Him she selected and saved, saying that another husband and other children she might have, *but another father never.* I have lost a sister; but I

---

[1] He thought more highly of Chancellor Kent's Commentaries at a later period, *post*, p. 120.

[2] Tower's father had died, March 15, at St. Augustine.

[3] Tower, Hopkinson, Stearns, and Converse wrote to Sumner letters of sympathy at the time of his sister Matilda's death.

still have other sisters and brothers, entitled to my instructions and protection. I strive to forget my loss in an increased regard for the living. . . .

Let me then remind you (of what I know there is no need of reminding you) that the cares and honors of your father's house devolve upon you. Serve all as you have served him. I have written with the freedom of a friend who takes an unfeigned interest in you and yours.

Death, this winter, has glutted himself among those to whom my acquaintance and regards extended, more than in all the rest of my life. Penniman, our classmate, died, — a calm and easy death, unconscious that he was sinking into a sleep longer than that of a night. Yesterday's paper told me of the death of Hale, from New York, who graduated the year after we did. What death may come next, — who can tell ? . . .

I have thought but little of the Bowdoin subjects, and it is from now just a month when the dissertations must be handed in. If I write at all, it will be upon the second subject. I shall choose that, because it will require but little immediate investigation. A general knowledge of the course of events, the progress of society, and the causes and effects of some of the principal revolutions, is all that is wanted for a discussion of this subject. To be sure, that is a good deal; but my historical studies have, in some degree, fitted me for reflection upon it. To discuss the third subject, I should be obliged to review in detail the history of Mohammedanism. I am now studying the law with some singleness, and should feel unwilling to give myself to any so serious study aside from those of my profession. I much doubt whether I shall touch either subject. Fifty dollars is an inducement, — great to me; for I just begin seriously to feel the value of money. Last January I was twenty-one. New feelings have been opened to me since I arrived at that age. I feel that I ought to be doing something for myself, and not to live an expense to my father, with his large family looking to him for support and education. Stearns is somewhat recovered. He is with his father at Bedford, and has the care of a suspended boy from college. I doubt whether many days be in store for him.

I am anxious to know the extent of your law-studies. You will be for five years a business man. Never forget that you are also a scholar. If I can ever be of use to you, on account of my access to the library or on any other account, fail not to command me. Any trouble you may put me to will be a pleasing one. . . .

Excuse my long scrawl, and believe me your true friend,   C. S.

TO JONATHAN F. STEARNS.

34 DIVINITY HALL, Friday Evening, 10 o'clock, May 18, 1832.

MY DEAR FRIEND, — I am grateful to you for the regard you have expressed for my sister. She is now beyond the show of my affection and regard. I will then transfer them, for her sake, to those who speak and think well of her. Matilda died on March 6. You were the last of my friends who saw her. If I remember, when you were last at my father's, you sat for a while in her chamber. She gradually became weaker and weaker, sinking by degrees, imperceptible except in their aggregate; always contented and cheerful, and, till the last two days of her tarry here, able to sit up a good portion of the day. It was evident, though, a fortnight — perhaps a month — before she died, that she could not live. It is, I believe, the nature of consumption to deceive its unfortunate victim into the belief that health may yet be regained, or, at least, life retained. It is accompanied with no decided pain, and thus leaves the mind to its hopes and anticipations. That such was the state of my sister's mind, I do not know. I never ventured to introduce my fears to her, and she seemed as studiously to avoid allusion to that topic. My mother, but a few days before her death, introduced the subject, and found her to be perfectly conscious of her situation and resigned to that Will which is the governor of our lives. She sank into death " calmly as to a night's repose," the last words she uttered being those of gratitude to one of her young friends who was watching her wants and comforts. My father's distress was very great. More than once I saw tears steal from his eyes. My mother is still dejected and comfortless. . . .

You have referred to my health, &c. I never was better; in fact, I never was unwell. I 've always been well. Who can have spoken to you of me such flattering words, as should imply that I was hurting my health with study? *Contra*, I reprove myself for lack of study. I am well-determined, though, that, if health is continued to me, lack of study shall not be laid to my charge. *Study* is the talisman.

Carter is trying to start a school in Boston. Browne is well. He does not *love* the law. He is a keen, direct, and close debater.

From your true friend,

CHAS. SUMNER.

TO CHARLEMAGNE TOWER.

BOSTON, Sunday, July 29, 1832.

MY DEAR FRIEND, — This is vacation, — if such time there can be to one who has doubled his twenty-first year, and is moderately aware of the duties of manhood, — and I am at home. I have not stirred within sight of the Boston boundary-line since I came into town, and probably shall not cross it during the whole six weeks, except perhaps to make a pilgrimage to Cambridge. I am grateful to you for your kind invitation to visit you and see your doings. The gratification of friendship aside, I should be much delighted to travel through your great and growing State, and look at and hear " Niagara's roar." But pockets not full, and an attention given to studies by which I must earn what of bread and credit may be my lot, prevent. . . .

I wrote a Bowdoin dissertation on the subject which I mentioned in my last to you as uppermost in my mind. I commenced one evening, and a fortnight after I wrote the last sentence, — some fifty pages. During all the while I attended closely to the exercises of the school. . . .

Your affectionate friend,

C. S.

TO CHARLEMAGNE TOWER.

CAMBRIDGE, Wednesday, Oct. 24, 1832.

MY DEAR FRIEND, — . . . Yesterday, Dane Law College (situated just north of Rev. Mr. Newell's church), a beautiful Grecian temple, with four Ionic pillars in front, — the most architectural and the best-built edifice belonging to the college, — was dedicated to the law. Quincy delivered a most proper address of an hour, full of his strong sense and strong language. Webster, J. Q. Adams, Dr. Bowditch, Edward Everett, Jeremiah Mason, Judge Story, Ticknor, leaders in the eloquence, statesmanship, mathematics, scholarship, and law of our good land, were all present, — a glorious company. The Law School have requested a copy for the press. It will of a certainty be given. I shall send you the address when published.

When you again visit Cambridge you will be astonished at the changes that have been wrought, — trees planted, common fenced, new buildings raised, and others designed. Quincy is a man of life, and infuses a vigor into all that he touches.

Commencement Day, — it was a good one; parts full of modest merit, nothing poor; orations not great, but thoughtful and pleasantly composed. There was no strong and salient merit, but there was an abundance of that respectable talent which excites our respect and gives earnest of future usefulness. The world is apt to judge of a day's performances by the few brilliant and striking parts that are heard. This is not the proper test.

There was a general rising against the Master's degree. Curtis,[1] by far the first man of his class, with the *highest* legal prospects before him, refused it, and stirred many of his class to the same conclusion. . . .

From your sincere friend,

CHAS. SUMNER.

TO CHARLEMAGNE TOWER.

CAMBRIDGE, Dec. 17, 1832.

MY DEAR TOWER, — A letter from you is now something of an event in my meagre life. Last year and the year before I had several correspondents, who occasionally favored me with their letters. But they have all shrunk away but yourself. Professional studies, and those cares which thicken upon us all as we gain in years, gradually weaned them from the pleasures of friendship, binding them to those labors which may secure them bread and fame. With you I have now held a long correspondence, which to me has been full of interest and instruction. Every letter brings up crowds of associations, in which I like to find myself. The bare sheet before me has an intrinsic interest, indeed, of its own; but it is doubly grateful as it calls to my mind all those college scenes in which I so much delighted, those friends in whom I have such pride, and all the pleasures and improvement which I

1 Benjamin R. Curtis.

received in their society. I sit oftentimes, after having read one of your letters, filled with that mingled melancholy and joy which comes over one when thinking of the enjoyments of the past, and of the too palpable certainty that those enjoyments will never again be met except by Memory in her pleasant wanderings. But stop! —

We truly are in a sad state. Civil war, in a portentous cloud, hangs over us. South Carolina, though the sorest part of our system, is not the only part that is galled. Georgia cannot, Virginia cannot, stomach the high Federal doctrines which the President has set forth in his proclamation,[1] and upon which the stability of the country rests. That is a glorious document, worthy of any President. Our part of the country rejoices in it as a true exposition of the Constitution, and a fervid address to those wayward men who are now plunging us into disgrace abroad and misery at home. Judge Story speaks much of its value; and so striking did its argument appear to him, that he has introduced it into a note to his work on the Constitution, in three volumes; which will be published by the middle of January.[2]

To change the tone, I hope you have not given up the idea of studying law. I believe that you will be happier in that profession than in any other. By it you will be enabled to gratify that laudable and honest ambition which you possess. You will be interested and fully employed by its study. If one does not wish to follow the profession, I need not tell you that he will still find the law a most profitable study, disciplining the mind and storing it with those everlasting principles which are at the bottom of all society and order. For myself, I become more wedded to the law, as a profession, every day that I study it. Politics I begin to loathe; they are of a day, but the law is of all time. Pray excuse my sermonizing. . . .

From your true friend,　　　C. S.

TO JONATHAN F. STEARNS, ANDOVER, MASS.[3]

CAMBRIDGE, Jan. 12, 1833.

MY DEAR FRIEND, — I have received and am grateful for your letter. The interest you manifest in my welfare calls for my warmest acknowledgments. I do not know how I can better show myself worthy of your kindness than with all frankness and plainness to expose to you, in a few words, the state of my mind on the important subject upon which you addressed me.

---

[1] Andrew Jackson's Proclamation of Dec., 1832, upon the occasion of the nullifying ordinance of South Carolina.

[2] Story on the Constitution, Vol. I. Appendix.

[3] This letter is a reply to one from Stearns, then a student at the Andover Theological Seminary, in which he pressed the Christian faith on Sumner's attention, and began thus: "My knowledge of your candid temper, and the terms on which we have been long conversant with each other, encourage the belief that you will suffer me for once to address you with great plainness. The sentiments of friendship I have so long cherished towards you; the high respect I entertain for your character and talents; the extensive influence which I foresee you are to have in the community; and, more than these, the immortality to which we both are destined, — all forbid me to be silent."

The last time I saw you, you urged upon me the study of the *proofs of Christianity*, with an earnestness that flowed, I was conscious, from a sincere confidence in them yourself and the consequent wish that all should believe; as in belief was sure salvation. I have had your last words and look often in my mind since. They have been not inconstant prompters to thought and speculation upon the proposed subject. I attended Bishop Hopkins's lectures, and gave to them a severe attention. I remained and still remain unconvinced that Christ was divinely commissioned to preach a revelation to men, and that he was entrusted with the power of working miracles. But when I make this declaration, I do not mean to deny that such a being as Christ lived and went about doing good, or that the body of precepts which have come down to us as delivered by him, were so delivered. I believe that Christ lived when and as the Gospel says; that he was more than man, — namely, above all men who had as yet lived, — and yet less than God; full of the strongest sense and knowledge, and of a virtue superior to any which we call Roman or Grecian or Stoic, and which we best denote when, borrowing his name, we call it *Christian*. I pray you not to believe that I am insensible to the goodness and greatness of his character. My idea of human nature is exalted, when I think that such a being lived and went as a man amongst men. And here, perhaps, the conscientious unbeliever may find good cause for glorifying his God; not because he sent his Son into the world to partake of its troubles and be the herald of glad tidings, but because he suffered a man to be born, in whom the world should see but one of themselves, endowed with qualities calculated to elevate the standard of attainable excellence.

I do not know that I can say more without betraying you into a controversy, in which I should be loath to engage, and from which I am convinced no good would result to either party. I do not think that I have a basis for faith to build upon. I am without religious feeling. I seldom refer my happiness or acquisitions to the Great Father from whose mercy they are derived. Of the first great commandment, then, upon which so much hangs, I live in perpetual unconsciousness, — I will not say disregard, for that, perhaps, would imply that it was present in my mind. I believe, though, that my love to my neighbor — namely, my anxiety that my fellow-creatures should be happy, and disposition to serve them in their honest endeavors — is pure and strong. Certainly I do feel an affection for every thing that God created; *and this feeling is my religion.*

> "He prayeth well, who loveth well
> Both man and bird and beast.
>
> He prayeth best, who loveth best
> All things both great and small;
> For the dear God who loveth us,
> He made and loveth all."

I ask you not to imagine that I am led into the above sentiment by the lines I have just quoted, — the best of Coleridge's "Rime of the Ancient Mariner," — but rather that I seize the lines to express and illustrate my *feeling*.

This communication is made in the fulness of friendship and confidence. To your charity and continued interest in my welfare, suffer me to commend myself as   Your affectionate friend,

CHAS. SUMNER.

P. S. — Browne has left Cambridge, and is for the winter at Salem. Hopkinson has also left, and is with H. H. Fuller in Boston. McBurney has a charge in Boston, which keeps him happy and busy, — the former *par consequence* from the latter. I feel quite alone. My chief company is the letters of my friends. Write me.   C. S.

TO CHARLEMAGNE TOWER.

SUNDAY NIGHT, May 5, 1833.

MY DEAR TOWER, — . . . Since my last, our junior professor [1] — as you have seen by the papers and by the eulogy I had the pleasure of sending to you — has died. His death, though for a long time anticipated, yet had a degree of suddenness about it. All deemed his days numbered; but few were prepared to hear that they were cut short when they were. I was with him, and was the only one with him, at his death. It was the first death-bed, not to say sick-bed, I ever stood by. If death comes as it came to him, surely in it there is nothing to fear, except in the thoughts of " going we know not where." Those thoughts will be oppressive according to the education and religious feeling and mental strength of the sufferer; but the physical pain need make no one dread his *ultima dies*. Most persons, I believe, have a vague fear of racking pains and torments that attend dissolution; but these are creatures of the brain.

A successor has been appointed to Mr. Ashmun, who will commence his duties here in July, or next September. You have seen him announced in the papers, — Mr. Greenleaf, of Maine; a fine man, learned lawyer, good scholar, ardent student, of high professional character, taking a great interest in his profession: add to this, a gentleman, a man of manners, affability, and enthusiasm, nearly fifty years old; now has a very extensive practice in Maine, which he will wind up before he starts upon his new line of duties. It were worth your coming from New York to study under Judge Story and Greenleaf next term. I shall not be here after this year; not but I should like to be here, — for I could spend my life, I believe, in this, as some call it, monkish seclusion, — but because it is necessary to obtain a knowledge of practice in a lawyer's office, to come down from books and theory to men and writs; and one year, which will alone remain to me after Commencement, is usually considered little enough for that purpose.

How do you progress in law? Write me. How do you like Kent? I owe him much. I have had from him a great deal of elegant instruction. His

---

[1] Professor Ashmun.

Commentaries are not wholly appreciated by the student upon a first perusal; they are hardly elementary enough. Ashmun said that they were written as the judgments of a judge. But when one is a little advanced or familiar with them, he sees the comprehensive views they take of the law of which they treat, and the condensed shape into which the law on their several titles is thrown. Kent is one of the glories of your State, whether you look at him as a commentator or a judge. In the latter capacity, his opinions, for learning and ability, stand almost unrivalled. Judges Marshall and Story alone, of any judges in our country, may be compared with him. . . .

Truly and faithfully your friend,   C. S.

TO CHARLEMAGNE TOWER.

WEDNESDAY, June 12, 1833.

MY DEAR TOWER, — I send by your brother for your acceptance a couple numbers of Professor Willard's Review, of which you may have heard, containing slight articles of mine; which I flattered myself might be interesting to you, not from any merit of theirs, but on account of our friendship. The article on impeachments was the result of some study of the impeachments under our Constitution, and is the fullest historical survey of that subject that I know of. The article on Blackstone is a meagre thing, written at five minutes' notice, to piece out the number for the month. The two numbers may have another interest to you, as reviving some recollections of Cambridge and those who live therein. The whole Review smacks strongly of the place of its publication. The article on Professor Stuart's classics [1] is rather a celebrated one; has excited much comment; is thought to be one of the most thorough and searching reviews (strictly *reviews*, for it is not a talk round "about and about" its subject) that has ever appeared in our country.

Preparations are making to receive General Jackson with the same college ceremonies with which Monroe was received, — namely, an address in English from the President, and a Latin address from the first scholar of the Senior Class, — Bowen. [2]

Believe me your faithful friend,   C. S.

TO CHARLEMAGNE TOWER.

DANE LAW COLLEGE, Monday, July 15, 1833.

. . . If you want a book which will be a light law-book, and a most instructive work as to the government under which we live, which shall be entertaining and informing, written in a more brilliant and elementary,

---

[1] By Professor James L. Kingsley, of Yale College.
[2] Professor Francis Bowen.

though less correct, style than Kent's " Commentaries," read Judge Story's
" Commentaries on the Constitution." They make an invaluable work to
every statesman and lawyer; in fact, to every citizen of views raised at all
above the ephemeral politics with which we are annoyed.

WEDNESDAY EVE.

Since I wrote the above, two whole days have passed. I have heard Webster's performance,[1] and like it much. He did himself honor with mature
men. As for undergraduates, I suppose they were dissatisfied, for they could
find no brilliancies or points or attractive allusions. It was characterized by
judgment, sense, and great directness and plainness of speech. It had no
exaggerated thoughts or expressions, but was full of simple thoughts expressed
in the simplest language.

Come on here at Commencement Day; and yet I know no reason why I
should wish particularly to be here on that day. Unless Hopkinson or Stearns
or you perform the master's part, I doubt whether I shall take the trouble to
attend the fatiguing exercises, or take myself from my every-day duties.

Faithfully yours,   C. S.

TO JOHN B. KERR, EASTON, MD.

DANE LAW COLLEGE, Wednesday, Aug. 14, 1833.

MY DEAR KERR, — I am thankful to you for the gratification afforded
simply by the sight of that handwriting, of which I was wont to see so much
when in the further entry of Holworthy, as it lay scattered over your tables
loaded with books, or was thrown into the yard with forgotten things, in the
shape of embryo theses or letters or parts. It was last evening that I took
from the post-office your friendly favor; and I at once recognized the familiar
strokes, as if my eyes had rested upon them but yesterday. . . .

You inquire of many of our class; where they are, and what their present
prospects, &c. I can answer some such questions; for, being of Cambridge,
I am naturally in the centre of all information obtainable as to the fortunes
of graduates. Three years have made many changes; have fixed the characters for life of many whose ages were too young to have fixed characters in
college; have scattered widely the whole of our little band, not to be again
gathered together except in the great final bourne; have conducted some into
the occupations by which, in the words of the subject of our last theme, they
are to earn their " bread and fame," and have left many like myself lingering by the wayside, looking forward to business and its cares, but at present
unprepared to meet them. It is interesting to take a view of the present
characters and situations of our old associates. One wants the " vantage-
ground " of Cambridge to see them all distinctly. . . .

---

[1] The class oration of Fletcher Webster, son of Daniel Webster, at the exhibition is
referred to.

As to the degree of A. M.; few took the degree last year, — but thirteen, I believe. Few will take it this year; not that there is any combination against it, but there appears to be a pervading sense of its utter worthlessness. I have not yet heard of one who will take it. . . .

Your true friend,

CHAS. SUMNER.

TO CHARLEMAGNE TOWER.

DANE LAW COLLEGE, Sept. 1, 1833.

MY DEAR TOWER, — This is the last night of Commencement Week, and college has assumed much of its wonted air. New Freshmen are seen in the streets, with new-bought articles of furniture and with youthful cheeks, — two strong signs of the first stage of college life. Our Law School has begun to fill with students. Already is gathered together, I believe, the largest collection of young men that ever met at one place in America for the study of the law. There are now upwards of fifty who have joined the school. So we expect the ensuing term will be a driving one.

Commencement Day passed off without any thing very worthy of note transpiring. There were about twenty of our class who appeared and shook hands with one another; and after services partook of dinner with the graduates, — on that day my first effort being made in the department of Commencement dinners. I doubt whether I shall ever patronize them again; for, first, in the performances of the day I shall no longer have an interest, the time having now gone by in which my own friends will take part in them; and, secondly, if I were ever induced to come to the performances, I hope I shall be able to snatch as good a meal elsewhere, away from the press and turmoil incident to a public dinner. To do the table justice, it was tolerably well served, and we had quite a pleasant time in divesting it of its many dishes.

Of our classmates who were here, few or none had undergone any alteration. They looked and talked the same as when we met one another every day in social and intellectual communion. . . .

Need I say that Everett did wonders on Phi Beta day?[1] Popkin has resigned. Felton will probably be his successor. Thank you for reading my article in the "Jurist;" but I want you to make allowances for the haste in which it was composed, and more for the inaccuracy with which it is printed.

Your faithful friend,

C. S.

---

[1] Mr. Everett repeated on this occasion, Aug. 29, the oration on the "Education of Mankind," which he had delivered, Aug. 20, at Yale College. "Orations and Speeches by Edward Everett," Vol. I. pp. 404–441.

CHAPTER VII.

STUDY IN A LAW OFFICE. — VISIT TO WASHINGTON. — JANUARY, 1834, TO
SEPTEMBER, 1834. — AGE, 23.

HAVING finished his studies at Cambridge in Dec., 1833, Sumner entered as a student, Jan. 8, 1834,[1] the law-office of Benjamin Rand, Court Street, Boston; a lawyer having a large practice, but distinguished rather for his great learning and faithful attention to the business of his clients than for any attractive forensic qualities.[2] He had access to the remarkably well-stored library of Mr. Rand, which was enriched on the arrival of almost every English packet. He followed very much his tastes while in the office, doing little drudgery as a copyist, and seizing every opportunity of conversation with his learned master. He was missed at Cambridge, where teachers and friends had parted reluctantly from him. Already Story and Greenleaf counted on him as an associate instructor, and spoke of the separation as likely to be but temporary. The judge wrote to him from Washington, Feb. 4: —

"Professor Greenleaf has written me a letter full of lamentations at your departure, and he complains of being now left alone. I grieve also, but not as those who are without hope; for, if the Law School succeeds, I am sure you will be with us again at no distant period. . . . It would have been delightful to have had Mr. Livermore's bequest incorporated into your excellent catalogue. But, as it is, we must have it in an appendix. I wish exceedingly for two or three copies of your catalogue to present to some gentlemen here. The preface will do you, as well as them, good."

Sumner's contributions to the "Jurist" at this time were an article on the "*Lex Loci*, — Can the Assignee of a Scotch bond maintain an Action in his own name in the Courts of this Coun-

---

1 His father noted the day in his interleaved copy of "Thomas's Farmer's Almanac." His classmate Hopkinson had desired Sumner to enter his office at Lowell, and Mr. Alvord also invited him to his office in Greenfield.

2 Mr. Rand in the autumn of 1834 visited England, where he was well received by lawyers and judges. His partner, Mr. A. H. Fiske, remained in charge of the office.

try?"[1] containing citations from the Roman and the French as well as from the common law, — a paper which grew out of his argument of a moot-court case before Professor Ashmun, the previous year; a "Review of 'Chitty's Pleadings,'"[2] in which some technical questions are treated; "Characters of Law Books and Judges,"[3] a voluminous collection of opinions; "Replevin of Goods taken in Execution, — Error in the Books,"[4] an elaborate discussion of a technical question; and a caustic notice of "Tayler's 'Law Glossary.'"[5] To the July number alone he contributed more than one hundred pages. In May, he became one of the editors. His classmate Browne, whose advice he sought in relation to this connection, did not think the effect of habitual writing for law magazines upon a lawyer's mind to be wholesome, and strongly urged that, if he accepted the offer, he should limit his engagement to a year and a half.

His studies with Mr. Rand were soon interrupted by a journey to Washington, with an absence from the office from Feb. 17 to April 4. He had for some time felt a strong desire to visit the national Capital. He wished to see and hear the eminent statesmen of the time, and particularly to attend a session of the Supreme Court. It would be a satisfaction also to see Judge Story, whom he had known so well as professor, performing his high duties as judge. The Supreme Court of the United States, with Marshall as chief-justice, held at that period, — when the States were few and the best professional training was confined very much to the Atlantic States, — a larger place relatively than it now holds among the judicial institutions of the country. Young lawyers then, more than at present, sought as pilgrims this fountain of learning and authority. National politics then drew to the seat of government the highest talent more than now, when intellectual power finds a larger opportunity than formerly at the bar of commercial cities, or in other fields of distinction. Neither before nor since in our history

---

[1] Jan. 1834, Vol XI. pp. 101–105.

[2] April, 1834, Vol. XI. pp. 320–338.

[3] July, 1834, Vol. XII. pp. 5–66. The materials for this article were largely furnished by a memorandum-book, in which, beginning with 1832, he had been accustomed to write, from time to time, opinions of law books gathered in his reading.

[4] July, 1834, Vol. XII. pp. 104–117. Browne wrote, July 24, "Your article on 'Replevin' was learned, and well and logically expressed. It was an extraordinary article for a young man; but it is not practical. You seem to delight in the speculative in the choice of your articles."

[5] July, 1834, Vol. XII. pp. 248–270.

have three men of equal fame as orators with Webster, Calhoun, and Clay ever contended with each other in our national
Senate.

The love of travel was with Sumner an inherited passion,
which his brothers also shared. The journey to Washington
now accomplished in seventeen hours, in a railway carriage
furnished like a drawing-room by day and provided with couches
at night, is at once an easy and a commonplace experience. It
was then made only by stage-coach and steamboat, except a
short railway ride from Amboy to Bordentown (thirty-seven
miles), and another from the Delaware River to the head of
the Elk (sixteen and a half). With the dispatch of these days
Sumner would, by the time he then reached Hartford, have been
some hours at his journey's end.

At Washington he passed a month, occupying a room in the
house of Mrs. Eliza Peyton, at the corner of Pennsylvania Avenue and Four-and-a-half Street. Among her guests were several
members of Congress and other persons of distinction; most
worthy of note among them was Dr. Francis Lieber, between
whom and Sumner a long intimacy now began.[1] Mrs. Peyton
recalls the tall youth from Boston, sitting with the guests who
gathered at the fireside in the large parlor. Dr. John B. Blake,
a fellow-boarder, still living in Washington, remembers him as
modest and deferential, attracting attention by his remarkable
attainments and manly presence, and receiving from the judges
unusual civilities. Dr. Blake went so far at the time as to pre-
dict for him the highest judicial station, unless he should be
diverted by literary tastes.[2]

The commendation of Judge Story opened to him the best
social opportunities. He dined with the judges; made the
acquaintance of Henry Wheaton; and "dined repeatedly with
Horace Binney, and received many marks of friendly attention
from him." [3] Richard Peters of Philadelphia, the official reporter
of the decisions of the Supreme Court, — whom he had previously

---

[1] They were introduced to each other by a note of Richard Peters, commending Dr.
Lieber to Sumner.

[2] Dr. Blake's reminiscences of Sumner at the time of this visit were printed in the
Washington "Weekly Republican," March 19, 1874.

[3] Sumner had through life a profound respect for Mr. Binney's character. In an
address to the Law School of Howard University, Feb. 3, 1871, he spoke of "the venerable
Horace Binney, as the living head of the profession in our country." Mr. Binney died,
August, 1875, at the age of ninety-five.

met at Cambridge, and who was a devoted friend of Judge
Story, — conceived a strong regard for him at this time, and a
frequent correspondence between them followed.[1] Mr. Peters
kindly said to him, in Washington, that he should before long
have occasion to print his name in his reports as counsel before
the Supreme Court. During this visit he first met Samuel
Lawrence, who afterwards showed him substantial kindness.
He undertook to serve a lawyer, a college friend, who was
prosecuting a claim against the United States, — and this
friendly agency brought him into personal relations with Rufus Choate, then a member of the House of Representatives.
He left Washington, after a month's sojourn, with little expectation of ever seeing the city again, with an increased love of
his chosen profession, and with a strong aversion to politics.

On his way home he passed some days in Philadelphia, where
he seems to have enjoyed himself heartily; dining one day at
the house of Joseph R. Ingersoll,[2] "in a large and splendid
company," and passing his evenings with the family of Mr.
Peters. He left the city with a lively impression of the hospitality of the people. One of the daughters of Mr. Peters
pleased/him much with her excellent imitation of Miss Kemble's
acting. With another daughter, then quite a young girl, he
talked much concerning her studies, and afterwards sought, by
his letters, to foster her literary inclinings. Her vivid recollections of him, as he appeared at this period, find a place in this
chapter.

His father wrote to him, while he was in Washington, a
letter as stately as it was paternal, sending a friendly message
to Governor Lincoln, enjoining upon his son to visit the grave
of Vice-president Gerry, and also that of William Wirt who
had died Feb. 18, and ending with "*macte virtute, puer.*"
His brother Henry and his sister Mary added playful postscripts
to the father's letter. Professor Greenleaf gratefully acknowledged his reports of his visit to Chancellor Kent and of life in
Washington.

One of the daughters of Mr. Peters thus describes him at this
time : —

[1] Mr. Peters was fond of society, entertaining in conversation, and full of wit and anecdote. He lived till May 1, 1848. His intimate relations with Judge Story appear in the
latter's "Life and Letters."

[2] 1786–1868. Mr. Ingersoll was a member of Congress, 1835–37, and again 1842–49,
and Minister to England, 1850–53.

" It was somewhere about 1832 I think, in the summer-time, that Charles Sumner led me — then a little girl — and my father over Harvard Library; and it has always been to me a beautiful memory, — the recollection of this slender, bright-eyed youth, with what seemed to me an adoring reverence for the hallowed spot, so that his voice was subdued and his touch rested tenderly on the dear books as he stood showing them to my father.

" When he came to Philadelphia in 1834, he had finished his course at the Law School, I think; but had almost put his eyes out with hard study, and was forced to come away for rest. He was then a great, tall, lank creature, quite heedless of the form and fashion of his garb, ' unsophisticated,' everybody said, and oblivious of the propriety of wearing a hat in a city, going about in a rather shabby fur cap; but the fastidiousness of fashionable ladies was utterly routed by the wonderful charm of his conversation, and he was carried about triumphantly, and introduced to all the distinguished people, young and old, who then made Philadelphia society so brilliant. No amount of honeying, however, could then affect him. His simplicity, his perfect *naturalness*, was what struck every one, combined with his rare culture and his delicious youthful enthusiasm.

" My mother became very much interested in him, and thought his mother must be very proud of him.

" He was almost beside himself then over Fanny Kemble's acting; used to walk, he said, that winter to and from Boston, through snow and storm, to see her act. One of my sisters had a singular ability in imitating this gifted woman's acting and reading, and it was Charles Sumner's delight to insist on this rather shy lady's ' performing ' for him. His exclamation was, ' By George, that's fine ! By George, that's fine, Miss S.! Give it to us again : now, Miss S.! The " Do it " point, — the " Do it " point ' (from Sheridan Knowles' ' Hunchback ').[1] And striking his great hands together and heaving them about like Dominie Sampson, and striding up and down the room, he would keep repeating, ' By George, that's fine ! '

" Every one was sorry when he left town, and from that time his name was really a household word with us. There was a sweetness and tenderness of character about him, and an entire unworldliness that won all hearts, while his delightful culture completed the charm.

" My father was exceedingly fond of Mr. Sumner from his youth. He knew all about him, sometime before the visit to Philadelphia in 1834, from Judge Story; and believed with that dear friend that all possibilities for a legal and literary career of great brilliancy lay before this young man, so gifted, so fond of culture, so persevering in the study of his profession, so appreciative of, and so enthusiastic for, all that is good and fine.''

Shortly after Sumner's return from Washington, Judge Story pressed him to accept a connection with the Law School as instructor; but the offer was declined. An extract from his

---

[1] Act V. Scene 3.

classmate Browne's letter, of May 2, shows the latter's view of Sumner's probable future : —

"In the concluding lines of your letter, which I received this morning, you seemed to see and lament the course which fortune and your stars appear to have marked out for you. I see no reason for lamentation, but rather much for congratulation and rejoicing. The course of events, or rather your own might and main, have opened to you the very path your feet were made to tread. Let me speak plainly what I plainly discern and feel. You are not rough-shod enough to travel in the stony and broken road of homely, harsh, every-day practice. You were neither made for it by the hand of Nature, nor have you wrought and fashioned yourself to it by that less cunning but still most potent artificer, — practice. All your inclinations (I do not see through a glass darkly) and all your habits set you on with a strong tendency toward a green eminence of fame and emolument in your profession; but you are not destined to reach it by travelling through the ordinary business of a young lawyer in the courts. You see that yourself, and you affect to be sad thereat. Instead of looking back with regret to the practice which you are to leave to other spirits touched less finely, and to far less fine issues, you should reserve both your eyes to look forward and see the reasons of rejoicing. By all means take up the offer of the judge, and never think of opening an office in the city. If, before the day of service upon your post, you have an offer from some established man with large business and a good library, then deliberate, then suffer yourself to institute comparisons between that and the station in the Law School; but not till then. If such a chance should occur, the judge would be one of the foremost to relinquish his hold on you."

A few weeks before Sumner's admission to the bar, the Ursuline Convent at Charlestown was burned, Aug. 11, by a mob. The authorities of Harvard College seriously apprehended a retaliatory attack by the Catholics upon the college buildings, and particularly upon the library, then kept in Harvard Hall. The students were absent upon their vacation; and Rev. Mr. Palfrey, Dean of the Divinity Faculty, undertook to collect a volunteer guard among the recent graduates. One of seventy men was gathered for one night, commanded by Franklin Dexter; and another of like number for the next night, commanded by David Lee Child and George W. Phillips, — and the two guards alternated. Sumner was a private in the second guard; and, armed with a musket, left his father's house at evening to do duty at Cambridge, while the alarm lasted. The story is told of him, that, as they were quartered in Harvard Hall for the night, he started the question whether the guard had been assembled and was acting under due corporate authority, — a legal inquiry, which, under the circumstances, somewhat amused his companions.

At the beginning of September, 1834, Sumner, anxious to enter at once on practice, — there being no court in session at Boston having authority to grant admissions to the bar, — applied to the Court of Common Pleas, sitting in Worcester (Chief-Justice John M. Williams, presiding), where on the third of that month he was admitted as an attorney, after a recommendation by the bar of Worcester County, of which Pliny Merrick and Charles Allen were then the leaders. D. Waldo Lincoln,[1] a fellow student in College and at the Law School, who was admitted at the same time, interested himself in the preliminary arrangements for Sumner's admission.

LETTERS.

TO HIS FAMILY AT HOME, BOSTON.

STEAMER "SPLENDID," FROM NEW HAVEN TO NEW YORK,
WEDNESDAY, Feb. 19, 1834.

To MY DEAR HOME, — The steamer is now fast going to New York, where I shall be at two o'clock this afternoon. There is something imposing in the thought, that one with so many accommodations as I now see about me is moving on his journey at the rate of twelve or fourteen miles an hour. The boat has about sixty passengers on board, and we have all just risen from a well-prepared breakfast at a table the full length of the cabin. It is thus that we enjoy the comforts and luxuries of the best hotels, and still keep moving on our way. The motion of the boat is delightful; nothing to occasion sickness; the sea is placid as a mirror; wild fowl (immense flocks of geese) are swimming upon its surface; the sun is bright overhead; the air is pure and the day clear. Such is the happy scene through which I am now hurrying, — a scene most unlike that of the last two days, which has been marred by all the fatigue and discomfort of the most wretched roads and, generally speaking, equally wretched conveyances. If the roads had been good, I should have probably been at this time on my way for Philadelphia. I have lost a day.

We started from Boston at half past three o'clock [2] Monday morning, with

---

[1] Lincoln was the son of Governor Lincoln, for whom Sumner's father cherished a lively gratitude. _Ante_, pp. 21, 22.

[2] Before leaving, that morning, he wrote a note to Professor Greenleaf, accompanying a copy of Story's "Conflict of Laws," just issued, which the judge had requested him to send as the author's gift.

twelve passengers and their full complement of baggage on board, and with *six* horses. The way was very dark; so that, though I rode with the driver, it was some time before I discovered that we had six horses. Light overtook us at Newton Falls, about ten miles from the city; breakfasted at Natick, sixteen miles; part of us, then, for thirty miles, rode in a crazy wagon; after that I rode sixteen miles alone in a gig, driving a horse that Rosinante would not have owned as a kinsman, over roads almost impassable to the best animals; every step my horse took was caused by a blow from my whip. It was thus I rode, — literally *working* my passage, as much as he did who drove the horse on the canal. My shoulder was lame from its excessive exercise in whipping the poor brute. I arrived at Thompson, the first town we enter in Connecticut, about three o'clock, P. M., — about sixty miles from Boston. Here we dined, and again started weary on our way, with forty miles of heavy travelling before us: changed horses every sixteen miles. The moon was up, making the road less gloomy than it otherwise would have been; but even this deserted us before we arrived at Hartford, which was not till three o'clock of Tuesday morning, having been on the road twenty-three hours. I sat with the driver all the time, and was only sick for an hour or so in the evening of Monday. The cold was benumbing during that night; so much so that the experienced driver complained. No sound could have been more grateful than that of the heavy tramp of the horses over the sounding covered bridge that leads into Hartford. Had we arrived in proper season, we should have jumped aboard the stage to New Haven, and gone directly there to take the steamer, Tuesday morning, at seven o'clock. Upon arriving at the hotel, I warmed myself, and then went to bed to snatch an hour of sleep. In a short time I was perfectly rested; enjoyed a good breakfast; walked through some of the fine streets of Hartford; visited the court, there holding by C. J. Daggett, to whom I sent the kind note and package, Mr. Greenleaf had furnished me. At eleven o'clock, A. M., started from Hartford for New Haven, — a route of forty miles, — where we arrived at eight o'clock in the evening, having a very pleasant journey so far as a good driver and good weather could make it so, and without feeling sick in the least. Wednesday morning attended prayers at Yale College, which act nearly cost me my passage to New York, — certainly fifty cents to get my baggage to the boat, the stages appointed to take me and it having gone. I ran till my wind was most gone, and thus secured my place. The boat started at seven o'clock in the morning.

CHAS.

☞ Travelling is very expensive, — thus far full thirty per cent above my calculations. This is owing to the delays, bad roads, and to the season of the year.

I am very thankful to Mary for her tippet; without it I should have frozen.

TO PROFESSOR SIMON GREENLEAF, CAMBRIDGE, MASS.

NEW YORK, Wednesday Evening, Feb. 19, 1834.

" That Mr. Greenleaf is a civil sort of a man," said Chancellor Kent, this afternoon, to me, after he had slowly and fully read your kind letter of introduction. " He was a great loss to the profession at Portland; makes a fine professor, I have no doubt," he continued. To all of which I of course sincerely responded.

I called upon the chancellor at his house, two or three miles from the heart of the city where I was, at about half-past four o'clock in the afternoon. I handed him your letter; he asked me to sit. It was in a parlor that I saw him, with a young lady and an infant, probably the family of his son. He received me cordially; talked fast and instructively, but without elegance or grammar (however, *falsa grammatica non vitiat*); praised the civil law highly; thought Livermore's bequest a splendid one; liked the civil law, all but that relating to husband and wife, — he would stick to the common law on that subject; spoke with warmth of the present politics; thought Jackson would ruin us; wanted to go to Washington, but if he went should be obliged to see much company, call upon Jackson, and dine with him perhaps, all of which he could not consent to do; were he there, he should associate with such men as Webster; trusted next spring that he should visit the great valley of the West, which he wished much to see, as he had a great passion for natural scenery; said he never wrote an article for a review in his life; had just written with considerable pains a life of General Schuyler for the " Portrait Gallery," which he had condensed as much as possible, to suit the dimensions required for that publication; spoke of the " North American " and the other reviews; said that he read them all, — he had nothing else to do now; invited me up into his room, so he called it, where he introduced me to Mrs. Kent, and showed me his library with a good deal of particularity; pointed out the " Waverley Novels," Miss Edgeworth's, &c., and long rows of the reviews bound; also a very large collection of pamphlets, making ninety-five volumes, which he had collected since he was a young man, — that is, said he, within the last fifty years; showed me also " Greenleaf's Reports; " said he set much by that man; showed me the blank leaves of the first volume, in which he had written the time of your appointment as professor, and the testimonial of their regard offered by the Portland Bar, including in quotation marks the comparison run between your reports and those of Johnson and Binney: he had wafered into the first volume of " Greenleaf's Reports " your letter to him presenting the book, which he said he had done to preserve how you had honored him. I bid him good-by. He told me to give his regards to Judge Story; but as to Jackson, he had none for him.

Kent has great simplicity and freedom of manners; he opens himself like a child. This, though, I attributed partly to a harmless vanity. He undoubtedly knows that he is a *lion*, and he therefore offers himself readily for exhibition. Indeed, he seemed to be unfolding his character and studies, &c., to me, as if purposely to let me know the whole bent and scope of his mind

I thought more than once that he was sitting for his picture. Many more things I can tell you when I see you.

As I passed through Hartford, I saw Judge Daggett on the bench. Not having time to stop, I enclosed your favor in a note, in which I expressed a wish to consider your letter as a *continuing* introduction, if, upon my return, I should find him at home and disengaged.

I am now in the great Babel. Every thing is in a whirl. Boston seems small and thinly peopled compared with this mammoth place.

Here, as elsewhere, I am

Yours affectionately,

CHAS. SUMNER.

TO HIS PARENTS.

PHILADELPHIA, Friday Evening, Feb. 21.

MY DEAR PARENTS, — Since writing you from the steamboat, I have flown many rapid miles further on my journey, tried a novel conveyance, and seen the two most extensive cities of this part of the world. Indeed, Boston is but a baby compared with the mammoth size of these two places. New York is one perpetual whirl and bustle; the streets flow with throngs, as thick and pressing as those of Boston on a gala day. Carriages of all sorts are hurrying by; omnibuses and Broadway coaches for the conveyance of citizens up and down their miles of streets are perpetually in sight. Stores, almost infinite in number and variety, line the long streets. One must be wide awake, or he will run over or be run over by some of the crowd. One minute after I had left the steamboat was enough to let me know that I was in a place under different influences from Boston; where business was pushed to its extremest points, and all the available energies of men were put in requisition. I fancy that I can see a vast increase since I was there five years ago. This may be attributed in part to my being more of an observer now.

I arrived at New York at two o'clock in the afternoon of Wednesday; had my baggage carried to the "American;" was cheated by the porter; changed my coat, &c., and sallied out to walk round the city, to drop my many letters into the post-office, and to call upon Chancellor Kent. It was with some difficulty that I found him, living as he does at an extreme part of the city, in a splendid house, where a year ago, as he told me, was a pasture. I jumped into a Broadway coach, and was conveyed somewhere near his residence. I found him in a parlor; was waited upon by him into his study; shown his law and miscellaneous library; his manuscript comments upon the books and reviews he reads, — and he reads every thing legal and literary that is published; his interleaved copy of his Commentaries, in which he is making additional references, explanations, &c.; was invited to tea, which I declined, and to call as I returned. Kent's conversation is lively and instructive, but grossly ungrammatical. It is a wonder which I cannot solve, that he is so correct a writer (I do not think very highly of his taste as a writer) and so incorrect a converser. The same evening, after my interview with

Kent, I wrote a full letter to Professor Greenleaf, giving him an account of it.

Thursday morning, at seven o'clock, my baggage was in the hands of a porter, to be conveyed to the Philadelphia boat. And here was a delightful passage. First, thirty miles in a fast-sailing, spacious boat to Amboy; thence, thirty-seven miles on the railway, which we travelled in about two hours, part of the way going at the rate of more than twenty miles an hour. The interval between landing from the steamboat and starting on the railway was but a minute. All the baggage was taken from the boat in one crate and put into a car; the passengers, about thirty, jumped into the different carriages, all attached to one steam-carriage, and were soon far on our way, — moving fast but very gentle, — bowling through the sandy desert or pine-clad plains of New Jersey. At distances of about twelve miles the machine stopped for three minutes to take in water; the bell rang, and we were again on our "winding way." At Bordentown — the residence of Joseph Bonaparte — we took the boat again. The crate of baggage was swung into the boat, the bell rang, and we were soon pushing the water away before us, and leaving a wake as far back as the eye could reach. At four o'clock — after going thirty miles — we were in Philadelphia, the city of straight streets and marble edifices. I called upon Mr. Walsh;[1] was received kindly, &c.: called upon Mr. Troubat;[2] on his invitation determined to stay one day in the city, to attend the courts. To-day have attended the courts; visited the waterworks; seen my old schoolmate Peabody, who is a merchant here and boards where I am stopping. I shall start for Baltimore to-morrow at seven o'clock.

Your prodigal son,

CHAS.

TO HIS PARENTS.

WASHINGTON, Monday, Feb. 24, 1834.

MY DEAR PARENTS, — Here I am in the great city, or rather the city of great design, of spacious and far-reaching streets, without houses to adorn them or business to keep them lively, with a Capitol that would look proud amidst any European palaces, and with whole lines of houses, which resemble much the erections at Cambridgeport and Lechmere Point, — poor, stunted brick houses, with stores beneath and boarding above. There is nothing natural in the growth of the city. It only grows under the hot-bed culture of Congress. There is no confluence of trade from different parts of the country, and no natural commercial or manufacturing advantages to induce persons to live here. So, for aught I see, it must for ever remain as it is now, — a place of winter resort, as the Springs are of summer resort, and be supported entirely by travellers and sojourners. I arrived here last evening, at about six o'clock, and as yet have only seen the outside of the Capitol;

---

1 Robert Walsh, then editor of the "National Gazette."
2 Francis J. Troubat.

have not seen, except from a distance, the President's house; and have not traversed the city. All these are the pleasures of to-day. I called first upon Judge Story; found him boarding, with the rest of the court, in a house near the Capitol; was most kindly received by him. He wished me to tell you that he should take good care of me.

I left Philadelphia Friday morning at seven o'clock, in the boat " William Penn," — a large and ample establishment, — sailed forty miles down the Delaware to Newcastle; jumped into a railroad-car, and in an hour and five minutes, by Henry's watch, passed through the State of Delaware to French-town, at the head of Elk River, — General Washington's headquarters, — a distance of sixteen and a half miles; then took the steamer " Charles Carroll " for Baltimore, down the Elk and Chesapeake and up the Patapsco, upon which Baltimore is situated, — a distance of sixty-four miles, — arriving at Baltimore at six o'clock in the evening, where I stopped at Barnum's till the next morning, being Sunday, at eight and a half o'clock, when I started for Washington, mounting my last stage. The distance is but thirty-eight miles, yet we were till night laboring over the road, — the worst I was ever upon. The whole country was barren and cheerless; houses were sprinkled very thinly on the road, and when they did appear they were little better than hovels, — mere log-huts, which father will remember, though none else of the family may be able to conceive them. For the first time I saw slaves, and my worst preconception of their appearance and ignorance did not fall as low as their actual stupidity. They appear to be nothing more than moving masses of flesh, unendowed with any thing of intelligence above the brutes. I have now an idea of the blight upon that part of our country in which they live.

At these headquarters of politics, I shall see the *men* of the land, and ascertain their relative standing. The present prospects are represented as unpromising in the extreme. The majority of the Senate, having the great weight of talent, are against Jackson and his measures relating to the deposits. In the House it is the other way. The Legislature of Pennsylvania have the question now before them; and it is said that upon their proceedings depends the fate of the measure. If they go against Jackson, their large delegation will swing round directly, and give the day to the opposition. Jackson is represented as uncompromising and violent, determined to hold on in his course till he can no longer.

The city is full of travellers. I am now at Brown's, but I hope to find some private boarding-place in the course of the day.

My expenses to this time have been something over thirty dollars. I wish I had twenty dollars more with me. I hardly think I shall have occasion for it, but it would make me feel more comfortable to think that there was no risk of my spending my last dollar before I arrived home. I wish, of course, to see Baltimore and also Philadelphia more than I have. While passing through the cities now, I should see them so as not hereafter to make a special visit with that view.   Affectionately, your prodigal,

CHAS.

TO PROFESSOR SIMON GREENLEAF.

WASHINGTON, March 3, 1834.

MY DEAR MR. GREENLEAF, — Mr. F. S. Key[1] is now speaking in the Supreme Court, where I write these lines. The case before the court is an important one, between Amos Binney and the Chesapeake Canal,[2] — Key, Walter Jones, and Webster on one side, and Coxe and Swann on the other. Key has not prepared himself, and now speaks from his preparation on the trial below, relying upon a quickness and facility of language rather than upon research. Walter Jones,[3] — a man of acknowledged powers in the law, unsurpassed, if not unequalled, by any lawyer in the country, — is in the same plight. He is now conning his papers and maturing his points, — a labor which, of course, he should have gone through before he entered the court-room. And *our* Webster fills up the remiss triumvirate. He, like Jones, is doing the labor in court which should have been done out of court. In fact, politics have entirely swamped his whole time and talents. All here declare that he has neglected his cases this term in a remarkable manner. It is now whispered in the room that he has not looked at the present case,[4] though the amount at stake is estimated at half a million of dollars.

The insurance case,[5] argued by Selden, of New York, at Boston last year before Judge Story, has been argued here since my being in town by Selden on one side and Charles G. Loring and Webster on the other side. It was Loring's first appearance in the Supreme Court, and he acquitted himself honorably, drawing from Webster a practical compliment, dictated probably as much by his own convenience as by his sense of the merits of the argument, though they were superlative. He declined arguing the question after the learned argument of his friend, though a very large property was at stake, — saying, that out of respect to himself and to the court he would not pass over superficially, as he necessarily must, what his friend had discussed so thoroughly and satisfactorily. Loring spoke from a very full brief; was very clear and full, delivering his argument in a calm, undisturbed manner, which was a beautiful contrast to the rhetorical, excited, disturbed, tinselled manner of Selden, who spoke as if addressing his constituents at the Park or at Tammany Hall. Loring's manner was that of *reason*. The court and all present were highly impressed.

We expect a very interesting case. Wheaton v. Peters, — an action brought by Wheaton (the old reporter) against Peters for publishing in his "Condensed Reports" the twelve volumes of Wheaton, thus, as is alleged, violating Wheaton's copyright. One of the grounds of the defence — and a very interesting one — is, that there cannot be a copyright in the *opinions of*

---

1 Francis Scott Key, 1779–1843, author of "The Star-Spangled Banner."

2 8 Peters' Reports, p. 201.

3 1775–1861. An eminent lawyer, for many years residing and practising his profession at Washington.

4 Mr. Coxe, counsel on the other side, so informed Sumner.

5 Hazard v. New England Marine Insurance Co., 8 Peters' Reports, p. 555; s. c. 1 Sumner's Reports, p. 218.

the court published in the Reports. This ground is strongly upheld by Ingersoll, Peters' counsel at Philadelphia, in a printed argument, which I have read. John Sergeant is Peters' counsel, and Webster, Wheaton's.[1]

Franklin Dexter made an argument here a few days before I came, which gained him a good reputation. The court this morning gave judgment for his side.[2]

At this moment, Isaac Hill has *moved* both Senators and spectators from their seats by undertaking a written speech about the deposits. The Senate do not listen; but the public, whom he will reach through the press, will listen. Every day's attendance in the *political part* of the Capitol shows me clearly that all speeches there are delivered to the people beyond, and not to the Senators or Representatives present. In the Supreme Court, the object of speaking is to convince. The more I see of *politics* the more I learn to love *law*.

Signs of the deep distress of the country are received every day and proclaimed in both Houses. Jackson is obdurate. Sanguine hopes are entertained that he will soon be in a minority in the House, as he is in the Senate.

Judge Story has shown me immense kindness. He sends his love to you. He has just come to me from the bench, and tells me to inform you *that he is tired*. You will sympathize, I have no doubt, with the fatigue of a wordy argument. My love to Mrs. Greenleaf, and hope your son is well of that cough.   Yours, as ever, affectionately,

CHAS. SUMNER.

TO HIS PARENTS.

WASHINGTON, March 3, 1834.

MY DEAR PARENTS, — Since last I wrote, I have seen many great men and attended at the Capitol every day, making the Supreme Court (which is on the lower floor, in a dark room, almost down cellar) my first object of attention, the Senate my next, and the House of Representatives my last. There have not been many cases of interest in the Supreme Court, either from the talents displayed by the counsel or the character of the questions raised. The best argument I have heard as yet was by *our* Charles G. Loring. You, father, may here see the vanity of my journey in travelling so many hundred miles at such cost, and living here at such cost, to confess that the best treat I have as yet had in the Supreme Court, to attend which was the main object of my visit, was from a *home* lawyer.[3] . . .

---

[1] The brief of Mr. Webster's argument in Wheaton *v.* Peters, 8 Peters' Reports, p. 591, was taken by Mr. Peters, the reporter, from Sumner's notes, made during the argument. Mr. Peters prevailed in the case.

[2] Carrington *v.* Merchants' Insurance Co., 8 Peters' Reports, p. 495.

[3] The omitted paragraph is a repetition of a part of the letter of the same date to Professor Greenleaf.

I could write a quire about the different lawyers and the appearance of the court, and more about the different judges, of whom I have seen considerable, having supped and dined with them once _en famille_, as it were, — if I may apply that term where there is no family. All the judges board together, having rooms in the same house and taking their meals from the same table, except Judge McLean, whose wife is with him, and who consequently has a separate table, though in the same house. I dined with them yesterday, being Sunday. Judges Marshall, Story, Thompson, and Duval were present, who, with myself, made up the company, with two waiters in attendance. Sunday here is a much gayer day than with us. No conversation is forbidden, and nothing which goes to cause cheerfulness, if not hilarity. The world and all its things are talked of as much as on any other day. Judge Marshall is a model of simplicity, — " in wit a man, simplicity a child." He is naturally taciturn, and yet ready to laugh; to joke and be joked with. Judge Thompson is a kind-hearted man, now somewhat depressed from the loss of his wife. Judge Duval is eighty-two [1] years old, and is so deaf as to be unable to participate in conversation.

I have spent considerable time in the Senate, to the floor of which I received an introduction from Mr. Webster; in other words, he gave me a card which gives me access at all times to the floor. The Senate is now employed entirely upon the deposits. This subject is directly before them by means of Mr. Webster's great report as Chairman of the Finance Committee, which appeared before I left Boston, and also through the various memorials which are pouring in from every part of the country. The presentation of one of these memorials gives occasion for some introductory remarks, descriptive of the sufferings of the country and of the memorialists, which often draws out a reply or counter-statement, and not unfrequently leads on an animated discussion. I was present at one last Tuesday, in which Mr. Clay took part. His eloquence was splendid and thrilling. Without notes or papers of any kind, he seemed to surrender himself entirely to the guidance of his feelings. He showed _feeling;_ to which, of course, his audience responded. There was not one there whose blood did not flow quickly and pulse throb quickly as he listened. He delivered a violent attack upon Jackson, and a vehement exhortation to the people to continue their memorials and remonstrances. His language, without being choice, is strong; but it is his _manner_, or what Demosthenes called _action_, — _action_, ACTION, — which makes him so powerful. The opposition have now a majority of numbers in the Senate and much the heaviest weight of talents. Van Buren sits like a martyr under the volleys of abuse that are poured upon his master and his followers. In the House there has been little to attract attention.

For the first two days I was in Washington I boarded at Brown's Hotel, where I was dropped by the stage. Since then I have taken private lodgings.

Affectionately, your son,

CHAS.

1 Gabriel Duval, 1752-1844. He resigned Jan., 1835.

TO HIS SISTER JANE, AGED FOURTEEN.

WASHINGTON, March 4, 1834.

MY DEAR JANE, — I wrote a letter home yesterday, which will be carried by Charles G. Loring, Esq. This letter will go by the mail at nine o'clock this evening. Mr. Loring left town this morning at nine o'clock. You will see how much quicker the mail goes than a private traveller. I have no doubt that you will receive this at least a day earlier than that first written. Letters are carried by mail with all the speed possible. No delay is allowed at any place. They are hurried from one post-office to another, till they reach their final destination. Letters are never tired, as travellers are. They require no sleep or food. Relays of horses and changes of drivers are arranged, so that there may be no stoppage. The post-office is a vast establishment, and is an invention of very modern times. The first appearance of any thing like it was as late as James I. Since then it has received constant improvement and enlargement. And here you will see the importance of the railroads and canals which are now building throughout the whole country. They cause a quick interchange of goods and products, and also of opinions. Steam is now the great and surely powerful agent of this intercommunication. Thirty years ago, its use for this object was hardly known. All transportation of goods and letters was then by horses or ships. But now steam, with a swiftness that never tires, and which literally outstrips the wind, is fast becoming the universal agent. In a year or two, one will be able to go all the way to Washington by steam. Indeed, there are now but seventy miles on which horses are used, and railways are constructing over these miles. I refer to the roads from Boston to Providence, and from Baltimore to Washington. There is something partaking of the sublime in the sense that you are going at the rate of fifteen miles an hour, drawn by an insensible agent, the contrivance of man, who " has sought out many inventions; " enjoying, if you are in a boat, all the comforts and luxuries of the finest hotel, walking over carpets or sitting at a table loaded with all the products of the season; or, if in a railroad car, enjoying at least a comfortable and easy seat, from which you may see the country over which you are flying as a bird. Steam will be a great *revolutionist*. You, Jane, will hardly understand this word in the sense in which I use it. Yet I am persuaded that the idea intended to be conveyed by it is correct. A journey to Washington now is but a trifle; not so great an affair as a journey to New York twenty years ago. And a voyage to Europe is fast becoming as common and as easy as a journey to Washington. Steamboats are now erecting at Liverpool (I think) to run between that port and New York. Steam, you will see, is destined to be the great link of nations.

Pardon the above dissertation. I have been betrayed into it by my desire to impress upon your mind something that, though it may not be entirely new, still may be slightly instructive; or, at least, show you that I think of your instruction at the distance now between us. I hope you continue to study your Latin. You will not care to be an accomplished Latin scholar; but I trust you will have an ambition to acquire enough of that noble language to enable you to understand the grammar and etymology of your own, and also to enjoy the numerous allusions to and quotations from the authors of old Rome, with which elegant composition is so often interspersed. Further, the study of Latin will be a very proper discipline to your mind. The value of French, as a part of female education, I do not think so high as that of Latin.[1] Fashion and custom, though, have settled this question against me; and, in fact, have required from every lady a knowledge of this tongue. You, therefore, should learn French, as it were, in *self-defence*, to show that you are not behind that standard of education fixed for ladies. Remember, further, that *books* will be constant friends, to relieve you from lonesomeness and perhaps sorrow. . . .

These are incoherent hints, my Jane, which I wish you to think of, and, if willing, to adopt. I might expand them into a treatise. I hope Mary — who is not so docile as you — will imbibe some of your spirit of study, some of your willingness to undertake labor. She has fine intelligence and an *inquisitiveness*, which I think a good omen. I hope she will not abandon any of that; though I wish she would try to bear her little disappointments, in not being able to have her questions answered, with more nerve. She must remember the fable of Hercules and the laborer. The laborer's complaints and Mary's tears are equally unavailing.

There is little in Washington to interest you, or I would have written you about what I have seen and heard here. There are many strangers here. Indeed, Washington is peopled by them. It is a great encampment, where some pitch their tents for the season, and others for a month or a week. The Capitol you have read a description of. It is a sumptuous edifice, worthy in every way its high object, as the place of meeting of the representatives of the greatest republic on earth. The President's palace is of equal attraction. The description given of it in your "Juvenile Miscellany" is correct. I have been in many of its rooms, and seen General Jackson (the old tyrant), who appeared very infirm. He seemed to have hardly nerve enough to keep his bones together. When I first called upon him, he had just gone out with some gentlemen to see a horse. He soon returned, and went into conference with Secretary McLane, who was with him when I was introduced. Judge Story has shown me great kindness and afforded me many facilities here, for which I am grateful. He sends his regards to father. I wish, Jane, you would ask father to send me, enclosed in a letter, twenty dollars, if convenient. If not convenient, I will try to do without. It would be a comfort to me to have more than I have. My expenses here are considerable, — board ten dollars a week, — and I wish to stop a day or two in Baltimore and Philadelphia on my return. The money will be remitted, of course, at my risk.

This letter is written in the Supreme Court, while F. S. Key is speaking in a case of great magnitude.

Your affectionate brother,

CHAS.

[1] His foreign travels changed his opinion as to the study of the French language.

TO HIS SISTER MARY, AGED TWELVE YEARS.

WASHINGTON, Tuesday Evening, March 18, 1834.

MY DEAR MARY, — I am thankful to father for his letter, and to you for yours, — which, by the way, I wish had been written a little fairer. I received them in due time, with their enclosures of fifty dollars from Mr. Rand [1] and of twenty dollars from father. I have intended every day to write to you, but have been prevented by some engagement or other. Time passes very quickly here, without affording much room for study or correspondence; and it would be often difficult to point out at the end of the day what all the hours had been devoted to. I rise usually about seven o'clock; read the newspapers till breakfast, which is at eight and a half o'clock. After breakfast, say at nine o'clock, I take a walk to view some object of interest, or to make a call on some gentleman of Congress; sometimes get to the Capitol at ten o'clock, when I pass the next hour in the Congress library, till eleven o'clock, when the Supreme Court opens. Here I pitch my tent generally till the hour of its adjournment, which usually takes place about three and a half o'clock.

The Senate and House of Representatives open at twelve o'clock, and continue in session till four and sometimes five o'clock. If I hear of any very interesting debate in either, and there is nothing of great interest in the court, I desert the latter; and after the court is over I wait the adjournment of the Senate and House. This brings me to dinner at four or four and a half o'clock. After dinner there is but little daylight left, which I occupy in making calls. The first part of the evening I spend in conversation with some of the gentlemen at home, or in visiting. The latter I most invariably spend with Judge Story, — say from nine o'clock till ten, that being the hour when he is free. Such, Mary, is a simple account of the course of my time. It will be hardly interesting or intelligible to you, though otherwise to mother and father. The end of the day generally finds me tired and willing to go to bed, or at least indisposed to much exercise of the mind. I have found time, though, to read an able work of Dr. Lieber on the Girard Seminary, and to run my eyes through a law-book on " Tenures," and to prepare a law-argument of four pages, to be laid before the Judiciary Committee of the Senate, on Mr. Ward's claim against the United States,[2] besides writing the few letters which I have written.

This letter will be carried by Judge Story, who leaves to-morrow morning, — the Supreme Court then adjourning. It was my intention to have started with him; but as I should stop, at his recommendation, a day or two in Baltimore, so that I should be obliged to quit him, — and as I should be but an unsocial companion on the road to Baltimore, he riding in the inside and I necessarily on the outside, — I have determined to remain a few days longer in this city of magnificent distances, to give an undivided attention to the debates in Congress, which are growing daily in interest. Mr. Webster

[1] Mr. Rand had forwarded the amount for the purchase of law books for himself.
[2] Joshua H. Ward, a lawyer practising in Danvers.

has this day presented, with an eloquent speech, the protest from Boston, and also introduced his bank-bill.[1] This last will excite great debate. Mr. McDuffie[2] told me to-day that he should endeavor to show, to-morrow or next day, that General Jackson has deliberately aimed to engross all the powers of the government; and, in short, to challenge little short of a "kingly crown."

I shall not start for home till the last of the week, — say Friday or Saturday or Sunday, — and shall be fully a week on my way. My dear Mary, I am ashamed of addressing such a letter as the above to you. It contains nothing, I feel, adapted to your age, and should rather be addressed to father.

Good night, by your affectionate brother,

CHAS

TO PROFESSOR SIMON GREENLEAF.

WASHINGTON, March 18, 1834.

MY DEAR PROFESSOR GREENLEAF, — I snatch a moment to express to you my joy at receiving the testimonial of your regard and recollection enclosed in the letter to Judge Story. The Supreme Court adjourns to-morrow, and Judge S. starts immediately on his "winding way" home, where I hope will be peace and happiness. Since I have been in Washington my debt of gratitude to him has been largely swelled. To him I owe an introduction to many of the interesting persons and scenes of the place, and especially what I may almost call a place in the court, — *persona standi in judicio*, as Lord Stowell would say. I shall remain a few more days in Washington, being anxious to attend the animating debate which impends on Mr. Webster's bank-bill. I probably shall never come to Washington again, and therefore I shall do myself best service by making the most of this visit. I wish to become acquainted with the manner and appearance of those gentlemen whose speeches I am to read for some years, and with whose fame the country rings from side to side. Notwithstanding the attraction afforded by the Senate, and the newspaper fame which I see the politicians there acquire, I feel no envy therefor, and no disposition to enter the unweeded garden in which they are laboring, even if its gates were wide open to me; in plain language, I see no political condition that I should be willing to desire, even if I thought it within my reach, — which, indeed, I do not think of the humblest.

The country is in a sad condition, without a discernible sign of relief. I cannot but have a sense or feeling that things cannot continue in this pass, and that the very extremity of our distress shows the day of redemption to be near. However, why write of this? Judge Story will fully, and more justly than I can, tell you all the impressions a Washington residence makes.

Judge Story's "Conflict of Laws"[3] was cited in argument in the Supreme Court last Saturday for the first time.

---

[1] Webster's Works, Vol. IV. pp. 82-102.
[2] Representative from South Carolina.
[3] This treatise was published early in the year.

I have paid a pilgrimage to Mount Vernon alone on horseback; seen the original Declaration of Independence; the snuff-boxes and royal presents to our ambassadors; the toys at the Patent-Office, &c.

My love to Mrs. G., and my ardent wishes for your health and happiness.

From your, as ever, affectionate

CHAS. SUMNER.

TO HIS FATHER.

WASHINGTON, March 19, 1834.

MY DEAR FATHER, — I have seen Governor Lincoln several times since he has been in town. He has treated me very kindly, and cordially invited me to see him. I presented your respects to him upon his first arrival, and he appeared much gratified. He has spoken, you will have seen by the papers, this week, on presenting a memorial from Worcester. The speech, I think, reads well, though it made little impression on the House. In fact, nobody can make himself there heard, nor, by consequence, gain the attention of the House. Members have too many facilities for writing and reading to give up these last to attend to a speech where the very attention is labor and weariness. Governor Lincoln is very constant in his seat, and attentive to all the speeches. Indeed, he seems to give a studied attention.

The spring has stolen upon me here unexpectedly in this southern latitude. The grass looks green in many fields within sight, and the days feel sultry; which, with the dust that sweeps up and down Pennsylvania Avenue, make the walk to the Capitol quite uncomfortable.

Calhoun has given notice to-day that he will speak to-morrow on Mr. Webster's bank-bill. I shall probably hear him, and he will be the last man I shall ever hear speak in Washington. I probably shall never come here again. I have little or no desire ever to come again in any capacity. Nothing that I have seen of politics has made me look upon them with any feeling other than loathing. The more I see of them the more I love law, which, I feel, will give me an honorable livelihood. Mr. Peters, who has treated me with great friendship, told me, when I was remarking to him as above, that before 1840 I should come on to Washington (if I were willing) to argue some causes in the Supreme Court. This anticipation, flattering of course, was dictated undoubtedly by Judge Story's friendly recommendations of me. However, I do not presume to indulge any such anticipations. When indulged by others, I let them pass for what they are worth. To-day is Thursday. Saturday morning I shall probably leave Washington for Baltimore, where I shall be, perhaps, Sunday and Monday; on Tuesday pass from Baltimore to Philadelphia, over the track of the unfortunate steamer "William Penn," one of the largest and handsomest boats I ever was in, where I shall stay a couple of days; pass to New York, there to stop a day; then through the Sound *via* Providence home, where I hope to find you all well and happy, as I have been and now am.   Affectionately, your son

CHAS.

TO PROFESSOR SIMON GREENLEAF.

WASHINGTON, March 21, 1834.

MY DEAR MR. GREENLEAF, — Let me congratulate you upon the presence of your fellow-laborer in instruction. I hope Judge S. is at home, well and in good spirits.

I leave Washington to-morrow morning for Baltimore. I feel happy in the prospect of soon seeing home and my friends in Cambridge, who stand next in my affections; and, indeed, I have sometimes feared more than divided them. That I may find you and yours in health and happiness is my ardent wish.

It will be vacation, I presume, when I arrive. I trust that you will make it vacation in reality.

I have nothing interesting to write from this big city. There is the same strong cry of complaint received every day from every part of the country; and, in return, there is the same stubborn indifference manifested by the administration.

Excuse this rude scrawl, and believe me

Yours, as aforesaid,

CHAS. SUMNER.

TO HIS FATHER.

WASHINGTON, March 21, 1834.

MY DEAR FATHER, — I start for Baltimore to-morrow morning at eight and a half o'clock, after one month's residence in Washington. I have seen many of the first men in the country, and heard most of the speakers. The excitement of the times has afforded me a good opportunity to hear our leading minds.

I feel a little melancholy at leaving, as I have become almost a denizen here; have habituated myself to the hours and style of living here, so that I shall feel the change. And yet there is nothing that I have met, either in the Senate or the court, or in the well-furnished tables of the richest hotels, that I would take in exchange for the calm enjoyments and employments to which I have been accustomed. I feel in an unnatural state, and I shall have joy in once more resuming my constant labors.

Mr. Calhoun has spoken to-day on Mr. Webster's bank-bill.[1] He is no orator, very rugged in his language, unstudied in style, marching directly to the main points of his subject without stopping for parley or introduction. His speech made a very strong impression upon a very numerous audience.

I bade good-by to Governor Lincoln to-day, who wished me to present his regards to you. He has obtained private lodgings now, and feels a little more contented. He was quite homesick a week ago. He is much discouraged by the size of the Representatives' Hall; he can neither hear nor be heard.

Perhaps you will not hear from me again till I come in person. I wrote

[1] Calhoun's Works, Vol. II. pp. 344-376.

letters while on my way *from* home, but those were Parthian shafts. I shall follow so close upon my letters, that it will be superfluous to write till I come home.   Good-by.

                                                                        CHAS.

You will see that this is written in a hurricane of haste.

TO DR. FRANCIS LIEBER, PHILADELPHIA.

                                                    BOSTON, July 17, 1834.

MY DEAR DOCTOR, — Yours containing the notice of "Mittermaier's Journal" was duly received. I thank you for it; it was what was wanted. Your friendly address to me I appreciate, and under your advice shall hasten to learn German as speedily as possible. Judge Story will attest to you that my time is not unemployed; if it had been in the least otherwise for the last three months, I should already have made some acquests of that difficult language. I have just, by the help of a dictionary, made out the meanings of half a dozen title-pages in German, to enter in the list of new publications on jurisprudence at the end of our journal. Set that down as a beginning.

You may see at Micklin and Johnson's, probably, the "Law Magazine," No. 23, which contains Mittermaier's article on German criminal law. I see he has just published another medical work on "Proofs," &c.

I was with Judge Story when he received your letter giving an account of Mittermaier's article on his "Commentaries on the Constitution." How long is that article, and what is its purport and point? Ought it not to be presented to *our* public, translated?[1] I burn to know German, that I may at once read all these things myself, and not pester with my ignorance my indulgent friends.

Can I help you about *towns?*[2] You will wish first to state in brief what *towns* are in England, — to get, as it were, a unit of measure; and because ours are fashioned more or less upon those models. You will then be led to state that towns are public corporations: and here explain a nice distinction of the common law between public and private corporations, — a distinction unknown to the civil law, and, I presume, to German or any continental jurisprudence. The early history of New England should be searched, in order, as it were, to go behind the statute-book; for, I take it, towns were established long before there was much systematic legislation. Indeed, I have always regarded the formation of New England into towns as one of the peculiarities of the first settlers, to be accounted for by a study of their circumstances and character. Can I assist you? I have several engagements

---

1 "American Jurist," July, 1835, Vol. XIV. p. 247.

2 Mittermaier had requested Dr. Lieber to contribute to a German magazine an article on "Towns." This was prior to the publication of Tocqueville's review of the "American System of Townships," and particularly of the towns of New England, in his "Democracy in America," Vol. I. ch. 5.

of my pen in different quarters, but there is no one I should be so happy to serve as you.

With sincere attachment, yours,

CHAS. SUMNER.

TO MISS PETERS, PHILADELPHIA.

BOSTON, Aug. 13, 1834.

. . . I am glad that you are so fond of what most young ladies call *dry reading*, — Hume, Sallust, &c. Novels, indeed, are delightful. They are the sources of exhilaration and pleasure; and especially those of Walter Scott and Miss Edgeworth often contain much instruction, either by furnishing sketches of historical characters, or of an age, or of a remarkable event, which are thus imprinted on the attentive mind with the vividness of a picture, or by illustrating and enforcing some beautiful moral truth. Miss Edgeworth's "Helen," which I have just read, is worth a score of dull sermons on this account. With what point and skill has she shown the miserable consequences of the slightest departure from truth! But notwithstanding all the fine qualities which some novels possess, they must not be received as the only aliment of the mind. . . .

I am glad you have taken the trouble to abridge Hume as you read, though I fear you have done it out of kind deference to my advice rather than from love of it. The making this abridgment will have a tendency to fasten your attention upon the history more than it would have been otherwise, while you will also accustom yourself to select the leading events, — a habit of great importance. Hume's style is easy and fascinating. It has not the stately and oratorical character which belongs to Robertson and Gibbon, but is much more intelligible than that of either. . . . When you have grown a good deal older, you will take a pleasure in reading some criticisms and strictures upon Hume, and also the volumes of Sir James Mackintosh on English history, which, though written in an involved and often crabbed style, abound in the finest thoughts and in the most correct views of the English Constitution.

Sallust is one of the most valuable authors spared to us from antiquity. He is remarkable for point, strong remark, and sarcasm; the last is especially directed against vice, though he himself was one of the most flagitious men that ever lived, — if I remember right, the plunderer of the province of which he was pro-consul, and a sensualist who set no bounds to his indulgence. His works, so caustic in the cause of virtue, and his character so defiled by vice, taken together present an anomaly which is a standing wonder. . . .

Remember me affectionately to your father, mother, sisters, and

Believe me as ever yours,

CHAS. SUMNER.

CHAPTER VIII.

EARLY PROFESSIONAL LIFE. — SEPTEMBER, 1834, TO DECEMBER, 1837. —
AGE, 23–26.

A YOUNG attorney's "first case" is always with him a well-
remembered event, and Sumner's happened to have some
points of public interest.[1] Suffolk County had then a Commonwealth's attorney, from whose strong gripe it was hard to wrest
any prisoner; but Sumner was fortunate in this attempt at a res-
cue. A few weeks after his admission to the bar he engaged, as
a volunteer, in the defence of one Waylen, indicted in the Municipal Court under a statute for sending a challenge to one Alles-
sandro Gherardi, — a case which probably came to him through
his father's connection with the jail. He was associated with
George S. Hillard, who was admitted to the bar in April of the
previous year. The grounds of defence at the trial were, that
the paper sent by the defendant was an invitation to a conference, with a view to a satisfactory adjustment, rather than a
challenge; and that the defendant's surname ended with an *n*,
instead of an *r*, as written in the indictment. The trial occupied part of the day, Oct. 13, 1834, and resulted in an acquittal.
A newspaper of the next day said: " The defence was conducted
with much ability by Messrs. G. S. Hillard and Charles Sumner.
This is the first essay of the latter gentleman, who is said to be
more deeply read in the law than any other individual of similar
age." [2] Sumner, as his preserved minutes show, argued at length,
citing numerous authorities on the question of misnomer and the
construction of the statute. He reviewed with his characteristic
fulness the celebrated duels in English and French history;
urged that they were peculiar to men of fashion, and rarely

1 His first professional charge, being for a writ, was made Sept. 13, 1834.
2 Daily Atlas.

resorted to by persons of humble life, like the accused; and contended, therefore, that his client's language should be construed as intending only an amicable meeting.

Early in November Hillard and Sumner became associated as partners, and rented two adjoining rooms on the second floor of the Brooks Building, then recently erected, being Number 4 Court Street, at the corner of Washington Street, — the site of the present Sears Building. Sumner occupied the room next to the hall, and Hillard the rear one. He kept one or the other for about twenty years, so long as he remained at the bar.

Number 4 Court Street gathered at this period several lawyers, since well known, and some who were destined to a permanent fame. On the same floor with Sumner and Hillard were Theophilus Parsons, Rufus Choate, Theophilus and Peleg W. Chandler; and later John A. Andrew, afterwards Governor of the Commonwealth. On the third floor were Horace Mann, Edward G. Loring, and Luther S. Cushing. When Hillard left the building, in 1856, having previously removed to another room, he wrote in verse a graceful " Farewell to Number Four," which called forth some happy rejoinders.[1]

Sumner and Cushing[2] rented together a single lodging-room on the third floor of the Brooks Building. Sumner took his meals at a restaurant — Kenfield's, on Wilson's Lane. Some two years later he changed his lodgings to the Albion, and dined there or at the Tremont.

The culture and friendliness of Hillard and Sumner attracted many callers, — not only the other tenants of Number 4, but, besides them, Judge Story, Greenleaf, Cleveland, Felton, Park Benjamin, and George Bancroft. Greenleaf deposited his " writing-desk, table, and chair " in the office, calling it " *our* office." Here, when he came to the city, he usually called upon his two friends, and met the clients whom he served while he was professor. Whether many or few suitors came to the young attorneys, they at least had rare enjoyment in their fellowships.[3]

In Feb., 1835, Sumner defended successfully, in the Municipal Court, a party indicted for a libel. Failing on his law-points, — an alleged defect in the indictment and want of jurisdiction in

---

[1] Law Reporter, March, 1856, Vol. XVIII. p. 653.

[2] Cushing was the well-known author of works on Parliamentary Law.

[3] Hillard, writing to Sumner from New York, July 4, 1836, recalls, in contrast with the law-offices of that city, " our cool and pleasant office, and the quiet and cultivated friends who drop in."

the court, — which he strongly urged, he made a vigorous
opening to the jury on the truth of the article complained of
and the motives of its author, and discussed at length the law
of libel.

The following December he was counsel, as junior, with Theophilus Parsons,[1] for the plaintiff, in the case of Pelby v. Barry,
tried in the Supreme Judicial Court before Mr. Justice Morton,[2]
— a novel action exciting public interest, in which the plaintiff
sought, by applying the rule governing the relation of master and
servant, to recover damages against the defendant for enticing
Miss Kerr and other actors from his service.[3] He made quite a
full opening argument, covering, as was usual with him, a wide
range, which included a review of the drama, and particularly
melodrama, this being the specialty of the actors enticed by the
defendant; bespeaking the favor of the jury for his client, as the
weaker party, and entreating them not to indulge in any preju-
dice against him because of his profession. The jury disagreed,
and the entry, "neither party," was made on the docket.

Sumner's first appearance before the Supreme Judicial Court
at law-terms was in 1837. He was junior counsel in the argument of two causes, one heard in March relating to a mort-
gage of personal property,[4] and the other, in June, being an
action of tort for wrongfully putting a party's name on certain
medicines.[5] He was called into the former case by Richard
Fletcher, and into the latter by Theophilus Parsons, — two
friends who watched with interest his professional career. He
prepared a brief for Mr. Fletcher in a case involving the question, whether an agreement to procure a certain location for a
railway-station is void as against public policy, and suggested the
point on which the case was decided.[6]

Among his papers is an elaborate opinion, written in 1835,
which reviews at length the authorities on a question arising
under the law of watercourses, — whether the proprietors of mills

---

1 Mr. Parsons, an early friend of Sumner, was afterwards for many years Dane Professor in the Harvard Law School, and is the well-known author of the "Law of Contracts" and other law treatises.

2 Evening Mercantile Journal, Dec. 24, 25, 1835.

3 It was held in England, in 1853 (Coleridge, J., dissenting), that such an action was
maintainable. Lumley v. Gye, 2 Ellis and Blackburn's Reports, p. 216 ; Lumley v. Wagner,
1 De Gex, Macnaghten & Gordon's Reports, p. 604.

4 Shurtleff v. Willard, 19 Pickering's Reports, p. 202.

5 Thomson v. Winchester, 19 Pickering's Reports, p. 214.

6 Fuller v. Dame, 18 Pickering's Reports, p. 472. Sumner's name does not appear in the
report of the case.

at Lowell on the Merrimac River, which is fed by the waters of
Lake Winnipiseogee, have a right of action against parties who
divert for mill-uses the waters of Merrymeeting Pond, which
flow into the Lake.

In June, 1835, he was appointed by Judge Story a commissioner of the Circuit Court of the United States,[1] and a year
later was admitted to practice in that court.

Sumner, at this period, succeeded as well as the average of
young lawyers; but he did not, like his classmate Hopkinson,
step into a lucrative practice, nor obtain the business which, with
his laborious studies and many friends, he had expected. His
docket was a slender one even for those days. He was too much
absorbed in amateur studies to become a shrewd and ready prac-
titioner; and his mind, while so employed, was the less inclined to the petty details of an office. His engagements at the
Law School, yet to be mentioned, for the first three months
of each year — the busiest season for a lawyer — seriously invaded
the regularity of office hours, keeping him at Cambridge every
alternate day at some seasons. Clients are quick to detect such
departures from the professional routine, and prefer some painstaking attorney who is always to be found at his desk. Sumner, not meeting at once with the success which he had hoped
for, confessed his disappointment to his intimate friends. But
while with continuous devotion to the profession he would
have doubtless attained a very respectable rank at the bar, it
may be questioned whether he had the qualities which draw to
a lawyer "litigious terms, fat contentions, and flowing fees."
According to tradition, he weighted his arguments with learning
where only a skilful handling of testimony would have been most
effective; and was not gifted with the quickness of perception
which is as essential in the court-room as in the field. His tastes
and qualities of mind fitted him rather for a position as judge or
teacher, where his chief duty would be the exposition of the principles of the law. But he expressed no discontent with his profession, and certainly had no thought of leaving it. His enthusiasm in the study of jurisprudence as a science was unabated.

In Jan., 1835, he began to give instruction in the Law
School in the place of Judge Story, who was absent at Washington on official duty. Judge Story wrote to him, Feb. 9, —

[1] Office resigned by letter, Dec. 9, 1853, but vacated by law on his acceptance of the
office of Senator, in 1851.

"I rejoice that you have gone through the ordeal of your inauguration, and fairly through, and are now acclimated in the Law School. I never had any doubt upon the subject. Your success (for so I learn from Mr. Greenleaf) has been complete and every way gratifying. I hope that this is but the beginning, and that one day you may fill the chair which he or I occupy, if he or I, like autocrats, can hope to appoint our successors." [1]

He rendered the same service in the winters of 1836–37, and in the last-named year had the chief responsibility for the school during the absence of both Judge Story and Professor Greenleaf, — the latter being engaged at Washington as counsel in the case of The Charles-River Bridge v. The Warren Bridge.

Like the two professors, Sumner taught by oral examinations and also by formal lectures. He used as text-books Kent's "Commentaries," — the first and second volumes, — and Starkie's "Evidence." The volumes of Kent which he used, particularly the first, are very much underscored, and marked with additional references. The first volume treats of the law of nations, the jurisdiction of the national courts, and the sources of municipal law. The thorough study of these topics, which his duties as instructor required, gave him thus early a facility in dealing with them, which was to be of great use to him in public life. He had a difficult place to fill in the school, — one always suggesting a comparison with Story and Greenleaf. Few recall his method as a teacher; and while he did not leave a strong impression of any kind on the students, he appears to have realized a fair measure of success for so young a lawyer.

Early in 1835,[2] Judge Story appointed him as the reporter of his opinions in the Circuit Court. His first volume (filled with cases decided in the time of the preceding reporter, Mason) was published in March, 1836, the second in 1837, and the third in 1841.

In 1835, he assisted Professor Greenleaf in preparing the General Digest of his "Reports of the Decisions of the Supreme Court of Maine," which is a part of Vol. IX. of the series. In 1835–36, he prepared the indexes to the two volumes of Story's "Equity Jurisprudence." Some literary work planned in 1835 was not executed, — a condensed series of English Parliamentary Cases, to be prepared by him in connection with

---

[1] Story's Life and Letters, Vol. II. p. 189. Sheriff Sumner entered in his "Farmer's Almanac," Jan. 6, 1836, "Charles, twenty-five years old, lectured on Common Carriers."
[2] Story's Life and Letters, Vol. II. p. 194.

Professor Greenleaf, and a similar series of the English Chancery Reports, ancient and modern, in connection with Richard Peters;[1] and a treatise on the " Law of Sales." In 1836, he was urged to edit Chitty's treatise on Criminal Law, but declined; recommending in his stead Mr. Perkins, of Salem.[2]

During the whole of this period of three years following his admission to the bar, he continued to write for the " Jurist," having, as assistant of Mr. Phillips, the editor, the main charge until April, 1836; when Sumner, Hillard, and Cushing were announced as the editors. Besides contributing articles on legal topics, the editorship involved much drudgery in digesting the recent reports and in preparing miscellaneous matter. One number, — that for Oct., 1835, — when just ready to be issued, was destroyed by a fire which took place at the corner of Devonshire and Water Streets, and Sumner was obliged to rewrite his own contributions to it. The magazine kept up its high character, but was not remunerative; and the small number of its contributors imposed a heavy burden on its editors. Much of the material prepared by the different editors cannot now be traced to the one who supplied it; but Sumner's longer articles are marked with his initials, and his correspondence with friends reveals his authorship of some briefer notices. The following are identified as written by him : —

" Are Challenges to Jurors in Massachusetts determinable by Triors? "[3] — an article which treats not only the particular point, but the broader question, to what extent the American colonists adopted the common law of England; review of Howe's "Practice;"[4] "Right to Sue the United States,"[5] — suggested probably by the private claim which, as a friendly act, he promoted on his visit to Washington in 1834; "Sketch of the Law School at Cambridge,"[6] — taking for its text Professor Greenleaf's inaugural discourse, and giving a history of the school, with a tribute to Nathan Dane, a living benefactor;[7] " The Advocates' Library in Edinburgh," [8] — which dwells upon the necessity of law libraries to meet the vast increase in law

---

[1] American Jurist, April, 1835, Vol. XIII. p. 490.

[2] He wrote a notice of the edition for the "Jurist," Jan., 1837, Vol. XVI. pp. 371, 372.

[3] Oct., 1834, Vol. XII. pp. 330–340.   [4] Oct., 1834, Vol. XII. pp. 554–567.

[5] Jan., 1835, Vol. XIII. pp. 34–39.   [6] Jan., 1835, Vol. XIII. pp. 107–130.

[7] Mr. Dane, author of "An Abridgment and Digest of American Law," and framer of the celebrated ordinance of 1787, for the government of the North-west Territory, died shortly after, Feb. 15, 1835, at the age of eighty-three.

[8] April, 1835, Vol. XIII. pp. 382–389.

literature, and the value of good catalogues, "the soul of libraries;" "The Juridical Writings of Sir James Mackintosh,"[1] — commending Sir James as author and magistrate, with liberal extracts from his writings; "The Library of the Inner Temple,"[2] — criticising the library for its indifference to American law-books, in contrast in this respect with the Advocates' Library in Edinburgh, and testifying to its richness in ancient manuscripts; "Barbour's 'Equity Digest;'"[3] "Phillips on the Law of Patents;"[4] "David Hoffman's 'Anthony Grumbler;'"[5] and "The Judgments of Sir Edward Sugden."[6]

As will be seen by reference to these articles, Sumner's tastes led him to write upon authors, books, and libraries, rather than upon the law itself. His learning and comprehension of the principles of the law were appreciated by his friends, who frequently applied to him for his views as well as for cases in point. Among these were Mr. Daveis, Mr. Appleton, of Bangor, now Chief-Justice of Maine, Mr. Parsons, and his classmate Browne.

Sumner's time was much occupied, in 1835-36, in revising and completing Dunlap's "Admiralty Practice." The author, Andrew Dunlap, had mainly written the text of his book; when, in the early part of 1835, he was obliged by failing health to resign his office of Attorney of the United States for the District of Massachusetts, and to commit the revision of the text, the correction of proof, and the preparation of precedents to another. Among the young lawyers of Boston he selected Sumner, with whom he had relations of friendship, as the fittest person for the service. His whole heart was in the book, which he longed to finish. He wrote or dictated many notes to Sumner, from January till the time of his death in July, the last, with the preface, only four days before that event. After his death, Sumner made the indexes and most of the appendix, and prepared the "Practical Forms." He obtained these forms — a valuable feature of the book — from manuscript pleadings which had been tested in this country, and from English forms which he abbreviated and simplified for American practice. Others he drew himself without such aid, to meet cases found in the reports. These forms, carefully and skilfully prepared as they

1 July, 1835, Vol. XIV. pp. 100-134.   2 Oct., 1835, Vol. XIV. pp. 310-316.
3 July, 1837, Vol. XVII. pp. 366-372.   4 Oct, 1837, Vol. XVIII. pp. 101-119.
5 Oct., 1837, Vol. XVIII. pp. 119, 120.   6 Jan., 1838, Vol. XVIII. pp. 328-334.

were, did much to remedy the looseness, inaccuracy, and want of uniformity which prevailed in those early days of admiralty practice; and even now, after an interval of forty years, they remain, with only slight changes, the standard forms. His preparation of the work consumed so much time, that he was obliged to defer its publication till a year after the author's death. His preface to the volume gives a brief sketch of the author's life and character.

Mr. Dunlap dictated, July 23, four days before his death, a preface, in which he said: —

" These remarks are all which the author would have offered to the profession respecting himself and his work, were it not that he is under obligations to another, which both inclination and justice require him publicly to acknowledge. About the time when the body of the work was completed, and the author was preparing to give it a last revision as it went through the press, he was attacked by a most severe illness, from which he has not recovered, except in a very slight degree. He was, therefore, under the necessity of committing all the care of the publication of this book to Charles Sumner, Esq., the reporter of the decisions of the Circuit Court of the United States for the First Circuit, who has discharged the kind service with the zeal of a sincere friend and the accuracy of an excellent lawyer."

In 1836, Sumner was much interested in the proposed codification of the common law, — a project then much agitated in Massachusetts. He was consulted with reference to taking a place upon the preliminary commission, — consisting of Judge Story, Theron Metcalf, Simon Greenleaf, Charles E. Forbes, and Luther S. Cushing, — which was appointed under a legislative resolve to consider its expediency, but was dissuaded from accepting it by some of his friends; they thinking his great intimacy with Story, who would be the soul of the commission, an objection to his serving upon it. This movement for law-reform did not advance beyond the report of the commission.

In 1837, Sumner contributed to the " North American Review " an article on Francis J. Grund's " Americans," [1] and some brief notices of books.

In the winter of 1834–35, he was announced for a lecture in

---

[1] Jan., 1838, Vol. XLVI. pp. 106–126. In sending the article to the editor, Dr. Palfrey, he wrote, Nov. 25, 1837, " The whole has been written in the loopholes which I could find while my mind was anxious with business and thrilling with anticipations of Europe." He wrote a notice of Blunt's " Shipmaster's Assistant," Oct., 1837, Vol. XLV. pp. 502–504; David Hoffman's " Anthony Grumbler," pp. 482–504, and Lieber's " Hermeneutics," Jan. 1838, Vol. XLVI pp. 300–301. In the " Daily Advertiser," Aug. 24, 1835, he published a brief notice of a recent publication by Dr. Lieber.

a course delivered before the Boston Lyceum, at Boylston
Hall; in which Mr. Choate gave the first, followed by the
brothers Everett, George S. Hillard, and Amasa Walker. Sumner read, Jan. 26, 1835, a lecture on "The Law of Master and
Servant, including Mariners," before the Mercantile Association,
at Amory Hall, corner of Washington and West Streets, and repeated the same lecture before the Charitable Mechanics' Association, at Masonic Hall. He read another lecture, Feb. 2, on
"The Law of Bailments" before the Mercantile Association, and
repeated it a few weeks later before a class in the Law School.
The two lectures are a simple statement of the rules of law per-
tinent to each topic, with familiar illustrations from business life.
He received an invitation, in Jan., 1836, which he does not appear
to have accepted, to deliver a lecture at Lowell, before the
Moral Lyceum. He read, Feb. 28, 1837, a lecture on "The
Constitution of the United States" in the Smith Schoolhouse,
Belknap Street, before the Adelphic Union Society, — a literary
association of colored people. Hillard delivered the introductory
lecture, and was followed by Wendell Phillips, Rev. John Pierpont, and Dr. Gamaliel Bradford.

Sumner was at this period an overworked man, doing, besides
the business of his law-office, altogether too much literary drudgery. George Gibbs wrote to him from Paris, Sept. 16, 1835,
"You do not do justice to yourself in some of your undertakings,
from the speed with which they are prepared." Mr. Appleton
wrote from Bangor, Dec. 6, of that year, "There is one word of
advice to you, my friend; that is, not to labor too hard." Sumner himself afterwards thought that he had given too much of
his time to writing for magazines. But his health did not fail
him. He was rarely ill; and notwithstanding his excessive
application he was able to write to a friend, Aug. 25, 1835,
when suffering from a headache, that it was his first experience
of the kind.

He gave at this time no promise of future distinction as an
orator. His few arguments in court were mere statements of the
law, with illustrations from history and literature. His style
as yet was only that of an essayist. The lectures before lyceums were didactic only, such as any professor might read from
his chair. Young men no older than himself had already won
favor on the platform. Hillard had spoken at Faneuil Hall, and
delivered, in 1835, the customary oration before the city author-

ities on the Fourth of July, and an address at a commencement
of Dartmouth College. Wendell Phillips was already a favorite
public speaker; and, in Dec., 1837, made his famous reply
to James T. Austin, in Faneuil Hall, on Lovejoy's murder at
Alton. Unlike most young lawyers, Sumner took no part in
politics. His letters written in 1836 make no reference to the
political canvass of that year, which ended in Van Buren's election. Young men of similar education — as Robert C. Winthrop and Hillard — were elected to the Legislature, then much
larger than now, soon after they entered on manly life;[1] but no
one seems to have thought of him in such a connection, and certainly he had no ambition for the place.[2]

In 1835, he took a share in a speculation, — his only venture
of the kind through life. He was duped by the assurances of
brokers into investing in the American Land Company, of New
York, the officers of which pretended to have made fortunate
investments in the West. He hoped to realize a handsome
sum; but he lost all he had advanced, — an amount which
he could ill afford to spare from his meagre revenues, — and was
left in debt. Smarting under the deception to which he was a
victim, he wrote to the friend whose investigations had opened
his eyes, " I have learned a valuable lesson; money and business
dissolve all the ties and bonds of friendship."

In August and September, 1836, he took a vacation, the only
one which he is known to have taken during his first three years
of practice. He visited Niagara Falls, going by the way of
New York City and the Hudson River, and returning by the way
of Canada, the White Mountains, and Portland. At New York
he called on Chancellor Kent,[3] who treated him with much courtesy; met William Johnson, the reporter, whom he found "gentlemanly, accomplished, and talented, truly a delightful character; "
and had pleasant interviews with his friend George Gibbs, and
his classmate Tower. Impressed with the contrast between the
street life of New York and that of Boston, more striking then

---

[1] Winthrop was elected to the Legislature in Nov., 1834. Hillard and John O. Sargent,
a classmate of Sumner, were elected to the same body in Nov., 1835; and his classmate,
Browne, in Nov., 1837.

[2] Samuel Lawrence, who knew him intimately at this time, writes: "He was devoted
to law and literature, and I do not believe that political life had once been in his thoughts."

[3] In the early part of July the Chancellor had made a visit to Boston, during which Sumner was attentive to him, taking him to Trinity Church on Sunday, to a party at Judge
Samuel Putnam's, and to points of interest in the city, and to Cambridge.

than now, he said to Tower, as they sat together in a parlor of
the Astor House, looking out on Broadway, and listening to its
tumultuous life, " Well, this is a noisy city. I don't know, however, but I could come to like it after a while, when I had become
used to the great bustle, and attuned, as it were, to the place."
On the Hudson River he became acquainted with Mrs. Clinton,
the widow of De Witt Clinton; and at Albany he was introduced by her to the aged Chief-Justice Ambrose Spencer, then
living in retirement. At Saratoga he met two well-known
jurists, — Chancellor Walworth and Judge Cowen.[1] In Canada
he travelled with a young Scotchman whom he had met at Ballston, — Thomas Brown, of Lanfire House, Kilmarnock, a nephew
of Lord Jeffrey, a friend of Talfourd, and a member of the
Garrick Club of London. Brown took life easily, unencumbered
with professional or family cares, and amused himself in travelling and frequenting clubs. His knowledge of English society, particularly of the personal life of English men of letters,
made him an interesting companion for Sumner. They corresponded from this time, and afterwards met in London and Scotland.[2] At Quebec Sumner dined with Chief-Justice Sewall, now
well advanced in years, and at Portland enjoyed an opportunity
of meeting his much-valued friend, Charles S. Daveis. This
journey is in scenery and association, perhaps, the most attractive
which the continent affords, — the Hudson River, the falls at
Trenton, Niagara, and Montmorency, Lake Champlain, which
Sumner had traversed in school-boy days, the St. Lawrence,
Montreal, and Quebec, both cities of ancient and foreign aspect,
and the White Mountains of New Hampshire. He reached
Boston, after five weeks' absence, "full of spirits, health, and
satisfaction with his journey."

Sumner took at this time a thoughtful interest in the slavery
question. This appears particularly in his correspondence with
Dr. Lieber.[3] To Miss Martineau, who was in Boston in 1835, he
showed his strong feelings on the subject by his denunciation of
pro-slavery mobs; and he was one of the class, as she afterwards said, to whom she referred, in her " Society in America," [4]
as expressing the determination to set themselves against such

---

[1] Of Walworth and Cowen he wrote: "Neither interested me. They are *mere book-men.*
Judge Oakley, of New York, whom I met, is abler than both."

[2] Brown died in Jan., 1873.

[3] *Post,* p. 173.

[4] Vol. I. p. 130. Harriet Martineau's Autobiography (Memorials), Vol. II. p. 295.

violence. He began the same year to read the " Liberator; " and it was the first paper for which he subscribed.[1]

Sumner's personal relations with Rev. Dr. William E. Channing were formed as early as this period, probably beginning with an introduction by George Gibbs, a nephew of Dr. Channing. The doctor, who always took a great interest in young men, was attracted to Sumner by the commendation of Judge Story, his college classmate (the class of 1798); and he had occasion to be grateful for Sumner's kindness and good sense in relieving a young kinsman from a personal difficulty. Sumner's thoughts and aspirations were doubtless much affected by his association with Dr. Channing at this time.[2] To this reformer, to his character, his great arguments for freedom,[3] and his moral inspiration, the world will ever pay deserved homage; and Sumner's tribute to his memory glows with the grateful enthusiasm of one who in youth had sat at his feet.[4]

The correspondence between Sumner and his college classmates had now almost entirely ceased. With new associations and divergent tastes they had drifted apart. There was no want of kindly recollection, nor, when they met, of hearty sympathy; but the student days, which had been the common topics of their correspondence, had receded into the past. His correspondents were now chiefly law reporters and writers for law magazines, of whom most were contributors to the " Jurist." Among them were Richard Peters, Charles S. Daveis,[5] John Apple-

---

[1] He wrote April 9, 1850: "I have read the 'Liberator' more or less since 1835. It was the first paper I ever subscribed for." Wendell Phillips, in a speech of Jan. 27, 1853, said: "My old and valued friend, Mr. Sumner, often boasts that he was a reader of the 'Liberator' before I was." Speeches, Lectures, and Letters of Wendell Phillips, p. 135.

[2] In Sept. 1842, Sumner wrote to his brother George then in Europe: "I know the latter [Dr. Channing] intimately, and my admiration of him grows constantly. When I was younger than I am now, I was presumptuous enough to question his power. I did not find in him the forms of logical discussion, and the close, continuous chain of reasoning, — and I complained. I am glad that I am wise enough to see him in a different light." In October, 1842, he wrote in relation to Dr. Channing's death: "He has been my friend, and I may almost say my idol, for nearly ten years. For this period I have enjoyed his confidence in no common way."

[3] Dr. Channing's book on "Slavery" was published in 1835.

[4] Oration before the Phi Beta Kappa Society, Aug. 27, 1846, — "The Philanthropist." Works, Vol. I. pp. 284–298.

[5] Mr. Daveis, of Portland, Maine, who was a friend of Sumner's father, was learned in equity and admiralty law. On his return from the Hague, where he went in 1830 to assist in preparing the case of the United States against Great Britain, involving the north-east boundary dispute, then pending before an arbitrator, he formed in England relations of friendship with some eminent persons, among them Earl Fitzwilliam. He died March 29, 1865, aged seventy-six. A sketch of his life may be found in the Memorials of the Massachusetts Society of the Cincinnati, of which he was a member. He was very fond of Sumner, and took a great interest in his career.

ton,[1] Dr. I. Ray,[2] Francis J. Troubat,[3] John B. Wallace,[4] David Hoffman,[5] and Jonathan C. Perkins.[6] He corresponded with Judge Story when the judge was at Washington, and, when himself absent from home, with Hillard. His letters were always rapidly written, were not easily read by those who were not familiar with his handwriting, and contained many verbal abbreviations. They expressed in an unstudied way his thought at the instant; and he gave to them none of the careful reflection and emendation which he bestowed on whatever he printed.

The beginning of the acquaintance of Dr. Francis Lieber [7] and Sumner at Washington has already been referred to. From 1834 until Dr. Lieber's death in 1872, excepting the period of 1851–61, when their correspondence was interrupted, they wrote often to each other, the letters of Dr. Lieber being much more frequent and longer than Sumner's.[8] At this early period he addressed Sumner in familiar and endearing terms, and appears to have cherished a real affection for him. He availed himself often of Sumner's friendly offices in negotiating with publishers in Boston, and bringing his works before the public. He had then partly ready for the press his translation of Feuerbach's "Casper Hauser," a German Grammar, a "Dictionary of Antiquities," a series of school-books, "Political Hermeneutics," [9]

1 The present Chief-Justice of Maine. In a letter of May 18, 1837, Sumner wrote: "Mr. Appleton is a writer of great nerve, boldness, and experience, with a Benthamic point and force."

2 Dr. Ray then resided at Eastport, Maine, and afterwards became superintendent of the Butler Asylum for the Insane, at Providence, R. I. In 1837, he submitted to Sumner for criticism the manuscript of his "Medical Jurisprudence of Insanity."

8 Author of a treatise on the "Law of Limited Partnerships," and editor of law reports. He died in 1868.

4 Reporter of Cases in the Court of the United States for the Third Circuit. He died in Philadelphia, Jan. 7, 1837.

5 Author of "A Course of Legal Study" and "Legal Outlines." He resided in Baltimore, and later in Philadelphia, and died in 1854.

6 One of Sumner's friends, younger in the profession than himself, then practising law at Salem, afterwards a Judge of the Court of Common Pleas, and the editor of "Daniell's Chancery Pleading and Practice" and other law books.

7 Dr. Lieber was born in Berlin, in 1800. Having been a student, soldier, and exile, he came to this country in 1827, and resided successively in Boston, New York, and Philadelphia. In 1835, he became professor of History and Political Economy in the South Carolina College, at Columbia, where he remained more than twenty years. In 1857, he was appointed to a similar professorship in Columbia College, New York, and held the position till his death, Oct. 2, 1872. He is well known by his Encyclopædia; but his fame is to rest permanently on his "Manual of Political Ethics," and his "Civil Liberty and Self-Government."

8 Sumner preserved nearly a thousand of Lieber's letters to him.

9 Sumner published the "Political Hermeneutics" in the "American Jurist," Oct. 1837, Vol. XVIII. pp. 37–101. Jan. 1838, Vol. XVIII. pp. 281–294.

and "Political Ethics." All these were topics of correspondence between them. Sumner furnished historical illustrations for the "Political Ethics," was the first friend to whose critical eye the manuscript was submitted, and was by the direction of the author, who sailed for the West Indies in the summer of 1836, to take charge of it in case of the latter's death. The careful revision of the work, before it was given to the public, was however performed by Hillard. Lieber wrote to Sumner, Aug., 1835, "I want you to give me all that you can from the well stocked stores of your head. Your letters are a real treat to me." And again, Feb. 15, 1837, referring to Sumner's proposed visit to Europe: "That you are to go will be a great impediment to me, for though you are but young I know how well esteemed you are; and being young you are active for my interest. When you are gone, I shall have no friendly agent in Boston." He wrote, Oct. 23, "I don't know how I shall thank you for all your kindness and assistance;" and again, Nov. 30, "I thank you for the care you have taken of my literary reputation." Judge Story wrote to Sumner, Dec. 2, "What poor Lieber will do without you, I know not. He will die, I fear, for want of a rapid, voluminous, and never-ending correspondence."

Dr. Lieber wrote, Sept. 23, 1837 : —

"Let me thank you, my dear friend, most heartily for your kind addition of stock to my work in your last. The interest I see you take in my book cheers me much. Contribute more and more. It will all be thankfully received; only I am afraid I shall be embarrassed how to use it. I cannot all the time say, 'contributed by a friend,' and yet I do not want to plume myself with your feathers. . . . Write me more of what you happen to think; and my dear fellow, if it were not asking too much, I would beg you to grant me a pigeon-hole in your mind while abroad: say, if you would, a memorandum-book with this title, 'All sorts of stuff for Lieber.' It would be a real service of friendship."

Dr. Lieber's brain was always teeming with projects of authorship; and, in order to carry them through, he set his best friends to tasks which it was not easy to perform, and sometimes put their good nature to a strain. But with his robust understanding, his vast knowledge, and his varied experience, he gave them as much as he received. His conversation, always fresh, original, and sparkling with reminiscences, charmed the young of both sexes, and stimulated thought and study. Sumner found in him an excellent guide in the departments of political ethics and philosophy; and, during our civil war, often sought his views on questions of international and public law. Lieber's answers, given with great promptness, were always conspicuous for their good sense and knowledge of precedents.

Sumner's correspondence and association with foreigners, always much enjoyed by him, began at this period. The editing of the "Jurist" brought him into relations with foreign writers upon jurisprudence. Among these were Foelix,[1] and Wolowski,[2] both of Paris; Dr. Julius[3] of Berlin; Professor Mittermaier[4] of Heidelberg; and Arthur J. Johnes of Lincoln's Inn, London. Mr. Johnes had recently written a small volume on the "Reform of the Court of Chancery," proposing the amalgamation of law and equity, which attracted Sumner's attention.[5] Dr. Julius was a student of penitentiary science, and made Sumner's acquaintance during his visit to this country in 1835.[6] Foelix, the editor of the *Revue Étrangère*, was afterwards to render Sumner substantial kindness during the latter's visit to Paris. Louis Wolowski[7] was the editor of the *Revue de Législation et de Jurisprudence;* of Polish birth, and an exile, he had become a French citizen. Political economy rather than jurisprudence was to give him his fame. In time of birth he differed from Sumner less than a year. Each began his career as the editor of a law magazine, and each ended it as a senator. Sumner met in a very friendly way Harriet Martineau at the time of her visit to Boston in 1835-36, and in a letter to Judge Story she spoke of him and Hillard as "glorious fellows." With his Scotch friend, Thomas Brown, he had much correspondence, both while the latter remained in America and after his return home. He was

---

1 American Jurist, April, 1834, Vol. XI. p. 495 ; Oct. 1835, Vol. XIV. p. 493.

2 American Jurist, April, 1835, Vol. XIII. p. 483; Oct. 1835, Vol. XIV. p. 489.

3 American Jurist, Oct. 1837, Vol. XVIII. pp. 254-258.

4 Karl Joseph Anton Mittermaier. 1787-1867.

5 American Jurist, April, 1835, Vol. XIII., pp. 459-465; a notice probably written by Sumner.

6 1783-1862. Dr. Nikolaus H. Julius. He resided at Hamburg the later years of his life. He gave his time largely to the inspection of prisons, and to writing upon prison systems. He was the German translator of "Ticknor's History of Spanish Literature."

7 1810-1876. Wolowski was chosen a member of the Chamber of Deputies in 1848-49, and 1871, and afterwards a senator for life. In 1839, he became a law professor in the Conservatory of the Arts and Trades ; and in 1855 was admitted to the Academy of Moral and Political Sciences. He founded the first *Crédit foncier* of Paris, which became the *Crédit foncier* of France. His funeral on Aug. 18, 1876, though simple in rites, was imposing in the attendance of distinguished men. The religious services were held at the Église de la Trinité, and a discourse was pronounced at Père La Chaise on behalf of the Academy. *Journal des Débats*, Aug. 19, 1876. "London Times," Aug. 17, 1876.

fond of reading letters from Europe, and was grateful for access to those written by Mr. Rand and Mr. Ticknor while they were abroad, and to those received by Mr. Daveis from his English friends. He corresponded with George Gibbs, who in 1835 passed some time in Paris, where through Sumner's introduction he was well received by Foelix.

In the early part of 1837, a strong friendship was formed between Cornelius C. Felton, Henry W. Longfellow, George S. Hillard, Henry R. Cleveland, and Sumner; they called themselves the " Five of Clubs." They were near to each other in age ; Longfellow being thirty, Felton twenty-nine, Hillard and Cleveland twenty-eight, and Sumner twenty-six. Of the five, Hillard only was married. All achieved an honorable place in literature. Cleveland [1] was a teacher by profession, and a scholar of a refined and sensitive nature ; and, after suffering several years from ill-health, he died at the age of thirty-four. The others lived to fulfil the rich promise of youth. Felton and Sumner became friends when the former was Greek professor at Harvard College,[2] and the latter a student in the Law School. The friendship of Hillard and Sumner began with their law-partnership. A single interview, in 1835, between Longfellow and Sumner, in Felton's room, was their only meeting before the former, having passed more than a year in Europe after his election as Mr. Ticknor's successor, assumed in Dec., 1836, the duties of his professorship at Cambridge. The " Five " came together almost weekly, generally on Saturday afternoons. They met simply as friends with common tastes and the fullest sympathy with each other, talking of society, the week's experiences, new books, their individual studies, plans, and hopes, and of Europe, — which Longfellow and Cleveland had seen, and which the others longed to see. They loved good cheer, but observed moderation in their festivities. A table simply spread became a symposium when Felton, with his joyous nature, took his seat among his friends ; and the other four were not less genial and hearty. There was hardly a field of literature which one or the other had not traversed, and they took a constant interest in each other's studies. Each sought the criticism of the rest upon his own book, essay, or poem

---

[1] Cleveland was born Oct. 3, 1808, and died June 12, 1843. A memoir, with selections from his writings, was prepared by Mr. Hillard.

[2] Felton was born Nov. 6, 1807, and died Feb. 26, 1862. He was, at the time of his death, President of Harvard University.

before it was given to the public. Their mutual confidence
seemed to know no limitation of distrust or fear of possible alien-
ation; and they revealed, as friends do not often reveal, their
inner life to each other. Rarely in history has there been a
fellowship so beautiful as that of these gifted young men.

The riot in Broad Street, June 11, 1837, brought on by a
collision between a fire-engine company and an Irish funeral
procession, was the beginning of a friendship between Sumner
and Dr. Samuel G. Howe.[1] Five hundred combatants were engaged, and a body of bystanders obstructed the streets. The
Irish were worsted, and pursued to their homes. Well-known
citizens—Abbott Lawrence, Robert C. Winthrop, Josiah Quincy,
Jr., and others — supported Mayor Eliot, who was on the ground,
in his efforts to restore order. Sumner went with them to
the scene, and, then as always unconscious of personal fear,
pushed into the thickest of the fight, where, his stature soon
making him a target, he was struck down by a heavy missile.
His intrepidity was so conspicuous as to draw the attention of
Dr. Howe, who was there on a like errand. Their friendly
acquaintance began then, but their intimacy belongs to the
period following Sumner's return from Europe.

Richard Fletcher,[2] who was then a member of Congress from
Boston, and afterwards a Judge of the Supreme Judicial Court
of Massachusetts, became much attached to Sumner at this time;
employed him to prepare briefs, and opened to him other professional opportunities. Sumner was always grateful for the kindness which Mr. Fletcher, some years his senior, rendered to him at
this period, and their warm regard was uninterrupted through life.

Horace Mann and Sumner were brought together as lawyers
and tenants of the same building. Mann was already interested
in temperance, education, and the care of the insane, — topics
then much agitated; and, like Demetz in France, he was soon to
enter on a service for mankind greater than any which is possible
at the bar. There are brief records of his interest in Sumner at
this time. In Feb., 1837, he urged the latter to deliver a temperance address.[3] He wrote, Nov. 6, in his journal, " Dined with

---

[1] Dr. Howe was born Nov. 10, 1801, and died Jan. 9, 1876. From 1824 to 1830 he was
in Greece, serving that country in the army and in other capacities. From 1832 until his
death he was an instructor of the blind, and engaged in philanthropic movements.

[2] 1788–1869.

[3] Life of Horace Mann, p. 54. Sumner in a letter of June 29, 1836, commends Mr.
Mann to Charles S. Daveis as "the President of the Senate of Massachusetts, and a distinguished member of our profession."

C. Sumner to-day, who is going to Europe soon. When he goes, there will be one more good fellow on that side, and one less on this."[1] They were afterwards to be fellow combatants in the causes of education and freedom. Among Sumner's papers was found a sketch, written during the last autumn of his life, of his friend's career. This tribute was intended for a municipal celebration in Wrentham, the birthplace of Horace Mann, but some circumstances prevented Sumner's attendance on the occasion.[2]

Sumner's social range in Boston was, at this period, quite limited; but the few families he visited were those on whose fidelity and sympathy he could always count. He was on a familiar footing in the houses of Hillard, Samuel Lawrence, Robert B. Forbes, and Park Benjamin, then living with his sisters, who afterwards became Mrs. J. Lothrop Motley and Mrs. Stackpole. Hillard's kind words had opened the doors of some of these houses to Sumner. Oliver Wendell Holmes, then a young physician, visited most if not all of these families. There was no want of good talking at a dinner or supper where Hillard, Benjamin, Holmes, and Sumner were gathered. Sumner was accustomed to call at William Sullivan's and Judge William Prescott's, both friends of his father; at Jeremiah Mason's, Samuel Austin's, and Mrs. James Perkins's.

He frequented the rooms of Mr. Alvord, his former teacher at Cambridge, who passed the winter of 1837 in Boston when serving as a member of the Legislature from Greenfield.[3] The latter used to say of him and Wendell Phillips, whom he called his "boys," that the State and the country would one day be proud of them.

Those who saw much of Sumner at this time recall him as appearing to be a very hard student, thoroughly informed on all topics of conversation, wanting in humor, never speaking unkindly to any one or of any one; and winning all hearts by his transparent nature, his absolute good faith, and his knightly sense of honor and fidelity in friendship.

---

[1] Life of Horace Mann, p. 91.

[2] Mr. Mann was born in 1796, and died in 1859. He was Secretary of the Board of Education of Massachusetts, 1837–48; served four years in Congress as the successor of John Quincy Adams; and was President of Antioch College, Yellow Springs, Ohio, from 1852 till his death. Sumner passed a day with him at the College in 1855.

[3] Mr. Alvord was the chief promoter of the "Personal Replevin" statute, intended for the protection of persons claimed as fugitive slaves, and wrote an able report in its behalf. Leg. Doc., House, 1837, No. 51.

A friend who knew him intimately, and whose knowledge of life has been various, referring to this period, says: "Taking him as a whole, he was the most attractive young man I have ever known."

At his office he was always found in the midst of manuscripts and heaps of law books, but never loath to break off his work for a talk with his friends. No one, whose life was so devoted to study, ever gave his time more freely to others, or guarded himself less from intrusion.

At Cambridge he kept up his visits at Judge Story's and Professor Greenleaf's. He as well as Felton, Longfellow, and Cleveland found genial society in the home of Rev. Andrews Norton, a learned divine whose scholarship was not confined to theology. He was a welcome guest at the house of Mrs. William Eliot, in whose son Samuel, a college student, he took a special interest.[1] With Mrs. Howe, at whose house on the Appian Way he at times lodged, and with Mrs. Greenleaf, who took a maternal interest in him, his favorite theme of banter was the perfect woman he was some day to wed.

Samuel Lawrence writes: —

"During this period Sumner was not in general society, and visited very few houses in Boston. He was an admirable talker, with off-hand, frank, natural manners, enthusiastic in his admiration of Judge Story, whose house at Cambridge he often visited, and devoted to law and literature; and I do not believe that political life had once been in his thoughts."

Dr. Oliver Wendell Holmes writes : —

"He had already a name for scholarship, especially for legal knowledge. He was an amiable, simple-hearted, blameless young man; pleasant, affable, cheerful, with little imagination, wit, or sense of humor. I remember Park Benjamin said of him, in his rather extravagant way, that, if one told Charles Sumner that the moon was made of green cheese, he would controvert the alleged fact in all sincerity, and give good reason why it could not be so."

A lady, afterwards the wife of one of his dearest friends, who knew him well at this time, as also after his return from Europe, writes : —

"As a young man he had a fresh enthusiasm; though never brilliant socially, he interested one from his genuine and hearty engrossment in the discussion or narration, to which he brought always many and accurate facts. He was less at ease with women than with men, and I think understood them less. He had a very marked and dutiful respect towards elder men, whom

---

[1] Mr. Eliot is the author of " The Liberty of Rome," and " History of Liberty."

he honored. Where he was so familiar as he was at our house, he had an affectionate confidence which knew no shadow or distrust, and which stamped him as an unchanging and faithful friend."

A lady who saw him during the evenings which he passed at Mr. Alvord's rooms, writes : —

" Mr. Sumner was an intimate acquaintance and frequent visitor. The talk varied; sometimes it was light and sparkling, at others upon the topics of the day, upon politics or law. How well I remember Mr. Sumner at that time, tall and erect, so genial and so joyous, his whole face lighting up with interest and enthusiasm! He was not then a reformer, but a student. Unlike most New England scholars he was not satisfied with the prescribed years for preparation, but longed to go abroad to perfect himself in his law studies; and when rallied about settling down in life, he used to say, ' I am married to Europa.' "

Sumner was at this time much attracted to law students and undergraduates with whom he was brought into association while performing his duties as instructor in the Law School. At Mrs. Howe's table, where he was accustomed to meet them, he talked with them of their studies; and with some he kept up a correspondence after they left Cambridge. One of these, with whom he became quite intimate, was William F. Frick, then an undergraduate, now a lawyer of Baltimore. Thomas Donaldson, of the same city, writes: " My acquaintance with him was while I was an undergraduate at Harvard. I remember that he was exceedingly kind and genial in his manners, and that he took pleasure in conversing with young` students who could give nothing in return for his copious stores of learning, except an admiring attention."

Judge Charles P. James, formerly of Cincinnati, now of Washington City, writes : —

" My acquaintance (if it can be called by that name) with Mr. Sumner was made when I was a Sophomore, messing at the same table with him at Mrs. Howe's. Rufus King, of Cincinnati, his cousin James Gore King, J. Frank Tuckerman, and one or two others, were of the mess.

" I cannot recall the particulars of our table intercourse, but remember very well the general fact that Sumner talked freely, and that we listened eagerly. As I remember, a good deal of his conversation was really addressed to us, although it was carried on chiefly with Mrs. Howe. One morning, Sumner was very silent at the breakfast table, and King complained afterwards of his being so stupid. You will perceive that his failure to tell us something was a grievance.

" I recall one little incident which let us into his habits of reading. After tea, when we were gathered in Mrs. Howe's parlor, Sumner took up from a table an engraved portrait of Wellington, and observed that it was 'too young.' Some one questioned that. 'Why,' exclaimed Sumner, 'I know his age perfectly; I've read a hundred lives of him.' We understood, of course, that he meant only whatever lives had fallen in his way. Most people would be likely to read only one, — which none of *us* had done.

"I remember that it was his habit to study and prepare lectures at the Law School until eleven o'clock at night, and that it was Mrs. Howe's habit to 'sit up' for him in order to have an hour's talk. She had what may be called an enthusiasm for him. I fancy the entertainment between them was almost wholly intellectual, as Mrs. Howe had a man's brain; but intellectual sympathy, you know, is very sure ground for friendship.[1]

"My impression at that time was that he was very good tempered, and that he was fond of youngsters, — at all events as listeners. William Story was his favorite, as he well might be; for he was very jolly and amusing, and at the same time respectful."

Rufus King of Cincinnati writes : —

"He had a warm sympathy and fellowship with the 'boys,' and assumed no professional airs. At the period referred to I and in fact all the parties boarding at Mrs. Howe's were undergraduates, and even that did not put us beneath his *penchant* for student life.

"The only distinct recollection I have of the incidents in our prandial exercises and meetings is of the fiery discussions over the then pending question in Congress, concerning the 'Right of Petition,' in which John Quincy Adams was contending with the Southern politicians; beginning, I think, in some interference by the Post-office authorities with the transmission of 'incendiary matter' through the mails.

"I forget just how we were divided, or who formed the other side; but remember how Sumner used to hurl his thunders against the opponents of Free Mails and Free Petitions, and how enthusiastically Mrs. Howe used to back him up when she thought the youngsters were becoming too much excited on the other side."

Judge Story wrote, Feb. 5, 1835, to Sumner, who had taken much interest in his son : —

"I hope you will allure William occasionally to your room to keep him on correct ground, for he has infinite confidence in your kindness and judgment on such subjects. He has written me respecting the late rebellion [2] in a very manly and just tone. A word from you will do more than an hour of my preaching."

---

[1] Several of Mrs. Howe's letters are printed in the Memoir of her sister, Mrs. A. J. Lyman, Cambridge, 1876.

[2] A college disturbance.

LETTERS.

TO DR. FRANCIS LIEBER, PHILADELPHIA.

BOSTON, April 7, 1835.

MY DEAR DR. LIEBER, — I have received so much pleasure from two of your late productions, that I cannot forbear letting you know it. Dr. Beck was kind enough to lend me your paper, read before the Pennsylvania Prison Society, properly vindicating our country against the bad logic of English politicians. You always seem to be ready in the harness, — as the nursery phrase has it, " All saddled, all bridled, all fit for the fight." I rejoice that our country has found a son — by adoption or birth is immaterial — so prompt to volunteer in her cause. I think your argument completely successful.

Your volume, entitled " The Stranger in America," I finished yesterday, having read it with deep interest. I followed you anxiously over every inch of the fields of Ligny, Waterloo, and Namur, and through all the perils that ensued, from hospital to hospital, till the joyous close of this cycle of misfortunes in the love of your fair nurse. Oh, human nature! war did not choke the delicate sensibilities which glow in either sex, or alter the nature of man, which indeed is indestructible. I think the Peace Society could do nothing better than to reprint your chapter on Waterloo as a tract, or at least as an article in one of their journals. It gives the most vivid sketch I ever read of the horrors of war, because it embodies them in the experience of one individual, without resorting to any of the declamatory generalities which are generally used with that view.

Most truly your friend,

CHAS. SUMNER.

TO CHARLEMAGNE TOWER, NEW YORK.[1]

BOSTON, June 28, 1835.

MY DEAR TOWER, — . . . I was truly gratified by the morsel of praise from Anthon;[2] to have one's writing remembered a year is no small gratification, especially if that is the only reward. My labors in the " Jurist " are pressing and heavy, and lack the exciting stimulus of pecuniary profit. Indeed, I fear that exertions like mine will meet with very slight return in the way of this world's gear. If you or any of your friends or the gentlemen of the bar in New York will contribute to the " Jurist," the assistance will be appreciated. Mr. Anthon has written for it. In the last number, you will see my name announced as enlisted in two projects of some consequence.[3]

---

[1] Tower had become a student in the law-office of Messrs. John L. and James L. Graham, of New York City.

[2] John Anthon had commended Sumner's review of Tayler's "Law Glossary."

[3] *Ante*, p. 151.

Since then, I have been appointed reporter of the Circuit Court of the United States for the first circuit (Judge Story's), and have a volume already in press, which will be published, I hope, in the course of a month or two.

Rand has returned from abroad, and is full of the men and sights he has seen. He has received as great, perhaps greater, attentions than any other private citizen from our country ever met with.[1] All the distinguished names of the law, the peers of the law, and the judges paid him distinguished honor. It is refreshing to me — strongly attached as I am to the law — to converse about these men of whom I read, and whose works are every day cited in our courts, with many of whom Mr. Rand became acquainted.

Don't become so absorbed in practice as to forget the law, or

Your sincere friend,

CHAS. SUMNER.

TO DR. FRANCIS LIEBER.

BOSTON, June 28, 1835.

MY DEAR FRIEND,[2] — . . . Judge Story showed me a letter from you, from which it appears that you have received Mittermaier's articles. I also received your " National Gazette " and the " United States Gazette," containing the annunciation of your appointment.[3] Have you translated the articles yet? How long are they? Do you propose to publish them? If you have not time to translate them, send them here and I will have them translated for the " Jurist." [4] Judge Story always speaks of you with the liveliest regard. He says you always, when he converses with you, set him *a-thinking*. I am glad you propose to publish your " Recollections of Niebuhr." I thought some time ago that you might profitably publish such a book. When do you enter upon your new duties?

Good-by.   Yours ever,

CHAS. SUMNER.

If Dr. Julius comes to Boston, I wish to have the honor of seeing him.

TO JONATHAN C. PERKINS, SALEM.

BOSTON, July 10, 1835.

MY DEAR SIR, — Come to Boston on Monday or Tuesday, and I will introduce you at once to Pickering,[5] who is no talker, and have you baptized in

---

1 Mr. Rand was indebted largely for his social opportunities in England to letters of introduction from Charles S. Daveis.

2 The omitted parts of this and other letters to Dr. Lieber relate largely to Sumner's efforts in obtaining the publication of Dr. Lieber's writings.

3 To a professorship in the University of South Carolina.

4 American Jurist, Oct., 1835, Vol. XIV. pp. 330–344.

5 Octavius Pickering, who was then preparing a new edition of his Reports.

the labor. I think in a few minutes, with the volumes before me, I can give you some hints which your own knowledge and experience, I doubt not, will improve upon, but which will launch you in your labor. Do not be distrustful; faint heart never won success in law more than in love. You are abundantly competent to the task, believe me, from my knowledge of you and of the labor. Mr. Choate beckons you to come up. He wished me to say that we had conferred together since he had sealed his letter, and that we agreed in all the premises, and also in the feasibility of your commencing the duty in Salem. Of course you must read the volume, and observe all the cases which would illustrate it, that have been decided in our State courts since its date.

Don't regard the *money* as the pay. It is the knowledge you will get, — the stimulus under which your mind will act when you feel that you are reading law for a *purpose* and an *end* other than the bare getting of information, — every spur and ambition exciting you; depend upon it, no engraver will trace the law on your mind in such deep characters. Abandon *pro tem.* all other legal studies, and enfold yourself, like the silk-worm, in your own web. If I augur right, the six weeks, in which I think you will accomplish it, will be the most productive of your whole life. In them you will feel more palpably your progress than ever before in the same amount of time.

Your extempore readiness to undertake the labor reminds me of Ledyard, the traveller, who was asked when he should be willing to start to explore the interior of Africa; he replied, "To-morrow."

I shall probably be, on Tuesday forenoon next, in Judge Story's court.

Pardon the haste in which I write, and believe me

Most truly yours,

CHAS. SUMNER.

TO CHARLES S. DAVEIS, PORTLAND.

BOSTON, July 22, 1835.

MY DEAR SIR, — Judge Story has told me several times that I must endeavor to obtain from you the sight of a letter which you have received within a few months from Dr. Haggard,[1] of Doctors' Commons. . . .

Judge Story's "Commentaries on Equity Jurisprudence" have gone to press. He thinks more highly of them than of either of his former works. I think that they will establish a new epoch in the study of chancery in our country. How much more of an honor to the office than to Judge Story would it be, were he made Chief-Justice of the United States![2] Indeed, posterity will notice his absence from that elevation more than they would his presence there, as the Roman people observed the absence of the favorite statues of Brutus and Cassius in the imperial procession more than they

---

[1] John Haggard, reporter of cases in the Consistory Court, and also in the Admiralty.

[2] Chief-Justice Marshall, who was appointed by President John Adams in 1801, died July 6, 1835, and was succeeded by Roger B. Taney, of Maryland, who held the office till his death, in 1864.

would have noted their appearance. Tacitus tells the story in his pregnant way somewhere, does he not? Judge Story has consented to deliver a eulogy on the late Chief. He will, of course, select his own time, which will be somewhere in October.

With great respect, I am yours truly,

CHAS. SUMNER.

TO JONATHAN C. PERKINS.

BOSTON, July 28, 1835.

MY DEAR SIR, — I am delighted that you are so pleased with your work. I felt anxious lest my recommendation should not be confirmed by your experience; but your letter removes all doubt on that score. I still feel that the *money* will be the least advantage that you will reap. The practice, the self-confidence (without which, if properly tempered by modesty, nothing great can be done), the habit of looking up cases and of looking down upon the opinions of judges, and the wide and various learning, — all of it applicable particularly to the business of our State, — will be worth more to you than a governmental office. I believe that you will feel yourself a *stronger man* when you have passed through this labor than before. . . .

Yours truly,

C. S.

TO DR. FRANCIS LIEBER.

BOSTON, Aug. 25, 1835.

MY DEAR DOCTOR, — The day has gone by for a degree for Mittermaier this season. He will probably receive it next year. . . . In the *Revue Étrangère*, edited by M. Foelix, of Paris (a correspondent of mine), is a long article on the translations of Beaumont and Tocqueville,[1] — yours, Dr. Julius's, &c., — written by Mittermaier. An analysis of your Preliminary Essay is given, and you are spoken of in the most flattering manner. I wrote an editorial notice of it in the " Advertiser " of yesterday.

I am determined to have your sketch of the battle of Waterloo published as a *peace* tract, or as an essay in some journal of the Peace Society; perhaps I shall write some introductory remarks.

I feel anxious to hear from your " Reminiscences of Niebuhr." Now is the harvest-time for American authors in England. Perhaps our books are now sought after as much more than they deserve as they formerly were less than their deserts. Put your sickle in while the sun shines and the golden sheaves extend their necks to the edge. You are one of the few men whom I wish to see with a fortune, because I believe you would *use* it as one who has God's stamp should. It will be only a *novum organon* for higher exer-

---

[1] Their Report upon the Penitentiary System of the United States.

tion. You love labor so lovingly, and drive it with such effect, that I would risk you with Crœsus's treasury. By the way, I have plans and schemes[1] (*speculations*, the world calls them) by which I hope to make a few thousands. If I succeed I will let you know.

Believe me, your sincere friend,

CHAS. SUMNER.

TO CHARLES S. DAVEIS.

BOSTON, Sept. 12, 1835.

MY DEAR SIR, — I received in due season your letter with its valuable contents, — the letter of Dr. Haggard. I am always delighted — it amounts almost to a monomania in me — to see any such missive from abroad, or to hear personal, literary, or legal news about the distinguished men of whom I read. . . .

Mrs. Guild very kindly read to me, a few evenings since, portions of late letters from Mr. and Mrs. Ticknor. They spoke of a dinner at Lord Holland's, where Mr. T. conversed much with Lord Melbourne about literature, *our* politics, &c., the latter giving the palm to our present chief-magistrate over all present and past statesmen of our country; also of a delightful concert at Lord Landsdowne's, and visits to Joanna Baillie and Mrs. Somerville.[2] They were to start the day after the date of the last letter (July 24) for Ireland. Perhaps you have heard these particulars from other quarters.

The Law School is flourishing beyond a parallel, containing now upwards of fifty students.

Believe me, with great esteem,

Most truly yours,

CHAS. SUMNER.

TO DR. FRANCIS LIEBER, COLUMBIA, S. C.

BOSTON, Dec. 2, 1835.

MY DEAR FRIEND, — Will you pardon my remissness, my long undutiful silence? Besides the usual stock of things to do, I have been compelled to prepare anew a whole number of the "Jurist," which was burnt up, — sheets, proofs, copy, and nearly all, on the morning when it was due. I begin, however, to descry land. *Italiam! Italiam!*

My chief anxiety now is to know that, in your journey South " nearer to the sun," you have not entirely turned your back upon me.

To-day I finished your " Reminiscences," a few minutes before I received the copy forwarded by you, for which receive my thanks. I had previously read all the extracts I could glean in the English journals, the " Spectator " and the " Literary Gazette," both of which contain highly favorable notices,

---

[1] *Ante*, p. 155.
[2] Life of George Ticknor, Vol. I. pp. 408, 412, 413.

some extracts from which I shall launch in the Boston " Atlas." Your introduction is admirable; the spirit is capital, the style and language of a high order, the thought instructive, and, above all, the view of Niebuhr lifelike. The character is very clearly displayed; it stands out like a king's head on a piece of coin. Your own observations, which introduce and explain a remark of the historian, and your conversation, which served to draw out his, are very fine; but I must confess that my impression of Niebuhr, from this table-talk, is not of a very high character. I love him and feel his amiability, not his power. There is little or no point or depth of remark; nothing epigrammatic or sententious; very little of a higher order than philological or antiquarian criticism; really little or nothing of general remark or philosophical deduction, which is brought up like a priceless pearl from the deep ocean of events, — particulars which always show themselves in your writings, and which give you the foremost place in the present *brochure*. To tell the truth, you appear better than Niebuhr. I know Niebuhr was great; I have full faith in him: but I opine he was not a great talker; that he did not speak for the press, and that his thoughts needed the ordeal and alchemy of his own study and inkstand to be in proper order for the world. You have done good by your publication; for it is well, in these days of dwarfish studies, to have some man presented to our eyes whose character and labors may shame our moderated steps, and whose example may teach us how necessary and how sweet labor is. Besides, your book will lead many to read his history, and will thus contribute to shut up one large book of fable, and substitute in its stead the wonderful deductions which have been wrought out from such various materials as those of Niebuhr, and which go to establish truth.

The " North American," you know, has passed from Alexander H. Everett to Dr. Palfrey, who is pushing it pretty hard, and, I think, may revive it. His first number will be the January one. . . .

Believe me, most faithfully yours,

CHAS. SUMNER.

TO DR. FRANCIS LIEBER.

JAN. 1, 1836.

MY DEAR FRIEND, — " A Happy New Year " to you and yours; and many thanks for your kind letter of Dec. 13. Judge Story sends his regards. I doubt the truth, somewhat, with all humility however, of your views in your letter with regard to brilliant conversation. You have made me love Niebuhr, and that's a great end gained; and your book must be regarded with great interest as giving an insight into the character of a truly great man.

Judge Story told me to write you that he was delighted with it, and particularly with your account of yourself in the introduction. John Pickering spoke of it to me in the highest terms. He thinks every thing of you, and longs to have you back among us; as does also my dear judge, who says that you must be with us soon; that Harvard College must have your aid.

Write me how you live, or rather how you keep from dying, in the literary Sahara where you are exiled; what dew-drops or small springs of refreshing water can you meet in such a parched and arid place; or do I misconceive your situation, and have you indeed literary and social advantages ? All of which I devoutly, though despairingly, hope.   When shall I receive your inaugural? How does your book come on?

I send herewith Judge Story's " Eulogy; " [1] also a prospectus of the *Revue Étrangère* which I have received from Foelix, and several prospectuses of the *Revue de Législation et de Jurisprudence* by a Paris correspondent of mine; also the sheets of Sparks's " Washington," containing the letter which you alluded to in your correspondence with me " auld lang syne." [2] . . .

Yours truly,

CHAS. SUMNER.

TO DR. FRANCIS LIEBER.

BOSTON, Jan. 9, 1836.

MY DEAR FRIEND, — Before you receive this letter you will receive a newspaper containing a slight notice of your " Reminiscences " with references to some English criticisms.[3] Since that was written, the magazines for November have been received at the Athenæum. The " Monthly Review," the old monthly of England, supported of old by the first scholars and writers, Burke and Mackintosh, — the same review which noticed your " Stranger in America " so handsomely, — has an article of fifteen pages on your " Reminiscences," written or rather compiled in a spirit of kindness and respect towards you. It will do you good in England. . If any other reviews or notices appear, I will promptly apprise you of them. The German Grammar has not yet shown itself above the rolling sea of publications. I am looking out for it, and shall probably descry it on its first kissing the light.

I omitted to send by my last letter and package the sheet from Sparks of Washington's letter to his nephew. It is not so much to the point as you hoped, I am inclined to think. You are in the midst of slavery, seated among its whirling eddies blown round as they are by the blasts of Governor McDuffie, fiercer than any from the old wind-bags of Æolus. What think you of it? Should it longer exist? Is not emancipation practicable? We are becoming abolitionists at the North fast; the riots, the attempts to abridge the freedom of discussion, Governor McDuffie's message, and the conduct of the South generally have caused many to think favorably of immediate emancipation who never before inclined to it.

---

[1] Upon Chief-Justice Marshall.

[2] Letter of President Washington to Bushrod Washington, of July 27, 1789. Sparks's "Life and Writings of George Washington," Vol. X. p. 23. Lieber's "Political Ethics" (1875) Vol. II. pp. 30–34. Bushrod Washington was the nephew of the President, and desired the appointment of District Attorney of the United States for the Virginia District. His application was not successful, but he was afterwards appointed a Judge of the Supreme Court of the United States by President Adams.

[3] Contributed by Sumner to "Daily Atlas," Jan 6, 1836.

I think your "Stranger in America" is not in the Boston market. A young friend of mine, a son of Professor Greenleaf, who read it on my hint, is ravished with it, and tried to get a couple of copies to present to his friends. His mother and father were delighted with it.

Yours ever,

CHAS. SUMNER.

TO REV. DR. JOHN G. PALFREY,[1] CAMBRIDGE.

BOSTON, Feb. 5, 1836.

MY DEAR SIR, — It will give me great pleasure to write an article on the Uses and Importance of History, considering several topics suggested by Dr. Lieber's inaugural, — especially when you and Dr. Lieber concur in inviting me; but I feel unwilling to pledge myself to do it for the July number. My professional engagements, my own editorial duties, *unsupported* by a full list of able contributors, and the several connections in which I find myself implicated with works in preparation or in press, to say nothing of lighter demands which society and the current literature of the day make upon my time, leave me with less opportunity than inclination for literary composition. History, however, is a theme I love; and I hope to be able to call the attention of the public to the importance of its study, through the pages of your journal, as early as the October number if not in July. There are two other subjects which I have at heart, and wish to consider in your journal, if agreeable to you; one, the particular features which distinguish Judge Story's law treatises from the English law books, presenting a condensed view of the distinctive character of his law writings rather than a review and analysis of an individual work. The other subject is *legal education*, with a view to correct some erroneous notions on the subject, and to suggest courses and methods of study. These can be made the matter of future conversation between us.[2] With my best wishes for your health,

I am, my dear sir,

Yours very truly,

CHAS. SUMNER.

[1] Dr. Palfrey was born in 1796, and is still a resident of Cambridge. He was professor of Sacred Literature in Harvard University, 1831–39; and a member of Congress, 1847–49. Among his various contributions to literature is a "History of New England." His article on Lord Mahon's "History of England," — printed in the "North American Review," of which he was for several years the editor, — was in Sumner's judgment "one of the best specimens of criticism which our country has produced." Allibone's "Dictionary of Authors," Vol. II. p. 1491. Sumner began his first political speech, Nov. 4, 1845, with a tribute to Dr. Palfrey for his manumission of inherited slaves, — the legal details of which Sumner had assisted in arranging. Works, Vol. I. p. 151. They were at this period, and for many years after, very closely associated with each other in the political movement against slavery.

[2] He did not write any of the proposed articles for the "North American Review," named in the letter.

TO MISS PETERS, PHILADELPHIA.

Boston, April 30, 1836.

My DEAR E., — I have often chided myself and sometimes you for suffering our correspondence to die away. Business and the absorbing calls of the world, to which you are a stranger, have laid their iron hands upon me, so that I find it very difficult, even for a short time and for the sweet indulgence of friendship, to disengage myself from their strong grasp. But this is the life of man. He grows up and salutes labor and responsibility on the threshold of manhood, and these continue his constant and inseparable companions during his whole pilgrimage, until at last the wayfarer is permitted to lay down his load. Pardon this vein, which I have accidentally struck upon, and which will certainly jar upon a young lady's ear. . . .

Are your school days over? If not, I suppose you are anxious for the last day to come that shall fully discharge you from the dominion of childhood. I know, however, that you have filled up your time with profitable studies, so that you will be well prepared for a change. I should be pleased to know what your studies have been, and to what pursuits you have turned your attention; for, believe me, I shall watch your progress with deep interest, and, if by my counsel I may be instrumental in guiding your pursuits, it will be to me a source of unfeigned pleasure.

What is there new in the fashionable world of Philadelphia? Mrs. Wood's illness cuts you off from one source of enjoyment. Boston and Philadelphia seem to have vied with each other to see which would excel in the praise of this vocalist. Everybody among us was stark mad, not excepting, perhaps, one of your friends.

After this long letter, melancholic and "thus saith the preacher" as is its tone, I think the law of reciprocity will dictate to you a proper course.

Let me not forget to thank you for the neat and well-braided watchguard which you sent me. It was a most acceptable present.

Truly and affectionately your friend,

CHAS. SUMNER.

TO PROFESSOR SIMON GREENLEAF, CAMBRIDGE.

June 29, 1836, half-past twelve o'clock, A.M.

My DEAR PROFESSOR, — I have walked safely to the city, and have done some study and browsed on some pages for a hint on your question to me. I do not remember any case which points your way; but I find that the rules of court throw some light. Rule twenty-seven of the First Circuit requires that the same property without waste should be restored by the stipulator. The rules of the Southern District of New York are much more to the point. . . .

I do not think of any thing further; and so good night, or rather good morning.

CHAS. SUMNER.

N.B. — There is an agreeable, romantic feeling in sitting up and trimming your solitary lamp when the whole world are stretched in repose. And this romantic feeling is especially heightened when one is writing law, as if the dry bones of our science at this dead hour sparkled with phosphorescent light. The palpable stillness about you, especially in a city, and the triumphing feelings which throb in your veins from the consciousness that you are one of a very few who, at that witching hour, are enjoying consciousness, enable you to work with ardor and attention. Abstraction at that time will visit you, and the thousand cares of the world seem to have passed away in that hum of business which some hours since died upon your ears. Night! I almost wish there were no day; that we could never " peep through the blanket of the dark," but always live under those genial influences which the spirits of the other world have selected as most agreeable, and as those under which they visit this earth, — " that witching hour when ghosts and goblins walk."

If I do not wish to hear the cock-crow I must to bed. Believe me, by night and by day, in darkness and light,

Especially yours,   C. S.

TO CHARLES S. DAVEIS.

Boston, 4 Court St., Aug. 8, 1836.

My dear Sir, — . . . Your opinion of my father's conduct and statement was grateful.[1] I have not yet had an opportunity of communicating it to him. I assure you, however, of his cordial thanks for your kind feelings. The public will have a victim, and his situation seemed to present him as the fit offering.

Let me ask pardon for the negligent detinue of your papers, amounting, I fear, almost to a conversion.

While I am writing now, Mr. Metcalf,[2] the best common-law lawyer in our State, enters. I propose to him your case, not stating the venue or the names of any interested in it. He says, in his sententious style, " The administrator will hold."

Yours faithfully,

Chas. Sumner.

---

[1] The slave-rescue case, ante, pp. 24–26. The omitted parts of letters to Mr. Daveis refer mostly to purchases of books which Sumner made for him in Boston, points of law on which he was consulted by Mr. Daveis, and letters received by either from Europe, which were interchanged.

[2] Theron Metcalf, the reporter, author of digests and law reports, and of " Principles of the Law of Contracts," and a Judge of the Supreme Court of Massachusetts. He died, Nov. 13, 1875, at the age of ninety-one.

TO GEORGE S. HILLARD, BOSTON.

SARATOGA, Aug. 19, 1836.

MY DEAR HILLARD, — It is not a week since I detached myself from Court Street and the demesnes that there adjacent lie, and I have lived fast and much, and crowded a space of less than five days with the incident and excitement of a month of common being. I just begin to recognize the sedative influences of the Spring water and Spring tedium, after the disturbing powers of steamboats and, greater still, New York City have ceased their exercise. I have not been able, though much observing these matters, to find any uncommon degree of life or elasticity in the society here, and, let me go further, of beauty either. Indeed, I have not seen a face since I have been here which invited my attention. Some pretty girls there are, because they are young and buoyant and innocent; but none that have beauty's signet. Abram Fuller still leads the dances. He and Martin Van Buren at this moment engross the attention of the United States Hotel.

I left Boston, you know, Monday at one o'clock; but a delay on the railroad prevented the steamboat leaving Providence as early as usual, and we did not arrive at New York till after ten o'clock Tuesday morning. Tuesday forenoon I saw the chancellor [Kent]; talked with him about Judge Story and Mr. Greenleaf, and accepted an invitation to take tea with him; dined with George Gibbs; saw the bookseller Halsted; took tea and passed the evening with the chancellor, and was invited by Mrs. Kent to take a family dinner next day. Wednesday forenoon, visited the burnt district; the Court of Errors, then in session; dined with the chancellor, and then rode in a carriage with him and his daughter and Mr. Ruggles [1] to see the outer portions of the city, where man's work gradually fades away into the clear country fresh from God. After that I took tea and passed a pleasant evening with Gibbs and his sister; returned to my lodgings and packed up for departure Thursday morning, at seven o'clock, for Albany, at which time I was duly on board the boat, where I met S. D. Parker, and had considerable pleasant conversation. By him I was introduced to Mrs. Clinton (the widow of Governor De Witt C.), her daughter, and niece, with all of whom I had much conversation, and made myself — but I will not say it, for they had such good manners as to appear pleased even if they were not. Mrs. Clinton invited me urgently to call and see Judge Spencer, — the old patriarch of the law, — with whom she proposed to spend some time in Albany.[2] I accordingly called, and was repaid for my visit. The judge looks exactly like Allston's Jeremiah. Friday morning I left Albany for Saratoga; and here I am, on the evening of that day, in a raw, ill-provided chamber, without a carpet and with a pine table, on which I now write. How are all friends? Bright eyes and fair faces?

With love to all my friends,

Ever yours,   C. S.

---

[1] Samuel B. Ruggles.

[2] Judge Ambrose Spencer married successively two sisters of De Witt Clinton. He died, in 1848, at the age of eighty-three.

TO GEORGE S. HILLARD.

CATARACT HOUSE (AMERICAN SIDE),
NIAGARA FALLS, Aug. 29, 1836.

MY DEAR HILLARD, — Your letter, postmarked Aug. 22, which I have just received, was full to repletion — if such a thing be possible of a friendly letter — with interesting facts, chronicling the circumstances of our little interests, and bringing me almost the company of the hours and days which have run their round in Boston since I left. Thank you for all, and am glad to know that my sister is no worse; that the judge is well; that Cushing is lord of my chair, and that all friends are as they were. I give you joy in Greenleaf's visits. While you have been easy and calm " as a summer's morning," I have been jolted over hundreds of miles of rough roads, and kept in a constant state of occupation and fermentation, by change of scene, accommodation, and objects of interest. I have literally not had time to sketch a word even to you or my sister before yester noon, except the scrawl of Saratoga Springs, which I trust you received *tanquam sero*. Since that note I have been to Ballston, where I passed two most agreeable days in company with several delightful women and men. Of the women, by far the most to my taste was Mrs. William Kent, with whom I could talk the livelong night, as she had that prompt, suggestive manner, combined of voice and expression, which would not suffer the springs of conversation to cease their flow. Mrs. De Witt Clinton, Judge Spencer, and many other interesting personages were there; also a young Scotch advocate,[1] who has since been my travelling companion, and is now writing at the same table with me. He is the nephew of Lord Jeffrey, and an intimate friend of Sergeant Talfourd and other Englishmen of whom we are curious. He is thoroughly educated, and is indifferent in his manners and dress, though you will perceive in your intercourse with him that unbought grace which is supplied by natural goodness of heart and a considerable mingling with refined society. He will go with me to Quebec, and perhaps continue on to Boston. He is deeply interested in the present English Ministry, inclining towards radicalism, as does his friend Talfourd. Not the least point of interest about him is his ignorance of many things and persons about which our curiosity is very lively. He has never been present at a debate in Parliament, though he has often gone up to Bellamy's at midnight, in order to ascertain the result of a division, not liking to await the intelligence in the morning papers. To my inquiry about Bulwer, he said, " It so happened that I have never read any of his works." I have seen a pleasant letter of friendship, written him by Talfourd. Another intimate, to whom he is now writing, is Keen, the Chancery reporter, of the firm of Mylne & Keen, reporters of Lords Lyndhurst and Brougham. Hayward, of Faust, he knows well. He will visit Boston, when you will see him, as I shall feel it my duty as well as pleasure to show him our lions.

We left Ballston for Saratoga last Monday; were whirled over the beautiful railway from Schenectady to Utica, a distance of eighty miles, in about

[1] Thomas Brown.

four hours; were crowded in a foul tavern at Utica; passed a most exciting, brilliant day at Trenton Falls, seventeen miles from Utica, — a natural curiosity, unsurpassed I believe by any in the country, where rocks and water and overhanging trees present all their strangest combinations (I wish you could see them), and fill the mind with the most beautiful ideas. My blood flowed quick, and my mind seemed exhilarated in no common degree, when I first descended from the lofty banks into the deep bosom of the rocks through which the stream tumbles along for several miles, descending from stratum to stratum. These falls alone are worth a journey. From Utica I took a canal-boat, in the evening, and the next forenoon found myself at Syracuse, a village in the interior of New York, — a distance of sixty-five miles. From Syracuse I have travelled, in company with four or five others, in extra coaches, hired by ourselves exclusively, through the vast interior of this State, to the great climax of Nature's majestic freaks, — Niagara. Here I arrived Saturday evening, and need not tell you that I felt, as it were, a deep weight — heavier far than lead — on my mind, from the overpowering majesty and sublimity of this falling water. I feel oppressed, as I walk round the banks and frequent the paths of travellers here, by the scene: I cannot look upon it tranquilly; the thoughts which it excites disturb the mind as much as the noise of its thunders and of its crashing against the rocks shakes the body. I here feel the force of Burke's " Theory of the Sublime," — referring it to the principle of *terror.* I will not attempt a description, for it would be lame and superfluous. I am now writing with its voice filling my ears, and in an atmosphere pleasantly cooled by the motion of its waters. This afternoon I shall pass over to the Clifton House, in Canada, where I shall stay a day, previous to embarking for Toronto, Kingston, and Montreal. While at Trenton Falls, I saw Tracy's [Howe][1] and his party's names on the book, three days before me. I next met their names at Niagara, which they left the morning of the day on which I arrived, much to my disappointment. I longed to see them. Timothy Walker [2] left there an hour or two before I arrived. I saw his open, smiling visage in the stage as I was within a mile of the falls. I met D. F. Webster,[3] for one minute, while changing horses at Geneva, in the centre of New York. It was a most agreeable *rencontre.* You may send this letter to my sister. A storm is rising and the rapids are raging.

With my love to all my friends, believe me affectionately

Yours,

CHAS. S.

[1] The son of Judge Howe, and a fellow-student of Sumner in the Law School.

[2] Of Cincinnati, author of "Elements of Geometry" and of "Introduction to American Law." He died, in 1856, at the age of fifty-three.

[3] Fletcher Webster, son of Daniel Webster, from whose name the first Christian name was afterwards dropped.

TO PROFESSOR SIMON GREENLEAF.

CLIFTON HOUSE, CANADA,
NIAGARA FALLS, Aug. 30, 1836.

MY DEAR MR. GREENLEAF, — Here am I in the dominions of "Mariner Bill," with a new government clasping me, and a new tone of manners, I fancy, about me. I have just established myself on this side of the wonderful cataract, and now would fain stretch the hand of friendship across its vast waters to meet yours. Its thunders shake the building in which I write, and its spray gives an additional dampness to a stormy evening. But now I think of quiet Cambridge and my dear friends there, I almost lose the sense of its awful presence. I hope you are well, and have laughed much, for Chancellor Kent feared that it was otherwise with you, and said that he regarded a laugh as a most healthy operation. A long and most grateful epistle, which I received to-day from Hillard, makes mention of your occasional calls at our office. "A visit from Mr. G.," says Hillard, "does me good for the rest of the day;" so I trust you will not cease doing what I know is so near your heart.

Since I have been here I have haunted every path and point of observation from which the falls can be seen; I have descended staircases, clambered over rocks, hugged along narrow and precipitous paths, crossed bending bridges, scaled elevated acclivities, penetrated caverns, and finally drenched myself utterly in venturing under the falling sheet of waters. I have seen the cataract in broad sunlight, and again by beautiful moonlight:

"If thou wouldst view fair Melrose aright,
    Go visit it by the pale moonlight;" —

and so I would have an observer look upon Niagara. The bow of Heaven seems almost perpetually to rest on its face, spanning its white foam and emerald green. It is not withdrawn now, even for the night, for the full orb of the moon creates a most beautiful arc, seen a little less distinctly than that of the sun, but full and marked by all the prismatic colors. I have sat for an hour contemplating this delightful object, with the cataract sounding, like the voice of God, in my ears. But there is something oppressive in hearing and contemplating these things. The mind travails with feelings akin to pain, in the endeavor to embrace them. I do not know that it is so with others; but I cannot disguise from myself the sense of weakness, inferiority, and incompetency which I feel. Many there are who play with a dog on the side of the falls, and amuse themselves by all the tricks which thoughtless merriment resorts to. But this tone might well become a sermon, if I were writing one, — and think of *my* sermonizing for your benefit!

The first two days I passed on the American side, having arrived there Saturday evening; and this afternoon have crossed, bag and baggage, to Canada, intending to spend a day here, previous to taking the steamboat for Toronto, Kingston, Montreal, and Quebec. Since I left home, which is just a fortnight, I have been constantly occupied with sight-seeing. New York first engaged my attention. There I saw the chancellor, who of course inquired about you, and especially of your laughing propensities, as to which

I made a favorable report.   He said he should rather sit to be scraped by a barber ten times than to have his portrait taken.   He, however, seemed to consent to the operation.   Mrs. William Kent, whom I afterwards saw at Ballston Springs, informed me that an artist in New York — I think it was Inman — had taken two portraits, one of which was for her, and the other the artist now had on hand, perhaps for sale; and she suggested whether it would not be agreeable to us to purchase that.   I intended to have stopped at Hyde Park on my way up North River, to see Miss Johnston and Miss Allen; but it would have detained me a day, so I passed on, admiring the beautiful situation of some of the houses of the village on the banks of the river.   While in Albany, I saw Judge Spencer, who received me kindly because he understood I was Judge Story's friend; also Johnson, the reporter, who is one of the most agreeable and gentlemanly men I ever met.   Indeed, I have had reason to think of Judge Story, and to be grateful to him every step.   My solitary trouble now, aside from the natural anxiety with regard to the condition of absent friends, is that my absence will delay the appearance of the judge's book, by putting off the index.[1]   I hope otherwise, however.   I hope you will enjoy Commencement and the great "Eighth,"[2] in neither of which I shall participate.

Give my love to Mrs. G., and believe me,

Ever yours,

CHAS. SUMNER.

TO GEORGE S. HILLARD.

MONTREAL, Sunday, Sept. 4, 1836.

MY DEAR HILLARD, — . . . The narrow streets and their utter darkness without the least show of lamps, and the rough and apparently disjointed pavè, reminded me of the description I have read of European cities; and when I came to look round by the light of day, and saw the ancient weather-beaten aspect of things, the tin covering of the roofs and especially the French names of all the streets, — *Rue Notre Dame, Rue St. Antoine, &c.*, — and heard French conversation all about me, you may suppose that for some moments I may have imagined myself where I so much long to be, in a foreign city.

I have been in court and seen the judges with clergymen's gowns, and white bands, and revolutionary three-cornered cocked hats, sitting under the armorial bearings of England.   All proceedings here are in French or English according to the desire of the parties, and the juries are sometimes addressed in one tongue and sometimes in another.   To-day I have visited the immense Catholic Cathedral, and worn my knees and patience by compliance with the devotional attitudes of the place.   The service, homily, &c., were in French.   I am obliged to stay in this place longer than I feel willing to, because no steamboat leaves on Sunday night; I shall start Monday even-

----

[1] Vol. II. of "Equity Jurisprudence," *ante*, p. 150.
[2] *Post*, p. 182.

ing at eight o'clock for Quebec, where I expect to arrive the next day at about three o'clock, it being a distance of one hundred and eighty-four miles.

I am still with my English friend, and like him immensely; he is full of knowledge and acquisition, without the least display.

Montreal is a stagnant place, without energy enough to keep up the appearance of life; with thirty thousand inhabitants, but without a directory; with close and crowded streets, but without lamps; and with many persons of apparent fashion but without a single hack. Holmes [1] I trust has succeeded. I long to hear about it. Quincy will speak while I am in Quebec; [2] I will endeavor to listen. My recollections to all my friends. The Misses Mason won all hearts at Ballston. I heard much of them while there. Judge Story I am asked about everywhere.

Yours,   C. S.

TO LUTHER S. CUSHING, BOSTON.

MONTREAL, Sept. 5, 1836.

MY DEAR CUSHING, — . . . I am at the Exchange Coffee House. I have been obliged to stay here three days, during which I have seen strange things, heard much poor French jabbered, seen a parade of the soldiery and visited the courts. Do I mistake or am I right, when I think that the judges and lawyers all look better fed than ours do, more replete with wine and other good things? You see none of the paleness and the disagreeable lines of study on their countenances.

I visited the Law Library for a moment with a gentleman of the bar, who, seeing that I was a stranger, offered to introduce me. There are some few American reports, — Peters and Wheaton, — but the bulk of the Library, I think, consists of French works. . . .

Dr. Barber [3] is in Montreal, where he proposes to deliver a course of lectures on phrenology; he is full of hope, and anticipates a considerable audience. I have had a good deal of pleasant conversation with him.

At eight o'clock this evening I start for Quebec.

Yours,   CHARLES S.

---

[1] Oliver Wendell Holmes's poem before the Φ. B. K. Society, entitled, "Poetry: a Metrical Essay."

[2] Celebration of the Second Centennial of Harvard College, Sept. 8, 1836, with an address by President Quincy. Quincy's History of Harvard University, Vol. II. pp. 689–708. See a sketch of the pavilion, erected on the college grounds for the dinner, in "The Harvard Book," Vol. I. pp. 51, 52.

[3] 1784–1864. Dr. Jonathan Barber, a teacher of elocution in Harvard College when Sumner was a law student.

TO GEORGE S. HILLARD.

QUEBEC, Sept. 7, 1836.

MY DEAR HILLARD, — After long wanderings, I have at length arrived at this great castle.   Never till now, wearied with travel and the state of perpetual unrest in which I have been kept, did I perceive the full weight of the curse upon the Wandering Jew.   Alas, too, for this sinner, he had no steamboats to facilitate his movements, and no hotels to relieve the natural rigors of travel.   I long for some of the rest afforded by long days, and late nights, of study.

You can have no idea of Quebec.   If I thought Montreal was foreign, I think Quebec is more so.   The upper part of the city, which is the court end, is entirely surrounded by a massive wall, over which cannons are bristling, and on which mortars are squatting in silent passiveness.

The citadel is an impregnable place of about five acres; but I will not weary you or myself by a description, for you may read many more faithful than I can pen in my present haste.   Soldiers meet you at every turn.

Sept. 8.   I have just returned from a visit to the Falls of Montmorency, nine miles from Quebec, a slender and rather beautiful single fall of water, said to be two hundred and forty feet high; but, to the visitor of Trenton and Niagara, Montmorency seems like a mill-dam.   And yet I am glad to have seen it, for it has enlarged my standard of comparison of Nature's works, and has satisfied a curiosity which I can date back to the time when I first studied geography under a woman's tuition.   The euphony of the name has perhaps lent some charm to the falling waters.

I have presented Judge Story's letter to Judge Sewall,[1] who lives about three miles from the city in a beautiful country seat, who treated me very civilly.   I am engaged to dine with him en famille to-morrow.   He is a very polite and sensible old gentleman.   His conversation was very agreeable.

When I shall arrive at Boston I can hardly tell, — perhaps next Saturday. Who knows but I may be finally baffled, and run the race of Peter Rugg?[2] That I am "the missing man" you are, I presume, ready to cry out.

I hope you have had comfortable weather; most delightful for travelling we have had, but cold.   Perhaps here on the frozen loins of the North, the weather, herald of icy winters, has appeared sooner than with us, nearer the sun as we are.   Remember me to my friends.   I rejoice with you in the Harvard celebration of to-day, and shall drink a glass of wine to you and old Harvard and Judge Story at my dinner, the bell for which will soon strike.   Yours,

C. S.

---

[1] Chief-Justice Jonathan Sewall died Nov. 12, 1839, in his seventy-fourth year.

[2] "Peter Rugg, the Missing Man," — a tale of which William Austin, a friend of Sumner's father, was the author.

TO GEORGE S. HILLARD.

MONTREAL, Sept. 12, 1836.

MY DEAR HILLARD, — Once again in this French place I send you greeting. I shall carry this letter into Vermont with me, where I shall commit it to the care of the hundred-handed giant who keeps up the intercourse between the different and most distant parts of the country, " and wafts a sigh from Indus to the Pole."

I have just received yours of Aug. 30, and am sorry that sickness has grappled hold of you. I trust to see you restored on my return. I sympathize with ———— in his affliction, but am accustomed to view life and the great change in such colors as to consider death very little to be mourned. But an only daughter and sister are a grievous loss.

I wish you had delayed your letter till the evening of Φ. B. K., that I might have heard the success of Holmes. I picture the success of our poet as complete, making him the cynosure of all eyes, and the observed of all observers.

I left Quebec Saturday night (twelve o'clock) Sept. 10, the most extensive conflagration which ever raged in that city not yet entirely subdued. The inefficiency of the fire department was ridiculous, without hose, suction apparatus, I may almost add, engines and firemen. Their efforts against the furious element reminded me, from their impotency, of Gulliver's aid in extinguishing the flames at Lilliput. While at Quebec I made the acquaintance of Conway Robinson, of Virginia, a friend of the jurist and author of the work on " Practice;" of his newly-married bride, the daughter of B. Watkins Leigh, and of Judge Gaston [1] (the famous William), of North Carolina. They arrived there on a tour, Judge Gaston having left his daughters behind on the Hudson. He, however, proposes to visit Boston next week with them. The judge is a very agreeable and talented man, of remarkable polish and blandness of manner, about fifty-six. I also dined with the venerable Chief-Justice of Lower Canada and his family, and had a very pleasant time. Starting from Quebec at twelve o'clock Saturday night, I arrived in Montreal Monday forenoon at half-past ten o'clock; being imprisoned (" Denmark is a prison," and so is a steamboat) for two nights on board an elegant and spacious boat with few passengers besides an agreeable Russian Count with mustaches, &c., I was heartily glad once again to tread *terra firma*. At Port St. Francis, a landing midway between Quebec and Montreal, I parted with my English friend Brown.

In Montreal to-day I attended court, and heard what I supposed was the calling of the docket, and the conversation between the lawyers incidental thereto, with quite an animated argument growing out of the filing of an affidavit, — all of which were in French. Indeed this is the language which meets you everywhere in Canada, reminding you of the origin of the Colony

---

[1] 1778–1844. Judge Gaston remained in office till his death. In the State Constitutional Convention of 1835, he opposed the proposition to deprive free negroes of the right to vote which they had previously enjoyed.

and of its conquest. I have felt humbled at my inability to speak French, and also to understand what I hear spoken.

To-morrow (Tuesday, Sept. 13, anniversary of Wolfe's great victory and death), I shall leave Montreal for the South, commencing or rather continuing my journey homeward.

STEAMER "WOLOOSKI," LAKE CHAMPLAIN.
Six o'clock, P. M., Tuesday, Sept. 13.

. . . In a paper which I have just found on board the boat I have read with infinite delight the debate in the British Parliament on Texas. A blow has been struck which will resound.

Yours,   CHAS. S.

P. S. I have studied Gray's poetry during my wanderings. His fame is a tripod, resting on those three wonders, — the "Elegy," "Bard," and "Progress of Poesy." The ode on "Eton" and "Hymn to Adversity" are fine, but comparatively inferior.

How my blood boils at the indignity to S. E. Sewall![1]

TO CHARLES S. DAVEIS.

4 COURT ST., Oct. 13, 1836.

MY DEAR MR. DAVEIS, — Behold me again in my office, "returned from the wars" of a long journey, and listening to the cases of clients and the dull whisper of law books. Work is pleasant after play; as most certainly play is precious after work. I have had a long play-time, and must now embrace labor as my mistress. My recollections of my long journey are tipped, as with silver and gold, by its last scenes at Portland. Your kindness and hospitality have deeply tinged my reminiscences of the place. . . .

Rand has received a long and cordial letter from Lord Denman, thanking him for books which he sent, and proposing to him for his answer a question upon which the King's Bench have divided, and judgment is suspended.[2] . . .

Believe me, very faithfully yours,

CHAS. SUMNER.

TO DR. FRANCIS LIEBER, NEW YORK.

BOSTON, Nov. 17, 1836.

MY DEAR FRIEND, — I thank you for remembering me so cordially after so absorbing an event as your letter spoke of; and I congratulate you and your wife, *ex imo pectore*, upon your deliverance from the perils of the sea. . . . I congratulate you, and wish I could take you by the hand and tell you my joy.[3]

---

[1] Mr. Sewall had been assaulted in Boston by a Southern slaveholder, on account of his appearing as counsel for fugitive slaves, *ante*, p. 25.

[2] A question of the measure of damages on the breach of warranty in the sale of a horse. The other omitted parts of the letter are an answer to inquiries of Mr. Daveis as to points of law arising in his practice.

[3] Dr. Lieber had just returned from a visit to the West Indies.

All your friends here are well. Dr. Palfrey is well; and Judge Story as ever is in an overflow of spirits. He is now on his circuit in Rhode Island, and will not return for several days. The second volume of his work on "Equity Jurisprudence" has appeared since you left our *terra firma*. He is now engaged in preparing the report of the Massachusetts Commissioners, of whom he is chairman, on the "Codification of the Common Law;" the report will aim to show that codification is at once expedient and practicable. It will make an era, perhaps, in the history of the law in our country; for, coming with the authority of Judge Story's name and with the cogency of his learning and reason, it will be calculated to have a very great influence throughout the country, and perhaps to flow back with a strong tide upon law-reform in England.

The subject of an international copyright law has been much discussed among us lately. Sargent,[1] of the "Atlas," has written some spirited articles, which assume the right ground. Willis [2] has returned home, and is full of this subject. A leading article in a late number of the London "Metropolitan" (Captain Marryatt's) calls upon the British government to take some steps in the matter. Longfellow has returned home, having arrived only three days ago, full of pleasant reminiscences and of health. He tells me that he called upon Mittermaier, with a letter from you. He is a very pleasant fellow, and will at once assume the charge of Ticknor's department. Judge Story has written to Mittermaier; so also has John Pickering. Harvard College gave Mittermaier the degree of LL.D. last Commencement, and I have the parchment diploma in my iron safe, to forward to him at the earliest opportunity. Mr. Pickering is about publishing another edition of his "Americanisms." He is well, and as kind as ever. He is truly your friend and admirer.

Longfellow left the Appletons in Switzerland. Mrs. Newton [3] is well and charming. I regret that you could not come to Boston. I shall pray that the next storm may send you into our harbor. What projects have you in hand?

John Lowell, Jr., who died in India, has left by will two hundred and fifty thousand or three hundred thousand dollars to trustees, the income to be expended in lectures on science, religion, politics, &c., to be delivered in Boston during six months of the year, by professors appointed for that purpose. It is calculated that each professor shall have at least three thousand dollars for his six months' work. None of the money to be expended in a building. Here is the place for you! You must have it. Of this more hereafter. Felton wrote the article on your "Reminiscences;" otherwise it would have been done by,

Affectionately yours,

Chas. Sumner.

---

[1] John O. Sargent, a classmate of Sumner, and afterwards associated with the New York "Courier and Enquirer."

[2] Nathaniel P. Willis.

[3] A daughter of William Sullivan, an eminent lawyer of Boston.

TO PROFESSOR SIMON GREENLEAF, WASHINGTON, D. C.

Boston, Jan. 25, 1837.

My dear Friend, — Many thanks for your cordial letter of the 11th from Washington; and much pardon do I need at your hands for the lugubrious, hypochondriacal epistle which I inflicted upon you. I write now to greet you on your way home. Pray stay, as long as your affection requires, with your daughter, and banish all thought of the Law School. All are cheerful, respectful, and contented, and seem to receive the law with perfect faith from their *pro tem.* professor. A murmur, slight as that of a distant brook, has reached me from a counsel against whom I decided in a moot-court case, with an expression of an intention to appeal to Cæsar on his return. The parties were, however, entirely respectful, and none have given me any reason to be uneasy. Starkie I hear three days in the week, while Kent I encounter every day. This week I have held two courts, and decided the question of partnership and statute of limitations; and also that of the Hindu witness. I held, in the first case, that the admission of one partner after a dissolution did not take a case out of the statute; and I took a technical distinction, which enabled me to evade the force of the late Massachusetts and English cases, so as to decide the case independent of them. The venue being laid in Rhode Island removed it from their influence; but I put it on grounds which may be maintained in Massachusetts even in the face of those cases. In the other case I held that the deposition of the Hindu priest was admissible, for reasons which I will explain fully when I have again the joy of your countenance.

The students inquire of me daily when you will be back, and enter earnestly into your forensic contest. I have explained again and again the nature of the question you have argued, and endeavored to enforce and illustrate your views: in short, to make the school "*Warren-Bridge men.*" I have been with you in your labors, and have hung with anxious confidence upon the accents of your lips. I have hoped that some of your points might reach our dear judge's prejudices, and bear them away. If such be the case, I shall have great joy with you. To convince him would be a greater triumph than to storm a citadel.[1]

Mrs. Greenleaf has a sorrowful widowhood. Your absence makes her desolate. Bereft of you, she seems as if deprived of the precious lustre of her eye or of the goodly light of the sun. I have passed as many hours as I could snatch for such pleasure from my various calls in Cambridge and Boston, in conversing with her on those topics which you know are often *vexed* between us. I have re-argued the case with her several times; and I believe

---

[1] Professor Greenleaf was attending the Supreme Court as counsel for the defendants in the celebrated case of The Charles River Bridge v. The Warren Bridge, 11 Peters' Reports, p. 420, — a case which settled the doctrine that public grants should be construed strictly. This view was supported by Professor Greenleaf against Mr. Webster, the counsel for the plaintiffs. Some conservative people (among them Judge Story, who dissented) regarded the decision as contrary to the Constitution and perilling rights of property. Story's "Life and Letters," Vol. II. pp. 262–273.

she thinks more favorably of me than she did of old. Indeed, I have thought
that she now entertains some hope that I shall eventually not be found
wanting.[1]

The students attend all the exercises promptly and constantly, and seem
to take an unabated interest in their studies, studying the cases referred to
in the marginal notes. I endeavor to stimulate them as much as possible,
and flatter myself that I have at least kept the old breath in the body, if I
have not succeeded in breathing into it any new afflatus. We shall all welcome you back; and we have long ago said —

"Ducite ab urbe domum, mea carmina, ducite Daphnim."[2]

But do not hasten from Litchfield, and remember me to your daughter, who,
I hope, is well.

Codification is at a *stand-still*. Nothing has been said about it yet, though
there is a prevailing impression that it will pass, at least so far as the criminal law is concerned. The Legislature have not yet plunged into mischief,
though they are floundering on. I have come to the end of my paper and of
my thoughts, and must hasten to take the "hourly" (on the outside) for
Cambridge.

Ever yours affectionately,   C. S.

TO REV. DR. JOHN G. PALFREY.

DANE LAW COLLEGE, Feb. 3, 1887.

MY DEAR SIR, — . . . I have lately received from Dr. Lieber the MSS.
of his German Grammar, which he is desirous that you should examine before it is offered to any bookseller. I enclose the letter, which explains its
nature and his desires.

And now let me excuse myself from a failure of contract on my part touching a certain article.[3] The absence of Judge Story and Mr. Greenleaf has
actually *swamped* the whole of the last month so far as I am concerned. Daily
lectures and moot-courts, and the calls of business and correspondence have
absorbed every minuté of my time, taking me to Cambridge every day, and
again taking me back to the city. To one, however, who grapples with such a
variety of labor as yourself, I feel that my excuse is very slender; but I most
freely confess my humiliation at thus finding myself a debtor. Mr. Greenleaf's return in a few days will leave me a freer man; and I shall at once
proceed to make a dividend on the various outstanding claims against me.

Very truly yours,

CHAS. SUMNER.

---

[1] A reference to banter concerning matrimony.
[2] Virgil. Ecl. VIII. 68.
[3] *Ante*, p. 174.

TO PROFESSOR MITTERMAIER, HEIDELBERG.

BOSTON (MASSACHUSETTS, U. S. AMERICA), March 27, 1837.

MY DEAR SIR, — My friend, Mr. Pickering,[1] has communicated to me the flattering terms which you have used in your letter to him with regard to the " American Jurist," a journal with which, for several years, I have been editorially connected.   I assure you of the high gratification afforded to myself and to my associates by your favorable opinion.

You kindly promised, in your letter to Mr. Pickering, to furnish our journal with information respecting the law in Germany.   Be assured that your communications will be highly valued.   The subject of codification is beginning to excite a strong interest in our country, and we naturally look to Germany for light.   Any views which you should be willing to furnish with regard to the present state of the controversy in Germany would be read with the deepest attention.   Among us, the *codification* proposed is simply *revision* and *redaction*, — the reduction of a portion of the vast mass of decided cases (*Jurisprudence des arrets*) to a written text, — thus establishing, as it were, a *stratum* of written law, which will give firmness and solidity to that portion which remains *unwritten*.   By such a course, it seems to me that we, in a great degree, avoid the evils pointed out by Savigny and the Historical School.   We still preserve the historical features of the law, not presuming to frame a *new* system from *new* materials without consulting the previous customs, habits, and history of the country.   The error of Jeremy Bentham and of John Locke was in supposing that they, in their closets, could frame *de novo* a code for a people.   Locke prepared a code, a century ago, for one of the North American colonies, which proved a signal failure.   The attempt to codify the law in the United States is now making only in the State of Massachusetts.   A resolve has just passed our Legislature, authorizing the Governor to appoint *five* commissioners to codify the *criminal law*, leaving the remaining portions untouched.   Upon the success of this experiment will depend, in a great measure, future exertion on the subject.   At the last session of the Legislature commissioners were appointed, at the head of whom was Judge Story, to consider the expediency and practicability of codification.   Their report I shall forward to you with the numbers of the " Jurist," [2] and also a report made to the Legislature at its present session on capital punishment.[3]

Some time ago I received from the Hon. President Quincy, of Harvard University, Cambridge, a diploma of LL.D., to be forwarded to you, with an accompanying letter from the President.   Allow me to express my great

---

[1] John Pickering.

[2] The Report of the Commissioners, drawn by Judge Story, which favors a limited system of codification of the common law, was printed as a legislative document.   1837, House No. 8.   Story's "Life and Letters," Vol. II. pp. 241–251.

[3] At this period, 1835–37, the death-penalty was much discussed in the legislature of Massachusetts, Robert Rantoul, Jr., strongly urging its abolition in reports which argued at length all the points in the controversy ; but the measure did not prevail.   Leg. Doc. 1837. House Nos. 4, 43.   Senate No. 69.

gratification that the oldest and best endowed literary seminary of my country has bestowed its *laurel* upon one whose labors and character have so well earned it.   The interest which you have ever shown in American jurisprudence, and the able expositions of it which have appeared in your " Critical Journal," have caused your name to be viewed by our jurists with great admiration and regard.   According to the direction of my friend, Dr. Lieber, I enclosed your diploma to Messrs. Perthes & Besser, Hamburg.   I hope that there will be no miscarriage.   If you should do me the honor to write to me, I should be glad to have you write in French.   I hope to see you within a year at Heidelberg, as I propose very soon to visit Germany, and feel desirous to bespeak your favorable notice and instruction, should I be so happy as to accomplish my proposed journey.   If I can be of service to you, please to command me; and believe me, with the highest consideration,

Very respectfully, your obedient servant,

CHARLES SUMNER.

TO DR. FRANCIS LIEBER, COLUMBIA, S. C.

BOSTON, June 17, 1837.

MY DEAR FRIEND, — I fear much that I shall not see Europe so soon as I anticipated.   The thought of going abroad makes my heart leap, and the gloomy fear that I must stay at home awhile longer plunges me in disappointment.   But, as you have said, these pinching times pinch me and have caused me to postpone my departure.   If I can possibly administer on my affairs, and be able to command the requisite funds, I shall leave in the fall. Then will my joy be great.   The thought of Europe fills me with the most tumultuous emotions; there, it seems, my heart is garnered up.   I feel, when I commune with myself about it, as when dwelling on the countenance and voice of a lovely girl.   I am in love with *Europa*.   May I have the success of Jove without his transformation!   I shall rely upon your friendly counsels before I depart and during my absence, and shall be anxious to serve you at all seasons and in all places.   The moment I see my way clear to the exact time of departure, I shall inform you, and hope that we may meet before I go.   How we would talk of Europe and its intellectual resources and excitements!   An hour with you would stimulate my mind on this favorite theme like the noises of the ancient Corybantes.

June 19.

Captain Marryat, of novel-writing memory, is in Boston, and has been for some days; but I think is very little noticed. . . . Miss Martineau's book will be published in a few days, and will make the feathers fly.   From the extracts published in the papers, her work will be of a most decided character, mowing to the right and left with keenness and effect.   I hope her castigation will do good.   Already calumny has beset her among us, and she is classed with Hall and Trollope.   Her comments on slavery are said to be scorching. I do not regret this.   I hope that through her some truths may reach the

South. Perhaps her book may be burned by the hangman; certainly it will
be placed on the *Index Expurgatorius* of the South. I wonder that your free
spirit can endure the bondage to which opinion at the South must subject
you, tying your tongue and taming all your expressions. I ask pardon for
this language, for perhaps I mistake your views and situation.

You speak of studying law. I should hesitate long before encouraging
you in such a step. Why study law? For money? Considering your age
and country of birth, is it not doubtful whether you could reap more from it
than from your present exertions? For office? There is no political office
in the United States worth your acceptance. I say in all sincerity that I
would take your *literary reputation* in preference to any office in my country.
For reputation? In my view, the reputation of no lawyer is equal to yours.
Then, you must not expose yourself to the imputation of fickleness, of changing your employment for ever, and of being, as Dryden says of some one,
" all things by starts and nothing long;" or, of the lines of Juvenal, —

> Grammaticus, rhetor, geometres, pictor, aliptes,
> Augur, schoenobates, medicus, magus: omnia novit.[1]

Your attainments and reputation are already quite *encyclopædic ;* but such
a change as you propose would excite surprise. Do not abandon your present vantage ground in the field of literature. At the bar you would be for
the present on a level with the vast herd. You would be obliged to push
your way through the thick and serried ranks of the profession, jealous perhaps of a new comer with such a reputation as yours. In literature you are
on your native heath, and your name is MacGregor.

Faithfully yours,　　　　　　C. S.

TO GEORGE S. HILLARD, PORTLAND, MAINE.[2]

4 Court St., Saturday, July, 1837.

My dear George, — Yours came to hand last evening, and I shall write
a line which I hope you will get on Sunday. All things are calm as a mirror. I sit, like Nicholas Biddle " of a summer morning," in the shaded
recess of an office, nor am I disturbed by many new or urgent applications.
The ———s vex me with daily notes and requests to call upon them, and
some little affairs — trustees-answers, &c. — consume much of my time.
There is an utter dearth of all event in our circle. The news from Europe
has filled all ears, and people talk foolishly about the Queen, Victoria, and
anticipate a chivalric court, because forsooth there is a youthful maiden
queen. The " Morning Chronicle " is in black lines, and all the papers abound
in those particulars of the death and character of the old king, and of the
proclamation of the girl, which you know are so greedily devoured by English
readers.

---

1 Juvenal. Sat. III. 76, 77.
2 Hillard was then passing a vacation in Maine.

Grund[1] is in Boston, fresh from England. I see him every day at the Tremont House. He is very able and bold. I am quite struck with his conversation. He talks sledge-hammers. He wishes to learn law of me, and offers me two hours of his day to read and talk German and French for one of mine on law.

I have concluded a contract with Little & Co. for my Reports, and they will commence printing on Monday. I shall drive the press like a fiery horse, and will be in England at the next election of members of parliament, which will be the most powerfully contested one which ever took place. I have nearly determined to make for England first, for reasons which I will explain when we meet. Cleveland was in the office this forenoon. It was my first sight of him for days. He is toying in the shades of Pine Bank, and sends his love to you.

Yours ever,   CHAS. S.

My love to Longfellow, and kindest recollections to Chas. Daveis. Felton thinks himself better.

TO CHARLES S. DAVEIS.

4 COURT ST., BOSTON, Aug. 4, 1837.

MY DEAR MR. DAVEIS, — I think a draft by one citizen of Massachusetts upon another citizen of Massachusetts, payable in another State, is clearly a foreign bill of exchange.[2] . . .

My second volume [Sumner's Reports] is now in press, and I am driving it with the speed of the Wild Huntsman, hoping to get it out in October; and then " I'm on the sea," &c. The visions of boyhood and of the lengthened shadows of youth and manhood will then be realized, and I shall see what has so often filled my mind and imagination. I wish your advice very much about my journey, and I shall rely very much upon your kind introductions. Before I go, I intend to visit Portland, in order to talk over the whole route, its objects and advantages. My journey will not be peculiarly legal. I shall aim to see *society* in all its forms which are accessible to me; to see men of all characters; to observe institutions and laws; to go circuits and attend terms and parliaments; and then come home and be happy. . . .

Believe me as ever most faithfully yours,

CHAS. SUMNER.

TO HENRY W. LONGFELLOW, PORTLAND.[3]

4 COURT ST., Aug. 15, 1837.

MY DEAR LONGFELLOW, — . . . Felton is very much better than when you left; so that to-day he dined with me at the Tremont. A good sign. Poor

---

[1] Francis J. Grund.

[2] The letter refers to the authorities on the question, and states the opinion of Judge Story as given in conversation.

[3] Professor Longfellow was then visiting his father at Portland.

fellow! He has been obliged to endure blisters which are as bad as tooth-pulling or usury. And yet he is as sociable, as pleasant, and full of *bonhomie* as ever. He has sat patiently in his room during the warmest and most sultry days, with all his windows closed, and with all the martyrdom of St. Lawrence on his gridiron.

I was glad to hear that you had so pleasant a time in the White Mountains. Hillard returned full of what he had seen or heard, *quorum pars magna fuisti.* Choate and Howe both joined in expressions. Dr. Lieber is in the city now, and is at our office a great deal, and is very interesting from the fulness and invention of his mind. He has inquired after you. I suppose we shall see you soon, returned to occupy your new rooms.[1]

Yours ever faithfully,

CHARLES SUMNER.

TO DR. FRANCIS LIEBER.

BOSTON, Sept. 11, 1837.

MY DEAR LIEBER, — On *Nepotism*, see a capital letter of General Washington, written in 1797, to John Adams.[2] The latter had solicited the advice of Washington with regard to a promotion of his son, J. Q. A., in the diplomatic line. Washington advises it, on the ground that he has already been appointed by government; and it is now proposed only to advance him another step. At the same time, he commends J. Q. A. in a way that does my heart good. Washington, in this letter, alludes to his own conduct on these subjects. Perhaps you have seen the letter. I do not know that it is preserved by Sparks. It probably is; at any rate, it is to be found in the renowned Cunningham correspondence, the publication of which is the most barefaced violation of confidence that I know of.

See the last number of the "London and Westminster Review" for articles on Taylor's "Statesman [3]" and Fonblanque's "England under Seven Administrations," [4] both of which touch upon some of your topics.

Don't publish by subscription; [5] don't make yourself a general beggar: it is enough to petition booksellers; do not offer prayers to the many-headed public for the sake of a paltry subscription. It is undignified, and betrays a want of confidence in your work. Study, ponder, and polish your work;

---

[1] Prof. Longfellow began in Sept., 1837, to occupy rooms at the Craigie House, Washington's headquarters, — an estate which he afterwards purchased, and where he has since resided.

[2] Works of John Adams, Vol. VIII. p. 530. Sparks's "Life and Writings of George Washington," Vol. XI. p. 188. Lieber had applied to Sumner by letter, Sept. 2, 1835, while writing his "Political Ethics," for information relative to the appointment of Bushrod Washington to an office. *Ante,* p. 173. Lieber's "Political Ethics" (1875), Vol. II. pp. 30–34. Sumner, in a speech in the Senate, May 31, 1872, treated at length of "Nepotism," with reference to the administration of President Grant, drawing historical parallels. He discussed it briefly in a speech intended to be delivered in Faneuil Hall, Sept. 3, 1872, entitled, "Greeley or Grant."

[3] April, 1837, Vol. XXVIII. pp. 1–32.

[4] Idem, pp. 65–98.   [5] Political Ethics.

then *select* a publisher and commit it to the world. If these times will not accept it, posterity will, — which is an *infinity*. Grotius did not solicit subscriptions; nor Bacon, nor Story, nor Kent. You may reply that you will not solicit them, but the bookseller will, — that is a distinction without a difference. Every time your paper is presented for a signature, the person, while reluctantly signing his name, will mutter some querulous tones, and will afterwards console himself for his extravagance by the remark that he did it to get rid of the applicant. Will you expose yourself to such shots? No! Your work is new, elaborate, important, great. Comport yourself with regard to it as becomes the author of such a work. Pardon this warmth. I may be wrong in judgment, but not in my friendly regard. . . .

Ever yours,   C. S.

TO CHARLES S. DAVEIS.

4 Court St., Boston, Sept. 12, 1837.

My dear Friend, — . . . Of Mr. Ingersoll's [1] oration I have heard much, and regret that he passed through Boston without presenting a vision to my eyes. When in Philadelphia, some years ago, he was very kind to me, and I dined at his house in a large and splendid company. I should, therefore, take great pleasure in paying my respects to him.

Whether I shall be able to visit you, on Oct. 1, I am uncertain. Within a short time of that date I shall certainly present myself, to indulge in the luxury of a full day's communion on Europe and the great scenes which I hope to look on. My reports are about two-thirds printed, but will probably be through the press about that time. Some professional engagements will detain me, I fear, beyond Oct. 1. If I could ride in the inside of a stage-coach, I would certainly go down with the judge; but as it makes me sick, — very sick, — it would be a mere mockery to go in his company, or afterwards in yours. . . .

Affectionately yours,

Chas. Sumner.

TO CHARLES S. DAVEIS.

4 Court St., Boston, Sept. 28, 1837.

My dear Friend, — I send you a hasty scrawl as a premonitory symptom of a firm determination to take the stage on Friday with the judge, or the boat on Friday night for Portland. I cannot seduce the judge to encounter the exposure to sea-sickness, confined quarters, and a prolonged trip by steamboat. He is of old Cato's mind, who never regretted but one thing, which was on one occasion going by water when he might have gone by land. But the horrid, blinding dust will suffocate a poor fellow like myself, who must consort the whole way with Jehu on his box.

---

[1] Joseph R. Ingersoll's Address at Bowdoin College.

Mr. Ingersoll spent about a week here, during which I was with him good portions of each day. We talked of you, and he thought that seeing you was seeing a large part of Maine.   Yours as ever,

CHAS. S.

TO PROFESSOR MITTERMAIER.

BOSTON (UNITED STATES OF AMERICA), Nov. 20, 1837.

MY DEAR SIR, — I feel grateful for your kind letter of 14th June last, and for the interest which you have expressed in the jurisprudence of my country. Your promise to furnish an article for the " American Jurist " has given me and my collaborateurs the greatest pleasure. We hope to receive it very soon. The subject of codification is deeply interesting to us at this moment. Commissioners in Massachusetts are now engaged in reducing to a code our criminal law. I think it will take them upwards of two years to accomplish this; and then the Legislature may reject their labors, as that of Louisiana did the code of Livingston.[1] While the attention of the bar and the public are directed to this subject, an article from a person so competent and distinguished as you are would be read with the greatest interest. Let me ask you to persevere in your promise. My associates and myself will be glad to send in return some contribution to your very valuable journal, on such subject as you would be pleased to have discussed. The exchange would, indeed, be unequal; like Diomed, we should give iron for gold.

I have directed my bookseller to send to you, through Perthes & Besser, Hamburg, my " Reports of the Decisions of Mr. Justice Story," in two volumes; also a work on " Admiralty Practice," which was edited and partly prepared by me. Allow me to refer you to the preface of the latter work as indicating my agency in it. The forms of proceedings, consisting of libels and answers, which I prepared, have been adopted in the practice of the admiralty courts of the United States, so far as my knowledge extends. I ask you to receive the foregoing works as a mark of my high regard. I have also directed to be sent, through the same channel, the last three numbers of the " American Jurist," which I fear you have not received.

I am now about to embark for Europe, partly with a view of acquainting myself with the jurisprudence of its different countries, and promise myself the pleasure of making your personal acquaintance at Heidelberg, where I hope to pass some time. I shall probably be in Paris during the months of January, February, and March, and shall then pass over to England; after which I shall visit Germany. My associate, L. S. Cushing, will have the chief management of the " American Jurist " during my absence; and he joins me in expressing an earnest desire that you would furnish your promised article.

I have the honor to be, with great regard,

Your most obedient, faithful servant,

CHARLES SUMNER.

---

[1] The "Report of the Penal Code of Massachusetts " was not made till 1844; it was then referred to the next legislature, and no further action taken.

CHAPTER IX.

GOING TO EUROPE.—DECEMBER, 1837.—AGE, 26.

FROM his boyhood Sumner had longed to visit Europe, and with his reading of history this desire grew into a passion. The want of the necessary funds compelled him to postpone its gratification until he had in part earned them, and won friends who would advance the rest. A circumstance gleaned from the letters of Browne and Hopkinson, which occurred during his last year in the Law School, is significant of his earnestness in this direction. He nearly completed, at that time, a negotiation by which a gentleman was to defray his expenses for a year's travelling abroad, in consideration of certain personal services to be rendered at home. Its details are not preserved; but the two classmates, who did not hear of the proposed arrangement until it had fallen through, upbraided him in a friendly way for proposing to assume an obligation which they thought would compromise his personal independence. This strong desire, increasing with his studies, became a definite purpose at the beginning of 1837. He fixed first upon October in that year as the time of sailing; but a pressure of engagements compelled him to postpone it for two months.

His purpose differed from that of an ordinary tourist, who seeks only relaxation from business, relief from the *ennui* of an idle life, and a view, grateful to the eye, of scenery, costumes, galleries, spectacles. He desired to see society in all its forms; to converse with men of all characters and representatives of all professions; to study institutions and laws, and to acquaint himself with courts and parliaments.[1] He had read many books, and wished to see the men who wrote them, and the men whose deeds they commemorated. The poem, the speech, the history, the judicial opinion, and the treatise would, he felt,

---

[1] See letter to Mr. Daveis of Aug. 4, 1837, *ante*, p. 192.

after such communion, charm with a new interest or light up with a clearer intelligence. He had read foreign law, and he aspired to comprehend fully its doctrines and spirit by attending its schools and observing its administration, with the view of using such knowledge in efforts to improve our own. To his cherished ideal, — the *jurist*, whether serving as lawyer, judge, or teacher, — he had been loyal as well in practice as when a student; and it was his purpose, after the further studies and wider observations abroad which he deemed essential to its attainment, to return to his profession better equipped for all its duties. He craved the faculty of reading and speaking foreign languages, and sought the opportunity of learning them, not merely from the drill of professional teachers, but as well from the lips of those whose words, written or spoken, had taught mankind.

He had not striven for social consideration at home, and had no expectation of that which awaited him abroad. But for a tour of the kind which he had in mind letters of introduction were essential; and like Milton, two centuries before, he had friends to supply them who were not less kindly than those now best remembered for their good offices to the pilgrim poet.

Mr. Daveis commended him to Earl Fitzwilliam and Lord Jeffrey, both having volunteered to receive any of his friends whom he might be pleased to introduce to them, and also to Lord Denman and others, with whom he was on less familiar terms. Mr. Rand gave him letters to Lord Denman, Baron Parke, and Solicitor-General Rolfe; Judge Story to Mr. Justice Vaughan and John Stuart Wortley; John Neal to Mrs. Sarah Austin; Washington Allston to Wordsworth; Ralph Waldo Emerson to Carlyle; Professor Parker Cleaveland, of Bowdoin College, to Sir David Brewster; Dr. Channing to the Baron de Gérando. Dr. Lieber did his utmost to make his journey agreeable at the time and permanently improving, warmly certifying of his character and acquisitions to continental jurists and *savans*, — notably Mittermaier and the younger Thibaut, as well as to his English friends. Such letters are keys useful for opening doors; but there, as many by experience know, their service ends; after that, he who bears them must, by his manners and gifts, vindicate his title to continued hospitality.

In his letter to Earl Fitzwilliam, Mr. Daveis, after referring to Sumner's professional learning, said: —

"I cannot, of course, be understood to exhibit these titles to your lordship, except as marks of those merits by which he is distinguished in the estimation of those who have the best opportunity of appreciating his personal and intellectual qualities. But what they especially prize and cherish in his character, is that ardor and enthusiasm in whatever is connected with the learning of his profession and the elevation of its office, which leads him to aspire to an acquaintance with all that is ennobling in itself or congenial to it in excellence. His studies and pursuits will carry him to the Continent, and cause him to pass some portion of his time in Germany, where there is so much to attract those who seek the highest intellectual cultivation."

Dr. Lieber, who joined heartily in Sumner's plans, gave him elaborate advice, specifying in detail points to be regarded, which were, being here abbreviated, as follows: —

"1. Plan your journey. 2. Spend money carefully. 3. Preserve newspapers, hand-bills, &c. 4. Concentrate your attention for lasting impressions. 5. Take views — as of Paris from Montmartre — from elevated places, steeples, hills, &c. 6. Keep steadily a journal; let it be the *carte* of the day. Never think that an impression is too vivid to be forgotten. Believe me, *time* is more powerful than senses or memory. 7. See every thing, including feasts, fairs, theatres. 8. Eat the dishes of the country. 9. Dress well, being specially careful as to linen. 10. Don't give introductions easily. 11. Draw diagrams of courts, buildings, &c. 12. Keep little books for addresses. 13. Write down first impressions of men and countries. 14. Note large and noble fabrics. 15. See the Vatican by torchlight. 16. [Names of various eminent persons in France, Germany, and other countries to be seen; including Mittermaier, the Thibauts, and Bunsen, — 'the last well worth knowing, and one of the best antiquarians in Rome.']"

He also urged Sumner to keep in mind during his absence a work of a forensic character (*iter forense*), treating of courts, parliaments, popular meetings, with descriptions, incidents, and anecdotes.

With the exception of Dr. Lieber and Mr. Daveis, Sumner's friends did not encourage his proposed enterprise.[1] Hillard, however, who knew how much his heart was in it, felt that he would be unhappy if defeated in his purpose, and bade him Godspeed. Judge Story and Professor Greenleaf feared — an apprehension well founded — that the foreign experiences he counted upon would wean him from his profession. President Quincy, in a parting interview, touched his sensitiveness by telling him rather bluntly that all that Europe would do for him would be

---

1 He recalled, in a letter to Hillard of Dec. 11, 1838, that he had undertaken his plan of travel "contrary to the advice of dear friends."

to spoil him, sending him home with a mustache and cane, — a remark meant in kindness, but, with Sumner's reverent regard for the President, disturbing him for months afterwards, whenever his memory recurred to his vacant law-office.[1]

Mrs. Waterston writes : —

" I perfectly remember Sumner's deciding to go to Europe, and that my father opposed it. He feared ' Sumner would be spoiled.' I do not recall what Judge Story's opinion was; but Sumner went, and was not ' spoiled.' I remember his last visit to us previous to his departure, and his face as he took leave of my mother and the President (as he always called him), — his earnest face, partly bright with expectation, partly grave with regret, especially regret at going against the President's approval."

Sumner's professional savings — and he had no other resource except borrowing — were quite inadequate to meet the expense of his journey. He was to spend during his absence five thousand dollars, or nearly that sum, of which he had laid aside from his earnings hardly more than a third. Three friends — Judge Story, Richard Fletcher, and Samuel Lawrence [2] — generously proffered loans of one thousand dollars each, which he accepted. They were repaid, some time after his return, chiefly, as is supposed, by his mother from the family estate.

The journey to Europe was not then as now a rapid and even cheap excursion, which every year is taken by a horde of tourists. It was confined chiefly to merchants who had foreign connections in their business, scholars bound for a German university to complete their studies before entering on a professorship, and to sons of wealthy parents, who, having finished an academic course, began a life of elegant leisure with a foreign tour. No steamer, carrying passengers, had as yet crossed the Atlantic. A young man who went abroad at such a period, with narrow means, with a profession which he had served too briefly to retain a hold on clients during his absence, and against the counsels of friends, was indeed stirred by no common aspiration.

Early in November he made a farewell visit of a day to his valued friend, Mr. Daveis, at Portland; taking the boat on the evening of Tuesday, the seventh, and leaving that city on his return the next evening. He dined, while in Portland, with Mr.

---

[1] The President's remark is referred to in Sumner's letter to Hillard of Jan. 30, 1838.

[2] Mr. Lawrence, — brother of Abbott Lawrence, who was at one time Minister to England, — is now a resident of Stockbridge, Mass.

Daveis, meeting at the dinner John Neal,[1] and later in the afternoon Stephen Longfellow, the father of the poet.

After leave-takings with his teachers, Story and Greenleaf, and President Quincy, at Cambridge, his family at home, his intimate friends, and among these, last of all, Hillard,[2] — one of the kindest and most devoted that ever a man had, — he left Boston late in November, making before he sailed a quick visit to Washington, where he obtained his passport and was made bearer of despatches, — an appointment which then brought some advantages to a traveller. On the way he stopped at Burlington, N. J., to bid good-by to a friend, — a lady recently betrothed to Cleveland, one of the "Five," — tarried a day in Philadelphia where he dined with Mr. Peters and spent the evening with Mr. Ingersoll, and passed a few hours in Baltimore with reference to some promised letters of introduction.

During his preparations for departure, and when about to embark, he received many letters from friends, expressing deep interest in his welfare, and full of benedictions.

Dr. Lieber, who addressed him as "Young man on the threshold of a great life," wrote from Columbia, S. C., Oct. 7, —

"How I would enjoy an intense, deep, and vast life could I accompany you, and learn, admire, adore with you, and initiate you in the great temple of the beautiful and good!"

And again, Oct. 17 : —

"Good-by, my dear friend. May God protect you on the deep and on the main! May he vouchsafe you good health, acute senses, a cheerful mind to observe and receive every thing that comes in your way! Keep an affectionate heart for your friends, and do not allow yourself to be torn every way by the many thousand different and interesting things. Keep steady and within bounds. I bless you as never friend blessed his friend."

Mr. Daveis wrote, Aug. 8 : —

"There will be a good many true hearts that will set up the Horatian strains over the ship that takes you in trust. I shall take pride and pleasure in giving you the best letters I can; and, besides the one to Lord Jeffrey,

---

1 Mr. Neal was through life a busy writer of poetry and prose. He was born Oct. 25, 1793, and died June 20, 1876. In early life, while in Europe, he lived for a time with Jeremy Bentham, an association which brought him into relations with the Benthamites, particularly the Austins. Mr. Neal, not long before his death, thus wrote with reference to Sumner's visit: "He appeared with a right royal presence, his countenance characterized by a genuine warmth and great readiness; in a word, it was that of a highly bred, well-informed gentleman of a somewhat older school than I was in the way of meeting."

2 Hillard gave him a *portemonnaie* with the inscription, "Coelum, non animum mutant, qui trans mare currunt."

one or two others at least. But the long and the short of it is that you
will be your best letter yourself. You are quite wild with your anticipations,
and it is enough to make anybody else so to read them."

And again, Nov. 2 : —

"And now, my dear friend, my heart goes with you. I could say, *Ventorum-
que regat pater, Obstrictis aliis;*[1] but the right winds and ·auspices and influences with my most fervent wishes will certainly follow you in all your
wanderings. Write to me soon after you arrive at Paris; and especially and
fully from England, where our admiration and affections fully meet. I have
commended you very cordially to Ticknor, and I authorize you to draw upon
him in my name to an unlimited extent.

" And now again, Farewell! *Vive et Vale!* Go, and God speed you! May
you live to be an honor and blessing to your friends and society even more
than you are now, and more than realize all our fondest wishes and anticipations. And so, Farewell! Always affectionately and faithfully yours."

Dr. Channing wrote : —

" I need not speak to you of the usual perils of travelling. Local preju-
dice and illiberal notions are worn off; but there is danger of parting too
with what is essentially, immutably good and true."

Rev. Andrews Norton, wrote, Nov. 6 : —

" You are, I trust, about to enjoy much and to learn much in Europe, to
lay up for life a treasure of intellectual improvement and agreeable recollections. You carry with you the cordial good wishes of Mrs. Norton and
myself. May God bless you, and make your life as honorable and useful as
you now purpose it shall be! "

Samuel Lawrence wrote, Dec. 6 : —

" And now, my dear friend, let me say you have many, many ardent
friends here who are sincerely attached to you, and who will look forward with
intense interest to your return home. In the mean time your letters will be
looked for with great interest. Mrs. L. begs me to say your note (parting)
she received, and will retain near her till we all meet. She regards you as a
brother, as does your friend."

Judge Story wrote from Cambridge, Dec. 2 : —

" We miss you exceedingly, for we were accustomed to derive a great deal
of comfort from your cheering presence. And already we begin to mourn
over you as one lost for the present, — a sort of banished friend, whom we can
ill spare at any time, and least of all just now. Depend upon it, the waves of
the Atlantic, as they waft you to France and England, will carry our warmest,
truest prayers, constant and fervid, for blessings on you. But no more of
this, or I shall relapse into sober sadness. . . . I saw Hillard yesterday. He

---

[1] Horace, I. Ode iii. 3.

seemed quite a lone man, and I am sure misses you exceedingly. Greenleaf is very well, and he and I talk you over constantly. . . . Farewell, my dear sir! May God preserve and bless you, wherever you are, on the restless ocean or the solid land! Believe me most truly and affectionately your friend.

Professor Greenleaf wrote, Jan. 28, 1838 : —

" And so, my dear friend, you are gone. We had so often made this enterprise of yours the subject of mirth, that I never regarded it real till the morning when I found your good father in the very article of leave-taking. The next day, as usual, I ran upstairs and rushed into your room with ' How fare ye? ' on my tongue; but alas, the executor and the appraisers were there; your writing table was dissected, and the *disjecta membra* scattered on the floor, ready to be taken into the sanctum of Mr. Hillard, which they now adorn.

> " One morn I miss'd him at the customed court (*scil.* Law Library),
> Along the (side) *walk*, and near his fav'rite tree;
> Another came, — nor at his known resort,
> Nor at the *Albion*, nor the *Dane* was he.

" I am almost tempted to murder the rest of Gray's ' Elegy,' and apply the epitaph, *mutatis mutandis.*

> "Thus left his home to wander o'er the earth
> A youth, to fortune and to fame *well* known:
> Fair Science frown'd not on his generous birth,
> And Jurisprudence mark'd him for her own.
>
> Large was his bounty and his soul sincere,
> Heaven did . . . *cœtera desunt.*

" . . . Here am I at the end of my paper, without saying any thing. But this is not composed for publication among the correspondence to be inter-larded in your biography; nor is it written like one of Charles Lamb's con-versations, by ' punch light,' for you know I am a tee-totaler. Wishing you with my whole heart the protecting care of Heaven during this pilgrimage, and its richest blessings for ever, yours affectionately."

Mrs. Greenleaf added a postscript : —

" MY DEAR FRIEND, — I cannot refrain from thanking you for your kind note, though it rang the knell of your departure. We entirely reciprocate all the kind regards which you express. We only wish that you may preserve inviolate all the feelings with which you left us, and that your cup may be filled to the brim with untold happiness. It will be a long time ere we cease to listen for your wonted footsteps, and to turn instinctively, when the door of our parlor opens, to see you enter.   Your affectionate friend."

Cleveland wrote from Philadelphia, Jan. 5 : —

" I got a very kind letter from you written from New York just before you sailed. I hope that you got a very kind one from me also, written about the same time. If you did not, I beg you to consider yourself as having received one, which will do just as well. I thought much of you after you sailed. The winds were fair and fresh, and the skies were bright, and the prayers and blessings of many kind hearts went with you."

Felton wrote to Sumner's father a few weeks later : —

" You judge rightly that any intelligence of Charles's welfare would be most acceptable to me, and I congratulate you from my heart on his safe arrival in France. He is now in the full enjoyment of eager and enlightened curiosity fully gratified, and if ever a young man merited such good fortune, by fine talents nobly employed, and generous feelings unceasingly cherished, that man is Charles Sumner. He has long been very dear to me; and no one of his numerous friends has sympathized more deeply in his honorable and brilliant career than I have, and no one will hear of his success and happiness in the exciting scenes he is now entering upon with livelier pleasure than I shall."

Hillard wrote Dec. 6, 1837 : —

" And now, my dear fellow, Farewell. May God bless you, and restore you to us with all your anticipations of enjoyment and improvement more than realized! May he be to you a pillar of fire by night and of cloud by day, and shield you from the perils of the land and the deep! If the good wishes of loving hearts were talismans of defence and protection, you would be well guarded indeed; for no one ever went away compassed about with a greater number. Once more, God bless you, and, Farewell."

At New York he passed an evening with Chancellor Kent, who gave him books for his voyage ; and had pleasant interviews with William C. Russell,[1] his classmate John O. Sargent, and other friends.

The night before he sailed, and early the next morning, he wrote many letters to relatives and friends, some of them covering several pages, — to his sister Julia, to young Frick, a law student in whose progress he had conceived an interest while the latter was an undergraduate, and himself an instructor in the Law School; to Mr. Daveis, Dr. Lieber, Professor Greenleaf, Longfellow, Cleveland, and Hillard. His luggage included a large number of books, copies of the " Jurist," of his Reports, and of the treatises of Judge Story, intended for presentation by himself or on behalf of the judge to English lawyers and judges.

---

[1] Professor Russell, of Cornell University, writes: "I saw him when on his way to Europe ; he called at my office in New York, handsomely dressed, — I remember the effect of his fashionable drab overcoat, — erect, easy, conscious of his strength; and when after a short visit he hurried off ' to see,' as he said, ' my man of business,' I felt that he had left childish things behind."

LETTERS.

BOSTON, Oct. 21, 1837.

Your last letters of Oct. 7 and Oct. 16 (last by express mail) have quite touched my heart by their fulness and warmth. I owe you a deep debt —

" The debt immense of endless gratitude " —

for your thorough interest in my travels, — a subject where my whole heart is. And yet our friendship is not to be measured by any reciprocity of obligation and performance. My heart throbs for you, and my mind thinks of your labors. What I can do to aid, encourage, and cheer you, I yearn to do. This you feel persuaded of, I know; and that is enough. I shall remember you at every step of my journey, and in your dear fatherland shall especially call you to my mind. Oh, that I spoke your tongue! My mortification and humiliation is great to think of my ignorance. In my own language — dear native English! — I am sometimes told that I excel; and how I shall be humbled by my inability to place myself *en rapport* with the minds which I shall meet! I shall write you in German from Germany. There, on the spot, with the mighty genius of your language hovering over me, I will master it. To that my nights and days must be devoted. The spirits of Goethe and Richter and Luther will cry in my ears, " trumpet-tongued." I would give Golconda or Potosi or all Mexico, if I had them, for your German tongue.

What I shall write abroad I know not. I shall keep a journal, probably a full one, and shall trust to circumstances to suggest and bring out a subject. I shall remember your suggestions; treasure them all. All your requests I shall remember, and let you know that I shall not forget you. Your good advice I shall ponder well.[1] Laertes did not receive better instructions from old Polonius, when he was about going abroad, than you have given me. My heart is full on account of your kindness.

It is now Oct. 21, and I shall be more than a week longer in Boston. I shall leave my home Nov. 1. My business is not all closed yet, and I sometimes fear that I may lose another week; but I must tear away. Then for New York, Philadelphia, Baltimore, and Washington. You will hear from me often before I go, and I shall send longing, lingering looks behind. You will hear my lamentations across the sea, and also my rejoicings. How I shall leap with joy at the sight of Europe; how I shall sigh over my ignorance; how I shall long for some of my American friends to sympathize with

---

[1] *Ante*, p. 198.

the deep sympathy of friendship and a common admiration! You will hear of me often.

Good-by for a few days.　　　　As ever yours,

CHAS. SUMNER.

TO DR. FRANCIS LIEBER..

BOSTON, Nov. 19, 1837.

MY DEAR LIEBER, — "Yet in Boston!" you will exclaim. Ay; perverse fates and various cares have conspired to keep me in my durance for some days longer than I anticipated. In two days more, and my course is ended here. I have taken leave of all my friends, even of my dearest judge, and of those fair acquaintances[1] whom I beheld under your auspices, — *auspice Teucro*. I have consummated all my professional business, and now only linger to arrange a few personal affairs, to equip myself for travel, and to scrawl a few letters and some writing to which I am bound before leaving. I am heart-sick of appointing the day on which I shall leave; for I have found that, in my eagerness to get away, I have constantly underrated the labor I was to perform. Monday after Monday has been fixed upon; and when the day has come, business, with its hydra-head, presented some unexpected impediment. But now the day is within my grasp, — a few hours, that may be counted soon, with their swift-running sands, are all that is left.

I yesterday talked with Fletcher[2] about your "Political Ethics." We debated the question, whether a citizen should be obliged, under a *penalty*, to vote, as he is to serve on the jury. If voting be a duty and not a privilege, should not the duty be enforced by law? At our recent election two of our wealthiest citizens, whose position in society is mainly accorded on account of their wealth, declined voting. Their immense property was protected by the law, and yet they would not interfere or assist in the choice of the law-makers. I wish you would ponder this question for your book. I promised Mr. Fletcher that he should some day read a solution of it from your pen.

I lately fell in with John Neal, of Portland, and told him of your work. I described it so as to enlist his interest and that of my friend and host, Mr. Daveis, of Portland.

I shall hear of your success across the ocean, and perhaps may be able to send an echo back. But let me repeat, do not be over-hasty. Take time. You have a good plan and good materials, and do not mar both by too great anxiety to rush before the public.

As ever, faithfully,

CHAS. SUMNER.

----

[1] The Misses Appleton, afterwards Mrs. Longfellow and Mrs. Mackintosh.

[2] Richard Fletcher, *ante*, p. 162.

TO DR. FRANCIS LIEBER.

NEW YORK, Dec. 7, 1837.

MY DEAR LIEBER, — I have returned from a flying visit to Washington, where I found the warm reflection of your friendship. Gilpin was very kind to me, and placed me at my ease in the little business which I had on hand. He carried me for a portion of an evening to the President, where I met Forsyth and Woodbury.[1] The conversation turned upon Canadian affairs, and I was astonished by the ignorance which was displayed on this subject. But in a farewell letter, let me not consume your patience or my own by unfruitful politics.[2] . . .

And now, my dear friend, we must part. The sea will soon receive me on its stormy bosom. To-morrow I embark for Havre, and I assure you it is with a palpitating heart that I think of it. Hope and joyous anticipations send a thrill through me; but a deep anxiety and sense of the importance of the step check the thrill of pleasure. I need say nothing to you, I believe, in justification of my course, as you enter with lively feelings into my ambition and desires. Believe me, that I know my position and duties; and though I trust Europe may improve me, and return me to my own dear country with a more thorough education and a higher standard of ambition and life, yet it cannot destroy any simplicity of character which I possess, or divert me from the duties of the world. If you find it so on my return, I wish you to show your continued friendship by acting as my mentor, and correcting my aberration. There will be many who will be willing to cry out during my absence, " Europe will spoil him." Let the future determine this. To my sight that future is full of promise and hope; but I will not seek to lift its veil. Farewell, my dear friend; your friendship has been to me a source of pride and pleasure, and I hope to enjoy it much more. Remember me cordially to your wife, whom I most highly regard; and may God bless you all.

Faithfully and affectionately yours,

CHARLES SUMNER.

TO WILLIAM FREDERICK FRICK, BALTIMORE, MD.

ASTOR HOUSE, NEW YORK, Dec. 7, 1837.

MY DEAR FRICK, — I feel unwilling to leave the country, not to return perhaps until after the completion of your professional studies, without venturing to say a word to you of advice and encouragement, which you will

------

[1] Henry D. Gilpin, of Philadelphia, was then Solicitor of the Treasury; John Forsyth, of Georgia, and Levi Woodbury, of New Hampshire, were members of President Van Buren's Cabinet, — the former as Secretary of State, and the latter as Secretary of the Treasury.

[2] The omitted part of this letter relates to Dr. Lieber's "Political Ethics," advising at length as to the revision of the manuscript and mode of publication, and giving an account of what Sumner had done to promote public interest in it, and assurance of a continued care for its success while in Europe.

receive as from a friend, I trust. My conversation with you during the delightful afternoon at Mr. Donaldson's has interested me much in your course, and as you then appealed to me, I feel anxious to avail myself of the privilege afforded.

Let me suggest, then, that you should not hesitate to propose to yourself the highest standard of professional study and acquirement. Be not deterred by its apparent impracticability; but strive zealously, and you will be astonished at the progress you make. If you place a low standard at which to aim, you will not surely rise above it, even if you reach it; whereas, failing to reach a higher mark may be full of honor. In plain language, determine that you will master the whole compass of law; and do not shrink from the crabbed page of black-letter, the multitudinous volumes of reports, or even the gigantic abridgments. Keep the high standard in your mind's eye, and you will certainly reach some desirable point. I am led to make these suggestions from knowing, from my experience with law students, that the whisperings of their indolence and the suggestions of practitioners, with more business than knowledge, lead them to consider that all proper professional attainments may be stored up with very slight study. I know from observation that great learning is not necessary in order to make money at the bar; and that, indeed, the most ignorant are often among the wealthiest lawyers: but I would not dignify their pursuit with the name of a profession, — it is in nothing better than a trade. And I feel persuaded, from the honorable ambition which characterizes you, that you would not be content to tread in their humble track. Pursue the law, then, as a science; study it in books; and let the results of your studies ripen from meditation and conversation in your own mind. Make it a rule never to pass a phrase or sentence or proposition which you do not understand. If it is not intelligible, — so, indeed, that a clear idea is stamped upon your mind, — consult the references in the margin and other works which treat of the same subject; and do not hesitate, moreover, to confess your ignorance or inability to understand it, and seek assistance from some one more advanced in the pursuit. In this way, you will gradually — *per intervalla ac spiramenta temporis* — make advances and clear the way. You may seem to move slowly at first; but it is like the tardy labor of fixing the smooth rails on which the future steam-car is to bowl through the country. I would not have you understand that I am a devotee of authorities. There are few, I flatter myself, who are more disposed than I am to view the law as a coherent collection of principles rather than a bundle of cases. With me, cases are the exponents of principles; and I would have you read them in order to understand the principles of the law and the grounds of them. The best way, therefore, of reading them is in connection with some text-book, following the different references in the margin to their sources, and thus informing yourself of the reasons by which the principles are supported. The most important cases, in which some principle has been first evolved or first received a novel application, are called "leading cases," and all these should be read with great attention. These are the caskets of the law, containing the great fundamental principles which are applied in numerous subsequent cases of less impression. There are not many who can be prevailed upon to study reports in this way; but all who have ever done it, within my knowledge, have reaped ample benefit therefrom. In this connection, let me renew my advice that you should diligently study the characters of reporters and judges. It may seem a hard task at first blush, but I assure you it is of comparatively easy accomplishment to familiarize yourself with the character of every reporter and of all the important judges in English history. To this end read legal biography, wherever you can lay your hands upon it, — Roscoe's " Lives," the collection in the " London Law Magazine," " American Jurist," &c. Study legal bibliography; acquaint yourself with the time of publication of every legal work, and the repute in which it has been held; examine its preface and look at the book itself, so that you may have it bodily before you whenever you see it referred to.

I hope you will not consider me as suggesting too much when I add, Study the Norman or Law French. A few hours a day for a few weeks will give you a competent knowledge of it. There is a dictionary of the language by Kelham, but it is very poor, and you must rely upon your good wits to assist you. At the beginning of the " Instructor Clericalis," you will find a list of the principal abbreviations which prevail in the black-letter. Commence studying Norman by reading Littleton in an old copy of Coke-Littleton. There the translation will serve for a dictionary. Then attempt " The Mirror " or Britton, and a few pages of the " Year-Books." Do not consider that you will never have any use for this learning, and therefore that it is not worth the time it costs to obtain it. A few weeks will suffice to make you such a proficient in it that you will never again be obliged to study it. I assure you that I have found occasion for my scanty knowledge of this; and that, slight as it is, at two different times it has given me opportunities of no little value.

I need hardly add to these desultory recommendations that you cannot read history too much, particularly that of England and the United States. History is the record of human conduct and experience; and it is to this that jurisprudence is applied. Moreover, in the English history is to be found the gradual development of that portion of the common law which is called the Constitution, — for the British Constitution stands chiefly on the common law. The history of legislation in England contains the origin, also, of portions of the Constitution. History is of itself such a fascinating study that it can need to your mind no such feeble recommendation as mine.

But, above all, love and honor your profession. If you become attached to it, all that you read will make a lively impression on your mind, as the countenance of his mistress upon a lover. You cannot forget it. And here let me say that you can make yourself love the law, proverbially dry as it is, or any other study. Here is an opportunity for the exercise of the will. Determine that you will love it, and devote yourself to it as to a bride. Adopt the Horatian declaration, —

> "Quid verum atque decens curo et rogo, et omnis in hoc sum." [1]

Among the old English ballads is one which I read a long time ago, the

[1] Epis. I. i. 11.

name of which I have now forgotten; but it is of a knight who was compelled to make love to a hideous lump of deformity, without seemliness or knowledge. The knight did his *devoir*, and espoused his unwelcome bride; when lo! she suddenly, on the marriage eve, underwent an entire change, and appeared to his admiring gaze a queen of beauty and love. And such, my dear Frick, is the law, — harsh and forbidding at first; but let the suitor summon resolution, and determine that he will woo and win this tough jade, and the transformation at once takes place. Jurisprudence appears before him with untold attractions, and he wonders that he could have hesitated in the pursuit.

If you conclude to go to Cambridge, — and I think you would be much benefited by studying there, — I would advise you to go in April and continue till January. I will add to this long letter a couple of letters of introduction, which you may be pleased to present if you should make up your mind to go. They will give you at once the confidence and regard of the professors.

And now, pardon this most hasty scrawl, written after midnight, with a mind teeming rather with thoughts of travel and foreign lands than the law. Out of the fulness of the heart I have written, and only hope that you may read it with the pleasure with which it has been penned. If any thing I have assumed to say should be of any service to you, I shall be happy; if not, I shall still have the happiness of my humble effort to do some good, unsuccessful though it be.

In a short time, and I shall descend upon the sea. Let me bid you good-by, and believe me,

> Faithfully and affectionately yours,
>
> CHAS. SUMNER.

TO PROFESSOR SIMON GREENLEAF, CAMBRIDGE.

ASTOR HOUSE, Dec. 7, 1837.

MY DEAR FRIEND, — My hours of *terra firma* are numbered. To-morrow, before this time, I shall be rocking on the water. Qualms of sea-sickness will be upon me; and more than these, the anxiety and regrets at leaving friends, kindred, and country. It is no slight affair to break away from business which is to give me my daily bread, and pass across the sea to untried countries, usages, and languages. And I feel now pressing with a mountain's weight the responsibility of my step. But I go abroad with the firmest determination to devote myself to self-improvement from the various sources of study, observation, and society; and to return an *American*. Gladly will I receive any of those accomplishments or modifications of character which justly proceed from an extended survey of the human family. I pray fervently that I may return with benefits on my head; and that the affectations of character and indifference to country, which are thought sometimes to proceed from travel, may not reach me. All this is in the unknown future, which I may not penetrate. To the candid judgment and criticism of my friends I shall submit myself on my return; and I shall esteem it one of the highest duties of friendship to correct me, and to assist in bringing me back to the path of sense and simplicity, if it shall be found that I have departed from it. Do not let it be said, then, that I shall be spoiled by Europe; but rather suggest that I shall return with an increased love for my country, an admiration for its institutions, and added capacity for performing my duty in life. My standard of knowledge and character must be elevated, and my own ambition have higher objects. If this is not so, then shall I have seen Europe in vain, and my friends may regret their generous confidence in me.

My pen trembles in my hand as in that of a culprit who sees before him the awful tree, and counts the seconds which remain to him. I have a thousand things to say, but no time in which to express them; so with love to Mrs. Greenleaf, farewell, and believe me

Your affectionate friend,

CHARLES SUMNER.

TO HIS SISTER JULIA, AGED TEN YEARS.

ASTOR HOUSE, Dec. 7, 1837.

MY DEAR JULIA, — I don't remember that I ever wrote you a letter. I feel confident, however, that your correspondence cannot be very extensive; and, therefore, I may flatter myself that what I write you will be read with attention, and I trust, also, deposited in your heart. Before trusting myself to the sea, let me say a few words to you, which shall be my *good-by*. I have often spoken to you of certain habits of personal care, which I will not here more particularly refer to than by asking you to remember all that I have told you. . . . I am very glad, my dear, to remember your cheerful countenance. I shall keep it in my mind, as I travel over the sea and land, and hope that when I return I may still find its pleasant smile ready to greet me. Try never to cry. But, above all things, do not be obstinate or passionate. If you find your temper mastering you, always stop till you can count *sixty*, before you say or do any thing. Let it be said of you that you are always amiable. Love your father and mother, and brothers and sisters, and all your friends; cultivate an affectionate disposition. If you find that you can do any thing which will add to the pleasure of your parents, or anybody else, be sure to do it. Consider every opportunity of adding to the pleasure of others as of the highest importance, and do not be unwilling to sacrifice some enjoyment of your own, even some dear plaything, if by doing so you can promote the happiness of others. If you follow this advice, you will never be selfish or ungenerous, and everybody will love you. . . .

Study all the lessons given you at school; and when at home, in the time when you are tired of play, read some good books which will help to improve the mind. . . . If you will let Horace read this letter, it will do the same, perhaps, as one addressed to him. Give my love to mother, and Mary, and the rest.

Your affectionate brother,

CHAS.

TO GEORGE S. HILLARD, BOSTON.

ASTOR HOUSE, Dec. 8, 1837.

MY DEAR GEORGE, — It is now far past midnight, and I sail to-morrow forenoon. But I must devote a few moments to you. Your three letters have all been received, and have given me great pleasure. I have a fresh copy of " Wordsworth " as my cabin companion, and I hope that I may be penetrated with his genius. Sea-sickness now stares me in the face, and the anxiety arising from the responsibility of my course quite overcomes me. I have in my letters to several of my friends alluded particularly to my feelings, and also defended my plan of travel; but to you I need start no such idea. Your mind goes with me; and your heart jumps in step with my own.

I passed a pleasant day in Philadelphia, where I dined with Peters and supped with Ingersoll, and met all the first lawyers; then a delightful *home-like* day in Burlington, where S. P. received me with sisterly regard, I may almost say; and the whole family made my stay very pleasant. In New York I have been exceedingly busy, for the day I have been there, in arranging my money affairs, and writing letters of all sorts.

Keep your courage up, my dear Hillard; have hope, and don't bate a jot of heart. The way is clear before you, and you will bowl along pleasantly and speedily. Be happy. Remember me affectionately to all my friends, and to your wife; and believe me

Ever affectionately yours,

CHAS. SUMNER.

TO GEORGE S. HILLARD.

ON BOARD " ALBANY," Dec. 8, 1837.

MY DEAR GEORGE, — We have left the wharf, and with a steamer by our side. A smacking breeze has sprung up, and we shall part this company soon; and then for the Atlantic! Farewell, then, my friends, my pursuits, my home, my country! Each bellying wave, on its rough crest, carries me away. The rocking vessel impedes my pen. And now, as my head begins slightly to reel, my imagination entertains the glorious prospects before me, — the time-honored sites and edifices of the Old World, her world-renowned men, her institutions handed down from distant generations, and her various languages replete with learning and genius. These may I enjoy in the spirit that becomes a Christian and an American!

My captain is Johnston, a brother of Miss Johnston, the friend of Mrs. Sparks, and a very good seaman-like fellow. Fellow-passengers are four in number, — one a young man about twenty, a brother of the captain who makes his first trip; another, Mr. Munroe,[1] a commission merchant of Boston; and two others who I am told are French, though I have not yet been

---

[1] John Munroe, afterwards a banker in Paris.

able to distinguish them among the number of strangers who are going down
to return in the steamboat.   No ladies are aboard.   Your father was kind
enough to come to the wharf and see me off.

I have said farewell to you and all my friends; you know how my heart
yearns to them all.   Let them know that while I was leaving my native land
I thought of them.   I have them all before me; and my eyes are moist while
I think of them.   I cannot help it, — "albeit unused to the melting mood."

Again, Farewell,

CHARLES SUMNER.

TO HIS BROTHER GEORGE.

ON BOARD PACKET "ALBANY," Friday, Dec. 8.

MY DEAR GEORGE, — I have longed for a moment to write you, and
seize the few moments before the steamboat will leave.   We are under tow;
but a smart breeze promises soon to relieve the steamer and bear us swiftly
to the Atlantic.   And now, at parting, bear with a brother's advice.   You
have talents and acquirements which are remarkable, and which with well-
directed application will carry you to any reasonable point of human distinction.   Follow commerce in a liberal and scientific spirit, and become one of
the traffickers of the earth; or follow law, and become a thorough and liberal jurist and advocate, who sees and regards mankind as much as the special interests of his client.   Follow, my dear boy, an honorable calling, which
shall engross your time and give you position and fame, and besides enable
you to benefit your fellow-men.   Do not waste your time in driblets.   Deem
every moment precious, — far more so than the costliest stones.   Make
a rule, then, that you will pursue some regular studies at all seasons; and
keep some good book constantly on hand to occupy every stray moment.   And
consider your evenings, — how full of precious time, with boundless opportunities of study!   Do use them.   I am no Puritan, and would not debar you
from innocent pleasures; but there is a moderation to be observed.   My head
swims so with the motion of the vessel that I cannot write much longer.
Preserve an affectionate heart for your family, friends, and society, and be
not forward or vain.   Believe that modesty and a retiring disposition are
better recommendations than the contrary.   The letter is called for to be
carried up by the steamer; and so good-by, and believe me affectionately
yours,

CHAS.

I wished much to write Mary, before sailing; but my engagements have
been so numerous that I could not.   Let her know this.

CHAPTER X.

THE VOYAGE AND ARRIVAL. — DECEMBER, 1837, TO JANUARY, 1838. — AGE, 26-27.

THIS memoir, for the period of Sumner's absence from the country, must be confined chiefly to selections from his letters, and a journal which he began on the voyage and continued nearly four months.

The journal begins thus : —

Dec. 25, 1837. — Christmas. It is now seventeen days since I left New York for Havre in the ship "Albany," Captain Johnston.[1] My passage had been taken, and my bill on the Rothschilds in Paris obtained, on the 7th December. On that day dined with a pleasant party at Mrs. Ledyard's,[2] — the last dinner of my native land. Left early, called on one or two friends, and spent the residue of the hours before retiring — running far into the watches of the night — in writing letters ; saying some parting words to the friends whom I value. And a sad time it was, full of anxious thoughts and doubts, with mingled gleams of glorious anticipations. I thought much of the position which I abandoned for the present; the competent income which I forsook; the favoring tide, whose buoyant waters were bearing me so well, which I refused to take even at its ebb, — these I thought of, and then the advice and warnings of many whose opinions I respect. The dear friends I was to leave behind all came rushing before me, and affection for them was a new element in the cup of my anxieties. But, on the other hand, the dreams of my boyhood came before me: the long-pondered visions, first suggested by my early studies, and receiving new additions with every step of my progress; my desire, which has long been above all other desires, to visit Europe; and my long-cherished anticipations of the most intellectual pleasure and the most permanent profit. Europe and its reverend history, its ancient races, its governments handed down from old time, its sights memorable in story; above all, its present existing institutions, laws, and society, and its men of note and mind, followed in the train, — and the thought of

---

[1] Described in a letter of Sumner to Judge Story, Dec. 25, as "a man of science and veracity."

[2] Mrs. Susan Ledyard, 53 Crosby Street; a friend of Judge Story, and the daughter of Brockholst Livingston, a judge of the Supreme Court of the United States, 1806-23. She died March 7, 1864; surviving her husband, Benjamin Ledyard, more than half a century.

these reassured my spirits. In going abroad at my present age, and situated as I am, I feel that I take a bold, almost a rash, step. One should not easily believe that he can throw off his clients and then whistle them back, "as a huntsman does his pack." But I go for purposes of education, and to gratify longings which prey upon my mind and time. Certainly, I never could be content to mingle in the business of my profession, with that devotion which is necessary to the highest success, until I had visited Europe. The course which my studies have taken has also made it highly desirable that I should have the advantage derived from a knowledge of the European languages, particularly French and German, and also a moderate acquaintance with the laws and institutions of the Old World, more at least than I can easily gain at home. In my pursuits lately I have felt the want of this knowledge, both of the languages, particularly German, and of the Continental jurisprudence. I believe, then, that, by leaving my profession now, I make a present sacrifice for a future gain; that I shall return with increased abilities for doing good, and acting well my part in life. The temptations of Europe I have been warned against, and am fully aware of. I can only pray that I may be able to pass through them in safety, and add my firmest efforts to guard my footsteps. May I return with an undiminished love for my friends and country, with a heart and mind untainted by the immoralities of the Old World, manners untouched by its affectations, and a willingness to resume my labors with an unabated determination to devote myself faithfully to the duties of an American!

Such were the thoughts which passed through my mind during the last night before sailing, while I was tracing the hasty lines which were to go to some of my friends. The letters were written; and late at night, or rather near morning, I went to bed.

The "Albany" left the wharf about noon, Dec. 8, and, while she was being towed by a steamer down the harbor, Sumner wrote letters to Judge Story, Hillard, and his brother George. A fresh breeze then took the vessel gayly along, and the spires of the city soon faded from view. He remained on deck, enjoying the splendid sight of "the ship bending to the wind," and keeping his eyes on the receding shore, "hill after hill and point after point," till all, except the Jersey headlands, "that met the most searching gaze was the blue line which marked the meeting of the waters and the land." Retiring then to his berth, he "thought of friends, and all that he had left behind, with confidence in their continued regard." "You cannot imagine," he wrote to Hillard, "the intensity with which my mind, during these moments, reverted to the old scenes and faces with which it was familiar."

The wind kept fair and strong, and the voyage, for one made in a sailing vessel and during the winter, was exceptionally rapid and agreeable.

JOURNAL.

Dec. 25.   On the fourth day I was rejoiced to find myself able to read, though lying in my berth.   Previously my time had passed without the relief which this at once afforded.   Chancellor Kent had been kind enough to advise me to take a stock of pleasant books, and I had provided myself with some on the morning of sailing.   I read the fourth and fifth parts of Lockhart's "Life of Scott," James's novel of "Attila," Cooper's "England," and the "Life of Burr," while stretched in my berth; and never were books a greater luxury: they were friends and companions where I was, in a degree, friendless and companionless.

At the end of the first week I was able, with some ado, to appear at the dinner-table.   I know no feeling which, in a small way, is keener than for a man disabled by the weakness rather than the nausea of sea-sickness, with his appetite returning upon him like a Bay of Fundy tide, to lie in his berth and hear the clatter of plates and the merry voices of his fellow-passengers, as they attacked a turkey or a duck, and as another cork briskly left the bottle.   Our dinners I found quite pleasant.   Our company was small, — Mr. John Munroe, a young merchant going to establish himself in Paris; Mr. Darlington, a midshipman on leave of absence for his health; M. Vasseur, a young Frenchman returning home after upwards of a year's absence; and a young man, a brother of the captain.   And though with none of these did I have any particular sympathy, — any thing, indeed, which under other circumstances would have led to more than a passing acquaintance, — yet I found them uniformly pleasant; and our dinners, between four and five o'clock in the afternoon, formed the *reunions* of the day.   Several times after dinner I revived my old and forgotten knowledge, first gained in college and with college abandoned, of whist and chess.[1]   A walk on the ever-wet deck, a talk with the captain, a hand at cards or at the chess-board, reading, and the study of French have occupied the week which has passed from the time of deserting my berth till now.   Our passage has been somewhat rough; but that was expected from the season.   We have, however, kept our course constantly, without being obliged to tack once.   We are now in the English Channel, passing over the grave of the Spanish Armada.   We have left Scilly and Lizard on our left, without however being able to catch a sight of them, and are now midway between the coasts of England and France.   My mind has felt a thrill under the associations of these waters; it is my first experience of the rich memories of European history.   On my left now are the chalky cliffs of England, — Plymouth, from which the Pilgrim ancestors of New England last started to come to our bleak places; also the Isle of Wight, consecrated by the imprisonment of the royal Charles; and the harbor of Portsmouth, big with the navies of England.   On my right is *la belle France* and the smiling province of Normandy; and the waters which now bear this American ship are the same over which Cæsar with his

---

[1] A letter to Hillard of Dec. 25 thus refers to these games: "Both of which acquired in college, I have found little time or inclination to pursue since; but, indeed, have put them away, with many other childish things of college life."

frail boats, and afterwards William of Normandy, passed to the conquest of England. Their waves dash now with the same foamy crests as when these two conquerors timidly entrusted themselves to their bosom. Civilization, in the mean time, with its attendant servants — commerce, printing, and Christianity — has been working changes in the two countries on either side; so that Cæsar and William, could they revisit the earth, might not recognize the lands from which they passed, or which they subdued. The sea receives no impress from man. This idea Byron has expanded in some of the most beautiful stanzas he has written in the " Childe Harold."

On Christmas Day, besides writing in his journal, he wrote letters to Hillard and Judge Story. To Hillard he wrote: " It is now seventeen days, and I am without news of you and your affairs, and of all our common friends; and I feel sad to think that many more days will elapse before I shall hear from you. When you write, dwell on all particulars; tell me about all my friends, give me every turn of the wheel." To Judge Story he wrote: " It is now about seven o'clock on the evening of Christmas; allowing about five hours for difference of time between this longitude and Cambridge, it will be about two o'clock with you; and your family, with Mrs. Story in restored health, I trust, are now assembling for the happy meal. I have just left the dinner-table, where I remembered all in a glass of Burgundy." In both letters, as in his journal, he dwelt upon the historic scenes which belong to the English Channel. While writing the letter to Judge Story, a French whaleman came in sight, " the tricolor flapping in the wind," the first sail seen during the voyage, — a refreshing sight, but momentary, as both vessels were speeding in opposite directions. On the evening of the 25th, the captain descried dimly Start Point, in Devonshire; and the next morning Sumner saw Cape Barfleur, about fifteen miles to the right, — his first glimpse of Europe, and " the first land he had seen since the afternoon of the eighth, when he went below while the headlands of New Jersey were indistinctly visible on the distant horizon."

On account of unfavorable winds encountered in the Channel, the " Albany " did not come to anchor at the Havre docks till early on the morning of the 28th, — less than twenty days from the time of sailing.

JOURNAL.

Dec. 26, 1837. At half-past two o'clock this afternoon a pilot from Havre came aboard. We were still off Cape Barfleur, and, as he informed me, fifty-four miles from Havre. I inquired after news, and particularly from England; to which his reply was, *tout est tranquille,* — his idea of news seeming to resolve itself into the question of peace or war.

Dec. 27. Still in Havre Roads, and anchored within three miles of the city. Adverse winds have disappointed our expectations, and doomed us to a longer imprisonment. The city may be dimly descried beneath a heavy mist; but every thing is so indistinct that I cannot form any definite idea of its size or general appearance. To-night I sleep on the waters of France.

He wrote to his sister Mary, the 27th, giving an account of the voyage, and expressing a brother's interest in her studies: —

Before leaving New York I intended to write you, and say a few words on your studies and education in other respects, which I felt assured you would not be unwilling to receive from an elder brother. But the multitude of letters which I felt called upon to write, and which kept me engaged into the watches of the morning, saved you from the homily. You will not forget what I have told you, either with regard to study, or, what is more important than study, health. I need not here particularize what I have said. Try to understand every thing as you proceed; and cultivate a love for every thing that is true, good, and pure. I need not exhort you to set a price upon every moment of time; your own convictions, I have no doubt, have taught you that minutes are like gold filings, too valuable to be slighted, — for a heap of these will make an ingot. Give my love to mother, and all the family. Tell George to write me a brisk, news-full letter.

Your affectionate brother,

CHAS.

JOURNAL.

Dec. 28, 1837. At length in Havre, with antiquity staring at me from every side. At four o'clock this morning weighed anchor, and drifted with the tide and a gentle wind to the docks; a noble work, contrived for the reception of vessels, and bearing the inscription of *An IX. Bonaparte 1ᵉʳ Consul,* — the labor of this great man meeting me on the very threshold of France. Dismissed from the custom house we went to the Hôtel de New York, where a smiling French woman received us, and we were shown each of us to a chamber. The house was small and narrow, and the stairs composed of tiles; but the chamber into which I was conducted harmonized with my anticipations of a French apartment. The room was of moderate size, with a floor of hexagon tiles partially covered with a neat rug-like carpet; with a bed plump and neat as imagination could picture, with a crimson coverlet and curtains; with curtains to the window of linen with a border of red, and with two engravings in the room of some of the glorious scenes of the French Republic. The whole was un-American. I should have known that I was in a foreign place, even if the reality of a sea-voyage had not given me the completest assurance of it. My apartment taken, for which I am to pay three francs per day, I at once escaped to view the city. And here I felt a gush of interest at every step. Nothing was like what I had been accustomed to. Every thing was old; and yet to me every thing was new. Every building which I passed seemed to have its history. Old Time himself seemed to look down from its roof. And yet there was little in the way of architecture; the single element of interest was antiquity combined with novelty. I saw but one street with a sidewalk. All others slanted from the side to the centre, *ad mediam filam viæ*, where there was the gutter; and all were slippery with mud and moisture, and uncomfortable to the feet from the large stones with which they were paved. Scrub horses with heavy and inconvenient harness; men and women with huge wooden shoes which clattered over the stones; women in caps and without bonnets; market women on donkeys and horses, with panniers containing their provisions on either side, — these constantly met my eye. I felt as I looked about me that I was in a country where custom and prescription were regarded; where changes, and of course improvements, were slow to be introduced, from the impression that what was established was for the best. In the United States the extreme opposite of this character prevails. Nothing is beyond the reach of change and experiment. There is none of the prestige of age about any thing, and we are ready at any moment to lay our hands on any custom or mode of business and modify it; and, though we may sometimes suffer by this proclivity, yet it is the means of keeping us constantly on the *qui vive* for improvements. The common people in Havre now clatter over the ground in the same shoes which their great-grandfathers wore, and harness their horses in the same clumsy style. It appears that women do more out-door work than with us. The market seemed full of them, and we met them in every street carrying articles of different kinds. In my walk I wandered into the cathedral at the hour in which they were celebrating Mass, and there found many market women, as they appeared to be, who had slipped in with their baskets on their arms, and for a few moments counted their beads, and, bending to the ground in the attitude of devotion, looked absorbed in prayer. There is something tangible and palpable in the Catholic faith which the common mind readily takes hold of, as a handle. I have never seen people in the United States of this grade, except at a Methodist meeting, so absorbed in devotion. Ascending the hill at Havre, which I did in company with Mr. Emerson,[1] I had a beautiful prospect over the city beneath, and passed in view of many of the country houses of gentlemen belonging to the city. I could distinctly observe the wall and moat which surrounded the city; though the city has now actually outgrown the military strait-jacket by which it was invested. Some of the best portions are without the walls.

After a considerable walk took breakfast, say at twelve o'clock, — a late one, even for France; and it was a delicious meal, with light wine and coffee clear as amber. After walking round the city, I dined with Mr. Emerson at his house, whose acquaintance I have made through the introduction of my friend Cleveland. Our hour was between six and seven o'clock; stayed till

[1] Ralph Emerson, an American merchant, then resident in Havre, now living in San Francisco.

ten o'clock, and then walked home over the dirty and slippery streets. The chimes of midnight have this moment sounded from some ancient steeple; and I expect a pleasant sleep in my neat bed, after the confined quarters to which I have been doomed for so many nights.

The chief features which I am able to recognize as distinguishing Havre from an American city are (1), antiquity; (2), dress of women with caps and without bonnets in the street; (3), labor of women; (4), presence of the military and police, a soldier or policeman presenting himself at every turn; (5), narrowness and dirt of the streets; (6), houses of stone, and narrow and chimney-like. Of course, these are merely the features which have met the eye during the observation of a few hours.

Dec. 29, 1837. New scenes have been rising upon me with each moment; I find myself now with midnight at hand, and new objects were breaking upon me until I closed the door of my chamber. I can hardly believe in my personal identity. Such is the intensity of my present experience, that all I have undergone to reach here seems obliterated.

I enjoyed my first sleep ashore last night, in sheets of linen and on a pillow of down, as much as my excited imagination would allow, and early in the morning I prepared for Rouen; breakfasted at nine o'clock, at the hotel where I was stopping, on a mutton chop, light wine, and coffee. Wine in France appears to be a drink as common at breakfast as coffee; and, from the experience of two days, I should not feel disinclined to adopt the usage. I repaired to the place of starting for Rouen, and found the diligence on the point of leaving. My place, however, had been secured on the day before, when I had paid five francs as earnest-money, or a sort of pledge, which I was to forfeit if I did not present myself at the proper time. As soon as I arrived I was addressed in the rapid French style, " Montez! montez! " and the diligence immediately started. I had taken the place on the top. My seat was protected by a heavy and cumbersome covering, like that of a chaise, and my first desire was to have that thrown back; but my French vocabulary would not enable me to express my wish, so that I was obliged to resort to the universal language of gesture and pantomime. My desire being understood, I was informed in French that the top should be turned back when we stopped to change horses. And it was done.[1] . . . I was alone on top and tried to enter into conversation with *le conducteur*. He took me for an Englishman, and sought to flatter me by pointing to the Seine, and calling it the Thames. When I undeceived him, he said, pointing to the snake-like stream, that it was the Mississippi of France. All the while he and the postilion were whipping their scraggy horses with constant lashes. It was an amusing sight to see the *empressement* with which they applied the lash, taking hold of the whip-handle with both hands and using it for several minutes together. There were sometimes five and sometimes six horses to the diligence, — all of them short and thick, with rough, un-

---

[1] The diligence is described at length, and particularly as " very much in the shape of a Boston Booby-hut on runners in the winter."

combed manes, and tails tied up; a practice which seems to be universal here with regard to horses. Their tails are not docked, but suffered to grow to their natural length, and then tied up to about the same shortness with the docked tail. On our way to Rouen, which was fifty-four miles, we changed horses as many as a dozen times. I succeeded on the way so well with my little French as to extract considerable information from *le conducteur*, and also to add to my facility in the use of the language. Now, indeed, I feel the situation of a foreigner, who cannot speak the language of the country where he is. He is cut off from society and from a great source of knowledge, and his thoughts are all imprisoned within himself. In the few hours during which I have been in France, my mind has been chafing in the chains by which it is now confined. I feel sensibly the advantages which I lose from not being able to speak the language, and I feel mortified at being restrained to the uttering of a few sentences, and that in such a stammering uncouth way, that the very postilion stares at me. However, I shall not be deterred. My rule is to practise upon everybody; to take every opportunity to speak the language, even if it be but a word; for every time of trial gives me assurance, and also adds to my stock of words or phrases. Accordingly I did not hesitate all the way from Havre to Rouen to interrogate *le conducteur* to the full extent of my knowledge; and he was pleased to endure me with great grace.

The road from Havre to Rouen (the upper one) which I travelled was mostly through a level champaign country. It was very smooth, and made easy going for the horses compared with our roads; though the lowness of the wheels of the diligence, and its general cumbersomeness, went far to counterbalance the facilities of the road. Within a few miles from Havre we passed through Harfleur, the same, I suppose, which Harry V. of England besieged. It is a small but very ancient place, with streets so narrow that it seemed as if I could span them, and surrounded by a decayed wall and moat. It was the last part of the month of December, and yet the plough and harrow were seen constantly in the fields, and sheep grazing, with a shepherd and dog in attendance. How the romance of poetry and bucolics was dashed by the appearance of these men! Their flocks did not appear to consist of more than forty or fifty sheep; and they were rude-looking men, who lounged about with a cane instead of a shepherd's crook. Their vocation arises from the absence of fences to separate different parcels of land. Here and there you may see a thin ridge or mound of earth, or a hedge, in the neighborhood of a house, and surrounding some choice field; but nearly all the lands are without any kind of fence. This gives the country a very open appearance to one accustomed to the stone walls and rail fences of New England. By the wayside I constantly saw cottages and barns covered with thatch, which was generally overgrown with moss. The thatch appears to be straw matted on the roof quite thickly. In observation of the country, and in reflection upon what I saw, the time passed away until, after descending a long and steep hill, we entered Rouen, — time-honored Rouen. If Havre appeared ancient, what shall I say of Rouen? I seemed among catacombs. Nothing but the living countenances and the merchandise at the windows appeared fresh.[1]

Next took lodgings at the Hôtel de Normandie, and dined; and then, having fixed some landmarks in my eye, walked by the lights of the shop windows through the principal streets of the city; passed by two theatres, and about eight o'clock visited one of them. My knowledge of French did not serve me so that I was able to take much interest in the play; and though every thing that I saw both on and off the stage had an interest for me, yet it was all blurred by my ignorance of the language. The audience appeared very respectable. The accommodations were different, as well as more various, than those in our theatres. Sentinels were on guard before the doors of both the theatres. During the play, I left the house and again wandered round the city before commencing this record of the day. I must not forget to mention that, while we were at dinner, a beautiful girl entered the room (there were about eighteen or twenty at table), and, having first touched her guitar, sang to its accompaniment several pretty French songs, and then handed her little tin box to each person at the table. She stood behind me, and first presented her box to me. I dropped into it a few sous, and regarded the whole scene as thoroughly and beautifully characteristic of France. She was listened to with pleasure and respect.

Dec. 30 (Saturday). A day at Rouen, the ancient capital of Normandy; and my eyes and mind have been constantly on the stretch with interest and observation. Shortly after breakfast, in company with a fellow-traveller, I took a *commissionnaire*, or guide, to conduct me to the interesting objects in the place. He spoke English, and, as a resident of the town, had a superficial acquaintance with it; and therefore was in a degree useful, though afterwards I learned from examining the guide-book (which I should have read at first) that many of his stories were vulgar errors. We first visited the cathedral, where we spent about three hours: as many weeks devoted to it would leave its immense fund of interest for the intelligent traveller unexhausted. The cathedral[2] is the great lion of the north of France, and is said to be the finest specimen of Gothic architecture on the Continent. Certainly it is immensely vast and elaborate, transcending all that my imagination had pictured as the result of this architecture, The minuteness of the workmanship testifies that it was done by those who commanded hands for labor with a facility not unlike that which summoned the thousands of laborers who raised the pyramids of Egypt. I can hardly imagine such a work at the present day. No building, unless it be Westminster Abbey, abounds more in historical associations. Enlarged, if not built, by the ancient dukes

---

[1] To Judge Story he wrote, Jan. 6, 1838: "The whole country was full of novelty. During the day I was kept at the highest pitch of excitement, and when, at dusk, we entered the ancient city of Rouen, it seemed as if all the dreams of my boyhood were to be realized." And again of his visit to the cathedral at Rouen: "Need I tell you that my whole frame thrilled with every step and every glance of my eye. I was fully recompensed for the expense of my journey and the imprisonment of a sea voyage. Such floods of feeling and reflection as were started in my mind made me forget all that had passed."

[2] Sumner visited Rouen and its cathedral some years afterwards, March 21 and 22, 1857.

of Normandy anterior to the conquest of England, it is the chosen place where the bones of many of them repose. Here are the remains of Rollo, the first duke of Normandy and the ancestor of the Conqueror, and over them a monumental effigy; of William of the Long Sword, his son; of Henry, the father of Cœur de Lion; and here the Lion-heart itself was deposited. At a later day, the remains of the Duke of Bedford — the English regent of France, discomfited by the Maid of Orleans — were deposited here; and an inscription behind the great altar marks the spot. Different parts, in the neighborhood of altars, are occupied by inscriptions and engraved effigies of bishops, archbishops, cardinals, and other eminent men, whose standing or character gave them admission after death to this company. Over all was the vast Gothic roof, stretching on with its ancient and numerous arches in imposing perspective; and the light which was shed upon this scene came through richly painted windows, where were martyrdoms and sufferings and triumphs, such as the history of Christianity records. And here was I, an American, — whose very hemisphere had been discovered long since the foundation of this church, whose country had been settled, in comparison with this foundation, but yesterday, — introduced to these remains of past centuries, treading over the dust of archbishops and cardinals, and standing before the monuments of kings and the founder of a dynasty, the greatest and best established of modern Europe. Now, indeed, may I believe in antiquity and in the acts which are recorded. Often, in fancy, have I doubted if such men as history mentions ever lived and did what we are told they did: if William of Normandy actually conquered England; and, indeed, if such a place as England existed for him to conquer. But this fancy, this Pyrrhonism of the imagination, is now exploded. These monuments and their inscriptions, with the traces of centuries upon them, in this holy place, bear testimony to what I have read.

In this immense building there are no pews, but simply a few chairs placed in the middle of the church. Every thing is stone; the floor, the pillars, and walls are all of stone. I ascended the highest tower, by a winding staircase which communicated apparently with a great number of other staircases, all of stone, running in every direction about the tower. Indeed, every step that I took showed the extent of the building. From the tower I saw the palace of the archbishop, and his gardens beneath; besides looking down completely upon the whole city and the adjoining country, with the Seine curling through the beautiful meadows, green at this very close of the month of December.

Next passed to a building scarcely less interesting or ancient, L'Église de St. Ouen. Beautiful rose-painted windows, tombs, and a splendid Gothic *coup d'œil* arrested the attention. From this we passed to the adjoining building, the Hôtel de Ville, or city hall. Here was the museum, a gallery of paintings and statues: we hardly paused long enough fully to study a single picture, much less several hundred; and yet I cannot but record the admiration, blind and untutored, which was excited by this first view of the arts in Europe. In the collection, a painting was pointed out as that of

Raphael: it was a picture of the Mother of the Saviour, with the infant in her arms; it did not, however, particularly arrest my attention. From the gallery we passed to the library, consisting principally of the books which formerly belonged to the church and monastery of St. Ouen. One of the books was a show-piece, very curious, being a splendid folio of vellum, splendidly illuminated and printed with the pen by one of the monks of St. Ouen, and which cost him the labor of thirty years. It was a collection, I think, of the music used in the monastery, — a monument of the time and labor employed for a trivial purpose. Thirty years of time spent in the manual operation of making a single copy of an unimportant work!

The Palais de Justice was a very interesting building, — ancient and finished with the elaborateness which seems to have been lavished upon public buildings in earlier times. One of the rooms was covered with a ceiling of oak, which had become black as ebony from age, and was studded with golden knobs. Several courts were in session; but my guide could not explain to me about them, and my knowledge of French was so imperfect that I could with difficulty ascertain even the general nature of the discussion which was proceeding. The judges appeared to be numerous; in one court, which seemed the highest, — perhaps La Cour Royale, — there were as many as half a dozen, all having a peculiar costume, consisting of a cap, bands round the neck, and gown. The lawyers wore gowns and caps, and the dresses appeared to be different in the different courts. In Paris I hope to make these matters more of a study; but at this time my means of getting correct information were so small, and my time so limited, that I passed to other objects, which possessed an interest into which I could more readily enter. Particularly among these was the market-place in which the Maid of Orleans was burnt;[1] and a building which the Duke of Bedford was said to have occupied, and which had a beautiful *relievo* on its wall of the meeting of Francis and Henry at the Field of the Cloth of Gold. Bridges, market-places, &c., we visited; also we passed in a narrow street the house in which Pierre Corneille was born, on which was printed in large characters, *La Maison du Grand Corneille*. It was a tall and well-looking house, the lower part of which, I think, was occupied by a brazier. A beautiful bronze statue of Corneille has been quite recently erected by subscription on one of the bridges. My guide spoke of him as one of the greatest men of France: the same in France, he said, as that great man that lived in England. Shakspeare, I said. "Yes," said he; "he died not many years ago"!

At dinner to-day we had the music of the harp instead of the guitar, and an attendant appeal to charity.

It seems that I could spend months in Rouen and still find interest. If I had time and fortune I should like, while here, to read the various histories of this wonderful cathedral, and master the romantic history of Normandy. From Normandy sprang the long line of kings that has governed England; and here are the tombs of the founders of this dynasty. Two of the finest specimens of Gothic architecture that exist in Europe are here to be seen,

---

[1] Place de la Pucelle.

also. However, to-morrow night is the last on which the "hells" of Paris are to be open, they being abolished after that time by law; and I wish, if possible, to see them, besides being in Paris on New Year's Day. To-morrow, therefore, I shall start for Paris.

Dec. 31, 1837. At a quarter before seven o'clock I found myself in the *coupé*, with a fellow-passenger from America, and a French lady. The apartment was small, being just large enough for three persons to sit snugly. The gray light of morning was beginning to prevail, and as we passed under the towers of the cathedral, it seemed to invest them with an additional air of antiquity. It was not the moonlight, which struck through the numerous trellises and interstices, but the dim light of morning, which brought them out by a sort of relief against the sky. We went at a rapid rate, the horses galloping much of the way, and the diligence having a motion which I must confess to be, independent of the smoothness of the roads, remarkably easy, and very much like that of our rail-cars. This easiness is caused chiefly, I think, by the lowness of the springs. On the way I taxed all my French to enter into conversation with the French lady; it was commenced by my inquiring if she would have the windows open or shut. On our making known that we were Americans, she inquired about our voyage, about the commerce and manufactures of the country, and listened with the politest attention to all that we said, and appeared to understand it. We talked of the cathedral at Rouen; and I told her that our forests were our cathedrals. Our fair companion was not yet beyond the age of considerable personal attractions. She was our *cicérone* on the route, giving us the names of the towns through which we passed, and pointing out some of the principal *châteaux*. It was Sunday; and yet, as we drove through the different towns, we could observe none of the signs which mark this day in New England. Here "Sunday shines no Sabbath day;" all things proceed as on week days. The roads were thronged with market women, with their heavy burdens; the markets, through which we passed, were full of them. The shops were all open; the windows full of various articles, — the baker rolling his bread; the carpenter at his plane; the smith at his forge; the farrier shoeing his horse. Upwards of forty miles from Paris we saw one mark of an approach to a great city: we there commenced with a paved road, over which we rattled for the remainder of the way; entering Paris between seven and eight o'clock in the evening by the Barrière du Roule.[1] And here I became absorbed with wonder at the throbbings of this mighty heart of France. We drove through long streets with great rapidity, through which innumerable other vehicles were driving with the same rapidity, building after building bursting upon us, and long lines of splendid shops, until at last we were landed at the bureau of all the *Messageries Royales* of France, — the focus of all the diligences from every quarter, situated in the Rue des Victoires. Here our baggage was inspected by an officer of the police. We gave our trunks to porters, who, by means of a sort of rack, took them, large and

---

[1] Situated at the intersection of the Rue du Faubourg Sainte Honoré and the Avenue de Wagram.

heavy as they were, on their backs to the Hôtel Montmorency, Boulevard Montmartre No. 12.

Dinner despatched, I went about ten o'clock to Frascati's, — the great "hell" of Paris. By law all public gaming-houses are forbidden after the first of January, which commences this midnight. Passing through an outside court, and then a short entry, we entered an antechamber, where there were a large number of servants in livery who received our hats and outside garments, no one being allowed to enter the gambling *salons* with either. The hats already hanging up and in the custody of the servants seemed innumerable, and yet the servants had no numbers or marks by which to indicate to whom each hat belonged; trusting entirely to recollecting the countenance. The door of the *salon* was then opened; and the first table of gamblers was before us, — men young, middle-aged, and old; with the bloom of youth yet mantling on the face, and with the wrinkles and gray hairs of age. This table was a *roulette*, I believe. It was about the size of a common billiard table, and it was completely surrounded by a double and triple row of persons; the first row sitting, and the others standing. Among those sitting were two or three women of advanced age; and moving about the room were several younger, undoubtedly Cyprians, possessing considerable personal attractions. Passing into the next *salon* through an open door, we found a larger table, with players more intent and more numerous, where the game turned upon cards. The silver and gold spread on the table was to a vast amount; and I saw one man, with a lip that quivered and a hand that trembled, stake his double handful of gold on a single throw, — amounting to many hundred dollars. Little wooden rakes or hoes were used to draw the money in. The third *salon* had a table where the chance turned upon dice. It was a scene which I am glad to have witnessed. The excitements of gambling have been said to be strong; and I can understand how persons have been drawn by its fascinations within its terrible maelstrom. They try once for experiment, and are seduced by a momentary success, or excited by a loss, and observing others, perhaps, winning large sums, they are finally absorbed in the whirling vortex. Several of the friends that I went with ventured several francs, and alternately lost and won. I am free to confess that I felt the temptation, but I restrained my hand. To-night being the last night, the rooms were very full, the gamblers wishing to have their last game. We left sometime before midnight, thinking that there might be some disturbance at that time, when the transforming wand of the law would exercise its power. I however walked the boulevards, which were splendidly illuminated by the shop windows till long after midnight, as well as thronged by people; and at twelve o'clock I stood before Frascati's. The people were retiring from within, and as the women came out they were subjected to the sneers and jeers of a considerable crowd who had collected in the street about the gateway. A few of the police were present, who at once interfered to prevent the uproar; and in a few minutes three horsemen rode into the crowd, and speedily dispersed them. Such was the last night of Frascati, and my first night in Paris.

CHAPTER XI.

DURING his first week in Paris, Sumner found no time to continue his journal. "In this hasty diary," he wrote, a few weeks later, "there is no memorial of my first week. Suffice it to say that I was kept in such an intoxicating whirl by the novelty which every thing had for my eyes, and every moment of my time was so intensely occupied, that I found not a fraction for this record. Of the letters which I brought to Paris I presented but few, feeling my utter incompetence for any French intercourse from my ignorance of the language."

His first call was upon Foelix,[1] the editor of the *Revue Étrangère*, with whom he had, before leaving home, exchanged letters. With him Sumner maintained, while in Paris, the most cordial relations. Foelix, by the place of his birth and early life which had passed from one sovereignty to another, combined in himself, as it were, two nationalities, — the German and the French. He was cosmopolitan in his learning and sympathies, and studied jurisprudence as a science. He had a large acquaintance with contemporary *savans*, and in conversation spoke unreservedly of their merits or pretensions. He was not above the everyday services which are invaluable to a foreign student not yet familiar with the country, its language, teachers, and authors. Sumner visited him freely, and seems to have regarded him, while in Paris, very much as he had regarded Lieber at home.

---

[1] Jean Jacques Gaspard Foelix, 1791–1853. He was born in the Electorate of Treves, and began, in 1814, the practice of the law at Coblentz. Upon the transfer of the Rhenish provinces from France to Germany, which soon followed, he had occasion to deal with questions involving a conflict between German law and the French code. He was thus led to the study of comparative jurisprudence, — a department in which he excelled all his contemporaries. Removing to Paris in 1826, and naturalized as a French citizen in 1829, he founded, in 1833, the *Revue Étrangère de Législation et d'Économie Politique;* the name of which was, in 1840, changed to the *Revue Étrangère et Française de Législation, de Jurisprudence, et d' Économie Politique:* aided by associates, he conducted this Review till 1850. He was the author of a treatise on the "Conflict of Laws" (*Traité du Droit International Privé*).

He was also indebted to Foelix for a personal introduction to Pardessus. Of comparative jurisprudence, which was the specialty of Foelix, Sumner spoke, some years afterwards, as " kindred to those other departments of knowledge which exhibit the relations of the human family, and show that amidst diversity there is unity." [1]

In a letter to Judge Story, Jan. 21, he wrote of his first call on Foelix : —

In No. 7 Rue de Verneuil, Foelix, with two maiden sisters, occupied an apartment on what we should call the second floor. On being shown into the room of the learned Pundit, I summoned all my French, and asked, " *Est-ce Monsieur Foelix, que j'ai l'honneur de voir?* " to which he replied in the affirmative. I then said, " *Je m'appelle Charles Sumner.*" His reply convinced me that I had pronounced my French so badly that he did not understand me, for he inquired if I had seen Mr. Sumner lately. Then ensued a series of *contretemps*. He did not speak a word of English; and my French was no more fit for use than a rusty gun-barrel, or than the law of a retired barrister. Then came to our assistance his sister, — a lady, say thirty-five or forty. She knew English so as to speak it pretty well, though rather painfully. With her as interpreter, I made known who I was, whence I came, &c. I presented my letters and answered ·Foelix's inquiries, particularly with regard to you. I very soon found, however, that our mutual ignorance of any language which could serve as a medium for conversation would render our intercourse of but little interest for the present. Foelix is a German by birth, you know, and retains those national features which have continued from the time of Tacitus. He is about the size of Dr. Follen, only somewhat stouter, with hair on his head quite thin but not gray. I should call him fifty-five years old. He is not a man of the world or of dress, but he is absorbed in his Review, upon which he works very hard, and seems full of the dignity and importance of his vocation. In his study, or office, which is a room about as large as your parlor, sat his eldest sister busily engaged in copying papers. I have understood that she is a perfect lawyer, having diligently read all the codes; and that she assists him very much in his Review. I was amused at the interest which he took in having me economically established. When I informed him where my lodgings were, — being in one of the hotels on the boulevards, — he expressed an orthodox German horror, and told me I must abandon them immediately; and he assisted me in getting lodgings on the same side of the river with himself. I have changed again since he established me, and am now in the same house with George Shattuck.[2] You may be glad to hear that he is doing more honor to himself and his country than any other young American has done since James Jackson.[3]

[1] Works, Vol. I. p. 270.

[2] Dr. George C. Shattuck, a physician of Boston, always a valued friend of Sumner. They were fellow-students in college, and also in the Law School.

[3] A young physician of Boston, who, after professional studies ín Paris, died in 1834, soon after his return home.

Travel and residence abroad have had their best influence upon him. . . .
Have you read Tocqueville's " Democracy in America "?

During his first two months in Paris, Sumner employed his
time almost solely in acquiring the capacity to speak the French
language. He had studied it in college, but could not use it in
conversation. Repeatedly, in his journal and letters, he lamented
this deficiency in his education. To Hillard he wrote, Jan. 6:
" I shall renounce every thing until I learn to speak French.
To that my first labors must be devoted. Think of me coming by childlike progression to the use of my tongue, hearing
sounds which convey no idea, and thus, in a degree, debarred
from the society and scenes of this great metropolis." Most of
the time he took lessons of two teachers; he became a subscriber
at Galignani's reading-room; frequented theatres, following the
actors with the printed play before him; and attended lectures,
not merely those which treated of his favorite studies, but those
also which related to other departments, in order to become
familiar with the sounds of the language. He postponed visits
to places of interest, and abstained from society, until he had
overcome the difficulty which he so much deplored. His perseverance met with a success which highly gratified him. When
he arrived in Paris, he could understand hardly a sentence in
French when spoken to him. In less than a month he could
follow a lecturer; in six weeks participate in conversation; and
at the end of three months he served as interpreter before a
magistrate on the examination of a fellow-countryman.

Of the one hundred and fifty or more lectures which he attended, nearly all were given by professors eminent in their
respective departments, — as Rossi, Ampère, Lenormant, Biot,
Jouffroy, Dumas, and Saint-Marc Girardin. In the hospitals he
saw Roux, Louis, Dubois, and Cloquet, attending to patients and
followed by students. At the theatres and opera he saw and
heard Mars, Georges, Déjazet, Rubini, Tamburini, Lablache,
Persiani, and Grisi ; in the church, Coquerel ; and in the Chambers of Peers and Deputies, Dupin, Berryer, Guizot, Thiers,
Odilon Barrot, Arago, and Lamartine.

During his sojourn in Paris, he wrote fully of his experiences to
Judge Story, Hillard, Greenleaf, Longfellow, Felton, Cleveland,
Charles S. Daveis, Dr. Lieber, and William W. Story. Most of
these letters, as well as some to his family, are preserved, — from

which extracts, in connection with the journal, will be given. One
remarks, in reading his letters, how warm was his affection for
his friends, and how much he craved tidings from them. He
wrote to Hillard, Jan. 6: "I do not forget you and our 'Five
of Clubs' on this my birthday. I wish that we could all meet
this evening and renew old scenes and recollections." And to
Judge Story, Feb. 7: "It is now two months since I left the
United States, and when I consider what I have seen, and the
new impressions I have received, it seems like two years. The
time is lengthened by another consideration, — the sense of
my solitude, and the cessation of intercourse with those friends
to whom I am so tenderly attached. Give me letters! A cup of
water was never more inspiriting to the battle-worn soldier than
is a letter to me at this distance from friends."

JOURNAL.

Jan. 8, 1838 (Monday). This morning went to lodgings on the other side
of the river, No. 3 Rue St. Dominique. I am now in a quiet apartment in a
quiet part of the town, distant from the attractions of the boulevards, and
hope to be able to devote myself to the study of French. In the house where
my chambers are there is a *table d'hôte*, at which I expected to meet Frenchmen alone. I had desired to place myself where I should hear French and
nothing else, and be compelled, if I wished to break silence at all, to express
myself in this language. But a young man, prepossessing in his appearance,
was by my side, who at once confessed that he was an Englishman, or rather
of the Isle of Jersey, and an attendant upon the law lectures in the École de
Droit. Conversation with him for a while distracted my attention, so that
but little of it was given to the French that was rapidly passing from the
various mouths about me. The little intercourse which I have had with him
gives promise of an amiable companion, but I fear may impair some of the
advantages which I looked for in my present quarters. For my room, which
has a large closet or *cabinet*, and another *cabinet* in which the bed is placed, I
have engaged to give seventy francs per month. The dinner at the *table
d'hôte* is thirty-five sous. Ordinary Burgundy wine is supplied and included
in this price. Every French dinner begins with soup; and at my place about
four other dishes followed, with cheese and nuts afterwards. The whole,
however, was quite unlike the repasts which I have had in the *cafés* and
restaurants on the boulevards, and in the Hôtel Montmorency.

Among the means which I hope to use for instruction in French is the
theatre; and I went to-night, for the first time at Paris, in company with my
young acquaintance at the table. I went to the old and famous Théâtre
Français. There were two plays of five acts each; one, *L'Inconnu*, or, *Mis-
anthropie et Repentir*, derived from the drama of Kotzebue, which was the
foundation of the English play of the "Stranger;" and the other, *L'Avare*,

in five acts, of Molière. I had a seat in the *parterre*, or pit, which cost two francs and twenty centimes; and also bought at the door copies of the two plays, for which I paid a franc each. With these I endeavored to follow the different performers. It was not a little difficult; they spoke, as it seemed, with such lightning rapidity; and, before the ten acts of the evening were performed, my eyes and attention had become quite weary. We left the theatre as the curtain fell and passed out between two soldiers at the door, and encountered sentinels every few rods. It was bitter cold, reminding me of the weather which I have left behind; yet these men, with their cold muskets, were pacing over the short spaces of their watch, some of them, I observed, without the protection of a cloak or outer garment; but the greater part with a heavy cloak, to which was attached a sort of hood that protected the head. As we passed through the Place du Carrousel, and in front of the Tuileries, we observed this royal residence splendidly lighted from end to end, and sentinels on the watch about it at all points. The Théâtre Français, where I have been this evening, is supported by the government at a considerable expense, and is the place where the classical drama of France is generally enacted. One may see Molière and Corneille here. The house is about the size of the Tremont House. The scenery did not strike me as at all better than that of American theatres. The curtain did not fall between the acts, and there was no change of scenery to-night from one end of each play to the other; a new scene was occasioned simply by one of the persons on the stage making his exit, or a new one his entrance.

Jan. 9. To-day commenced reading and conversing in French with Madame Laboust, — an English lady who has lived in France fifteen years, and, I believe, is the widow of a French officer.

Jan. 10. This morning had a lesson or conversation with my teacher; and after breakfast went, with my friend Shattuck, to visit some of the interesting objects of *Le Pays Latin*, as the district of the schools is called, and entered the École de Médecine, and the Musée Dupuytren. Thence I passed to the Sorbonne, entering only the court-yard of this ancient and famous seat of science and learning, and to the old church of St. Étienne. We next passed to the Bibliotheque de St. Geneviève, a large library, containing upwards of two hundred thousand volumes and thirty thousand manuscripts, — like every thing in Paris open to the public. We entered without ticket or introduction of any kind, and yet without let or hindrance. A long table was surrounded by readers and students, who had the use of books innumerable, for the asking. What is authorship? Here are two hundred thousand volumes. Who knows the names of the wise and learned and laborious who built on them confident hopes of immortality on earth? The pages of an unread catalogue are the only roll of fame on which most of their names are inscribed; and dust gathers over the leaves of the works on which long lives have been consumed. It seems like passing through tombs and a city of the dead, to walk through a large library; for here how many aspirations, — proud and high-reaching as the stars, — hopes, and longings lie buried! From this library we passed by the Panthéon, the depository of the dust of the great men of France, without however going in, and entered the École de Droit. After wandering round the corridors of the spacious building for some time, after inquiry we found ourselves in the lecture-room of Rossi,[1] who, according to the programme, lectured upon *Droit Constitutionnel Francais*. The lecture-room was in the shape of an amphitheatre, the professor's chair being in the chord of the arc which formed the room. The seats of the hearers were semi-circular and without backs. I should think there were as many as one hundred and fifty hearers of all ages present, many of them too old for students. By far the larger part appeared very attentive, and took ample notes; having a little portfolio for the purpose, in which a certain quantity of paper was fastened, and also a small inkstand. The professor sat while lecturing, and appeared to have a fluent and interesting manner, though not at all elegant. He was dressed in a black gown, with a scarf of red over his shoulders, and a high, round, red cap of cloth. I was at some distance from him, and hardly within the range of his voice; but I did not understand fully a single sentence that he uttered, though I was able to catch many detached words and phrases here and there. The lecture did not continue more than fifteen or twenty minutes after I entered; and the moment the professor closed his lecture he jumped from his seat, and, without so much of a "good-by" to his audience as an oath (according to the *jeu d'esprit* about Lord Thurlow), hastily left the room. Rossi appeared to be about forty years old. He is an Italian by birth, and is one of the most celebrated of the professors. He is also the author of several volumes of law, which have met with considerable success. This short incursion into the quarter of the lectures and schools admonishes me of the great fund of interest which exists there. Here are lectures at every hour of every day on every part of science, literature, and law, which may be attended *gratis*. And the buildings and streets in this vicinity are marked by great antiquity and historical association. The Panthéon and the Sorbonne are within a stone's throw of each other.

I kept at home this evening, studying my French grammar. Received a card to-day from Mrs. Cass, informing me that, in consequence of the ball at the Tuileries this evening, her *soirée* would be postponed from to-night to the next Wednesday. If it had been to-night, I should not have gone. I feel unwilling to go anywhere till I know more of the language which I hear about me. I feel tempted to follow the example of the ancient, and shave one side of my head, so that I may be restrained from showing myself abroad.

Jan. 11 (Thursday). Yesterday I attended a lecture which was open

---

[1] Count Pellegrino Luigi Odoardo Rossi was born at Carrara, July 13, 1787. He was at first a lawyer at Bologna, but went to Geneva, in 1814, where he became a professor of law; published a treatise on the "Penal Law;" was associated with Sismondi in publishing "Annals of Legislation and Political Economy;" and was a member of the Diet and Council. Removing to Paris, in 1832, he was appointed Professor of Political Economy in the College of France; and, in 1834, Professor of Constitutional Law. He became the political associate of Guizot and the Duc de Broglie, and was made a peer of France and a member of the Council of State. From 1845, when he was sent as ambassador to Rome, until his death, he remained in Italy, taking part in political movements; though at one time in retirement at Carrara. While the Pope's chief minister, he was assassinated, Nov. 15, 1848.

to all who chose to attend. To-day I spent several hours in another
place presenting interests of a different kind, but open *gratis* to the citizen
and stranger. This was at the Museums of the Louvre, — a royal palace, and
truly royal it is, converted into a receptacle for collections of paintings, antiquities, and curiosities. I had not been there before, as my time had been
so much occupied by some necessary arrangements for my sojourn in Paris. I
had often read and heard of the Louvre, but I had no adequate idea of its vast-
ness, or of the extent of its collections. Here were upwards of three thousand
pictures, of the French, Dutch, German, and Italian schools, — with a Spanish gallery also, which was just opened, — containing numerous productions of
the first masters, Raphael, Leonardo da Vinci, Rubens, Caracci, Murillo, &c.
A portion of these galleries was open to all, both citizens and strangers,
without question of any kind. At what is called the long gallery, however, containing the principal collection of paintings, strangers were required
to exhibit their passports and sign their names in a book preserved at the
porter's lodge. In this gallery numerous artists, many of them women, were
employed in making copies of the paintings, liberty being always given for
this purpose on proper application. I will not here record the impressions
produced on my mind by the sight of this magnificent palace and its numerous apartments devoted to such purposes. I passed through all the rooms, —
those of painting, antiquity, designs, and of the marine, — taking merely a
hasty *coup d'œil* of the varied scene, and reserving for subsequent visits
a more minute examination.

    Jan. 12. Went again to the scene of lectures. At the Sorbonne, heard
Geoffroy Saint-Hilaire [1] on natural history; he appeared to be considering the subject of comparative anatomy. He was a man apparently about
thirty-five years of age, not over-careful in dress; in manner earnest and apparently interesting. The room in which he lectured was similar in size and
shape to the old Circuit-Court room [2] at Boston, and the professor's tribune
not unlike the bench of the judge. He sat during his lecture, as have all
the professors whom I have heard; and his audience (the greater part of
them) kept their hats on. Many of them were men considerably advanced,
certainly beyond the age of students. At the Sorbonne I also heard Constant Prévost [3] on geology, and Lenormant on ancient history. The former
lectured in the same room that had been occupied by Geoffroy Saint-Hilaire.
He appeared to be about forty-five years old, and was a pleasant lecturer.
The room was full, and many were taking notes. I forgot to mention that
when Saint-Hilaire closed his lecture there was applause by stamping the
feet. Lenormant [4] lectured instead of Guizot, who has become absorbed

  1 1805–1861. Author of works on zoölogy, and son of the naturalist of the same name.
  2 The United States Circuit-Court room, formerly in the Court House in Court Square.
  3 1787–1856.
  4 Charles Lenormant was born in Paris, June 1, 1802, and died in Athens, Nov. 24, 1859.
He accompanied, in 1828, the younger Champollion to Egypt; was chosen, in 1835, Guizot's
substitute (*suppléant*) in the professorship of History, and in 1848 Professor of Egyptology,
in the College of France. He was learned in antiquities, particularly the Asiatic. His wife
was the niece of Madame Récamier, of whose " Memoirs " she is the author.

in politics, and thus lost to his professorship. He was a spruce-looking man, with well-adjusted hair, a neat coat, pantaloons, and boots, to say nothing of the fresh hat in his hands as he entered the room. The attendant had placed a decanter of water, a tumbler, and some pieces of white sugar on the table before he entered; and his first act was to prepare a drink, which is very common in France, from a combination of these. While lecturing he stirred his water and sugar, and occasionally moistened his lips. His subject was Sidon, and its commercial prosperity. He had notes before him, and a black-board behind him on which he chalked some dates showing the contempo-raneousness of Sidon with the Jewish government. Constant Prévost also used notes for his lecture. Saint-Hilaire did not appear to have any. Un-like the professors at the École de Droit, those of the Sorbonne whom I have seen had no dress or badge, except a piece of red ribbon in one of the upper button-holes on the left lapel of their coats. At the École de Droit to-day I heard Delzers [1] on *Procédure Civile.* He was a man with hard features, of about fifty-five years of age, and with the black gown, red scarf, and red cap which I had before observed as the garb of Rossi. His manner was very plain and deliberate. He read an article in the code, having the book before him, and then proceeded in a plain way to expound it. In the course of an hour he expounded about a page of the code, relating to the formalities of recording the judgment. I was happy to find that I could understand nearly all that he said, as I could a good deal of what the other lecturers said to-day. This is to me an encouraging sign that I am gradually acquiring a French ear.

This evening went to the Théâtre Odéon to see Molière's *Les Femmes Savantes*, and Mademoiselle Mars in the part of *Henriette;* and the evening was a feast. I had previously prepared myself by reading the play, and I also carried a copy with me, by means of which I followed the actors easily through the whole of this brilliant production. Mars [2] is now nearly sixty, and yet she had the appearance of thirty. Her voice was clear as silver and exquisitely modulated, and her movement on the stage thoroughly graceful. I have seen no performance, by any actor, which was so eminently pretty and graceful as that of this evening by Mars: the part did not call out those stronger traits which she is said to possess. The poetry of Molière fell from her lips with honeyed accents, and all the players did well; there was noth-ing bad. After this play, Mars appeared in a pretty little piece called *Le Château de ma Nièce.* The theatre of the Odéon is situated in the region of the students, and the *parterre* or pit was, of course, crowded with these. They ranged from the ages of sixteen or seventeen to twenty-one or twenty-two, and like American students were noisy and uproarious, crying to the orchestra for the Marseilles Hymn, &c. While looking at them ranged in

---

[1] Joseph François Casimir Delzers, 1787- ; a writer upon criminal law and criminal and civil procedure, and a professor from 1823 to 1857.

[2] 1779–1847. Her first success, which was at the beginning of this century, was achieved in the personation of a deaf and dumb girl in the *Abbé de l'Épée.* She was for thirty years without a rival on the French stage in genteel comedy, and retired in 1841. Her favorite plays were those of Molière.

rows in the pit, I might have mistaken them for Cantabs, if the sounds of French from all quarters, penetrating my ear, had not keenly reminded me that I was not in my own country. Mademoiselle Mars was, I should think, rather under the common height, and of a neat and beautiful figure. Her eyes were brilliant; and her teeth, hair, and bust all good, — though nobody can tell what of these is the gift of God, or of the dentist or milliner. The theatre of the Odéon is very pretty.

TO GEORGE S. HILLARD.

PARIS, Jan. 13, 1838.

MY DEAR GEORGE, —. . . You can imagine my feelings in such a scene as I passed through to-day [the Louvre], when you think that Mr. Sears's house was my type of a palace, the Athenæum Gallery, of a collection of paintings, and the plaster casts in the Athenæum reading-room and Felton's study, of a collection of antiques. My voyage has already been compensated for — sea-sickness, time, money, and all — many times over. It was fully paid for at Rouen. All that I have seen since is clear gain. But still I cannot forget dear Boston and friends there, and long much to hear of you. I sadly fear that all of you will delay writing me until you hear from me, which will serve me badly, as I shall then be without letters from you for many months. Tell my friends to write; let me know all the news, — law, literature, politics, love, and matrimony. Before this letter can reach you Cleveland will be a married man; give my love to him, if he is in Boston. I have already written him to the care of Bishop Doane, Burlington. Tell Miss Austin that I had the happiness of placing her little packet in Mrs. Ticknor's hands on New Year's morning. Mrs. T. is delightful, and it does me good to see her. Every evening of my first week in Paris I passed with her.　　　　　　　　　As ever, affectionately yours,

C. S.

Have seen Mademoiselle Mars in Molière's *Les Femmes Savantes*. It was a treat which I shall never forget. Her voice is like a silver flute; her eye like a gem. Have met several professors.

JOURNAL.

Jan. 13, 1838. Called on my friends the Ticknors, — it being the first time I had been to the boulevards since I left them last Monday: it is now Saturday. Found Mrs. T. as agreeable and friendly as ever; full of kindness to me. Mr. T. was not at home at first; he however returned soon, having in the mean time been to my lodgings in search of me. While with them I saw Count Circourt,[1] a Frenchman, who though young has great attainments, and speaks many languages. He was the private secretary of Prince Polignac, and of course, with the prostration of that mad minister, lost his chances of advancement for the present. I was not formally presented to him, as it is not the usage to introduce strangers to each other; all in the room are privileged to address each other without an introduction.

Went to Cutter's, an American tailor established in Paris, to be measured for a surtout; was struck by the close attention paid to the shape of my person by the measurer. It was noted, among other things, that my right shoulder was slightly higher than the left. Of course, the appearance of this was to be counteracted. So the tailor makes the man!

Next read the papers at Galignani's, where I have subscribed for two months, paying twelve francs. Here are all the English and French newspapers covering two large tables, and all in constant demand. When, however, I looked for American papers, it was with difficulty that I could find them: they were put away in the dark. Such is the interest excited by our affairs! But I must confess, that, as I perused the columns of these papers, — being fresh from the perusal of the elaborate sheets from the English press, and the smaller but piquant and vigorous papers of France, — I felt strongly the pettiness of the politics of my country, their provincialism, and their lack of interest for the cosmopolite, besides also the ordinary character of their editorial matter. There is not so good a market for editorial talent in our country as here; in other words, the talents which will make a good editor with learning, comprehension, and rhetorical ability will find better situations with us than at the desk of a newspaper. *Au contraire* in France, Thiers steps from the chair of his printing office to that of prime minister; and Armand Carrel, as a simple journalist, in the pages of the *National*, exercises an influence on the destinies of his country, greater than the most favored minister of the crown. In America the profession has not the same high regard which it has in Paris; and men of distinguished talent, before whom the world is opening, hesitate to engage in it, except as an *agrément* of youth, or to piece out the narrow income of a profession. However, I will not speculate upon the reasons; it is sufficient that there is a great difference. The French press, so far as I have been able to comprehend its spirit, is vigorous, keen, constant, watchful, and full of ability, with force of rhetoric and argument in great store. The papers are not more than half as large as ours; indeed, they are of about the same size with a half-sheet of an American newspaper, folded in the middle, — being, therefore, in the folio form; still they contain as much, and indeed more, interesting matter than our papers. Their four pages are full of discussion, reports, or news, with but a few lines for advertisements; which latter form the bulk of an American newspaper.

---

[1] Count Circourt was born in 1809. He is the author of historical works on "The Arabs in Spain" and "The Battle of Hastings." He was one of Tocqueville's intimate friends. In 1872 he became a Councillor of State. Sumner on his visit to Paris, in 1857, received attentions from the Count and Countess.

Next dined at one of the restaurants at the Palais Royal, for two francs. Then went to the Théâtre Vaudeville in the street running from the Palais Royal to the Place du Carrousel; heard two short pieces, of which I understood very little. They were unpublished, and of course I could not procure a copy; so I was left to my ear, which served me quite badly. Indeed, I despair of ever following the rapid and idiomatic expressions of French conversation.

Jan. 14 (Sunday). This morning M. Foelix called upon me before breakfast, — that is, before eleven o'clock; kindly inquired about my situation, and invited me to go with him to-morrow evening to a *soirée* at the Baron de Gérando's.[1]

Notwithstanding it was Sunday, I went with some friends to the Italian Opera. The opera for the night was *Don Giovanni*, one of the most famous, if not the most so, of the productions of Mozart. The performers were the famous Italians, who now stand the highest in the musical world, — Signori Rubini[2] (Don Ottavio); Tamburini[3] (Don Giovanni); Lablache[4] (Leporello), the latter with the most powerful bass voice I ever heard; Madame Grisi[5] (Donna Anna); and Madame Persiani[6] (Zerlina), the latter a *débutante* of the season, and to my taste equal to Grisi herself in many points, though not in fierceness and power. I have no knowledge of music, and but little, scarcely any, ear for it; but I felt the singular power of these performers.[7] Their voices, attuned to such various and subtle harmonies, entered the chambers of my heart. At times the notes were soft and delicate, touching gently on the sense as a linnet's feather; and then again they would rise, and, borne by the powerful music of the orchestra, thunder in the ear with the voice of one who was taking a city. In one of the back boxes, sitting out of the range of the light, so that, like Xerxes at his feasts, they could see well themselves but not be seen by others, were two of the younger sons of the King; with light hair, and looking not unlike other boys of their age, say from fourteen to seventeen. They are dukes or princes of something, but I do not know of what. The house was crowded with a brilliant audience; and it was a sensation different from what I had yet experienced, to find myself, as it were, between two foreign languages, — Italian on the stage, and French sounding from every voice about me. As we left the theatre, we

---

[1] He declined the invitation because of his inability as yet to speak French.

[2] Giovanni Battista Rubini, 1795–1854; reputed the first Italian tenor of his time.

[3] Antonio Tamburini, 1800–1876. After singing in Italian theatres, he appeared first in Paris in 1832. He retired from the stage in 1854.

[4] Luigi Lablache, 1794–1858; the celebrated basso. He succeeded both in the serious and the comic opera. He came to Paris in 1830, and performed there and in London. He is said to have given music lessons to Queen Victoria.

[5] Giulia Grisi, 1808–1869. Her first appearance in Paris was on Oct. 16, 1832, at the Théâtre Italien in *Semiramide*. She performed in the principal cities of Europe, and in 1854 in the United States.

[6] Madame Persiani (*née* Fanny Tacchinardi), 1818–1867. Her first appearance was at Leghorn, in 1832. She appeared in Paris, in 1837, in *Francesca da Rimini*.

[7] Grisi, Malibran, Tamburini, Lablache, Rubini, and Ivanhoff were united in a concert at Stafford House, in 1835. Gréville's "Memoirs," ch. xxviii.; July 15, 1835.

passed through a small file of the military who stood in the entry, and encountered in the street five dragoons mounted in front of the theatre. I sat in what is called the *stalles d'orchestre*, being some of the front benches of the pit, which have been parted off from the remainder and subdivided into seats, like arm-chairs. The ticket was twelve francs, — a most costly amusement.

Jan. 15 (Monday). This morning, while taking my breakfast at a café, and reading a newspaper, I found that the building of the Italian Opera had been burned on the preceding night. This was the very house that I had left, but an hour or so before the flames were discovered. The powerful musical company will undoubtedly be transferred to some other house, as their talent is unrivalled in the whole world; but I am glad to have heard them in their own splendid theatre. The fire was a bad one, and has extended to other buildings. I visited the spot this forenoon, and found the adjacent streets full of spectators, with numerous soldiers on guard protecting the property, and also preventing spectators from approaching the engines, which were manned by bands trained by the government for this purpose, and in uniform.

Walked from the boulevards near the Opera to the Sorbonne, and heard for a few minutes Dumas [1] on chemistry, and Fauriel [2] on Spanish literature. I understood very little of what either said. The former, a very neat gentlemanly person, was talking and experimenting to a large audience, of several hundred. Fauriel, rather an elderly gentleman, say fifty-five or sixty, considered in his lecture the remains of the ancient Phœnicians in Spain.

To-night is the anniversary of Molière's birth, and it was celebrated at the Théâtre Français. *Le Tartuffe* and *Le Malade Imaginaire* were both performed, Mars performing the part of Émile in *Le Tartuffe*. I had not had time to read the plays before going; but carried them with me to the theatre, and followed the actors throughout. After the plays ensued a ceremony, annually repeated, I believe, on this night, — the crowning of Molière's bust with bays by all the performers, who successively approach it with a laurel crown in their hands, which they place on the head of the statue, amidst the applause of the audience. And this is in honor of the man who was refused burial, on his death, in consecrated ground, because he had been a player!

As I passed from the theatre, after midnight, my walk home carried me through the Place du Carrousel, and in front of the Tuileries. This splendid palace of kings was resplendent with lights, and its ample court-yard, the scene of much Revolutionary incident, filled with lines of carriages awaiting

---

[1] Jean Baptiste Dumas, a celebrated chemist and author of works on his specialty, was born July 14, 1800. He was minister of agriculture and commerce, 1850–1851, and has held other public offices. He was elected, Dec. 1875, member of the French Academy as successor of Guizot. His efforts have been directed to the promotion of scientific agriculture.

[2] Claude Charles Fauriel, 1772–1844. He was a nephew of the Abbé Sieyès; the intimate friend of Guizot, Manzoni, and Madame de Stael; a professor of foreign literature, taking, in 1830, a chair which the Duc de Broglie, then Minister of Public Instruction, had created for him; and a writer upon historical and literary subjects.

the gay and the honored who were enjoying the festivities within. Sentinels were on their silent watch, in view of this scene. Little indeed did they, while holding with benumbed hands their muskets, enjoy the cheer and music and hilarity of their King. The weather was intensely cold, so as to remind me of a New England winter. The situation of these poor soldiers strikes me every evening that I walk the streets. They are never out of sight; the gleam of their arms is seen at every turn that one makes, and they are always walking at the same slow pace over a short patch of ground. They are especially in the neighborhood of all theatres, of all the public offices, public buildings, public libraries, bridges, and generally of all places of public amusement and gathering.

Jan. 16 (Tuesday). To-day I enjoyed a treat at the Sorbonne and at the College of France. I heard at the former Jouffroy,[1] well known through the world for his writings on philosophy and international law; and at the latter Lerminier, a man of different character, but of considerable celebrity as an author, and great popularity as a lecturer. Jouffroy is now a distinguished member of the Chamber of Deputies, and during the last week made an able speech in that body. He lectured in the same room in which I had already heard Lenormant and Fauriel. The room was crowded before he entered, with young and old, who appeared to be watching eagerly for his appearance, and who broke into applause when he was seen advancing to the desk. He was tall, with a slight stoop in his shoulders, and appeared to be about forty-five or forty-eight years old. His hair was thin, and was suffered to grow long on the back of his head, so as to cover the collar of his coat. His eye was mild but striking; and, together with the pallid countenance, showed the student. Like all the professors, he sat while lecturing. He had neither volume nor notes of any kind before him. His subject was generally philosophy, and to-day he was presenting a tableau of the principal faculties of the human mind. So far as I could understand him, with my poor French ear, he presented a beautiful view of the subject. His language was close and precise, and yet fluent, elegant, and animated. His voice was soft and well-managed; his gestures frequent and graceful. His own interest in the subject seemed to be great. When he closed there was considerable applause. I have seldom, if ever, heard a lecturer who pleased me more than Jouffroy.

From Jouffroy to Lerminier [2] was a great change. The former was sim-

---

1 Théodore Simon Jouffroy, 1796–1842. He was distinguished as a philosopher, particularly for his studies in morals and metaphysics. He translated into French the works of Thomas Reid, and Dugald Stewart's "Moral Philosophy." In 1833 he became a Professor of Greek Literature and Philosophy, in the College of France, and in 1838 resigned his chair to become Librarian of the University. In 1831 he was elected to the Chamber of Deputies. In 1840 he was appointed on the royal commission of public instruction. His plans for radical improvements not being seconded, he withdrew disheartened into complete solitude, in which he remained until his death.

2 Jean Louis Eugène Lerminier, 1803–1857. He was at first an advocate, but left the bar to study literature and jurisprudence. He became a professor in 1831. His lectures were singularly attractive for their eloquence and animation of style. He contributed to journals and reviews, particularly the *Revue des deux Mondes*.

ple, modest, unaffected, and almost conversational; the latter loud-voiced, rhetorical, and ambitious in his delivery. In personal appearance the contrast was great. Jouffroy looked every inch the scholar; Lerminier more like a disciple of Anacreon. His hair was sleek and long, not unlike Nicholas Biddle's, and his size and general appearance reminded me very much of the bank-president. He appeared to be about thirty-eight years of age. Like Jouffroy, he had a large and attentive audience, notwithstanding the lecture-room was uncomfortably cold; and (*mirabile dictu*) there was a considerable number of ladies in the room. I have since been told that his lectures always attract ladies, many or few. His subject, according to the programme, was the history of comparative legislation; but he was occupied this morning in considering the effect of the conquest of the North of France by the Normans upon the conquerors themselves, since they received Christianity and feudalism from the conquered. His enunciation, though it appeared to be distinct, was so rapid as to make it difficult for me to follow him. His manner was animated, and even excited in the extreme; and frequently, by way of additional emphasis, he gave the desk before him a bang with his hands in time with his voice. There is but one step from the sublime to the ridiculous; and the eloquent and absurd are often separated by thin partitions. Had I been left this morning to my own unassisted judgment, I should have been in great doubt how to regard Lerminier, — whether as an eloquent lecturer or a vapid declaimer. Foelix, the editor of the *Revue Étrangère*, has told me that he was nothing better than a charlatan; and I must confess that what I heard this morning has not disturbed this opinion. I shall keep my mind open with regard to him, and hope to hear him repeatedly after I shall be better able to understand him.

Jan. 17 (Wednesday). Called on the Ticknors and Walshes,[1] and attended to some little affairs in the city, and thus exhausted the day. So much for the distances of Paris! In front of the Théâtre Italien, which was burnt, was the funeral of an unfortunate who was destroyed in the conflagration. The house which contained his remains was covered, at the lower part of it, with black cloth; and a hearse was in waiting with black plumes nodding on the top and horses decorated with black. Mourning carriages were also in attendance. In the street were several persons — I took them for hired mourners — dressed in black, with cocked hats and deep weeds. They were engaged in smoking pipes and enjoying jokes, as if they were to assist at a wedding and not at a funeral. I observed to-day the ruins of the building. Its walls and beautiful portico still stand, apparently strong and unaffected by the fire which destroyed the interior of the building. I do

---

[1] Robert Walsh was born in Baltimore in 1784, and died in Paris in 1859. His career was miscellaneous, both as to residence and literary occupations. He studied in the Catholic colleges of Baltimore and Georgetown. Then he resided several years in Europe. Returning to this country, he studied law in Philadelphia, but did not follow the profession. In 1821, he founded, and for fifteen years edited, the "National Gazette" of that city. He published various papers on American politics, biography, and literature. In 1837 he went to Europe for a permanent residence. From 1845 to 1851 he was Consul of the United States at Paris. In 1834, Sumner met him in Philadelphia. *Ante*, p. 133.

not wonder that fires do so little injury in Paris. The houses are all built close together, but they are of stone. There is no such thing as a wooden house; and in the stone houses there is very little inflammable matter. The roof is tiled or slated; the entries and most of the stairways and floors are of stone. Besides, the walls of all buildings are so thick that, if a fire broke out in a building, it would be confined there. The engines are ridiculously small and filled by buckets; there does not appear to be any such thing as a suction-hose here. The engine companies consist of six hundred men, trained and drilled by the Government, called the *sapeurs-pompiers*, who are on watch in different parts of the city constantly. Americans could teach the Parisians how to put fires out.

Jan 18 (Thursday). Heard Tissot[1] at the Collége Royal de France, and also Ampère. The former is quite a classic name. He is the translator of some of Virgil's Eclogues, and has been connected with other literary labors. His subject was Latin Poetry. After exhorting his hearers to its study, and in very animated language telling them what companions and friends they would find in the classics, he read from Virgil's "Æneid," second book, the description of the death of Priam, translating line for line as he proceeded, and then commented upon it. He was an old and venerable man of sixty or more, and spoke rather indistinctly; so that I was unable to follow him, except now and then; and I found it more difficult to understand him while reading Latin poetry than when speaking French. He gave the French pronunciation to his Latin, so that at first I should have mistaken it for French. M. Ampère,[2] at the same college, lectured on chivalry. He was a man apparently of not more than thirty-five, with quite a distinct manner, though he could hardly be called fluent. He considered the elements of chivalry, — Christianity and Germanism, according to him, — and pointed out the features referrible to each of these elements. I was able to follow him pretty well, — much better than Tissot.

To-night I have engaged the assistance of a new teacher for French, — M. Debidas,[3] who has been recommended from many quarters. I am to have lessons from him three times a week, in the evenings. I shall also continue with my instructress; so that, between them both, I shall be pretty well supplied with French.

To-day is very cold, and several preceding days have been so likewise. I hardly expected such inclement weather when I left home. Wood is very

---

[1] Pierre François Tissot, 1768–1854. He was a student of the ancient classics; wrote also upon French literature and history, and was in public life under the first empire.

[2] Jean Jacques Ampère (son of the scientist, André Marie Ampère, who died June 10, 1836) was born at Lyons in Aug., 1800, and died at Pau, March 27, 1864. From May, 1833, to the time of his death, he was Professor of French Literature in the College of France. He travelled widely, and, in 1851–52, visited the United States and Mexico. He is celebrated for his friendship with Tocqueville and his passion for Madame Récamier. See "North American Review" for Oct., 1875, and "Galaxy" for Nov., 1875, for articles, both entitled "The Two Ampères."

[3] On Sumner's next visit to Europe, he sought at Paris, March 23, 1857, first of all, his former teacher at 52 Rue St. Dominique, but could find no trace of him.

dear; it is doled out like wax candles, and my landlord looks with absolute amazement upon the quantity which I use.

Jan. 19 (Friday).　The long gallery of the Louvre will close to-morrow, in order to prepare for the annual exhibition of the productions of modern artists, which takes place in it, — the new pictures being placed before the old.　I went there to-day, to snatch a hasty view of these numerous specimens of art and genius.　I felt " cabined, cribbed, confined," from my ignorance of the principles of art and of its history, except in its most prominent traits.　There are about a dozen pictures here by Raphael, and as many by Leonardo da Vinci, which at once attracted my attention.　There was the stamp of genius upon them.　If I should attempt to describe their effect or appearance, I should probably make some blunder.　They touched my mind, untutored as it is, like a rich strain of music.

To-night had an exercise with my new Frenchman; found him the very man I wanted.　The cold continues intolerable; and my chamber, notwithstanding all my exertions, frigid beyond endurance.　I go to bed to-night earlier than usual — the clock this moment striking midnight — in the hope of escaping the cold.　My French grammar will be my companion.

Jan. 20 (Saturday).　Waked in the full determination with which I went to sleep; namely, to find a warmer place for my body.　In America I am accustomed to cold weather; but there I find a comfortable shelter from its inclemency.　My present quarters do not afford it.　With a large fire in front and my surtout on, I freeze behind; and my hair is so cold that I hesitate to touch it with my hand.　Of course, I cannot endure this; and I have taken neat and comfortable quarters at No. 25 Rue de l'Odéon, where Shattuck and Benjamin are, at the rate of sixty francs a month.

To-day I heard at the Sorbonne the substitute of Cousin, M. Poret, a gentleman very plain in his appearance, who appeared to be about forty-five.　His lecture was written, — the first written one I have heard, — and he seemed to be so little acquainted with its text, and was so near-sighted, that he was obliged to stoop his head constantly in order to read it.　It was on the philosophical theory of Heraclitus.　I did not stay long to hear it; but went to the École de Droit, where I found Ducaurroy [1] in the midst of a lecture on the " Institutes of Justinian."　He was an old gentleman of sixty, with gray hair and a mild manner, with a slow enunciation, and in the black-and-red dress which I first noticed as that of a professor; but which, now, I believe to be peculiar to the schools of medicine and law.　He had quite a large audience, among whom I noticed two or three blacks, or rather mulattoes, — two-thirds black, perhaps, — dressed quite à la mode, and having the easy,

[1] Adolphe Marie Ducaurroy de la Croix, 1788–1850.　The "Institutes of Justinian" were the study of his life.　His distinctive aim was to set aside the Commentaries, and restore the Institutes themselves to their just place as a study and an authority.　His chief work — which is a classic — was " The Institutes of Justinian newly Translated and Explained " (Institutes de Justinien nouvellement Traduites et Expliquées), which, first published in 1835, had reached an eighth edition in 1851.　He was also a contributor to the Revue Étrangère.

jaunty air of young men of fashion, who were well received by their fellow-students. They were standing in the midst of a knot of young men; and their color seemed to be no objection to them. I was glad to see this; though, with American impressions, it seemed very strange. It must be, then, that the distance between free blacks and the whites among us is derived from education, and does not exist in the nature of things.

Dined with Mr. Harrison, where I met a young Russian, Mr. Chichacheff; who is quite a cosmopolite, having been absent from his country nearly five years, and speaks a multitude of languages with perfect fluency, — English, so that I mistook him for an Englishman when he first entered. I talked with him a great deal about Russia, and found him intelligent and communicative. From him I learned much about the real state and policy of his country. He was fond of American institutions, and yet he gloried in being a slave under his own despot. After dinner, we went to one of the concert rooms (Rue St. Honoré), where you get the finest music — for *one franc*.

Jan. 22 (Monday). I went to the École de Droit to hear M. Rossi again, but found that he was prevented by indisposition from lecturing; then visited the Panthéon, which overshadows the Law School, and returned home. My present plan is, for a fortnight or more, to stick to my French, and of course to keep within doors considerably. Much should I like to be abroad, seeing some of the thousand sights which constantly present themselves; but my first desire is to speak French.

Jan. 23. Heard part of Jouffroy's lecture, but did not arrive in season to have a seat; and so lost an opportunity of listening with attention.

Jan. 24. Went to the Sorbonne and the École de Droit; found the professors I intended to hear at the former place indisposed, so that their lectures were adjourned. At the latter place heard Demante [1] on the *Code Civil*. He appeared to be about forty-five, with rather a low forehead and black hair. His manner was very hurried; so much so that I was able to apprehend very little that he said. From there, walked down the narrow streets that lead to the river, to the ancient structure of Notre Dame. After the cathedral at Rouen this seems tame; though, if I had not seen the former, I should be very much struck by Notre Dame.

This afternoon I engaged another French master, who will come every day in the week, except Sunday, and talk and read with me. He is an old gentleman, who was recommended to me by Mr. Brent, our consul.

Jan. 25. Went again to the Sorbonne; found the professor I wished to hear sick with a cold, so that his lecture was adjourned. Then went to visit the Palais des Thermes, a relic of the Roman occupation of Gaul. The building is, of course, at this date only a wreck; but you there see the very bricks and arches of that great people, whose eagles pervaded all the ancient world; and you stand more distinctly in the presence of antiquity than in the Cathedral of Rouen, though the grandeur of the latter and the historical associations connected with it give it a more thrilling interest.

[1] Antoine Marie Demante, 1789–1856. He became, in 1819, a substitute (*suppléant*) professor in the École de Droit. In 1848, he served in the Constituent Assembly and in the Legislative Assembly. He wrote upon the *Code Civil*.

My French master came to-day, and I talked with him an hour or more.
I found myself interested in him, and we kept up the ball of conversation
very well.

Jan. 27. At the Sorbonne heard a portion of the lecture of Poret on
the history of Philosophy, in which he considered the philosophical opinions of Heraclitus, and concluded by promising to discuss those of Anaxago-
ras. After this, in the same room, I heard a long lecture from Guigniaut,[1]
on Geography. The professor appeared to be about forty or forty-two years
old, neatly dressed, with rather a dark countenance and dark hair. His
manner was any thing but fluent, and yet he was very much excited by his
subject. He treated of the first population of Greece, so that his lecture
savored of an historical as well as a geographical character. Some idea of
the extensive way in which he treated the subject may be formed from the
fact that this point alone — namely, the first population of Greece — was to
be treated in three or four lectures.

This evening received an invitation from M. Foelix to dine with him
to-morrow; after some hesitation, accepted it.

Jan. 28. In the morning went to the other side of the river for the forenoon. Saw my friends, the Ticknors; read newspapers at Galignani's; and
punctually, at half-past five, presented myself at the apartments of M. Foelix.
I was shown into the *salon*, which was without a carpet, where I found the
younger of the two sisters of Foelix, and also a gentleman, whom I afterwards
found to be a member of the Chamber of Deputies, — I could not catch his
name. My French was sadly taxed to make my salutations in a proper
way. I succeeded without any very great offence against grammar or propriety, and entered into conversation. Very soon appeared the elder sister,
who speaks a little English, and M. Foelix, and a German of quite striking
and attractive appearance, about fifty years of age; I could not catch his
name, — I think it was Mohl. When dinner was announced, the German
offered his arm to the elder sister and the deputy to the younger, and I
walked into the *salle à manger* alone. All the rooms were cold as the arctics,
but there was a little stove for this apartment, which came near the table,
by the side of which I was placed, as a mark of attention. There were cards
with the names of each guest placed at their respective plates. In the course
of the dinner I talked with the elder sister, by my side, in English, — sometimes both speaking English, and sometimes I speaking French and she speaking English. In the course of the dinner, however, I was appealed to by the
deputy with regard to the Constitution of the United States and those of the
different States; the qualifications of electors, the terms of office, &c.; the
present state of parties, slavery, banks, &c. Excited by the occasion, I threw
myself upon my resources and spoke. I felt conscious of continual blunders;
but I also felt that I was understood, so that I was making language serve
its principal purpose, — namely, to convey thought. I often spoke little better

---

[1] Joseph Daniel Guigniaut was born May 15, 1794. His studies were at first in the
ancient mythologies, and afterwards in geography and history. He took the lead in found-
ing the French School at Athens.

than gibberish; but still I spoke on. This was a triumph to me, and I began to feel, for the first time, that I was gradually acquiring the language.

At table to-day nobody drank healths, — this practice being peculiar, I believe, to England and the United States. The wines were all light; the dinner was an ordinary one, hardly better than that which is served every day at the house where I am. As I sat next to Mademoiselle Foelix, I offered to relieve her of carving; and did the greater part of the carving for the table. I was astonished that my host allowed it; but he was much absorbed in the conversation, and is evidently very little a man of the world. The knives and forks were not changed for the different dishes, though the plates were; and Mademoiselle informed me that it was not the custom to do so here. We all left the table together, and entered the *salon*, where we had coffee, — the poorest I have found in France. My friends here are all Germans, and probably have not the mysterious secret which all French seem to possess of making this beverage. The *salon* was cold, and very soon we all adjourned to the *cabinet* or study of M. Foelix. Here the deputy inquired of me with regard to the law of alluvion in the United States. There was music and singing of German songs by one or more of three young men who now formed part of the company, two of whom, indeed, were at the dinner-table. The guitar was offered to me for a song! The gentlemen left about ten o'clock, not shaking hands when they parted. I sat an hour longer, and answered the inquiries of the ladies with regard to Boston society, about which they were very curious. I promised Foelix to go with him to see Baron de Gérando to-morrow evening. So much for my first evening in *foreign* society!

Jan. 29. At the École de Droit heard Perreyve [1] for a few minutes, at the conclusion of his lecture. He was quite a young man, and did not interest me much. Next heard Rossi, who was the first lecturer that I heard in Paris, less than three weeks ago. Then I could not understand a sentence that he uttered. To-day I was able to follow him through the greater part of his lecture, which was on the proper qualifications of a deputy and the term of service. His enunciation was occasionally indistinct; but his manner was interesting and his matter good. In the course of his remarks he sketched the history of the English Parliament with regard to duration, and quoted Blackstone. I felt much at home while he did this; it seemed as if household words were in my ears. In the evening, dressed for Baron de Gérando's; Foelix called for me with a cabriolet. We found that the baron was ill; so I returned home and took a French lesson.

Jan. 30. Jouffroy's lecture was adjourned on account of indisposition. Many of the professors seem to find occasions for adjournments, for every day some advertisement appears indicating that a lecture is postponed. To-day the Professor of Geography advertised that his would be postponed, because he had been drawn to serve in the National Guard. My French instructor also apologized for not visiting me this evening, that he was obliged to do duty then in the National Guard. Heard an interesting lecture from Geoffroy Saint-Hilaire on zoölogy, in which he considered the subject of the

---

[1] Henri Perreyve, 1799–1869.

physical adaptation of different animals to their peculiar circumstances, — their teeth, for instance, harmonizing with the food, whether flesh or vegetable, which their appetite leads them to choose.

In the evening heard the _Tartuffe._ Mademoiselle Mars did not play; but it was nevertheless exceedingly well acted. I followed the actors with the book in my hand.

TO GEORGE S. HILLARD.

PARIS, Jan. 30, 1838.

MY DEAR HILLARD, — . . . Since I have been here my time has been almost entirely employed in learning to speak French, and in attending the lectures of the Sorbonne and the École de Droit.

I have not attended the courts or the Chamber of Deputies yet, because I wish to reserve these till my knowledge of French shall enable me to attend them with the most advantage. I attend the lectures, as a good opportunity of hearing French spoken, and accustoming my ear to its sound. For this purpose I have also been to the theatre, with the play in my hand to assist me in following the actors. As yet I have not seen one-quarter of the interesting sights in Paris. Distances are so gigantic, and time is so precious, that I cannot accomplish more than one a day. The Chamber of Deputies, the courts, Versailles, and Père La Chaise (Judge Story will start at this) are still unvisited. I have delivered but few of my letters, because I was unwilling to subject myself to the chance of civilities and the time they necessarily take up. All these I reserve for my last month. In fact, I have not lived, for a great while, so cheaply and college-like as at present. . . . Paris, beyond my anticipations, presents opportunities to a studious young man, which he may improve at small cost. You know the supremacy of its schools of medicine: they have not been overrated. But there are opportunities afforded for knowledge in other departments, which are hardly less important. Besides, here, more perhaps than elsewhere in the world, the human heart is laid bare; you see people more as they appear in Angelo's representation of the great Judgment Day. On this I might enlarge: _sat verbum._ Though I have seen much to interest and instruct me, I have seen nothing which has weakened my attachment to my country; neither have I yet procured mustaches or a club cane, as President Quincy predicted.

Why did the Northern members of Congress bear the infamous bullying of the South? Dissolve the Union, I say.

Affectionately yours,   C. S.

JOURNAL.

Jan. 31, 1838. At seven o'clock this morning went with my friend Shattuck to the Hôtel Dieu, an immense hospital where there are twelve hundred beds. Visited the wards of Roux;[1] a very distinguished surgeon, who was making his morning circuit. Students followed in his train from bed to bed, and observed his examination of each patient, some of them taking notes of the results of the examination. Here I saw wretchedness indeed, in the shape of sores of all kinds and broken limbs, which made me shudder. Roux appeared to be about fifty years old, rather stout and of a robust appearance, but of about the common height. He was quick in his speech, and seemed to be quite passionate. He was scolding right lustily one of the students attached to the hospital, who was tardy. He did not always address the patients in the mildest terms. From this set of wards we passed to the wards of Louis,[2] where were patients who required simply medical treatment, or rather whose complaints were internal. Louis is considered the great medical light of the age. He has revolutionized, perhaps, the study of medicine, by introducing the study of particular cases, and combining them and arriving at general results with regard to the nature of different diseases. He has devoted himself with great zeal to the hospitals, and accumulated a vast deal of knowledge from his minute observation of a great number of cases. His manner of examining a patient is said to be admirable. He is a tall man, with a countenance that seems quite passive. His questions to the patients were numerous and rapid. After this examination was over, the students descended to a lecture room in the Hôtel Dieu, where Louis gave a lecture (clinical) on two or three of the cases which they had observed upstairs. I was able to understand but little. It was spoken of as an admirable lecture. Louis is not a professor, but delivers lectures at his hospital gratuitously and for the mere love of science, — suâ sponte. From this lecture room I passed to the operating room; the operations were by Roux.

Received to-day a letter from Hillard, — my first token from Boston since I left. It is to me like the leaf of olive in the mouth of the dove. In the midst of the satiety which Paris affords, I hunger for news of home.

Feb. 1 (Thursday). Took the eldest son of Madame, with whom I board, — a lad of fifteen years, — as my companion in my walks, for the sake of having somebody with whom to talk French; and made my first excursion to-day through the Faubourg St. Germain, the residence of the nobility and the wealthy of France, to the Hôtel des Invalides, the retreat of broken-down soldiers, — the Greenwich of France. The establishment is vast and splendid beyond the imagination of an American, and betokens the munificence of its ambitious founder, Louis XIV. Here was a kitchen, where carrots were preparing for some fricassee, which seemed large enough for an army.

Feb. 2. Visited for a few moments the other side of the Seine, and returned to my French.

Feb. 3. At eight o'clock this morning visited the church of the Sorbonne, which is only open at this early hour; heard a priest in the rich

---

[1] Joseph Philibert Roux, 1780–1854; an eminent surgeon and successor of Dupuytren at the Hôtel Dieu.

[2] Pierre Charles Alexandre Louis, 1787–1872 ; an eminent pathologist and author of various works on medical subjects. He retired from practice in 1854.

livery of the Catholic Church, who stood near the altar muttering the matin service, with but one other person in the house, and that the official who had charge of the building.

From the church I passed to the Collége Royal de France, where I heard Burnouf [1] on *Éloquence Latine*. He is a gentleman of fifty-five or sixty, short and thick, without any particular marks of intelligence. I counted in his lecture room thirteen students. These all sat round a long table at the head of which was the professor, while he read and expounded in a sufficiently humdrum manner some passages of Sallust's Jugurthine War. He had Sallust before him; first read a few sentences, and then presented a translation, commenting as he went along. Nearly all the students took notes; they seemed to range from seventeen to twenty-one or twenty-two years of age. From this amphitheatre I passed to the École de Droit, where I first heard Berriat Saint-Prix,[2] a name well known in French jurisprudence. He had the red costume of the law professors, and kept his red hat on his head during his lecture. A reason for this may be found in the intolerable coldness of the apartment. He is an old man, — I should say sixty-five or seventy, — with hair white with age, and of an interesting appearance. His manner was interesting, and he sprinkled his legal commentary upon the Code of Procedure with some *plaisanteries*, the exact bearing of which it was difficult for me to comprehend. I sat at some distance from him; and he spoke so low that I could hear but little of what he said. After him I heard in the École de Droit Royer-Collard,[3] a younger man, — say thirty-eight or forty, — full in body and face, and looking as if well-fed and content with the world. His subject was the *Droit des gens;* and he was considering this morning the *quality* of Consuls. He commenced by reviewing the history of antiquity to see if there were any persons recognized, anterior to modern times, as consuls. His manner was clear; his arrangement seemed to be natural, consecutive, and just; and his voice was so full and his enunciation so distinct, that I lost scarcely a sentence. After this, returned to my breakfast and gave the rest of my day to French.

Feb. 4. Visited the other side of the river, and studied French.

Feb. 5. At the Collége de France, at eight o'clock this morning, heard De Portets on the *Droit des gens*. He was a man apparently about fifty, stoutly and substantially built, with iron-gray hair. His lecture had no elegance of manner, but was distinct. There were only four or five persons present. His object appeared to be to show that all the races of men have a common origin, that of course they must be substantially alike at

---

[1] Jean Louis Burnouf, 1775–1844. He was a student of the Greek and Latin classics, and became a professor in 1817. He translated into French Cicero's orations against Catiline, his "Brutus," and "De Officiis," and the works of Tacitus.

[2] Jacques Berriat Saint-Prix, 1769–1845. He became a teacher of the law as early as 1796, and a lecturer at the École de Droit in 1819. He taught law as a science, and expounded it in many publications.

[3] Albert Paul Royer-Collard, 1797–1865; nephew of the eminent French statesman (Pierre Paul). His favorite study was the law of nations. He was, 1845–1847, the dean of the Law Faculty.

present, and that the principles of the law of Nature, therefore, must be universal. From his lecture room I passed to the École de Droit, where I found an audience of five hundred listening to a thick, black-headed man, M. Bugnet;[1] who was speaking on the code, commenting on some sections of the title relating to marriage.

This evening, was persuaded by a friend to sacrifice a French lesson and visit the French Opera, to witness the opera of the *Huguenots*, founded on the massacre of St. Bartholomew. The French Opera was large and brilliant beyond my anticipation, the stage extensive, the scenery imposing, and the whole machinery of the piece a wonderful spectacle. The Duc de Nemours,[2] a tall youth of about twenty-three or twenty-four, the second son of the King, was pointed out to me in a conspicuous box near the stage. This theatre, like many others, is under the patronage of Government, its expenses being included in the civil list.

Feb. 6. Jouffroy was to-day again prevented from lecturing, on account of indisposition. I heard again Geoffroy Saint-Hilaire on zoölogy. He was pursuing the subject which he treated when I last heard him, — the harmony between the different parts of animals. He seems to be very popular; the close of his lecture is invariably attended by applause, and sometimes there is a straggling "bravo."

Feb. 7. Dined by invitation to-day with Mr. O'Donnell, to whom I brought a letter of introduction from Mr. McNally of Baltimore. He was a simple man in his appearance, about forty or forty-two years old, who I believe lives at Paris for the sake of economy. He is a constant writer in "Blackwood," being the author of all the articles of late in that journal on the subject of France. I talked with him considerably in relation to the duties of the editor, &c. He told me that Wilson had fifteen hundred pounds a year as editor, and that contributors received sixteen guineas a sheet; that the duty of the editor is to write for the journal, and lend his name to it, and to examine or read a contribution from an untried hand; that the editor never reads the contributions of one of the regular corps, but that these are sent direct to the printer: further, that the editor never alters the manuscript of an article, but preserves the *ipsissima verba* of the writer; and, if the article in the shape presented is not worthy of publication, it is returned, without any troublesome attempt on the part of the editor to put it into shape. I have noted these things, as they are different somewhat from the practice in America. The *Noctes Ambrosianæ* Mr. O'Donnell told me had been discontinued, on account of the death of Ambrose, in whose tavern they were represented as taking place, and also of Hogg and some others.

Feb. 8. Heard this morning before breakfast Royer-Collard and Poncelet[3] at the École de Droit. The former continued his review of the

---

[1] Jean Joseph Bugnet, 1793–1866. He was remarkable for the clearness of his expositions of the *Code Civil*. He edited Pothier's works.

[2] The Duc de Nemours, the second son of Louis Philippe, was born Oct. 25, 1814. He was an exile from 1848 to 1871.

[3] François Frédéric Poncelet, 1790–1843. He translated German works on the Roman law, which he also illustrated by his own writings.

character and situation of Consuls. The latter lectured on the history of law, and was speaking to-day upon customary law. His voice was indistinct, so that I was not able to gather much from him. He was a man of about thirty-five or thirty-eight, with nothing striking or prepossessing in his manner.

Feb. 9.   Heard Magendie [1] this morning, at the Collége Royal de France. He is renowned for killing cats and dogs, as well as for thorough scientific attainments, I believe. He is a man apparently about fifty, rather short and stout, with a countenance marked by the small-pox. There were no less than three murdered dogs brought upon his table while I was there, in order to illustrate the different appearance of the blood at certain times after death. From Magendie I went to the École de Droit, where I stumbled accidentally upon an examination of a law student for some degree, whether that of Bachelor of Laws, Licentiate, Avocat, or what, I could not tell. The examination was conducted by M. Oudot, a professor whom I have not heard lecture as yet, but who in manner and figure seemed not unlike Henry VIII. Before the examination was concluded three other professors entered, all in their robes and red hats. The student under examination was habited in a black gown of some woollen stuff.

Next heard M. Rossi, whom I have already heard repeatedly, on administrative law. He considered the House of Peers; and, by way of illustration, glanced at that of England. To-day also visited, for the second time, the church of St. Étienne, where are the tombs of Pascal and Boileau, and of St. Geneviève, the patron saint of Paris.

Feb. 10.   Before breakfast went to the Hôpital de la Charité, one of the great hospitals which make Paris such a profitable resort for the student of medicine. The buildings were quite old and rugged, but vast and with spacious courts. The great surgeon, Velpeau, [2] has charge of the surgical wards at this institution, and, as professor, lectures. He is followed through his wards in the morning by an army of students with their note-books. Every kind of hurt, swelling, and loathsome complaint seems to collect here; at all of which these students and their teacher look with an undisturbed countenance. Blessed be science, which has armed man with knowledge and resolution to meet these forms of human distress! From the wards we passed to the lecture room connected therewith, where Velpeau, in a plain way, explained some of the cases which they had just seen in the wards; this being done, he took up the thread of his regular course of lectures, which at this stage related to the eye and its complaints. He appears to be about fifty, of the middle size, and with a mild gentle countenance. From the lecture room passed to the consultation room, where the poor called and exhibited to him their ailments and received gratuitous attention, the students forming a circle around, and of course observing the patient.

Feb. 11 (Sunday).   Dined with Mr. Ticknor. After dinner an Italian

---

[1] François Magendie, 1783–1855. He was eminent as a physiologist, and tested the science by experiments. More than his predecessors he used living animals for the purpose.

[2] Alfred Armand Louis Marie Velpeau, 1795–1867. He wrote upon surgical anatomy and obstetrics, and was eminent in the clinical art.

came in, who was a literary man of some rank, — Ugoni.[1] He was upwards of fifty, and spoke with a strong Italian accent.

Feb. 12. This morning rose before seven o'clock; first went to that immense receptacle of all diseases, the Hôtel Dieu, where I witnessed, for a second time, the rapid and fierce manner of Roux in his surgical wards, and the slow and exact philosophical examination of Louis. From the Hôtel Dieu I passed through the Ile de la Cité, and the part of the city in front of that to the Hôpital St. Louis, situated at the other extreme of the city, and devoted chiefly to diseases of the skin.

Feb. 13. Early went to the Sorbonne; heard Saint-Marc Girardin [2] on the character of Jean Jacques Rousseau, the favorite author of the French. There was something in Rousseau's conduct and mind which is not an unfit type of the French character. In both we behold the rankest vegetation of vice intermingled with the most brilliant flowers of the intellect. The lecturer to-day evidently loved his subject. He treated it with eloquence and ardor. The room was a little cold, and he kept his hat on (a common hat) during his lecture. He was quite simple and unadorned in his person, and about thirty-seven. From the Sorbonne to the École de Droit, where I heard Royer-Collard again, on the subject of Consuls.

Visited this forenoon the Palais du Luxembourg, which was built by Marie de Médicis, though it still retains the name of the palace whose ancient site it occupies. It is now occupied by the Chamber of Peers; but there are several large rooms which are not needed for the purposes of the peers. Here is the collection of paintings by the modern artists of France. Classical scenes seem to be more taken than Scriptural now-a-days; and Helen and Paris are instead of the Virgin and the Infant. The painting seems to be of an extremely sensuous character; the forms of women and men are displayed with great freedom, and the most careful tints from the pencil invest them with more than flesh-like attractiveness. I do not know enough to compare these artists with the giants, some of whose pictures still charm from the walls of the Louvre; and I feel unwilling, without making an effort at judgment, to fall in with the current which seems to set against the present school. In the modern productions there are great beauty, brilliancy, and finish of coloring, — whether it will endure is another question, — and all the persons and scenes represented are very much idealized. There seems none of the roughness of Nature which the older artists often hit upon; all is smooth and gilded. I visited the ancient chapel of Marie de Médicis, in which, as my *cicérone* (a gabbling old woman) told me, the daughters of peers are married at the present

---

[1] Camillo Ugoni, 1784–1856. He was a translator of Horace and Cæsar; but his chief work was a "History of Italian Literature." He was an exile from 1821 to 1838.

[2] Saint-Marc Girardin, 1801–1873. In 1830, he succeeded Guizot as Professor of History. From 1834 to 1863 he was Professor of French Poetry at the Sorbonne. He was a contributor to the *Journal des Débats* and the *Revue des Deux Mondes*. His writings related chiefly to French literature. As Minister of Public Instruction in 1848, and as a member of the Chamber of Deputies, he interested himself to promote education. After twenty years' retirement from politics, he entered the National Assembly in 1871, and was chosen its Vice-President.

day; also visited some other apartments, beautiful indeed, which are used as committee-rooms by the peers, particularly the bedchamber of Marie de Médicis, which was a truly royal apartment, decorated in the most sumptuous style, with panels richly gilt and painted in compartments by Nicolas Poussin, and with the ceiling richly painted by Rubens and Champagne. Such aid did the arts lend to the luxury of palaces; and such splendors were displayed in the bedchamber of a princess!

Called on Mr. Warden [1] this morning, with a letter of introduction from Mr. Sparks. He treated me quite civilly. He was formerly American consul, and is at present a member of the French Institute. In the evening, called upon Foelix; he was just going out upon business, and without any ceremony left me to talk with his sisters. I spent about two hours or more "airing" my French in this conversation.

Feb. 14. Heard this morning, at the École de Droit, M. Oudot,[2] whom I had formerly seen presiding at an examination of students. He lectured on hypothecation. His manner was uninteresting.

This forenoon, took a walk through the Faubourg St. Germain, the seat of the old *noblesse* of France. The houses are large and magnificent; but they stand back from the street, and have in front a high stone wall, say ten feet high. There is a wide *porte-cochère*, the entrance to the court on which the houses stand.

This evening visited Foelix, where I met the German gentleman whom I had formerly met at dinner. He has kindly invited me to pass a week with him at his house on the banks of the Rhine, and I have accepted his invitation. I talked with Foelix of Judge Story. He told me that there was no lawyer in France equal to him, though there were some in Germany. I was astonished when he further told me that the Bibliothèque du Roi did not contain all the books cited in the "Conflict of Laws;" and that, of the thousand lawyers at Paris, there were nine hundred and ninety-nine who did not even know of the existence of all these books. Thus has Judge Story beaten them on their own ground. After this, talked with regard to the rules for admission to the bar; and also about several of the law-writers and professors. Foelix thought the greater part of the books of the present day were absolutely good for nothing. He excepted Toullier [3] and Pardessus; [4] but Duranton [5] and his twenty volumes he abused heartily, characterizing him as

---

[1] David B. Warden, M.D., was born in Ireland, in 1778, and died, in 1845, in Paris, where he had resided as Consul of the United States for forty years. He wrote upon the "Faculties and Literature of Negroes" and "Consular Establishments," and was the author of miscellaneous papers on America.

[2] François Julien Oudot, 1804-1864.

[3] 1752-1835; author of a work in fourteen volumes on "The French Çivil Law according to the Order of the Code Napoleon."

[4] Jean Marie Pardessus, 1772-1853. His works on commercial and maritime law are of high authority. He took the chair of Commercial Law when it was established, in 1810. He was in the Corps Législatif from 1807 to 1811, and again from 1820 to 1830. He remained loyal to the Bourbons after the Revolution of 1830, and was then deprived of his professorship.

[5] Alexandre Duranton, 1783-1866; author of a treatise on Contracts, and also of Commentaries on the *Code Civil*, in twenty-two volumes, entitled, *Cours de Droit Français suivant le Code Civil*.

a charlatan, who knew nothing of principles, and who was very much disliked by his brother professors; Oudot, also, whom I had heard this morning, was a charlatan, — and this I believe; M. Rossi, an able man, but *paresseux*.

All were kind enough to remark this evening that I had gained a great deal of French; that they were astonished at my progress. I just begin to enjoy conversation, and the sensation is delightful. My greatest difficulty is promptly to command the proper form of salutation when I enter a room. After I am once started, I find myself able to run on with some comparative facility, but of course with constant blunders.

TO JUDGE STORY.

Paris, Feb. 14, 1838.

My dear Judge, — . . . I have not yet heard Duranton, though I have heard nearly all the other professors at the Sorbonne and the École de Droit. I generally hear two or three lectures of an hour or more each before breakfast. I am particularly attending to the style of lecturing on different subjects, — law, literature, mathematics, philosophy, &c., — and when I have completed my observations I shall let you have the results. Then for the courts, which at present remain unvisited. Time flies, and it seems as if I had seen nothing of the immense store of interesting objects at Paris. All my hours are occupied far into the watches of the night. So far as labor is concerned, I should much prefer to be again in my office dealing with clients and familiar law books. Travelling, with my desires and determinations, is no sinecure. I am obliged to husband all my minutes. . . . Has William written me yet? He must tell every thing about Cambridge and your family. I hope Mr. Greenleaf will not forget me because I have not lately written him.

As ever, affectionately yours,   C. S.

JOURNAL.

Feb. 15, 1838. In the morning before breakfast, heard Berriat Saint-Prix at the Law School. He did not appear less venerable this time than when I saw him before. He held his snuff-box in his hand during all his lecture, and occasionally rapped with it for silence, calling out, *Un peu de silence !* About the middle of his lecture, he stopped for a moment, rose, and walked backwards and forwards, — to rest, perhaps, his ancient limbs, — and then proceeded. After his lecture, he said he would attend to examinations; and about half-a-dozen students came forward, handed their names, and then resumed their seats, when the professor called them, one by one (Monsieur A., &c.), and proposed questions, apparently in the law of Procedure, upon which he lectured. Each student answered to four or five questions. I presume that this examination is one of the many which a student undergoes preparatory to admission to the bar.

In the afternoon visited the Anatomical Museum and the dissecting rooms. In these rooms are about fifty subjects constantly, presenting the amplest opportunities for the student. There were five different rooms, in each of which were twelve iron tables; and each, in the two rooms which I entered, had one or more subjects. With gladness did I drink a long draught of fresh air when I passed from these shambles of death; the air within was worse than that of a tomb.

In the evening dined with Mr. Cass,[1] at 17 Avenue Matignon. Mrs. Cass did not appear at table, being ill. The company consisted of about fifteen or sixteen; and among them the Mexican ambassador and an Englishman with a title, and a star on his coat, whose name I did not catch. The table was splendid, and the attendance perfect; servants in smallclothes constantly supplying you with some new luxury. I sat next to the lady of "Milord English," and found her good-natured rather than sensible or informed; a far superior lady from the South of my own country was on my other side. This being the evening of the *soirées* of General Cass, I stayed after dinner for that. I should say that all left the table together, and gentlemen did not linger behind to drink wine and tell stories, or discuss politics. Of course, much less wine was drunk than at an American table; though there was offered some of almost every kind. General Cass's Hôtel is furnished sumptuously. On entering, your name is received by a servant, who announces it. We were received in a small *salon*, to reach which we passed through, besides the antechamber, a billiard room, and a large and splendid *salon;* the dinner was in yet another *salle*. In the evening company was received in both the *salons*. Mr. Cass is a man of large private fortune, and is said to live in a style superior to that of any minister ever sent by America.

Feb. 16. In the morning before breakfast visited the wards of Dubois [2] in the Hospice de la Faculté. These are devoted to *accouchements*. Dubois appeared an admirable man for this duty. He was mild, attentive, and I should think quite intelligent and experienced. After the progress had been made through the wards, he delivered a clinical lecture on some of the cases which had passed under observation. As a lecturer he was good. The day being rainy, I stayed in the house the remainder of the time.

Feb. 17. This morning again followed Dubois in his wards; and also Jules Cloquet [3] in some of his. He is a surgeon of considerable eminence, and an author. He appeared to be rather a young man for his position, say thirty-five; but he must be older. After he had gone through his wards, he repaired to the lecture room; where, in presence of the students, he gave gratuitous advice to *Malades* who presented themselves. In the afternoon

---

[1] Lewis Cass, 1782–1866; afterwards United States Senator and Secretary of State.

[2] Baron Paul Antoine Dubois, 1795–1871; celebrated both in the practice and teaching of his profession, and as a writer upon obstetrics. He was *accoucheur* to the Empress Eugénie at the birth of the Prince Imperial.

[3] Baron Jules Germain Cloquet, 1790–. He succeeded in 1831 to the chair of Clinical Surgery. He was the author of a treatise on "Human Anatomy," and the inventor of surgical instruments. He published "Recollections of Lafayette."

dined with Mr. Draper [1] at the Rocher de Cancale.[2] There are several restaurants at Paris that claim pre-eminence, — Grignon's, Véry's, Véfour's, Périgord's, and, *primus inter pares*, the Rocher de Cancale.

Feb. 18. To-day, visited the hall of the Chamber of Peers; after this drove to the Bois de Boulogne. . . .

Feb. 19. This morning, heard M. Bugnet at the École de Droit, who spoke to a very full audience, — the large amphitheatre being completely filled. At half-past two went with Mr. Warden to attend a meeting of the far-famed Institute of France. The building devoted to the sittings of this memorable body is quite large and ancient. The meeting to-day was of the Academy of Sciences. Their hall is not so large as either of our court-rooms in Boston. It is a parallelogram. The walls are adorned by portraits of men eminent in science and literature in France. At three o'clock the session commenced. The *procès verbal*, or journal, of the last meeting was read, and then memoirs upon different subjects; one upon steamboats, the person reading the memoir sitting at a table in front of the president. After the memoirs had been read, the secretary, M. Arago (a man whose personal appearance reminded me of Mr. Bailey,[3] the schoolmaster of Boston), read the different communications, amounting to a dozen or more. It was then announced that the Academy would go into secret session; and all strangers retired. I was honored with a seat, by invitation of the president, within the bar, directly by the side of the persons who read memoirs.

In the evening went to the Baron de Gérando's.[4] I had a letter of introduction to him from Dr. Channing; and on Saturday last I left it with my card. On the next day I received M. de Gérando's card and an invitation to his *soirées*. I went this evening with M. Foelix. De Gérando is an old gentleman, full of goodness of heart, and he gave me a most cordial reception. He presented me to his niece, who appeared to be the mistress of the house; and who did the honors with great grace and cordiality. The *salon* was of about the size of an American parlor; and the walls were hung round with pictures. There were about as many ladies as gentlemen; and the appearance of things was little different from that of a small party in our country. Ladies do not, as with us, enter the room on the arm of a gentleman, or take a gentleman's arm to walk across the room. I think they were

---

[1] The banker.

[2] Then the most celebrated restaurant of Paris, and situated in the Passage du Saumon.

[3] Ebenezer Bailey, who died in 1839.

[4] Baron Joseph Marie de Gérando, philosopher and publicist, was born in Lyons in 1772, and died in Paris in 1842. During the French Revolution he was by turns soldier and exile. Under Napoleon he was in public service at home and in Italy. He became a Councillor of State in 1811, and retained the office, with a brief interruption, until his death. He was made a Peer in 1837. In his youth he developed a faculty for metaphysics, winning a prize from the Institute for an essay on the influence of signs on the formation of ideas; and in this science he attained a deserved distinction. His department in the École de Droit was administrative law. He investigated, both in books and visits to institutions in France, Switzerland, and Germany, philanthropic schemes for the improvement of public health, industry, and education, and for the administration of charities. He published in 1839, in four volumes, the work which he was writing when Sumner was in Paris, on "Public Beneficence," — *De la Bienfaisance Publique*.

more neglected at this *soirée* than ladies are with us. They sat on the sofas, almost entirely by themselves; and at the latter part of the evening another room was opened, and they went in to get some *confitures*, I think, a whole troop, with scarcely a single gentleman. Among the gentlemen I met here was M. Pellat,[1] the professor who lectures on the "Pandects" at the École de Droit, and with whom I had considerable conversation; and another gentleman, whose name I do not recollect, who has just published a work upon the establishments for *Enfants Trouvés* in Europe. Several others I was introduced to, and conversed with, but cannot remember their names. De Gérando was so kind as to authorize me to use him in any way in which he could be of service. He expressed a great interest in Dr. Channing.

Feb. 20. Visited the Observatory, where is the meridian line of France, a building which seems made for immortality. There is hardly any thing in it but stone; neither wood nor iron; the floors are of stone, and also the stairs. After this, visited the Hospice des Enfants Trouvés, an institution at which an American might well be astonished. This is the receptacle of the foundlings of Paris; and upwards of one hundred are left here each week, making more than six thousand during the year. The argument for such establishments is that they prevent infanticide by furnishing an asylum for infants. There is a little box with a green cushion, about large enough for an infant, which opens on the street; into this the child is put by the parent or other person intrusted with it, and at the same time the box is turned round, a bell being made to ring by the act of turning, and the little thing is received into its new asylum.[2] If the infant is well, it is very soon put out to nurse in the country. There were about one hundred and fifty in the Hospice. It was a strange sight to see so many children all of an age, ranged in rows, in their little cradles. There was a large number with sick eyes, and many with other complaints. The curtains of many were drawn aside that I might see them. In one cradle I observed that the countenance was pallid and the mouth open, and I said to my attendant, *Elle est morte*. The attendant doubted, and thought that she perceived a breath from the mouth. I touched the cheek; and it was very evident that the poor child was dead, — it was cold as marble. It was melancholy to see even an infant that had died without any attendant affectionately watching; and who breathed its last, with the curtains of its little cradle closed against all sight. Every thing appeared neat and well-managed in this institution. I next went to the church of the Val de Grâce, which was built by Anne of Austria, the mother of Louis XIV. It is a beautiful architectural relic of those times.

In the evening visited Foelix, where I passed three hours in conversation. I met there M. Bravard,[3] one of the professors of law, — a man forty years

---

[1] Charles Auguste Pellat, — a learned commentator on the Roman Law, and dean of the Law Faculty, 1847–1868, — was born at Grenoble in 1793.

[2] The *tour* has been discontinued in Paris.

[3] Pierre Claude Jean Baptiste Bravard-Veyrières, 1804–1861. His specialty was Commercial Law. He served in the Constituent Assembly of 1848, and in the Legislative Assembly of the next year, and rendered service in perfecting measures relating to this

old, with black hair, very agreeable and good-natured. We spoke of jurisprudence in France and America, and of slavery in the latter country; also of several French juridical works. He treated the work of his brother-professor Duranton with great contempt; he said it was good for nothing. He told me that there were upwards of three thousand students of law at Paris; and that they were from all parts of the world, — Poland, Austria, Prussia, Italy, Spain, England, and even Greece. From this he drew, perhaps justly, some strong inferences in favor of the supremacy of Paris as the literary and juridical capital of the world. M. Bravard further observed that there were very few Frenchmen who gave any attention to foreign languages.

Feb. 21. Heard M. Duranton this morning; and I am disposed, from his lecture and appearance, to believe what I have been told of him. He is about fifty years old, with thick, uncombed iron-gray hair, and with a very vulgar look and manner. His voice was harsh and querulous, and there seemed no kind of grace in any thing he did. The subject of his lecture was "Testaments and Donations *inter vivos* under the *Code Civil.*"

Feb. 22. This morning first heard, at the Sorbonne, Lefébure de Fourcy[1] on the differential and integral calculus. He lectures in the place of the venerable Lacroix. Perhaps there was an audience of twenty-five. Almost all had their note-books, and took down the explanations of the professor. He stood at his blackboard, and in a plain business style went through his calculations. The chalk and sponge were his chief implements. Of course I could not follow him into the regions of mathematics, whither his involved and complex figures carried him; but I could observe the manner, which was entirely practical, without any show or apparent desire to do any thing but make his hearers understand the calculations. The professor was a large-sized and rather rough-looking person. From him I passed to the lecture-room of Pellat at the École de Droit. The latter lectures upon the "Pandects." He had a copy of the *Corpus Juris* before him, and was expounding the part relating to *servitudes*. He read, in the first place, a clause of a few lines in Latin, and then expounded its meaning with fulness and plainness, and in an entirely conversational manner. Almost all the students had their copies of the *Corpus Juris* resting on their knees, and followed the professor as he read, besides taking notes of his exposition. Pellat I have met at the Baron de Gérando's. He is apparently about forty or forty-five, and is modest in his manner. He did not produce the impression of remarkable talent. After Pellat, I heard, at the Sorbonne, a part of the lecture of Géruzez[2] on some French author, — I could not catch the name; and after

---

branch of jurisprudence. Sumner wrote to Judge Story, April 21: "I have spent a long evening with Bravard, Professor of Commercial Law, and successor of Pardessus who vacated his chair at the time of the Revolution of July, being a great Carlist. Bravard says that Boulay-Paty's work is very much superior to that of Pardessus."

[1] Louis Étienne Lefébure de Fourcy, 1785–1869. In 1838 he succeeded Lacroix in the chair of Differential and Integral Calculus. He is the author of books on geometry.

[2] Nicolas Eugène Géruzez, 1799–1865. He was, from 1833 to 1852, the substitute of Villemain in the chair of Literature. His writings related mostly to the history of literature and eloquence.

this, at the École de Droit, heard Ducaurroy, on the "Institutes." I have already spoken of his manner. He was more animated than Pellat; he had his copy of the "Institutes" before him, and read and expounded.

From the scene of lectures I went to the Musée d'Artillerie, which in one respect corresponds to the Tower of London. Here are the coats of arms of many of the kings and marshals of France, and of many of her renowned knights and commanders. . . . I was astonished by the weight of the armor, many of the suits weighing a hundred pounds, and some more, without including the sword or any offensive weapon, or even the buckler. No one who sees these remains of armor can wonder that many a knight fainted under the load. To bear a knight armed in complete steel must have required a steed of uncommon stoutness, especially when we consider that he was often loaded with armor as heavy as that of his master.

Feb. 24. Visited the manufactory of the Gobelin tapestry.

Feb. 25. To-day I ascended the monument in the Place Vendôme, conceived and built by Napoleon. It is composed of the cannon taken at Austerlitz. There is genius characteristic of Napoleon in making the conquered cannon into a monument of victory; and the monument is a most beautiful one. It is an imitation of the pillar of Trajan at Rome, of which it preserves the proportions on a scale larger by a twelfth. Its elevation is one hundred and thirty feet, and from its top there is a fine view of Paris.

Feb. 26. This morning heard Biot[1] at the Sorbonne. He is an old gentleman, sixty-five perhaps, full of life and animation, and using his chalk and sponge with as much ardor as others do the dance. He was engaged at the blackboard making explanations and calculations with regard to the sun and moon. Astronomy, in its mathematical relations, seemed to be the subject. In manner, in quickness of expression and self-abandon, he was not unlike Professor Farrar.[2] Also heard Poisson,[3] another mathematician, who was equally animated, and who stood at his blackboard with his sponge and chalk. Next heard Valette[4] at the Law School, — a man of about thirty-five, without having any thing particularly interesting about him. After that, took a long walk to the immense Hôpital Salpêtrière, where there are five thousand infirm and aged women, it being a great almshouse. As I left this establishment, I met on the sidewalk a person of rather humble appearance, of whom I asked some question, which enabled him to detect me as a foreigner. It seems that he understood a little English, and had read Sterne's

---

[1] Jean Baptiste Biot, 1774–1862. He was one of the most eminent men of the century in mathematics, astronomy, and natural philosophy. He became a professor at the College of France as early as 1800. In 1804 he ascended in a balloon with Gay-Lussac, and, in 1806, accompanied Arago to Spain on a scientific expedition with which they were charged by the Government. He won fame in authorship as well as by his experiments and discoveries.

[2] John Farrar, 1779–1853; Professor of Mathematics and Natural Philosophy in Harvard College when Sumner was a student.

[3] Siméon Denis Poisson, 1781–1840; a scientist of the highest attainments, specially distinguished in mathematical physics. He published several treatises, and contributed many articles to periodicals. In 1837 he was made a peer.

[4] Claude Denis Auguste Valette, Professor of Civil Law, was born in 1805. In the National Assembly he was active in law reform.

" Sentimental Journey,"—a book, by the way, which appears to be read a great deal in France,—and he wished to understand more. He frankly told me that he was a mechanic, who could only find time to study on Sundays, and that he could not afford to hire an instructor in English. He accordingly proposed to render me assistance in acquiring French, if I would return the same assistance to him with regard to English. The whole *rencontre* was so odd that I at first feared some deception, and buttoned my surtout so as to protect my pockets; but I was soon convinced that I did my friend injustice, and I gave him my card that he might know where to call upon me, if he saw fit. I talked with him perhaps three-quarters of an hour. Is this a specimen of the new-born zeal for knowledge in the humbler orders of Paris?

After this passed through the Jardin des Plantes, an immense establishment devoted to botany, mineralogy, zoölogy, and comparative anatomy. My visit was short, so that I only saw the outside of a small portion. This place will necessarily require several future visits.

TO PROFESSOR HENRY W. LONGFELLOW, CAMBRIDGE.

PARIS, Tuesday, Feb. 27, 1838.

MY DEAR LONGFELLOW,—. . . I wish that Hillard and Felton could enjoy Europe. They need it, and their minds are ripe for it. How often have I thought of the thrill with which they would survey the objects I daily see. Tell Felton to come out immediately and pass a good half-year at Paris; there is enough to consume all that time in one round of pleasant study.

There is no news stirring at Paris. You know that the Warrens and Cabots are in Italy, to return to Paris or London in May; and the Farrars are there also. Mrs. Sears is here. The Ticknors and Mr. Gray leave for London in a week or fortnight. Walsh and his family of daughters are here. Walsh himself has been quite sick, having been confined to his chamber for some time. Thiers says he is engaged upon a history of Florence at present; but he is notoriously so immersed in politics that I should doubt if he had time or inclination for writing a quiet book. Mrs. Fry has been at Paris, exciting some attention on the subject of prisons. The French, by the way, are just waking up on that subject; and also on that of railroads. A good letter, my dear Longfellow, to the care of the Barings, London, is the amend to be made for past negligence.

As ever, faithfully yours,

CHAS. SUMNER.

JOURNAL.

Feb. 27, 1838. This is *Mardi Gras*, or Fat Tuesday, the last day of the Carnival, the day before Lent. In all Catholic countries this is one of the great *fête* days of the year. Commenced the morning by a visit with Dr. Shattuck to one of the distant hospitals, full of the most disgusting sights and the most impressive moral lessons, — the Hôpital des Vénériens. About two o'clock, went over the river to the thronged boulevards; in the streets met the fat ox, which was escorted by a band of butchers on horseback, dressed in the most fantastic costumes. The boulevards and the Rue St. Honoré were crowded literally for miles with equipages, with groups of maskers and spectators. An ever-present and most numerous police kept this immense and inflammable multitude in the most perfect order. For several hours I walked or stood on the boulevards, and during all the time saw not a single instance of collision either between those on foot or those in carriages. The people on foot moved on by easy swells without jarring upon each other; the carriages were all kept in regular files or *queues*, and moved on slowly as a funeral procession. There were many maskers on horseback; others in carts and carriages. This is the Saturnalia of France, and all are privileged for this once to play the fool. I was told that formerly, on this occasion, the young men, the *élite* of society, appeared habited in fantastic dresses; this is now left chiefly, I think, to the lower orders. Nevertheless, there were many to-day in costume who had gentle blood. Among the fantastic dresses was a man habited like a bear, with an iron collar about his neck, and another man leading him. He sprawled upon the ground, and then reared himself very much like the hugging animal.

Dined at Grignon's, one of the renowned restaurants of Paris; then read at Galignani's reading-room; and at midnight went to the masked ball at the house of the French Opera. On this evening, or rather night, Paris is full of balls; every hall, every musical saloon, and almost every theatre, with its pit floored over, has its ball and its set of maskers. At the French Opera the dancing commenced about one o'clock, or a little after; when I left at four o'clock, the spirit of the dancers and *intrigantes* had not abated. Nearly all the women were in masks and in fancy dresses; there were many in black dominos. The *coup d'œil* was beautiful of the brilliantly dressed assemblage, under a sun-like stream of light from numerous chandeliers, moving in the mazy dance or in the volatile waltz, while the powerful band was pouring out a flood of music. The words for the figures were given through a speaking-trumpet. At four o'clock in the morning, with some friends, I took a carriage, drove over the boulevards still brilliant with the light of the lamps and the windows of the *cafés* and restaurants, all of which were open to receive and entertain the maskers. Little rest was there in Paris this night, I should think. We stopped about five o'clock at a restaurant on the Boulevard du Temple, where we took something, whether breakfast or supper it would be difficult to tell; and then drove outside the barriers of Paris to what is called the Courtille, — a village the other side of the wall, where, on this night, all the common people assemble to enjoy *their* dance and *their* mask. We entered three or four balls, where dancing was proceeding as vigorously as if the streaks of morning had not begun to appear. In some of the corners, leaning on the tables, were some sleepers; but the main assemblage seemed to be unconscious of the peep of day. The noise was considerable, but I saw no quarrel, and indeed no disturbance of any kind. There was, indeed, the deep stamp of low life upon the appearance of every thing; but there was nothing to justify the interference of the police. Here the police was also in great force; horsemen were constantly riding up and down the street, and within each *bal* there were stationed several *gendarmes.* Shortly after, when morning had finally penetrated the darkness, and many of the dancers, excited from the labors of the long night, had rushed into the street, squads of troops of the line were posted in the street, at intervals of a few rods, for the space of a third or half a mile. It was towards seven o'clock when we left; the light of day had already filled the streets, and was struggling with the lamps in the dancing halls; the music, however, was still sounding, and there were many who danced on in obedience to its time. As we came away we passed a train of carriages and *citadines,* a mile long, of persons, some maskers and some not, going from the city to see the scene which we had left. This is usually the last scene of the Saturnalia of *Mardi Gras.* Flour is liberally thrown from and into the carriages without offence being taken. Glad was I, after struggling for a mile or thereabout over muddy pavements, through the dense crowd which attended these carriages, to find a cabriolet, and set my face homeward. At half-past seven o'clock of the morning went to bed so thoroughly fatigued, that I did not recover consciousness till three and a half o'clock of the afternoon. So much for *Mardi Gras* and the last day of a Parisian Carnival. I have forgotten, in my account of this day, to mention that, after dinner and before the ball, I visited what is called the Café des Aveugles, — a café in the Palais Royal in which there is a small band of blind musicians, and also a little stage on which there is some acting. No price is charged for admission, but you are expected to call for something at the bar, — a cup of coffee or beer; and you sit sipping your liquid while the blind men play.

March 1. This forenoon heard Bravard at the École de Droit. He is the author of one or two books, and is a professor much liked, I believe. He appears to be about forty, with eyes inflamed by study. His subject is the *Code de Commerce.* To-day he was lecturing on bankruptcy. His audience was quite large. Late in the afternoon went to see my friend Shattuck off for Italy in the *malle-poste,* as it is called.

In the evening went to the Théâtre Français, to hear the *Horaces* of Corneille; and it was a treat. The sublime and powerful verse of this great author from the studied enunciation of a French actor produced a great and constant effect. The audience were attentive all the time, and not, as with us, only when a single well-graced actor is on the stage. And the interest of the piece was in the recitation, not in the *action;* there was not even a single change of the scene from the beginning to the end, neither was there any combat or battery or disturbance. And yet the interest of the audience was unflagging throughout. This presents certainly a marked difference between England and America and France. After the *Horaces* came a pleasant piece, translated from the German of Kotzebue, called *Les Deux Frères.*

CHAPTER XII.

PARIS. — SOCIETY AND THE COURTS. — MARCH TO MAY, 1838. — AGE, 27.

EARLY in March, Sumner changed his lodgings from the Latin quarter to the vicinity of the boulevards, with the view of seeing more of French society, and mingling in the various scenes of the metropolis. His intercourse with Demetz, Chevalier, Cousin, Sismondi, and Pardessus belongs to the months included in this chapter: two weeks earlier he had been brought into relations with De Gérando. He still frequented the Sorbonne and the College of France; but his attendance on the courts, both in Paris and at Versailles, is also an interesting feature of this period.

JOURNAL.

March 4, 1838. The last three days I have wearied myself in search of other lodgings on what is called the fashionable side of the river near the boulevards. For my last few weeks in Paris I wish to be where I may see more of the world than I can in my present comfortable, but retired, quarters. I have been pleasantly situated on this quiet side of the river, hearing lectures, studying French, and familiarizing myself with the objects of interest here. It was amusing to call at so many houses, as I did, to inquire for lodgings, and to practise my French upon all the women who kept them. It was a good exercise, — better, perhaps, than that with a French master.

March 5. Some days ago received an invitation to dinner with the Baron de Gérando. There were at the table an Italian poet, a Spanish Procureur-Général, several Frenchmen, including a proper quota of Counts, and Colonel White and lady of Florida. I was placed between these two, unfortunately; and so lost the opportunity of talking French, except across Colonel White with Mademoiselle, the niece of our host, who did the honors of the house with great grace. There appeared to be no head or foot to the table. It was a parallelogram. Mademoiselle sat at one end, and the Baron in the middle of one of the sides. After dinner we adjourned to the drawing-room, where we had coffee, and joined the soirée of our host. Here I talked with several persons. There were Spanish, Italians, Germans, French, and Americans present, and through the medium of French I talked with all. The Baron, our host, was kind enough to give me a ticket to the House of

Peers, to sit in the box set apart, I think, for the eldest sons of Peers. In the *salon*, during the *soirée*, I could not but observe that the ladies were more herded together than among us. Gentlemen stood in groups talking with each other, and did not seem to feel obliged to entertain the ladies. Some ladies, indeed, asked me to bring them a book or pamphlet from the table to read; and this was in a room almost crammed with people. I should remark that these were German ladies.

March 6. To-day I left my quarters in the Rue de l'Odéon, and entered my new *apartement* in the more thronged and fashionable quarter. It is No. 5 Place des Italiens, looking on the square in front of the Italian Opera House. It is a neat, comfortable room, with a thick carpet, and chairs and sofas of red plush. French taste always selects something of this kind. I have not seen in Paris our simple hair-bottom chairs.

March 7. Took a cab and drove in various directions, leaving letters of introduction, which I had retained till the present time because I could not speak French enough to justify presenting them: and now I do it with the greatest distrust; but, if ever done, it is necessary to do it quickly, as the days which remain to me in Paris are few. After leaving my cards I attended a sitting of the Peers. I entered the room between soldiers, and found myself in a small place, hardly larger than the box of a theatre. I have already made mention of the chamber, which I had seen before to-day; though this is the first view I have had of the Peers in session. The session was pretty full. The dress of the Peers was a blue coat with a standing collar and cuffs trimmed with gold. The assembly appeared highly respectable. Most of the Peers were considerably advanced in years, and the snows of age seemed liberally scattered among them. The subject under discussion was a law regulating the number of horses and the weight of vehicles allowed to pass on the public roads. All the members, who spoke at any length, left their places and mounted the tribune. If they only spoke by way of explanation, they did not leave their seats. Several Peers who spoke had their remarks apparently written out, and read them from the paper in their hands. The style of debate was entirely creditable; it was animated and courteous. Indeed, I can hardly imagine an assembly appearing more respectable, or a debate conducted with more of that spirit by which truth and the public good are best advanced. Yet I cannot help recording, that I observed a Peer standing in a most prominent place, on the elevation of the President's chair, and in conversation with the President, with his thumbs stuck in the arm-holes of his waistcoat, — which I remember hearing years ago was a Yankee trick.

After the debate in the Peers, dined, and called on Foelix; spending several hours of the evening in conversation with him. It seems that, like many others, he has been banished from Prussia, his native country. He described the state of Prussia to me as very bad, its government as *false* (that was his word) and detestable.

March 8. Spent a large portion of the day in preparing some law papers for a friend. Among the letters of introduction which I left yesterday was one to M. Érard.[1] I received from him this morning a ticket to one of the concerts at his *salon*, which I attended, and heard most delicious melody. I regretted that some of my friends with ears better attuned to harmony were not in my place.

TO GEORGE S. HILLARD, BOSTON.

PARIS, March 8, 1838.

MY DEAR HILLARD, — A month has passed since I have written you; and your two letters have been running through my mind every day. How I long for news of distant Boston, and how I picture all its clean streets, its sensible people, and my dear friends! Stands my office where it did; and all Court Street, is it still firm on its foundations? . . . I rejoice to hear from various quarters of the reception of Prescott's book in our country. I have seen a copy and glanced through it. By the way, the American edition is every whit as well printed as the English, and has some plates more appropriate than those prefixed to the English. The book reads beautifully, and I am glad that we have produced a work with so much of research, learning, suavity, and elegance. A few days since, at dinner at the Baron de Gérando's, I met the Procureur-Général of Spain. I was full of Prescott's book, and took the occasion to endeavor to scatter some seed in Spanish ground. I described the work and the labors of Mr. Prescott to the Spaniard, who appeared particularly interested and inquired the name of the author. He was quite astonished when I told him that the historian had drawn from unpublished manuscripts and documents. Ticknor has placed a copy of the book in the hands of one or two French *littérateurs*, who have promised to review it in some of the French journals. Ticknor leaves for London in a few days. I am sorry to lose him and his family. . . . Write me about the "Jurist" and all other things. I shall stay in Paris till the middle of April. I find ten times as much here to interest me as I anticipated. The lectures, the courts, the arts, — each would consume a year, to say nothing of the language which I am trying after very hard. Love to all.

As ever, affectionately yours,

CHAS. SUMNER.

TO DR. FRANCIS LIEBER, COLUMBIA, S. C.

PARIS, March 9, 1838.

MY DEAR LIEBER, — I was longing to hear from you when your agreeable letter of Jan. 18 came upon me. Here at Paris I have to satiety the richest fare for mind, and body also; that is, when I choose to extend my hand for it: but that does not make me wish any the less for a cup of refreshing drink

---

[1] Jean Baptiste Pierre Orphée Érard, 1794–1855; manufacturer of musical instruments and nephew of Sébastien Érard. Both, and particularly the uncle, were distinguished in their art.

from the distant waters of my own country. A word from a friend, when it has traversed so many ridges of the sea, becomes tenfold consecrated. All that you have promised for me in Europe has been more than realized. I have seen new *lives;* and the life of life seems to have burst upon me. Cicero could hardly have walked with a more bounding and yet placid joy through the avenues of his Elysium, and conversed with Scipio and Laelius, than I, — a distant American, of a country which has no prescription, no history, and no association, — walk daily in the places which now surround me.

. . . There is no individual about whom I have more changed my mind by coming to Paris than Louis Philippe. I had hitherto esteemed him a sensible, prudent, but ordinary sovereign. I find him a great one, truly great; mingling in business as much as his ministers, and controlling them all. He is more than his cabinet. Measures emanate from him. With skill that is wonderful, he has reined in the revolution of July. He stands now, with the Republicans pressing on one side and the Legitimists on the other, both complaining of broken oaths and promises: the first, of his promise to surround his throne with republican institutions; the second, of his ancient relations with his cousin, Charles X. His habits are very industrious. He rises so early as to be in his study at eight o'clock; breakfasts at ten with his family; from twelve to four attends to public business, receives, &c.; from four to six takes his exercise; at six dines with his family, with whom he passes the evening till ten o'clock; when he retires to his study, and writes till two o'clock, his hour of retiring. It is supposed that he is engaged upon some book, — memoirs, perhaps. . . . Tocqueville has been absent from the city till last week. I shall call on him to-day.

As ever, faithfully yours,

Chas. Sumner.

JOURNAL.

March 9, 1838. Assisted about law papers; called on M. Érard, who invited me to dine with him on Sunday next. Visited Foelix, and examined his library; with most of the books on French law I am already more or less acquainted. Next tried to find Tocqueville, but he has left the city; returned to my room, and was in *déshabillé*, preparing to go out to dine with a French lawyer, when my door opened and a gentleman in black, of about the middle size, rather thin, with sharp black eyes, black hair brushed smoothly, entered my room. He announced himself as M. Cousin.[1] I offered him a chair, and he was good enough to sit with me for more than an hour. He

---

[1] Victor Cousin, 1792–1867. In 1815 he became a professor at the Sorbonne. His writings on morals and metaphysics have been studied in all civilized countries. His translation of Plato was completed in thirteen volumes; a collected edition of his works, in twenty-two volumes, was published in 1847. Under Louis Philippe he was for a while Minister of Public Instruction, and engaged in the debates of the Chamber of Peers. His connection with public affairs ended in 1848.

inquired after Mr. Henry,[1] Mr. Ripley,[2] Mr. Brooks.[3] Mr. Bancroft, but particularly Mr. Brownson;[4] of the latter he spoke as a man of a great deal of talent, and indeed as a most remarkable person. He had received the *brochure* of Mr. Brownson, lately published. Mr. Ripley he described as a man of talent, and great activity of mind; Mr. Brooks as a man of enthusiasm; and Mr. Henry as a person he hoped would soon be established in another professorship. His interest in Mr. Brownson appears to be unfeignedly great. I mentioned Dr. Channing's name, and he simply said, in his measured manner, "*C'est un homme bien respectable.*" He spoke at considerable length of his interest in the subject of education, and I cannot but confess that he was eloquent beyond most men whom I have met. He avowed his entire devotion to this cause, and his faith in its paramount importance; that other causes admitted, perhaps, of two sides; that this did not; that it was one in support of which all persons could unite. It might be otherwise, he said, with slavery. He did not wish office from Government, he said; but simply to devote himself to the great cause of education. In avowing this dedication of his life he used language as elevated as the sentiment itself. He appeared very well informed with regard to the United States, and even with regard to the present proceedings in Massachusetts on the subject. I described to him Mann's labors and character; he seemed grateful to hear of them, and asked particularly about Mr. Mann. He spoke of his own recent work on Holland, which he seemed very much to desire might reach the United States; he added that there was a vast similarity between the institutions of the United States and those of Holland. His manner of conversation was ardent, almost burning, with a great deal of emphasis and a loud voice; his sentences, nevertheless, were quite measured. He does not speak English. He did not appear amiable; and, though he spent upwards of an hour with me, his countenance and manner did not once assume an appearance of liveliness and gayety; it was sombreness that prevailed throughout. I must add that, though he stands high at present, being a peer of France and a man of great talents, he does not appear to be a favorite with any party; it is surmised that he is selfish and loves money He told me that his translation of Plato had pro-

---

[1] Caleb S. Henry; a clergyman born in Rutland, Mass., in 1804. In 1834 he published "Cousin's Psychology," being a translation of Cousin's lectures on Locke's "Essay on the Human Understanding." He was one of the founders of the "New York Review," and from 1839 to 1852 Professor of History and Philosophy in the University of New York.

[2] George Ripley was born in Greenfield, Mass., Oct. 3, 1802. He published, 1838–1842, "Edited Specimens of Foreign Standard Literature," which contained his translations of Cousin, Jouffroy, and B. Constant. He was one of the "Brook-Farm" community in Roxbury, Mass., of which Hawthorne's "Blithedale Romance" was written. In 1849 he became, as he still continues, the literary editor of the "New York Tribune." He edited, with Charles A. Dana as associate, the "American Cyclopædia."

[3] Rev. Charles T. Brooks, of Newport, R. I.; author of several translations from the German. He was born in Salem, Mass., June 30, 1813.

[4] Orestes A. Brownson, 1803–1876. He was by turns the partisan of various theologies; finally entering, in 1844, the Catholic communion. He was the editor and almost the sole writer of the "Boston Quarterly Review," established in 1838. He entered on metaphysical and philosophical discussions at an early period of his career, and embraced with little modification the views of Cousin.

ceeded to the eleventh volume which was already published, and that he was now engaged upon the twelfth. He concluded his visit by inviting me to visit him at his "cabin" at the Sorbonne.

After M. Cousin left I hurried to my dinner, which was to be with M. Ledru, a French lawyer, who appeared to be rather young. He was, nevertheless, the counsel of Alibaud,[1] the person who was executed for attempting to kill the king; and, as he told me himself, the most intimate friend of Armand Carrel. The latter died in his arms, he said. He added, that Louis Philippe was accustomed to say that the two persons in his kingdom whom he most detested were Ledru and Carrel.[2] As for law he appears a charlatan; but he is a character. I talked with Ledru about Cousin; he did not like him, and regarded him as a man who had deserted republican principles, which he professed ardently before the Revolution of July.

March 10. Saw the neat, modern, and beautiful church of Notre Dame de Lorette; entered the immense Library of the King, seeing however but one apartment, as the whole library was not open to-day; then visited my new acquaintance Ledru, talked French, examined his library, and gave him advice on some matters of American law; dined with the Ticknors; and then went to the Théâtre des Variétés where I heard a very amusing and neat vaudeville, *Le Père de la Débutante*. I found myself able to follow the thread of the whole piece, though there were many particular passages that I lost.

March 11. Saw the review of troops of the line and national guards in front of the Tuileries, and then went to church in the chapel of Colonel Thorn.[3] The colonel lives so *en prince* that he has his private chapel and chaplain; and all the world are at liberty to enjoy them. The room is not larger than a good-sized *salon;* it is furnished very neatly, with a handsome carpet and chairs, and a pretty desk and pulpit. The American Episcopal service was used; the prayer ran for the "President of the United States, the King of the French, and the Queen of England," — in that order. Afterwards went to the Chamber of Deputies, which not being in session, I was allowed to see the hall; it was beautiful, indeed: I must say more about it, when I attend a debate. Walked to the Arc de Triomphe and went to the top, from which I had a beautiful view of Paris. This is a wonderful work,

---

[1] Louis Alibaud attempted the assassination of Louis Philippe on June 25, 1836, at the Pont Royal, and was guillotined the next month. His counsel was M. Charles Ledru. Louis Blanc has given an account of the attempt, and of the trial and execution. "History of the Ten Years," London, 1845; Vol. II. pp. 415-424.

[2] Nicolas Armand Carrel, a French journalist, who was born in 1800. In 1830, he founded with Thiers the "National," of which he became, after Thiers entered the ministry, the sole editor. He was killed by Émile de Girardin in a duel, in July, 1836. "History of the Ten Years," Vol. II., pp. 424-430. See article, "Armand Carrel," by J. S. Mill, in "London and Westminister Review," Oct., 1837, reprinted in Mr. Mill's "Dissertations and Discussions."

[3] Herman Thorn, a purser in the United States Navy, who became rich by his marriage with Miss Jauncey, of New York. In Paris, he took a lease of the Hôtel Monaco, the property of Madame Adelaide, sister of Louis Philippe, once occupied by Talleyrand, and extending from the Rue St. Dominique to the Rue de Varennes; where in style of living and entertainments he vied with royalty. He died in New York.

intended to commemorate the victories of Napoleon, and indeed worthy of them.   It is the largest triumphal arch ever built.   The train of carriages in the Champs Élysées to-day was immense.   Dined by invitation with M. Érard; and at dinner sat between two French ladies.   Two or three eminent musical persons were present.   The dinner was neat and pleasant.   I must record M. Érard's ignorance with regard to America.   He asked me, with the greatest simplicity, if our noblest and most respectable families were not the descendants of Montezuma!   And yet he is a man of considerable position; and at the head of his business in Paris, perhaps in the world!

March 12.   To-day commenced a struggle in the Chamber of Deputies, in order to unseat the ministry.   The English ministry have just passed through their trial; and now a similar one awaits the French.   The contest took place on the question of secret funds, which the ministry demanded as usual in their budget, and at the same time gave out that they wished to regard the vote on this subject as a vote of confidence.   A large number of spectators were drawn together by this annunciation.   I had a ticket to one of the reserved tribunes, and yet was obliged to repair to it full two hours before the house opened, which was at two o'clock.   The house is beautiful, larger than that of the Peers; but not so large as ours at Washington.   The President's seat is in the axis of the radii of the semi-circumference of which the chamber is composed; and directly in front of it is the tribune, from which all speeches, other than mere explanations, are made.   The *banc des ministres* is the middle of the front row of seats.   The members all had desks before them.   At the foot of the tribune sat a whole row of *huissiers*, — corresponding perhaps to our serjeant-at-arms, — with swords, and also with chains about their necks.   They appeared to have little or nothing to do, except to receive a letter or billet occasionally from a member; a service which might have been done by one boy.   Over the President's chair is a large painting representing the king, Louis Philippe, receiving the charter in 1830, in which are portraits of most of the leading men of that period, — Lafayette, Constant,[1] Guizot,[2] Laffitte, &c.   The picture is historically interesting, but as a work of art there is little in it to excite admiration.   Each of the ministers had a red portfolio, which gives occasion to the newspapers to speak of the contest for the "portfolios" of office, &c.   At two o'clock I heard a sound of drums, and immediately M. Dupin,[3] the President, entered the chamber, having been attended from his house,

---

[1] Henri Benjamin Constant (Constant de Rebecque), 1767–1830; a distinguished political writer and editor.

[2] 1787–1874.

[3] André Marie Jean Jacques Dupin, 1783–1865; the eminent lawyer and statesman. He defended Marshal Ney in 1815, and was much engaged in political trials while he remained at the bar.   His career in the Chamber of Deputies was long and distinguished. He was elected its President eight times.   As an orator he was remarkable for striking expressions.   "At times his *bon-mots* have created a majority or upset a cabinet."   He was appointed Procureur-Général in the Court of Cassation, after the Revolution of 1830, of which he was one of the leading promoters; and, resigning at one time, was reappointed in 1857.   He wrote many books upon jurisprudence and politics, but gave too little time to their preparation.

which adjoins the chamber, by a municipal guard. I was infinitely disappointed in his appearance. It was ordinary, and almost vulgar; and yet he is the famous M. Dupin, the editor of Pothier, the writer of sundry matters of law, and the sayer of several smart and memorable things. His head was partially bald, and the hair left was brushed smooth and sleek. Perhaps, on seeing this famous man nearer, I might alter the above impressions; but they are those of a first sight. I noticed in the Chamber of Peers what I thought was a Yankee trick; in the Chamber of Deputies I noticed others. For a good part of the debate, a *huissier*, whose place was very conspicuous, being directly on a level with the President, sat with his chair on its hind-legs. Another, — M. Salvandy[1] the Minister of Public Instruction, — sat for some time, cutting with his pen-knife the mahogany desk before him. There were a good many speakers, one of whom was quite prominent, being able, eloquent, and humorous. This was the Count Jaubert.[2] He made a severe attack on the ministry, which produced a sensible effect. He was very witty and caustic, and was constantly interrupted by exclamations of "*très bien*," or by murmurs of dissent, or more frequently by laughs at his sarcasm. I observed all the distinguished members of the House, and scanned their features. Guizot is justly eminent. His literary labors have been immense, and his political elevation is now as distinguished as his literary. He is no longer in the ministry, but he is intensely regarded by all parties for the expansion of his views and their deep philosophical reflection. In his personal carriage, as I saw him at a distance, he reminded me of Mr. Theron Metcalf,[3] of Dedham. His forehead is high; but he is not bald, though his hair is thin. His face is mild and gentle in its expression. M. Thiers,[4] the celebrated author of the "History of the French Revolution," is a most distinguished member of the Chamber. I did not hear him speak; but I narrowly regarded him. He is but little above the middle size, with sleek black hair, and with a bright countenance which seemed to content itself with short and momentary looks. Laffitte[5] sat on the extreme *gauche;* that is, at the extreme of the liberal section. He was the great leader of the Revolution of July. His appearance is prepossessing. One would hardly expect to find in the gentlemanly person with silver locks, who sat so quietly during an exciting debate, the leader of a revolution. Odilon Barrot[6] sat by his side; and his whole frame

---

[1] 1795–1856.

[2] Count Hippolyte François Jaubert was born in 1798. He was in the Chamber of Deputies from 1831 to 1844. In 1840 he received the portfolio of Public Works. He was one of the four members of the National Assembly, who, in the vote of July 10, 1872, opposed the treaty of evacuation with Germany. He is noted as a botanist. He died in 1875 or 1876, while a member of the Chamber of Deputies.

[3] *Ante*, p. 176.

[4] 1797–1877. In 1873, Sumner was the guest at dinner of Thiers, then President of the Republic.

[5] Jacques Laffitte, 1767–1844.

[6] Camille Hyacinthe Odilon Barrot, 1791–1873. He shared in the Revolution of 1830. In the Chamber of Deputies he opposed the administration of Guizot; just before the Revolution of 1848 he was appointed Prime Minister. He was Minister of Justice in 1848–49, under Louis Napoleon, then President of the Republic. He opposed with vigor the *coup*

and features seemed to be in constant motion. His appearance was neat, attractive, and gentlemanly; but I saw him from such a distance that I could not discern his particular features. The great astronomer Arago,[1] who has mingled very much in politics, and who is an extreme liberal, sat by his side. On the opposite side of the house was Lamartine, — a tall, thin man, looking like a poet, of whom I had but an imperfect view; also Berryer,[2] the eloquent Carlist, with his blue coat buttoned high up in his neck, and his burly face full of blood and passion. The members of the Chamber sat with their hats off, and generally preserved a respectful deportment; but they interrupted the speaker at pleasure, with notes of admiration or dissent, to as great an extent, I should think, as in the English parliament. The Chamber did not rise till six o'clock.

March 13. To-day, through the kindness of M. Pierron, a deputy of some distinction on the Liberal side, I had a seat in the reserved tribune. M. Montalivet,[3] the Minister for the Interior, — a man celebrated in the Revolution of July, — commenced from the tribune a reply to the attacks which had been made upon the ministry. A scene occurred which will probably be quite memorable. The speaker was interrupted in his speech several times by members of the opposition; and finally, all at once, became ill, nearly fainted and fell in the tribune, from which he was led by several of the *huissiers*, who were near at hand. All the ministry and many of the deputies followed him into the antechamber, and the House was thrown into a great deal of confusion. It was very soon adjourned. After this went to view the Palais de l'Élysée Bourbon, — the palace which Murat with his wife, the sister of Bonaparte, occupied and adorned, and in which Bonaparte spent the last days of his reign. I was shown the chamber in which he slept, and in which he made his last abdication. This morning I called, with Mr. Ticknor, on the Duc de Broglie,[4] the late prime-minister of France. He is emphatically a gentleman, — his manners smooth and even, without any thing particularly striking, and yet calculated to inspire respect. He is,

d'état, and then retired from public life. In 1872 he was appointed by Thiers Vice-president of the Council of State.

[1] Dominique François Arago, 1786–1853. The astronomer was through his long career a faithful partisan of liberty. He refused, after Louis Napoleon's *coup d'état*, to take the oath of allegiance. He is buried at *Père La Chaise*, and his monument is conspicuous to the visitor not far from the principal entrance.

[2] Pierre Antoine Berryer, 1790–1868. From his participation, with his father, in the defence of Marshal Ney, in 1815, until his death, he was associated with the most celebrated causes, civil and political. He was a steadfast adherent of the Legitimist cause and its foremost champion in the Chamber of Deputies. Sumner met M. Berryer in social life on his visit to Paris in 1857.

[3] The Comte de Montalivet, son of a French statesman, was born at Valence, April 25 1801, and is now living. He bore a part in the Revolution of 1830, and was devoted to the Orleans family. He was, for some years, in the cabinet of Louis Philippe, as Minister of Public Instruction or of the Interior.

[4] 1785–1870. He descended from an ancient family of Piedmontese origin, and married the only daughter of Madame de Staël. His honorable efforts for the abolition of slavery deserve commemoration. In politics he affiliated with Guizot. He was for a time, under Louis Philippe, Minister of Public Instruction or of Foreign Affairs. His son Albert, born in 1821, has had a conspicuous place in recent French history.

perhaps, fifty years old. He was kind enough to promise to give me some introductions and facilities for seeing the distinguished lawyers of Paris.

March 14. This morning the Ticknors left Paris for London; and sorry indeed was I to part with them, since their house has been as a home to me in Paris; and I have had their constant counsel and advice, and the results of their long travel and experience. It was with a heavy heart that I saw their carriage roll away. I felt solitary and sad, and endeavored to walk off my gloom by a long stroll; so I visited the churches of St. Eustache and St. Germain l'Auxerrois, the Marché des Innocents, the house where Molière was born, the Mazarine Library in the building of the Institute, and finally the exhibition of paintings of modern French artists in the Louvre. For two months of each year the old masters, crowned by the laurels of many generations, are veiled from view, and the vast gallery of the Louvre is devoted to the exhibition of paintings by living artists. Here was an immense assemblage, but how immeasurably below the old masters! Acres of canvas and paint literally spread themselves before the eye. In all this quantity I saw little that fixed my attention; and the verdict of others better instructed in the subject of paintings than myself has confirmed my untutored judgment. Spent a long evening with Foelix, talking French and law.

March 16 (Friday). Took the diligence this morning at eight o'clock for Versailles, there to attend a criminal trial and to view the palace. An acquaintance, which I have made among the advocates, invited me to be present at a trial in which he was to appear as counsel,[1] and which promised to be very peculiar and important. I was unwilling to let this occasion of commencing my initiation in French criminal procedure pass by. The court opened at ten o'clock. It was a room of quite moderate size, in a very ancient building which, at the same time, contained the prison. It was the Court of Assize, having three judges. The presiding judge, who sat in the middle, conducted the whole trial, neither of the other two once opening his mouth. He was dressed in robes of black and red, the side judges in robes of black; and all of them had high caps, which they wore or not, according to the inclination of the moment, during the trial. The Procureur-Général for the district conducted the case on the part of the Government. The court entered with the jury in their train, and also with the prisoner between several of the police. The twelve persons of which the jury consisted had been drawn by the prisoner immediately before entering. A large number of the police, and also of the troops of the line, were in attendance. Three or four or even more of the police sat by the side of the prisoner. The arrangement of the court was entirely different from ours.[2]

[1] M. Ledru, *ante*, p. 266. Sumner, in his letter to Hillard of March 21, speaks of this advocate as "the greatest friend of perhaps the greatest man France has had for the last ten years, unhappily now dead. I mean Carrel."

[2] The Journal contains other diagrams than that of the court-room. The advice of Dr. Lieber will be remembered in this connection. *Ante*, p. 198.

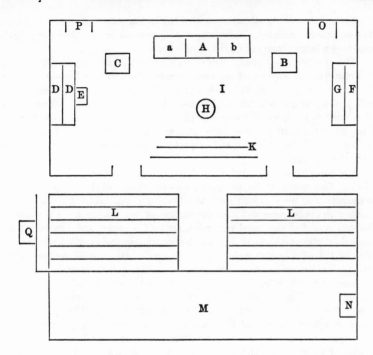

A, the principal judge, with *a* and *b*, the side judges, the seat slightly raised.

B, seat and box of the *greffier*, or clerk of the court.

C, the little box and seat of the Procureur-Général.

D D, the seats of the jury.

E, seat of the chief *huissier*, who had the charge of keeping order in court.

F, seat of the prisoner, directly in face of the jury and considerably elevated, say three or four feet.

G, seat of prisoner's counsel, directly under the prisoner, as a clerk is under the judge in one of our courts.

H, stove in the centre of the court-house.

I, place where the witnesses stood during their testimony.

K, some reserved seats.

L, other reserved seats, where the witnesses sat after examination.

M, place open to the public, and full of old women and vagabonds, who stood up.

N, door for the public.

O, private or privileged door.

P, door of the judges' room, and by which the court entered.

Q, little door, through which the witnesses were brought in one by one; also by which the prisoner was brought in, and through which the jury retired to deliberate: it communicates with the prison.

There was nothing attractive or striking in the construction of the room; it was, indeed, ordinary. The seats were of common wood. Over the judge's seat was a large picture of Christ on the Cross.

The prisoner was a young man of eighteen, who was charged with killing his mistress. It seems that the two, according to a French fashion, tired of life, agreed mutually to kill each other. The pistol of the prisoner took effect, and the girl was killed; but hers did not take effect. The prisoner then tried to kill himself, but was finally arrested before he had consummated his project. I shall preserve the printed account of the trial. Here I shall only mention a few things that I observed, and which will not appear in the published account.

The first step was the reading of the *act of accusation* or indictment by the clerk. The names of *all* the witnesses were then called. They were very numerous, and were all sent into an adjoining room. Among them was the mother of the prisoner and also the mother of the deceased. The prisoner himself was *first* examined very minutely by the judge, and detailed all the important circumstances of his life, his education, and of his final commission of the offence with which he was charged. He gave all the particulars fully. This examination was conducted entirely by the senior judge. The prisoner cried while telling his story, and did not speak loud enough to be distinctly heard by the jury. He was then removed from the witnesses' stand. The judge next read the *procès verbal* of the examination of the prisoner on his first apprehension, and then the testimony given by physicians at the first examination. Witnesses were then introduced one by one; first the *mother* of the accused: she was sworn. The oath was very much like ours; so much so, that I think it must have been borrowed from England. The witness holds up his hand while the judge repeats the oath (the judge not rising); and, at the close of the oath, kisses his hand. The mother sat while giving her testimony, and was in tears all the while. She frequently fortified what she said by adding that it was given upon her "*parole d'honneur*," — which sounded a little curious when she was already under oath. The second witness was a man. He stood up and was examined, as were all after him, by the judge. The few questions put by counsel on either side were through the mouth of the judge; and there were not half-a-dozen during the whole trial, and to, perhaps, thirty witnesses. The first set of witnesses proved the previous character of the accused; the second set the same of the deceased. Next came the doctors, and then the persons who found the body and the prisoner. Members of the jury asked questions when they pleased; and all, or nearly all, had a little piece of paper on which to make notes. The examination of witnesses was completed the first day, and the court adjourned at about five o'clock in the afternoon. The jury separated without any injunction not to converse on the subject of the trial; but on the adjournment mingled among the crowd.

March 17. At ten o'clock the court again convened. One of the morning papers contained a full report of the doings of yesterday. My friend, the counsel of the prisoner, anticipating it last night, enjoined upon his servant to bring from Paris a dozen copies of the paper containing the report to distribute among the jury. I told him he would commit a crime, according to English and American law, — "Embracery;" but he laughed at the idea. This forenoon the Procureur-Général first spoke, then the counsel for the prisoner; then again the Procureur, and again the counsel for the prisoner. I understood that they had a right to speak as many times as they chose, the counsel for the prisoner always having the last word. In the arguments there was nothing such as I have been accustomed to; every thing was different. The defence was theatrical, brilliant, *French*. The counsel grasped the hand of his client, and worked the whole audience into a high pitch of excitement. At the close of his argument, he called upon his client to promise, in the face of the court and of God, that, if he were restored to liberty by the verdict of the jury, he would hasten to precipitate himself upon the tomb of the unfortunate girl he had destroyed and pray for forgiveness; and the prisoner, by way of response, stretched his hand to his counsel, who seized it with a strong grasp, saying at once, "*J'ai fini.*" Women screamed and fainted, strong men yielded, and tears flowed down the cheeks of the jury and even the grim countenances of the half-dozen police, or *gendarmes*, who sat by the side of the prisoner, elevated and within the observation of all the audience. The arguments concluded, the judge, sitting (and the jury sitting), read a very succinct statement of the case, and the law which bore upon it. This occupied perhaps five or ten minutes. The jury then retired, and within less than ten minutes returned. The prisoner, in the mean time, had been conducted to a room out of the court-room. The jury rendered their verdict, "Not guilty;" the prisoner was then brought in, and the judge communicated the decision to him, dismissing him with an impressive admonition. The greatest excitement prevailed in the court-room when the verdict was announced. Women, and men too, cried for joy. So much for a French criminal trial! [1]

March 18 (Sunday). Stayed in Versailles another day, to view the wonderful palace, now opened as an historical museum, and the former scene of the Arabian Nights' magnificence of Louis Quatorze. I had previously, on the days of the trial, stolen some peeps at the garden; but I gave to-day entirely to this object. All that my imagination pictured fell infinitely short of what I found to be the reality. [2]

March 19. Was at the *soirée* of De Gérando this evening.

March 20. Again went to the Collége Royal de France and heard Lerminier. His audience was quite crowded, and he was excessively animated. He discussed the relations of France with the Church, under Philip Augustus; the character of Pope Innocent III.; and the crusade against the Albigenses. Americans are accused of national vanity; but certainly they must yield the palm on this account to the French. This whole lecture was calculated to pamper the national vanity of Frenchmen, and to fortify them in a belief, which needs no additional support among them, that they are and

---

[1] The printed report of the trial noted Sumner's attendance.

[2] He described at length the visit to the palace in a letter to Hillard, of March 21, 1838.

always have been the first nation of the earth. Lerminier's manner is very brilliant and energetic. It is not pure, and he abounds in words; but I must confess that his lecture this morning presented an instructive view, which riveted the attention of a large audience.

Passed through the Place de la Bastille; saw Napoleon's huge elephant; the foundation for the monument to the victims of July; the Boulevard du Temple; and the house, No. 50, from which Fieschi's infernal machine was directed against the king. Spent a quiet evening *chez moi*.

TO GEORGE S. HILLARD.

PARIS, March 21, 1838.

MY DEAR GEORGE, — I have received all your letters, and, did you know the thrill with which I opened them, you would not write grudgingly. Give me a glass of water from the New England springs, I say, amidst the plenty of all kinds which surrounds me. You do not know what it is to be in a foreign land, where the sounds which salute you are of a strange tongue, and the voices of friends are not heard. With what zealous attention do I devour every word! And when I have read the letter several times I strive again to alchemize from its exhausted page some new meaning, — to drain from it another drop of its precious wine.[1] . . . On my return to the city from Versailles, I found an invitation to a *soirée* for the same evening. I went and enjoyed a most delicious private concert, where there was the choicest music of the voice, the piano, the harp, and the violin, by the most brilliant performers. Adelaide Kemble,[2] the sister of Fanny, was there. She has appeared in public but once; and that was some time ago, when her friends deemed it advisable to withdraw her. She sang, another playing the accompaniment; and then she took her place at the piano, and played and sang at the same time. Of course it was Italian music. You know that I am no judge of music, but still I have a heart and pulses which throb under manifestations of human feeling. Her music affected me deeply, and I cannot describe to you how much impressed was the beautiful and crowded circle by which she was surrounded, who interrupted her at every pause by a gush of "bravas." After her two songs she soon retired. In her singing she had great force, but I thought lacked variety and softness. She was a singing Fanny Kemble. There was no American but myself at the *soirée*, and Miss Kemble will not appear in public for some time yet. She goes forthwith to Italy to continue her training. . . Consider that my time is all employed from seven o'clock in the morning till twelve or one at night, and then give me a generous return for this letter. I shall not be in London till May. Tell Cushing to write me there. How often do I think of all of you,

---

[1] In the omitted part of this letter is a description of the trial at Versailles, already given in the Journal.

[2] She was born in London in 1820, and retired from the stage in 1843, on her marriage to Mr. Sartoris.

and of the quiet circles where I was received in Boston and Cambridge!
My heart is with you.

As ever, affectionately,

CHAS. SUMNER.

JOURNAL.

March 21, 1838. Took a long ramble through parts of the Parisian
world which I had not yet visited; saw the pigeon-shooting in the gardens
at Tivoli, chiefly by young counts, viscounts, and the like; went through
the Cemetery Montmartre, situated beyond the walls of the city, and near
the barrière of the same name, and in the evening dined with M. Ledru, the
advocate, at Véfour's. The scene at the cemetery was thoroughly French.
Long before I approached it I saw persons on the sidewalk with wreaths to
sell, and I was pressed several times to purchase them. Mourners, when they
resort to the cemetery, throw one of these wreaths, purchased at the gate, on
the tomb of the lost one. Here was a large graveyard, not so large as Mt.
Auburn or one hundredth part as beautiful from Nature, filled to crowding
with monuments. There were literally thousands, being close to each other;
and almost all had the common French offering of wreaths hung over them.

March 22. To-day is another of the ridiculous show-days of France. It
is mid-Lent, and the rigors of this holy time are relaxed for this day, and the
follies of Carnival renewed. Maskers were in the streets, and this evening,
or rather night, all the balls are again open to the masks. The balls commence at midnight. By accident strayed into the famous church St. Germain l'Auxerrois, and saw the Archbishop of Paris, — perhaps of France,
for I do not know his exact style, — and heard a sermon from one of the
most eloquent preachers of France. It was a sermon for charity to the poor,
expressed with a good deal of eloquence. The preacher, I thought, part of
the time sat in his pulpit. It was a strong appeal to the rich. Alms were
received afterwards at the great door of the church; all the other doors were
closed, and everybody passed through this avenue of charity, on either side
of which were two young matrons, marchionesses or countesses, who held the
beautiful bags which received the alms, and recognized the charity with a
smile. The archbishop was clad in simple but rich vestments; and on one
of his hands, which were gloved with purple silk, glittered a most brilliant
ring. Should he not have thrown this ring into the alms for the poor; since
the preacher in his sermon characterized him as *le pontife et le père des pauvres?*
As he walked through the audience, with his hand at his face, by a sort of
motion from his face he scattered blessings among the people, who most
devoutly crossed themselves as he passed along. His rich vestments touched
me, so near was I; but the jewel on his hand could be seen at a great distance, gleaming most resplendently.

In the evening, dined, by invitation received some days ago, with M. Filas-
sier. The company consisted of twelve, and my seat was on the right of
Madame. The gentlemen were of good social position, but I do not know

their names; because, in the first place, they do not introduce persons in
society here as a general rule, and when they do, it is very difficult to catch a
French name so as to remember it.   After twelve o'clock went to one of the
balls at Musard's.   It was literally crammed with dancers and spectators.

March 23.   This morning visited the Bibliothèque du Roi; saw its immense collections of books, medals, plates, and maps, and its great museum
of manuscripts.   Here are eighty thousand manuscripts.   In the evening
went to the Theatre of the Palais Royal, where I saw Mademoiselle Déjazet [1]
(a woman famous for libertinism, as well as spirit as an actress) in one of
the popular pieces of the day, called a *folie*, — *La Maîtresse de Langues*.
Her manner was very easy, graceful, and lively.

March 24.   Visited the Conservatoire des Arts et Métiers. . . . Attended
Lerminier's lecture at the Collége Royal; his subject was the contest of
Frederick II. of Germany with the power of the Pope, with a sketch of the
character of the former.   As usual he was animated, and drew the atten-
tion of a large audience.   In the evening heard Le Sage's best comedy, —
Turcaret, — at the Théâtre Francais.

March 26.   In the course of the day I called upon Mrs. Florida White ;
while I was there, among a good deal of company, I met the Countess Guiccioli.[2]   She was rather short, inclined to *embonpoint*, with a light complexion,
and a touch of red in the cheek.   I did not notice her particularly, because
I did not catch the name when she was announced, and I left very soon after
she entered the room.

March 27.   Walked much, and went to the top of Notre Dame ; the day
was beautiful, and I saw all Paris beneath my feet. . . . Heard Lerminier
at the College of France; as usual, brilliant, rambling, excited, with a full
and attentive audience of young men.   His subject was St. Louis, — his
crusades, and his character.   After the lecture again walked; penetrated
through all the small streets between the Place de la Bastille and the Rue
St. Martin. . . . Dined at Meurice's *table d'hôte;* this is the great English
hotel, and English is the prevalent language at table.   The dinner is well
served.   I sat, of course, between two Englishmen.   Tired of silence, by
and by I presumed to break it with my next neighbor, who seemed not
sorry ; we talked very happily together, and he opened his heart in the
fulness of sympathy, as to a compatriot.   I deemed it my duty, however, to state that I was not an Englishman, — he started with astonishment ; I added that I was of the United States.   All at once he became
cold ; his countenance was averted, and the little conversation which we
afterwards had was measured, tame, and insipid.   Cooper would build an
argument on this incident to show the deep-seated antipathy on the part of
Englishmen to our country!   In the evening attended for a short time the

---

[1] Pauline Virginie Déjazet, 1798–1873. She went upon the stage when only five years
old, and left it in 1868.

[2] The Countess Guiccioli, *née* Teresa Gamba, 1801–1873. Her *liaison* with Lord Byron,
whom she met, in 1819, at Venice and Ravenna, Pisa and Genoa, gave her great notoriety.
In 1851 she married a Frenchman, the Marquis de Boissy, who died in 1866. Late in life
she published "Recollections" of the poet.

Théâtre des Jeunes Élèves, in the Passage Choiseul. I believe all or the greater part of the actors were boys and girls. I was so fatigued after my walks that I did not stay long.

March 28. Again walked; penetrated beyond the Barrière du Combat [1] to the Boyauderie, so called, where is deposited all the filth of Paris.

Dined with Foelix, where I met M. West, an _avocat_, and his collaborateur in his Review. I spent a long evening, during which I learned much of the studies and duties of _avocats_, and of the practice of courts. Indeed, the object of our meeting to-day was to converse on these subjects.

March 29. Saw the beautiful exhibition of Sèvres porcelain. In the evening went to the Italian Opera. The Opera was _I Puritani;_ the music was certainly delicious, but I am not competent to admire it according to its merits.

March 30. This evening attended a meeting of the Société de Géographie, at which M. Guizot did not preside as expected. The meeting was in one of the halls of the Hôtel de Ville. Some old gentlemen sat round a desk, and read reports and papers, while spectators or humbler members of the society sat on benches. The meeting was dull enough, and I left about ten o'clock, while a gentleman was in the midst of reading a fragment of his travels in Bolivia.

TO JUDGE STORY, CAMBRIDGE.

PARIS, March 30, 1838.

MY DEAR JUDGE, — . . . I have made the French language a study with all the assistance I could derive from French masters. With these I have been extravagant, having had two almost all the time I have been here. What is worth _doing_ is worth _well doing_, and I wish to obtain such a knowledge of French as to be able to preserve it all my life, and also to use it as a medium of intercourse in Germany. I have now heard almost all the lectures of the metropolis; perhaps I have attended one hundred and fifty, — no small labor. Of the manner and character of the professors I must write you at large. At present I am attending the courts. Indeed, a French court is a laughable place. To me it is a theatre, and all the judges, advocates, and parties " merely players." In those particulars in which they have borrowed from the English law, they have got hold of about half of the English principle and forgotten the rest. Thus, they have juries. These they imported from England; but with them none of the regulations by which the purity of our verdicts is secured. The jury, with a capital case in their hands disperse and mingle among the citizens. [Here follows a description of the criminal trial at Versailles, already given in the Journal.] In answer to the interrogatories of the judge, the prisoner gave a detailed account of the whole affair, of his connection with the girl, and their mutual agreement to kill each other, and of the unfortunate result. One would think

---

[1] Situated at the end of the Rue Grange aux Belles.

that the case might stop here; but no! the same facts were extracted, by means of question and answer, from the mouths of more than thirty witnesses. There was nothing like *cross-examination;* and I have reason to believe that this test of truth is entirely unknown to the French procedure. All the questions were put by the presiding judge, who, however, took no notes of the answers: and the questions were general, such as, names and times being altered, would apply to all cases. All persons are admitted as witnesses. Parents and near relatives of parties are not admitted if objection is made; neither is a person *infamous,* — namely, one who has been condemned for robbery, &c. These are the only exceptions I know of at present. Papers of all kinds are admitted. You will see from these few words that the duties of the judge and advocate are infinitely abridged; the lawyer giving his chief attention to his pleading (*plaidoyer*), and the presiding judge putting a series of questions which have been digested beforehand. Neither judge nor lawyer is obliged "to watch the currents of the heady fight," as with us, where almost every word of testimony makes its way against the serried objections of opposing counsel.

As ever affectionately yours,

CHAS. SUMNER.

JOURNAL.

March 31, 1838. A day or two since I received an invitation to breakfast with M. Demetz,[1] a *Conseiller de la Cour Royale,* — namely, a magistrate or judge. At a quarter before eleven o'clock I found myself with him. He is a man of about forty, who has visited the United States and written a book about the country; and yet he does not venture to speak English, or did not to-day. His wife received me cordially. The *salon* was — perhaps I may say, in Yankee phrase — splendidly furnished, and yet there was no carpet; the walls were all covered with silk, and the chairs also. We sat down to break-

----

[1] Frédéric Auguste Demetz, 1796–1873. In 1836 he visited the United States, accompanied by an architect, for the purpose of inspecting our prisons; and became a convert to the cellular system of Pennsylvania. In 1840 he renounced the profession of the law, in order to found and administer the famous Reform School for Boys at Mettray, upon the family system, known as "The Agricultural and Penitentiary Colony;" and he remained steadfast in this work until his death. Lord Brougham, in Parliament, pronounced Mettray in itself sufficient for the glory of France. His institution has been the model of many others, not only in Europe but in this country. In Sept., 1873, the writer met M. Demetz at his lodgings in Paris. Though somewhat bent with age, his intelligence and good sense were as vigorous as ever. He died a few weeks later, Nov. 2, 1873. Sumner visited Mettray and had an interview with M. Demetz, on May 26, 1857. He was much touched by a remark of the philanthropist, made in the conversation, that he had renounced his position as judge, thinking that there was something more for him to do than to continue rendering judgments of courts (*faisant des arrêts*); that he had the happiness of being a Christian, and that it was of much more importance to him what the good God should think of him than what men thought. Funeral services were celebrated in Paris in the Église de la Trinité, at Dourdan, the place of his burial, and at Mettray, where he directed his heart to be deposited. On May 3, 1874, the busts of Demetz and his colaborer, Courteilles, were inaugurated at Mettray, with an address from M. Drouyn de Lhuys.

fast at about half-past eleven o'clock. I was asked to give my arm to Madame in passing from the *salon* to the *salle à manger*, and was placed at her right. The company consisted of six, besides Monsieur and Madame, my hosts. The breakfast was truly sumptuous: seldom, if ever, have I seen such a repast for dinner. There were certainly half a dozen wines, and a long retinue of the richest and subtlest dishes.[1] Among the guests was Michel Chevalier,[2] one of the editors of the *Journal des Débats*, and author of a recent work on the United States. He is a man of about thirty-five, modest, not handsome, but intelligent, with a prominent but expressive eye. I conversed with him considerably, partly in French and partly in English. From what I hear said of him, from what I have read of his writings, and from having seen him, I think he will take an eminent stand in France.[3] There was a magistrate present, with whom I conversed; he seemed proud of the thorough police of Paris, and of the almost dictatorial power of the Prefect of Police, as he said, over the *intentions* as well as acts of persons. I left at about half-past one o'clock, having passed a very agreeable time and met some very agreeable people, and also finding that I had at last got French enough to carry on something of a conversation. After this, called on Mr. John Wilkes, — the famous "O. P. Q." of the London press, — a large, gross man, who notwithstanding told me that he took but one meal a day, and that his dinner. The conversation accidentally turned on Chevalier, whom I had just left. I observed that there was a savage cut-up of Chevalier in a January number of "Frazer." "Yes," said Mr. Wilkes, "I wrote it." Singular accident that I should pass from one man to the very person who had flayed him, as it were, through the public press!

April 1. This evening went to the Théâtre Porte St. Martin to see Mademoiselle Georges,[4] famous for her *liaison* with the emperor, as everybody here calls Napoleon. She is now quite advanced, and is very large and heavy, almost gross; still she must have been attractive in days gone by. Her playing was good, and drew a full house; but I think it was her history and ancient fame which kept the large audience attentive.

[1] M. Demetz, speaking of the culinary talent of the French, said at the dinner: "*Notre cuisine est la cuisine du monde.*"

[2] M. Chevalier was born Jan. 13, 1806. After the Revolution of 1830, he became editor of the *Globe.* In 1833–35, under an appointment from Thiers, then Minister, he visited the United States for the purpose of investigating our railroad system, and later published his "Letters on North America," which had already appeared in the *Journal des Débats.* In 1840, he succeeded Rossi in the chair of Political Economy at the College of France. He is among the most eminent economists of his age, and the head of the free-trade school in his country. Sumner received many attentions from M. Chevalier, on his visit to Paris in 1857; and a friendly correspondence from that time was continued between them.

[3] Sumner, in his letter to Hillard of April 10, speaks of M. Chevalier as "an active-minded, talented man of thirty-five, who is culminating fast, and I think will run the career of Thiers, Guizot, and Carrel."

[4] 1787–1867. She began to perform in Paris, in 1802 in "Clytemnestra." She was attached, at one time, to the Imperial Theatre at St. Petersburg. She played at Dresden and Erfurt before Napoleon and Alexander. From 1821 to 1847 she performed chiefly in Paris at the Odéon and Porte St. Martin theatres. She retired in 1849, but reappeared in 1855. Among her personal admirers were princes and the Emperor Napoleon.

April 2. Commenced in earnest following the courts. M. Demetz called for me at nine o'clock in the morning, and conducted me to that venerable pile where the courts convene, — the ancient residence of the kings, — the Palais de Justice. I went into the different court-rooms, but finally rested for the day in the Cour d'Assises, where M. Demetz himself was to preside as one of the judges. There were three judges on the bench, habited in black robes, with high black caps with a gold band. The arrangement of the court was not materially different from that I had already seen at Versailles. The room was old and venerable, and the ceiling was painted by one of the celebrated artists of France.

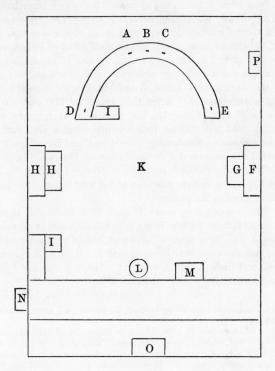

A B C, the three judges at a circular table, raised considerably above the level of the court.

D, Procureur-Général at one end of the same table.

E, *greffier* at the opposite end.

F, accused and *gendarme*.

G, counsel of accused.

H H, the jury.

I I, *huissiers*.

K, place where the witnesses stood when giving testimony.

L, stove.

M, little door by which to enter the bar.

N, door for witnesses and lawyers.

O, door for the public.

P, door to the judges' room.

I had a good seat, and heard several trials with the greatest pleasure. As among us, the defences chiefly fell to the hands of very young members of the bar; persons who are, as it were, in their *apprentissage*. I was much interested in seeing the application of the French criminal code. Its provisions were followed completely, and I sat with it in my hand while the trials proceeded. The arguments of the Procureur-Général and of the counsel in defence were shorter than with us, and the charge of the judge much shorter and less elaborate.

In the evening went to the grand Opéra Français, and saw the splendid ballet-pantomime of *Le Diable Boiteux*, and the dancing of Fanny Elssler.[1] I did not think before that scenery and spectacle could be carried so far as they were in this piece.

April 3. Again at the Palais de Justice and in the Cour d'Assises; feel more and more interested in the administration of justice here.

April 4. At the Cour d'Assises. Have now heard many cases; am much pleased with the French penal code in many particulars, — its definitions of crimes are much more natural and intelligible to common persons than ours; do not see that the habit of examining the accused works badly; like the system of the jury's expressing an opinion on different circumstances which attend the crime, but am not so much pleased with the requisition of a majority of *seven*. Cross-examination seems unknown. I have heard a very few questions put to witnesses by counsel, but of all the witnesses that I have seen not one has been insulted or treated with harshness. Always, as the judges enter or retire, the spectators, lawyers, and jury rise; but neither the judges nor jury rise during the charge. The verdict is given while the prisoner is out of the room, and he is immediately called in and it is announced to him. If it be "*Coupable*," the judges rise and confer together (on one occasion I saw them retire to their room and agree upon the sentence, having regard to the code); if it be "*Non coupable*," the accused is discharged, the judge perhaps giving him some good moral advice.

In the evening, heard Corneille's great production, *Cinna*, at the Odéon.

April 5. At the Cour d'Assises; also was at the exhibition of the *Sourds-Muets*, — the deaf and dumb.

April 6. At the Cour d'Assises; heard part of a rather complicated case for forgery. At three o'clock, went with Mr. Wilkes ("O.P.Q.") to visit David,[2]

[1] Fanny Elssler (sister of Therese, who was born in 1808) was born in Vienna in 1811. She won great applause as a dancer in European cities, appearing in Paris in 1834. She, with her sister, visited the United States in 1841. She took leave of the stage in 1851, and has since resided at her villa near Hamburg.

[2] Pierre Jean David, 1789–1856. His first great work was a statue of the Prince of Condé. He was an earnest Republican, and his genius delighted most in commemorating in busts and statues the benefactors of mankind, — as scholars, men of science, patriots, and liberal statesmen. Sumner wrote to Hillard, April 10, of his visit to David: "I was presented to him as a Republican and an American, which at once opened his heart."

the great sculptor, the author of the piece in front of the Panthéon, and of many of the statues which have been lately erected in France. He has just completed a statue of Riquet,[1] the engineer who, in the time of Louis XIV., started the idea of the canal of Languedoc. I spent a long time in his *atelier*, during which the great artist was kind enough to show me the casts of his principal works. The statue of Riquet is colossal; it was just completed in the clay, and was to be modelled in marble by another hand. In one part of his *atelier* a workman was engaged on the statue of Cuvier: it was thus that I witnessed a practical illustration of what I had heard, that great artists confine themselves to modelling, leaving the heavy working in marble to other hands. David is a great Republican. He talked much about Republicanism; and to his views on this subject I was doubtless indebted for some of the cordiality with which I was received. Dined with Mr. Wilkes at Passy, the residence of Benjamin Franklin; find Wilkes a striking illustration of the literary Swiss, who lets his pen out for hire to any side that will pay well; formerly the vigorous correspondent of the "Morning Chronicle," and now that of the "Standard," and writing for "Tait" and "Frazer" at the same time.

April 7. Had a treat to-day at the Cour de Cassation. A very important case was to come on, involving a question of French constitutional law, in which Dupin, the Procureur-Général and President of the Deputies, was to speak. I was in the *queue* at the *entrée* of the *avocats* for half an hour before the door opened. While there, a gentleman and lady approached; the gentleman was tall and rather loosely put together, — not unlike, in this particular, Henry Clay. I looked at him for one moment, and at once knew him to be Lord Brougham, who is now in Paris, from the resemblance to the caricatures, though all these are immensely exaggerated. He inquired for the office of M. Dupin, and subsequently entered the court in his company, and had a chair by his side. I watched him during the whole sitting; he appeared much at his ease, first putting one leg across the other and then changing; gaping, and talking with his neighbor. After the first counsel had concluded, there was a recess of five minutes, during which Brougham left his seat, and came among the spectators to talk with a Frenchman whom he recognized. He appeared to talk *right and left*, without any consciousness that people were watching and observing. His motion and step reminded me of Judge Story's, as also did his animated voice and manner. The cause that was argued was very important. M. Laborde, on one side, made what I thought a very beautiful speech, — animated, flowing, *French*. He used a brief, which appeared to contain the quotations only which he made; I think the whole argument had been written out and committed to memory. Dupin was dry and quiet in his delivery, having his whole argument *written out*, and reading it without pretending to look off his paper.[2] He appeared here, as in the Chamber of Deputies, vulgar. The room in which the Cour de Cassation met was quite rich. The judges, as I counted them, were fifteen.

[1] Pierre Paul Riquet, 1604–1680. He was the engineer as well as projector of the canal.
[2] Sumner wrote to Judge Story, April 21, that "Dupin, the first lawyer of France, is not equal to Webster."

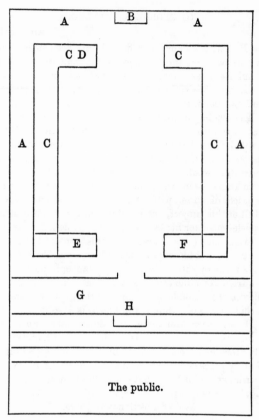

A, a desk and bench not occupied on ordinary occasions; reserved, I believe, for the presence of the king.

B, the king's seat.

C, the benches occupied by the court ordinarily.

D, the seat of the President.

E, the seat of the Procureur-Général, at the left of whom was Brougham.

F, *greffier*.

G, aisle between the part for the judges and the rest of the court.

H, the advocate who speaks (except the Procureur-Général, who by office has a seat within).

Over the king's chair in this court-room is an excellent portrait of Louis Philippe.

April 8. Had a treat to-day of an opposite kind from that of yesterday, — heard M. Coquerel[1] preach, and thought him truly eloquent, and much superior as a preacher to M. Dupin as a lawyer.

[1] Athanase Laurent Charles Coquerel, 1795–1868. This French Protestant divine, born in Paris, preached twelve years in Holland, and returned to Paris in 1830. He served, in

TO GEORGE S. HILLARD.

PARIS, April 10, 1838.

MY DEAR HILLARD, — For some days I have been steeped in law to the very lips. I have attended the courts every day, and in the Cour d'Assises have had a comfortable and honorable seat assigned me by the court; and I assure you that the observations I have made are not unimportant. I am diligently studying the operation of the French Code, in which I find much to admire. The whole *procédure* has struck me most favorably. I will only say at present, that those who have spoken and written about it in England and in the United States have not understood it; or else have calumniated it grossly. A *tertium quid* which should be the result of the French and English manner of procedure would be as near perfection as I can imagine; but I am inclined to think, — indeed, I am convinced, — that if I were compelled to adopt the *whole* of either without admixture, I should take the French. My mind is full of this subject, but I will not enlarge upon it at present. . . .

Dupin [1] is celebrated for his terseness of expression, for his epigrams and points, and he sustained his character in this respect; but his manner was dull and inanimate, and his appearance vulgar, — in French I should say, *grossier.* He was more subtle than broad, — an opinion which Brougham expressed to a friend of mine after the argument. In writing out his argument, he followed the example of Cochin and the great lawyers in France of one and two centuries ago. Dupin, you know, is President of the Chamber of Deputies; I have seen him there, and do not like him. He has made some rulings on points of order this winter in the Chamber, which would have properly proceeded from the Czar of Russia or the Sultan of Turkey; but parliamentary proceedings are not understood at all in France. I shall fatigue you with law and politics, but out of the fulness of the mind the pen moves. . . .

As ever affectionately yours,

C. S.

JOURNAL.

April 10. To-day was presented by Colonel White [2] to Madame Murat, [3] the sister of Napoleon and ex-queen of Naples, and widow of the great captain of cavalry. She is now at Paris to prosecute a claim against the

1848 and 1849, as a moderate Republican, in the Constituent and Legislative Assemblies. He withdrew from politics upon the *coup d'état* of Louis Napoleon, and thereafter devoted himself exclusively to his profession.

[1] Referring to Dupin's argument in the Court of Cassation, *ante,* p. 282.

[2] Joseph M. White, delegate to Congress from Florida from 1823 to 1837. He died at St. Louis in 1839.

[3] Caroline Bonaparte, Napoleon's youngest sister, was born at Ajaccio, March 26, 1782. As the wife of Murat, whom she married in 1800, she became Queen of Naples in 1808. After his execution, in 1815, she assumed the title of Countess of Lipona. She lived at Trieste many years, and died in Florence, May 18, 1839. In 1838, the French Assembly granted her a pension. Her son, Napoleon Achille, died in Florida in 1847.

Government for the Palais de l'Élysée Bourbon. She is full sixty, but appears to be forty-five. She received me quite cordially in her bedroom, where there were already three or four ladies, and, in the true French style, was pleased to compliment me on my French; when, indeed, I spoke wretchedly, — not speaking as well as I might, for I felt a little awe at the presence in which I found myself. She is rather stout, with a free, open, pleasant countenance and ready smile. Presently some marquis or other titled man was announced, and she said, " *C'est terrible*," and rose and passed to the *salon*, where she received him. Her countenance had the roundness which belonged to Napoleon's, but none of his marble-like gravity. In the evening went to a dinner.[1]

We hardly found ourselves at table before eight o'clock. The American minister, the Greek ambassador, and a large company of a hundred or more were there. After the dinner, what was my astonishment to hear my name introduced into some remarks of the President, with terms of praise, which, though disguised in a foreign language, sounded most strange and undeserved. An ambassador could not have a longer or more richly-embroidered paragraph devoted to his merits. And then the company applauded.

April 12. Heard a singular admission of hearsay evidence in court to-day. The accused was partly identified as the person who committed the alleged theft through the medium of a handkerchief, which had been found in the place where the theft had been committed. The evidence was quite strong that this handkerchief belonged to the prisoner. His advocate, in his defence, stated that he had seen the washerwoman of the accused and described to her the handkerchief in question, and she had said that *she had never washed such a handkerchief* for the prisoner. The court at once admitted the advocate as a witness, to state what the washerwoman had told him!

April 14. To-day heard a case of *avortement* against two females. The trial lasted from eleven o'clock in the forenoon till seven o'clock in the evening. The two were acquitted, much to the astonishment of many. When their acquittal was declared, they both threw themselves on their knees and raised their clasped hands to Heaven in thankfulness, and then kissed each other. After the trial, dined with one of the successful advocates. Agreeably to a provision of the code, at the commencement of the examination of the witnesses, the public were dismissed from the court, as the evidence concerned the public morals.

April 15. This evening saw an interesting personage, — a *commissaire de police*, at his house. One of my friends was robbed, and had complained to the police, who had been indefatigable in their search. I called with my friend upon the *commissaire* this evening. His conversation showed remarkable *expertness* in his business, and what a *trade* it is in Paris to detect thieves. He drew from his pocket a white, red, and blue sash, which he told me he always carried with him, and in any emergency put it on, when

---

1 " Dîner Encyclopédique de l'Union des Nations." The President was Jullien de Paris, who was born in 1775, and died in 1848. He was a Jacobin during the Revolution. In 1818 he founded the *Revue Encyclopédique*.

at once his person became *sacred*. He spoke with something approaching contempt of our laws; and said, " *Dans votre pays il n'y a pas de justice du tout* " : if he could have the making of the laws, he would make a law by which *all thieves* should be hung!

Here the Journal ends.

TO SIMON GREENLEAF, CAMBRIDGE.

PARIS, April 13, 1838.

MY DEAR FRIEND, — Your letter was a green leaf cast up by the ocean, — fresh, cheering, and full of goodly tokens. Would that I could take the wings of the morning, — or of the evening rather, — and cross for one day the depths of water that part me from Cambridge and Boston! One draught from the deep fountains of home would be better than all the rich sources which are open about me. And yet I have renounced the former willingly, ay, joyously for the time, and have found no occasion to repent of my choice. Since I have been in Paris my every moment has been occupied; and one of the subjects which has interested me much is the lectures and the manner of lecturing at the Law School (where there are four thousand pupils from all the countries of the world except the United States), and at the Sorbonne, and the College of France. I have heard, perhaps, one hundred and fifty or two hundred lectures in all branches of jurisprudence (*droit*), belles-lettres, and philosophy.[1] . . .

Most of the lectures at the Law School consist of commentaries on the French Codes, and the Institutes and Pandects of the Roman law. The professor has before him the law which forms the subject of his lectures; he first reads a section, and, if it be the French Code, takes clause by clause, and in a free, easy, and conversational manner expounds it, illustrates the importance of the provision, and the reasons which led to its adoption. Judge Story's Commentaries on the Constitution are executed in precisely the style of these lectures, except that there is in them more unction and more research than in any law-lecture I have heard in France. If the subject of the lecture be the Roman law, the professor reads one section and then translates it critically, giving occasionally some of the different readings. The lectures on the Roman law were excessively dry, — almost repulsive. There is but little in the manner of these professors that differs from that at Cambridge, except that the examination of the students is not intermingled with the exposition of the professors. But I would not have you understand that the students escape examination; if they desire the diploma of Bachelor of Laws, which is necessary in order to be admitted to the bar, they must undergo repeated examinations, — not as with us, for the sake of strengthening and confirming their knowledge, but in order to test it, and ascertain if it

[1] A description of the lecture rooms and of the dress of the professors, similar to that already given in the Journal, is omitted.

actually exist. The students almost invariably take notes, and for this purpose have portfolios containing an inkstand and paper which they bring into the lecture room. I have seen them very often taking down what I did not think was worth noting, and which they would have known, if they had read faithfully the codes, even without the assistance of the commentators. Some of the students are attentive; others again are quite indifferent. There seems to be about the same proportion of black and white sheep that you find in your fold. The professors are all, or nearly all (there are fifteen), authors, and some of them rather celebrated; but no man among them has struck me as a distinguished *jurist*. One of the most eminent — perhaps the most eminent — is the Baron de Gérando, whom I know personally very well; but he does not appear to take any interest in his place, though he takes a deep and lively interest in all the great causes of humanity and virtue. Of all, I prefer M. Rossi, who lectures on constitutional law; he is a man of broad and liberal views, and of more various studies, I suspect, than the others. I have heard him quote Blackstone in his lectures, and I can assure you it sounded at once ridiculous and agreeable. The *horizon* of the French lawyer is extremely limited. Foreign nations, with their various laws, are nothing to him. Strong in the Chinese conceit that France is the celestial nation, he neglects with a truly Mohammedan indifference all but his own peculiar jurisprudence; and in the study of this I am strongly inclined to believe that he generally bounds his labors by the perusal of the codes, and some few of the commentators. I write this with some hesitation, — not however because what I have seen has left any doubt upon my mind, but because I am reluctant to judge foreigners. But one of the most distinguished of their professors (M. Bravard, Professor of Commercial Law) made a confession to me, similar to what I have stated above.

The manner of lecturing in the departments of belles-lettres and of philosophy is similar to that I have already described. The most eminent men, — Biot, whose works are used at Cambridge, and Baron Poisson, — take the chalk and sponge and stand for an hour at the blackboard; and other eminent professors expound a section of Sallust or of Herodotus to perhaps a dozen young men, who, with the classics in their hands, sit round a table of the size of those in our rooms at Cambridge. And yet these manipulations at the blackboard, and these familiar expositions of a classic (often made at eight o'clock of the morning), are called *lectures*. You will see, therefore, that you were never wrong in styling the exercises at the law school *lectures:* according to the vocabulary in use here, they are such without doubt. I have much to say with regard to this subject, but cannot compass it within the bounds of a letter. At present, another subject of even greater importance is engrossing my mind, — I mean the courts, and the operation of the codes. I have only time to say that I have been most agreeably disappointed in the penal code. There is much in it which we must adopt. Would that I could draw a sponge over all our criminal law, whether by statute, custom, precedent, or however otherwise evidenced! When I see the simplicity, neatness, and common sense of the procedure here, I sigh over the cumbrous, antiquated forms and vocabulary which we persist in retaining. But this is not to be discussed at the end of a letter. I shall return, not simply a codifier, but a *revolutionist;* always ready however, I trust, to be illuminated by the superior wisdom of my friends.

I regret daily that I have not a *credit* in behalf of the College for the purchase of books; with two hundred dollars, I could fill up many little chasms of French law. Our collection is very good, but it is not complete. You have not even the continuation of Toullier, by Troplong, which a French judge told me lately was as good as the work of Toullier itself — great praise. I have not yet heard from the Judge, and know nothing about the Supreme Court, and the decisions during the last winter. Write me about these. With affectionate regards to Mrs. G., as ever your affectionate friend,

CHAS. SUMNER.

TO JUDGE STORY.

PARIS, April 21, 1838.

MY DEAR JUDGE. . . . Your communications about the Supreme Court were most interesting, because in that body have I garnered up all the hopes which I build for my country. And let me tell you, my dear Judge, that the sentiment of patriotism, of love of country, is called out most strongly by contact with foreigners. I have never felt myself so much an American, have never loved my country so ardently, as since I left it. I live in the midst of manners, institutions, and a form of government wholly unlike those under which I was born; and I now feel in stronger relief than ever the superior character impressed upon our country in all the essentials of happiness, honor, and prosperity. I would not exchange my country for all that I can see and enjoy here. And dull must his soul be, unworthy of America, who would barter the priceless intelligence which pervades his whole country, — the universality of happiness, the absence of beggary, the reasonable equality of all men as regards each other and the law, and the general vigor which fills every member of society, besides the high moral tone, — and take the state of things which I find here, where wealth flaunts by the side of the most squalid poverty, where your eyes are constantly annoyed by the most disgusting want and wretchedness, and where American purity is inconceivable. . . .

I have attended court every day, and am delighted with the operation of the French penal code. There are many particulars in which they have immeasurably the start of us, and I shall never rest content until I see some alterations in our criminal jurisprudence. Here is an immense topic of discussion, and I desire much the light of your counsel. I have talked with all sorts of professional men with regard to the operation of the code, and am glad to find that the enemies of codification in England and America have calumniated its plan because they did not understand it. By the way, one of the most distinguished jurists of France, — M. Victor Foucher,[1] — spent

<hr style="width:30%">

[1] Victor Adrien Foucher, 1802–1866.

some time with me at my room yesterday, during which we talked much of you.

As ever affectionately,   C. S.

Since writing this, I have spent a long evening talking with Bravard, Professor of Commercial Law and the successor of Pardessus.

TO PROFESSOR SIMON GREENLEAF.

PARIS, May 6, 1838.

MY DEAR FRIEND, — I think you have hardly yet lost your interest in *inaugurations*, particularly of law-professors. I will, therefore, tell you how this affair is ordered in France. Another professorship, in addition to the *fifteen* already existing in the School of Law, has just been established to treat of *comparative penal legislation;* and M. Ortolan has been chosen professor. His first or inaugural lecture took place last week. Now the inaugural lecture is nothing more than the *first* lecture of the course, in which the professor salutes his audience and gives an outline of his subject. I presented myself in proper season at the door of the lecture room, and was refused entrance by the janitor because I had no ticket, which was required on this occasion from some motives of *police*, but which could have been procured beforehand. Determined not to lose the inaugural, I stepped into the porter's lodge, demanded a morsel of paper, and wrote something like the following: " *M. Sumner, avocat des Etats-Unis, a l'honneur de saluer Monsieur Ortolan, et de lui exprimer son empressement à entendre la première leçon de M. Ortolan aujourd'hui. M. S. attendra chez le concierge un billet d'entrée.*" I handed this note to the porter, and asked him to carry it to the professor, who was then in his robing-room, just assuming the red gown and cap. The porter at once returned with M. Ortolan's compliments to me, and ushered me into the robing-room of the professor, who received me with great distinction; and astonished me by saying that he had been apprised beforehand of my intention to honor his lecture by my presence, and directed the attendant to show me into the lecture room by the professors' entrance; and I soon found myself seated in the circle of the great lawyers of France, near Dupin, the Procureur-Général, Troplong, the continuator of Toullier, &c. Soon, the professor entered, — a short, modest, dark-haired man of thirty-five or forty. His countenance trembled with anxiety; but his entrance was received with a shout from the students. He took his seat, and then, *ex cathedra*, delivered his lecture, putting on his hat immediately after the utterance of the first sentence. In his lecture he discussed the importance of comparative penal legislation, and gave an outline of the manner in which he proposed to treat the subject. Several times was he interrupted by a shout of applause from the students; and when he ceased the shout was redoubled. He immediately left the room, and so ended the inauguration.[1] You see that an in-

----

[1] The legal journals which gave an account of the ceremonies noted Sumner among the distinguished persons present.

auguration is a simple affair; but I believe that this man met it with as great anxiety as a friend of mine on the other side of the salt sea. The students here form such a numerous and powerful body, and are under so little restraint, that a professor feels much solicitude with regard to his reception until he has actually met them face to face. You see, from this account, that there is no solemnity, no squeezing out of reluctant Latin; but the Latin must be exhibited before. In order to be chosen professor, one must *contest* before certain judges certain topics of law in Latin! The judges, after this *concours*, as it is called, make the election.

In a bundle of books which I shall send home will be a letter, written by a friend of mine, the Professor of Commercial Law, to the Minister of Instruction, making fun of this old usage, and asking for its abolition. I got the author to give me some copies, for I thought it might do good in helping to explode the practice among us of using Latin at inaugurations.

I find much more to interest me at Paris than I expected. I have been here four months; but I leave much unseen, and many pursuits neglected. I wish that I were able to spend three or four more months here, immediately before my return. I am excessively anxious to make myself master of the operation of the code and of the system of legal instruction. The last I think I have done pretty well; but the first is a great work which it would take months, perhaps years, to accomplish. I shall be in England soon, — the great theatre of a different jurisprudence. You shall hear how that affects me. This is a dull letter for Mrs. G.; but my recollections are not the less affectionate on this account.

Yours as ever,

CHAS. SUMNER.

TO GEORGE S. HILLARD.

PARIS, May 11, 1838.

MY DEAR HILLARD, — After repeated efforts, during which we have exchanged cards several times, I have seen Sismondi,[1] who is now in Paris to superintend the publication of a new book. He received me almost like an old friend, with great ardor and simplicity of manner, at once speaking English, and not allowing me to speak French. He is a stout person, of about fifty-five, perhaps sixty; of great vivacity and cheerfulness, and without the least affectation. His countenance does not denote the student, but there is in it that quickness of motion and peculiar brightness of expression which rather mark the man of affairs: I might take him for the steward or manager of a large concern in the country. His wife has much more the air of society; she is as graceful as simple, and both exhibited towards each other a loverlike attachment. She speaks English very prettily. I spoke of Mr. Prescott's book, which I have had an opportunity of reading cursorily at

---

[1] Sismondi was born at Geneva, May 9, 1773, and died in that city in 1842. He is best known by his two works, the "History of the Italian Republics" and the "History of the French." His wife was an English lady, and a sister-in-law of Sir James Mackintosh.

Paris. It seems that Sismondi had just received a copy without note or any indication from whom it came; but he supposes it, perhaps rightly, from the author. He requested me, when writing home, to let Mr. Prescott know that he had received it; that he had glanced through its pages with the greatest pleasure, and had found masses of authorities cited in the notes with which he had been hitherto entirely unacquainted. He added that, as he was in Paris for only a short time, he should not read the work till his return to Geneva, when he should address the author a letter. I recounted to him the circumstances so discouraging under which the work had been composed, and I assure you he received them with the liveliest interest. He said that he could never have struggled against such difficulties himself, and that he should fall asleep at once on hearing a foreign language read. I trust you to mention to Mr. Prescott what Sismondi requested I should write him. I regret that I have not been able to procure here a couple of copies of Prescott's book, as there are two Spaniards now here, whom I have met several times and feel considerably acquainted with, who are prepared from my conversation to be interested in the work; one is the Procureur-Général of Spain, and the other is a Deputy of the Cortez. If I could sow the seed with them, it might add to the author's just reputation and to the character of our country. This last consideration is one which I bear not a little in mind in my intercourse with foreigners. Much were my Spanish friends astonished, that the great sovereigns of their country should find a historian on the other side of the water.

Sismondi talked much and with great ardor of slavery. He is a thorough abolitionist, and is astonished that our country will not take a lesson from the ample page of the past and eradicate slavery, as has been done in the civilized parts of Europe. The serfs of the feudal system have entirely disappeared, and a better state of society has taken their place. I had heard in America that the little history of the Italian Republics in Lardner's "Cyclopædia" had been composed in English by him; he told me that it was translated under his eyes, but not by him, for that he cannot write English. The "Decline and Fall of the Roman Empire" was translated by Mrs. Austin. He inquired after Dr. Channing particularly, and expressed his admiration of his sermons, but, above all, of his work on slavery. The *brochure* on Texas he had not yet received. He is anxious for some provision in our country securing a copyright to authors, but he would be content with a moderate allowance; he says there is a middle ground on which the rights of the public might be respected, as well as those of authors. He thought Sergeant Talfourd had gone too far.

Have I written you that De Gérando is preparing a large work in three volumes on the "Charitable Institutions of the World?" What he says about those of the United States I was asked to read in manuscript. I have no doubt the work will contain much valuable matter. De Gérando has been made a *peer* this winter. He is rather old, and appears (if I may use the expression) a little *fussy* in his manner. His mind seems filled by his book, whether he is in his professor's chair, his seat as peer, his *salon*, or at the head of his table; in all of which places I have seen him. He is quite an ancient professor in the Law School; but his lectures are now listened to with but little interest, and I am inclined to think justly. I have heard one of his brother professors make not a little fun about him. This, I must remark, is quite consistent with the French character. I have hardly met a Frenchman who spoke well of another; and I have heard a professor of the Law School take up his brethren, professors at the same school, and deal judgment upon each in succession. . . .

As ever affectionately yours,

CHAS. SUMNER.

TO JUDGE STORY.

PARIS, May 10, 1838.

MY DEAR JUDGE, — My letters are the hurried effusions of the moment, written with a racing pen; but still the opinions which I have expressed are not the less deliberately formed. I have already told you something with regard to French politeness; now for the learning of the French bar. I do not wish to pronounce rashly, though I write quickly; but I cannot hesitate in saying that the learning of the profession is of the most shallow kind. The old fields beyond the time of the code, out of which so much corn has been gathered, are seldom or never entered. One French judge with whom I conversed told me that all lawyers who studied the science of their profession resorted to Dumoulin and Cujas; but when I asked him whether Faber was studied, — an author whose works form *nine folios* in our library, — he replied, "*Je ne connais pas cet auteur.*" And Bravard, the successor of Pardessus as Professor of Commercial Law, and one of the ablest of their writers and professors (indeed, the foremost), told me that there were five-sixths of the bar who had never read a page of Cujas, Dumoulin, Domat, Cochin, or D'Aguesseau; and Bravard added that he didn't think it at all useful to read them: and Foelix told me further that he didn't believe Bravard himself had ever read a page of them! So there you have the chain of ignorance or indifference. The code is the *vade mecum*, the "be-all and end-all," with the French *avocat;* this he possesses in a neat pocket edition, the different codes designated by the different color of the leaves, and carries with him to court. Among the younger lawyers whom I have met, I have found the greatest ignorance with respect even to the modern authors of France. One lawyer, who was introduced to me as a young *avocat* of great promise, had never heard of the work of Boulay-Paty on the Maritime Law; and another, whose library I examined, had a copy of Toullier, of which the leaves were yet uncut. Now I do not give these little straws as decisive; but still they are indications on which you will build, as well as myself. I can assure you without vanity (for between us there is no such thing), that I have several times felt that my acquaintance with the literature of French jurisprudence, and with the character and merits of its authors, was equal if not superior to that of many of the Frenchmen with whom I conversed. With them now it is indeed *Nil præter edictum prætoris,* — the code and nothing but the code. Ignorant as they are of their own jurisprudence, it would seem superfluous to add that they know nothing of foreign jurisprudence, nothing of English and American in particular. One object of Foelix's journal has been to promote a knowledge of the science of the law, and to show its growth abroad; but his journal, though enjoying much consideration, has only a small and goodly company of readers.

You will understand that I have enjoyed some advantages for finding out the actual gauge and measure of the French *avocat*, when you know that I have had the friendship and confidence of Foelix, who is a Prussian by birth, and with whom I can always speak of the French with perfect liberty; because, not a Frenchman born, he has none of the sensitiveness of a native. His residence in France, and his acquaintance with French society, have given him an insight into the actual state of things. I find that we rarely disagree. I compare my impressions constantly with his matured opinions. You may well wonder then, since such are my views, that I wish to stay longer in Paris. But, after all possible abatement, the French are a great nation, with a versatility and activity of intellect almost wonderful. There is no science to which they have not brought contributions; even the science which we cultivate owes to France a Pothier, an Emerigon, and a *Code*. And it is the operation of this code that I am particularly anxious to study. You will understand that this is not an off-hand labor; it requires months to follow the different courts, and to get any thing like a precise idea of the actual course of things. With the criminal courts I am considerably *au courant;* with the other courts much less, though I have attended all. When I return home, I shall wish to discuss a thousand things with you, and I long for the daily benefit of your learning and judgment. If I find, then, that my arrangements will permit, I shall, before my return home, pass through Paris and stop here yet longer.

May 12, 1838.

I have seen Pardessus to-day, — an old gentleman of sixty or upwards, with thorough French *politeness*. When I left him he made a sweeping bow, saying he felicitated himself upon the honor of my visit, and then thanking Foelix for introducing me. He told me that the Spanish " Code of Commerce " (a copy of which I shall send home) is much better than the French, for several reasons: (1) because it came after the French Code; (2) because they had the benefit of his, Pardessus's, Commentaries; and (3) because it was made by *one* man, and not by a commission. He told me that his translation of the *Consolato del Mare* was the only one to be relied on; that Boucher's (which we have at Cambridge) is full of mistakes; that Boucher did not understand Catalan, and has fallen into the worst blunders. When I asked him how many volumes his collection of sea laws would make, he replied: " *O mon Dieu! six tomes et même plus que cela.*"

Affectionate remembrances to all your family, and

As ever yours,

CHAS. SUMNER.

TO JUDGE STORY.

PARIS, May 14, 1838.

I have just come from that immense city of the dead, Père La Chaise. I have wandered round among its countless monuments; have read its characteristic inscriptions, and gazed on the memorials raised to genius, virtue, and merit. . . . You may ask then how Père La Chaise compares with Mt. Auburn. I can answer easily. There is an interest which Père La Chaise possesses which Mt. Auburn has not yet acquired, and I hope long years will pass away before it can assume this melancholy crown. Everywhere, in the former, you see the memorial which marks the resting-place of some man whose very name causes the blood to course quickly through the veins. Your eyes rest on the modest tomb of Talma, and then on the more attractive monument of Laplace. . . . And yet, as a place of mourning to be visited by the pious steps of friends and kindred, give me our Mt. Auburn, clad in the russet dress of Nature, with its simple memorials scattered here and there, its beautiful paths and its overshadowing groves. Nature has done as much for Mt. Auburn as man has for Père La Chaise, and I need not tell you how superior is the workmanship of Nature. In the French graveyards there is an actual surfeit of gravestones; the sense is fatigued by the number of monumental inscriptions.[1] . . .

I am on the point of leaving Paris, where I have already passed several months, and yet I have just seen Père La Chaise for the first time. From this fact you may conceive the number of interesting and engrossing objects in this wonderful city. I leave Paris with the liveliest regret, and feeling very much as when I left Boston, — with a thousand things undone, unlearned, and unstudied which I wished to do, to learn, and to study. I start for England, — and how my soul leaps at the thought! Land of my studies, my thoughts, and my dreams! There, indeed, shall I " pluck the life of life." Much have I enjoyed and learned at Paris, but my course has been constantly impeded by the necessity of unremitted study. The language was foreign, as were the manners, institutions, and laws. I have been a learner daily; I could understand nothing without study. But in England every thing will be otherwise. The page of English history is a familiar story; the English law has been my devoted pursuit for years, English politics my pastime, and the English language is my own. I shall then at once leap to the full enjoyment of all the mighty interests which England affords; and I shall be able to mingle at once with its society, catch its tone, and join in its conversation, attend the courts, and follow all their proceedings as those at home. Here then is a pleasure which is great almost beyond comparison, — greater to my mind than any thing else on earth, except the consciousness of doing good; greater than wealth and all the enjoyments which it brings. In England I shall find a *vacation*, — the first I have had for years. And yet, there I must keep up my study of French and German; and I propose to devote the early part of my mornings to these languages.

---

[1] A detailed account of the approach to the cemetery and of its monuments is omitted.

May 21.

Still in Paris, and still longing to stay here. I have promised many persons that I will return, and I must return. I find myself on a track which no American, perhaps no Englishman, has ever followed. I wish to master the judicial institutions of this great country; and for this purpose to talk with the most eminent judges, lawyers, and professors, and to get their views upon the actual operation of things. How I shall use the materials I may collect remains to be seen, — whether in a work presenting a *comparative view of the judicial institutions* of France, England, and America, particularly with a view to the theory of proofs and the initiation of causes, I cannot tell; but certainly there is a vast amount of invaluable information which I may harvest in future years. In collecting this information, I see before me the clear way of doing good and gratifying a just desire for reputation. You will understand me when I write as I do, my dear Judge. And here let me congratulate myself upon your friendship, and the influence it has ever had upon me to make me cultivate science rather than practice.

Much joy do I find in my present exile in the acquaintances I have been able to make; but still I send my thoughts back to home and the quiet talks in which I have so often indulged with my friends. I think every day — ay, every hour — of ancient scenes, and I long to be able to unbosom myself to well-familiar hearts.

I cannot conclude without alluding to a very remarkable conversation which I had with Cousin yesterday, particularly about philosophy in America. He takes a deep and I believe sincere interest in it, and is very anxious with regard to the professorship at Cambridge. He has read some productions of Mr. Brownson, whom he thinks one of the most remarkable persons of the age, and wishes to see placed where he can pursue philosophy calmly, thinking his labors will redound to the advance of science throughout the globe.

Give one look at old Cambridge for me; remember me affectionately as ever to your family. I hope to find news of you on my arrival in London, and to hear of Mrs. Story restored in health and spirits and again the life of your fireside. My next will salute you from England. I can imagine that you thrill with me at the thought of that jewel of the sea. Farewell.

As ever affectionately yours,

CHAS. SUMNER.

TO REV. DR. WILLIAM E. CHANNING, BOSTON.

PARIS, May 21, 1838.

MY DEAR SIR, — One of the last times that I had the pleasure of conversing with you, we spoke of Jouffroy and Lerminier, two French writers now among the most conspicuous on philosophical subjects. I have heard them both very often, — the former at the Sorbonne, and the latter at the Collége Royale de France; and I have thought that I could not better redeem my promise to you than to present a hasty sketch of them. As you enter the lecture room of Jouffroy, you find it crowded with young and old, who appear to be watching eagerly for the appearance of the lecturer. . . . He has been considering psychology this winter, and presented in one of his lectures a beautiful tableau of the principal faculties, capacities, and susceptibilities of the human mind. I fear that he will be lost to philosophy and the Sorbonne, for he is already a deputy, and this winter delivered, according to my judgment, one of the best speeches of the season. He is so ill that he has been obliged to drop a portion of his course. A French gentleman shrewdly remarked to me that he was ill for his *cours*, but not for the Chamber of Deputies; his friend Cousin, however, told me that he was verily ill. His lectures are *facile princeps* among all that I have heard in France, and I have heard many. I look back upon them with great pleasure. I think, however, that I place a higher estimate on all his labors than is generally placed here.[1] . . .

De Gérando has inquired with great friendship after you, and requested me to apologize to you for his long silence. Sismondi is now in Paris to superintend the publication of a work on political economy. He requested to be kindly remembered to you. In Paris I have met a Mr. Gibbs, of South Carolina, a resident here for some years. He is a slaveholder, and yet is against slavery, and believes it can be and ought to be abolished. I have conversed with him, and found him full of philanthropic views. He informs me that some time since he sent a letter to America for publication, — I think in the New York " American," — signed a " Slaveholder," and pointing out a way in which slavery might be abolished. Let me invite your attention to this production, if you meet with it; I have not seen it myself. Allow me to be remembered to your family, and believe me

Your faithful friend,

CHAS. SUMNER.

Sumner, in his later writings and addresses, referred to his visit to Paris, as also to his subsequent visit to Germany. In his tribute to Judge Story, of Sept. 16, 1845, he said : —

" It has been my fortune to know the chief jurists of our time in the classical countries of jurisprudence, — France and Germany. I remember well the pointed and effective style of Dupin, in one of his masterly arguments before the highest court of France; I recall the pleasant converse of Pardessus, to whom commercial and maritime law is under a larger debt, perhaps, than to any other mind, while he descanted on his favorite theme; I wander in fancy to the gentle presence of him with flowing silver locks who was so dear to Germany, — Thibaut, the expounder of Roman law, and the earnest and successful advocate of a just scheme for the reduction of the unwritten law to the certainty of a written text; from Heidelberg I pass to Berlin, where I

---

[1] Descriptions of Jouffroy and Lerminier, already given in the Journal, are omitted.

listen to the grave lecture and mingle in the social circle of Savigny, so stately in person and peculiar in countenance, whom all the Continent of Europe delights to honor: but my heart and my judgment, untravelled, fondly turn with new love and admiration to my Cambridge teacher and friend. Jurisprudence has many arrows in her quiver, but where is one to compare with that which is now spent in the earth? " [1]

In his argument before the Supreme Court of Massachusetts against the constitutionality of separate schools for colored children, Dec. 4, 1849, he said : —

" And let me add, if I may refer to my own experience, that at the School of Law in Paris I have sat for weeks on the same benches with colored pupils, listening, like myself, to the learned lectures of De Gérando and Rossi; nor do I remember, in the throng of sensitive young men, any feeling toward them except of companionship and respect." [2]

During his last few weeks in Paris, he endeavored to promote the election of Judge Story as a member of the French Institute, and for that purpose prepared in French a memoir of the judge's career and writings, which he delivered to Mr. Warden, already a member.

Sumner left Paris for London, May 29, having remained nearly two months longer than he had intended before leaving home. As he himself states, in his letters and Journal, he left much unseen, and regretted that he could not prolong his sojourn, particularly with the view of conversing with eminent French jurists. He had, however, accomplished what he most desired, — he was able to speak the French language, and through it to come into personal relations with educated Europeans of whatever country.

[1] Works, Vol. I. p. 144.
[2] Works, Vol. II. p. 375.

CHAPTER XIII.

ENGLAND.—JUNE, 1838, TO MARCH, 1839.—AGE, 27-28.

SUMNER arrived in London on the evening of May 31, and remained in England nearly ten months. He came by the way of the Thames, and was a guest temporarily at the Tavistock Inn,[1] Covent Garden. He soon took permanent lodgings at 2 Vigo Street, near Charing Cross and the Strand, and within ten minutes' walk of Westminster Hall and the Abbey. Leaving cards with Earl Fitzwilliam, John Stuart Wortley, and Mr. Justice Vaughan, he soon found himself embarrassed by conflicting invitations, and his time taken up by society. He was admitted as a foreign visitor, — a qualified membership, — to four clubs;[2] the Garrick, Alfred, Travellers', and Athenæum. He was present in court dress at the coronation of Queen Victoria in the Abbey, receiving the courtesy of two tickets, — one from Lord Lansdowne, and the other from Sir Charles Vaughan. He attended the sessions of the courts and the debates in Parliament, reserving till the London season was over the remarkable sights, — the Tower, Tunnel, British Museum, and Abbey. He sat on the bench at Westminster Hall, and dined with the judges at the Old Bailey, where he spoke at the call of the Lord Mayor. Following the plan of his journey, he observed with the keenest interest " men, society, courts, and parliament."

Having been invited to many country-seats, he was well provided with facilities for visiting different parts of England, as also of Scotland and Ireland. He left London, July 24, to

---

[1] Recommended by his Scotch friend, Brown, and by John Wilkes. The latter, an active writer in his day, seems to have been much attracted to Sumner; and at Paris they were often together. Wilkes bade Sumner good-by, as he left for London, in a note closing thus: "So now a pleasant voyage to you; for you are a right good sample of a thoroughly good-hearted, hard-headed, able, well-informed American." Wilkes soon after returned to London, where he became editor of the " Church and State Gazette," and died in 1844 or 1845. He was the grandson of a Methodist clergyman, and son of John Wilkes, of Finsbury Square, M. P. for Boston.

[2] To the Garrick through Brown, and the Travellers' through Sergeant D'Oyly.

attend, by invitation of the judges, the circuits, and to visit
places of interest on the way. His route was from London to
Guilford, where Lord Denman was holding the Home Circuit,
Winchester, Salisbury, Exeter, and Bodmin in Cornwall, where
the Western Circuit was then in session, and where, with Wilde
and Follett, he was the guest of the bar; then to Plymouth in
the carriage of Crowder, Queen's counsel, afterwards judge; to
Combe Florey, where he was for two days the guest of Sydney
Smith; to Wells, where he met the Western Circuit again, Bristol and Cheltenham; to Chester, where Mr. Justice Vaughan,
then holding court, called him to his side upon the bench; and
reaching Liverpool Aug. 11, during the session of the Northern
Circuit, where he met with the same courtesy from Baron Alderson. He dined with the bar and the court, and responded to
toasts at Bodmin, and more at length at Liverpool. To Judge
Story he wrote, Aug. 18: "Never did I enjoy so much happiness
as has been my lot within the last few weeks. I have had a
constant succession of kindnesses and attentions of the most
gratifying character." To Mr. Daveis he wrote, Sept. 2: "At
times I was honored with a seat on the bench by the side of
the judge, and at times I mingled with the barristers. I have
made myself master of English practice and English circuit-life.
I cannot sufficiently express my admiration of the heartiness and
cordiality which pervade all the English bar. They are truly a
band of brothers, and I have been received among them as one
of them."

Leaving Liverpool, he visited Robert Ingham, M. P. for South
Shields, at his residence, Westoe Hall, near the mouth of the
Tyne. Late in August, he was present at the annual session of the
" British Association for the Advancement of Science," and was
called up at the dinner by the Bishop of Durham, Dr. Maltby.
Then followed visits to the bishop at Auckland Castle; to George
H. Wilkinson, the Recorder of Newcastle, at Harperley Park,
with a view of Brancepeth Castle on the way to Harperley, and
of Raby Castle[1] while at Harperley; to Christopher Blackett,
M. P., at Oakwood; to Archdeacon Scott, with whom he played
the sportsman for the first time since his college vacations; to Lord
Brougham at Brougham Hall, and John Marshall at Hallsteads,
on Ulleswater Lake. He enjoyed greatly some hours with Words-

---

[1] Wytton and Ravensworth castles were visited about this time.

worth, at Rydal Mount; but missed Southey, then absent on the
Continent. From Keswick he went to Penrith, where he was
for a day with Sir George Back, the Arctic voyager. Passing
into Scotland, he was at Melrose the guest of Sir David Brewster. Here he conversed with companions of Sir Walter Scott,
and made an excursion to Abbotsford. He was in Edinburgh
nine days, meeting some of its most famous men; dining with
Sir William Hamilton and Sir John Robison, Secretary of the
Royal Society, enjoying the society of Jeffrey, who was assiduous in attentions, and entertained by Sir James Gibson Craig at
Riccarton House. Next he visited his friend Brown at Lanfire
House, Kilmarnock, and joined in the rude festivities of a Highland wedding. While lodging at an inn at Dumbarton, he
passed a day with Talfourd, then living in a cottage near by.
He was the guest of John A. Murray, the Lord Advocate, at
Strachur Park, near Inverary. He visited Stirling and Glasgow, and crossed to Dublin, where he was welcomed by Lord
Morpeth, then Chief Secretary of Ireland, and received civilities from Thomas Lefroy, M. P. for the University.[1] Returning to England, he passed the rest of October at Wortley Hall
(Lord Wharncliffe's), Fairfield Lodge near York (Mr. Thompson's), Holkham Hall in Norfolk (Earl Leicester's), with visits
to Hull, Boston, and Lynn on his route from York to Holkham. He arrived in London early in the morning of Nov. 4,
after an absence of nearly three months and a half. Among
many expressions of satisfaction with his journey is the following, written to Dr. Lieber, Nov. 16: —

"I arrived in town ten days ago, after a most delightful and thrilling
journey through various parts of England, Scotland, and Ireland. I have
been received with a kindness, hospitality, and distinction of which I truly
felt my unworthiness. I have visited many — perhaps I may say most —
of the distinguished men of these glorious countries at their seats, and
have seen English country life, which is the height of refined luxury, in
some of its most splendid phases. For all the opportunities I have had I
feel grateful."

He remained in London till March 21, — four months and a
half, — making three brief excursions; one in December to Oxford,[2] where he lodged at All Souls as the guest of Sir Charles

---

1 The record of this part of his journey is not complete, none of his letters between Oct. 7
and Oct. 24 being preserved, except a brief one to his sister Mary, written Oct. 14.

2 He was accompanied by Robert Ingham, Sir Gregory Lewin, and John Stuart Wortley.

Vaughan, then in residence at the college; another, later in the same month, to Cambridge, where the attentions of Professor Whewell awaited him, and to Milton Park, where he shared in the festivities of Christmas with Earl Fitzwilliam, and joined with his son, Lord Milton, the present earl, in a fox-hunt; and the third, in January, to Stratford-on-Avon, and Warwick and Kenilworth castles. He attended the Lord Mayor's dinner at Guildhall, and responded to a toast; was present at the opening of Parliament, and heard the young Queen's speech; and passed a day at Windsor Castle, by the invitation of one of the lords-in-waiting.

While in London, or journeying in other parts of the British Islands, he mingled with the best society. His associations were not confined to any one set, but embraced persons widely divergent in professional callings, politics, tone of thought, and rank, — judges, lawyers, and divines; scholars eminent in literature, metaphysics, and science; titled persons who combined good breeding and intelligence; statesmen, Whig, Tory, and Radical, some of whom were aged, and full of reminiscences of great orators; women, whose learning, cleverness, or grace enriched the thought and embellished the society of their day. He was received as a guest, sometimes with the familiarity of a kinsman, into the houses of Denman, Vaughan, Parke, Alderson, Langdale, and Coltman, among judges; of Follett, Rolfe (Lord Cranworth), Wilde, Crowder, Lushington, and D'Oyly, among lawyers; of Hayward, Adolphus, Clark, Bingham, Wills, Theobald, Starkie, and Professor Bell, among law-writers and reporters; of Hallam, Parkes, Senior, Grote, Jeffrey, Murray, Carlyle, Rogers, Talfourd, Whewell, and Babbage, among men of learning, culture, and science; of Maltby, Milman, and Sydney Smith, among divines; of Robert Ingham, John Kenyon, Monckton Milnes (Lord Houghton), Basil Montagu, and Charles Vaughan, among genial friends who wrote or loved good books; of Brougham, Durham, Inglis, Cornewall Lewis, Campbell, Labouchere, Hume, and Roebuck, among statesmen and parliamentary chiefs;[1] of Fitzwilliam, Lansdowne, Wharncliffe (and his son, John Stuart Wortley), Leicester, Holland, Carlisle (and his son, Lord Morpeth), among noblemen. He met on a familiar footing Charles

---

[1] At Joseph Parkes's he met Richard Cobden, who was not as yet a member of Parliament.

Austin, Macaulay, Landor, Leigh Hunt, Thomas Campbell, and Theodore Hook. He talked with Wordsworth at his home, and looked with him on the landscapes which had inspired his verse. Among women to whose society he was admitted were the Duchess of Sutherland, Mrs. Montagu, Joanna Baillie, Mrs. Jameson, Mrs. Sarah Austin, Miss Martineau, Mrs. Shelley, Mrs. Marcet, Mrs. Grote, Lady Morgan, Mrs. Norton, and Lady Blessington. With some of these persons the acquaintance was only temporary; with others there followed a correspondence more or less frequent, and a renewal of intercourse in later visits to Europe: and there were those, like Lord Morpeth, Robert Ingham, Joseph Parkes, and Mr. and Mrs. Montagu, with whom a lifelong friendship was established.

The persons already named are referred to more or less frequently in his letters. There were many others not mentioned in them with whom he had more or less association, and from whom he received hospitality or civilities.[1]

Sumner's acquaintance with English society was wider and more various than any previously enjoyed by an American, and even exceeded that of most Englishmen. The remarkable favor which he everywhere met was noted at the time, and is still remembered, by those who witnessed it. It was said of him, that "when an American gentleman, the gifted Charles Sumner, was in England, his popularity in society became justly so great and so general, that his friends began to devise what circle there was to show him which he had not yet seen, what great house that he had not yet visited."[2] A few months after his return home, Mr. Hayward referred to him in the "Quarterly Review,"[3] as the reporter of Judge Story's decisions, "who recently paid a visit

---

[1] Some of these are the following: George Peabody, American banker, 1795-1869. W. Empson, son-in-law of Lord Jeffrey (Hertford). Thomas Longman, Jr. (2 Hanover Terrace, Regent's Park). Arthur J. Johnes, of Lincoln's Inn (4 South Bank, Alpha Road). Petty Vaughan (1788-1854), son of Benjamin Vaughan, of Hallowell, Me. (70 Fenchurch Street). Sir George Rose (Hyde Park Gardens). Robert Alexander (13 Duke Street, Westminster). J. N. Simpkinson (21 Bedford Place, Russell Square). J. Guillemard (27 Gower Street). Graham Willsmore, of Plowden Buildings Temple (1 Endsleigh Street, Tavistock Square). John Washington, of the Royal Geographical Society. John P. Parker, Secretary of the Temperance Society (Aldine Chambers, Paternoster Row). Frederick Foster, whom Sumner met at Wortley Hall. Alexander Baillie Cochrane (4 Burlington Gardens). Lady Mary Shepherd.

[2] Autobiography, Memoir, and Letters of Henry Fothergill Chorley, Vol. I. p. 180.

[3] Dec., 1840, Vol. LXVII. pp. 33, 34. Article on "American Orators and Statesmen." This reference to Sumner was copied by the "Law Reporter" in a notice of the third volume of his Reports. Feb., 1841, Vol. III. p. 403.

of some duration to this country, and presents in his own person a decisive proof that an American gentleman, without official rank or widespread reputation, by mere dint of courtesy, candor, an entire absence of pretension, an appreciating spirit, and a cultivated mind, may be received on a perfect footing of equality in the best English circles, social, political, and intellectual; which, be it observed, are hopelessly inaccessible to the itinerant note-taker, who never gets beyond the outskirts or the show-houses."

His letters of introduction opened to him his opportunity; but that was all. The greater number of those which he took with him he withheld. A letter of introduction, given with due authority, usually entitles the bearer to an invitation to dine, or to some similar courtesy; but its function is then exhausted. If he cannot contribute his part to the circle to which he has been admitted, his career will be short-lived. This is true of the best society everywhere; and it is most true of English society.

Sumner abstained from seeking introductions, and awaited the advances of others. The persons whom he first met were pleased with him, and their good words soon gave him currency in London society. In many instances he bore no American letters to those with whom he became most intimate. At a dinner or party he met other guests, who, attracted by his manners and character, invited him to visit at their houses. In this way, English society in different directions was 'opened to him. The Attorney-General, afterwards Lord Campbell, introduced him to Dr. Lushington. Through Joseph Parkes he was brought into relations with Lord Brougham, the Montagus, and Roebuck. Robert Ingham, who conceived a strong affection for him, met him at the Judges' dinner at Liverpool. Sydney Smith commended him to Baron Alderson; the baron introduced him to the Bishop of Durham; and at the bishop's he met Sir David Brewster, who invited him to Melrose.

To Hillard he wrote, Dec. 4, 1838: —

" The acquaintance which I have made, various and extensive, has been volunteered to me. It has grown out of casual meetings in society, and has been extended in a spirit of kindness and hospitality which makes my heart overflow as I think of it. I now hardly call to mind a person in England that I cared to see whom I have not met under circumstances the most agreeable and flattering to myself." [1]

---

[1] Sumner's fancy for collecting autographs was developed at this period. He was supplied with many by Kenyon, Morpeth, Sir David Brewster, Hayward, Talfourd, Brown, Miss

Sumner's success in English society was due to the same characteristics which had secured for him at home strongly attached friends, as well among his seniors as among persons of his own age.   He had the genuineness and enthusiasm which always charm, alike in the oldest and the newest society.   His rare intelligence on all topics most interesting to Englishmen, — their history, politics, law, and literature, and the personal life of their authors and public men, — was doubtless an advantage to him.   If he was wanting in the wit and brilliancy which sparkled in the conversation of some of the eminent writers who then mingled in London society, he everywhere won favor by his thoughtful spirit, his fulness of knowledge, his amiable disposition, and the catholic temper with which he observed foreign customs and institutions.   Of the large number of persons whom he then met in a familiar way, generally older than himself, most have died, — including his dearest friends Morpeth, Ingham, Parkes, and Mr. and Mrs. Montagu.   The few who survive have, in most instances, contributed for this memoir their recollections of him, still vivid after an interval of nearly forty years.   Their testimony accords with that of those who knew him as a student and in the early years of his manhood.

Hon. James Stuart Wortley writes: —

"I have great pleasure in responding to your appeal for information, for I have a lively recollection of the early visits of Mr. Sumner to my father and his family, both at Wortley Hall in Yorkshire and afterwards in London, where he was a frequent and much valued guest.   I was then in the early years of my practice at the bar, and I well remember the pride I felt in introducing your amiable and cultivated countryman to the leaders of the Northern Circuit, and taking him to a seat among the barristers in court when he joined us at York, to observe the procedure and practice of our courts.   He was also invited to the bar mess; and, in the several times that he dined with our body, he won golden opinions by his most amiable manners and abundant resources of conversation.   Both there and in private society he was always genial, though modest; and all that fell from him was agreeable and intellectual, and often instructive.

"Mr. Sumner was introduced to my father's house by my dear brother John, who was four years older than myself, and who, having succeeded my father in his title and estates, unhappily died some years ago, at a comparatively early age.   You are right in supposing that my brother was one of a

Martineau, and the Montagus. These, together with others, some rare and costly, which he purchased late in life, and notes written to himself by distinguished persons, he bequeathed to Harvard College. Kenyon gave him those of Southey, Faraday, Landor, Miss Mitford, Coleridge, Malthus, and Thomas Campbell.

small band who visited the States in 1824–25; consisting besides himself of the late Prime-Minister, Lord Derby (then Mr. Stanley), Mr. Labouchere, who was afterwards a member of Lord Melbourne's cabinet and died as Lord Taunton, as well as Mr. Evelyn Denison, who eventually became Speaker of the House of Commons, and died only two or three years ago in retirement as Lord Ossington. They were, in fact, the pioneers of the class to which they belonged; and, being all known as members of the British House of Commons of more or less distinction, were received by your countrymen with even more than their wonted courtesy and hospitality: and their example led to the more frequent and happy intercourse of our public men with those of the United States.

" I wish I was able to give you more ample reminiscences of the interesting subject of your inquiries; but, in the mean time, I beg you to be assured that it is a most interesting pleasure to our family if we are able to contribute any thing of value to the record of a life so distinguished as that of Senator Sumner."

Mr. Henry Reeve writes : —

" It will give me sincere pleasure to assist you in preserving any recollections of my old friend Charles Sumner, for whom I entertained the greatest regard. I cannot remember how our acquaintance began, but I presume that it was in 1838; very likely it was at the house of Baron Parke (afterwards Lord Wensleydale), with whom he was a great favorite. His legal attainments, his scholarship, his extensive knowledge of English literature, his genial and unaffected manners, but above all the enthusiasm and simplicity of his character, opened to him at once not only the doors but the hearts of a large circle of persons eminent in this country. I think I still hear him repeating a passage of Burke, or engaging in debate on some nice question of international law. English society was flattered and gratified by the strong regard he showed for the leading members of what was then one of the most intellectual and cultivated bodies of men in Europe; and he was not insensible to the attentions which were paid to him. . . .

" At the bottom of his heart, I believe Charles Sumner loved the old country next best after his own.

> But to be wroth with those we love,
> Doth work like madness in the brain;

and I am sure that nobody would have hailed with greater satisfaction the restoration of feelings of cordial amity in the great Centenary of Independence. He ranks among us with those Americans whom we would most willingly recognize as our countrymen, — Everett, Ticknor, Adams, Longfellow, Motley, and Winthrop, — all, I think, citizens of Massachusetts, and all equally welcome to England. In some respects, Sumner was the most genial of them all. He came here young; he had no stiffness or reserve in his character; and he will always be remembered and regretted by us as one of the most agreeable companions we have known."

Dowager Lady Wharncliffe, who survives her late husband, John Stuart Wortley, second Lord Wharncliffe, writes : —

"I never knew an American who had the degree of social success he had; owing, I think, to the real elevation and truth of his character, his *genuine* nobleness of thought and aspiration, his kindliness of heart, his absence of dogmatism and oratorical display, his general amiability, his cultivation of mind, and his appreciation of England without any thing approaching to flattery of ourselves or depreciation of his own country."

Mr. Abraham Hayward writes : —

"My recollections of Charles Sumner are scanty, although in the highest degree favorable. When he first came to England, he was the editor of a law magazine published on the same plan as that of which I was the principal founder in 1828, and which I edited till 1844. We had, therefore, many common topics of interest from the commencement of our acquaintance. He also brought letters of introduction from Mr. Justice Story, with whom I was in constant correspondence till his death. Sumner's social success at this early period, before his reputation was established, was most remarkable. He was a welcome guest at most of the best houses both in town and country, and the impression he uniformly left was that of an amiable, sensible, high-minded, well-informed gentleman. But his powers of conversation were not striking; and when you ask me to recall the qualities which account for his success, I most frankly own that it was and is to me as much a puzzle as the eminent and widespread success of your countryman and townsman, George Ticknor.[1] At the same time, I feel satisfied that, in each instance, the success was indisputable and well deserved."

Lady Monteagle, daughter of Mr. John Marshall, writes : —

"I have a distinct recollection of the pleasant intercourse which I enjoyed with Mr. Charles Sumner in my father's house, both in London and at Hallsteads in the year 1838, when he visited the English lakes. His intelligent inquiries respecting any thing that differed from either habits or opinions to which he had been accustomed, and the candid and genial manner in which he was ready to consider such differences, made his society very attractive and interesting. In his later visits to this country, — when I know that my husband, Lord Monteagle, saw him frequently, — I had not so much personal intercourse with him, excepting in the large meetings of London general society. I am sorry that I cannot supply any more definite information respecting a distinguished man whose society was so much prized in this country."

Mrs. Grote writes : —

"My recollections of Charles Sumner when he first came amongst us are still fresh and lively. We first met him at the house of William Ord, M. P.,

---

[1] Mr. Hayward contributed an article on Mr. Ticknor's Life to the "Quarterly Review" for July, 1876; pp. 160–201.

and after that at Mr. Senior's, and other places. His company was sought and valued by several families of the English nobility and gentry, with whom he became a favorite guest; and I may safely affirm that no visitor from the United States ever received more flattering attention than Mr. Sumner from both English and Scottish houses. His extensive knowledge, polished manners, and genial cast of character recommended him to all circles of society; and deep was the sympathy inspired amongst us when this philanthropic citizen was assailed in the savage manner so well recollected by all, in 1856. When the historian and myself received Mr. Sumner at St. Germain en Laye, in 1858, he was undergoing the severe treatment adopted by Dr. Brown-Sequard for the cure of his spinal injuries. Subjugated as he was by the pain and irritation of the injured organs, Mr. Sumner's conversation still preserved its charm and even animation, when topics interesting to his mind came up between us."

Mrs. Parkes writes : —

" It was said, after Mr. Sumner's northern journey, that he made the acquaintance of all the principal Whig families going north, and of the Tories on his return. He was wondrously popular, almost like a meteor passing through the country. Young, agreeable, full of information and animation, he enchanted every one; and he bore the ovation well and modestly. I recollect him as he then was perfectly. I used to think he had the good fortune to dispel personally any lingering prejudices which might exist in the British mind respecting their transatlantic brethren. American-born myself,[1] and having known much of the disfavor felt towards our unjustly maligned country, I was very proud of the young champion who could so well exhibit what well-educated, well-bred young Americans were, in contrast to the mercantile specimens whom business objects had more frequently brought over; and who, being wealthy without the previous advantages of education and social culture, excited unfavorable remarks. They had had time to get rich, but not time for the usual concomitants of wealth in an old country like England; and it made me very indignant that so much that had been done should be ignored, and no allowance made for the impossibilities of doing more. My excuse for imposing this episode upon you must be my grateful feeling to the object of your interest, for assisting to dispel the prejudices of those less enlightened days."

Sumner became acquainted with the well-known publishers, Colburn, Maxwell, Bentley, Longman, William Smith, and Clark of Edinburgh ; and, by means of his friendly relations with them, endeavored to promote the reading of American books in England. He obtained an English publisher for Lieber's " Politi-

---

[1] Mrs. Parkes is the granddaughter of Dr. Priestley, and in early life resided in the United States. The change in the character of American visitors to England is referred to in the " Personal Life of George Grote," pp. 123, 124.

cal Ethics," and sought to interest in the work the managers of the leading reviews. He also rendered a similar service for some of Judge Story's law treatises. He was assiduous in commending Prescott's first great work, the "Ferdinand and Isabella," then recently issued, and in obtaining for it fair criticism in the reviews, — a service which the author gratefully acknowledged.[1] He sought the publication of Longfellow's poems,[2] who was as yet known in England chiefly by his "Outre-Mer;" and made similar efforts for Richard Hildreth's "Archy Moore," and Sparks's "Washington." He purchased books for the Harvard Law School, and for Judge Story, Professor Greenleaf, and Luther S. Cushing; and caused copies of original manuscripts of Lord Hale and Hargrave to be made for the judge. His interest in the peculiar toils and pursuits of his friends was constant, and he spared no pains to serve them.

While in England, he was much occupied with correspondence, writing often and at great length to Judge Story of lawyers, judges, law-writers, law-books, and courts; to Hillard of scholars, society, and personal experiences; and with less frequency and detail to Professor Greenleaf, Felton, Cleveland, Longfellow, Dr. Lieber, Mr. Daveis, and a few others. These letters were written with no view to publication or even preservation, but simply for the gratification of friends; and, having only this purpose in view, he sometimes mentioned in an artless way the kind things which were said to him, and the unusual courtesies he received. He reclaimed none of them on his return, and his only solicitude concerning them was lest by accident

---

1 Mr. Prescott, not then personally known to Sumner, wrote to him, April 18, 1839: "Our friend Hillard read to me yesterday some extracts from a recent letter of yours, in which you speak of your interviews with Mr. Ford, who is to wield the scalping-knife over my bantling in the 'Quarterly.' I cannot refrain from thanking you for your very efficient kindness towards me in this instance, as well as for the very friendly manner in which you have enabled me to become acquainted with the state of opinion on the literary merits of my History in London. It is, indeed, a rare piece of good fortune to be thus put in possession of the critical judgments of the most cultivated society who speak our native language. Such information cannot be gathered from reviews and magazines, which put on a sort of show-dress for the public, and which are very often, too, executed by inferior hands. Through my friend Ticknor first, and subsequently through you, I have had all the light I could desire; and I can have no doubt that to the good-natured offices of both of you I am indebted for these *prestiges* in my favor, which go a good way towards ultimate success. . . . Thanks to your friendly interposition [referring to a forthcoming review of the 'Ferdinand and Isabella' in the 'Quarterly'], I have no doubt this will be better than they deserve; and, should it be otherwise, I shall feel equally indebted to you." — Prescott's "Life," pp. 339, 340.

2 The "Voices of the Night" was not published till 1839.

they might reach the newspapers.[1]   Those received by Story and Hillard were passed round at the time among his friends in Boston and Cambridge.

William W. Story writes concerning Sumner's European journey : —

" I was still in college when he first went to Europe. He longed to enlarge his horizon, and to meet face to face the men who ruled the world of letters, politics, law, and government. The Houses of Parliament, Westminster Hall, Doctors' Commons, the Temple and Inns of Court were magical words to him. He could not rest till he had seen them. Furnished with good introductions, he set forth to the Old World; and his lively letters show the enthusiasm with which he walked in this new region. I remember well the impression I received from them as they came back to us over the ocean, and how I longed to be with him. Every thing and every person interested him: he seemed to walk in enchanted air. The commonest things in the commonest habits of a foreign people delighted him: he was in a constant state of astonishment and delight. He was exceedingly well received everywhere, and he left on the minds of all whom he met a most agreeable impression. That visit opened to him a new life; and when he returned he poured forth a torrent of talk about all that he had seen, which was delightful to hear. The letters he then wrote to my father give an admirable picture of his mind at this time. They are fresh, lively, anecdotical, enthusiastic, — just as he was."

With the members of his family he kept up a correspondence : with his brother George, who, in the early part of 1838, sailed for Russia *via* Elsineur and Copenhagen, and at St. Petersburg met with remarkable favor from the court; with Albert, the captain of a merchantman, who was now at New York and then at New Orleans, Liverpool, and Marseilles ; with Henry, who, to Charles's regret, accepted the appointment of deputy-sheriff in Boston; with Horace and Mary and his mother, at home.[2] With much earnestness and repetition, he urged his younger brothers and sisters to zeal in their studies, insisting most on their learning to speak the French language ; and pressed his sister Mary, whose complete education he had greatly at heart, beyond the limitations which, unknown to him, her physical weakness imposed. In the midst of scenes which filled his

[1] He never came into possession of any of the letters which he wrote from Europe, except a part of those written to Judge Story.

[2] His father, while taking a paternal pride in his success abroad, expressed the fear that he was wearing himself out with social dissipation, and unfitting himself for work on his return.

whole soul with delight, there was no forgetting of home and kindred.

The few American tourists sojourning in London in those days were generally brought into personal relations with each other. Sumner welcomed heartily, as a fellow-lodger at 2 Vigo Street, Dr. Shattuck, his companion in Paris, who had in the mean time visited Italy and Germany. He met, in a friendly way, Rev. Ezra S. Gannett, a well-known Unitarian divine, Joseph Coolidge, Mr. and Mrs. Henry Cabot, and their daughter, afterwards Mrs. John E. Lodge, — all from Boston. The Cabots had chambers in Regent Street, near his own, and he found it pleasant to talk with them of social experiences in London.

Thoughts of his vacant law-office disturbed him at times in the fulness of his enjoyments; and he revealed to friends his anxiety as to his future success in his profession, recurring to the prediction of President Quincy in their parting interview, that Europe would only *spoil* him.[1]

To Mr. Daveis he wrote, Dec. 6 : —

"I begin to think of home and my profession. Tell me, as my friend, what are my chances at home. Will it be said that I have forgotten that law which some have given me the credit of knowing; that I am spoiled for practice and this work-a-day world? True, I should be glad to be able to hold constant communion with the various gifted minds that I nightly meet; to listen daily to the arguments of Talfourd and Follett: and so, indeed, should I rejoice in more ennobling society still, — to walk with Cicero over Elysian fields, and listen to the converse of Plato and Socrates. But I well know that I have duties to perform which will be any thing but this. Welcome, then, labor in its appointed time!"

As he left for the Continent, uncertain whether he should return to England on his way home, many kind words were said to him. Lord Denman wrote from Guildhall, Feb. 27, 1839 : —

"Allow me to express the hope that you like England well enough to pay us another visit. No one ever conciliated more universal respect and goodwill. Far from deserving your acknowledgments to myself, I have regretted that my varied engagements have prevented me from paying you the attentions to which you are entitled."

---

[1] *Ante*, p. 198. Such thoughts appear in letters to Judge Story, Aug. 18, 1838; Dr. Lieber, Nov. 16 and Dec. 13, 1838; Hillard, Dec. 11, 1838, March 13, 1839; and Professor Greenleaf, Jan. 21, 1839.

John Kenyon wrote, March 17 : —

" Your time has been well employed in the best society of every sort which we have to offer to a stranger; and you seem to me to have passed through the ordeal — for such it is — with balanced foot and mind."

Robert Ingham wrote, Jan. 19 : —

" Let us, I beg of you, continue friends. I will not multiply speeches, nor dilate on the many causes I have to look back with thankfulness on that casual cup of coffee at Baron Alderson's, at Liverpool, which introduced us to each other. Only be assured (without palaver) that it will be an abiding pleasure to me to hear of you, and above all to hear *from* you."

In another note, without date, he wrote : —

" I have an irksome presentiment that we shall not meet in London again this year. 'This year,' I repeat, for it would indeed grieve me that the grave was to close over us without another meeting; but friendship lasts where intercourse fails, and you must not forget me. God bless you, my friend, and do not neglect to write."

In a tribute to Judge Story, Sept. 16, 1845, Sumner referred to English judges and lawyers whom he met at that time : —

" Busy fancy revives the past, and persons and scenes renew themselves in my memory. I call to mind the recent Chancellor of England, the model of a clear, grave, learned, and conscientious magistrate, — Lord Cottenham. I see again the ornaments of Westminster Hall, on the bench and at the bar; where sits Denman, in manner, conduct, and character 'every inch' the judge; where pleaded the consummate lawyer, Follett, whose voice is now hushed in the grave; — their judgments, their arguments, their conversation I cannot forget: but thinking of these, I feel new pride in the great magistrate, the just judge, the consummate lawyer whom we lament." [1]

During his stay in England, Sumner, as has been seen, enjoyed a rare opportunity of observing closely the men of that day who had been distinguished in Parliament or in the Cabinet. Their broad culture, their delight in classical studies, their large knowledge of history and international law, their high-bred courtesy and finished address in debate, impressed his imagination and shaped his ideal of a statesman. Near the end of his life, when set upon by public men who envied his fame but could not comprehend his elevation of spirit, he must have recalled, in contrast with them, these exemplars of his youth.

[1] Works, Vol. I. p. 144.

CHAPTER XIV.

FIRST WEEKS IN LONDON. — JUNE AND JULY, 1838. — AGE, 27.

LETTERS.

TO HIS BROTHER GEORGE, ST. PETERSBURG.

LONDON, June 1, 1838.

MY DEAR GEORGE, — I write you my first lines from London, and that with the especial object to reclaim sundry letters which the Barings have had the folly to despatch to St. Petersburg after you. . . .

Last night I entered London, having passed just five months in Paris; and, when I found myself here, I seemed at home again. Paris is great, vast, magnificent; but London is powerful, mighty, tremendous. The one has the manifestations of taste and art all about it; the other those of wealth and business. Public buildings here seem *baby-houses* compared with what Paris affords. Go to Paris, you will see art in its most various forms; you will see taste in the dress of everybody, in the arrangement of the shop-windows, and particularly in the glories of the opera. I have been to Drury Lane to-night. I went late; and yet I could not stay through the evening, so dull and tasteless did it seem. The last night I was in Paris I attended the French Opera, and the wonders of that scenic display are yet thrilling my mind. But I have not come abroad to see theatres, though these, as one phase of society, I see with interest always. I was much absorbed while in Paris with observing the administration of *justice*, and endeavoring to master the system of the French law, — a subject to a foreigner of much difficulty ; and I confidently think that I have reaped not a little advantage from the pursuit, and that I may be able to apply my knowledge to some profit hereafter: perhaps I shall write some work on the subject, though I hardly venture to think of it. It is more probable that I shall endeavor to use the knowledge I have acquired and the opinions I have formed in influencing some changes and improvements in the laws of my country. If you conclude to visit Paris, do not fail to let me know beforehand; for I can give you instructions with regard to your management there which are the result of five months' study and mingling with a great variety of people. . . .

I have been here one day; have seen much already; have been proposed as an honorary member of one of the clubs, and cordially received by Earl Fitzwilliam, — one of the first peers of the realm. As yet, however, I have not presented one of my letters of introduction; that I shall not do till I have selected lodgings. After these I am in full chase; but I wish my letters even more than lodgings, though I despair of comfort until I have both. Send back my letters, then, my dear George; send back my letters, and believe me

As ever, affectionately yours,   CHAS.

TO JUDGE STORY, CAMBRIDGE.

GARRICK CLUB,[1] LONDON, June 4, 1838.

MY DEAR JUDGE, —. . . My pulses beat quick as I first drove from London Bridge to the tavern, and, with my head reaching far out of the window, caught the different names of streets, so familiar by sound, but now first presented to the eye. As I passed the Inns, those chosen seats of ancient Themis, and caught the sight of " Chancery Lane," I felt — but you will understand it all.

I send now my memoir of your life and writings, which I have prepared to be laid before the Institute with an accompanying letter. Of course, I was very much cramped by writing in a foreign language; but yet I have contrived to say one or two things which, I hope, are as just in fact as they are appositely introduced. Writing in the country of Cujas and D'Aguesseau, I could not forbear making an allusion to those great minds.

As ever, my affectionate recollections to all your family and to yourself.

C. S.

P. S. London teeming with interest will naturally form the subject of many letters.

TO GEORGE S. HILLARD, BOSTON.

GARRICK CLUB, June 4, 1838.

MY DEAR HILLARD, — From Paris to London is but a span in distance on the globe, and yet what spaces separate them when we regard manners, morals, character, and external appearances! I thought that five months' study of one great city teeming with life, animation, and gayety would take off the edge of my wonder, and throw over all other places that I may visit a secondary character. But here I am in "famous London town," and my wonder still attends me; but it is of an entirely different quality from that

---

[1] Established in 1831, in King Street, Covent Garden, for literary men, and particularly for those who were by profession or tastes specially interested in the drama. Its collection of pictures contain several painted by Sir Peter Lely, Gainsborough, and Reynolds. The club was frequented by Theodore Hook and Albert Smith.

born of Paris. I have a sense of oppression as I walk these various streets, see the thronging thousands, catch the hum of business, and feel the plethora of life about me. The charm of antiquity, so subtle and commanding, — at least I confess to its power, — the charm of taste, and then the excitement produced by a constant consciousness that one is in a foreign land: these belong to Paris. Here I seem again at home; I start as I catch English sounds in the streets; and for the moment believe that I am in New York or more loved Boston when I see the signs over shop-doors staring me in the face. The style of building is American; or rather ours is English. Everywhere I see brick. I do not remember a house in Paris of that material. If I enter a house, I find the furniture like ours; and then, over and above all, is the common language, which, like the broad and "casing air," seems to be perpetually about me.

I left Paris, May 29, in the diligence, early in the morning; rode all day and night and all the next day, when, at six o'clock in the evening, I entered the old fortifications of Calais. Here I gave my French a considerable "airing," — the last it will receive for some time, — in scolding at the twenty servants and agents of different inns, who, as I alighted, besieged me and my luggage in a style of importunity which I think you cannot conceive. Sharp-set, indeed, are these European tide-waiters; those of New York might take some lessons in this school. From Calais I sailed at three o'clock the next morning, bound direct for London. My friends, English and American, advised me to take this route, and enter London by the gate of the sea;[1] and I feel that the advice was good. I waked up in the morning on board the small steamer, and found her scudding along the shores of Kent. There were England's chalky cliffs full in sight, — steep, beetling, inaccessible, and white. Point after point was turned, and Godwin's Sands — where was buried the fat demesne of old Duke Godwin, the father of Harold — were left on the right. We entered the Thames; passed smiling villages, attractive seats, and a neat country on the banks, and thousands of vessels floating on the river. For eighty miles there was a continuous stream of vessels; and as we gradually approached the city, then did the magnitude, the mightiness, of this place become evident. For five miles on either side, the banks were literally lined with ships, their black hulls in gloomy array, and their masts in lengthening forests. We were landed at London Bridge, and my eyes recognized at once " London's column pointing to the skies," and, as I drove up to lodgings, St. Paul's. When I landed I first supposed myself in the centre of the city; but I subsequently found that I hardly reached this point, when, driving two miles, I was set down at the Tavistock Hotel, in Covent Garden.

They have made me an honorary member of the Garrick Club, where I dine, and now write, with the magazines and papers within reach, and the most perfect picture-gallery of the British stage which exists, adorning the walls of the *salon*. Here Talfourd takes his *negus* on passing to Westminster Hall in the morning, and also his midnight potation on returning from Par-

---

[1] John Wilkes ("O. P. Q.") was one who advised this route.

liament; here Poole takes his cheese and salad, and tells stories which would do well in " Paul Pry," and redeem the degenerate numbers of " Little Peddlington." I have also been nominated for another club. All this is well, as it opens to me various ways of meeting society. I must tell you more at large of London club-life. The two nights that I have been at my club, I have been all unconscious of the progress of time, and midnight has been far advanced before I thought of retiring. Such are London hours!

What was my disappointment on arriving at London, when I found no letter from you! The Barings had sent all my letters, except one or two, to my brother at St. Petersburg. Do thank Longfellow for his capital letter, which by good luck stayed behind; also Lawrence, for his hearty, friendly lines; and Greenleaf for his lamentation over the changing spirit of the times. I shall write them all in due time; but at present my hands and time are so full that I cannot.

I find, as I get into the atmosphere of the wits of London, that I see many literary characters in different lights from those in which we view them at a distance. In the short time that I have been here I have heard a flood of anecdote and gossip, but must reserve all these things for conversation in future years. No, I will forget it; for you will have the Ticknors with you, to whom all things have been revealed: I can only hope to follow humbly in their wake. I assure you, they have seen the prime of England; and I promise you a treat in the reminiscences which they can pour out: their autographs and little memorials of that kind alone would not be of slight consequence; but above all these is the living spring of knowledge and of actual experience of London life, and of all the wits that sparkle in its deep waters.

I have not time to write; and so I say, Good-by. I am startled by the expenses here; but, *prudence. Nullum numen abest*, &c.

Yours affectionately,

CHAS. SUMNER.

TO JUDGE STORY, CAMBRIDGE.

LONDON, June 14, 1838.

MY DEAR JUDGE, — Three places have I seen which you would like to see, and which I have longed to see, — the House of Commons, Doctors' Commons, and Westminster Hall. Do you not start at the thought ? I can assure you, I did not enter either without a thrill. My first night at the Commons was very dull. I happened there, led by some barrister friends, at ten or eleven o'clock at night, when nothing was in hand except some matters of ordinary business. For half an hour the novelty of the situation, and the thronging fancies which possessed me, kept me wide awake; but after that I found sleep stealing gradually over my eyelids and — you will read it with astonishment — I slept under the gallery of the House of Commons! Another night was full of thrilling interest. Mr. Whittle Harvey [1] took me under his wing, and I was admitted to the floor of the House, the evening of the twelfth of

---

[1] M. P. for Southwark; born in 1786.

June, during the discussion of the Irish Municipal Corporation Bill; and there I sat from six o'clock till the cry of " divide " drove me out at twelve.[1] Need I tell you that the interest was thrilling during the whole time ? Peel [2] made a beautiful speech, — polished, graceful, self-possessed, candid, or apparently candid, in the extreme. We have no man like him; in some respects he reminded me of William Sullivan,[3] but he made more of an effort than I ever heard Mr. Sullivan make; and yet there was rather a want of power. Lord John Russell [4] rose in my mind the more I listened to him. In person diminutive and rickety, he reminded me of a pettifogging attorney who lives near Lechmere Point. He wriggled round, played with his hat, seemed unable to dispose of his hands or his feet; his voice was small and thin, but notwithstanding all this, a house of upwards of five hundred members was hushed to catch his slightest accents. You listened, and you felt that you heard a man of mind, of thought, and of moral elevation. Sheil [5] then broke forth with one of his splendid bursts, full of animation in the extreme; in gesture and glow like William Sturgis; [6] in voice, I should think, like John Randolph. He screamed and talked in octaves, and yet the House listened and the cheers ensued. Sir Edward Sugden [7] tried to speak, but calls of " question," " divide," and all sorts of guttural, expectorating sounds from members in a corner, or outstretched on the benches of the gallery, prevented my catching a word of what he said during the half-hour he was on his legs. Sir John Campbell, the Solicitor-General,[8] and Follett, all spoke; and of these Follett was by far the best. O'Connell spoke several times, but only long enough to give me a taste of his voice, which is rich in the extreme, more copious and powerful than Clay's, though less musical. But I have not space to write you all my impressions. I must reserve them for conversation.

The first court I entered was Doctors' Commons. The Prerogative Court was sitting, and Sir Herbert Jenner [9] was on the bench. I was taken by one of my friends among the doctors (there are but fourteen or fifteen in all) into their seat, where I sat a solitary *wigless* man. In one case I heard Doctors Adams and Haggard,[10] with an opinion from Jenner. All

---

[1] Hansard's Parliamentary Debates, Third Series, Vol. XL. pp. 617–655.

[2] 1788–1850. Peel was at this period the leader of the Conservatives. In 1835 he had been succeeded by Lord Melbourne as Prime-Minister; afterwards, in 1841, he succeeded Lord Melbourne.

[3] 1774–1839; an eminent lawyer of Boston, and a Federalist in politics. As an author, he wrote upon the characters and events of the American Revolution. *Ante*, p 83.

[4] Lord John Russell (now Earl) was born in 1792. In 1838 he was the Secretary of the Home Department. Sumner wrote to Lieber, Sept. 3, 1838: " You are right in your supposition about Lord John Russell. He is one of the greatest men I have seen in England."

[5] Richard Lalor Sheil, 1793–1851.

[6] 1782–1863; a merchant of Boston.

[7] 1781–1875; author of law treatises on "Vendors and Purchasers" and "Powers;" entered Parliament in 1828; Solicitor-General in 1829; Lord Chancellor of Ireland, 1834–35 and 1841–46; and, in 1852, Lord Chancellor of Great Britain, with the title of Baron St. Leonards.

[8] Rolfe.

[9] Died Feb. 20, 1852, aged 75.

[10] John Haggard; reporter of cases in the Consistory, Admiralty, and Ecclesiastical Courts.

these advocates were as dull as possible : the whole business of this court is conducted in a conversational style. Phillimore [1] and Lushington are the two chief men. You cannot conceive my gratification at hearing Dr. Harding, my friend and attendant, say, even before he knew my relation to you, " Your countryman Story, I think, has written the best law-book in the English language after Blackstone; " and I must not omit to add that, before going to Doctors' Commons, I breakfasted with a friend of the common-law bar, Mr. White,[2] in King's Bench Walk, Temple, and found in his library your " Conflict of Laws." All the courts of Westminster I have seen. Mr. Justice Vaughan was kind enough to quit the bench during a hearing, and speak with me. He has treated me with the greatest distinction. Day after to-morrow I dine with him to meet the Vice-Chancellor [3] and Alexander,[4] the old Chief Baron, with several other judges. Mr. Justice Vaughan has already mentioned my visit to Tindal and Denman, and they have been pleased to say that they shall be glad to see me. I am struck with the spirit of comity which prevails between barrister and barrister, and between bench and bar. But I should write a volume if I expressed all that is in my mind. I have heard Campbell, Follett (the best of all), Talfourd (I dine with him next Sunday), Sergeant Wilde, Erle, Williams, Platt, &c. I wish to talk with you about all these. I am going a circuit.

As ever, yours most affectionately,

CHAS. SUMNER.

P. S. Sir Charles Vaughan [5] has been very kind, and made the most friendly inquiries after you. He wrote me a very warm-hearted note. Stuart Wortley has been quite civil.

TO GEORGE S. HILLARD.

LONDON, June 14, 1838.

MY DEAR HILLARD, — The Ticknors are gone, and I am in this great world all alone. To be sure I already know multitudes; I frequent public places and clubs, and have been kindly received by judges and lawyers, members of Parliament and others; but I am without the sympathies of

---

[1] Joseph Phillimore, 1775–1855; Regius Professor of Civil Law in the University of Oxford; a contributor to the "Edinburgh Review;" member of Parliament, 1817–30; reporter for the Ecclesiastical and Prerogative courts; appointed, in 1834, King's Advocate in the Admiralty Court; and, in 1846, Judge of the Consistory Court of Gloucester.

[2] William Frederick White, with whom Sumner breakfasted June 5.

[3] Sir Lancelot Shadwell.

[4] William Alexander, 1761–1842; Lord Chief Baron of the Exchequer, 1824–31.

[5] Sir Charles Richard Vaughan, 1775–1849: Fellow of All Souls' College, Oxford; Secretary of Legation in Spain in 1810; Minister Plenipotentiary to Spain, 1815–16; to Switzerland in 1823; and to the United States, 1825–35 (with an absence, 1831–33). His friendly relations at Washington with Judge Story brought the latter into a correspondence with Mr. Justice Vaughan, a brother of Sir Charles. Story's "Life and Letters." Sumner, while in England, was indebted to Sir Charles for many civilities.

home: and yet I need not complain; I have found so much kindness, and particularly from my old friend Brown. I belong to two clubs, — the Garrick, and the Alfred. The Garrick is the chosen place of the wits: dining quietly there, you may see and enjoy the society of many of the men whose scintillations we catch even across the Atlantic. There is poor James Smith, one of the handsomest men I ever saw, tall and well-proportioned, with a clear, bright eye, and the white silver crown of age; and yet observe his hand, and you see the horrid marks of gout, and on his foot the large soft shoe; often he calls the waiter to cut his meat, his hand is so lame. Hayward I saw there yesterday talking earnestly with Stephen Price,[1] the author, you will remember, of that redoubtable punch commemorated in the " Quarterly." Poole,[2] of " Paul Pry " memory, sits very quietly, eating moderately and using few but choice words; I have heard him say some very clever things. Forster, of the " Examiner," formerly dined there often. Talfourd is a night-bird; he does not appear till midnight or thereabouts. Then a quantity of barristers congregate here, so that I am always sure to find somebody with whom to have a good talk; further, the charges are the most moderate in London. In the " Alfred "[3] there is more style, a larger library, better cooking, and less society. A delightful place it is to read the reviews and new publications; you will find them all there in a beautiful suite of drawing-rooms, full of chairs the most variously contrived for comfort that I ever saw; you will hardly find two alike, so that when your body is tired of one position, you may fall into another. It was here that I read Brougham's article in the last " Edinburgh " on George IV., in parts excessively able, and full of democratic tendencies.[4] I am told it has excited a greater stir than any other article which ever appeared in any journal, and it is considered his Lordship's best production in point of style. Poor Lord Brougham! how fallen! He is, indeed, fallen: you know my gauge of men's position and my admiration of his career, and you will understand *me* when I say he is fallen. I shall undoubtedly see him while here.

I heard Carlyle lecture the other day; he seemed like an inspired boy; truth and thoughts that made one move on the benches came from his apparently unconscious mind, couched in the most grotesque style, and yet condensed to a degree of intensity, if I may so write. He is the Zerah Colburn of thought; childlike in manner and feeling, and yet reaching by intuition points and extremes of ratiocination which others could not so well

---

[1] He was for many years one of the proprietors of the Park Theatre, New York, and afterwards manager and lessee of the Drury Lane Theatre, London. He died in New York, Jan. 20, 1840, while in charge of the Park Theatre. He was the inventor of the gin punch, made with iced soda water, in which Theodore Hook indulged freely. The recipe is given in "Timbs's Club Life of London," Vol. I. pp. 263, 264.

[2] John Poole, 1786-1872 ; author of farces, of which "Paul Pry," published in 1825, is the most famous. He died poor and neglected.

[3] In Albemarle Street ; founded in 1808, with a membership composed largely of travellers and men of letters.

[4] April, 1838, Vol. LXVII. pp. 1-80. "George the Fourth and Queen Caroline Abuses of the Press."

accomplish after days of labor, if indeed they ever could. I have received from him a very kind note inviting me to pass an evening with him;[1] but another engagement prevented my accepting. To-morrow I dine with Mr. Justice Vaughan, to meet the Vice-Chancellor and other judges; the next day with Stephen Price; the next with Talfourd, &c. My forenoons are at Westminster Hall, — that glorious old Hall, the seat of the richest and most hallowed associations. I can hardly believe, as I look about me, that it is I who have been permitted to enjoy the rich tapestry of society and thought and history which is now about me. I can say nothing of the House of Commons; I have written of that to Judge Story. Whittle Harvey, of great parliamentary fame, has been offered the British Consulate at Boston. The Ministry will be glad to get rid of him.

As ever, yours affectionately.	CHAS. SUMNER.

TO HENRY W. LONGFELLOW, CAMBRIDGE.

ALFRED CLUB, LONDON, June 15, 1838.

DEAR LONGFELLOW, — I found your cheering letter, welcome-like, on my arrival in London. It did me good to read it, for it carried me back to times of converse, when we have talked over some of the things and sights which are now challenging my admiration. But books and conversation, — what do they do towards initiation into the real mysteries of travel? It is a Freemasonry, which is only revealed to those who have taken the traveller's staff and scrip. Before my starting, I had read much of Europe and talked much with those who had enjoyed it, and my imagination withal had done business enough in picturing the reality; but what spaces did my imagination halt behind the reality! To you I may write all this, for your own experience will verify what I say. Is it not great and glorious to walk the teeming streets of magnificent capitals, — to see the productions of art at every turn, — to gaze on some time-honored erection, from every stone of which issues some reverend history, — then to observe foreign manners, and mayhap to catch the unwonted tones of a language which you heard not in your cradle?

---

[1] The following is the note: —

5 CHEYNE ROAD, CHELSEA.

"DEAR SIR, — Your card and Emerson's letter lay waiting for me yesterday, when I got back to my little room. I had not understood till then that it was New England friends; that it was other than 'two foreign gentlemen, Germans most probably,' who wanted to see me, and hear me. To hear me they were welcome ; but I could see no one at that time. I hope you, as my friend's friend, understood it all and excused it. Perhaps now, as it has gone so, you will come down and see us here. We are generally at home; we are to be at home specially on Saturday evening for one date ; tea at 7 o'clock: that evening will be safer than another. We will expect you if we hear nothing to the contrary. Along with your card lay cards of Mr. Gannett and Dr. Warren, both Boston men. If they are friends of yours and will come on such unceremonious terms as these, we shall be right glad to see you all. I had another letter from Emerson, forwarded by you (I think) from Paris. Hoping to know you better soon,

Faithfully yours,	T. CARLYLE.

At Paris I ever felt the romance of travel, for I never could deceive myself into the belief that I was not abroad; but here in London, with everlasting brick before my eyes, and English reaching my ears, I sometimes start and fear that I am at home! I tremble for my visions, my hopes, and anticipations, and look round almost expecting to see a client or a printer's devil; and in the night, when touched but lightly by the leaden sceptre of sleep, I dream that 1 am in Boston, — that an early breakfast awaits me, and some heavy technical work will absorb the whole of the coming day. And yet you know that I love that dear city, and hope again to live there among my cherished friends; but the thought of returning before my time, with an unsatisfied mind, and desires still raging, — I will not think of it.

Before this reaches you, Felton will be a married man![1] Poor fellow, he can never travel! All this great book in which I am reading, and with whose leaves I sport daily, is to him closed. He would enjoy its broad magnificent page, and should come and look into it if he can. But that house which report says he has builded, and that Lexicon which he has not yet finished, and the wife he has taken, will all keep him at home. You will be the better for his society; but he will live with unsatisfied longings, till from the eminence of death (shall I be serious? — I start at the word I have traced) he looks down upon all the things of earth, and nations are to him as Greek particles now. I really wish Felton could come abroad.[2]

—— is here, where he has sported himself for a year or more; living on nothing, writing in the "Athenæum," tramping in the country, calling on anybody he fancies with or without introduction. He has an article in the forthcoming "Quarterly Review,"[3] on "Atlantic Steam Navigation." Lockhart, when he presented it, growled a ghastly smile, fretted about the handwriting as being infinitely the worst he had ever seen, and left poor —— in *nubibus* with regard to its acceptance or rejection. Our author takes a tramp in the country, and on his return finds a very civil note from Lockhart, and the article advertised to be in the forthcoming number for June. *Très bien.*

Old Harvard, stands it where it did? Quincy Hall, does it peer above the foundations? And prejudices against the college and the present order of things, — where are they? And what are you about? Do keep me informed of all that you do. I hope to return home and resume the threads of society and friendship and business, losing nothing in the way of either by my absence; and I must rely upon my friends keeping me informed of what passes.

What has become of Hillard? He is alive and well I trust? And the "North American Review," I hope it thrives. I wish you would be kind enough to say to Dr. Palfrey that I shall write him on the different points of his letter as soon as possible. And Mr. Sparks, how is he? Remember

---

[1] He was married July 19, 1838.

[2] Professor Felton visited Europe twice; first in 1853–54, and again in 1858, each time extending his journey to Greece. The fruits of his travels and studies on these visits appear in his "Familiar Letters from Europe," and "Greece, Ancient and Modern."

[3] June 1838, Vol. LXII. pp. 186–214.

me to him and all friends, not omitting Felton, to whom I send all possible felicitations. Can I do any thing for you here? I shall see Bentley about your books. Write soon, and believe me as ever your sincere friend.

Chas. Sumner.

P. S. As I fold this, it occurs to me that it will reach you in vacation. A happy vacation to you with all my heart!

TO JUDGE STORY.

Alfred Club, June 27, 1838.

My dear Judge, — I cannot recount (time and paper would both fail) the civilities and kindness which I have received in London. You know I have learned by your example and by some humble experience to husband time; and yet, with all my exertions, I can hardly find a moment of quiet in which to write a letter or read a book. But I cannot speak of myself: my mind is full of the things I hear of you from all quarters. There is no company of lawyers or judges, where your name is not spoken with the greatest admiration. Mr. Justice Vaughan feels toward you almost as a brother. He has treated me with distinguished kindness; invited me to his country seat, and to go the circuit with him in his own carriage; he placed me on the bench in Westminster Hall, — the bench of Tindal, Eldon, and Coke, — while Sergeants Wilde and Talfourd, Atcherley [1] and Andrews argued before me. He has expressed the greatest admiration of your character. At dinner at his house I met Lord Abinger, the Vice-Chancellor, Mr. Justice Patteson, &c. With the Vice-Chancellor I had a long conversation about you and your works; he said that a few days ago your "Conflict of Laws" was cited, and he was obliged to take it home, and to study it a long evening, and that he decided a case on the authority of it. Shadwell is a pleasant, — I would almost say, — jolly fellow. With Mr. Justice Patteson I had a longer conversation, and discussed several points of comparative jurisprudence; he is a very enlightened judge, the most so, I am inclined to think, after Baron Parke, who appears to be *facile princeps*. [2]

[1] David Francis Atcherley, 1783–1845. The "Annual Register" of 1845 (his death was on July 6) gives an account of his professional career.

[2] James Parke, 1782–1868. He assisted the Crown officers in the prosecution of Queen Caroline; was made a judge of the King's Bench in 1828, and of the Exchequer in 1834; resigned in 1855, and was upon his resignation raised to the peerage with the title of Baron Wensleydale. A second patent was issued to remove a disability from sitting and voting in Parliament, which arose from the limitation of the first patent to the term of his natural life. See reference to Baron Parke's subtlety and eccentricity in Arnould's "Life of Lord Denman," Vol. I. p. 329, Vol. II. p. 250. In 1872, Justice Blackburn referred to him as "probably the most acute and accomplished lawyer this country ever saw." Brinsmead *v.* Harrison, Law Reports, 7 C. P. pp. 547, 554. Sumner during this visit dined several times with Baron Parke. Eight years later, when an insurance case was cited in the Court of Exchequer from "Sumner's Reports," the Baron asked, "Is that the Mr. Sumner who was once in England?" An affirmative reply being made, he said, "We shall not consider

Patteson spoke of your works, with which he is quite familiar. Abinger is not a student, I think. Coltman was an ordinary barrister with a practice of not more than five hundred pounds a year, and his elevation gave much dissatisfaction; but he has shown himself a competent judge. Only last evening I met Baron Parke at a delightful party at the poet Milman's;[1] there was Taylor,[2] the author of "Philip Van Artevelde," Babbage, Senior, Lord Lansdowne, Mrs. Lister,[3] Spring Rice's[4] family, and Hayward of the "Law Magazine." Parke inquired after you, and said that in the Privy Council your work was of great resort. Baron Parke is a man with a remarkable countenance, intellectual and brilliant. The Solicitor-General[5] honored me with a dinner, where I received the kindest attentions. He inquired about you, and Mr. Rand,[6] as did the Attorney-General.[7] With the latter I had a great deal of conversation (for several hours), and he has asked me to dinner ten days ahead; all invitations are for a long time ahead. I have just been obliged to decline a subsequent invitation from Lord Denman for the same day.

It would be impossible for me to give you a regular account of the persons I see. I may say that I am in the way of seeing everybody I desire to meet; and all without any effort on my part. Most of the judges I personally know, and almost all the eminent barristers. When I enter Westminster Hall, I have a place (I decline to sit on the bench) in the Sergeants' row of the Common Pleas, with Talfourd and Andrews and Wilde; or in the Queen's

it entitled to the less attention because reported by a gentleman whom we all knew and respected." Sumner, when visiting England in 1857, received courtesies from Baron Wensleydale.

[1] Rev. Henry Hart Milman, 1791–1868. After this period he was better known as historian than as poet. In 1849 he became Dean of St. Paul's. Sumner, when visiting England in 1857, renewed his acquaintance with the Dean.

[2] Henry Taylor, born about 1800; author of "The Statesman," and other works in poetry and prose. He has been for some years one of the senior clerks of the colonial office. He married, in 1839, a daughter of Lord Monteagle (Thomas Spring Rice).

[3] Mrs. Lister (Maria Theresa), a sister of Lord Clarendon, was first married to Thomas Henry Lister, who died in 1842. She married, in 1844, Sir George Cornewall Lewis, and died in 1865. She is the author of "Lives of the Friends and Contemporaries of Lord Chancellor Clarendon."

[4] Thomas Spring Rice, 1790–1866. He represented Limerick in Parliament from 1820 to 1832, and Cambridge from 1832 to 1839; was Under-Secretary of State of the Home Department in 1827; Secretary of the Treasury from 1830 to 1834; Secretary of State for the Colonies in 1834; Chancellor of the Exchequer from 1835 to September, 1839, when he was appointed Comptroller-General of the Exchequer. He was made a peer, Sept. 5, 1839, with the title of Baron Monteagle. In Parliament he advocated liberal measures. He married for his second wife, in 1841, a daughter of John Marshall of Hallsteads. In 1857, Sumner met Lord and Lady Monteagle in London.

[5] Robert Monsey Rolfe, 1790–1868. He was appointed Solicitor-General in 1834; was succeeded in a month, on a change of government, by Sir William W. Follett, but was re-appointed six months later, and continued to hold the office until November, 1839, when he was raised to the Bench of the Exchequer. In 1850 he became Vice-Chancellor, and in the same year was created Baron Cranworth. He was Lord Chancellor from 1852 to 1858, and from 1865 to 1867. Sumner was his guest at dinner several times in 1838, and was entertained by him again in 1857.

[6] Benjamin Rand, of Boston.

[7] Sir John Campbell.

Counsel row of the Queen's Bench, with Sir F. Pollock, and the Attorney-General. Then I know a vast number of younger men, whom I meet familiarly in the court room or at the clubs. Not a day passes without my laying up some knowledge or experience, which I hope to turn to profit hereafter. In another walk of life, I am already acquainted with many literary men. Among the peers I have received great kindness from Lords Wharncliffe (with whom I have dined), Bexley, Fitzwilliam, and Lansdowne. I have just been with Lord Lansdowne [1] in his study; I met him last evening at a party. He had previously been kind enough to call upon me, and presented me with a card for his great ball in honor of the Coronation, and also with a card of admission to the Abbey; the latter I gave away to a friend,[2] as I was already provided with a better ticket, being that of a privy-councillor. A few nights ago I was at the great ball at Lord Fitzwilliam's; I started from my lodgings at eleven o'clock, and such was the crowd of carriages that I did not reach the door till one o'clock in the morning. When I first saw Lord Fitzwilliam, he was leading the Duchess of Gloucester on his arm; the Duc de Nemours came in immediately after me. As I stood in the hall, waiting for the carriage (it rained torrents), I seemed in a land of imagination, and not of reality; carriages drove up to the door in quick succession, and twenty servants cried out the name of the owner. There was the *élite* of England's nobility, — it was all "lord" or "lady," except "Spring Rice;" the only untitled name I heard pronounced was that of the Chancellor of the Exchequer. I stood there an hour with dowager duchesses pressing about me, and Lady John Russell, in delicate health, and beautiful, waiting with submission as great as my own.

If other engagements allow me, I go to the House of Lords or Commons. In the former I have had a place always assigned me on the steps of the throne, in the very body of the house, where I remain even during divisions. I was present at a most interesting debate on the 20th June, on the affairs of Spain.[3] I heard Lyndhurst; and I cannot hesitate to pronounce him a master orator. All my prejudices are against him; he is unprincipled as a politician, and as a man; and his legal reputation has sunk very much by

---

[1] Lord Henry Petty, third Marquis of Lansdowne, 1780–1863. He was the son of William, the second Earl of Shelburne (who is honorably identified with the opposition to coercive measures against the American colonists). He became a successful debater in the House of Commons; was Chancellor of the Exchequer, 1806–7; Lord President of the Council, 1830–41 and 1846–52. He was an enlightened statesman; supported the abolition of slavery, and Catholic Emancipation. He was the friend of men of letters, — notably of Macaulay. Henry Wheaton, the publicist, introduced Sumner by letter to Lord Lansdowne. Sumner received attentions at Lansdowne House on his second visit to England, in 1857.

[2] Ralph Randolph Wormeley, afterwards Rear-Admiral of the British Navy, 1785–1852.

[3] The debate of Tuesday, June 19, 1838, in the House of Lords upon intervention in favor of Don Carlos, is reported in Hansard's Parliamentary Debates, Third Series, Vol. XLIII. pp. 806–867. The peers who spoke at length were the Marquis of Londonderry, Viscount Melbourne, Lord Lyndhurst, Earl of Carnarvon, Marquis of Lansdowne, and Duke of Wellington; the Earls of Minto and Ripon spoke briefly.

the reversal of his judgment in the case of Small *v.* Attwood,[1] in which it is said Brougham exerted himself with superhuman energy: notwithstanding all this, Lyndhurst charmed me like a siren. His manner is simple, clear, and direct, enchaining the attention of all; we have nobody like him: he is more like Otis[2] than any other, with less *efflorescence*, if I may so say, and more force. Wellington is plain and direct, and full of common-sense; all listen with the greatest respect. Brougham is various, — always *at home*, whether for argument or laughter. The style of debate is different in the Lords and in the Commons; in the latter I have heard the two discussions on the Irish Corporation Bill.

I have alluded to my opportunities of seeing various shades of life and opinion. I may add that I know men of all parties. With Lord Wharncliffe I have talked a great deal about toryism and the ballot; while Lord Lansdowne expressed to me this morning his strong aversion to the King of Hanover as King of England. Sir Robert H. Inglis,[3] one of the best men I ever met, has shown me great kindness; I breakfasted with him, and then partook of a collation with the Bishop of London. At the Solicitor-General's I heard politics much discussed; and Mr. Duckworth[4] of the Chancery Bar, in going home with me, told me in so many words that he was a *republican*. Opportunities I have also of meeting the best and most philosophical of the radicals. And now, my dear Judge, do not believe that I have given this long detail of personalities and egoism, from vanity; but in the freedom of friendship, and because I have no other way of letting you know what I am about. I must reserve for conversation after my return my impressions of the bench and bar, of politics and society. Let me say, now, that nothing which I have yet seen has shaken my love of country, or my willingness to return to my humble labors. I am grateful for the opportunities afforded me, and congratulate myself that I have come abroad at an age when I may rank among men, and be received as an equal into all society; and also, when, from comparative youth, I may expect many years of joyous retrospection, and also of doing good. Your advice and friendship I rely upon; and you know that your constant kindness has been my greatest happiness. I hope Mrs. Story is well; I shall write her an account of something that may be interesting; but imagine that every moment of my time is absorbed, and my mind almost in a *fever*. I have averaged, probably, *five* invitations a day. To-morrow is the Coronation.[5] That I shall see.

[1] Clark and Finnelly (House of Lords), Vol. VI. pp. 232-531. The Lords read their opinions on March 22, 1838. The case involved the right to rescind a contract on account of fraud.

[2] Harrison Gray Otis, 1765-1848; a prominent leader of the Federal party; Mayor of Boston; United States Senator from Massachusetts. *Ante*, p. 83.

[3] Sir Robert H. Inglis, 1786-1855. He entered Parliament in 1824, and represented the University of Oxford from 1829 to 1853. He was a finished scholar, and much identified with literary and charitable associations. Sumner dined with him several times, and attended parties at his house, 7 Bedford Square.

[4] Samuel Duckworth, M. P. for Leicester, brother-in-law of Mr. Justice Coltman.

[5] A letter to Mrs. Story giving an account of the Coronation on June 28 has not been found. It is referred to in Judge Story's letter to Sumner of August 11, 1838. "Story's Life and Letters," Vol. II. pp. 297-300.

Unsolicited on my part, I have received two tickets; and kind offers of others. Thanks for William's letter.

As ever, affectionately yours,   C. S.

P. S. I shall write you about the " Law Magazine " and Hayward, whom I know intimately. He is a curious fellow, of much talent.

TO PROFESSOR SIMON GREENLEAF, CAMBRIDGE.

TRAVELLERS' CLUB,[1] July 1, 1838.

MY DEAR FRIEND, — I have thought of you often, but particularly on three occasions lately; and what do you think they were? When, at a collation, the Bishop of London asked me to take wine with him; when I was placed on the bench of the Court of Common Pleas in Westminster Hall; and lastly, when, at the superb entertainment of the Marchioness of Lansdowne, I stood by Prince Esterhazy [2] and tried in vain to count the pearls and diamonds on the front of his coat and in his cap. You will not remember it; but it was you who first told me of the extravagant display of this man. That I should call you to my mind on the two other occasions you will readily understand. And so here I am amidst the law, the politics, the literature, and the splendors of London. Every day teems with interests; and I may say, indeed, every moment. Minutes are now to me as valuable as Esterhazy's diamonds.   Imagine me in Westminster Hall where I sit and hear proceedings and converse with the very counsel who are engaged in them.   I hardly believe my eyes and ears at times; I think it is all a cheat, and that I am not in Westminster Hall, at the sacred hearthstone of the English law. With many of the judges I have become personally acquainted, as well as with many of the lawyers. I have received cordial invitations to go most all the circuits; which I shall take I have not yet determined. Mr. Justice Vaughan says that I shall take the coif before I return. I cannot express to you how kind they all are. You know that I have no claims upon their attentions; and yet wherever I go I find the most considerate kindness. They have chosen me as an honorary member of three different clubs, in one of which I now write this letter.

I know nothing that has given me greater pleasure than the elevated character of the profession as I find it, and the relation of comity and brotherhood between the bench and the bar. The latter are really the friends and helpers of the judges. Good-will, graciousness, and good manners prevail constantly. And then the duties of the bar are of the most elevated character. I do not regret that my lines have been cast in the places where they

---

1 In Pall Mall; founded soon after 1814 specially for the convenience of Englishmen who had travelled, and of foreigners sojourning in London. It was frequented by Talleyrand during his residence in England.

2 Paul Anthony Esterhazy de Galantha, 1786–1866; a Hungarian nobleman, who was the proprietor of vast estates, then Austrian Minister at London; his loyalty to the national cause, in 1848, led to the sequestration of his possessions.

are; but I cannot disguise the feeling akin to envy with which I regard the noble position of the English barrister, with the intervention of the attorney to protect him from the feelings and prejudices of his client, and with a code of professional morals which makes his daily duties a career of the most honorable employment. Grateful I am that I am an American; for I would not give up the priceless institutions of my country (abused and perverted as they are), the purity of morals in society, and the universal competence which prevails, in exchange for all that I have seen abroad; but still I see many things in other countries which I should be glad to have adopted among us. Let us then not sigh that we are not Europeans, but cling to our own institutions and model of society, and endeavor to engraft upon it all that is good and fitting in other countries. Such infamous professional sentiments as I have heard avowed by lawyers at our bar, and by a man like ———, would bring a brand upon an English lawyer as bad as Cain's. I remember here, with a thrill of pleasure, the beautiful lessons on this subject contained in your Inaugural Discourse. I long for an opportunity of discussing this subject with you face to face, and pouring out to you the various results of my observation. In a hurried letter, written while my mind is distracted by various excitements, I cannot go into detail. All this I must reserve for the " thousand and one " nights after my return, when I hope to fight all my battles o'er again; to conduct you to Westminster Hall; to point out its vast proportions, its heaven-aspiring roof, its deep echo, its prints of antiquity; to enter the different court-rooms, small in size but full of reminiscences, which open on one side of the great hall; to gaze on the impressive figures before us, in judicial robes and wigs, seeming rather the personation of the law than flesh and blood; or, perhaps, I may in my story marshal you to the Coronation, admire its gorgeousness, and dream again of feudal glories; or enter the *salons* of some of the fashionable and elevated, and see again the array of beauty and bravery. But I am dreaming. When will that future come? Believe I am more than happy at present; but I look forward with a thrill to the day that shall once more let me see my friends, and in the enjoyment of quiet and confiding friendship give me the truest happiness. Thanks for your letter (I have forgotten the date, — 1848, I think) in which you have looked into the future. I have much to say on that subject. But how can I write it all?

Affectionate recollections to Dane Hall, and to Mrs. Greenleaf and all your family, and to yourself.

CHAS. SUMNER.

TO GEORGE S. HILLARD.

LONDON, July 3, 1838.

MY DEAR HILLARD, — You love literature better than law, and I know will be better pleased to hear of the men who move in the quiet walks where haunt the poet, the author, and the artist, than of the gowned and wigged followers of the law. Of judges and lawyers I see enough daily; much, also, of politicians; perhaps I may say the same of literary men. I have already written you some hasty lines on some of the wits I meet at clubs. There are others and worthier that I have met under other circumstances. There is Walter Savage Landor.[1] I know you admire his genius. I first met him at Mr. Kenyon's;[2] he was there at dinner with a considerable party. I could not dine there, as I was already engaged for the same evening with the Solicitor-General; but I was very kindly asked to stop there a little while till they went down to dinner. Landor was dressed in a heavy frock-coat of snuff color, trousers of the same color, and boots; indeed, he wore a morning dress, which one is more inclined to notice here than among us where the distinction between a morning and evening dress is less imperiously settled. He is about fifty-five, with an open countenance, firm and decided, and a head gray and inclining to baldness. We got into conversation; dinner was announced, and Landor and myself walked down stairs together. In the hall I bade him "good evening." "But where are you going?" said he; "you dine with us, surely." I then explained to him the necessity I was under of dining elsewhere; when he asked where he should call upon me. I told him that I would rather, with his permission, have the honor of calling upon him (at Lady Blessington's). But our host at once arranged the difficulty by inviting us both to breakfast a few days ahead. At breakfast he was in the same dress as before. I was excessively stupid; for I had been up at Lord Fitzwilliam's ball till four o'clock, and the breakfast was very early. Landor's conversation was not varied, but it was animated and energetic in the extreme. We crossed each other several times: he called Napoleon the weakest, littlest man in history; whereas you know my opinion to the contrary. He considers Shakspeare and Washington the *two* greatest men that ever lived, and Cromwell one of the greatest sovereigns. Conversation turned upon Washington; and I was asked why he was still suffered to rest in the humble tomb of Mt. Vernon. I then mentioned the resolution of Congress to remove his body to the Capitol, and the refusal to allow it to be done on the part of his legal representatives. In making this statement, I spoke of the "*ashes* of Washington," saying "that his ashes still reposed at Mt. Vernon." Landor at once broke upon me, with something like fierceness: "Why will you, Mr. Sumner, who speak with such force and correctness, employ a word which, in the present connection, is not English? Washington's body was never *burnt;* there are no ashes, — say, rather, *remains.*" I tell this story, compliment and all, just as it occurred, that you may better understand this eccentric man. I think we were all jaded and stupid, for the conversation rather

---

[1] 1775–1864. In 1856, Mr. Hillard edited "Selections" from Landor's writings.

[2] John Kenyon, 1787–1856; the inheritor of a large fortune, and friend of many men of letters; the author of "A Day at Tivoli," and other poems. He distributed his fortune among eighty legatees, among whom were Elizabeth and Robert Browning and Barry Cornwall. Several notes from Kenyon to Sumner are preserved; one from 4 Harley Place, of June 15, 1838, saying: "You are hardly a stranger among us; you were hardly a stranger when you had been here only three days;" another, inviting him to meet Southey; another inviting him to dine, Jan. 19, 1839; and another regretting a previous engagement of Sumner, and adding, "I give you *ten* days' notice, and cannot have you."

flagged. Forster [1] was there, whom you well know as the great writer in the "Examiner" and the author of the "Lives." He is a very able fellow, and is yet young. Landor takes to him very much. His conversation is something like his writing. I had a good deal of talk with him. You must know, also, that our host, Mr. Kenyon, is a bosom friend of Southey and Wordsworth, and is no mean poet himself, besides being one of the most agreeable men I ever met.

Dining at Lord Lansdowne's a few evenings since, I met another literary man, whom I saw with the greatest pleasure. There was Lord Lansdowne, with the blue ribbon of the garter across his breast and the star on his coat, — kind, bland, amiable; Lady Lansdowne, — neat, elegant, lady-like. Next me was the daughter, about nineteen, — pale and wan, but, I am glad to say, extremely well-informed. I conversed with her during a long dinner, and we touched topics of books, fashion, coronation, &c.; and I found her to possess attainments which certainly do her honor. She was kind enough to mention that she and her mother had been reading together the work of a countryman of mine, Mr. Prescott; that they admired it very much, and that the extraordinary circumstances under which it was written [2] made them take a great interest in the author and desire to see him. During the dinner, I was addressed across the table, which was a large round one, by a gentleman with black hair and round face, with regard to the United States. The question was put with distinctness and precision, and in a voice a little sharp and above the ordinary key. I did not know the name of the gentleman for some time; till, by and by, I heard him addressed by some one, — "Macaulay." I at once asked Lord Shelburne, who sat on my right, if that was T. B. M., just returned from India; and was told that it was. [3] At table, we had considerable conversation; and, on passing to the drawing-room, it was renewed. He is now nearly or about forty, rather short, and with a belly of unclassical proportions. His conversation was rapid, brilliant, and powerful; by far the best of any in the company, though Mr. Senior was there, and several others of no mean powers. I expect other opportunities of meeting him. He says that he shall abandon politics, not enter Parliament, and addict himself entirely to literature.

I may say here, that among acquaintances you never hear the word "Mr." Lawyers at the bar always address each other without that prefix. It is always "Talfourd," "Wilde," "Follett;" and at table, "Landor," "Forster," "Macaulay," "Senior," &c. I did not hear the word "Mr." at Lord Lansdowne's table, except when he addressed me, — a stranger. My time is hurried and my paper is exhausted, but I have not told you of the poet Milman, and the beautiful party I met at his house, — Lord

---

[1] John Forster, 1812–76; contributor to reviews, and author of the biographies of Oliver Goldsmith, Charles Dickens, Walter Savage Landor, and Dean Swift (the last incomplete).

[2] Referring to the author's loss of sight.

[3] 1800–1859. Macaulay arrived from India in June, 1838, and was returned to Parliament from Edinburgh the same year, and served till 1847, when he lost a re-election. He was returned again in 1852, and served till his resignation in 1856. Sumner met him at Lord Belper's in 1857, and wrote of him as "so altered that I did not know him."

Lansdowne, "Van Artevelde" Taylor, Babbage, Senior, Mrs. Villiers, and Mrs. Lister, who talked of Mrs. Newton[1] with the most affectionate regard; nor of the grand *fête* at Lansdowne House, where I saw all the aristocracy of England; nor of the Coronation; nor of Lord Fitzwilliam's ball; nor of the twenty or thirty interesting persons I meet every day. This very week I have declined more invitations than I have accepted; and among those that I declined were invitations to dinner from Lord Denman, Lord Bexley, Mr. Senior, Mr. Mackenzie, &c.

As ever, affectionately yours,   C. S.

TO JUDGE STORY.

LONDON, July 12, 1838.

MY DEAR JUDGE, — I have now been in London more than a month; but have not seen the Tower or the Tunnel, the British Museum or the theatres, the General Post-Office or Westminster Abbey (except as dressed for the Coronation): I have seen none of the sights or shows at which strangers stare. How, then, have I passed this time, till late midnight? In seeing society, men, courts, and parliaments. These will soon vanish with the season; while "London's column" will still point to the skies, and the venerable Abbey still hold its great interests, when men and society have dispersed. In a few days, this immense city will be deserted; the equipages which throng it will disappear; and fashion, and wealth, and rank, and title will all hie away to the seclusion of the country. Have I not done well, then, to "catch the Cynthia of the minute"? One day, I have sat in the Common Pleas at Westminster; then the Queen's Bench and Exchequer; then I have visited the same courts at their sittings at Guildhall; I have intruded into the quiet debate at Lincoln's Inn before the Chancellor; have passed to the Privy Council (the old Cockpit); have sat with my friend, Mr. Senior,[2] as a Master in Chancery; with Mr. Justice Vaughan at Chambers in Serjeants' Inn; and lastly, yesterday, I sat at the Old Bailey. This last sitting, of course, is freshest in my mind; and I must tell you something of it. Besides the aldermen, there were Justices Littledale, Park (James Allan), and Vaughan. I was assigned a seat on the bench, and heard a trial for arson, in which Payne (Carrington & Payne) was the counsel in defence. I was waited upon by the sheriff, and invited to dine with the judges and magistrates, at the Old Bailey. I was quite dull,

---

[1] *Ante,* p. 186.

[2] Nassau William Senior, 1790–1864. He was appointed Master in Chancery, in 1836. His writings, on topics of Political Economy, are various; and he was for several years professor of that science at Oxford. Among his publications was one upon "American Slavery," which reviewed Sumner's speech, of May 19 and 20, 1856, on "The Crime against Kansas," and the personal assault which followed it, being a reprint with additions of his article in the "Edinburgh Review," April, 1855, Vol. CI. pp. 293–331. In 1857 they met, both in Paris and afterwards in London, and enjoyed greatly each other's society. Mr. Senior invited Sumner to dine several times in 1838–39.

and really ill (being beaten out by dining in society, and often breakfasting and lunching in the same way every day for more than a month); but they treated me very kindly: and Sir Peter Laurie, the late Lord Mayor, proposed my health in a very complimentary speech, in the course of which he "hoped that he might have the honor of calling me his friend," &c. I rose at once, and replied in a plain way, without a single premeditated thought or expression, and found myself very soon interrupted by " hears; " and Littledale and Park and Vaughan all gave me more hearty applause. As I sat down, Vaughan cried to me: " Sumner, you've hit them between wind and water! " I should not omit to mention that I simply expressed, in my remarks, the deep affection which all educated Americans owe to England; that we look upon her with a filial regard; that in her church-yards are the bones of our fathers: and then I touched upon the interest which I, a professional man, felt in being permitted to witness the administration of justice here; and concluded by proposing the health of the judges of England, — " always honorable, impartial, and learned." Mr. Charles Phillips [1] (the notorious Irish orator), was at the table. I wish I were at home, to give you personal sketches of the lawyers and judges. My heart overflows when I attempt to speak of them; their courtesy and high sense of honor you have never overrated. The bench and the bar seem to be fellow-laborers in the administration of justice. Among the judges for talent, attainment, and judicial penetration, the palm seems to be conceded to Baron Parke, — a man of about fifty or fifty-five, with a very keen, penetrating, chestnut eye, and an intellectual countenance. At his table I met the chief barristers of the Western Circuit, — Erle, Manning, Bompas, Rogers, Douglas, &c.; and they have invited me, very kindly, to visit their circuit. At table, after Lady Parke had left, I put to the Baron and the bar the question on which you have expressed an opinion, in the second volume of my " Reports," [2] with regard to the power of a jury to disobey the instructions of the court on a question of law in rendering a general verdict; and on which, you know, Baldwin [3] has expressed an opinion opposite to yours. Parke at once exclaimed, and Erle and Bompas chimed in, that there was no possible ground of question; that a court should instruct a jury to take the law absolutely as it is laid down from the bench; and that a jury should not presume, because it has the physical power, to pronounce upon the law. I was quite amused to see how instantaneously they all gave judgment in the matter, and what astonishment they expressed when I assured them that some persons held otherwise in America.

I have recently breakfasted with Lord Denman, as I was so engaged as not to be able to accept his invitation to dinner. Bland, noble Denman! On the bench he is the perfect model of a judge, — full of dignity and decision,

---

[1] 1787–1859. He was born in Sligo; removed to London in 1821, where he was often counsel in criminal trials, and became, in 1846, Commissioner of the Insolvent Debtors' Court.

[2] United States *v.* Battiste, 2 Sumner's Reports, p. 240.

[3] United States *v.* Wilson, Baldwin's Reports, p. 78.

and yet with mildness and suavity which cannot fail to charm. His high
personal character and his unbending morals have given an elevated tone to
the bar, and make one forget the want, perhaps, of thorough learning.   In
conversation he is plain, unaffected, and amiable.   I talked with him much
of Lord Brougham.   He assured me that Brougham was one of the greatest
judges that ever sat on the woolsack, and that posterity would do him justice when party asperities had died away.[1]   (Of Lord B. by-and-by.)   I
told Lord Denman the opinion you had formed of Lord B., from reading his
judgments; and his Lordship said that he was highly gratified to hear it.
Denman called the *wig* "the silliest thing in England," and hoped to be
able to get rid of it.   He is trying to carry a bill through the Lords, allowing
witnesses to *affirm* in cases of conscientious scruples,[2] and inquired of me
about the practice in America; but he said he could not venture to allude to
any American usage in the Lords, for it would tell against his measure.
Think of this!   I must not omit to mention that Lord Denman has invited
me to visit him on the Home Circuit, where I shall certainly go, as also to
the Western; and to the North Welsh Circuit, — perhaps also the Oxford;
and, the greatest of all, the Northern.   To all of these I have had most
cordial invitations.

I have heard Lord Brougham despatch several cases in the Privy Council;
and one or two were matters with which I was entirely familiar.   I think I
understand the secret of his power and weakness as a judge; and nothing
that I have seen or heard tends to alter the opinion I had formed.   As a
judge, he is electric in the rapidity of his movements: he looks into the very
middle of the case when counsel are just commencing, and at once says,
"There is such a difficulty [mentioning it] to which you must address
yourself; and, if you can't get over that, I am against you."   In this way
he saves time, and gratifies his impatient spirit; but he offends counsel.
Here is the secret.   I have heard no other judge (except old Allan Park)
interrupt counsel in the least.   In the mean time, Brougham is restless at
table, writes letters; and, as Baron Parke assured me (Parke sits in the Privy
Council), wrote his great article [3] in the "Edinburgh Review" for April
last at the table of the Privy Council.   I once saw the usher bring to him a
parcel of letters, probably from the mail, — I should think there must have
been twenty-five, — and he opened and read them, and strewed the floor
about him with envelopes; and still the argument went on.   And very soon
Brougham pronounced the judgment in rapid, energetic, and perspicuous
language, — better than I have heard from any other judge on the bench.
I have already quoted the opinion of Denman.   Barristers with whom I

---

[1] See "Life of Lord Denman," Vol. I. p. 257, for Denman's opinion expressed in the
House of Commons, Dec. 16, 1830, in relation to Brougham's probable success as an equity
judge.

[2] He brought the bill forward, first, in 1838, again in 1842, and again in 1849, — each
time without success.   The measure became a law in 1854, — the year of his death, — by
virtue of the twentieth clause of the Common Law Procedure Act, which was extended to
other courts by later acts.   "Life of Lord Denman," Vol. II. pp. 72, 106, 216, 217.

[3] *Ante*, p. 318.

have spoken have not conceded to him the position accorded by the Lord
Chief-Justice, but still have placed him high.   Mylne, the reporter,[1] an able
fellow, says that he is infinitely superior to Lyndhurst, and also to Lord
Eldon, in his latter days.   In the Lords I have heard Brougham, — with
his deep, husky notes, with his wonderful command of language, which keeps
you in a state of constant excitement.   I found myself several times on the
point of crying out "Hear!" — thus running imminent risk of the polite
attentions of the Usher of the Black Rod!

I am astonished at the reputation which is conceded to Follett [2] (I have
not yet met him, except in court).   He is still a young man for England,
— that is, perhaps, forty-five, — and is said to be in the receipt of an immense income, much larger than that of any other lawyer at the bar.   I have
heard Sir William Alexander and Mr. Justice Vaughan, who remembers
Lord Mansfield, say that Follett reminds them of him; but, with all the
praise accorded to him from judges, lawyers, and even from Sir Peter Laurie
(ex-mayor), who thought him the greatest lawyer he ever knew, it does not
seem to be thought that he has remarkable general talents or learning.
They say he has "a genius for the law;" but Hayward, of the "Law Magazine," says he is "a kind of law-mill; put in a brief, and there comes out an
argument," without any particular exertion, study, or previous attainment.
I have heard him several times.   He is uniformly bland, courteous, and
conversational in his style; and has never yet produced the impression of
power upon me; in this last respect, very unlike Serjeant Wilde, — who is,
however, harsh and unamiable.   Wilde has an immense practice.   The Solicitor-General is one of the kindest and most amiable of men, with a limited
practice, and is a bachelor.   The Attorney-General is able, but dry and uninteresting.   I have been more pleased with his wife, than with any other
lady I have met in England.   You know she is the daughter of Lord
Abinger, and is a peeress in her own right, by the title of Lady Stratheden.[3]
She is beautiful, intelligent, and courteous.   The Attorney-General has

---

[1] J. W. Mylne.   Mr. Mylne's note of June 16, 1838, referring to Sumner's being in the
Rolls Court that day, regrets that he did not come to his "den" in Lincoln's Inn, and invites
him to attend a breakfast the next Wednesday, and to hear an unfinished argument in a
copyright case before the Lord Chancellor.

[2] Sir William Webb Follett, 1798–1845.   He was elected to Parliament in 1835, 1837, and
1841; was Solicitor-General, 1834–35, under Sir Robert Peel, and again in 1841, and became
Attorney-General in 1841.   Miss Martineau said of him that he "wanted only health to
have raised him to the highest legal and political honors," — History of England, Book VI.
ch. xvi.   Lord Campbell, who was present at his burial, which was attended with much
solemnity in the Temple Church, bore an affectionate tribute to his memory, — "Lives of the
Lord Chancellors," Vol. VII. ch. clxi. note.   Follett wrote, Nov. 17, 1838, from Duke Street
to Sumner: "If you are not tired of English lawyers, will you do me the favor of meeting
some of them at dinner at my house on Saturday, the 24th, at seven o'clock?"   Nov.
25 he again invited Sumner to dinner on the following Saturday; and on Feb. 10, 1839,
sent him a note accompanying some briefs and referring to "Story on Bailments," which
he had just read.   His note of Nov. 11, 1838, to Sumner, on receiving Story's "Law of
Agency," is printed in Judge Story's "Life and Letters," Vol. II. p. 305.

[3] She was married to Sir John Campbell in 1821; was made a peeress in her own right
in 1836, with the title of Baroness Stratheden; and died in 1860.   See reference to her being
raised to the peerage in "Life of Lord Denman," Vol. II. p. 27.

invited me to meet him at Edinburgh, when he goes down to present himself
to his constituents.

This morning, Lord Bexley[1] was kind enough to invite me to "Foot's
Cray," his country seat. Many invitations of this kind I already have; one
from Lord Leicester (old Coke), which I cannot neglect; also from Lord Fitzwilliam, Sir Henry Halford, Mr. Justice Vaughan, Lord Wharncliffe; and
besides, from my friend Brown in Scotland, Mr. Marshall at the Lakes,
Lord Morpeth in Ireland; and this moment, while I write, I have received
a note from the greatest of wits, Sydney Smith,[2] who says, "If your ram-
bles lead you to the West of England, come and see me at Combe Florey,
Taunton, Somersetshire." Thus you see that there is ample store of means
for passing an interesting two months, when you consider that I shall take
the circuits, with all these.

Mr. Justice Littledale[3] is a good old man, simple and kind, but without
any particular sagacity. Patteson, who appears to stand next after Baron
Parke in point of judicial reputation, is still young,[4] — that is, near fifty;
he is about as deaf as Mr. Ashmun was, and yet Lord Denman says that
he would not spare him for a good deal. Patteson was much annoyed by
the report some time ago of his intended resignation.

TRAVELLERS', Sunday, July 15.

Have I told you the character of Mr. Justice Vaughan?[5] He is now
seventy, and is considerably lame from an accident; and is troubled with
rheumatism, possibly with gout. Otherwise he is in a green old age; is
tall and stout; in his manners, plain, hearty, and cordial; on the bench
bland, dignified, and yet familiar, — exchanging a joke or pleasantry with
the bar on all proper occasions; in book-learning less eminent than for

1 Nicholas Vansittart, 1766–1851. He was chosen to Parliament in 1796; was in the
foreign service at Denmark; Lord of the Treasury in Ireland; Chancellor of the Exchequer
from 1812 to 1823; and then raised to the peerage as Baron Bexley. He was distinguished
for his capacity in financial administration. He promoted religious and charitable enter-
prises with much zeal, and was President of the British and Foreign Bible Society. His
card admitted Sumner to the gallery of the House of Lords, on July 16, 1838. In
June he invited Sumner to attend a meeting of the Bible Society, at which he was to
preside.

2 1771–1845. He invited Sumner to dine March 6, 1839, at 33 Charles Street, Berkeley
Square; and, after Sumner's return from the Continent, to breakfast at 56 Green Street.

3 Joseph Littledale, 1767–1842. He was appointed a judge of the King's Bench in
1824, and resigned in 1841. His distinction is confined to the law. Sumner dined with
him in Dec., 1838.

4 John Patteson, 1790–1861. He was made a judge of the King's Bench in 1830; resigned
on account of deafness in 1852, and sat five years after his resignation on the judicial committee of the Privy Council. His second wife was the sister of his colleague, Sir John
Taylor Coleridge. See reference to him in "Life of Lord Denman," Vol. I. p. 330.

5 John Vaughan, 1768–1839. He became a baron of the Exchequer in 1827, and a
judge of the Common Pleas in 1834. He was supposed to be indebted for his advancement
to his brother, Sir Henry Halford, the court physician. "Life of Lord Denman," Vol. I.
p. 45. He was very courteous to Sumner, inviting him several times to dine at his house,
9 Mansfield Street, on one occasion in company with distinguished judges; and also
to attend the circuits. His death took place, Sept. 25, 1839, while Sumner was on the
Continent.

strong sense and a knowledge of the practice of courts, and of the human character. Yet I have always found him apt in apprehending legal questions when raised, and in indicating which way he should instruct the jury. His wife is Lady St. John,[1] the origin of whose title I do not remember, though I think he explained it to me. She is of the family of Sir Theodosius Boughton, whose murder by Captain Donellan[2] makes such a figure in the history of crime. I have met at dinner the present Sir William Boughton,[3] who is the successor of Sir Theodosius. Sir Charles Vaughan is living quietly, as a bachelor, quite at his ease. I expect to meet him at dinner to-night with Serjeant D'Oyly.[4]

Tindal[5] is a model of a *patient* man. He sits like another Job, while the debate at the bar goes on. I may say the same of the Lord Chancellor,[6] who hardly moves a muscle or opens his mouth during the whole progress of a cause. But turning from the bench to the bar (you see how I jump about in my hasty letters), a few days ago I strayed into a committee room of the House of Lords. Several counsel were busily engaged. I observed one with a wig ill-adjusted, with trousers of a kind of dirty chestnut color, that neither met the waistcoat nor the shoes; and I said to myself, and then to my neighbor, "That must be Sir Charles Wetherell."[7] "Yes," was the answer; and very soon a reply of the witness under examination confirmed all. The witness (a plain farmer) had been pressed pretty hard, and was asked by the counsel whether he thought many articles of *fashion* would be carried on a proposed railway; to which the witness promptly replied, "As to articles of *fashion*, — I do not think they much concern either *you* or I, Sir Charles." The whole room was convulsed with laughter, in which Sir Charles most heartily joined.

Hayward,[8] of the "Law Magazine," I know very well. Last evening I met at dinner, at his chambers in King's Bench Walk, some fashionable ladies

[1] Louisa, daughter of Sir Charles William Boughton Rouse, and widow of Lord St. John, was married in 1823 to Sergeant Vaughan, and died in 1840.

[2] By poison, August 21, 1780. The facts are given in Wills on "Circumstantial Evidence," ch. iii. sec. 7; and more at length in James Fitzjames Stephen's "General View of the Criminal Law of England," pp. 338–356.

[3] Sir William Edward Boughton, son of Sir Charles William Boughton Rouse, died in 1856. He was the successor, but not the immediate or lineal successor, of Sir Theodosius.

[4] Thomas D'Oyly died Jan. 14, 1855, at the age of eighty-two years. He became a Sergeant at Law in 1819. He was attached to the Home Circuit, and was for many years Chairman of the Quarter Sessions for the western division of the County of Sussex. He often invited Sumner to dine at his house, 2 Upper Harley Street, and once to attend with him a play of Terence (Phormio) performed by the boys of the Westminster School, Dec. 12, 1838.

[5] Nicolas Conyngham Tindal, 1776–1846. He was counsel for Queen Caroline, Solicitor-General from 1826 to 1829, and Chief Justice of the Common Pleas from 1829 until his death.

[6] Lord Cottenham.

[7] Sir Charles Wetherell, 1770–1846. He was a member of Parliament for a considerable period, Attorney-General in 1826 and 1828, and Recorder of Bristol.

[8] Abraham Hayward, born about 1800; author of several legal publications; editor of the "Law Magazine," from which he retired in 1844; translator of Goethe's Faust, and of one of Savigny's works; and contributor to the "Quarterly Review." Among his articles pub-

and authors, and M.P.'s. There we stayed till long after midnight, and —
shall I say with Sir John? — " heard the chimes of midnight in this same
inn," — though it was Clifford's Inn and not the Temple, which was the
scene of Falstaff's and Shallow's mysteries. Hayward is a fellow of a good
deal of talent and variety. He is well known as the translator of " Faustus,"
and as one of the constant contributors to the " Quarterly Review," in
which he wrote the articles on " Gastronomy " and " Etiquette." I have
talked with him very freely about his journal, and hope before I leave
England to do something in a quiet way that shall secure a place in it for
American law. He has acknowledged to me that " the Americans are ahead
of the English in the *science* of the law." He speaks well of you, but
evidently has only glanced at your works. It seems that his friend Lewis,
who is the author of some of the best articles in his journal, as that on
Presumptive Evidence,[1] had undertaken to review your works, but has since
gone to the Continent.

And thus I have rambled over sheets of paper! Do you, my dear judge,
follow me in all these wanderings? . . . Then think of my invading the quiet
seclusion of the Temple; looking in upon my friends in King's Bench Walk;
smiling with poetical reminiscences as I look at the " No. 5 " where Murray
once lived; passing by Plowden Buildings, diving into the retirement of Elm
Court to see Talfourd, or into the deeper retirement of Pump Court where
is Wilkinson, or prematurely waking up my friend Brown from his morning
slumbers, at two o'clock in the afternoon, in Crown-Office Row.

You may gather from my letters that I have seen much of the profession,
and also of others. Indeed, English lawyers have told me that there are
many of their own bar who are not so well acquainted with it already as I
am. And if I am able to visit all the circuits, as I intend, I think I shall
have a knowledge and experience of the English bar such as, perhaps, no
foreigner has ever before had the opportunity of obtaining. I shall be glad
to tell you further that since I have been here I have followed a rigid rule
with regard to my conduct: I have not asked an introduction to any person; nor a single ticket, privilege, or any thing of the kind from any one;
I have not called upon anybody (with one exception) until I had been
first called upon or invited. The exception was Mr. Manning,[2] of the
Temple; the author of the " Digest," and the translator of the newly found
" Year-Book." I met him at Baron Parke's. He is a bachelor of about
fifty, of moderate business, of very little conversation, who lives a year without seeing a soul that takes any interest in his black-letter pursuits. I took
the liberty, on the strength of meeting him at Baron Parke's, to call upon
him; and was received most cordially.

Your friend, Stuart Wortley, has called upon me several times and has intro-

---

lished in this periodical is one on " American Orators and Statesmen," Dec., 1840,
Vol. LXVII. pp. 1-53. See a letter of Judge Story to him, which furnished suggestions
for the article, — Story's " Life and Letters," Vol. II. pp. 324-327. Sumner was indebted
to Mr. Hayward for many civilities, among them an introduction to Mrs. Norton.

[1] Vol. VI. p. 348.

[2] James Manning, the reporter.

duced me to all his family. I owe him my thanks for his kindness. Lord
Wharncliffe has treated me with no little attention; and I have been delighted
by the plain, unaffected simplicity which characterizes the whole family. I
am glad that it has fallen to my lot to become acquainted with two such
Tories as Lord Wharncliffe and Sir Robert Inglis (from the latter I have a
standing invitation to breakfast whenever I am not otherwise engaged).
Their strong Tory principles no one can doubt; and their beautiful private
characters have invested these principles with a charm for my mind that they
never had before. Not that I am a Tory; but meeting Tories of such a character has made me charitable and catholic, and convinced me that every thing
that proceeds from them is from the purest hearts and most cultivated minds.

And now, my dear Judge, I will bring this letter to a close. I have
written with the most entire frankness; for to whom should I pour out my
heart if not to you? You may show this to Hillard and Greenleaf; but I
doubt if any stranger would not think this narrative a tissue of vanity instead
of the offering of affectionate friendship.

I have received your "Equity Pleadings," and have been reading what I
had not read before. The day the copies were on sale two were purchased,
— one by Sutton Sharpe and the other by Joseph Parkes, the "Birmingham
Solicitor." The latter I know quite well;[1] he is an able fellow.

You will receive this in the middle of a hot month. It will be a good
afternoon's work to go through it. William will be on the point of quitting
the quiet haven of college and trying another sphere of life. Success be with
him! I shall write him probably by the same packet with this.

As I leave town soon for the circuits and for Scotland, I do not know when
you will hear from me again. I shall, however, think of you in the beautiful
west of England, in the mountains of Wales, the lakes of Scotland, and while
I hear the *brogue* of Ireland. And now, good-by, and believe me

As ever, most affectionately yours,

CHAS. SUMNER.

TRAVELLERS', July 17.

P. S.   To this already "Alexandrine" letter I add an "Alexandrine"
postscript. . . .

I have not spoken of arguments before the Lords. I have attended one,
and sat in conversation with the Attorney-General, Lushington, and Clark,
the reporter.[2] The Chancellor sat at the table below the woolsack; the
benches of the Lords were bare; only two unfortunate members, to whom by

---

[1] Joseph Parkes, 1796–1865. He was first a solicitor at Birmingham; removed to London
in 1832, and was taxing master of the Court of Exchequer from 1847 until his death. He
published a "History of the Court of Chancery," and was a writer for Reviews. The "Memoirs of Sir Philip Francis, with Correspondence and Journals," published in 1867, was
commenced by him, and completed after his death by Herman Merivale. He was much trusted
in the councils of reformers. Sumner, who bore a letter to him from John Neal, was indebted
to him for several of his best introductions, — as to Brougham, Charles Austin, the Montagus, and Cobden.

[2] Charles Clark, reporter (in association with W. Finnelly) of cases in the House of
Lords.

rotation it belonged to *tend-out* in this manner, were present in order to constitute the quorum. These happened to be, as Dr. Lushington explained to me, Lord Sudeley, who is quite skilled in architecture, and Lord Mostyn, who is a great fox-hunter. There they sat from ten o'clock in the morning till four o'clock in the afternoon, with their legs stretched on the red benches, and endeavoring by all possible change of posture to wear away the time. The Attorney-General told me that "it would be thought quite indecorous in either of them to interfere by saying a word." You have asked about the characters of judges. I should not omit that of the Lord Chancellor.[1] He did not once open his lips, I think, from the beginning to the end of the hearing. I am astonished at the concurring expressions of praise which I hear from every quarter. He has been all his days a devoted student of the law; and, I believe, of nothing else. Clark, the reporter, also author of the book on Colonial Law, told me that he had "most magnificently disappointed the profession;" and that Tories as well as Whigs would be sorry to see him obliged, by any political change, to abandon the great seal. Dr. Lushington also spoke of him in the highest terms, as did the Attorney-General. When I pressed Lushington into a comparison of Cottenham with Brougham, he evidently gave the former the preference. Lushington[2] himself is a great man; one of the ablest men in England. I owe his acquaintance to the Attorney-General. Dr. L. told me that Brougham, when Chancellor, nearly killed himself and all his bar; that, during the passage of the Reform Bill in the Commons, he sat in the Lords from ten o'clock in the forenoon till ten at night; and Lushington was in constant attendance here, and was obliged to repair from the Lords to the Commons, where he was kept nearly all night. The consequence was that Lushington did not recover from the effects of this over-exertion for fifteen months. Dr. L. told me that he had practised a great deal before Lord Stowell,[3] and that he was the greatest judge he ever knew; that he was rapid as lightning, — more rapid even than Brougham, besides being more uniformly attentive, and of course safe; he comprehended the whole of an argument before it was half uttered. I incidentally mentioned your name to Dr. L., when he exclaimed: "Dear me! I have used his book constantly, — an admirable book, which we could not get along without." He said that you had raised some questions about marriage, which he did not

[1] Charles Christopher Pepys, 1781–1851. He became Solicitor-General in 1833, Master of Rolls in 1834, Lord Chancellor in 1836, and a peer with the title of Baron Cottenham. He held the seal, with a brief interval, until June, 1850, when he resigned; having the same month been advanced in the peerage to the title of Viscount Crowhurst and Earl of Cottenham. He died in Italy, while travelling in the hope of regaining his health which had been broken by the too great labors of his office. See account of his appointment in preference to Brougham in Campbell's "Life of Lord Brougham," Chap. VI.; Greville's "Memoirs," Chap. XXX., Jan. 20, 1836.

[2] Stephen Lushington, 1782–1873. He served in Parliament from 1817 to 1841, advocated the abolition of slavery and the slave-trade; was one of Queen Caroline's counsel, and was appointed Judge of the Admiralty and a Privy Councillor in 1838. He was Lady Byron's counsel in her domestic difficulties. Sumner visited him in July, 1857, at Ockham Park, in Surrey.

[3] William Scott, 1745–1836. He was the brother of Lord Eldon, and distinguished as Judge of the High Court of Admiralty.

know how they should solve. Lushington is about fifty or fifty-five; a tall,
thin man, with an intelligent, open, smiling countenance.

I have already mentioned in this letter that Lord Denman calls the wig
the silliest thing in England. I took the liberty of telling this to Justice
Allan Park, who at once exclaimed that it was all a piece of Denman's cox-
combry; that he wished to show his person. A few years ago, when an invention came out by means of which wigs were made, with the appearance of
being powdered, and yet without powder and the consequent dirt, Park resisted the change as an innovation on the Constitution; and he actually
refused to recognize his own son at the bar, when he had appeared in one of
the new-fangled wigs!

I have alluded to the familiarity between the bench and the bar. I am
assured that the judges always address barristers, even on a first introduction,
without the prefix of " Mr."; and that a junior would feel aggrieved by the
formality, if his senior should address him as " Mr." This same freedom I
have observed between members of the House of Commons, and Peers. Indeed, wherever I meet persons who are at all acquainted, I never hear any
title, — which is not a little singular in this country of titles.

And now, good-by again.   C. S.

P. S. I have forgotten to say that Lord Langdale has as much disappointed the profession as the Chancellor has gratified them.[1] This is, however, partly attributed to the extravagant expectations formed with regard
to him; being such that it was next to impossible for any man to fulfil them.

TO JUDGE STORY.

BOSTON —— think of that !

MY DEAR JUDGE, — I have just written Boston, and would not alter it,
because I preferred to leave it, that you may see how I think of home, — how
present it is in my mind, and how unbidden it rises. I write these lines as
a supplement to the volume I have already written by this same steam-packet;
but some matters have occurred to my mind that I have failed to mention, I
believe. You will, doubtless, be pleased to hear about Lord Abinger. I have
written you that I have met him in society, and was not particularly pleased
with him: he was cold and indifferent, and did not take to me, evidently;
and so I did not take to him. Neither did I hear him, during a long evening,
say any thing that was particularly remarkable; but all the bar bear testimony to his transcendency as an advocate. Indeed, James Smith — the
famous author of " Rejected Addresses " — told me, last evening, that Erskine was the most eloquent man he remembered at the bar, but Scarlett[2]
by far the most successful advocate. You will perceive that this stretches

----

[1] As to the appointment of Langdale, see Campbell's "Life of Lord Brougham," Chap.
VI.; Greville's "Memoirs," Chap. XXX., Jan. 20, 1836.

[2] Lord Abinger.

over more than a quarter of a century. Abinger is said to be rich, and to love money very much. How is he as a judge now? *Deplorable !* I hear but one opinion; and recently I was with a party of lawyers who compose the Oxford Circuit, on which Lord Abinger is at this moment, and of which my friend Talfourd is the leader, when they all deprecated Abinger on their circuit. . . .

As ever yours,　　　　　　　　　　　　C. S.

TO JUDGE STORY.

London, July 23, 1838.

My dear Judge, — I start on my circuits to-morrow morning; but, before I go, I have a request to which I wish to call your attention at the earliest convenient time. My friend, Joseph Parkes, — the author of the famous work on "Chancery Reform," and one of the ablest and best informed men that I have met, — is engaged in preparing a work on the ballot and the extension of the elective franchise. In Rhode Island they have lately discussed, in newspapers, pamphlets, and public meetings, the extension of the suffrage. I feel anxious to get what there is for Mr. Parkes, as he is a thorough man, and most friendly to our country, and has the confidence of the first men of England, — I may say, the special confidence of Brougham and Durham.

The present ministry is quite liberal; but still it does not adopt the great radical measure of the ballot and the extension of the suffrage. . . . Peel is prudent, and with his forty thousand pounds a year can afford to wait; whereas Lyndhurst is desperately poor, and wishes office for its lucre. Peel is feared by the Radicals, on account of his prudence. I told the editor of the " Spectator " (Mr. Rintoul) [1] that I thought the better way was to work on under the present ministry, constantly getting liberal peers and bishops, as long as possible, rather than to make war against them.

Day before yesterday, I was regretting that I was obliged to decline a second invitation to dinner from Lord Denman, on account of a previous engagement. At my dinner, however, I met the old Earl Devon, [2] — the representative of the great Courtenay family, celebrated by Gibbon, [3] — Lord Plunkett, [4] the Attorney, the Solicitor, Sir Frederick Pollock, and Sir William Follett. I sat between Follett and Pollock. To the first I talked about

---

[1] Robert S. Rintoul, 1787–1855; the founder of the "Spectator." He was previously editor of the Dundee "Advertiser."

[2] William, eleventh Earl of Devon; he died in 1859, aged eighty-two.

[3] The "Decline and Fall," Chap. LXI.

[4] William Conyngham Plunkett, 1765–1854. He was successively Solicitor and Attorney General in Ireland; became a peer and Chief Justice of the Common Pleas in Ireland, in 1827, and was Lord Chancellor of Ireland, with a brief interval, from 1830 to 1841. He opposed in the Irish Parliament the union with England, and subsequently took very high rank in the British House of Commons as an advocate of Catholic Emancipation. Martineau's "History of England," Book II. ch. x. Sketch of Lord Plunkett in Brougham's "Autobiography," ch. xxviii.

law, and his cases; to the latter, about Horace, and Juvenal, and Persius, and the beauty of the English language. Pollock is a delightful scholar: Follett is a delightful man, — simple, amiable, unaffected as a child. Said Follett: "I have often cited, before the House of Lords, the work of one of your countrymen, — Dr. Story;" and he inundated me with questions about you. He has been so kind as to call and see me. You would have been pleased by the cordiality and friendship between the present Whig and the old Tory law-officers. When Lord Plunkett inquired of me the meaning of "*locofoco*," and I defined it to be "a very ultra Radical," Follett and Pollock both laughed, and cried out to the Attorney: "Campbell, you are the '*locofoco!*'" They appeared so pleased with the term that I should not be surprised if they adopted it. This cordiality is indescribably pleasant. Plunkett is old, and has lost his powers; in the Lords, he speaks like an old man, and they very seldom report what he says. He was very kind to me; and when I told him that I had often declaimed at college one of his speeches (his most eloquent speech in the Irish Parliament), and I added a word from Juvenal, — "et declamatio fias," — the old peer brightened, and at once quoted the whole line, —

"Ut pueris placeas, et declamatio fias."

But I have seen another, — Lord Brougham. I was at Parkes's yesterday, when he said: "Get into my cab." I got in, and then asked where we were going. "To Lord Brougham's," he said; and so to Brougham's we went. His Lordship received me cordially, inquired earnestly after your health, and invited me to come down and pass some time with him at Brougham Hall, in Westmoreland; and I have promised to go. He flattered me, by saying that he knew me by reputation (the Lord knows how!); and, as I was leaving, he took me by the arm and conducted me to the door, repeating his invitation again, saying: "Come down, and we will be quiet, and talk over the subject of codification." In the course of conversation, when I told him I was going on the circuit, he offered me letters to Lord Denman, which I apprised him I had no need of, as I already knew his Lordship sufficiently well. "Then," said he, "I must give you a letter to Alderson, at Liverpool." I am at a loss to account for my reception from Brougham; for he is a person almost inaccessible at present, who sees very little society, but occupies himself with affairs and with composition.[1] From Brougham Hall you will hear from me. Tell Hillard of this, as I cannot write him now. The Solicitor-General has urged me to stay longer in London, in order to meet the Chancellor of the Exchequer at dinner, who would like to talk with me on American affairs; but I must go.

Affectionate regards to your family, as ever, from affectionately yours.

C. S.

---

[1] He was then preparing an edition of his "Speeches," with historical introductions. His translation of the "De Coronâ," composed about this time, was a failure; but his "Sketches of the Statesmen and Philosophers of the Reign of George the Third," also composed during the same period, has found much favor. Campbell's "Life of Brougham," ch. vi.

CHAPTER XV.

THE CIRCUITS. — VISITS IN ENGLAND AND SCOTLAND. — AUGUST TO
OCTOBER, 1838. — AGE, 27.

LETTERS.

TO GEORGE S. HILLARD, BOSTON.

LIVERPOOL, Aug. 12, 1838.

MY DEAR HILLARD, — Yours of June 26 and various dates greeted my
arrival in this place after a most delightful ramble in the South and West
of England, — first to Guilford, where I met Lord Denman and the Home
Circuit, and dined with his Lordship and all the bar; then to Winchester
and Salisbury, stopping to view those glories of England, the cathedrals.
Old Sarum, and Stonehenge, — that mighty,unintelligible relic of the savage
Titans of whom history has said nothing; then to Exeter, and down even to
Bodmin in Cornwall, where the Assizes of the Western Circuit were held.
Serjeant Wilde and Sir William Follett were there, having gone down special, not being regularly of the circuit; and we three formed the guests of
the bar.   Our healths were drunk, and I was called upon to make a reply,
which I did on the spur of the moment.   From Bodmin, I went still
farther in Cornwall to visit the high-sheriff, and his mines, — the largest
that are there; his seat is the palace of the old Cornish kings, — you have
doubtless seen pictures of it repeatedly; it is a perfect castle, and has a
most romantic situation.   I then travelled in the carriage of a friend, —
Crowder,[1] one of the Queen's counsel, — through portions of Cornwall, and
that most beautiful county, Devon, stopping at Plymouth; being received by
the commander of the largest ship in port, a barge placed at my orders to
visit any ship I wished, and an officer designated to show me over the dock-
yard.   From Exeter I went up through the green fields of Devon and Som-
erset to the delicious parsonage of Sydney Smith,[2] Combe Florey, where I

---

[1] Richard Budden Crowder, 1795–1859.   He became Recorder of Bristol in 1846, and a
Judge of the Common Pleas in 1854.   Sumner dined with him in February, 1839, at his
house, 11 Pall Mall East.
   [2] The following note is preserved: —

COMBE FLOREY, TAUNTON, Aug. 16, 1838.
   MY DEAR SIR, — I have a great admiration of Americans, and have met a great number of agreeable, enlightened Americans.   There is something in the honesty, simplicity,

passed a good part of two days, and most reluctantly left in order to go north to Wells, to meet the Western Circuit again; here I dined one day with the bar, and the other with the judges, — Baron Parke and Mr. Justice Coltman. From Wells I passed to Bristol and Cheltenham; and then, by a ride of one hundred and twenty-five miles on the outside of the coach, between six o'clock in the morning and six at night, to Chester, where Mr. Justice Vaughan was holding the Assizes. On my coming into court that evening, his Lordship addressed me from the bench, and called me to his side, where I sat for two hours. In the mean time, orders had been given to have lodgings provided for me in the castle, with the judges. This I firmly declined, but dined with them; and all this after my long ride. From Chester I have come to Liverpool. It so happens that I have not met Baron Alderson, — a most remarkable man, who holds the Assizes here; but I bring introductions, which were entirely unsolicited on my part, from Baron Parke, Mr. Justice Coltman, Mr. Justice Vaughan, Sydney Smith, and Lord Brougham. Brougham's I found at the post-office. I shall not present it, but keep it as an autograph: it is quite odd. Such is a mere skeleton of my progress. It were vain for me to attempt to record all the kindness and hospitality I have received. Sir William Follett has extended the hand of friendship to me in a most generous way. His reputation in the profession is truly colossal, second only to that of Lord Mansfield; in his manners he is simple and amiable as a child: he is truly lovable. My visit to Sydney Smith was delicious. He gave me a book on parting, as he said, to assist in calling to my mind his parsonage. I have written to Felton about this visit. From Liverpool I shall go north to attend the British Association, and shall then visit Lord Brougham at Brougham Hall, where I have been most kindly asked. I am in the way of thoroughly understanding his character; for I know well some of his most intimate friends. The Duke of Wellington says of him, "Damned odd fellow, — half mad!" And Brougham, who is now vexed with the Duke for interfering to save the ministry so often, says "Westminster Abbey is yawning for him!" . . .

I hope I do not repeat myself; but writing as I do, at inns and clubhouses, and with my mind full fraught with what I have seen or heard, I hardly know what I write. You will not count me vain for communicating to you what I have with regard to the kindness extended to me. I pour out my heart to my friends, and I doubt not I shall have their sympathy. I should be glad to have Cleveland, Felton, Cushing, Longfellow, Lawrence, and Greenleaf see my letters, if they care about it. All this, however, I confide to your discretion.

Perhaps you will not hear from me again for a month; for I am going north, and probably shall not write till my return to Liverpool on my

and manliness of your countrymen which pleases me very much. We were very grateful to you for believing in us and coming to see us; and it will be pleasant to me to think that I am remembered and thought well of on the other side of the world, by a gentleman as honorable and as enlightened as yourself.

Very truly yours,

SYDNEY SMITH.

MR. SUMNER.

embarkation for Ireland. I hope you will write me about all the matters mentioned in my last despatch to you, at length, and in your most closely-written hand. Would that I could imitate you. Good-by.

As ever, affectionately yours,

CHAS. SUMNER.

TO JUDGE STORY.

LIVERPOOL, Aug. 18, 1838.

MY DEAR JUDGE, — . . . [1] From Chester I passed to the great Northern Circuit at Liverpool, with various letters of introduction to the judges. The first day I was in Liverpool, I dined with the city corporation at a truly aldermanic feast in honor of the judges; the second, with the judges, to meet the bar; the third, with the Mayor at his country seat; the fourth, with the bar; the fifth, with Mr. Cresswell (the leader and old reporter), Sir Gregory Lewin, Watson [2] (author of a book on Arbitration), the sheriffs, &c., Rushton [3] (Corporation Commissioner), Wortley, &c., at a private dinner; and to-day, in a few minutes, I dine with Roebuck,[4] who has just entered upon the Northern Circuit. At the Judges' dinner, Baron Alderson alluded to me, and gave the health of the President of the United States. I made some remarks, which were well received. Mr. Ingham, an M. P. who was present, I observed, was quite attentive, and seemed pleased. At the bar dinner, Adolphus,[5] the reporter, proposed my health, which drew me out in a speech of considerable length, — the longest I have yet made. I should not fail to say that your health was proposed and drunk, and that you are known very well. I have a thousand things to say to you about the law, circuit life, and the English judges. I have seen more of all than probably ever fell to the lot of a foreigner. I have the friendship and confidence of judges, and of the leaders of the bar. Not a day passes without my being five or six hours in company with men of this stamp. And can you say that this will do me no good, — that I shall be *spoiled*? My tour is no vulgar holiday affair, merely to spend money and to

---

[1] The omitted part of this letter is mainly a repetition of one written to Hillard, Aug. 12.

[2] William Henry Watson.

[3] A friend of Dr. Julius and G. H. Wilkinson.

[4] John Arthur Roebuck was born in Madras, in 1802. He lived in Canada from 1815 to 1824; and then went to England to study for the bar. He joined John Stuart Mill's "Utilitarian Society," and was an early writer for the "Westminster Review." Autobiography of Mill, pp. 81, 96. He represented Bath in Parliament from 1832 to 1837, and from 1841 to 1847; and Sheffield from 1849 to 1869; and, after a defeat in 1869, was chosen again for Sheffield in 1874. He is the author of a book on "The Colonies of England," and a "History of the Whig Ministry of 1830," and has contributed to the "Edinburgh" as well as the "Westminster" Review. Allying himself in later life with the cause of American Slavery in its final struggle, he became intensely hostile to the United States during the Civil War, and was the partisan of the Southern Confederacy. Sumner was introduced to him by Joseph Parkes.

[5] John Leycester Adolphus, 1793-1868; Reporter of the Queen's Bench in association with Thomas Flower Ellis (Macaulay's friend). In 1820, he maintained in a pamphlet Scott's authorship of the Waverly Novels. "Life of Lord Denman," Vol. II. p. 244.

get the fashions. It is to see men, institutions, and laws; and, if it would not seem vain in me, I would venture to say that I have not discredited my country. I have called the attention of the judges and the profession to the state of the law in our country, and have shown them, by my conversation (I will say this), that I understood their jurisprudence.

I know Roebuck, and I like him much. He is young, ardent, ambitious, and full of great things; accomplished, and republican. He is one of the few men ever called for in the House of Commons in the course of debates. Perhaps you will not hear from me for some time, as I go to Scotland.

Ever affectionately yours,   C. S.

TO GEORGE S. HILLARD.

WESTOE HALL, DURHAM, Aug. 24, 1838.

MY DEAR HILLARD, — From my chamber window I look upon the mouth of the Tyne and the German Ocean, and the venerable ruins of Tynemouth Priory, coeval with the Conquest, and the foam of the sea breaking on this rock-bound coast, and lashed into great fury by a raging storm. Think of this picture: the white sea I am well accustomed to; but these reverend arches, the sturdy and graceful witnesses of centuries, I know much less about. I am the guest of Mr. Ingham,[1] the M. P. for South Shields. I was brought out by a toast from Baron Alderson at a dinner in Liverpool, and some remarks which I made secured the favorable attention of the honorable and learned member, who invited me to visit the British Association at Newcastle as his guest, offering to me apartments in town, and also at his seat, about ten miles from Newcastle. I cannot describe to you the heartiness of my reception. The style of English country life I must talk of on my return: I cannot give you any thing like a complete picture of it. I am struck by the elegance which I find in such a quiet retreat. Yesterday my host invited some company, fourteen gentlemen, to meet me and another friend staying with him, who all passed the night in the house. You sit down to dinner usually between seven and eight o'clock; and one

---

[1] Robert Ingham, M. P., 1832–1841 and 1852–1868, for South Shields near Westoe, where he was born and died. He was educated at Oxford, and in 1820 joined the Northern Circuit. He was not eminent at the bar or in Parliament, but he was a man of sterling worth and attractive personal qualities. He was a bencher of the Inner Temple, and had chambers in King's Bench Walk. In politics he was a moderate liberal. When he withdrew from public life, his neighbors and constituents gave him a testimonial in the form of an infirmary erected by public subscription in his honor. He delighted in hospitality, and was very cordial to visitors from this country, several of whom — Rev. Dr. Francis Wayland, Rev. Dr. Palfrey, Mr. Hillard, and Richard H. Dana, Jr. — were commended to him by Sumner, his first American guest. Mr. Ingham died Oct. 21, 1875, at the age of eighty-two. Tributes to his memory were published in the "Boston Advertiser," Nov. 8 and 19, 1875, — one by Clement H. Hill, and the other by Mr. Hillard. Sumner visited Mr. Ingham at Westoe, in October, 1857, and made the memorandum at the time, "Rambled about, hoping to recognize old spots which I had known nineteen years ago."

would sooner commit the unpardonable sin than appear in boots: these will do for Paris, but not for England.

The meeting of the British Association is passing off very well. I have visited all the sections, and received particular attentions; I do not, however, think the benefits from it to be exactly of the nature usually attributed. I doubt if any important suggestions are here made, or new lights struck out. It affords a stage on which men like Babbage, Lardner, Whewell, &c. may fret their hour, — and I have verily seen some fretting from all, — and it helps to excite the public interest in the great concerns of science. In this point of view I hold it good. Three thousand people are collected together, who are all filled with notions — more or less vague — of the greatness and importance of science, and of the value of the honors won by its successful cultivation; but I doubt if many go away much instructed by it, or with any positive addition to their stores. Miss Martineau is here on a visit to her sister married in Newcastle; Dr. Lardner seems a coxcomb and pertinacious fellow.[1]

My present arrangements are to pass from here to Harperley Park, the seat of a retired barrister of fortune; then to Auckland Castle, the seat of the Bishop of Durham, and, as you well know, one of the great feudal residences of England; then to the seat of Mr. Blackett,[2] the member for the County of Northumberland; and probably then to Lord Brougham's and the Lakes. My friend at Harperley Park has invited me particularly to shoot grouse on his moors. You will understand that all these places are very near each other. I must take another look at that time-worn priory, standing on a jutting rock, with the lighthouse close by, and then to bed.

As ever, your affectionate friend,

CHARLES SUMNER.

TO GEORGE S. HILLARD.

OAKWOOD, Sept. 2, 1838.

MY DEAR HILLARD, — Yours of several dates, July 23 and 27, found me at Newcastle. Glad was I, even in that feast of wise men, to hear of you and home and my home friends. The British Association had just concluded its sittings, but the philosophers had remained to attend the festival of a local society, at which the Duke of Northumberland or the Bishop of Durham has to preside. I was also invited; but went, as it were, *incog.*, being unwilling to make myself an object for attention. What was my surprise when the Bishop of Durham,[3] proposing the health of the distinguished foreigners present, singled me as the object of some particular remarks, which were received with no little applause. In the most unpremeditated manner

---

[1] Dionysius Lardner, 1793–1859. After his escapade in 1840, he came to the United States, and delivered lectures until 1845, when he took up his residence in Paris.

[2] Christopher Blackett.

[3] Edward Maltby, 1770–1859. He became Bishop of Durham in 1836. A note of the Bishop, written Dec. 22, 1838, refers to Sumner's visit to Auckland Castle, and desires it to be repeated. Another, of March 15, 1839, invites him to dine at 28 Curzon Street, London.

I expressed my thanks. I observe that my remarks have been reported in a variety of journals. The "Newcastle Courant," however, contains the best report or abridgment. I have sent that paper to you, and from its report you may form some idea of the tone of the Lord Bishop's remarks about me, and my reply. You will understand that the occasion was a capital one for an extended speech; but when you consider the briefness of my remarks you will observe that I spoke in the presence of all that was most distinguished in science in the British Empire, — Herschell, Babbage, Whewell, Sedgwick, Peacock, Buckland, &c.; and that it well became me to confine myself to the strict duty of returning thanks.

[The "Newcastle Courant" of Aug. 31, 1838,[1] reported the speeches at a dinner of the British Association for the Promotion of Science, at which Professor Bache, of Philadelphia, and Sumner were guests, together with Professor Ehrenberg, of Berlin. The Bishop of Durham presided at the dinner. In the course of his remarks, he said: —

"There was such an identity of feeling and good sense, — such an identity of every thing that had been considered almost peculiar to Britain in America, — that they could not consider each other as aliens or foreigners. They lived in distant parts of the world, it was true; but improvements in science have brought Philadelphia and New York within a short distance of this country; almost as short, in point of time, as within a century ago people could have gone from Newcastle to London. It was, therefore, with great satisfaction he brought before them Professors Bache and Ehrenberg; and he had likewise peculiar pleasure, on this occasion, in mentioning the name of Mr. Charles Sumner, who had been travelling in England, not perhaps for improvement in the abstract sciences, in which he had no doubt he would be well qualified to shine, but for the important object of making himself acquainted with our laws. He had been introduced to his learned friend and pupil, Mr. Baron Alderson, who spoke of him as he (the chairman) would not repeat in his presence. So great had been his zeal, that he had travelled part of the circuit with some of our best judges, — Lord Denman, Mr. Baron Parke, and Mr. Baron Alderson. He rejoiced to add that he was here among them at last, and he should endeavor individually to testify to him the high sense which he attached to any recommendation of such a man as Mr. Baron Alderson. In the mean time, it was gratifying to know that he was among them, profiting by their labors and partaking of the enlightened entertainment which it was their pride and gratification to give, together with a hearty welcome to their learned friends (applause)."

After replies by the two professors, Mr. Sumner said: "After the remarks which had been made by his learned friend who had just sat down, he felt that to add any thing would place him under the imputation of attempting

---

[1] The "Law Reporter," Nov., 1838, Vol. I. pp. 244–245, edited by P. W. Chandler, republished this report with a brief preface, in which it said that Mr. Sumner "has been everywhere received in a manner highly gratifying to his American friends, but not in the least surprising to those acquainted with him." The report was also printed in the Boston "Advertiser" of Nov. 28, 1838.

to 'gild refined gold.' But still the remarks which the venerable chairman had done him the honor to make regarding himself, required the sincere acknowledgments of his heart. He thanked his Lordship that he had not held him as a foreigner; for, indeed, if any one thing above another could give an American pleasure, he might say it would be to come to Great Britain and find himself authorized to claim kindred here, and have his claims allowed (applause). Speaking their language, derived from them, enjoying their laws, and, he might say, almost their political institutions, — for all that had been held sacred during all their constitutional history remained with his countrymen, and Magna Charta was perpetuated in the liberal institutions of America, — were they not, he would ask his Lordship, their brothers (applause)? Might not an American come here, and find, indeed, that he was coming home, — coming, as it were, to his father's hearthstone? He went to their churchyard, and there, perchance, he found his father's monument. Such men indeed were relations, and on such accounts he rejoiced that the chairman had not held them as foreigners, but greeted them as brothers. Might he say then, in this presence, so learned and so honorable, that of all countries England was the pride of Americans? They all rejoiced that they came from her and of her; they all rejoiced in her glory, and in her devotion to the sciences; and they gladly came up to such a high festival as this, — such a liberal association, where the good of mankind was consulted in its most important aspect. Might he presume to look still further toward the gradual strengthening of the intercourse between the two countries; and, indeed, anticipate the day when the Association would not merely travel from Liverpool to Newcastle, and from Newcastle to Birmingham, but have the whole world for its arena (loud applause); when they might see the meeting passing over from Birmingham to Philadelphia, and from Philadelphia back to Newcastle? Then, indeed, they would have an alliance greater and stronger than parchment or treaties; an alliance producing a scientific union, practical and theoretical, between both countries (applause). He had been betrayed into saying more words than he ought; but the very kind manner in which his Lordship had done him the honor to speak of his humble self, had so tempted him that personally he could not say less, while the manner in which his country had been mentioned would have justified him in saying more. Might he conclude by expressing to his Lordship personally his sincere acknowledgments, and likewise his thanks to the gentlemen present, in common with his learned friends (loud applause)? "]

From Newcastle I went in the coach of the Bishop of Durham to Auckland Palace.[1] This is the celebrated seat of the most powerful bishop of England. It is a venerable castle, with a beautiful park about it, stocked with deer. Here I was hospitably entertained for two days, and pressed to stay longer, and cordially invited there whenever I could come, on this visit

[1] Auckland Castle is described in Howitt's "Visits to Remarkable Places," Vol. I., pp. 252, 253; and Murray's "Handbook for Durham and Northumberland," pp. 71–73. Among its pictures are Titian's "Cornaro Family," and Spagnoletto's "Jacob and the Twelve Patriarchs."

or any future visit to England. You know that this bishop is the venerable Dr. Maltby, the friend of Parr, so renowned in Greek. Chantrey, the sculptor, once killed two woodcocks at one shot at Holkham. Old Coke was so delighted that he vowed a monument on the spot to be made by Chantrey himself; and all the classical world were invited to offer epigrams in Greek, — or, at least, all came forward. Alderson, Wellesley, Brougham, Maltby, &c. contributed; and the venerable bishop told me that Brougham was writing his while he was Lord Chancellor; and, on writing a line, used to send an express with it to his (Maltby's) house, to know if it was correct. The frequency and urgency of these messages from the Lord Chancellor excited the attention of Dr. M.'s neighbors, who thought that one of the archbishoprics was to be vacated, and that arrangements were making for the promotion of Dr. Maltby. The venerable bishop told me that he believed his (Dr. M.'s) verses were considered the best. I cannot repeat all the interesting classical and personal anecdotes which I hear. I left this venerable castle with regret, and went to Harperley Park; where I was engaged to pass a couple of days with Mr. Wilkinson,[1] the Recorder of Newcastle (he is no relative of Mr. Wilkinson, Judge S.'s correspondent). Here I rode on horseback with young ladies, visited castles in the neighborhood, listened to hunting stories and the accounts by the ladies of the leaps over hedges and fences which they took in pursuit of the fox; and then passed on to Oakwood, the seat of C. Blackett, Esq., the M. P. for the County of Northumberland. This is on the Tyne, and is about twelve miles from Newcastle. After passing a couple of days here, I shall go to Archdeacon Scott's, in Northumberland, on his urgent invitation to shoot grouse. The sport of shooting with a distinguished clergyman, who assured me that he had the best moors in all England, and his interesting conversation, have tempted me to this visit. Scott is an old friend of Parr and Horne Tooke, and is one of the *dramatis personæ* intended in the colloquies of the "Diversions of Purley." From there I pass to Brougham Hall; then to Mr. Marshall's, &c.; then to Melrose, near Abbotsford, on a visit to Sir David Brewster. I cannot enumerate the number of invitations which I have received — more than *thirty* — from men of all opinions and stations. I have written Felton from Auckland Castle. He will tell you about the place.

As ever, affectionately yours,   C. S.

P. S. Crowd your letters with accounts of all my friends and every thing in which I take an interest.

TO GEORGE S. HILLARD.

BROUGHAM HALL, Sept. 6, 1838.

MY DEAR HILLARD, — It is now midnight, and I have just said " good night " to my noble host, after a long evening filled by incessant conversa-

---

1 Mr. Wilkinson invited Sumner, Dec. 21, 1838, to pass Sunday at Harrow, and see the school and church; and later renewed the invitation.

tion. Yesterday I passed at the Rectory of the venerable Archdeacon Scott, — a friend of Horne Tooke and Parr, — and, on his invitation and in his clerical company, disguised in old clothes loaned for the occasion, and weighed down by heavy shoes, went on the fells and moors in his neighborhood to shoot grouse and partridges. Our dog started several coveys; but my gun missed, as also did that of the dignitary of the Church, and I contented myself with peppering to death a poor hare! I am no Nimrod, — as you well know, — though my parson is, and I can well bear the mortification of an empty game-bag in such company.[1] While we were on the moors it rained constantly, and the shower has been descending all day. In the rain, however, I left the archdeacon this morning, and mounted on his horse, and with his groom in attendance (my luggage being previously sent on), spattered over the moors and valleys of Northumberland, then took an open gig, and at three o'clock drove into the court-yard — all surrounded by battlements — of Brougham Hall.[2] I was thoroughly wet, and covered with mud. On my mentioning my situation to his Lordship, who kindly received me in the hall, he himself at once showed me to my bed-room, where I enjoyed the comfort of a complete change of dress. After I came downstairs, he left me in the library, and went about writing letters, which were to leave by the mail before dinner. He wrote more than the number which he could frank, — that is, ten, — and at six o'clock was in the library dressed for dinner. The only person besides myself was an old familiar friend, a clergyman (who brought with him as a present to the

[1] Archdeacon T. H. Scott wrote, Feb. 5, 1839, from Whitfield Rectory, Haydon Bridge, Northumberland: "If you received any pleasure here, either in shooting *at* grouse or in killing a hare, I do assure you the pleasure I enjoyed in your company, when you were kind enough to favor a poor mountain curate with a visit, was as great. I not only yield to you as a matter of courtesy, being my guest, the important question as to who killed the hare, but I have another reason for doing so. For the first time, I believe, in the Annals of the Parish since it was granted by Ada, Countess of Northumberland, in the reign of Henry II., to her almoner, Matthew de Whitfield, there now stands recorded in the Game-Book, 'One hare: Mr. Sumner, *a Republican born.*'" The archdeacon volunteered a letter of introduction to Count Albrizzi, of Venice, in which he commended Sumner as "a man of great talent, and in search of literature and all that is worth seeing;" and another to Tomaso Morenigo Soranzo, of an ancient Venetian family; but neither letter was used.

[2] Lord Brougham was born in 1779 and died in 1868. His mother, Eleanora, the only child of Rev. James Syme, and on her mother's side the niece of Robertson the historian, died Dec. 31, 1839, at the age (as given in Burke's Peerage) of eighty-nine. His Lordship's daughter, an only child, died Nov. 30, 1839, at the age of seventeen. He bought, in 1840, an estate near Cannes, France, and built upon it a house which he called "Château Eleanor Louise," in memory of his daughter, to whom tributes on its walls were inscribed by himself and his friends. Campbell's "Life of Brougham," ch. vi. and viii. He died at this retreat, where he was accustomed to pass the winter season. In 1838, he was writing "Sketches of Statesmen of the Time of George III.," which were published, 1839–43. He invited Sumner to dine with him at 4 Grafton Street, London, in February, 1839. In the letter introducing him to Baron Alderson, he said: "This will be delivered by C. Sumner of the American bar, whose reports I have read with satisfaction; who is also editor of the 'Jurist.' He is an estimable man, and I am desirous of his being known to you." Sumner received from Lord Brougham many courtesies in June and July, 1857, and in October visited him at Brougham Hall, when his Lordship gave him some souvenirs, — a medal portrait of himself, and colored prints of Edmund Burke when young (Sir Joshua Reynolds), and of the Madonna (Raphael).

ex-chancellor a bottle of rum upwards of fifty years old), though Lord Chief-
Justice Tindal and Lord Moncreiff [1] (the latter the great Scotch judge and
lawyer) were expected.   The truly venerable and interesting mother of his
Lordship, — now eighty-six years old, — was in the dining-room when we
entered, and presided at the table.   Never did I see a person who bore her
years so well.   She seemed a fit mother for a distinguished son.   Her manners were easy and even graceful, with very little of the constraint of age.
She refused my proffered assistance in helping the soup, though she afterwards condescended to allow me to mangle a partridge.   She is tall, has
sharp features, and an aquiline nose.   Her countenance is much more refined
and intellectual than her son's.   You doubtless know that she is the niece
of the historian Robertson.   Lady Brougham and her daughter are at a
watering place at the south.   During the dinner, his Lordship was constant
in his attentions to his mother, addressing her as " Mother," and urging her
to eat of particular dishes.   I heard Mrs. Brougham address her son as
" Lord Brougham."   I could hardly make up my mind and my tongue to
address this venerable woman as " Mrs. Brougham," which is all that belongs
to her, and then speak to her son as " My Lord."   At table the conversation
turned on light matters, — the great scarcity of game, the merits of some
old Madeira (the gift of Cutlar Fergusson), of a black cock (the gift of Lord
Anglesey), and of the rum (the valuable contribution of the clergyman).
Besides these there was a variety of topics arising from familiarity with the
parson, and reminiscences of common acquaintances.   Mrs. Brougham retired very soon after the cloth was removed.   His Lordship took very little
wine, less than I have seen any gentleman take at the head of his table in
England; but if he have not that vice, which has been attributed to him, —
and I fully believe that he has it not, — he has another which is, perhaps,
as bad; certainly it is bad and vulgar beyond expression, — I mean *swearing*.   I have dined in company nearly *every day* since I have been in
England, and I do not remember to have met a person who swore half so
much as Lord Brougham; — and all this in conversation with an aged
clergyman!   His manner was rapid, hurried, and his voice very loud.   He
seemed uneasy and restless; and, of course, made me feel the same.   His
language, as you may well suppose, was vigorous and to the point.   He
told some capital stories of King William, from which I should infer, notwithstanding all the reports to the contrary, that he was on good terms
with that monarch.   You remember Denman's famous appeal on the
Queen's trial, alluding to the slanders of the Duke of Clarence, " Come
forth, thou slanderer! " [2]   Brougham said that the Duke of York, sitting
in one corner of the house, said to a peer near him, " There is my brother
William! he is always in some scrape; " while the Duke of Clarence, sitting
on the other side of the house, whispered to his friend, " My brother Frederick is always saying some d——d absurd thing," — each supposing the other

<hr>

[1] Sir James Wellwood (Lord Moncreiff), 1776-1851; a Lord of Session and Justiciary of
Scotland.   His son has been Lord-Advocate, and held other high posts, judicial and
political.

[2] Life of Lord Denman, Vol. I. pp. 136-138.

referred to by Denman! After dinner the conversation turned upon politics, and upon Canadian affairs in particular. His Lordship seemed to exult over Lord Durham, and to think that he had him " on the hip." He praised Roebuck as a person of great talent; and spoke of Erskine as a very great man. When I asked who at the bar now was most like him, he said: " Nobody: there is a degenerate race now; there are no good speakers at the bar, except Sir William Follett and Mr. Pemberton." He spoke of Lord Langdale as a person who had never done any thing, and who never would do any thing, and who was an ordinary man. He said that Mr. and Mrs. Austin,[1] — who had just returned from Malta, where Mr. Austin went to reform the law, — would probably cease to be reformers, having experienced the practical difficulties of reform, and would retire disheartened from the cause. In making this remark, he obviously intended to allude to a supposed want of perseverance and resolution on the part of these persons. A dinner at Lansdowne House, he said, was a great cure for radicalism. He thought Ballantyne had refuted Lockhart, and that the latter as well as Scott would suffer in reputation. Money affairs were Scott's weak point. The illness of Lord Derby, of which we received the intelligence to-day, and his expected death, he characterized as great news; " for," said he, " Ned Stanley [2] goes into the Lords." It was thus that he passed from topic to topic, expressing himself always with force, correctness, and facility unrivalled; but, I must say, with a manner not only far from refined, but even vulgar. He had no gentleness or suavity; neither did he show any of the delicate attentions of the host. He _professed_ an interest in America, but did not seem to care to speak about it. He said that he should certainly visit us, for, with the present facilities of intercourse, it were a shame in an Englishman to be ignorant of the practical working of our institutions. " I am a republican," said he; " or rather, I am for entrusting to the people the largest possible degree of power." I doubt if he knows much about our affairs or our public men. When I mentioned Webster's name, he said, " Yes, I have understood that Webster is a clever man;" and Clay's did not seem to call up any particular idea. Of Judge Story he spoke more at length than of any other, and expressed the strongest regard for him; and yet I do not think that he is aware of the Judge's position among us, and I know that he is ignorant of several of his works. He did not speak of the law, though when I saw him at his house in Belgrave Square he said, " Come and see me, and we will talk about codification and the law;" though I had never opened my mouth to him about either.

I have not sketched the foregoing lines in the hope of tracing the conversation of this remarkable man; but simply to give you by flashes, as it were,

---

[1] John Austin, 1797–1860; author of " The Province of Jurisprudence Determined; " and Mrs. Sarah Austin of the Taylor family of Norwich, the translator of Ranke's " History of the Popes," and other German works. Mrs. Austin died in 1867. Their daughter, Lady Duff Gordon, well-known in literature, died in Egypt, in 1869.

[2] The fourteenth Earl of Derby, 1799–1869 ; eminent as statesman and scholar, serving many years in the House of Commons before entering the Peers in 1844 as Baron Stanley; three times Premier; and the translator of the " Iliad." His father survived till 1851.

a momentary view of his manner and character. The result of my intercourse with him thus far is that I like the *man* less, though I admire his powers as ever before. I could not fail to perceive, in the rapidity of his thought, the readiness of his language, and the variety of his topics, no slight confirmation of the received opinion with regard to his versatility and universal attainments. The gentleman, who is now staying here, assured me that he had often received long letters from his Lordship, written, *currente calamo*, in correct Latin; and a friend told me that he once stood behind him, when a barrister on the Northern Circuit, and saw him scrawl a Greek ode on his desk in court. You may say *credat Judaeus.* I have been told that the sketches of character, which form such a remarkable ornament of the new publication of his speeches (do read these), were written in his carriage while posting to the south of France; and I happen to know from another source that he was paying his postilions double, and I doubt not swearing at the same time, to make them go faster!

I am almost sorry that I have seen Lord B., for I can no longer paint him to my mind's eye as the pure and enlightened orator of Christianity, civilization, and humanity. I see him now, as before, with powers such as belong to angels: why could I not have found him with an angel's purity, gentleness, and simplicity? I must always admire his productions as models of art; but I fear that I shall distrust his sincerity and the purity of his motives. I think that he is about throwing himself again among the people, and accepting their leadership. Two letters that I have received from Lord B. have been signed "H. Brougham," and I have heard of his signing so frequently. He spoke to me in the most disparaging terms of the aristocracy; but I shall be afraid that he will not speak so much for truth's sake as to promote his own fame and power, or perhaps to gratify a personal pique.[1] Certainly, in the society in which I have moved I have heard but one opinion expressed with regard to the dishonesty and malevolence which have characterized his late conduct; and his spite towards Lord Durham is represented as diabolical. In illustration of this, I have heard anecdotes which I have neither time nor space to relate. One of these is striking. Last winter it was supposed for a while that an invention had been found out which would supersede the use of coal, upon which Lord Durham's immense income depends. Brougham is said to have gone about telling of it, and rubbing his hands, saying: "Old Durham is a beggar! Old Durham is a beggar!" Perhaps all these idiosyncrasies may be better understood and more charitably viewed, when it is known, as it is not generally in England, that Brougham's father died insane, and that he has a sister who is so still. I am disposed to believe that there is in him a nervousness and immense activity which is near akin to insanity, and which at present jangles the otherwise even measures of his character.

FRIDAY MORNING, Sept. 7.

I write this in Brougham's library and study, — a most beautiful apartment, with panels of old oak black with age, and with a rich ceiling of the same

---

[1] The unlovely side of Lord Brougham's character is brought out quite distinctly in the account of his treatment of Macaulay. Trevelyan's "Life of Lord Macaulay."

material, emblazoned with numerous heraldic escutcheons in gold. It is a room that you would love; and I now sit in a beautiful bow-window, which commands the fair lawn and terraces about the house, and the distant mountains which give a character to the scenery of this country, and in whose bosom lie the far-famed lakes of England. At breakfast the next morning I was gladdened by your letter of Aug. 10 and its enclosure, and Judge Story's generous double letter of Aug. 11; also Cushing's and Lieber's. Think of these meeting me at the breakfast-table of Lord Brougham! I took the liberty of reading to his Lordship what Judge S. said of his judicial opinions, — namely, that they were remarkable monuments of judicial reasoning, — and his Lordship seemed much gratified, and repeated the kind expressions which he had employed last evening about Judge S. He added, that his work on the "Conflict of Laws" enjoyed a reputation and authority here which caused it to be cited almost as a judgment of court. His mind, however, did not rest on law or on America; but quickly reverted to topics of interest between him and his friend, and which were of great interest to me, inasmuch as they illustrated the character of this wonderful man, and as they brought out much personal anecdote. Nothing was discussed, and no opinions expressed, except about individuals; and of these he expressed himself with the greatest freedom. The late Duke of Gloucester he styled "a d—d bore and fool," and told an odd story of the duke extracting at table from Wilberforce, by means of blunt and princely impertinence, the account of Necker offering his daughter, Madame de Staël, in marriage to Pitt. He also mentioned that, at the time Lord Chatham made his celebrated speech against employing Indians,[1] Lord Bute had in his possession letters from Chatham, when William Pitt, in which he boasted of employing Indians successfully, and exclaimed, "Sing *Io Pæan!* by means of Indians we have got the trick." Brougham, you know, is the author of the article in the last "Edinburgh" on Chatham.[2] He spoke of the article at table this morning, and seemed to be quite interested in the character of that statesman. He thought that the authorship of "Junius" would never be discovered, and said that Horne Tooke said "the author must have been a man in office, and a damned rascal." The Duke of Gloucester, pleased with his success in extracting the above affair of Necker from Wilberforce, at the same table turned round to Lord Grenville, and said, "My Lord, they say you know the author of 'Junius.'" No answer; and the question was impertinently repeated. "I have never said so," was the reply of Lord Grenville in a very decided manner; and silence reigned in the company for more than five minutes. After breakfast, I sat in the library talking with Mrs. Brougham, who told me that she was eighty-six. She said that she thought "the efforts for slave emancipation were the greatest and most honorable thing of Henry's life." When I said that I had the pleasure of hearing his last speech on that important subject, she added, "And a good speech it was." Was it not delightful to listen to

---

[1] Speech of Nov. 18, 1777, in reply to Lord Suffolk, who had justified "the use of all the means which God and Nature put into our hands." Goodrich's "Select British Eloquence," p. 138.

[2] July, 1838, Vol. LXVII. pp. 436–460, "Character of Lord Chatham."

such words from the mother of such a son? She very kindly sent for his purse as Lord Chancellor (you know the purse is a perquisite of office), a richly wrought bag, which costs one hundred pounds, and in which the Chancellor puts the great seal and the petitions which he presents to the King. She said that once the Chancellor apologized to his Majesty for troubling him with so many petitions, when the King promptly replied, "I shall be glad to see you take any thing out of the bag except the great seal." She was afraid that I should be dull; and was pleased to regret that there was not more company in the house to amuse me. My recollections of this woman will be of the most charming character.

HALLSTEAD'S, Sept. 7 (Evening).

I am now at the beautiful seat [1] of Mr. John Marshall, the former member for Yorkshire, and the father of the present member for Carlisle. Lord Brougham was engaged to pass this evening and to-morrow with the Bishop of Carlisle, about seventeen miles off; so I took my leave. He was busied in his studies, with a quire of manuscripts before him, and with five or six books open on top of each other, the upper one being Greek; I thought it the "Orations of Demosthenes." [2] He franked this letter to you, shook me cordially by the hand, thanked me for visiting him, apologized for not waiting upon me to the door, and bade me good-by. Before I had reached the door of the room where he was, his head was down and he was absorbed in his studies. I have forgotten to tell you that he will have an article in the next "Edinburgh," following out his former one, and replying to the strictures upon it, particularly those of Sir Herbert Taylor. Such was my visit to Lord B. and the impression it has made on my mind. I have written, as you will perceive, with great haste as well as freedom, and cannot write to any of my other friends on this same theme; you will, therefore, in your discretion, show this letter to those who may take an interest in it, remembering carefully that nothing in it is for publication, and that not a word must escape to the public.

Hallstead's, where I now am, is a beautiful seat on the banks of the Ulleswater Lake. From here I shall make excursions to see Wordsworth and Southey, and then pass on to Sir David Brewster, at Melrose.

As ever, most affectionately your friend,

CHAS. SUMNER.

P. S. Brougham made great fun of the thirty-nine articles, and told the story of a naval officer, who, in the House of Commons, said: "I am for the sixty-nine articles." "Thirty-nine, you mean," was the cry. The gallant officer replied: "Thirty-nine or sixty-nine, I am for the articles." Old

---

1 Patterdale Hall, where one of the best views of Ulleswater Lake may be had. Murray's "Handbook for the Lakes," p. 107. Mr. Marshall is honorably mentioned in Mill's "Autobiography," p. 117. His note, in March, 1839, written from 41 Upper Grosvenor Street, London, invites Sumner to visit with him pictures of English artists, Collins's paintings, and Wilkie's "Napoleon."

2 He was then preparing his translation of the "De Coronâ."

Pigott used to say, in answer to all questions about his belief, "I believe in the Church, *as by law established.*"

I have never seen Lord B.'s only child, a daughter of fifteen; but I know several of her friends, and I have been told that her situation is lamentable. She has been so sickly always as to have grown up without education or intercourse with the world.

Mr. Marshall was gazetted a baronet at the Coronation; but he declined the honor. He told me that he and Lord Fitzwilliam spent fifty-three thousand pounds in preparing to contest the county of Yorkshire; no contest, however, took place. This was in 1824.

I can see Helvellyn from the windows of my chamber at Hallstead's.

TO GEORGE S. HILLARD.

KESWICK, Sept. 8, 1838.

MY DEAR HILLARD, — I have seen Wordsworth![1] Your interest in this great man, and the contrast which he presents to that master spirit[2] I have already described to you, induce me to send these lines immediately on the heels of my last. How odd it seemed to knock at a neighbor's door, and inquire, "Where does *Mr.* Wordsworth live?" Think of rapping at Westminster Abbey, and asking for Mr. Shakspeare, or Mr. Milton! I found the poet living, as I could have wished, with worldly comfort about him, and without show. His house was not so large or so elegant as to draw the attention from its occupant; and more truly did I enjoy myself, for the short time I was under its roof, than when in the emblazoned halls of Lord Brougham. The house is situated on the avenue leading to Rydal Hall; and the poet may enjoy, as if they were his own, the trees of the park and the ancestral cawing of the rooks that almost darkened the air with their numbers. His house and grounds are pretty and neat; and he was so kind as to attend me in a turn round his garden, pointing out several truly delightful views of the lakes and mountains. I could not but remark to him, however that the cawing of the rooks was more interesting to me than even the remarkable scenery before us. The house itself is unlike those in which I have been received, lately; and in its whole style reminded me more of home than any thing I have yet seen in England. I took tea with the poet, and, for the first time since I have been in this country, saw a circle round a table at this meal; and, indeed, it was at six o'clock, when always before in England I have been preparing for dinner. I mention these little things, in order to give you a familiar view of Wordsworth. I cannot sufficiently express to you my high gratification at his manner and conversation. It was simple, graceful, and sincere; it had all those things, the absence of which in Brougham gave me so much pain. I felt that I was conversing with a superior being; yet I was entirely

[1] 1770–1850.   [2] Brougham.

at my ease. He told me that he was sixty-nine, — an age when, in the course of nature, the countenance loses the freshness of younger years; but his was still full of expression. Conversation turned on a variety of topics: and here I have little to record; for there were no salient parts, though all was sensible, instructive, and refined. He spoke warmly on the subject of copyright and of slavery. He showed me the American edition of his works in one volume,[1] and expressed the great pleasure it had given him; he thought it better executed than any work of the kind in England or France. I amused him not a little by telling him that a Frenchman recommended himself to me, on my arrival in Paris, as a teacher of French, by saying that he had taught the great English poet, Wordsworth. The latter assured me that he had not had a French instructor since his dancing-master! He spoke in the kindest terms of Mr. Washington Allston, and inquired earnestly after his health and circumstances. He regarded him as the first artist of the age, and was attached to him by two-fold relations, — first, as his own friend, and then as the affectionate friend of Coleridge.[2] He desired me to convey to him his warm regards, and those of Mrs. Wordsworth and all his family. He was pleased when I told him that the Ticknors had arrived safely among their friends, and spoke of them in a manner that did my heart good. He asked me to " spare a line in one of my letters to convey to them his affectionate regards." He added that such a line might be dull and uninteresting to them. I ventured to reply that it would be to them and their friends the most interesting part of my letter. I rely upon your conveying to Allston and the Ticknors the kind messages of Wordsworth.

Such was Wordsworth. My visit was one of unmingled pleasure, until I rose to depart; then, taking my hand, he said: " Some of your countrymen are in the habit of publishing sketches of the persons and conversation of literary men they meet; and one of them, ———, once called upon me with a note of introduction from young Hemans, and went away and wrote about my appearance, and what I said. He was very unprepossessing in manner; and *did* not, and *could* not, understand what I said. In his publication, he has foully misrepresented me." The venerable poet went on to say that such conduct was dishonorable, and a flagrant breach of confidence; and that, if continued, it would oblige himself and others to deny themselves to strangers. What, think you, were my feelings on hearing this? I felt grieved and indignant that a man like Wordsworth should have been wounded from our country; and I feared lest I should fall under the suspicion of seeking his society in order to fill the page of a book, or the corner of a newspaper. What I said, I will leave you to imagine.

As ever yours,

CHAS. SUMNER.

---

[1] By Henry Reed. Philadelphia: 1837.

[2] Coleridge and Allston became intimate friends at Rome, between 1804 and 1808. Sumner referred, in his oration of Aug. 27, 1846, to their intimacy at this time. Works, Vol. I. 276.

TO GEORGE S. HILLARD.

ALLERLY, MELROSE, Sept. 12, 1838.

AGAIN, MY DEAR HILLARD, — I am now the guest of Sir David Brewster,[1] and am writing in my bed-room, which looks upon the Tweed and Melrose Abbey and the Eildon Hills. Abbotsford is a short distance above, on the opposite side; while the cottages of Lockhart, and that fast friend of Scott, Sir Adam Ferguson,[2] are within sight. I spent the whole of to-day in rambling with Sir David about Melrose, noting all the spots hallowed by Scott's friendship or genius, and finally paying my pilgrimage to his tomb at Dryburgh Abbey. At dinner we had Sir Adam Ferguson himself and Mr. Todd, — the latter a Scottish judge, and an old friend of Sir Walter, as well as Sir Adam. I need not say to you how inexpressibly interesting was the whole day, passed in such company, — observing house after house in whose hospitality Sir Walter had taken pleasure, and whose plantations he had watched; then regarding, with melancholy interest, the simple sod, in the midst of some venerable ruins, which covers his precious dust. And what a crown was it, of the whole day, to dine among his chosen friends, — to hear their simple, heart-touching expressions of regard, and the numerous narrations, all untold in print, which serve to illustrate his character and genius! Sir Adam, with whose relation to Scott Lockhart's ungraceful biography must have made you familiar, is nearly seventy, but with an appearance at once hale and broken. The buoyancy of his spirits and the freshness of his countenance give him an aspect which is belied by his faltering step. He took great pleasure in a story, whether told by himself or another, and had a ready and exciting laugh always at command. He is certainly a capital story-teller himself, and, where Sir Walter was concerned, was supremely interesting. He told me a story of Scott and himself seeing the devil once, when they were taking some oysters and port wine; and assured me that Scott never saw *Melrose by moonlight* during all his life: and Sir David added that he had heard Scott say that twenty times. The truth was, Sir Walter would not go there by night for fear of *bogles*. Sir Adam vindicated his friendship with Scott by his love of whiskey; and because I did not show a strong relish for his potations of that liquor, he said that my palate was not yet *Scotified*. In truth, whiskey is the Scotch drink; and Brewster, — a most temperate man, — who has just returned from England, complained that, during a visit of more than a fortnight, he got nothing but wine. As Sir Adam left us, at the close of the evening, he most kindly invited me to come and see him, if I should again visit this part of the country.

---

[1] 1781–1868; an experimental philosopher, biographer of Sir Isaac Newton, and Principal of St. Leonard's College at St. Andrew's.

[2] Sir Adam Ferguson was the eldest son of Dr. Adam Ferguson, the Professor of Moral Philosophy in the University of Edinburgh. At his father's house he and Sir Walter Scott became friends in boyhood, and the friendship continued till Sir Walter's death. Sir Adam served as a captain in Wellington's Peninsular campaigns. He was a prisoner for some time, and returned home when Scott was building Abbotsford. His friends were charmed with his wit and gallantry. He died Jan. 1, 1855, at the age of eighty-three. He is frequently referred to in Lockhart's "Life of Sir Walter Scott."

What think you of a visit to Abbotsford? I have seen this confused pile, — a folly made sacred by the memory of its great author. To one fresh from America, who had not seen the baronial seats of England, Abbotsford might appear large and interesting in an architectural point of view; but to me it seemed little more than a large baby-house, with its keep and towers, on which were mounted boys' guns, — weak imitations of the proud and impregnable towers which actually compose the old castle. As I saw this building, I felt the fatal weakness of Scott's character more than ever, and sighed to think that he could not have had the simple tastes which I found in Wordsworth. Here was this child of the Sun, who might have left a path of unmixed light behind him, degrading and enslaving himself, in order to accumulate what Wordsworth rightly called to me " a few dirty acres," and to become a country squire, — setting no price upon his immeasurable possessions of renown, and coveting the sterile fields of his neighbors. The house is in wretched taste; and the entrance-hall, which makes such a figure in all descriptions, is a small apartment, filled with arms and relics which would be in their place in a museum, but which are not in keeping with a house of the size of Abbotsford.

I hear much said of the *injudiciousness* of Lockhart, in his biography. He has mortally offended many persons. I have not time or space to repeat the stories I have heard; but when you know that I am now in the midst of all Sir Walter's neighbors, you will understand that I cannot be misinformed. The fatal affair of the Ballantynes [1] has plunged his friends into great difficulty. Sir David Brewster read me a portion of a letter just received from Napier, the editor of the " Edinburgh Review," in which the latter complains of the difficulty of the subject, and says that an honest dissection of Scott's character may present him in a light in which his friends would be very unwilling to view him; and so the editor proposed to be silent. It is said that Lockhart did not submit his pages to any critical friend before publication, and that his publisher (Cadell) actually struck out some expressions which offended even his uneducated ear. Lockhart, as you are aware, asked for Scott's letters from all his correspondents. Rogers sent a large packet, without examining them; and among them, it is said, was one or more informing Rogers that Lockhart was about to become the son-in-law of Sir Walter, and expressing for him the greatest detestation. And yet I am assured that they appeared to harmonize very well; and I believe that Lockhart was always kind and attentive to his wife. Lady Brewster — who is herself the daughter of Macpherson Ossian — told me that she was the intimate friend of Mrs. Lockhart, whom she believed to be entirely happy with her husband.

What an odd thing that I, fresh from Lord Brougham, should have passed into another circle where I hear that about him which he does not know himself! Brewster read me a part of Napier's letter, in which the editor says: " Brougham is pestering me to death. I am afraid we shall be

---

[1] Publishers, for whose debts, amounting to one hundred and ten thousand pounds, Scott as a partner had become liable.

obliged to split; and yet I hope that we may get along." This refers to Brougham's articles in the " Edinburgh Review." He is trying to push the Review further than its editor wishes to go.

My last to you left me at Keswick. Southey was away on a tour upon the Continent. He has a young and lovely daughter, whom I saw at Words-worth's. From Keswick I went to Penrith; passed a day with Sir George Back;[1] came up through Carlisle; noted on my left the road to Gretna Green; drove by the side of the Ettrick and the Tweed, and under the very shadow of Branksome Hall to Melrose, where I now am under the hos-pitable roof of one of the ablest, best-informed, and most amiable men I have ever known, — Sir David B., — with the thick-coming fancies filling my mind, and my whole soul absorbed in the hallowed associations of the place. With the Eildon Hills staring into your windows, and old Melrose full in sight, could you sleep? I wish that you could enjoy this scene; but I hope that my sketch may give you a small idea of what it is.

As ever yours,   C. S.

TO GEORGE S. HILLARD.

RICCARTON HOUSE, Sept. 19, 1838.

Again I send you greeting, from one of the pleasantest houses in which I have had the fortune to be entertained. I am now the guest of Sir James Gibson Craig,[2] an old staunch Whig, the friend of Fox, who received his baronetcy from the present ministry. His place is about seven miles from Edinburgh. He is at the head of the Whigs of Edinburgh, and is the Keeper of the Signet; but his great worth and political influence are compara-tively local, and you will doubtless feel more interested in one whose labors have passed the bounds of countries and territories, as have Lord Jeffrey's.[3] I was at Craigcrook Castle last evening, and passed a good portion of to-day with his Lordship in his study. Never have I heard any one express himself with such grace, beauty, precision, and variety of word as did Jeffrey, when I introduced the name of Jeremy Taylor; to catch and send you his language would be like wreathing into this scrawl the brilliant colors of the rainbow. I am tired — as doubtless you are — of my descriptions of the persons and conversations of those I meet. I will not give you another sketch, and yet I

---

[1] 1796–1857; an Arctic voyager.

[2] Sir James died in 1850, at the age of eighty-four.

[3] Francis Jeffrey, 1773–1850; one of the founders of the "Edinburgh Review," and one of its writers for nearly fifty years. He visited New York in 1813, where he married his second wife, Charlotte Wilkes, the grand niece of the celebrated John Wilkes. A note of Lord Jeffrey is preserved in which he invites Sumner to dine with him on Sept. 18, at 24 Moray Place, and regrets that people are out of town and that the courts are not in ses-sion. He says, " You have come to Edinburgh at the time of its greatest desertion, and when all our courts are in vacation and all our lawyers shooting grouse. I am afraid, therefore, that I can offer you only a family party and a hearty welcome on Tuesday."

cannot help saying that Jeffrey is superlatively eminent as a converser, — light, airy, poetical, argumentative, fantastical, and yet full of the illustrations of literature and history. He indulged me with reminiscences of his old Boston acquaintances, when he visited us in 1814, — G. Cabot, whom he thought a shrewd, powerful man, and also Mr. Lowell (John undoubtedly), both of whom, he said, inclined against republics to such a degree that he thought it his duty, in conversation, to say something in behalf of them; Otis, quite a superficial man; and another person, with a very handsome wife, who he would venture to say was quite a fool! I supplied the name at once, and his Lordship recognized it. But it would be impossible to follow his graceful tongue. Our English did, indeed, fall mended from his lips. Words the most apt, and yet out of ordinary reach, came at his bidding, like well-trained servants. He spoke of anciently passing along the streets of Edinburgh, and having water *ejaculated* upon his head. But I shall become a Boswell, and will check this theme. What a different man is Lockhart, with whom I dined at Lady Gifford's,[1] the dowager, last Sunday; he is without words, conversation, heart, or a disposition to please, throwing nothing into the stock of social intercourse, and keeping himself aloof from all the hearty currents of life. I ought to tell you that my host at present is a lineal descendant of Robert Bruce (of which he boasts much), and also of the famous Sir Thomas Craig, of the times of James I., who wrote that venerable folio on *Jus Feudale*, in which I have whilom moiled, and who died in the house where I now am. His accomplished family have all read Mr. Prescott's book with the greatest interest, and have made earnest inquiries after his health and the present condition of his eyes. They first read the book, being interested in the subject, without knowing it to be that of an American.

LANFIRE HOUSE, AYRSHIRE, Sept. 24.

Jeffrey against all the world! While in Edinburgh I saw much of him, and his talent, fertility of expression, and unlimited information (almost learning), impressed me more and more. He spoke on every subject, and always better than anybody else. Sydney Smith is infinitely pleasant, and instructive too; but the flavor of his conversation is derived from its humor. Jeffrey is not without humor, but this is not a leading element. He pleases by the alternate exercise of every talent; at one moment by a rapid argument, then by a beautiful illustration, next by a phrase which draws a whole thought into its powerful focus, while a constant grace of language and amenity of manners, with proper contributions from humor and wit, heighten these charms. I have been fortunate in knowing as I have known, — ay, in knowing at their hearths — the three great men of the "Edinburgh Review," — Smith, Brougham, and Jeffrey. But there is a *fourth*, — John A. Mur-

---

[1] Lady Harriet Maria Gifford, daughter of Rev. Edward Drewe, and sister of the wife of Baron Alderson. She died in 1857, surviving many years her husband, Lord Gifford, who was successively Solicitor-General, Attorney-General, Lord Chief-Justice of the Common Pleas, and Master of the Rolls.

ray, the present Lord-Advocate of Scotland.[1] It was Murray who gave the
motto, at which Sydney Smith laughed, — _Judex damnatur cum nocens absol-
vitur_, — from Publius Syrus, though he was innocent of having read Syrus.
I forget the motto which Smith offered.[2] From here I go to Strachur Park,
by Inverary, in the Highlands, to visit the Lord-Advocate; and thus see
the other of that association which gave such a new character to periodical
literature.

I passed nine days in Edinburgh,[3] and was received with the greatest
kindness; though Lord Jeffrey in one of his letters to me said that I was
unfortunate in my time of coming, as everybody was away shooting grouse,
and that he could only promise me a hearty welcome. The first day I dined
with Sir John Robison (Secretary of the Royal Society); next with Lady Gifford, where I met Lockhart; then with Captain Moore; then with Lord Jeffrey; then with Sir James Gibson Craig; then with Sir William Hamilton;[4]
then with the officers of the Horse-Guards stationed at Edinburgh; then with
Mr. Guthrie Wright, to meet the Attorney-General and my most attractive
friend, Lady Stratheden; and last with Mr. Fergusson, the author of the
work on Divorce, and a venerable friend of Scott, — to say nothing of breakfasts. Add to this, that I was obliged to decline as many more invitations,
and those from the Solicitor-General of Scotland, two from Lord Jeffrey, and
also from the Attorney-General and Lady Stratheden. The last lady I admire very much, — the daughter of a peer, and moreover a peeress by creation
in her own right; beautiful, accomplished, amiable, bland. I do not remember that I have met another lady of her age, the mother of a considerable
family, equally attractive. Sir William Hamilton is the brother of Cyril
Thomas Hamilton; he is quite learned, but _brusque_ and _gauche_ in his manners. Wilson I did not see. He was invited once or twice to meet me
where I dined or breakfasted; but he took no notice of the invitations, nor
of a letter of introduction to him from Sir David Brewster. He was spoken
of as very odd, almost mad. Some of my friends wished me to call upon
him; but I resolutely declined, having determined never to put myself forward to make an acquaintance in Britain. I find that Willis is much laughed
at for his sketches; and Wilson says that he never said what is attributed to

---

[1] John Archibald Murray was in Parliament from 1832 to 1835; succeeded Francis Jeffrey, in 1834, as Lord-Advocate, and, losing the office in a few months, resumed it in 1835,
and was raised to the bench in 1839 as a Lord of Session. He died March 7, 1859, in his
eighty-first year, at his residence on Great Stuart Street, Edinburgh. Save Brougham, he
was the last survivor of that company of men who distinguished the society of Edinburgh
during the first third of the present century, — Jeffrey, Brougham, Playfair, Sydney Smith,
Francis Horner, Thomas Brown, and Henry Cockburn. A note of Sydney Smith, introducing
Sumner to the Lord-Advocate, was forwarded to the latter, and was at once recognized by wel-
coming Sumner to Strachur Park, near Inverary, with directions to come by Loch Lomond,
Tarbet, and Cairnclan. In London, he afterwards invited Sumner to take tea at 1 Parliament Place, with Sydney Smith and Harriet Martineau as expected guests.

[2] Sydney Smith offered, _Tenui musam meditamur avenâ_, — "We cultivate literature on a
little oatmeal," — which was rejected as coming too near the truth. Lady Holland's "Memoir of the Rev. Sydney Smith," Chap. II.

[3] He lodged at Tait's Hotel, Princes Street.

[4] The metaphysician, 1788–1856.

him about Lockhart, and also the review of Hamilton. Some of my friends
were at Gordon Castle when Willis was there, and describe his visit in
amusing colors. It was supposed that he would write a book; and all the
ladies agreed to take turns in riding with him, &c., so *all* might be *equally*
booked. Sir William Hamilton wished to be particularly remembered to
Governor Everett. Will you be kind enough to do this?

I am now visiting my friend Brown. His house stands about a mile from
the road. You approach it by either of two lodges, which are quite pretty
and are a mile apart, and go by a shaded path a mile either way to the house.
There are woods in abundance in every direction. I am now writing in the
library, — a pleasant room with a beautiful prospect, — which is covered with
books from the floor to the ceiling. Mrs. Brown, the mother of my friend,
looks very much like her brother, Lord Jeffrey. I find myself so much engaged by the hospitalities of my friends that I shall not get back to town till
Nov. 1, in order to sit out the next Michaelmas Term.

As ever, affectionately yours,

CHAS. SUMNER.

TO JUDGE STORY.

LANFIRE HOUSE, Sept. 28, 1838.

MY DEAR JUDGE, — Your *double-sheeter* of Aug. 11 saluted me at Lord
Brougham's breakfast-table, at Brougham Hall, in the mountains of Westmoreland. I read it with deep interest at the time, and have carried it with
me, reading it anew at every resting-place. I have just read it over, and again
feel thankful that you devoted so much time to me. In all my present happiness a letter from a friend comes to gild my joy. Let me first answer the
matters suggested by your letter. I will examine Lord Hale's manuscript,
and will have a copy taken only in the event that I find it contains views
and arguments which I think important in illustration of the Admiralty
jurisdiction. . . .

Baron Alderson [1] is the first Equity judge in the Court of Exchequer, and
unquestionably a very great judge. [2] I do not think you do him justice. I
have sat by his side for three days on the bench, and have constantly admired the clearness, decision, and learning which he displayed. In one case
of murder, where all the evidence was circumstantial, I sat with him from
nine o'clock in the morning till six at night. His charge to the jury was a
luxury. I wish you could have heard it. It was delightful to hear an important case, so ably mastered by one who understood his duty and the law, and
did not shrink from laying before the jury his opinions. Alderson's voice

---

[1] Edward Hall Alderson, 1787–1857; a reporter with Barnewall, 1817–1822; a judge of
the Common Pleas, 1830–34; and of the Exchequer, 1834–57. Sumner dined with him at
his house in Park Crescent, and by his invitation with the bar of the Northern Circuit. In
a note, he proposed to call for Sumner and show him "our business in Chambers, of which
few people know any thing, either in England or America."

[2] Sumner wrote to Hillard, Aug. 18, 1838: "I do not know but what I should place him
[Alderson] before Parke. . . . He is a great Tory."

and manner remind me of Webster more than those of anybody I have seen here; his features are large, but his hair, eyes, and complexion are light.

You ask why does not some one interfere and put Lord Brougham right. If you had ever seen him, you would not ask that. As well might you try to turn aside Boreas in his swift career as Brougham when he once has conceived a line of action. I doubt if he counsels with anybody. His intimates are persons far below him in station, — Charles Phillips, Matthew Davenport Hill,[1] and Dr. Shepherd,[2] a Unitarian clergyman at Liverpool. . . .

I am with my friend Brown at Lanfire House. One may ride in his grounds twelve, perhaps twenty, miles. I sit and read in the library and ramble in the shady paths of the woods, which for more than a mile on either side surround his house. He wishes to be kindly remembered to you. Enclosed is an autograph of Sir Walter Scott, given me by Sir John Robison, the Secretary of the Royal Society at Edinburgh, of which Scott was President.

I am glad Mrs. Story is so well, and hope I shall not be forgotten in your house; and am,

As ever, most affectionately yours,

CHARLES SUMNER.

———

TO GEORGE S. HILLARD.

DUMBARTON, Oct. 1, 1838.

I now write you, my dear Hillard, from the foot of the far-famed Dumbarton Rock, which has withstood sieges without number and witnessed so many deeds of chivalry. It is a huge hunk of stone, precisely like the picture above,[3] with sides nearly perpendicular. You may well imagine that under the ancient system of warfare it was nearly impregnable. In our days, when the force of artillery is so well understood, I doubt much if it " would laugh a siege to scorn.'' I am now at the comfortable inn in the place, having declined the hospitable shelter of Talfourd's roof. He has taken for the summer the beautiful Glenarbuck Cottage, about four miles from here, and I have just returned from passing the afternoon in rambling in his wild grounds and in dining with him, following the windings of the Clyde, with the romantic castle in sight. Talfourd is moaning that he must so soon desert these sweet places and hurry back to town and business.

I write you now particularly, in order to answer a question, which hangs upon my mind, in one of your former letters. You ask how will it do to pub-

---

[1] Of Birmingham; an active member of the "Society for the Diffusion of Useful Knowledge," and a promoter of juvenile reformatories.

[2] Rev. William Shepherd, of Gateacre, Liverpool; author of the "Life of Poggio Bracciolini," a copy of which was given by Edward Rushton to Sumner. Mr. Shepherd was a schoolmaster of reputation, and belonged to the same literary set with Roscoe. Sumner wrote on a copy (the author's gift) of Mr. Shepherd's "History of the American Revolution" the memorandum, "The author, whom I met at Brougham Hall, Aug. 1838, told me that this little history was read in manuscript and approved by Lord John Russell. C. S."

[3] Referring to a vignette at the top of the sheet.

lish a collection of Macaulay's writings? [1] Very well. I thought otherwise at first. There is a sameness in his style, — balance and counterbalance, gun answering gun, parterre casting the shadow of parterre, — so that I at first feared that a *volume* of his composition would not have the same relish that we find in an *article*. But I am now convinced that there is withal so much thought and generalization, and historical argument and illustration, in all that he has written, that it must challenge and fix the attention. Think of your idea seriously. When I get back to town I will sound Macaulay upon it, if I am so fortunate as to find him there. He has promised me a book; and I doubt not I shall meet him. I have heard much that is good about him; and he is one of the few men who have risen as I have entered the sphere in which they move. Who could be a better judge of one like Macaulay than Lord Jeffrey? — Jeffrey, a critic of thought and composition for years; a speaker, and a student of the proprieties of Parliament. He told me that no man spoke like Macaulay in the Commons; and that the great proof of this was to be found in the remarkable fact that, during the discussions on the Reform Bill, the views of Macaulay, advanced perhaps at the fifth or sixth day's debate, formed the topic of discussion for the remainder of the time that the subject was under consideration. The Tories were occupied, each and all of them, in the endeavor to answer some view that he had launched. Macaulay went to India with a view to gain an independence that should enable him to be, not simply above party subservience, but above the *imputation* of it. He wished to be able to support his sisters. He has happily accomplished his objects, and is now undoubtedly worth some thirty thousand pounds. He declines to return to Parliament, and avows a determination to surrender himself to literary pursuits. He has already commenced a history of England from the Revolution of 1688 to the passage of the Reform Bill; [2] and this, I understand, he is pledged to complete. Lord Jeffrey thought he would be persuaded to return to Parliament. If you should edit a collection of his writings, do not forget his speeches, which form some of his most striking productions. His article on Bacon is a masterpiece. [3]

I observed to Lord Jeffrey that I thought Carlyle had changed his style very much since he wrote the article on Burns. "Not at all," said he; " I will tell you why that is different from his other articles: *I altered it.*" Carlyle was quite vexed at this interference. Could you not publish one or two volumes of the articles of Sydney Smith? I have a list of them all, given me by himself; and he said when he gave it to me, "If you wish to read liberal sentiments expressed always with some humor, look at these." They would make a volume of infinite fun.

[1] The American edition of Macaulay's essays first led him to consider the expediency of an English edition. See his letter to Napier, Aug. 25, 1842, — Trevelyan's "Life of Lord Macaulay," Vol. II. p. 100.

[2] Macaulay, in his letter to Napier of July 20, 1838, first mentions his project of a history. From his journal it appears that he wrote a portion of the introduction on March 9, 1839. The first two volumes were published late in 1848. Trevelyan's "Life of Lord Macaulay," Vol. II. pp. 19, 215.

[3] Written in India, and published in the "Edinburgh Review," July, 1837.

I have passed five days with Brown in rambling round his grounds and in reading in his library. He wished to be remembered kindly to you. The smack of Edinburgh society still remains on my lips. There I saw, in a short time and in a most unfavorable season, many men of interest, — old companions of Scott, — and also those whose characters speak sufficiently for themselves. Tait asked me to meet De Quincey, the opium-eater; but I was engaged to ride with Lord Jeffrey, and could not go.

STRACHUR PARK, Oct. 3, 1838.

I close this letter at the seat of the Lord-Advocate of Scotland, in Argyleshire, in the very midst of the Highlands.

As ever, yours affectionately,   C. S.

P. S. Lord Jeffrey and Sydney Smith both spoke of Macaulay as a talker who *said too much*, — so much that Jeffrey thought he was not a popular diner out; and Sydney Smith said, when I told him that I had met Macaulay, " Well, you had talk enough for once in your life." Now I distinctly say that I saw nothing of this. He kept himself within bounds.

Sir David Brewster told me that he received several letters from Lord Brougham, written in court when Chancellor, on *light*, one of them fourteen pages long.

TO JUDGE STORY.

STRACHUR PARK, Oct. 4, 1838.

MY DEAR JUDGE, — I am the guest of the Lord-Advocate,[1] — a kind, agreeable gentleman, of about sixty-six. We are in the recesses of the Highlands, with mountain peaks about us in every direction; glassy lakes, in which are mirrored the surrounding objects; and far, far away from " the madding crowd's ignoble strife." Here is the great Temple of Nature; and none but her devout worshippers enter in. On the opposite shore of the *loch* is the castle of Inverary, — the celebrated seat of the Duke of Argyll, and the scene of some of the adventures of Captain Dalgetty in the " Legend of Montrose." After the ladies left the table at dinner, his Lordship inquired of me as to the extent of *Lynch law* in America. He said that it was the great stain of our country, and that it tended to create a distrust in the security of life, freedom, and property;[2] for if you once recognize a right in any persons to take the law into their own hands, or if, when they have taken it into their own hands, you do not perseveringly pursue them, you take away all security. This consideration is, by no means, new to you or to me. It is the palpable view, which is as plain as the road to mill; and yet why is it not enforced? Why will respectable men at home stand by and smile while the

----

[1] John A. Murray.

[2] Instances of summary popular justice were then somewhat frequent; they were the incidents of slaveholding or frontier communities, imperfectly civilized, in which citizens failed to obtain protection through the ordinary methods of justice.

law is prostrated? I do assure you, my dear Judge, this matter assumes a gigantic importance at the distance from which I survey it. Solon well said, that was the *best government* where an injury to a single citizen was resented as an injury to the whole State. Tried by this standard, how miserably poor is our government! The Lord-Advocate and some of his guests had read Judge Lawless's charge to the grand jury of Missouri, on the occasion of some infamous murder; and all expressed, justly I think, the utmost abhorrence of its doctrines. And the Lord-Advocate argued, with great power, that we ought to have some way of at once turning a judge out of office, who should lay down such law; and, further, that there should be a provision in our national Constitution securing to *Congress* some supervision of State judges and State laws; "otherwise," said his Lordship, "a citizen of Massachusetts, who happened to be in Missouri, might be tried and executed for matters which, in his own State, were no offence; or he might lose his life, and no punishment ensue to his murderers." You will at once perceive that these views, ingenious as they are, originated in misconceptions with regard to the nature of our Union, a matter which no foreigner clearly understands; but I think you will be struck, as I was, with their theoretic soundness, and perhaps regret that they cannot in some way be adopted. His Lordship further said that Congress (and here, of course, he went on mistaken notions of its powers) should appoint a committee at the next session to inquire into the number of cases of Lynch law, and all the circumstances attending their occurrence. Cannot something be done? All the good and sound part of the community should address themselves to this. I have always (with one exception) been treated with great forbearance and delicacy, when this subject has been brought on. There was a gentleman at Riccarton House, with Sir James Gibson Craig, who pressed me so hard as to vex me, and nearly put me out of temper. Sir James himself was perfectly serene and just.

STIRLING, Oct. 7, 1838.

I continue this letter beneath the towers of Stirling, — so famous in Scotch history, and which have witnessed the ebbs and flows of so many bloody tides. The castle must have been impregnable before the art of war, and particularly the science of artillery, had introduced such great changes. Since I commenced this letter, I have passed through Loch Lomond and Loch Katrine, the pictures of which will give an added value to this sheet. I have been rowed by moonlight on this last beautiful lake, — a distance of ten miles, — while Ben Lomond towered in the distance; and, by the light of day, have visited the island of the "Lady of the Lake;" have seen the spot where Fitz James wound his horn, after his "gallant grey" had sunk exhausted to the ground; have followed his course beyond "Clan-Alpine's outmost guard, as far as Coilantogle's ford." And now I am on the rock of Stirling, — one of those natural fastnesses which, in early days, were so much regarded by all soldiers. Among the adventures which I have had in the Highlands, amidst these weird hills and glassy lakes, was a Highland wedding. Let me tell you of this on my return. It was one of the richest scenes I ever enjoyed; and I was a kind of Guy Mannering in the whole affair.

I have long wished to write you of Edinburgh and its society, and now find only the fraction of a letter for what several units would hardly suffice. I doubt not that you have already heard something of what I saw there from Hillard. It was a season when everybody was out of town, so that I saw only comparatively a few persons; but they were the *élite*. Among others, I saw Professor Bell, the venerable author of the work on Commercial Law.[1] He came out to Lord Jeffrey's at dinner, though, poor man, he eat nothing, as his physicians had cut him off from dinner: he afterwards came to Sir William Hamilton's, where he eat nothing. I breakfasted with him; and he was so good as to go with me over the courts, and explain to me their different jurisdictions. I assure you a worthier or more warm-hearted old gentleman does not exist in either hemisphere. He is advanced in life, — say seventy, — and, I fear, quite weak, even for his years. He told me that he was the first person in Scotland who imported a copy of Pothier. His works, in a pecuniary sense, I understand, have been losing affairs. He was well acquainted with Kent's "Commentaries," and inquired after the Chancellor as if for an old friend. I shall not fail to write the Chancellor the agreeable inquiries which have been made with regard to him by Mr. Bell, and also by Pardessus at Paris. You are perhaps aware that Clark, the bookseller, has published a neat volume, containing the *commercial* parts of Kent's "Commentaries;" but, though he received highly commendatory letters from Lord Denman and Lord Chief-Justice Tindal, the book has not succeeded. On the other hand, your "Conflict of Laws" has entirely succeeded. Of that he published an edition of one thousand copies. Clark is a gentlemanly, intelligent, pushing man. I dined one day in Edinburgh with Fergusson,[2] the author of the "Consistory Reports," who is a bland, noble gentleman, of seventy. He and Bell are both clerks of Session, as Scott was; so that they are entirely comfortable. Robertson, who has written a work on "Personal Succession,"[3] had it all printed and just ready to be published, when he met your work: being a man of fortune, he determined not to go before the world without the lights derived from you; and accordingly cancelled all his sheets, and rewrote them, embodying the new considerations suggested by the "Conflict of Laws." They tell strange stories of Fergusson's absence of mind, some of which I hope to remember to tell you when I get home.

As ever, affectionately yours,

CHAS. SUMNER.

[1] George Joseph Bell, 1770–1843.

[2] James Fergusson, at one time one of the Judges of the Consistory Court of Edinburgh, author of "Recent Decisions by the Consistorial Court of Scotland in Actions of Divorce," and of "A Treatise on the Present State of the Consistorial Law in Scotland, with Reports of Decided Cases."

[3] David Robertson; his work was published at Edinburgh in 1836, and dedicated to Lord Brougham.

TO HIS SISTER MARY.

DUBLIN,[1] Oct. 14, 1838.

MY DEAR MARY, — I write now in the coffee-room of a hotel in the capital of Ireland. . . . Learn to understand your own language, my dear sister; make it a study, and fix upon it your serious thought. Most of the world speak their mother tongue unconsciously; and, like Monsieur Jourdain in Molière's delicious comedy, would be astonished if they should be told that during all their lives they had been talking *prose !* Read the *Bourgeois Gentilhomme,* if you have not read it before now; it is easy French, and is full of pleasant turns.

This sheet is enriched by a picture of Abbotsford and of Melrose Abbey. I hope that you know all about these already. The life of Scott must have made you acquainted with Abbotsford; and Melrose Abbey is the scene of his earliest — I am inclined to think his best — poem.

When you have a moment's leisure, catch up the "Lay of the Last Minstrel;" read its sounding lines, which enter the ear like the reverberating hoofs of the fast-going horse. There is much that is stirring in Scott. His poetry is martial music: and I always feel when reading it (though for the thousandth time) as if stirred by a trumpet.

I have visited Abbotsford, and seen those towers which you may see in the picture. It was with deep melancholy that I contemplated this structure, to rear which the distinguished author had enslaved his mind and life. Every stone, and all those towers and fantastic monuments, proclaimed his vanity. Foolish man! why could he not have lived in contentment in an ordinary house, built after common designs, without aping those great baronial models, to equal which all his fortune was of course incompetent? Abbotsford looks well enough in a picture; perhaps it would seem imposing to one who had not seen the larger castles of England. I approached it, after having visited Lambton Castle, Auckland Castle (or palace), Raby Castle, Brancepeth Castle, Wytton Castle, Ravensworth, &c., in the North of England, in four of which I have been as a guest. And, after these proud piles, I cannot express to you the littleness of every thing about Abbotsford. Melrose is a beautiful ruin. I passed two days with Sir David Brewster at his seat, directly opposite the Abbey, with the silver Tweed — that river so illustrious in Scottish history — flowing between; and from my chamber window, while the moon was riding aloft, I looked out upon this venerable ruin, illustrated by poetry and association, and upon the towering Eildon Hills, which, with their majestic bodies, stood like two grand sentinels over the scene.

God grant that you and all the family may be well, with happiness as a sunbeam in your paths! Study, my dear girl; employ your time; catch the priceless moments, and believe that they are better than gold and silver.

As ever, affectionately yours,   CHAS.

---

[1] Sumner visited Glasgow, and probably took a steamer from Liverpool for Dublin; but no letter covering this week of his tour, Oct. 7-14, has been preserved.

TO JUDGE STORY.

WENTWORTH HOUSE,[1] Oct. 24, 1838.

MY DEAR JUDGE, — From Wortley Hall I have passed to this magnificent palace; and, as my Lord Fitzwilliam [2] said to me to-night, I have dined under the shadow of Lord Bute, and now of the Marquis of Rockingham. I arrived after dark, and therefore have not seen the immense proportions of this edifice. They were going in to dinner as I drove up. I was at once shown to my room by the groom of the chambers; dressed, and got into the dining-room just after the disappearance of fish, and found a place vacant for me by the side of the Lady Charlotte, who is his Lordship's eldest daughter, and does the honors of the house. There were twenty-five or more at table.

I have passed three agreeable nights at Wortley. Before I came here, Lord Morpeth told me that I should find Wentworth magnificent and Wortley comfortable. And you may conceive an English peer's idea of comfort when I tell you that Wortley Hall is a spacious edifice, built by the husband of Lady Mary Wortley Montagu.[3] I do not know an edifice like it in the United States, with extensive domains. Wharncliffe Park, which belongs to it, contains of itself eighteen hundred acres, in which the deer are ranging. Every thing about it is elegant. But you will wish to hear of the noble family. Lord Wharncliffe is now about sixty-five.[4] He was troubled during my stay with severe rheumatism. He is a man of great simplicity of manners and of strong common sense, with a great practical turn. Sir Robert Inglis told me that I must not fail to see Lord Wharncliffe presiding at the

---

[1] Murray's "Handbook for Yorkshire," pp. 448, 449, has a description of Wentworth Castle.

[2] Charles William Wentworth, fifth Earl Fitzwilliam, 1786–1857. He was a liberal peer and a supporter of the Reform Bill. His father was the friend of Fox until the controversy concerning the French Revolution divided them, and the nephew of the Marquis of Rockingham, Burke's friend. Earl Fitzwilliam survived his eldest son, William Charles, Viscount Milton, who died in Nov., 1835. The Earl was, on his death, succeeded in the peerage by his second son, the present earl, William Thomas Spencer, who was born in 1815, and who married, in September, 1838, Lady Frances Douglas, daughter of the Earl of Morton. One of the seats of Earl Fitzwilliam was Wentworth House, Yorkshire, and another, Milton Park, near Peterborough. Sumner bore a letter of introduction to him from their common friend, Charles S. Daveis, of Portland.

[3] Murray's "Handbook for Yorkshire," p. 468.

[4] James Archibald Stuart Wortley Mackenzie, 1776–1845; descended from the third Earl Bute, and created a peer as Baron Wharncliffe in 1826. Lady Wharncliffe survived him till 1856. Their eldest son, John Stuart Wortley, 1801–1855, who succeeded to the peerage on his father's death, travelled in his youth in the United States. He was the author of pamphlets on political topics, and the editor and translator of Guizot's "Memoirs of George Monk." His widow, the Lady Georgiana, survives him. Her recollections of Sumner are given, ante, p. 306. John Stuart Wortley, June 14, 1838, invited Sumner, who brought a letter to him from Judge Story, to dine at his house in Curzon Street, and meet Lord and Lady Wharncliffe. He wrote to Sumner, Nov. 9, 1838: "I think you will have taken a pretty good survey of English country-houses, and will know more of our mode of life in them than most foreigners, though this word seems scarcely to suit a person who has so many points of identity with us as yourself. It gave us all great pleasure to be able to receive you here [Wortley Hall], and I think I may take the opportunity of saying as much for Lord Fitzwilliam, if I may judge from a few hurried words which we had together after some business in Sheffield the other day."

Quarter Sessions, which are held with a jury, and dispose of all crimes where the punishment is under transportation for life, and also of all the cases under the poor laws. For thirty years his Lordship has been chairman, and is said to have discharged these important duties in such a manner as to distinguish him among all the magistrates of England. I have had the good fortune to sit by his side on the bench. I need not tell you that Lord W. is a thorough Tory, and so are all his family. He inquired about you, and said he wished you would visit England. Lady Wharncliffe is one of the handsomest women of her age I ever saw. She is a daughter of the Countess of Erne, and a sister of the late Countess of Liverpool. John Stuart Wortley is amiable, intelligent, and gentlemanly. He has expressed the warmest regard for you. Of course he is a Tory. He has contested unsuccessfully many places, so as to get the *soubriquet* of the " standing member." Lady Georgiana, his wife, is a tall and striking person, with a good deal of brilliancy in conversation and quickness of mind. She is a daughter of the Earl Harrowby, and, I need not add, a very strong Tory. Next is Charles,[1] who is in the army; but who was not at home, so I will say nothing of him. Then comes James Stuart Wortley.[2] He is the young member of the bar to whom your works have gone; and, you will be glad to hear, without question one of the most promising and rising members of his profession. If his party shall be able to get and keep power, he may expect no inconsiderable promotion; indeed, the " keeper's seals," as of old, " may dance before him." He is now about thirty-two. He would, however, pass as much younger than I am. I know James Wortley very well. Next is the daughter Caroline, who is married to Mr. Talbot, the third son of the Earl Talbot. They were at Wortley while I was there. Such is the family: never have I seen more good sense, pure toryism, simplicity, and affectionate intercourse than among them. The park about the house is famous as the scene of the opening of Scott's " Ivanhoe." It is also supposed to have been infested in ancient times with a dreadful dragon; and an old English ballad, preserved in Percy's " Reliques," commemorates this.

To return to Wentworth. In the chapel to-night at prayers there were about fifty servants, constituting the household establishment. Young Lord Milton has just married a very pretty little wife, a daughter of Earl Morton. The earl arrived to-night, and was pleased to express his regret that I had not visited him when in Scotland. You may find pictures of Wentworth and descriptions enough. I will, therefore, not fatigue you by my sketch. It is truly vast. All the country places round Boston put together would not equal it; and it contains some very remarkable paintings, — among others the famous Vandykes of Strafford. This house and estate once belonged to the great Strafford, and many of the books in the library have his name. Lord Fitzwilliam has all the papers of Burke, — letters, essays, and unpublished manuscripts. I have taken the liberty of urging his Lordship to give these to the public; and I think he is disposed to do it.

[1] 1802–1844.

[2] Born in 1805. He has been a member of Parliament; was Recorder of London in 1850, and Solicitor-General in 1856-57. His recollections of Sumner are given *ante* p. 304.

I cannot conclude this letter without letting you know the splendid hospitality and friendly notice which I received from Lord Morpeth[1] when I was in Ireland. His position is eminent; but he is as good and simple as he is eminent in the government and aristocracy. From Wentworth I go to York, to see the Minster; and then to visit Lord Leicester, in the grandest house in England, as he told me; then to London, to sit in Westminster Hall.

As ever, affectionately,

CHARLES SUMNER.

TO GEORGE S. HILLARD.

WENTWORTH HOUSE, Oct. 26, 1838.

MY DEAR HILLARD, — You know all about this vast place from books. It will therefore be quite vain for me to send you a sketch, even if I had the disposition to do so, — writing, as I now do, after dinner in the long gallery, where are many of those paintings by Vandyke, Reynolds, and Raphael, of which all the world has heard, and where also the ladies are assembled for the evening's diversions. I cannot content myself, however, without saying that nothing which I have previously seen in Paris, or other parts of England, in Scotland or Ireland, had prepared me for the vast and magnificent scale of this establishment. The house is certainly the largest private edifice I have ever seen; and, I think, larger than any public one, except the Palace of Versailles. The front is unquestionably the finest specimen of architecture I have looked upon. I shrink from going into details; but you may conceive the extent of the establishment in some degree, when you know that there are upwards of two hundred horses. I have had an opportunity here of witnessing, under favorable circumstances, English races, and seeing the conduct of the younger portion of the aristocracy of this great country. I assure you it has been deeply interesting. But more interesting, by far, was it to look upon the wonderful features of Strafford, — the original owner of these estates, and the ancestor of Lord Fitzwilliam, — perpetuated by Vandyke. Here are several of the productions of this renowned artist; and the whole place, when you consider that it has passed through the hands of that great lord and of the Marquis of Rockingham, so memorable in the time of our Revolution, breathes an air of deep historical interest. Lord Fitzwilliam is one of the mildest and purest of men. You will be glad to hear that Prescott's book was in his Lordship's hands, and also in those of several of the ladies of the house; and Lord Fitzwilliam told me that Earl Grey expressed to him the highest opinion of its merits. I should not fail to add that Lord Morpeth — whose distinguished position you well know, and to whom I am indebted, not simply for hospitality, but for the greatest and most friendly kindness — inquired with great interest about Mr. Prescott; and Mr. Labouchere,[2] whom I met at his Lordship's table, spoke of his work

---

[1] This is the first mention of Lord Morpeth in his letters.

[2] Henry Labouchere, 1798-1869. He was a member of Parliament from 1826 to 1859, became Privy Councillor in 1835, and was Vice-president of the Board of Trade from 1835

as *the* history of the period.   I passed three days at Lord Wharncliffe's, — one day longer than I intended to stay.   If I had not passed this day at Wortley Hall, I should have met Lady Francis, the widow of Sir Philip, at Wentworth.

As ever, affectionately yours,

CHAS. SUMNER.

TO GEORGE S. HILLARD.

FAIRFIELD LODGE, near YORK, Oct. 27, 1838.

MY DEAR HILLARD, — It was only last night that I wrote you from Wentworth House.   I failed, doubtless, to give you an idea of that immense establishment, where you find persons of every trade, — a baker, with his rooms and apparatus; a confectioner; a butcher; a brewer; and, of course, his majesty the cook.   In the stables you find farriers, carpenters, joiners, and the like.   Then there are conservatories and hot-houses, by the side of which those of our Botanical Garden and of Mr. Cushing [1] — the two together — are quite small things; and, more than this, there is an aviary, where you may see more strange birds than I have ever seen together in any collection in America: in one place you may see the eagle in his spacious cage, and in another that rarity of antiquity, the *black swan*, sailing on an artificial lake, while sea-gulls and other aquatic birds are splashing about him.   Somewhat used, as I have now become, to the country-life of this wonderful island, I am astonished at the extent of all that I have seen at Wentworth.   I would gladly have stayed longer, according to his Lordship's kind invitation; but my other engagements would not permit.   I however indulge the hope of being able to visit him at his other seat, — Milton,— during the hunting-season, that I may not leave England without seeing one of her great national sports.   I am now the guest of a sportsman, — Mr. Thompson, whose acquaintance I made at Wentworth, — at his pretty place in the neighborhood of York, where I have come simply to see the Minster. I should tell you that I had a good opportunity at Wentworth to observe the way in which the wealthy sons of the aristocracy pass their time.   The young Lord Milton had invited some of his friends, of about his own age, and keen in their love of horses, to visit him, and have some private races. Milton offered, among various prizes, a gold cup and a dessert set.   Among the young men were the future Lord Scarborough and Lord De Mauley. They were all dressed as *jockeys*, with the cap, the close blue or red or yellow silk jacket, the leather breeches, and the white-top boots.   I observed a

----

to 1839, and again from 1847 to 1852; Chief Secretary for Ireland from 1846 to 1847; Colonial Secretary from 1855 to 1858, and was raised to the peerage as Baron Taunton in 1859.   His second wife, to whom he was married in 1852, was Lady Mary Matilda Georgiana, a daughter of the sixth Earl of Carlisle, and sister of Sumner's friend, Lord Morpeth. His visit to this country has been mentioned already, *ante*, p. 305.   Sumner visited Lord Taunton in July, 1857, at his seat at Stoke.

[1] Of Watertown, Mass.

strong habit with them all: a remark could not be made without an offer to support it by a *bet*. If they were walking in the garden, one observed on the distance of a certain object, and straightway a bet was offered and taken with regard to it; and on one occasion the young De Mauley — who, besides being the heir of a peer and at present a member of the House of Commons, has just married one of the handsomest women I ever saw in any country — offered to bet that he could run a certain distance within a given time. The bet was taken, the ground measured: he took off his boots and coat and waist-coat, ran, and gained the bet. At cards, they were always disposed to make the sum played for quite high. I have found it universal in England to play for money; sober persons make the sum sixpence on each point, — a term which I do not understand, though I have gained several points, as I have been told. I played one evening with Lord Fitzwilliam as my partner; and we won between us about a pound, which was duly paid and received. Another evening, I played with the young Scarborough and De Mauley and a *clergyman*. I then won; and the clergyman paid me five shillings. Now, I must confess that I have disliked all this very much. I do not fancy cards in their best estate, — especially do I not fancy them when so nearly allied to gaming. I however took my seat at the tables in order to make a set, and fell in silently and without any question with what appeared to be the received usage. Indeed, so strong is the custom in this regard as to give rise to another, which is quite different, I believe, from that in America. Among us, man and wife never are partners, — are they? Here, as I heard Lord Fitzwilliam observe, they always are partners, — because, otherwise, they would *gain nothing:* it would do a man no good to win from his wife. You know very well that Lord Fitzwilliam is a person of the greatest purity of character and religious feeling. I will not abandon my reminiscences of Wentworth without speaking of the young lady who was so beautiful, — beautiful, in my sight, beyond most that I have ever seen. She was a daughter of Lord Duncannon, and newly married to the young personage I have mentioned. I do not remember any face in England, except that which passed before my eyes at Ravensworth Castle, so captivating. English ideas of country-life you will somewhat understand, when I tell you that she said, " London at this season is intolerable; and even a *villa* is not to be endured." Now, a villa is a neat, pretty spot, with fifteen or one hundred acres of land occupied by a garden, — being precisely what all the " places " and " seats " round Boston are. Nothing here is dignified as a *place* or *seat*, unless the grounds are so extensive that one may take his drive without cross-ing the borders of his own property, and the ladies may, with their own hands, drive their pony-phaetons through the winding paths of its woods.

I have seen York Minster. These wonderful piles of Gothic architecture fill my mind with an intenser glow than aught else I have seen or felt in England. Is not that saying a good deal? My happiest moments in this island have been when I saw Salisbury and Durham cathedrals. Much hap-piness have I enjoyed in the various distinguished and interesting society in which I have been permitted to mingle; but greater than all this was that which I felt when I first gazed upon the glorious buildings I have mentioned. Then it was that I was in communion with no single mind, — bright and gifted though it be, — but with whole generations. Those voiceless walls seemed to speak; and the olden time, with its sceptred pall, passed before me. Oh! it was with a thrill of pleasure that I looked from the spire of Salisbury, and wandered among the heavy arches of Durham, which I can never forget. At Durham I was with a most distinguished ornament of the Church, — Dr. Gilly,[1] — and with my namesake, the Lord Bishop of Chester,[2] with Gally Knight,[3] the old college friend of Byron, and with Dr. Buckland;[4] but those venerable walls were more interesting, by far, than all that these men could say. And I remember no feast so rich in elevated pleasure, — not those where the contributions of wit and learning have " outdone the meats, outdone the frolic wine." Let me say, however, that York did not produce this fine effect. I saw it on a rainy day, and with my mind full of my journey to the South.

                                                  BOSTON, Oct. 29.

Not from "famous Boston town," where I first drew breath, do I write, but from the small place on the distant coasts of Lincolnshire, whence John Cotton, "whose fame was in all the churches," went to settle our New England. I saw the old parsonage which Cotton left for the woods of America, and tapped at the back door with a venerable, triangular knocker, — which, I doubt not, the hands of the Puritan preacher had often known, before he forsook the soft cushion of the Established Church and the shadow of that fine Gothic pile, on which, even in his day, so many centuries had shed their sunshines and showered their storms. And a glorious pile is this parish church of Boston, built in the time of Edward III.! I wish we could remove it to our city. In every thing else we have immeasurably outstripped the English town, which numbers about thirteen thousand people, and has all the air of a provincial place. There is a windmill, which, with its broad vans, is so like that which once stood at the South End, that I would have sworn to its identity.

                                    HOLKHAM HOUSE,[5] Nov. 2, 1838.

This house has not the fresh magnificence of Chatsworth (the princely residence of the Duke of Devonshire), the feudal air of Raby and Auckland

---

1 William Stephen Gilly, 1790–1855; canon of Durham and vicar of Norham; author of publications concerning the Waldenses. He wrote a pleasant note to Sumner, Nov. 26, 1838, expressing regret that he could not visit Norham, and see country curates and English people in farm-houses and cottages.

2 John Bird Sumner, 1780–1862. He was made Bishop of Chester in 1828, and Archbishop of Canterbury in 1848. His younger brother, Charles Richard Sumner, 1790–1874, was first Bishop of Llandaff, and then of Winchester; resigning his see in 1869, which he had held forty-one years.

3 Henry Gally (or Galley) Knight, 1788–1846; poet and traveller, member of Parliament; referred to in Moore's "Life of Byron" (London: 1860), pp. 60, 218, 245.

4 William Buckland, 1784–1856; professor at Oxford, and Dean of Westminster; distinguished for his studies in geology and mineralogy. He invited Sumner to dine with the Geological Society Club, Dec. 19, 1838, at the "Crown and Anchor" Hotel.

5 Murray's Handbook, — "Essex, Suffolk, Norfolk, Cambridgeshire," — pp. 254–261.

castles, or the grand front of Wentworth; but it seems to me to blend more magnificence and comfort, and to hold a more complete collection of interesting things, whether antiques, pictures, or manuscripts, than any seat I have visited. The entrance hall is the noblest I have ever seen; and the suite of apartments is the best arranged for show and comfort that can be imagined. With the doors open, you may look through a vista of eleven spacious rooms; and these of the most agreeable proportions, and adorned by the choicest productions of the pencil. Here you may admire the luxurious tints of Titian, the landscapes of Claude, the magnificence of Vandyke, and the soul-touching canvas of Raphael and Da Vinci. The painting by Vandyke of the Duke of Aremberg, which, large as life — and the duke on his courser — adorns the principal saloon, Lord Leicester considers the best picture in the world. He has refused twenty thousand pounds for it. Here is the "Leo X." by Raphael, — an engraving from which you will find in Roscoe's "Life of Leo;" and a "Holy Family," by Raphael. A large "Joseph and Mary," with the infant Saviour, going into Egypt, by Rubens, I do not admire. It has that tawdry coloring which flames so along the walls of the Louvre, where his canvas is spread for several rods. As you pass from these rooms to the dining-room, you go through a gallery of surpassing grace and proportions, which is occupied by a collection of antique statues and busts, the completest in England, — a "Pythian Apollo," a "Venus" with a veil, a "Meleager," a "Faun" in most beautiful preservation, a "Neptune," a "Diana" (for sending which from Rome the old Lord Leicester was thrown into prison), with busts of Seneca and Cornelius Sylla, — the latter said to be the only one that has come down to us. I have only mentioned some of the principal ones. And you dine with noble and almost colossal heads of Juno and of Lucius Verus looking from their high niches down upon you. You have heard much of the manuscripts at Holkham, which were arranged and put in order by the late Mr. Roscoe;[1] this also is called the completest collection of the kind in England. Some of the illuminations are beautiful beyond imagination; and some of the manuscripts are invaluable. They relate to all branches of learning; and here I have found the handwriting of Sir Edward Coke, and have for hours pored over the crabbed page which bears the marks of his pen. In the library there are many works with his annotations.

Lord Leicester[2] is now old and infirm. He is a very ardent friend of

---

[1] Roscoe's "Life of William Roscoe," Vol. II. pp. 256, 262.

[2] Thomas William Coke, Earl of Leicester, 1752–1842. He inherited the estates of his uncle, Thomas Coke, who was Earl of Leicester and a descendant of Sir Edward Coke. He represented the County of Norfolk in Parliament from 1776 to 1832, and was known as "the first Commoner of England." He was faithful to the Whig party. In 1837 he was created a peer, with the title of Earl of Leicester of Holkham. He was distinguished for his zeal in promoting an improved cultivation of the soil, and was reputed to be "the first farmer of England." Miss Martineau records the remarkable changes which he wrought on his estates, — "History of England," Book VI. ch. xvi. His estate and mode of living are described in "Life of Lord Denman," Vol. I. pp. 237–239; also a visit to him when he was in his eighty-second year, Vol. II. pp. 5, 7. His widow married, in 1843, Edward Ellice, M. P. for Coventry, and died in 1844. Sumner wrote on an autograph of the Earl of Leicester, " The above autograph of the Earl Leicester, formerly known as Mr. Coke, and the mover

America, and recounts as the proudest event of his life the motion he made for the recognition of our Independence. He speaks of Fox with the warmest friendship; of George IV., who had visited him at Holkham, in no measured terms. This pedantic monarch used to call Fox "Charles," and Mr. Coke (now Lord Leicester) "Tom." Brougham was once a great favorite of my host; but his recent conduct seems to have estranged everybody from him, even Lord Leicester and also Lord Spencer, who is now here, though I have not heard the latter speak of him. There is a large party about assembling to enjoy shooting. Lord Spencer and his brother and Lord Ebrington have already come, with the Ladies Anson and Elizabeth Stanhope.[1] You would be amused to see Lord Spencer,[2] — once the leader of the House of Commons, and perhaps the most distinguished member of the Ministry, and now looked to as a future Premier, if he will consent to have greatness thrust upon him, — in a rough dress, with thick hob-nailed shoes, duck-painted gaiters, and a mackintosh, — his whole dress defying the wet, — going round the barnyards, and feeling of cows and oxen and bulls, in order to determine their comparative merits, or with his gun and well-trained dogs wandering through fields of turnips and stubble to shoot pheasants and partridges; and after dinner, not wotting of the affairs of state, but talking about his dogs and of the fifteen brace of partridges he has shot, and then sitting down to a silent game of whist. There is a register kept of all the birds killed; and Mr. Stevenson, our Minister, who once visited here, is remembered for often missing, and for charging his gun so high as to blow off its lock, and nearly to blow himself to pieces. But the shot never to be forgot-

of the recognition of the Independence of the United States, was given me by his daughter, Lady Elizabeth Stanhope, at Holkham, Nov., 1838.'' In March, 1839, Lord Leicester, by his secretary, expressed himself as "most happy to see Mr. Sumner again at Holkham, whether alone or with any friend,'' and thanked him for Felton's Greek epigrams on Chantrey's woodcocks.

[1] Lord Leicester's second daughter, Anne Margaret, was married to Thomas (Viscount) Anson in 1794, and died in 1843. His third daughter, Elizabeth, was married, in 1822, to John Spencer Stanhope, of Yorkshire, and both herself and husband died in 1873. William Roscoe, the historian, while visiting Holkham, celebrated Lady Anson's birthday, Jan. 23, 1831, in verse: —

> "When Anson's natal day returns,
> And Holkham's halls resound with joy," &c.

Roscoe's "Life of William Roscoe," Vol. II. pp. 265–268. Sumner first made the acquaintance of Lady Anson in London, who introduced him, at an interview specially arranged, to her father. She also interested herself to have him see the Bridgewater and Grosvenor collections of pictures. Her note of Oct. 20, 1838, welcomed him to Holkham.

[2] John Charles, third Earl of Spencer, 1782–1845. As Lord Althorp, he served in the House of Commons from 1804 to 1834, and was Chancellor of the Exchequer from 1830 to 1834. His integrity and good sense won him a leading position in Parliament. Miss Martineau, referring to his retirement, says: "Lord Althorp, now become Lord Spencer, was thus soon at liberty to enter upon the privacy he sighed for. He never returned to office. Perhaps no man ever left the House of Commons and an official seat, about whom there was so little difference of opinion among all parties. Nobody supposed him an able statesman; and nobody failed to recognize his candor, his love of justice, his simplicity of heart, and his kindliness and dignity of temper and manners.'' "History of England," Book IV. ch. xii. He was foremost among English noblemen in promoting the improvement of agriculture.

ten, and which has been commemorated in a most classical way, was that of
Chantrey, the sculptor.   He killed two woodcocks at one shot, — a thing not
known in the memory of man in these parts; and Lord Leicester was so delighted that he vowed that Chantrey must make a monument of his own
achievement.   A beautiful marble tablet adorns the library, on which are two
woodcocks falling together, — the offering of the sportsman and the sculptor
to his noble host.   Inscriptions for this tablet came in from various quarters,
and I have derived so much pleasure from them that I send you some which
I have copied on the spot.   From these you may catch an idea of the "diversions" of Holkham.   The idea that was sought to be expressed was that the
sculptor and the sportsman were one and the same, and Chantrey further
wished that his *name* should appear in the inscriptions.   Several, you will
see, are faulty in this last respect.   As none seemed to satisfy the sculptor
entirely, he finally put on the tablet a simple *prose* inscription, which is
quite well expressed: "Two woodcocks killed at Holkham, Nov. 1830, by
Francis Chantrey, sculptor, at one shot; presented to Thos. Wm. Coke, Esq.
1834."   There is a space, however, on the marble for the addition of an
inscription, if they should ever get one that suited.   If you and Felton will
write inscriptions, I will most gladly send them to Lord Leicester; indeed, I
should like to make such a contribution.   I was asked to offer some of my
own; but I never wrote Greek or English verses, and my Latin would not
flow very smoothly now.[1]

> Vixerunt, vivunt, O vîs quanta entis! eâdem
> Ad vitam reduces quâ periere manu!
>
> MR. CHILDREN, F.R.S.

This last is quite epigrammatic.

> We fled from Norway o'er the German wave,
> And pilgrims here we found an early grave;
> Hard fate was ours; for here, at Holkham farm,
> We deem'd the stranger had been safe from harm.
> But Heav'n consol'd us with our victor's name,
> And he that slew us gave us deathless fame!
>
> W. G. COOKESLEY, a Master at Eton.

I like the versification of these very much.

> Let passing sportsmen hail the favor'd spot
> Where fell two woodcocks at a single shot;
> Fell by a hand for different deeds more known,
> Imparting grace and breath to shapeless stone.
> Once more he bids them die, and once again
> Start into life, demanding to be slain.
> Master of either art, this vase to fame,
> Chantrey! shall give thy chisel and thine aim.
>
> SIR ROBERT ADAIR.

Very good.

[1] The inscriptions have been printed in "Winged Words on Chantrey's Woodcocks,"
edited by James Patrick Muirhead, M. A., with etchings. London: John Murray. 1857.
A copy of the volume is in the Boston Public Library. Only a few of the seventeen, as
copied by Sumner, are given here; in some instances they differ from Mr. Muirhead's
version.

From kindred cocks, when robb'd of life,
  How wide the fate we boast!
Their chisel is the carving-knife,
  Their bed, a bed of *toast;*
Whilst Chantrey's hand, by which we fell,
  Of magic power possessed,
Bids us — our wondrous tale to tell —
  On marble bed to rest.
        SIR HUSSEY VIVIAN, Master-General of Ordnance.

These are pleasant and humorous.

In sport immortal as in art,
  Chantrey is gifted to outgo
All others; 'tis his happy part
  To double all that they can do.
        R. W. BACON.

I was told that these last verses were pronounced very good by a company of Cantabs at Sir Francis Chantrey's table. I am not of that opinion.

. . . .

I hope these may please you and my friends, particularly Felton, as much as they have me; though, perhaps, they strike me more as I am on the spot of the achievement, and in view of the marble tablet. As I have walked down that glorious gallery and suite of apartments, and looked on the lifelike marble and the breathing canvas, I have had you in my mind, and observed for you, — "spirits twain have passed with me."

The term is commencing at Westminster Hall, and I must renounce these things to plunge again into the haunts of the law. I go to London to-morrow, leaving a most brilliant company which is now assembling at this favored seat.

    As ever, affectionately yours,

        CHARLES SUMNER.

P. S. I hope Felton did not burn my letter recounting my Guy Mannering adventures in the Highlands before you read it. I think William Story will be pleased by this woodcock episode.

[Professor Felton wrote six inscriptions in Greek (see *post*, letter of March 1, 1839), which Sumner sent to Lord Leicester, one of which was the following: —

Οἵηπερ Νιόβης μοίρη τοιῆδε καὶ ἡμῖν
Ἐστιν ὀϊζυροῖς καὶ μακάρεσσιν ὁμοῦ·
Ἡμεῖς γὰρ θάνομεν Χαντροῖο βέλεσσι δαμέντες,
Κἂν λίθῳ ἀθανάτους αὐτὸς ἔθηκε πάλιν.

It is thus translated by Mr. Muirhead, the compiler of the "Winged Words on Chantrey's Woodcocks," p. 37: —

"Happy at once and miserable, we
Seem to partake the fate of Niobe;
For, perishing by Chantrey's dart, we die,
And in his marble live immortally."]

TO PROFESSOR SIMON GREENLEAF, CAMBRIDGE.

HOLKHAM HOUSE, Nov. 2, 1838.

MY DEAR GREENLEAF, — Which is the older of the two, — you or I? There cannot be much disparity of age, I feel; for you write so freshly as to respond to all the little of youth there is left in me, or I have grown so grave as to be climbing prematurely to the dignity of your years. But time has moved faster with me, since I left your planet. I certainly can hardly make up my mind, or find voice or even pen-strokes, to call you " Mr." or " Professor." There is no feature in English social life, particularly in the intercourse of the bar, that has more struck me than the familiarity and brotherly tone in which all acquaintances — I do not say simply friends — address each other. At the bar, as a general rule, all barristers address each other simply by their surnames, without any prefix; and there are many of the English bar, who are old enough to be my father, whom I address with that familiarity. I wish I could talk with you now; there are a thousand things on my mind that I fear I may lose in the Lethean waters of Germany, where I go from England, and which I should like to discuss with you and the Judge, and others of the goodly fellowship.

I am now the guest of the Earl Leicester, — the famous " old Coke," as he has been called for years, — who was offered a peerage four times before he accepted it. His house is beautiful beyond expression, and is adorned with the choicest antiques and paintings. The rooms are spacious, magnificent, and comfortable. His library of manuscripts is said to be the richest in England; it contains MSS. of most of the classics; also Italian and ancient English ones. They are all beautifully bound, and occupy the shelves which surround a room nearly as large as your study in Dane Hall — how my pulse throbs as I write this word! Lord Leicester is the descendant of no less a person than our Sir Edward Coke, whilom Lord Chief-Justice of the Common Pleas; and to him have come the manuscripts and library of the distinguished lawyer. Little did I think when I moiled in the pages of this writer, and almost felt my eyesight fail before his stern black-letter, that I should ever be the guest of his descendant, — one of the most distinguished peers of England, — in one of the most remarkable private dwellings in the world, and permitted to see and examine the very books — the *Registrum Brevium, Statuta Antiqua*, &c. — that our great master once used, to study his crabbed handwriting, and to pore over the darksome notes and memoranda which he made on the margin of the volumes he read. Lord Spencer and Lord Ebrington are here; while they are wandering through fields, with their faithful dogs to bear them company, after partridges and pheasants, I have been scanning these gloomy pages. On the title-page of many of these books is written, *Edward Coke*, — being the autograph of the grim lawyer. In one of the drawing-rooms of the house is an original portrait of Lord Coke, by Janssen. You may imagine that I have felt no common thrill in being thus permitted to look upon these things. Have I not cause for great gratitude in the opportunities of gratifying so many of my fondest desires, in enjoying the society and confidence of so many of the learned in the law, in mingling with the good and great in such various walks of life? I have feasted from silver, and lived among nobles; but I believe that you would find me at the present moment not less desirous of getting knowledge and doing my duty, than I have ever been during the few years in which I have had the happiness of your friendship. I look forward to my return with no little anxiety; and hope, after a few days of quiet intercourse with my friends, to renew the labors which I have for the while forsaken; to grasp resolutely the plough which I have left in the furrow.

Tell me frankly; do you and the Judge think it would have been better for me had I stayed at home? This broad page of human life which I have been studying has been full of instruction; and I feel that I know more, and can do more, than before I forsook my affairs for Europe. You have thrown out some hints with regard to my occupying a place with you and the Judge at Cambridge. You know well that my heart yearns fondly to that place, and that in the calm study of my profession I have ever taken more delight than in the pert debate at the bar. I shall only wish to see some distinct and honorable line of duty marked out for me, and I shall at once enter upon it. I should observe, however, that, for various causes, I shall feel a strong obligation to devote myself to my profession on my return, in such wise as will insure me the most considerable income, — those principles of duty and honor being regarded which you have taught me never to lose sight of. I shall of course be always obliged by your advice and suggestions, and hope to hear from you at length before my return with regard to the best way of recovering the place in my profession which I have left. Lord Brougham said to me, " It is very strange that men in your profession in America can abandon their clients and go abroad, without entirely breaking down, — Mr. Pinckney did it." I added that Mr. Pinckney was a *student* of his profession when in Europe, and that *I was myself*. " That alters the case," said his Lordship; " and I doubt not you will go home better prepared than before." This is a case in point, certainly a *dictum*, by an ex-chancellor of England. The court is about to commence its labors, and I leave this retreat to-morrow for Westminster Hall.

As ever, affectionately yours,

CHAS. SUMNER.

END OF VOL. I.